NEW WORLD ARCHAEOLOGY

Readings from

SCIENTIFIC AMERICAN

NEW WORLD ARCHAEOLOGY: THEORETICAL AND CULTURAL TRANSFORMATIONS

Selected and with Introductions by

EZRA B. W. ZUBROW

Stanford University

MARGARET C. FRITZ

California State University, San Jose

JOHN M. FRITZ

University of California, Santa Cruz

W. H. Freeman and Company

San Francisco

Some of the SCIENTIFIC AMERICAN articles in *NEW WORLD ARCHAEOLOGY* are available as separate Offprints. For a complete list of more than 975 articles now available as Offprints, write to W. H. Freeman and Company, 660 Market Street, San Francisco, California 94104.

Library of Congress Cataloging in Publication Data

Zubrow, Ezra B. W. comp.
New World archaeology.

1. Indians—Antiquities—Addresses, essays, lectures.
2. America—Antiquities—Addresses, essays, lectures. I. Fritz, Margaret C., joint comp. II. Fritz, John M., joint comp. III. Scientific American. IV. Title.
E61.Z82 1974 970.1 74–7028
ISBN 0–7167–0503–6
ISBN 0–7167–0502–8 (pbk.)

Printed in the United States of America

9 8 7 6 5 4 3 2 1

PREFACE

Once a poet was granted a choice: to know all that had happened and was to happen, or to know nothing with certainty, but to pursue knowledge of all. He chose the latter. Archaeologists pursuing knowledge of the prehistory of the New World have been given no such choice. We must seek to know the past with no certainty that the shadowy events and patterns we see are real. Yet the pursuit is exciting. In this book of articles from *Scientific American*, New World archaeology brings to light the material remains that once formed part of the lives of native American peoples, that is, the events and patterns in which these remains figured. This book also indicates the methods and techniques, the day-to-day work-filled routine, the occasional hazard, and the rare discovery by which we attempt to know the past.

The articles reprinted here reflect two kinds of changes in knowledge of New World prehistory. On the one hand, native cultures underwent changes as dramatic as those in the Old World from the end of the last Ice Age to the fall of Rome. From relatively simple ways of life based on the gathering and hunting of wild foods, some New World Cultures evolved into complex civilizations with pronounced social differentiation and frequently with urban centers. Possibly as much as 25,000 years are represented in these articles, during which there were major transformations in the population, technology, means of subsistence, society, religion, and art of native American cultures.

On the other hand, the ways in which archaeologists think about these cultures, their changes, and their material records have also changed. The articles themselves span twenty-five years, during which there have been significant theoretical changes in the discipline that attempts to know these cultures by recovery and analysis of their material remains. We would like to believe that these changes have resulted in better ways of thinking—more sophisticated, more inclusive, better confirmed. Although these new theoretical approaches have changed the focus and concerns of previous ones to greater or lesser degrees, we also believe that each approach has contributed valuable techniques, data, and insights to our subject.

We have organized these articles to reflect the theoretical transformations of New World archaeology. Four theoretical perspectives are considered: the Romantic Vision; Time-Space Systematics; Reconstruction of Events, of Sequences, and of Strategies; and the Analysis of Systems and Processes. Articles that reflect characteristics of each perspective are grouped together. The introduction to each section discusses the objectives, the theoretical perspectives, the methods, the disadvantages and advantages, and the wider relevance of each approach.

This book may be used in a variety of courses. Students being introduced to the results of archaeology will find information about a major "experiment" in recent human evolution. Paired with *Old World Archaeology: Foundations of Civilization* (Readings from *Scientific American*, with Introductions by C. C. Lamberg-Karlovsky), students can compare and contrast developmental processes throughout most of the world. They can also compare and contrast the methods and theories employed by Old and New World archaeologists. Some instructors may prefer to use the book to introduce archaeology as a process, focusing on the dynamic interplay of perspective, technique, and data in recent archaeological history. This book may also be used in advanced courses on New World prehistory, on archaeological theory, or on archaeological method.

Realizing that the users of this book may wish to organize the articles in other ways, we include Tables I and II (pages ix and x), which provide information on alternative arrangements. First, articles can be read for information on the history of cultures within particular subcontinental regions, e.g., the Arctic of North America or the arid west coast of South America. Second, the diversity of cultural forms and adaptations, or the interrelations between cultures in adjacent regions, e.g., Mesoamerica and the Southwestern United States, at particular times can be seen. And third, variations within or between adaptive strategies in particular regions or throughout the Americas can be analyzed.

We hope that students of New World archaeology will gain from these readings not only a sense of the achievements of native New World peoples, but also a sense of the excitement that an archaeologist may feel in pursuing knowledge of these achievements. The poet was right. We assume that today's perspectives will be modified or replaced tomorrow. What will remain is the perspective on ourselves and on our fellow human beings.

March 1974

Ezra B. W. Zubrow
Margaret C. Fritz
John M. Fritz

CONTENTS

Note on cross-references: References to articles included in this book are noted by the title of the article and the page on which it begins; references to articles that are available as Offprints, but are not included here, are noted by the article's title and Offprint number; references to articles published by SCIENTIFIC AMERICAN, but which are not available as Offprints, are noted by the title of the article and the month and year of its publication.

Table I. The Articles Arranged by Theoretical Perspective, Chronological Coverage, Geographical Area, and Adaptive Strategy

Author	Theoretical perspective	Time	Area	Strategy
1. Flannery (1967)	Changing theoretical perspectives	—	—	—
2. Steward (1956)	Changing theoretical perspectives	—	—	—
3. Schaedel (1951)	Romantic	A.D. 1–1500	Western South America	Civilization
4. Von Hagen (1952)	Romantic	A.D. 1500	Western South America	Civilization
5. Lanning and Patterson (1967)	Time-space systematics	10,000 ± 2000 B.C.	Western South America	Hunting-gathering
6. Mayer-Oakes (1963)	Time-space systematics	6–8000 B.C.	Western South America	Hunting-gathering
7. Anderson (1968)	Time-Space systematics	Pre-6500 B.C. to A.D. 1000	Arctic Alaska	Hunting-gathering
8. Cruxent and Rouse (1969)	Time-space systematics	5000 B.C.–A.D. 1500	West Indies	Hunting-gathering
9. Giddings (1954)	Reconstruction by event or period	15,000–10,000 B.C.	Arctic Alaska	Hunting-gathering
10. Meggers and Evans (1966)	Reconstruction by event or period	3000 B.C.	Coastal South America	Hunting-gathering
11. Tuck (1970)	Reconstruction by event or period	2000 B.C.	Arctic Newfoundland	Hunting-gathering
12. Millon (1967)	Reconstruction by event or period	A.D. 1–1000	Mesoamerica	Agricultural civilization
13. Proskouriakoff (1955)	Reconstruction by event or period	1168–1263 A.D.	Mesoamerica	Agricultural civilization
14. Dozier (1957)	Reconstruction by event or period	A.D. 1500–1950	Southwestern United States	Agricultural
15. MacNeish (1971)	Reconstruction of an historical sequence	20,000–1 B.C.	Western South America	Hunting-gathering and agricultural
16. MacNeish (1964)	Reconstruction of an historical sequence	10,000 B.C.–A.D. 1500	Mesoamerica	Hunting-gathering and agricultural
17. Ford (1954)	Reconstruction of an historical sequence	2500 B.C.–A.D. 1200	Western South America	Hunting-gathering and agricultural
18. Martin (1951)	Reconstruction of an historical sequence	2500 B.C.–A.D. 1300	Southwestern	Hunting-gathering and agricultural
19. Borhegyi (1959)	Reconstruction of an historical sequence	1000 B.C.–A.D. 1500	Mesoamerica	Hunting-gathering and agricultural
20. Schwartz (1958)	Reconstruction of an historical sequence	A.D. 600–1800	Southwestern United States	Agricultural
21. Tuck (1971)	Reconstruction of an historical sequence	A.D. 1100–1800	Northeastern United States	Hunting-gathering
22. Haynes (1966)	Reconstruction of a strategy	10,000–5000 B.C.	North America	Hunting-gathering
23. Wheat (1967)	Reconstruction of a strategy	6500 B.C.	Southwestern United States	Hunting-gathering
24. Prufer (1964)	Reconstruction of a strategy	100 B.C.–A.D. 550	Eastern United States	Hunting-gathering and agricultural
25. Coe (1964)	Reconstruction of a strategy	A.D. 500–1964	Mesoamerica	Agricultural
26. Parsons and Denevan (1967)	Reconstruction of a strategy	Pre-Columbian	Tropical	Agricultural
27. Easby (1966)	Reconstruction of a strategy	Pre-A.D. 1400	New World	Hunting-gathering/ agricultural civilization
28. Haag (1962)	Systems	100,000–15,000 B.C.	Arctic	Hunting-gathering
29. Sjoberg (1965)	Systems	5500 B.C.–A.D. 1965	New and Old World	Agricultural/industrial
30. Hammond (1972)	Systems	A.D. 570–730	Mesoamerica	Agricultural
31. Kemp (1971)	Systems	Feb. 14, 1967–Mar. 1, 1968	Arctic	Hunting-gathering
32. Roberts (1948)	Issues	—	United States	—
33. La Farge (1960)	Issues	A.D. 1600–1960	United States	—

Table II. The Articles Arranged by Geographic Area and Cultural Transformations.[a]

	Arctic and subarctic North America	Eastern and central North America	Western and southwestern United States	Various Meso-american highlands	Mesoamerican lowlands and/ or Maya	South and Central America	Theory and generali-zations
Commentary and issues	La Farge VI	Roberts VI La Farge VI	La Farge VI				Flannery I Steward I
Contemporary societies and ethnographies	Kemp V	La Farge VI	Dozier IV				Sjoberg V
Civilizations				Borhegyi IV Millon IV Coe IV	Hammond V Proskouriakoff IV Easby IV	Easby IV Schaedel II Von Hagen II Ford IV	Sjoberg V
Agricultural peasants and the formative		Tuck (21) IV Prufer IV Easby IV	Martin IV Schwartz IV Easby IV	Borhegyi IV Coe IV Millon IV Easby IV	Hammond V Proskouriakoff IV Easby IV	Meggers & Evans IV Ford IV Easby IV	Sjoberg V
Archaic	Tuck (11) IV Anderson III	Easby IV	Schwartz IV		MacNeish (16) IV Easby IV	Ford IV Meggers & Evans IV Cruxent & Rouse III	
Early man	Anderson III Giddings IV Haag V		Haynes IV Wheat IV		MacNeish (16) IV	MacNeish (15) IV Lanning & Patterson III Mayer-Oakes III Cruxent & Rouse III	

a. Roman numerals refer to sections; numbers in parentheses give the article number.

NEW WORLD ARCHAEOLOGY

I

CULTURAL AND THEORETICAL TRANSFORMATIONS

I CULTURAL AND THEORETICAL TRANSFORMATIONS

INTRODUCTION

Transformations are dramatic changes in the organization, the interrelations, and even the content of a set of phenomena. We have chosen to highlight theoretical transformations in this reader, because we believe that the *way* we conceive the past is as important as, and in fact strongly conditions, *what* we conceive. The perspectives we consider—the Romantic Vision, Time-Space Systematics, Reconstructionism, and Analysis of Systems and Processes—tend to address different problems, to conceive of past events and processes and of present archaeological data differently, and to employ different methods and techniques. When cultural transformations are considered, different qualities are emphasized, so that in a sense each perspective conceives of different transformations.

The romantic vision establishes links between those living today and particular events of the past. The magnitude of these events and of objects recovered by archaeologists from the past catalyzes the experience, as may qualities of archaeologists and of their work. The age or antiquity as well as products of transformations—the earliest cultures, the great art styles—are emphasized. The romantic vision does less to provide verified information about the past than to satisfy contemporary personal needs and to validate contemporary social attitudes, values, and symbols.

Today the romantic experience is of relatively small import within New World archaeology. Much more significant is placement of artifact form and cultural characteristics in space and time. Grids locating forms and characteristics according to these dimensions have been important both as descriptive devices and as raw data for the reconstruction of cultural histories. Both the products of transformations and the time and place that they occurred in particular instances are emphasized.

Paleoethnography, or the description of past cultures and their histories with the same detail as other anthropologists describe contemporary non-Western cultures, has been a goal of New World archaeology for over six decades. It was reiterated forcefully in 1948 by Walter W. Taylor in his *Study of Archaeology*. The result has been a set of speculative reconstructions of prehistoric events and sequences of events more or less supported by documented archaeological data. Reconstructions normally have been done within the intellectual framework that Kent Flannery, in the review reprinted below, terms Cultural History. When cultural sequences that resulted in transformations are considered, the qualities of events at particular times and places are emphasized.

Reconstructions of the material and behavioral strategies by which prehistoric populations adapted to their natural and social environments have led away from this framework. Cultural standards for ideological, social, or material behavior either are ignored, as irrelevant to the understanding of adaptation, or are incorporated as simply one of a set of material constraints on or determinants of particular adaptations. In this sense, the reconstructionist approach is similar to the perspective of the process school defined by Flannery. However, the *description* of *particular* adaptations has been emphasized by the reconstructionists, whereas the process school has emphasized the explanation of adaptations and their transformations. Sometimes such explanation is attempted by means of elaborate description of complex mutual relationships between and among a large set of variables at particular times and places, i.e., through definition and descriptions of systems. Explicit use has been made of theories about the nature of systems in general or about smaller sets of relations between restricted cultural or ecological variables. It would be premature to claim that the process school has thus developed a comprehensive and systematic theory of human adaptations and their evolution. But many New World archaeologists are turning to explicit attempts to create such an understanding. Undoubtedly, new theoretical transformations will create new understandings of the cultural transformations of the New World.

As Flannery points out, there is a tendency for more recent perspectives to replace older ones. Yet we would hopelessly distort the case if we suggested that these perspectives form a unilinear sequence of stages. Not only are each of these perspectives taken by different contemporary New World archaeologists, but also the work of particular archaeologists may incorporate particular mixes. In this sense these perspectives represent changes both in the intellectual content of schools of archaeologists and in the relation among objectives and emphases of each of us. Thus, although each article here evidences a particular perspective, it may indicate others as well.

We urge readers to note the date of publication of each article in this anthology. Changing perspectives, as well as changing knowledge in the form of newly recovered data, may have altered interpretations found in earlier articles. In this sense, each article should be considered a document not only of a culture at a particular place and past time, but also of archaeological theory at the time of writing.

THE READINGS

Kent Flannery uses the occasion of the publication of a major synthesis of the culture history of the Americas to discuss a theoretical transformation in North American archaeology in his review "Culture History vs. Culture Process." He defines salient characteristics of the cultural historical school, of which Willey's book is archetypical, and of the process school.

Since this article appeared, debate on the issues discussed by Flannery has continued. In one sense, the objectives of the process school have been attained. Its research problems and vocabulary are widely shared. Yet increasingly more sophisticated defenses of the goals, if not the methods, of culture history have appeared. And debate has developed within the process school regarding effective means for attacking problems. Some advocate the simultaneous analysis of large numbers of variables, some of more restricted sets. All these developments, chronicled by Flannery in his article, "Archaeology with a Capital S," in Charles L. Redman's reader, *Research and Theory in Contemporary Archaeology* (1973), underscore the current renaissance in the field. The sophistication and diversity of approaches has never been greater. The potential for the understanding of cultural transformations also has never been greater.

Julian Steward's article, "Cultural Evolution", chronicles the career of cultural evolutionary thought from the mid-nineteenth century through its "dark ages" of the first decades of this century to its revival at mid-century.

As a central figure in this revival, he writes with special force. He argues for the validity of an evolutionary perspective, particularly of one that is concerned with particular adaptations and evolutionary transformations. Not only does he use the data of New World archaeology, but also his hypotheses have stimulated further work in its prehistory.

His method compares reconstructions of particular historical sequences in order to derive common characteristics of the stages through which they pass and the common conditions which produced common changes. He emphasizes the variability among developmental sequences as well as the diversity that may obtain in adaptive solutions to particular environmental pressures.

Subtle differences distinguish his approach from that of the process or systems school. First, by emphasizing the evolution of culture, which he defines as a characteristic of an aggregate of individuals, he deemphasizes the role of the individual in producing the variability upon which stability and change depend, and the conditions that produce this variability. Second, members of the systems school tend to seek explanations in much more complex interrelationships than Steward considers. There is a strong movement away from monocausal relationships, such as irrigation and the rise of theocratic states. Some disagree (and some agree) with his emphasis on the technological and economic relations within cultures as "core" determinants of other characteristics. Finally, many New World archaeologists believe that human adaptations and their transformations should be understood and explained in terms of the mutual interdependence of human biological, cultural, and environmental variables. From the perspective of human ecology, stability and change cannot be understood simply by reference to culture. Nonetheless, Steward has helped to revitalize the study of cultural transformations in the New World and has given us provocative generalizations and explanations.

Culture history versus cultural process: a debate in American archaeology

1

by Kent V. Flannery
August 1967

A review of An Introduction to American Archaeology, Volume I: North and Middle America, *by Gordon R. Willey.*

A dominant characteristic of American archaeology has been its long history of reaction to American ethnology. When ethnology was little more than the collecting of spears, baskets and headdresses from the Indians, archaeology was little more than recovery of artifacts. When ethnology increased its attention to community structure, archaeology responded with studies of settlement pattern—an approach in which Gordon Willey was an innovator. Publication of works by Julian H. Steward and others on "cultural ecology" was answered by great archaeological emphasis on "the ecological approach." When the concept of cultural evolution emerged triumphant after years of suppression, archaeology showed great interest in evolutionary sequences and in the classification of "stages" in the human career. The interaction of these two disciplines has been increased by the fact that in the U.S. both are housed in departments of anthropology; as Willey remarked some 10 years ago, "American archaeology is anthropology or it is nothing."

And now, in 1967, Willey—Bowditch Professor of Mexican and Central American Archaeology and Ethnology at Harvard University—has written a monumental synthesis of New World prehistory. There is nothing like it. Recently we have had several edited volumes on the New World with contributions by regional specialists, but this book is written cover to cover by one man. Thus the inevitable lack of firsthand familiarity with certain areas is partially offset by the advantage of having one consistent approach and writing style throughout. Although aimed at the student, the book's costly format almost prices it out of the student range. It is a centerpiece for the coffee table of the archaeological fraternity, at least until an inexpensive paperback edition can be produced.

Willey's archaeological career is reflected in monographs and articles on every major land mass of the New World, from the region of the Woodland culture in the U.S. Northeast to the Maya area, the shell mounds of Panama and the coastal border of the Andean civilization. He is a perennial favorite who for a variety of reasons has never come under attack. One reason is his avoidance of any one polarized theoretical position; the other is his adaptability in the face of continual change. While other members of the establishment have clenched their fists and gritted their teeth when their formerly useful theories dropped from favor, Willey has shown no such hostility; younger archaeologists sense he would rather join them than lick them. And he is always free to join them as long as he maintains no vested interest in any comprehensive theory that needs defending.

This book, well organized from the primary literature and from constant conversations with Willey's colleagues, is no exception. It is unlikely to stir up controversy except where Willey commits himself to one of a series of possible theories proposed by others—for example, siding with Emil W. Haury rather than Charles C. Di Peso on the interpretation of the U.S. Southwest, or with Henry B. Collins rather than Richard S. MacNeish on the American Arctic. It is not Willey's aim to intrude his own theories into the synthesis. Indeed, he tells us that he is "not demonstrating or championing any one process, theory or kind of explanation as a key to a comprehensive understanding of what went on in prehistoric America." Clearly Willey feels that it would be misleading to do more than present the student with the facts as most of his colleagues agree on them in 1967. Hence "the intent of this book is history—an introductory culture history of pre-Columbian America."

This statement by Willey makes it appropriate to consider one of the current theoretical debates in American archaeology: the question of whether archaeology should be the study of culture history or the study of cultural process. In view of this debate it is interesting to note that in practically the same paragraph Willey can brand his book "culture history" and yet argue that he is "not championing any one point of view."

Perhaps 60 percent of all currently ambulatory American archaeologists are concerned primarily with culture history; this includes most of the establishment and not a few of the younger generation. Another 10 percent, both young and old, belong to what might be called the "process school." Between these two extremes lies a substantial group of archaeologists who aim their fire freely at both history and process. And although Willey himself belongs to this group, his *Introduction to American Archaeology* also constitutes a massive restatement of the accomplishments of the culture-history school.

Most culture historians use a theoretical framework that has been described as "normative" (the term was coined by an ethnologist and recently restressed by an archaeologist). That is, they treat culture as a body of shared ideas, values and beliefs—the "norms" of a human group. Members of a given culture are committed to these norms in different degrees—the norm is really at the middle of a bell-shaped curve of opinions on how to behave. Prehistoric artifacts are viewed as products of these shared ideas, and they too have a "range of variation" that takes the form of a bell-shaped curve.

In the normative framework cultures change as the shared ideas, values and beliefs change. Change may be temporal (as the ideas alter with time) or geographic (as one moves away from the center of a particular culture area, commitment to certain norms lessens and commitment to others increases). Hence culture historians have always been concerned with constructing "time-space grids"—great charts whose columns show variation through the centuries. Some have focused an incredible amount of attention on refining and detailing these grids; others have been concerned with discovering "the Indian behind the artifact"—reconstructing the "shared idea" or "mental template" that served as a model for the maker of the tool.

While recognizing the usefulness of this framework for classification, the process school argues that it is unsuitable for explaining culture-change situations. Members of the process school view human behavior as a point of overlap (or "articulation") between a vast number of *systems*, each of which encompasses both cultural and noncultural phenomena—often much more of the latter. An Indian group, for example, may participate in a system in which maize is grown on a river floodplain that is slowly being eroded, causing the zone of the best farmland to move upstream. Simultaneously it may participate in a system involving a wild rabbit population whose density fluctuates in a 10-year cycle because of predators or disease. It may also participate in a system of exchange with an Indian group occupying a different kind of area, from which it receives subsistence products at certain predetermined times of the year; and so on. All these systems compete for the time and energy of the individual Indian; the maintenance of his way of life depends on an equilibrium among systems. Culture change comes about through minor variations in one or more systems, which grow, displace or reinforce others and reach equilibrium on a different plane.

The strategy of the process school is therefore to isolate each system and study it as a separate variable. The ultimate goal, of course, is reconstruction of the entire pattern of articulation, along with all related systems, but such complex analysis has so far proved beyond the powers of the process theorists. Thus far their efforts have not produced grand syntheses such as Willey's but only small-scale descriptions of the detailed workings of a single system. By these methods, however, they hope to explain, rather than merely describe, variations in prehistoric human behavior.

So far the most influential (and controversial) member of the process school has been Lewis R. Binford of the University of California at Los Angeles, and it is interesting to note that Binford's name is confined to a single footnote on the last page of Willey's text. It is Binford's contention that culture historians are at times stopped short of "an explanatory level of analysis" by the normative framework in which they construct their classifications. Efforts to reconstruct the "shared ideas" behind artifact populations cannot go beyond what Binford calls "paleopsychology"—they cannot cope with systemic change. And where Willey says that "archaeology frequently treats more effectively of man in his relationships to his natural environment than of other aspects of culture," Binford would protest that most culture historians have dealt poorly with these very relationships; their model of "norms," which are "inside" culture, and environment, which is "outside," makes it impossible to deal with the countless systems in which man participates, none of which actually reflect a dichotomy between culture and nature. The concept of culture as a "superorganic" phenomenon, helpful for some analytical purposes, is of little utility to the process school.

As a convenient example of the difference in the two approaches, let us examine three different ways in which American archaeologists have treated what they call "diffusion"—the geographic spread of cultural elements. It was once common to interpret the spread of such elements by actual migrations of prehistoric peoples (a view, still common in Near Eastern archaeology, that might be called the "Old Testament effect"). The culture historians attacked this position with arguments that it was not necessary for actual people to travel—just "ideas." In other words, the norms of one culture might be transmitted to another culture over long distances, causing a change in artifact styles, house types and so on. A whole terminology was worked out for this situation by the culture historians: they described cultural "traits" that had a "center of origin" from which they spread outward along "diffusion routes." Along the way they passed through "cultural filters" that screened out certain traits and let others pass through; the mechanics of this process were seen as the "acceptance" or "rejection" of new traits on the part of the group through whose filter they were diffusing. At great distances from the center of origin the traits were present only in attenuated form, having been squeezed through so many filters that they were almost limp.

Since process theorists do not treat a given tool (or "trait") as the end product of a given group's "ideas" about what a tool should look like but rather as one component of a system that also includes many noncultural components, they treat diffusion in different ways. The process theorist is not ultimately concerned with "the Indian behind the artifact" but rather with the system behind both the Indian and the artifact: what other components does the system have, what energy source keeps it going, what mechanisms regulate it and so on? Often the first step is an attempt to discover the role of the trait or implement by determining what it is functionally associated with; some process theorists have run extensive linear-regression analyses or multivariant factor analyses in order to pick up clusters of elements that vary with each other in "nonrandom" ways. When such clusterings occur, the analyst postulates a system—tools *X*, *Y* and *Z* are variables dependent on one another, constituting a functional tool kit that varies nonrandomly with some aspect of the environment, such as fish, wild cereal grains, white-tailed deer and so on. By definition change in one part of a system produces change in other parts; hence the process theorists cannot view artifacts *X*, *Y* and *Z* as products of cultural norms, to be accepted or rejected freely at way stations along diffusion routes. When such elements spread, it is because the systems of which they are a part have spread—often at the expense of other systems.

Thus the archaeologist James Deetz recently presented evidence that the spread of a series of pottery designs on the Great Plains reflected not the "acceptance" of new designs by neighboring groups but a breakdown of the matrilocal residence pattern of a society where the women were potters. Designs subconsciously selected by the women (and passed on to their daughters) ceased to be restricted to a given village when the matrilocal pattern collapsed and married daughters were no longer bound to reside in their mothers' villages. In this case, although each potter obviously did have a "mental template" in her mind when she made the pot, this did not "explain" the change. That spread of design could only be understood in terms of a system in which designs, containers and certain female descent groups were nonrandomly related components. The members of the process school maintain that this is a more useful explanatory framework, but even they realize that it is only a temporary approach. They are becoming increasingly aware that today's human geographers have ways of studying diffusion that are far more sophisticated and quantitative than anything used by contemporary archaeologists.

One other example of the difference in approach between the culture historian and the process theorist is the way each treats the use of "ethnographic analogy" in archaeological interpretation. The culture historian proposes to analyze and describe a prehistoric behavior pattern, then search the ethnographic literature for what seems to be analogous behavior in a known ethnic group. If the analogy seems close enough, he may propose that the prehistoric behavior served the same purpose as its analogue and then use ethnographic data to "put flesh on the archaeological skeleton."

The process theorist proposes a different procedure. Using the analogous ethnic group, he constructs a behavioral model to "predict" the pattern of archaeological debris left by such a group. This model is then tested against the actual archaeological traces of the prehistoric culture, with the result that a third body of data emerges, namely the differences between the *observed* and the *expected* archaeological pattern. These differences are in some ways analogous to the "residuals" left when the principal factors in a factor analysis have been run, and they may constitute unexpectedly critical data. When the archaeologist sets himself the task of *explaining* the differences between the observed archaeological pattern and the pattern predicted by the ethnographic model, he may come up with process data not obtained through the use of analogy alone.

Willey is certainly alert to the current debate, and although he summarizes the New World in a predominantly culture-history framework, he concludes Volume I with a discussion of the hopes and promises of the process school. These he leaves for the future: "I shall be less concerned with process or a search for cultural 'laws,'" he says, "than with at times attempting to explain why certain cultural traditions developed, or failed to develop." Certainly the process school would argue that he cannot explain, within a culture-history framework, why such traditions developed or failed to develop; yet, as he explicitly states, explanation is not the purpose of this volume but rather history.

Let us hope, as Willey seems to, that there is a place in American archaeology for both approaches. Certainly we can use both the historical synthesis and the detailed analysis of single processes. By no stretch of the imagination do all process theorists propose to reject history, because it is only in the unfolding of long sequences that some processes become visible.

In fact, what does the difference between the two schools really amount to? In terms of the philosophy of science, I believe the process approach results in moving "decisions" about cultural behavior even farther away from the individual. It is part of a trend toward determinism that the culture historians began.

It was once common to hear human history explained in terms of "turning points," of crucial decisions made by "great men." This view proved unacceptable to the culture historians, with their normative framework of shared ideas, values and beliefs. They argued convincingly that this body of shared norms determined the course of history—not the individual, who was simply a product of his culture. Possibly the most devastating critique of the individual as decision-maker was due to Leslie A. White, who in one brilliant polemic concluded that the course of Egyptian history and monotheism would have been the same "even had Ikhnaton been a bag of sand."

Now the process school would like to move crucial decisions still farther from the individual by arguing that systems, once set in motion, are self-regulating to the point where they do not even necessarily allow rejection or acceptance of new traits by a culture. Once a system has moved in a certain direction, it automatically sets up the limited range of possible moves it can make at the next critical turning point. This view is not original with process-school archaeologists—it is borrowed from Ludwig von Bertalanffy's framework for the developing embryo, where systems trigger behavior at critical junctures and, once they have done so, cannot return to their original pattern. The process school argues that there are systems so basic in nature that they can be seen operating in virtually every field—prehistory not excepted. Culture is about as powerless to divert these systems as the individual is to change his culture.

Obviously individuals *do* make decisions, but evidence of these individual decisions cannot be recovered by archaeologists. Accordingly it is more useful for the archaeologist to study and understand the system, whose behavior is detectable over and over again. Obviously this approach is too deterministic for some purposes, but for others it is of great theoretical value.

But then if both historical and processual approaches are useful, why should there be a debate at all? I believe the debate exists because of two basically different attitudes toward science.

The previous generation of archaeologists, who did mostly culture history but also laid the foundations for the process school, were often deathly afraid of being wrong. Many of them felt (and many still feel) that if we will only wait until all the facts are in they will speak for themselves. They spoke in awe of the incompleteness of the archaeological record and of the irresponsibility of speculating on scanty data. Somehow they seemed to feel that if they could get together a few more potsherds, a few more projectile points or a few more architectural details, their conclusions would be unshakable. There has not been, however, any convincing correlation between the quantities of data they amassed and the accuracy of their conclusions.

The process theorists assume that "truth" is just the best current hypothesis, and that *whatever* they believe now will ultimately be proved wrong, either within their lifetime or afterward. Their "theories" are not like children to them, and they suffer less trauma when the theories prove "wrong." Their concern is with presenting developmental models to be tested in the field, and they have noted no consistent relationship between the usefulness of a given model and the absolute quantity of data on which it is based. To be useful a model need only organize a body of disorganized data in such a way that hypotheses can conveniently be tested, accepted, modified or rejected. Thus the process school will continue to present model after model on the basis of returns from the first few precincts, and at least some of the culture historians will continue to accuse them of being "hasty," "premature" and "irresponsible." And the issue will be settled years from now by another generation that will probably not belong to either school.

Willey's synthesis sums up nearly 100

years of American archaeology, and it comes at the start of one of the most exciting archaeological eras yet begun. My prediction for the next decade is that we shall see general systems theory, game theory and locational analysis all applied successfully to American archaeology in spite of the loudest mutterings of the establishment. I also predict that, in spite of his decision to concentrate his own efforts on producing reliable culture history, we shall hear all these subversive approaches applauded by Gordon Willey.

Cultural Evolution

2

by Julian H. Steward

May 1956

The 19th-century idea that cultures evolve in the same way as plants and animals was abandoned when anthropologists found that it did not jibe with their observations. Now the evolutionary approach is revived

It is almost 100 years since evolution became a powerful word in science. The concept of evolution, which Charles Darwin set forth so clearly and convincingly in his *Origin of Species* in 1859, came like a burst of light that seemed to illuminate all of nature—not only the development of the myriad forms of life but also the history of the planet earth, of the universe and of man and his civilization. It offered a scheme which made it possible to explain, rather than merely describe, man's world.

In biology the theory of evolution today is more powerfully established than ever. In cosmology it has become the primary generator of men's thinking about the universe. But the idea of evolution in the cultural history of mankind itself has had a frustrating career of ups and downs. It was warmly embraced in Darwin's time, left for dead at the turn of our century and is just now coming back to life and vigor. Today a completely new approach to the question has once more given us hope of achieving an understanding of the development of human cultures in evolutionary terms.

Before considering these new attempts to explain the evolutionary processes operating in human affairs, we need to review the attempts that failed. By the latter part of the 19th century Darwin's theory of biological evolution had profoundly changed scientists' views of human history. Once it was conceded that all forms of life, including man, had evolved from lower forms, it necessarily followed that at some point in evolution man's ancestors had been completely without culture. Human culture must therefore have started from simple beginnings and grown more complex. The 19th-century school of cultural evolutionists—mainly British—reasoned that man had progressed from a condition of simple, amoral savagery to a civilized state whose ultimate achievement was the Victorian Englishman, living in an industrial society and political democracy, believing in the Empire and belonging to the Church of England. The evolutionists assumed that the

CHINESE BAS-RELIEF of the second century A.D., here reproduced from a rubbing of the original stone, depicts a battle scene on a bridge. Organized combat of this sort is characteristic of one stage in the evolution of cultures based on irrigation farming. The development of irrigation farming led to the specialization of labor, the centralization of authority and, when agricultural production had leveled off, to aggressive warfare of the state against its neighbors. In China such warfare began around 1000 B.C.

universe was designed to produce man and civilization, that cultural evolution everywhere must be governed by the same principles and follow the same line, and that all mankind would progress toward a civilization like that of Europe.

Among the leading proponents of this theory were Edward B. Tylor, the Englishman who has been called the father of anthropology; Lewis H. Morgan, an American banker and lawyer who devoted many years to studying the Iroquois Indians; Edward Westermarck, a Finnish philosopher famed for his studies of the family; John Ferguson McLennan, a Scottish lawyer who concerned himself with the development of social organization, and James Frazer, the Scottish anthropologist, historian of religion and author of *The Golden Bough*. Their general point of view was developed by Morgan in his book *Ancient Society*, in which he declared: "It can now be asserted upon convincing evidence that savagery preceded barbarism in all the tribes of mankind, as barbarism is known to have preceded civilization." Morgan divided man's cultural development into stages of "savagery," "barbarism" and "civilization"— each of which was ushered in by a single invention.

These 19th-century scholars were highly competent men, and some of their insights were extraordinarily acute. But their scheme was erected on such flimsy theoretical foundations and such faulty observation that the entire structure collapsed as soon as it was seriously tested. Their principal undoing was, of course, the notion that progress (*i.e.*, toward the goal of European civilization) was the guiding principle in human development. In this they were following the thought of the biological evolutionists, who traced a progression from the simplest forms of life to *Homo sapiens*. Few students of evolution today, however, would argue that the universe has any design making progress inevitable, either in the biological or the cultural realm. Certainly there is nothing in the evolutionary process which preordained the particular developments that have occurred on our planet. From the principles operating in biological evolution—heredity, mutation, natural selection and so on—an observer who visited the earth some half a billion years ago, when the algae represented the highest existing form of life, could not possibly have predicted the evolution of fishes, let alone man. Likewise, no known principle of cultural development could ever have predicted specific inventions such as the bow, iron smelting, writing, tribal clans, states or cities.

The Facts

When, at the turn of the century, anthropologists began to study primitive cultures in detail, they found that the cultural evolutionists' information had been as wrong as their theoretical assumptions. Morgan had lumped together in the stage of middle barbarism the Pueblo Indians, who were simple farmers, and the peoples of Mexico, who had cities, empires, monumental architecture, metallurgy, astronomy, mathematics, phonetic writing and other accomplishments unknown to the Pueblo. Field research rapidly disclosed that one tribe after another had quite the wrong cultural characteristics to fit the evolutionary niche assigned it by Morgan. Eventually the general scheme of evolution postulated by the 19th-century theorists fell apart completely. They had believed, for example, that society first developed around the maternal line, the father being transient, and that marriage and the family as we know it did not evolve until men began to practice herding and agriculture. But field research showed that some of the most primitive hunting and gathering societies, such as the Bushmen of South Africa and the aboriginal Australians, were organized into patrilineal descent groups, while much more advanced horticultural peoples, including some of the groups in the Inca Empire of South America, had matrilineal kin groups. The Western Shoshonis of the Great Basin, who by every criterion had one of the simplest cultures, were organized in families which were not based on matrilineality. Still another blow to the evolutionists' theory was the discovery that customs had spread or diffused from one group to another over the world: that is to say, each society owed much of its culture to borrowing from its neighbors, so it could not be said that societies had evolved independently along a single inevitable line.

The collapse of the theory that cultural evolution had followed the same line everywhere (what we may call the "unilinear" scheme) began with the researches of the late Franz Boas, and the *coup de grâce* was dealt by Robert H. Lowie in his comprehensive and convincing analysis, *Primitive Society*, published in 1920. When the evolutionary hypothesis was demolished, however, no alternative hypothesis appeared. The 20th-century anthropologists threw out the evolutionists' insights along with their schemes. Studies of culture lost a unifying theory and lapsed into a methodology of "shreds and patches." Anthropology became fervently devoted to collecting facts. But it had to give some order to its data, and it fell back on classification—a phase in science which F. S. C. Northrop has called the "natural history stage."

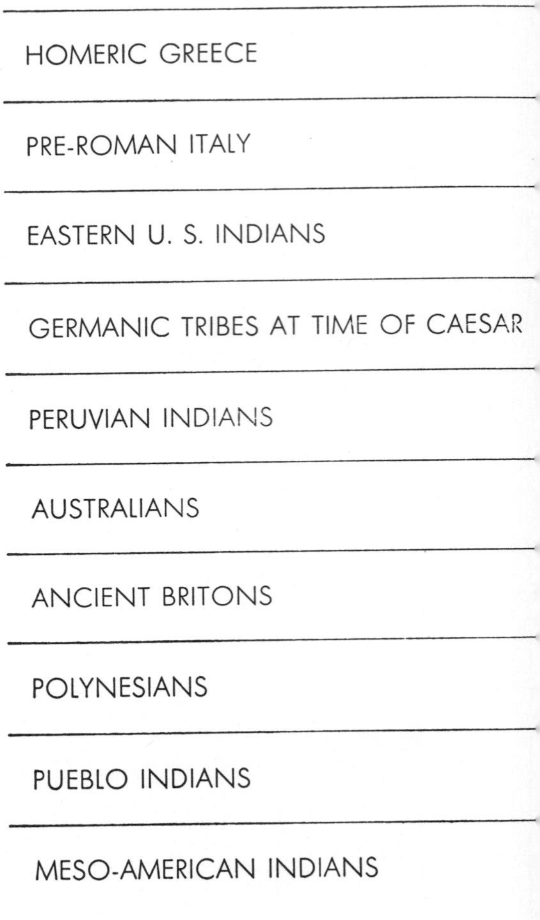

The "culture elements" used as the classification criteria included such items as the bow and arrow, the domes-

EARLY THEORY of cultural evolution is depicted in this chart based on the scheme

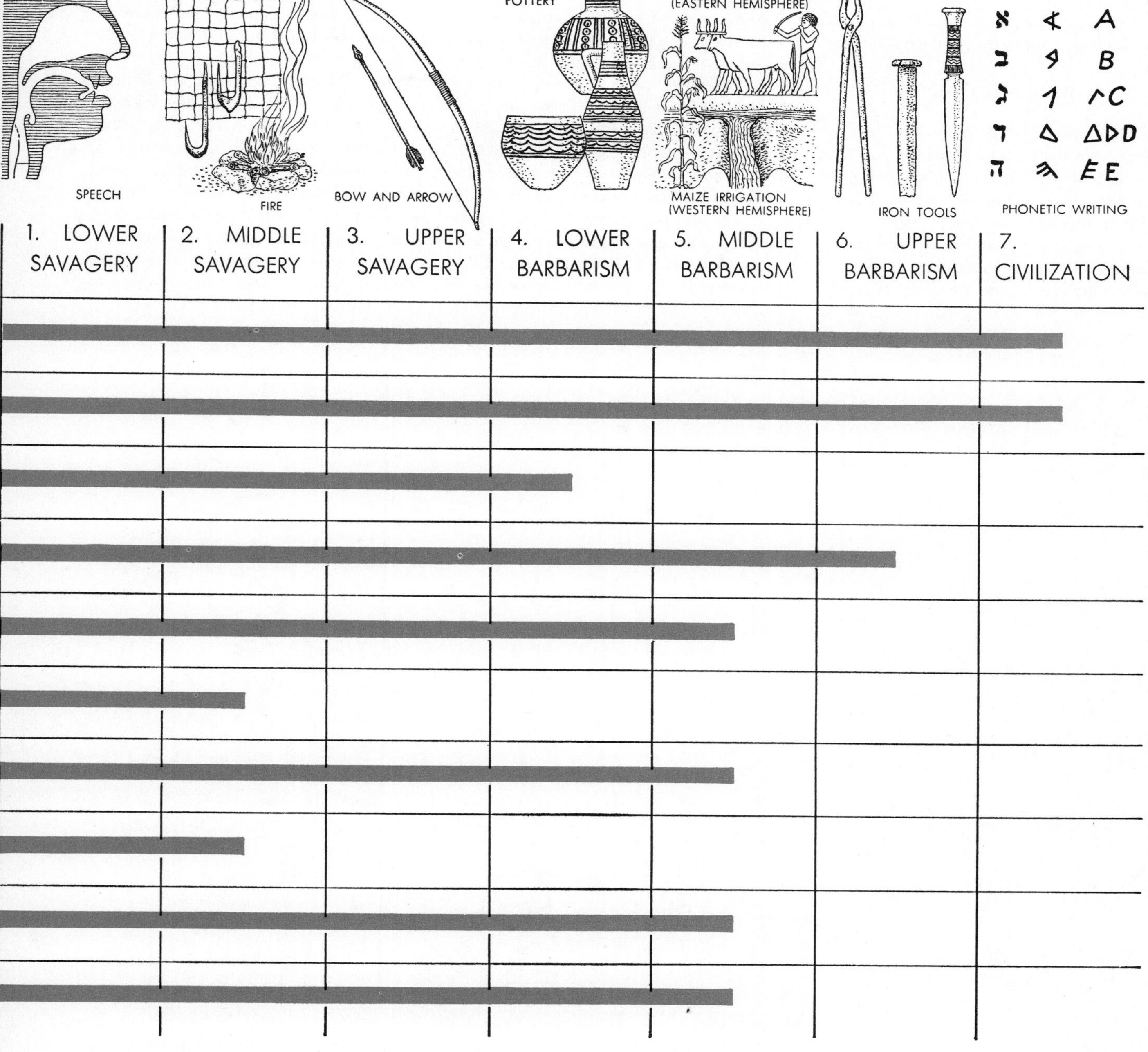

of Lewis H. Morgan, a 19th-century anthropologist. Ten cultures are listed at left. The putative stages of their evolution are at the top. Above the name of each stage is its cultural criterion. The bars represent the stages through which each culture passed.

ticated dog, techniques and forms of basketry, the spear and spear thrower, head-hunting, polyandrous marriage, feather headgear, the penis sheath, initiation ceremonies for boys, tie-dyeing techniques for coloring textiles, the blowgun, use of a stick to scratch the head during periods of religious taboo, irrigation agriculture, shamanistic use of a sweat bath, transportation of the head of state on a litter, proving one's fortitude by submitting to ant bites, speaking to one's mother-in-law through a third party, making an arrowhead with side notches, marrying one's mother's brother's daughter. Students of the development of culture sought to learn the origin of such customs, their distribution and how they were combined in the "culture content" of each society.

Eventually this approach led to an attempt to find an over-all pattern in each society's way of life—a view which is well expressed in Ruth Benedict's *Patterns of Culture*. She contrasted, for example, the placid, smoothly functioning, nonaggressive behavior of the Pueblo Indians with the somewhat frenzied, warlike behavior of certain Plains Indians, aptly drawing on Greek mythology to designate the first as an Apollonian pattern and the second as Dionysian. The implication is that the pattern is formed by the ethos, value system or world view. During the past decade and a half it has become popular to translate pattern into more psychological terms. But description of a culture in terms either of elements, ethos or personality type does not explain how it originated. Those who seek to understand how cultures evolved must look for longer-range causes and explanations.

Multilinear Evolution

One must keep in mind Herbert Spencer's distinction between man as a biological organism and his functioning on the superorganic or cultural level, which also has distinctive qualities. We must distinguish man's needs and capacity for culture—his superior brain and ability to speak and use tools—from the particular cultures he has evolved. A specific invention is not explained by saying that man is creative. Cultural activities meet various biological needs, but the existence of the latter does not explain the character of the former. While all men must eat, the choice of particular foods and of how they are obtained and prepared can be explained only on a superorganic level. Thanks to his jaw and tongue structure and to the speech and auditory centers of his brain, man is capable of speech, but these facts do not explain the origin of a single one of the thousands of languages that have developed in the world. The family is a basic human institution, but families in different cultures differ profoundly in the nature of their food-getting activities, in the division of labor between the sexes and in the socialization of the children.

The failure to distinguish the biological basis of all cultural development from the explanation of particular forms of culture accounts for a good deal of the controversy and confusion about "free will" and "determinism" in human behavior. The biological evolutionist George Gaylord Simpson considers that, because man has purposes and makes plans, he may exercise conscious control over cultural evolution. On the other

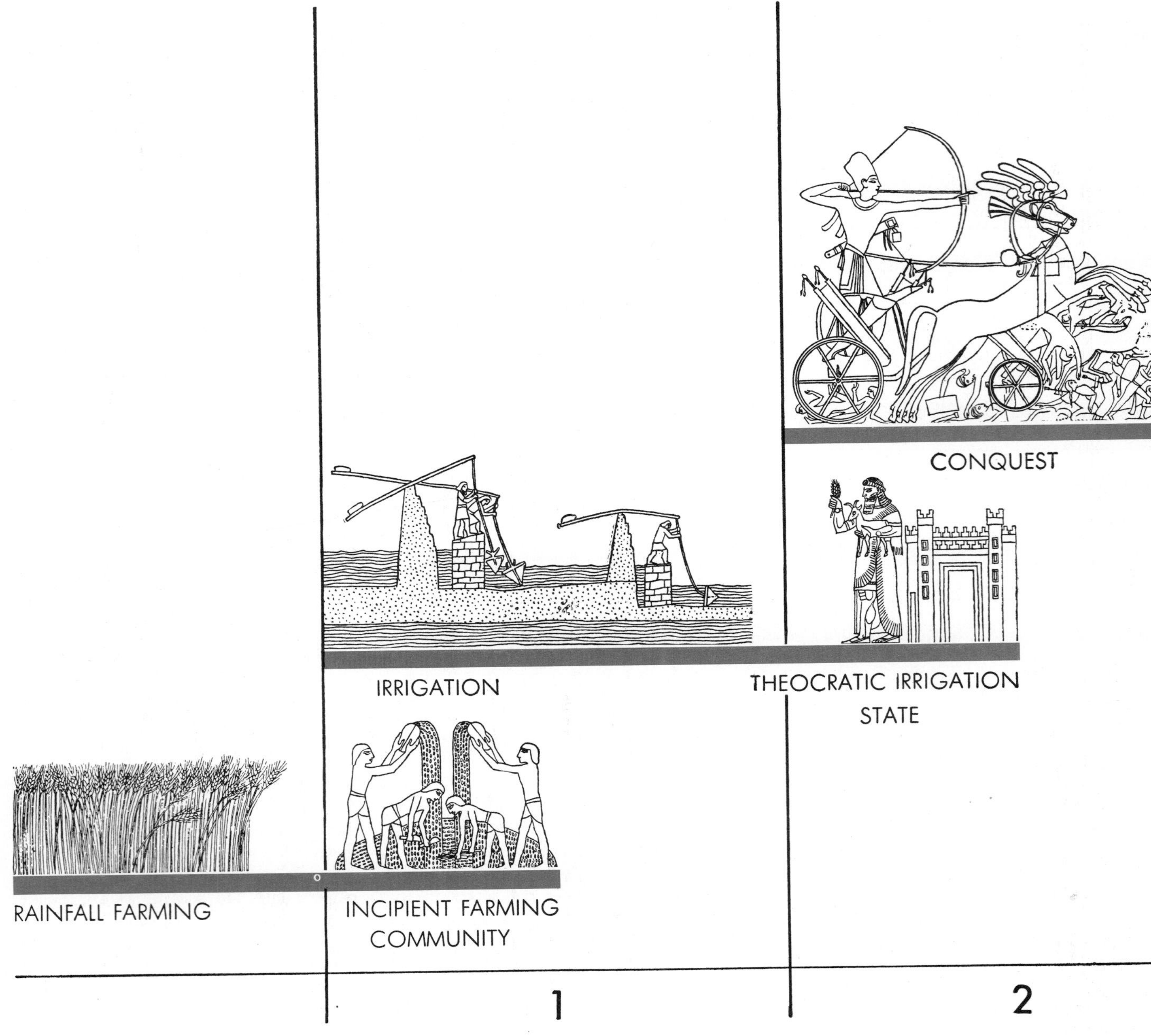

MODERN THEORY of cultural evolution is depicted for the special case of cultures in Egypt, Mesopotamia, China, Meso-America and Peru. In these cultures rainfall farming led to the incipient farming community. Such communities made possible irrigation

hand, the cultural evolutionist Leslie A. White takes the deterministic position that culture develops according to its own laws. Simpson is correct in making a biological statement, that is, in describing man's capacity. White is correct in making a cultural statement, that is, in describing the origin of any particular culture.

All men, it is true, have the biological basis for making rational solutions, and specific features of culture may develop from the application of reason. But since circumstances differ (*e.g.*, in the conditions for hunting), solutions take many forms. Moreover, much culture develops gradually and imperceptibly without deliberate thought. The growth of settlements, kinship groups, beliefs in shamanism and magic, types of warfare and the like are not planned.

This does not mean that there is no rhyme or reason in the development of culture, or that history is random and haphazard. It is possible to trace causes and order in the seeming chaos. In the early irrigation civilizations of the Middle East, Asia and America the inventions were remarkably similar and ran extraordinarily parallel courses through several thousand years. There was clearly a close connection between large-scale irrigation agriculture, population increase, the growth of permanent communities and cities, the rise of specialists supported by agricultural workers, the appearance of unprecedented skills in technology, the need for a managerial class or bureaucracy and the rise of states.

There have been other patterns in the development of man's institutions, each adapted at different times and places to the specific circumstances of a specific society. The facts now accumulated indicate that human culture evolved along a number of different lines; we must think of cultural evolu-

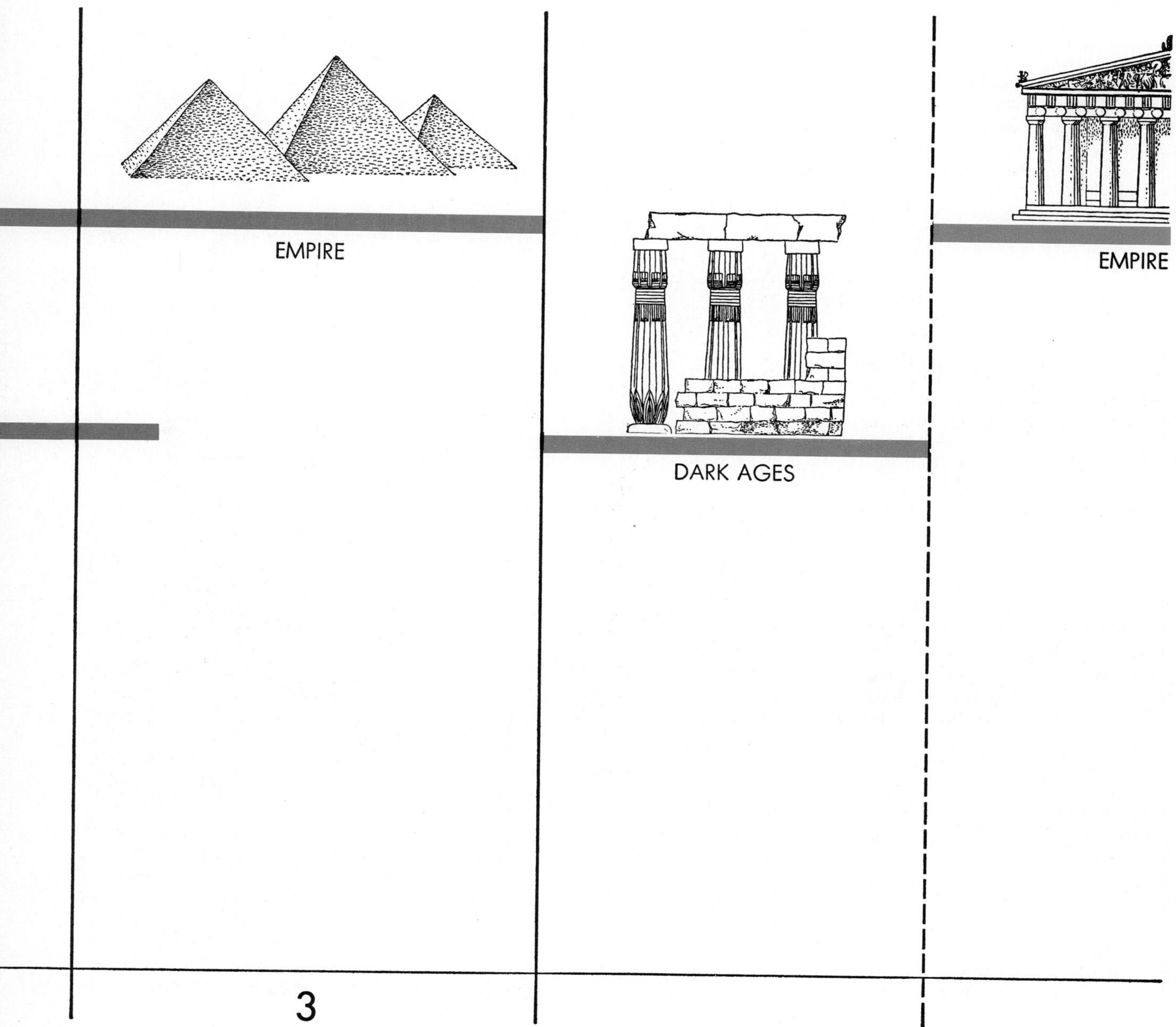

farming, which culminated in the theocratic irrigation state. When the state outstripped its resources, it turned to conquest and empire. Periodic revolutions then caused oscillations of empires and dark ages. The horizontal bars depict the overlap of these various stages.

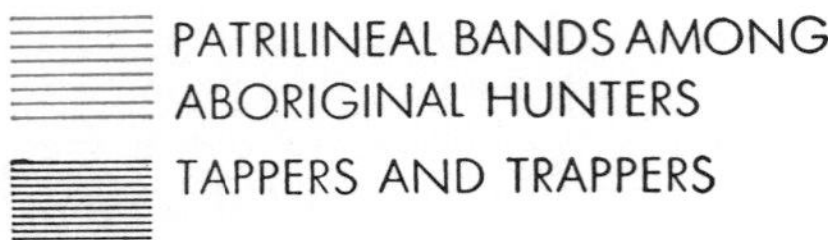

TAPPERS AND TRAPPERS

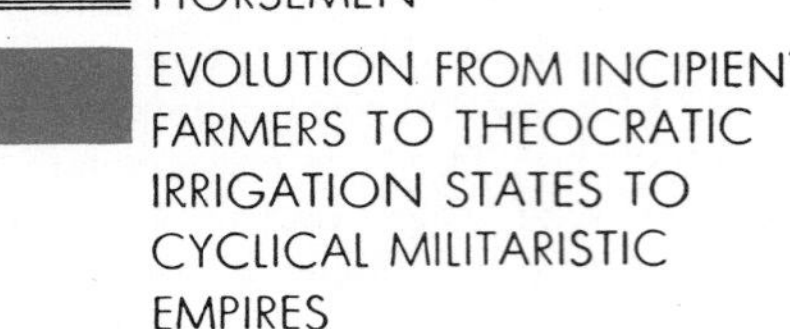

LOCATION of cultures in five lines of evolution is mapped. The cultures shaped by irrigation farming were, from left to right, in Meso-America, Peru, Egypt, Mesopotamia, the Indus Valley of western India, and China. The predatory bands of horsemen rose in inner Asia during the 11th and 12th centuries, in the western U. S. from 1850 to 1880 and in South America from 1700 to 1850. The feudal states are premercantile Europe and preindustrial Japan.

tion not as unilinear but as multilinear. This is the new basis upon which evolutionists today are seeking to build an understanding of the development of human cultures. It is an ecological approach—an attempt to learn how the factors in each given type of situation shaped the development of a particular type of society.

Multilinear evolution is not merely a way of explaining the past. It is applicable to changes occurring today as well. In the department of sociology and anthropology of the University of Illinois my colleagues and I are studying current changes in the ways of rural populations in underdeveloped areas of the world: it is called "The Project to Study Cross-Cultural Regularities." During the past three years my colleagues—Eric Wolf, Robert F. Murphy, F. K. Lehman, Ben Zimmerman, Charles Erasmus, Louis Faron—and I have constructed research models to be tested by investigations in the field. These models consist of several types of populations—peasants, small farmers, wage workers on plantations and in mines and factories, primitive tribes. The objective is to learn how the several types of societies evolved and how their customs are being changed by economic or political factors introduced from the modern industrial world. Such studies should obviously have practical value in guiding programs of technical aid for these peoples.

Hunters, Trappers, Farmers

To illustrate the ecological approach let us consider very briefly several different types of societies, using the ways in which they made their living as the frame of reference. The first example is the form of society consisting of a patrilineal band of hunters. This type of organization was found among many primitive tribes all over the world, including the Bushmen of the deserts in South Africa, the Negritos of the tropical rain forest in the Congo, the aborigines of the steppes and deserts in Australia, the now extinct aboriginal islanders in Tasmania, the Indians of the cold pampas on the islands of Tierra del Fuego and Shoshoni Indians of the mountains in Southern California. Although their climates and environments differed greatly, all of these tribes had one important thing in common: they hunted cooperatively for sparsely scattered, nonmigratory game. In each case the cooperating band usually consisted of about 50 or 60 persons who occupied an area of some 400 square miles and claimed exclusive hunting rights to it. Since men could hunt more efficiently in familiar terrain, they remained throughout life in the territory of their birth. The band consequently consisted of persons related through the male line of

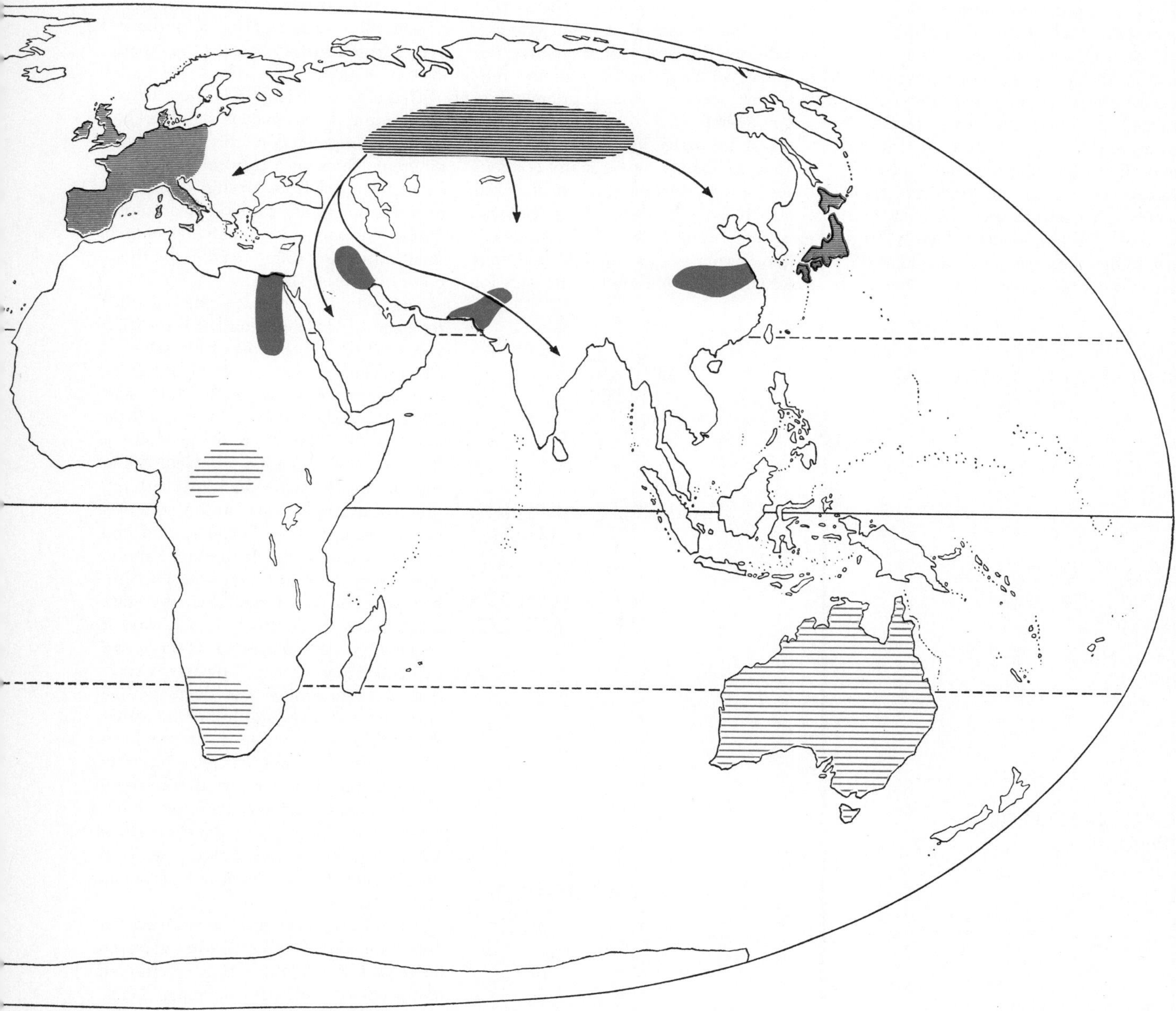

descent, and it was required that wives be taken from other bands. In sum, the cultural effects of this line of evolution were band localization, descent in the male line, marriage outside the group, residence of the wife with the husband's band and control by the band of the food resources within its territory.

Another line of evolution is exemplified by rubber-farming Mundurucú Indians in the Amazon Valley and fur-trapping Algonquian Indians in eastern Canada, of whom Murphy and I recently made a comparative study. The common feature in these two groups is that both were transformed by contact with an outside economy from simple farmers or hunters to barterers for manufactured goods. Although the aboriginal Mundurucú villagers and the Algonquian bands had had very different forms of social organization, both converged to the same form after they began to pursue similar ways of making a living. As the Indians came to depend on manufactured goods, such as steel axes and metal utensils, obtained from traders, they gradually gave up their independent means of subsistence and spent all their time tapping rubber trees and trapping beaver, respectively, eventually depending upon the trader for clothing and food as well as for hardware. Since tapping and trapping are occupations best carried out by small groups on separate territories, the Indians' villages and bands broke down into individual families which lived in isolation on fairly small, delimited areas. The family became part of the larger Canadian or Brazilian national society, to which it was linked through the trader. Its only relations with other families were the loose social contacts created by dealing with the same trader.

Irrigation Civilizations

Irrigation farming is the major organizing factor of another line of evolution, which covered a considerable span of the early prehistory and history of China, Mesopotamia, Egypt, the north coast of Peru, probably the Indus Valley and possibly the Valley of Mexico. This line had three stages. In the first period primitive groups apparently began to cultivate food plants along the moist banks of the rivers or in the higher terrain where rainfall was sufficient for crops. They occupied small but permanent villages. The second stage started when the people learned to divert the river waters by means of canals to irrigate large tracts of land. Irrigation farming made possible a larger population and freed the farmers from the need to spend all their time on basic food production. Part of the new-found time was put into enlarging the system of canals and ditches and part into developing crafts. This period brought the invention of loom weaving, metallurgy, the wheel, mathematics, the calendar, writing, monumental and religious architecture, and extremely fine art products.

When the irrigation works expanded so that the canals served many communities, a coordinating and managerial control became necessary. This need was met by a ruling class or a bureaucracy whose authority had mainly religious sanctions, for men looked to the gods for the rainfall on which their agriculture depended. Centralization of authority over a large territory marked the emergence of a state.

That a state developed in these irrigation centers by no means signifies that all states originated in this way. Many different lines of cultural evolution could have led from kinship groups up to multicommunity states. For example, feudal Europe and Japan developed small states very different from the theocratic irrigation states.

The irrigation state reached its florescence in Mesopotamia between 3000 and 4000 B.C., in Egypt a little later, in China about 1500 or 2000 B.C., in northern Peru between 500 B.C. and 500 A.D., in the Valley of Mexico a little later than in Peru. Then, in each case, a third stage of expansion followed. When the theocratic states had reached the limits of available water and production had leveled off, they began to raid and conquer their neighbors to exact tribute. The states grew into empires. The empire was not only larger than the state but differed qualitatively in the ways it regimented and controlled its large and diversified population. Laws were codified; a bureaucracy was developed; a powerful military establishment, rather than the priesthood, was made the basis of authority. The militaristic empires began with the Sumerian Dynasty in Mesopotamia, the pyramid-building Early Dynasty in Egypt, the Chou periods in China, the Toltec and Aztec periods in Mexico and the Tiahuanacan period in the Andes.

Since the wealth of these empires was based on forced tribute rather than on increased production, they contained the seeds of their own undoing. Excessive taxation, regimentation of civil life and imposition of the imperial religious cult over the local ones led the subject peoples eventually to rebel. The great empires were destroyed; the irrigation works were neglected; production declined; the population decreased. A "dark age" ensued. But in each center the process of empire building later began anew, and the cycle was repeated. Cyclical conquests succeeded one another in Mesopotamia, Egypt and China for nearly 2,000 years. Peru had gone through at least two cycles and was at the peak of the Inca Empire when the Spaniards came. Mexico also probably had experienced two cycles prior to the Spanish Conquest.

Our final example of a specific line of evolution is taken from more recent times. When the colonists in America pre-empted the Indians' lands, some of

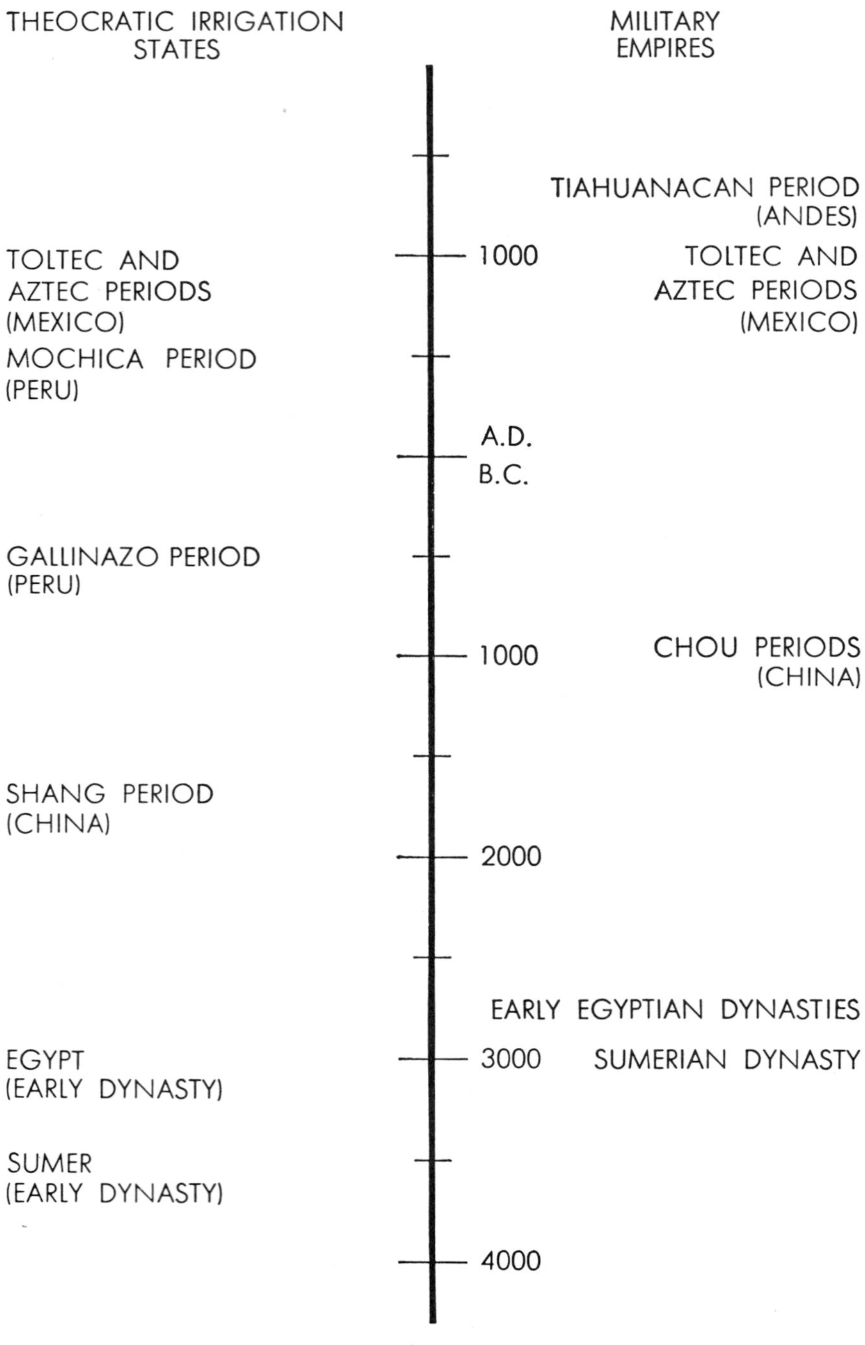

THEOCRATIC IRRIGATION STATES		MILITARY EMPIRES
		TIAHUANACAN PERIOD (ANDES)
TOLTEC AND AZTEC PERIODS (MEXICO)	1000	TOLTEC AND AZTEC PERIODS (MEXICO)
MOCHICA PERIOD (PERU)		
	A.D. / B.C.	
GALLINAZO PERIOD (PERU)		
	1000	CHOU PERIODS (CHINA)
SHANG PERIOD (CHINA)		
	2000	
		EARLY EGYPTIAN DYNASTIES
EGYPT (EARLY DYNASTY)	3000	SUMERIAN DYNASTY
SUMER (EARLY DYNASTY)		
	4000	

TIME SCALE of theocratic irrigation states and of military empires is compared in this chart. In general the theocratic irrigation states appeared before the military empires.

the Indian clans formed a new type of organization. The Ute, Western Shoshoni and Northern Paiute Indians, who had lived by hunting and gathering in small groups of wandering families, united in aggressive bands. With horses stolen from the white settlers, they raided the colonists' livestock and occasionally their settlements.

Similar predatory bands developed among some of the mounted Apaches, who had formerly lived in semipermanent encampments consisting of extended kinship groups. Many of these bands were the scourge of the Southwest for years. Some of the Apaches, on the other hand, yielded to the blandishments of the U. S. Government and settled peacefully on reservations; as a result, there were Apache peace factions who rallied around chiefs such as Cochise, and predatory factions that followed belligerent leaders such as Geronimo.

The predatory bands of North America were broken up by the U. S. Army within a few years. But this type of evolution, although transitory, was not unique. In the pampas of South America similar raiding bands arose after the Indians obtained horses. On an infinitely larger scale and making a far greater impression on history were the Mongol hordes of Asia. The armies of Genghis Khan and his successors were essentially huge mounted bands that raided entire continents.

Biology and Culture

Human evolution, then, is not merely a matter of biology but of the interaction of man's physical and cultural characteristics, each influencing the other. Man is capable of devising rational solutions to life, especially in the realm of technical problems, and also of transmitting learned solutions to his offspring and other members of his society. His capacity for speech gives him the ability to package vastly complicated ideas into sound symbols and to pass on most of what he has learned. This human potential resulted in the accumulation and social transmission of an incalculable number of learned modes of behavior. It meant the perpetuation of established patterns, often when they were inappropriate in a changed situation.

The biological requirements for cultural evolution were an erect posture, specialized hands, a mouth structure permitting speech, stereoscopic vision, and areas in the brain for the functions of speech and association. Since culture speeded the development of these requirements, it would be difficult to say which came first.

The first step toward human culture may have come when manlike animals began to substitute tools for body parts. It has been suggested, for example, that there may have been an intimate relation between the development of a flint weapon held in the hand and the receding of the apelike jaw and protruding canine teeth. An ape, somewhat like a dog, deals with objects by means of its mouth. When the hands, assisted by tools, took over this task, the prognathous jaw began to recede. There were other consequences of this development. The brain centers that register the experiences of the hands grew larger, and this in turn gave the hands greater sensitivity and skill. The reduction of the jaw, especially the elimination of the "simian shelf," gave the tongue freer movement and thus helped create the potentiality for speech.

Darwin called attention to the fact that man is in effect a domesticated animal; as such he depends upon culture and cannot well survive in a state of nature. Man's self-domestication furthered his biological evolution in those characteristics that make culture possible. Until perhaps 25,000 years ago he steadily developed a progressively larger brain, a more erect posture, a more vertical face and better developed speech, auditory and associational centers in the brain. His physical evolution is unquestionably still going on, but there is no clear evidence that recent changes have increased his inherent potential for cultural activities. However, the rate of his cultural development became independent of his biological evolution. In addition to devising tools as substitutes for body parts in the struggle for survival, he evolved wholly new kinds of tools which served other purposes: stone scrapers for preparing skin clothing, baskets for gathering wild foods, axes for building houses and canoes. As cultural experience accumulated, the innovations multiplied, and old inventions were used in new ways. During the last 25,000 years the rate of culture change has accelerated.

The many kinds of human culture today are understandable only as particular lines of evolution. Even if men of the future develop an I.Q. that is incredibly high by modern standards, their specific behavior will nonetheless be determined not by their reason or psychological characteristics but by their special line of cultural evolution, that is, by the fundamental processes that shape cultures in particular ways.

II

THE ROMANTIC VISION

THE ROMANTIC VISION II

INTRODUCTION

The romantic vision is incorporated into the archaeology of the New World in many ways. The articles in this section contain phrases that indicate, illustrate, and indeed catalyze the romantic experience. "The first," "the oldest," "the origins," "early man," "ancient," and "prehistoric" emphasize the remoteness of distant time and the unique seminal events. "Vanished people," "huge funeral mounds," submerged "Maya offerings," "gold buried in . . . prehistoric tombs," "more impressive than . . . the Romans," and "tides of civilizations and conquest" tell of the grandeur and mystery of the past. "Enigmatic subject," "lost cities," "surprising discovery," "our excitement was great" emphasize not only the elusiveness of the record of the past and the difficulty that archaeologists have in knowing it, but also the drama when the little-suspected is suddenly known. "Rubbish heap," "meager . . . archaeological evidence," "intensive archaeological expedition," "prepare accurate maps," "careful study," "history as we read it, layer by layer" indicate that archaeologists gain knowledge of the past by diligent technical analysis, focusing on minute details, of the abandoned and discarded materials of past people.

When archaeologists excavate sites, they are frequently visited by curious or interested people. Some watch; some ask questions. More often than not their questions indicate the romantic foundation for their interests and motivations. "How do you know where to dig?" "I've walked over this many times and never seen anything." "Did you find any gold?" "How old is it?" "Aren't you afraid to dig up these skeletons?" Such questions reveal a sense of wonder and mystery about the subject of the archaeologist's endeavors—the dig and the past—and about his knowledge and skills. For some visitors the excavation of a prehistoric site and the construction of a skyscraper have the same appeal. Both may be complex operations, involving several participants and a great deal of equipment, and governed by rules that are not immediately obvious but which may be discovered by careful observers. But archaeology can be much more than a fascinating technical game.

OBJECTIVES

Romanticism is an attempt to push beyond the limits of everyday experience. Everyday lives may contain the unpleasant, the unexpected, and the painful. Or they may be unrelieved continua—flat planes with landmarks and no monuments. In the romantic experience, rationality and common sense are pushed aside. The self is extended and linked to the uncommon, the remote, and the exotic. The part is one of many stages upon which self-extensions may be performed. The past, like the night, is the dominion of the gods and the dead. It is the seat of emperors, the stage upon which empires rise and fall. This stage is shrouded in mist, but we can see forms and masses moving in the twilight. Unrelieved plains are filled. Ancient cities, armies, rituals, the works of great artisans, and monuments are placed there. The unpleasant and painful facts of everyday life are lost sight of in the presence of events that are so ancient, so mysterious, so powerful, or so grand as to immerse us in awe.

In the past—during the last century and the beginning of this century—the quest for the romantic vision gave strong impetus to New World archaeology. Financed by wealthy private foundations and individuals, expeditions were mounted to explore and describe the most spectacular remains of the historic Indian cultures—the civilizations and near-civilizations. The remote fastnesses of the Americas—the U.S. Southwest, Central Mexico, Yucatan, and the Andean Highlands—were illuminated not only by expedition reports, but also by examples of rare and beautiful objects recovered. These were displayed in private collections and public museums. Thus the most immediate and striking features of these areas became known. And objects were provided that are now the subject of the discipline of primitive art.

In one sense the impetus for the romantic vision lies not in the discipline of New World archaeology, but in those who attempt to forge links with the remote and the otherworldly. Archaeology simply provides one view of other experiences. But archaeologists are sensitive to their role. When they write or speak to audiences that are innocent of the nuances of archaeological data, problems, or theories, they are often forced to try to create interest—even excitement—by telling of discoveries, rare objects, ancient happenings, and exotic places. For this reason, most articles dealing with New World archaeology in *Scientific American* during the past 25 years have focused either on the earliest occupations or on the most complex accomplishments of the prehistoric American Indians—the civilizations. By sparking the romantic vision, archaeologists can create a path to lead the educated public toward an understanding of the complexities and details of archaeological data and theory and of their views of the past.

THEORETICAL PERSPECTIVE

In one sense, there is no theory in romantic archaeology. Each person's recreation of the past is idiosyncratic. It is based on one's present needs and preconceptions about objects and events that might be exciting, valuable, and mysterious. Most important, the romantic focus is on the particular. The discovery of the tomb of a particular Maya priest, the excavation of *the* earliest artifacts, the fall of this city or that civilization, are powerful and immediate experiences, whereas general and abstract statements about such events may be no more exciting than statistical summaries of artifact frequencies. All the articles we might have reprinted here deal with particular events, and almost none of them attempt to transcend the particular to reach a more general understanding of man.

In quite another sense, there *is* a romantic theory for archaeology; it can be defined in terms of the kind of events and objects that catalyze the romantic experience. All are extraordinary. All are beyond the common and everyday. Simply to be of the past, for example, is not enough. Events were extraordinary because power was exercised by great political agencies, as during the construction of the Inca roads, the conquests of the Aztecs, or the collapse of the Maya civilization. Or power was exercised by those who spoke for the gods—the cultists, the priests, the builders of temples. Ancient gods extend their power to the present through our dread of the dead. Burial mounds and the death of civilizations produce an aweful fascination.

The mysterious power of archaeologists to reveal the past through the intricate ritual of excavation and analysis is part of romantic theory as well. By exercise of superhuman patience and care, they achieve contact with the supernatural forces of the past and link them to us in the normal world. That archaeologists do not normally have any such image of themselves is irrelevant. Romantic theory is based on views of the world that derive from present states and needs. The real world of archaeological research is no more pertinent than the real world of the past. The principle of uniformitarianism does not apply. The past was not like the present. Romantic theory cannot be tested; it is not disproven; it is simply reiterated. Change comes not from the attempt to fit theory to data, but from changing needs and definitions of the romantic.

METHOD

In the past archaeologists sought out the remote and exotic remains of the past by techniques that few, if any, would advocate or employ today. Prehistoric sites were often mined for the "goodies" they contained. Large labor forces, sometimes with little prior training, were employed whenever possible to uncover the greatest number of rare objects from the richest parts of the sites. Impoverished areas and sites were ignored. Little or no attention was given to details of the context in which objects were found. Designation of the room from which they were recovered, for example, would suffice at best. Associations with other objects, particularly if not beautiful or mysterious, were not noted. In fact, the latter were frequently discarded.

Actually, the romantic gains his "knowledge" of the past by introspective speculation, but archaeological data or work may be necessary to kindle the romantic experience, the speculation, in him. People may contact data in many ways. They may visit or join a "dig." They may visit a museum, leaf through a coffee-table folio, read a book about the past or the discovery of the past, attend lectures, see movies, or watch television. All these media depict and present objects, plausible events, and archaeological processes. Speculations can be of the moment, for the moment. They deal with what is at hand and may not extend beyond it. This *ad hoc* quality makes test and proof irrelevant. The validity of the momentary experience suffices.

DISADVANTAGES AND WIDER RELEVANCE

To the New World archaeologist, the Romantic Vision has certain disadvantages. Although it may contribute to our knowledge of ourselves in an artistic sense, such knowledge is unsystematized and unverified in a scientific sense. We may feel that a romantic reconstruction of the past seems to tell us about the condition of all men. We may feel that qualities of the past are also qualities of the present, or even that our need to experience the past in certain ways tells us of our present state. But this is a highly individual matter. Different individuals reach equally valid but quite different visions, starting from the "same" past events or objects.

A more compelling disadvantage is the destruction of the very evidence that archaeologists need to develop and verify their reconstruction of the past. The desire to possess physical links with the past in the form of objects made and used in the past has led to wholesale and thoughtless destruction of prehistoric sites, monuments, and objects. In the United States the problem is severe, but at least the "pot hunting" and "relic collecting" are usually carried out on a small scale, being individual efforts using hand tools. But in Latin America, as elsewhere in the world, our archaeological heritage is being destroyed by looters, using dynamite, helicopters, and bulldozers, despite stringent laws against the smuggling of artifacts. Wealthy American and European collectors, who perhaps are supporters of "law and order" at home, directly or indirectly support theft and vandalism abroad. This is the ugly side of the romantic vision.

Nevertheless, the romantic vision provides a sense of participation in the work of archaeologists. It attracts many to courses, to books, to films, to museum exhibits on archaeological method and on New World prehistory. It is a fact of life that at least some of the support that archaeology enjoys from the public, from institutions, and from popular journals can be traced to its romantic impact. Enjoyment, exercise of creativity without the burden of responsibility, the healthy outlet of fantasy, and the reinforcement of contemporary views of the world also are benefits of the romantic vision. Finally, let us frankly admit that New World archaeologists participate today in a vision that is no less romantic (albeit rather more abstract) than those of their predecessors: the belief that our understanding of the past will contribute to our understanding of the present and of the future.

TABLE III. Articles Employing the Romantic Perspective.

Author	*Time*	*Area*	*Strategy*
Schaedel (1951)	A.D. 1–1500	Western South America	Civilization
Von Hagen (1952)	A.D. 1500	Western South America	Civilization

THE READINGS

"The Lost Cities of Peru" by Richard P. Schaedel is only partly about cities. To be sure, Schaedel describes and depicts several temple centers and cities. Like von Hagen he refers to the grandeur of ancient Peruvian civilizations and the massive character of their material remains. But the heroes of the story are archaeologists and the excitement of the plot is in the doing of archaeology. The romantic vision of archaeology is manifested, first, in the innovative use of sophisticated technical equipment. The scientific glamour of aerial photography was still great in 1951. Today the glamour, but not the tool, has been replaced by the computer. Second, the dramatic discoveries of hidden cities during analyses of photographs and field observation are described. Archaeologists' mysterious, but technically based, expertise enables them to know what even natives had not known. Finally, archaeologists are portrayed as having superhuman endurance in the face of extraordinary difficulties—bulls, "pot holes," and presumably heat and dust. Superhuman as well is their extraordinary skill and patience. It is irrelevant that archaeologists too "sometimes must stand naked."

The work described here sheds light not only on the architectural development of religious and political centers in prehistoric coastal Peru, but also potentially on the conditions that effect urban development. Like the cases discussed in Sjoberg's article (p. 271), these data can be related to general concepts for urban form and growth. Although technically not the first cities of the New World (see Millon's article, p. 115), planned urban settlements like Chan Chan are physical indicators of complex systems of behavior. And like the Inca roads that eventually would link such centers physically, the regularity of many of these plans reflect the simplifications necessary for the evolution of complex systems.

The subject of von Hagen's article, "America's Oldest Roads," is a rare object indeed: the roads that make up an imperial highway. Von Hagen describes these roads, compares them with the roads built by the ancient civilizations of the Near East and Mediterranean, and briefly discusses the rise and fall of the Incas, builders of the roads. A sense of awe is created by the use of superlatives. Wonders of the human world, they are fabulous, the oldest. They span 10,000 miles and hundreds of bridges, hundreds of abysses. They are creations of an empire, the routes of conquerors. The Inca engineers' great expertise and the extraordinary conditions in which they and, undoubtedly, countless thousands labored express the magnitude of the accomplishment. So does the comparison with Rome—that symbol of technical skill, power, and imperial grandeur.

Von Hagen notes that the roads are related to many facets of Inca history that we do not understand well. Spanish accounts give us particulars of their use and appearance with an immediacy that archaeological accounts have not attempted. From a systematic perspective, these roads indicate the role of monumental public works, thought to be a universal characteristic of civilizations, as both the products and the creators of social and political integration. As a symbol of the ability of a central authority to mobilize resources, including personnel, for construction and maintenance and of the special extent of this authority, the roads are material reminders of political control. They also indicate the importance of rapid and unambiguous communication for the growth and maintenance of large complex systems. Without such relatively simple and "linear" mechanisms, large systems tend to flounder in their own complexity. The rapid movement of goods, personnel, and information is greatly facilitated when agents of central control invest in such mechanisms. Finally, these roads, like all roads, are physical manifestations of the social, political, and economic relationships that existed, or that the Royal Inca hoped to establish, between settlements and other "nodes."

3 The Lost Cities of Peru

by Richard P. Schaedel
August 1951

How aerial photography and the jeep combined to give an overall view of the many cultures that flourished on the north Peruvian coast before the Inca conquest

TWO technological conveniences developed in recent years have become highly useful tools in archaeology. They are the jeep and aerial photography. The jeep, a "mechanical burro" that can go almost anywhere, gives the archaeologist a relatively rapid means of reaching and reconnoitering archaeological sites in out-of-the-way places. Aerial photography adds a new dimension to exploration. Not only does it bring to light ruins in unexplored areas that might never have been discovered otherwise, but it allows the archaeologist a bird's-eye view in addition to the worm's-eye view with which he has had to be content in the past. Exploring the labyrinthine structures of an ancient civilization on the ground, he is apt to become entangled in the details and be unable to see the picture as a whole. Aerial photographs now make it possible to see the shape and scope of entire cities and civilizations of the prehistoric past.

I shall describe here how we used these two new aids to investigate the early civilizations of northern Peru, where Spanish explorers found the home of the fabulous Incas when they first came to South America in the 16th century.

Let us first sketch in what was known about ancient coastal Peru before we began our study. For at least 3,000 years before Europeans discovered them, American Indians who had settled in Peru had been building civilizations of higher and higher complexity. The North Coast of Peru is a 400-mile strip of coast, bounded on the west by the Pacific Ocean and on the east by the bleak, steep foothills of the Andes. It is a narrow ribbon of desert crossed at intervals by small rivers that flow from the hills into the Pacific. The peoples of ancient Peru lived in these river-valley oases, and the small valleys are crowded with the remains of their civilizations.

The earliest permanent settlements in the area were small fishing villages; they were in existence by 1500 B.C. or earlier. By about 800 B.C. a new people had come into the region, presumably from the highlands, and introduced an agricultural economy, based on the staples maize and yuca. This phase of the region's civilization is called Chavín. We do not know how long it lasted, but it had practically disappeared by the year A.D. 1, and during the next 1,000 years or so a number of different local cultures developed in the individual valleys. Toward the end of this period one of these cultures, called Mochica because it is believed to have originated in the valley of the Moche River, expanded and conquered much of the region. But about A.D. 1000 it in turn was overthrown by an aggressive culture from the south known as Tiahuanacoid. That occupation was short-lived. The next 200 to 300 years of Peru's history, known as the "middle period," is obscure. By about 1300, however, the picture again becomes clear: under a dynasty called the Chimu the people of the Moche Valley once more conquered the coastal lands. The Chimu empire attained splendid heights, but by 1470 it was subdued by a new invasion from the south, this time by the redoubtable Incas. The Inca occupation of the region lasted until the arrival of Pizarro in 1532.

FROM THE GROUND Galindo, a Chimu ruin near the Moche River, is hard to find. Until it was located on aerial photographs (*see opposite page*) it was unknown to archaeologists or to some people who lived nearby.

In short, the chief phases in the chronology of Peru's North Coast were the early fishing settlements, the Chavín period of the first truly agricultural communities, the development of local cultures, the emergence of the Mochica as the dominant culture, a time of invasion and conflict lasting several hundred years, unification of the entire region by the Chimu empire and finally conquest by the Incas.

IN 1948 I was called to organize an Institute of Anthropology at the University of Trujillo, the provincial capital city in the center of this region. The Peruvian authorities gave me *carte blanche* to do as I pleased, provided that my work shed more light on Peru's past. I came to the conclusion that we should take stock of the total picture before burying our noses too deeply in any one excavation. Most of what was known about the sequence of Peru's civilizations had been constructed from stratigraphic studies of pottery types. We

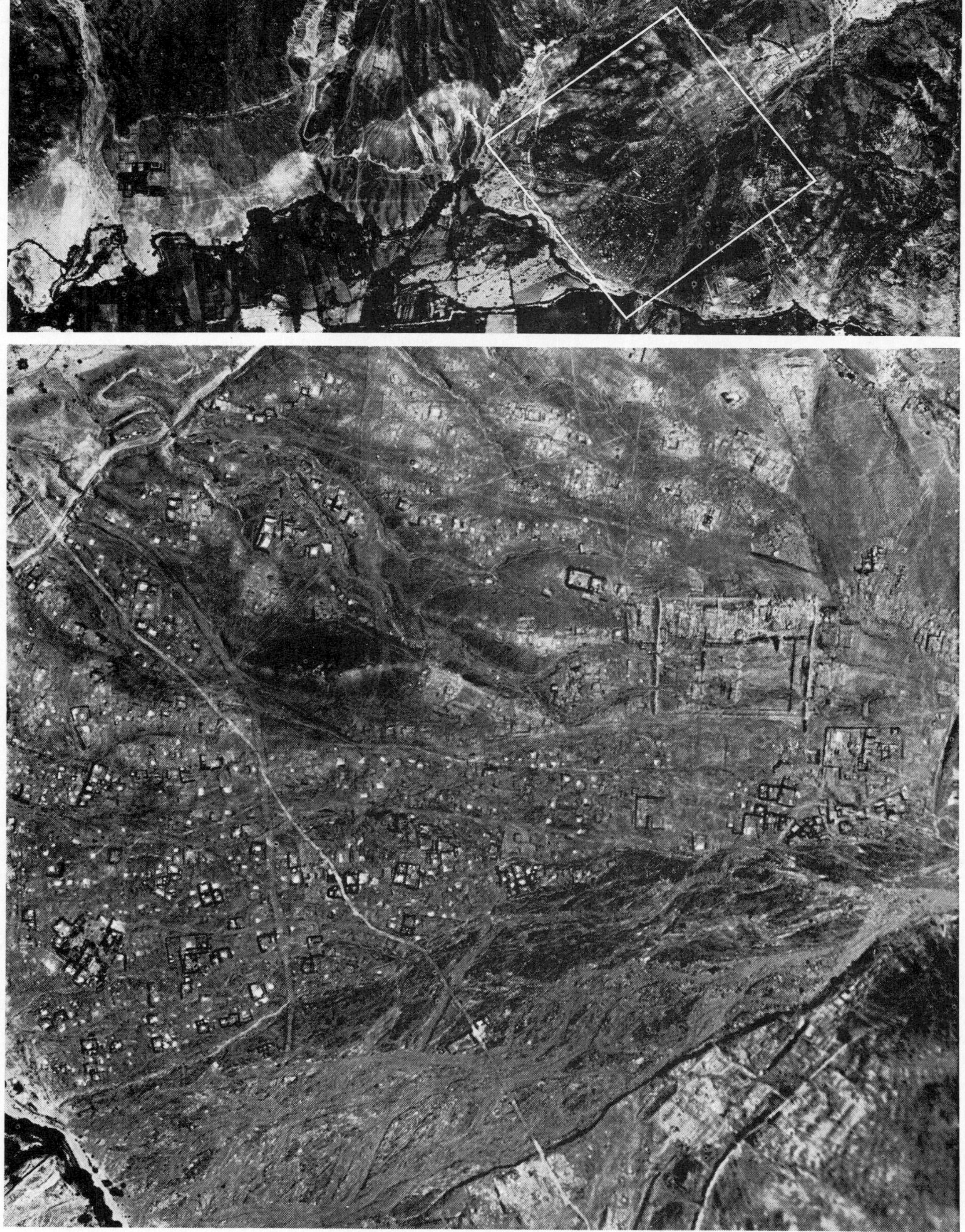

FROM THE AIR Galindo is the ruin of a teeming city. At the top of the page is the large aerial photograph on which the ruin was discovered; at the bottom is an enlargement made from the same negative. The low ramp in the photograph on the opposite page is in the large rectangular structure at upper right in the enlargement.

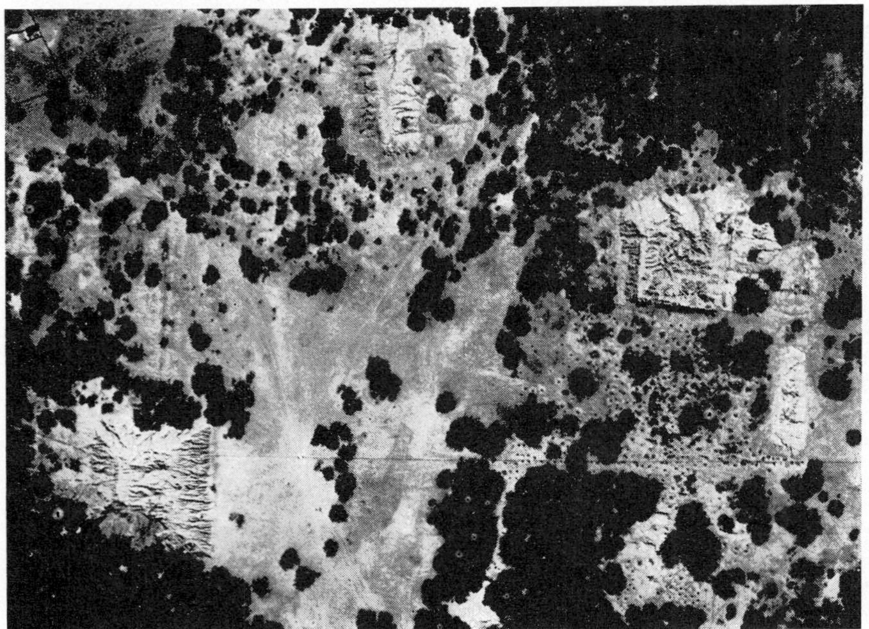

BATAN GRANDE was occupied during Chimu times but was built earlier. The photograph at the bottom is an enlargement of the one at the top. The small pits at the lower right of the enlargement were dug by grave robbers.

undertook to make a large-scale survey of the ancient settlements, temples, towns and cities with the aim of determining to what phase each belonged and placing them all in the chronological framework. Fortunately the blueprints from which this broad-scale history might be read were already in existence. Peru had an Aerial Photographic Service which had photographed or was in the process of photographing all but one of the valleys in the North Coast region.

The first phase of the survey—a reading of these photographs to locate all possible ruins in 11 coastal valleys of the North Coast—was carried out in Lima, where the photographs were kept, by Paul Kosok, chairman of the history department of Long Island University, and his son Michael. They were in Peru to study prehistoric irrigation in the very region in which we were interested. For several months the Kosoks, father and son, labored day and night over the photographs until their patience and eyesight were well-nigh exhausted. They examined thousands of prints and wherever they found what looked like walls, buildings or other signs of an ancient community they located the site with the aid of a map and ordered enlargements of the photographs. The work took great patience and skill, but it was richly rewarded; when they had finished, they brought me enlarged photographs of a tremendous number of large ruins, most of which had not been known to archaeologists before.

WITH the photographs in hand, I set out with a field crew in the jeep, which the University had provided, to find the sites and examine the ruins at closer range. Our expedition blazed a trail of many miles of jeep tracks through dense forests, across rock-strewn river beds, along old canal bottoms and over barren wastes of desert. The aerial photographs helped us to avoid most of the natural obstacles, but we had trouble with man-made ones. One of these hazards was bulls (raised for bullfighting) that were pastured near some of the ruins. Another was the numerous craterlike holes dug by "huaqueros," Peru's time-honored grave robbers, who have left few ancient ruins uninvestigated. We found also, to our surprise, that farmers had turned some of the old ruins to their own use. In some places they utilized ancient pyramids as observation towers for watching the progress of crops in the surrounding fields. Occasionally we discovered that a pyramid which had stood for 1,000 years without major alterations had been provided in the 20th century with a circular ramp for the ascent of horse or automobile.

It was surprising how seldom the aerial photographs betrayed us into visiting something that was not a ruin. To be sure, some of the ruins were not

CAJAMARQUILLA, a huge ruin near Lima on the central coast of Peru, was inhabited as late as the Inca conquest. It sheltered some tens of thousands of people. Although the many walled structures of the city appear to be separated by streets, they are not; the people probably moved about by walking on top of the walls.

as impressive on the ground as they were from the air. We were somewhat disappointed, for example, when we reached one ruin in the Lambayeque Valley which the photograph had indicated to be of enormous extent. Its main pyramid proved to be gutted, little was left of its ancient walls and some of the old lines that showed in the photograph were virtually invisible on the ground.

On the other hand, in many places we were very pleasantly surprised to find the structures much more magnificent on the ground than they had seemed in the photographs. One of these was a ruin, previously unknown, in the Nepena Valley. This site, called Punkuri Alto, showed only as a vague outline in the aerial photograph. It stood on a hilltop, and the ruins of its adobe buildings blended with the bare rock on which it was reared. But when we reached it in our jeep, we found an impressive, palace-like building with terraced platforms and a series of corridors leading to upper rooms. We were delighted to discover the remains of a geometric frieze lining one of the corridors.

Among our problems was the fact that it was sometimes not easy to distinguish ruins from farms in the aerial photographs. The farmers of modern Peru have unintentionally camouflaged some of the old ruins by using well-built ancient walls to mark off sections of their fields. Their newer fences and boundary walls often merge with the walls of the old compounds.

WE WERE struck by the fact that often one might ride to within a few hundred feet of truly huge ruins and still be unaware of them. This is partly due to the fact that many of the ancient hillside towns were built on the leveled terraces of the hill, either of adobe or of stone and rubble from the same hill, and few of them had walls high enough to cast large shadows until late afternoon. Thus they were often hard to pick out from the natural hillside, and were also difficult to photograph. Only in late afternoon do Peruvian coastal ruins become photogenic.

Perhaps the most striking case of a large hidden city is the one named Galindo. The main highway to the north highlands in Peru today passes close by these ruins, and the site is within 20 miles of Trujillo. Yet no archaeologist had ever before laid eyes on this ancient town, which runs for about five miles beside the highway. It is effectively blocked

PHOTOGRAPH OF EL PURGATORIO, a massive ruin on the Leche River, shows some structures in sharp outline and others as shapeless masses. The elevated structure at the upper left is some 1,200 feet long.

from view by a high fence that borders the highway, and it is also screened off by vegetation, so that the ruin is visible only from one rise in the road, and then only if the observer knows it is there.

After I had shown slides of Galindo before a class of students in the University of Trujillo, one of the girls came up after class to inquire where this town really was. It turned out she had lived within 10 minutes' walk of the ruin all her life and had never heard of it!

By the time we had finished our reconnaissance, we were able to answer some of the questions we had set out to study. We defined the geographical extent of the Mochica culture and of the later Tiahuanacoid conquest, located the main provincial capitals of the Chimu empire and mapped the locations of the Inca garrisons on the North Coast. We were also able to determine that three main cultures had fought for control of the region during the confused "middle period," and to identify these cultures.

In addition, our reconnaissance yielded some information on a more interesting and important matter—the origin of the first cities in America. The Mochicas and their contemporaries did not build cities, although they did construct some of the largest pyramids in South America. Their typical capital consisted of several large adobe pyramids grouped around a central plaza. Only a limited group of priests, chiefs and artisans lived in these ceremonial centers; the rest of the population dwelt in the countryside. True cities did not arrive until several hundred years later, when the Chimus erected their magnificent metropolis called Chan Chan. The Chimus were the first civilization in the Western Hemisphere to cross the threshold of urbanization.

The towns of the "middle period," between the fall of the Mochicas and the rise of the Chimus, represent the be-

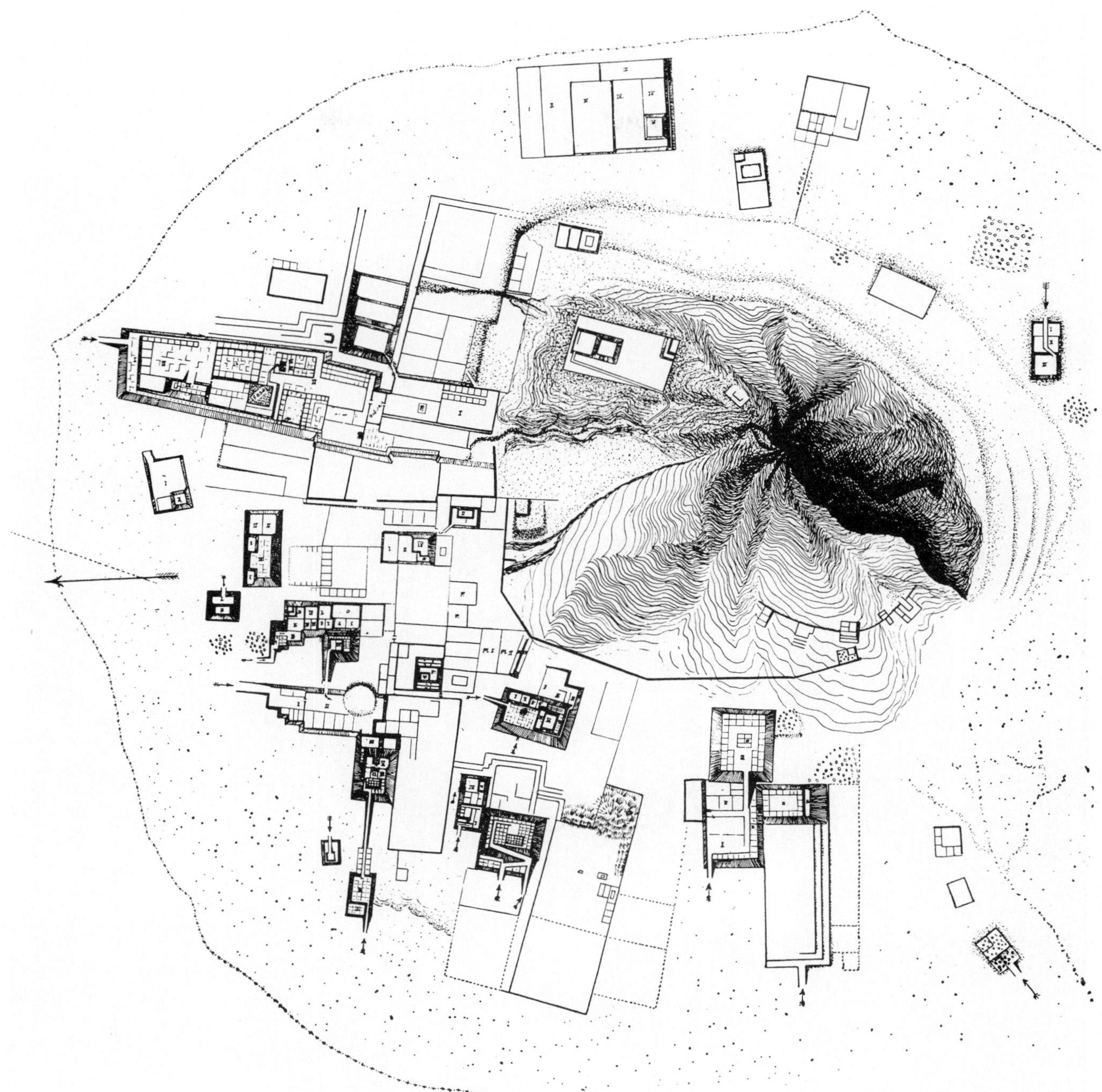

DRAWING OF EL PURGATORIO is a partial reconstruction based on ground surveys and the aerial photograph on the opposite page. The elevated structures of El Purgatorio were built with an eye to defense.

ginnings of city life. And here in coastal Peru we had an unusual opportunity to study how cities began, for the sites of the towns and of the metropolises that came later stand side by side, whereas in the Old World the former are buried beneath the latter. Thus from the data revealed by the aerial photographs we could work out the origin and development of city life in more detail in Peru than anywhere else in the world.

On the basis of these photographs and first-hand reconnaissance at the sites we have been able to draw ground plans of some of the town sites. One of these is illustrated in the photograph and drawing above. This town, called El Purgatorio, is built around a large natural hill in the center of the well-watered plain of the Leche Valley. The main buildings, dating from the "middle period," are clustered at the north end. These large pyramids with numerous room divisions are transitional building types between the solid pyramids of the earlier Mochica period and the later truly urban compounds, in which all the building space was given to rooms. It is likely that they were palaces housing several families of the ruling class, along with servants and craftsmen. At the southern and southwestern sides of the ruin are remains of what appear to be old pyramid complexes.

Until the last decade the quantity, size and complexity of ancient Peruvian towns and cities could only be guessed at. Aerial photography has made it possible for us to comprehend them for the first time in their large-scale significance. Let us hope that the sandy mantle that has covered them for centuries will be lifted soon to reveal the internal functioning of these thriving metropolises of prehistoric Peru.

GREAT WALL runs up into the Peruvian highlands near the Veru River. The wall marked the boundary between the Inca empire and Chimu kingdom. In the 15th century the Incas attacked and absorbed the Chimus.

America's Oldest Roads

by Victor W. von Hagen
July 1952

The highways of the Incas, which are in many respects more impressive than those of the Romans, are now to be explored for the light they shed on the life of the Peruvian empire

THE BRIDGE of San Luis Rey, which snapped its cables on the morning of July 20, 1714, and hurled a company of travelers into the gorge of the Apurímac River below, was part of a road system that is one of the wonders of human history. This 200-foot suspension bridge and hundreds of others like it had been built by the ancient Incas of Peru to carry their fabulous roads over the abysses of their mountainous empire. The Incas had a network of 10,000 miles of paved highways, stretching from Chile to Colombia and from the Pacific across the Andes to the jungle headwaters of the Amazon, that ranks with the road systems of Rome, Persia and other ancient empires. Though far less celebrated than the famous roads of Rome, the Inca highways are in many respects even more remarkable. A century and a half ago the explorer Alexander von Humboldt, retracing the remnants of the Inca roads, rapturously pronounced them "the most stupendous and useful works ever executed by man."

All great conquerors have perforce been great road builders, and when an empire dies, its roads may be its most durable and revealing monument. Much that we know of the political and social structure of the Roman empire we learned from the Roman roads. The Inca highway system, which so far has been little studied, may similarly hold answers to many of the still unanswered questions about the Inca civilization: its engineering and commerce, its geographical and political organization, its relations with the tribes conquered by the Inca rulers. Within a few months an expedition under the author's direction will begin a two-year exploration of the ancient Peruvian roads to seek light on these questions.

There was a period of some 400 years (before Napoleon reconstructed the Roman roads in Europe) when the royal road of the Incas was, so far as we know, the only decent highway system in the world. For centuries the culture of Europe was literally bogged down in mud, and it was said that a traveler needed "a falcon's eye, an ass's ears, a monkey's face, a merchant's words, a camel's back, a hog's mouth, a deer's feet" to survive his journey. By contrast, in South America during that period Inca couriers were carrying messages from Quito to Cusco, a distance of 1,500 miles along the ridges of the Andes, in five days. What makes the ancient Peruvian road unique, however, is not its extent nor its excellence but the fact that it was built by a people who had

SEACOAST HIGHWAY of the Incas runs past a pyramid in the Peruvian desert of Chicama. Here the road is 30 feet wide. On either side of it are adobe walls that were built to keep the sand from blowing over the road.

INCA CAPITAL of Cusco was the focus of the roads. Shown here in the center of the city is the Square of Huakypata that has survived since the time of the Incas. From it roads ran to the north, south, east and west.

SUSPENSION BRIDGE across a stream in the Andes is typical of the larger structures that were built by the Incas. The bridges were suspended from heavy cables of vegetable fiber that were anchored to stone piers.

never heard of the wheel. The Incas built the greatest footpath in history.

It is not to be supposed from this that the Peruvian system was an affair of mountain tracks and jungle trails. It was built broad, straight and solid, and it carried a heavy traffic: llama trains laden with produce and tribute and gold, soldiers on their way out to guard or extend the boundaries of the realm, relays of messengers trotting from one center to another on a schedule not unlike the pony express of the American West.

IN MAIN PLAN the Peruvian road system took the form of two parallel turnpikes—one along the ocean, the other high in the mountains. The two roads, running the length of the empire, were connected at intervals by laterals that knifed through the hills at terrifying grades. The coastal road, 30 feet wide, ran 800 level miles through a desert so dry that rain falls there only once in 25 years; it was bordered on either side by a waist-high wall of sun-baked adobe to hold back the drift of sand. The mountain road, about 15 feet wide, traversed territory of such overpowering difficulty that its engineering feats were not duplicated until the railroad builders of the 19th century opened up much of the same region.

The Inca construction engineers followed a simple rule in laying out their roads: they ignored all obstacles and ran their lines over the shortest route, straight across the face of the land. Over marshes the road became a causeway, so well built that parts of it are still in use. When the road came to a lake, it was securely floated on balsa pontoons. When it came to a chasm, the engineers flung a bridge across it. They made no concession to steep rock walls; when they encountered one, they either tunneled right through it or cut steps and went over the top. And all this was built in a clime as inhospitable as the moon—at an average altitude of about 13,000 feet, where the thinness of the air exhausts men and the glare of the sun on the snowcaps blinds them. The labor gangs that built the road were drafted from the villages along its route, and the state levied a special tax (in produce; the Incas had no money) for the road's maintenance.

Perhaps the greatest achievements of the Inca engineers were their suspension bridges. These spans look gossamer-frail, but they were strongly made of six-inch fiber cables anchored in solid masonry and laid with a floor of wooden laths lashed together and covered with coarse matting. Marvelously well wrought also were the paved sections of the roads near cities; the paving blocks, laid without mortar, fitted so perfectly that a knife blade could not be forced between them.

At intervals of 4 to 12 miles along the entire 2,000 miles of the system, the engineers put up wayside houses—like the refreshment stations along today's turnpikes. These large, single-roomed caravanserais were always stocked with food and kept in repair against the weather. There was also a separate chain of posthouses, maintained for the royal messengers, who were specially selected and trained to travel at high speed in the thin atmosphere.

In 1545 a young Spanish soldier named Pedro Cieza de Léon rode the whole length of the main road. He kept a travel diary on the journey, and it is from his notes that we know so much of what the system was like at the time of the Incas. Cieza de Léon began his journey at Quito, near the northern terminal, and traveled south 2,000 miles over the mountain route, stopping nights at the roadhouses. He describes these houses as being "the width of 21 feet and the length as much as a horse's gallop, all made of stone, embellished with huge wooden beams, over which a straw-thatch is laid with much skill." He found that where the "mountains were rocky, the road was made in steps, having great resting places and paved ways which are so strong that they will endure for many ages." Approaching the bridge of San Luis Rey over the Apurímac, the road was "much broken by mountains and declivities so that those Indians who constructed it must have given much labor in breaking up the rocks and leveling the ground, especially where it descends to the river. Here the road is so precipitious that some of the horses, overladen with gold and silver, have fallen in without the possibility of their being saved. There are two enormous stone pillars to which the bridge of the Apurímac is secured." Throughout the whole extraordinarily hostile terrain, the young traveler noted that the road was "level and paved, along mountain slopes well excavated, by the mountain's edge well terraced, through the living rock cut, along the rivers supported by walls, in the snowy heights with steps and resting

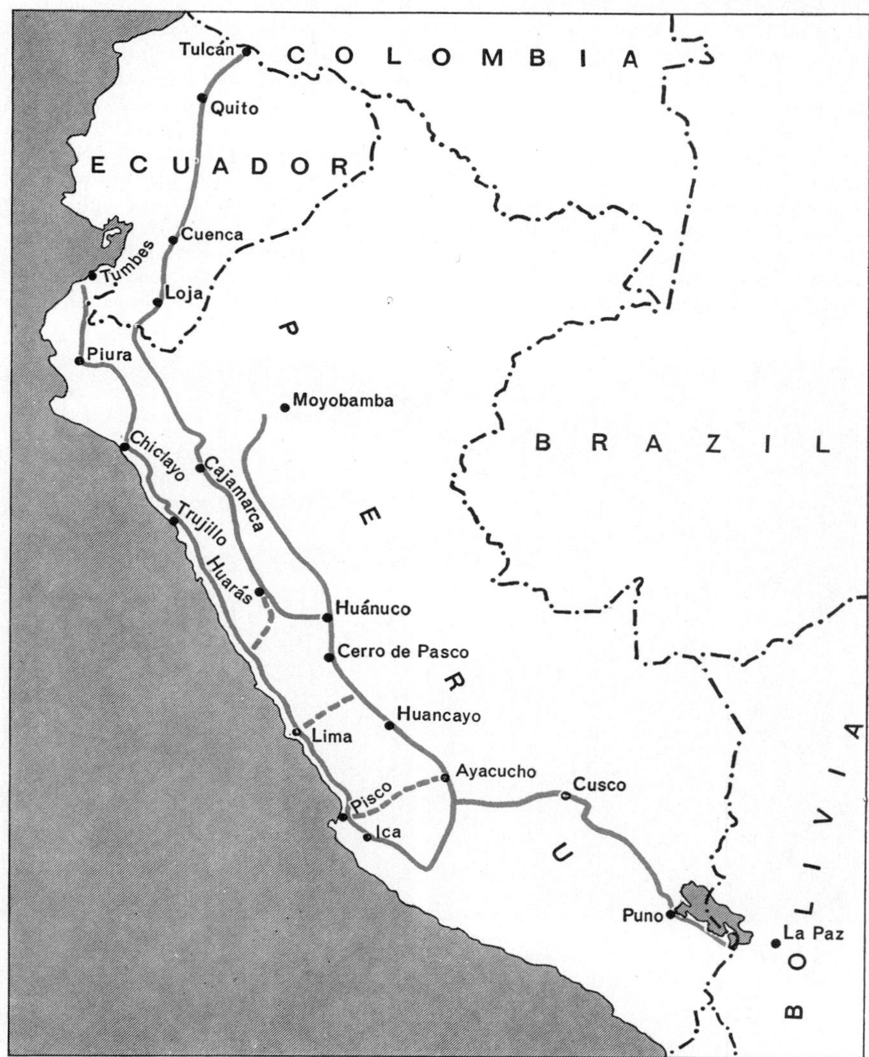

PRINCIPAL ROADS *(solid red lines)* **ran along the seacoast and through the Andes. At several places the systems were connected** *(dotted lines)*.

places, in all parts clean, swept clear of debris, with stone storehouses and temples of the sun set at intervals."

THE BUILDERS of this road, the Inca rulers, came from a tribe that had lived on the shores of Lake Titicaca. They were large-lunged, short, stocky Indians with coarse jet-black hair and jet-black eyes set at a Mongolian slant. They cultivated the bean, the potato and other tubers, and built their houses of adobe and their temples of well-cut stone. The Incas were originally only one small tribe among many spread up and down the range of the Andes. Then in the 11th century, about the time of the Battle of Hastings, this tribe began to expand. By the year 1200 they had moved into a large fertile valley north of their birthplace and had built their first city, which they called Cusco. There the dynasty of the divine Incas was established, and from their capital the Peruvians spread out steadily for a period of 300 years. One after another the smaller Andean tribes tumbled into the empire, until by 1500 the Incas controlled a vast region, now occupied by Peru, Ecuador, Bolivia and substantial parts of Chile, Argentina and Brazil.

The Peruvians built their cities mostly of stone. They perched fortresses on the mountaintops, and from the profits of empire they raised sun temples whose exteriors were faced with beaten gold. They greatly extended the fertile terraces on the slopes of the Andes, inherited from an earlier culture, and built large, complicated irrigation systems to water them. Granaries against famine were spotted throughout the realm. And wherever the Inca extended his empire, his road followed the conquest. It became at last a gigantic network weaving the disparate regions of South America—the desert coast, the high Andes and the humid jungle—into a unity of empire.

All the great roads of antiquity are somewhat akin: they were all royal roads, built at the command of the ruler, dedicated to the service of the ruler and traveled upon only by permission of the ruler. Roads began to appear in Asia Minor soon after the wheel was invented around 3500 B.C. By 1200 B.C. road engineers were attached to the army of the Assyrians and built a road "made shining like the light of day" for military and ceremonial purposes. The royal road to Jehovah in the Talmud had bordering trees pruned to the height of a camel's head; Herodotus knew from old documents that Darius in the fifth century B.C. built a stone-paved road from Susa to Babylon and that on it the journey was marked by milestones and broken by posthouses. Egypt began her formal roadbeds—as did the Incas—by building them to the stone quarries. By the 12th century B.C. Ramses II had run them throughout Egypt. In Karnak there was a stone avenue lined by sphinxes and lotus-crowned columns and "glistening with marigolds at its sides."

It was the Romans, however, who wrote the great epic of road building in the ancient world. As early as 500 B.C. Roman tracks and gravel beds were common, and by 100 B.C. the double pressure of conquest and commerce had developed the system to the point where highways spread throughout Italy, Asia Minor and into the kingdom of the Franks. The Roman roads and the Inca roads were much alike: both systems had night stations at approximately the same intervals, both were kept up by public levies and both were so well constructed that extensive sections of them today provide the beds for modern highways. However, unlike the Romans, who allowed everyone to travel freely over their highways, the Incas reserved theirs for royalty's purposes; common people traveled on them only at the monarch's pleasure and had to use separate bridges, paying a toll each time for the privilege.

LIKE THE ROMANS, the Incas built their roads primarily for conquest, then for tribute and finally for commerce and communication. In the end their superb highway system became the avenue for easy conquest of the Incas themselves. The Spanish invader found the Incas' excellent roads an open route to the heart of the country. After the coming of the *conquistadores* in 1537, the main Inca road fell rapidly into disrepair. Its destruction was begun by heavy Spanish oxcarts (for which the road was not intended), was continued by the beat of horses' hoofs, and was made permanent by lack of upkeep. The Spaniards, intent on funneling out the riches of the country, were interested primarily in the laterals that would take them quickly out of the mountains and down to the rivers and the sea.

When Cieza de Léon traveled over the road eight years after the conquest, Cusco was still the center of Inca culture and the main source of wealth for the Spaniard. It was also the hub from which the road's branches spread out through the empire. The land, Cieza de Léon noted, "was called *Tahua-ntin suyu*—literally, the-land-of-the-four-directions." Toward the end of his journey, this conscientious soldier burst out: "I believe that since the history of man has been recorded, there has been no account of such grandeur as is to be seen in this road which passes over deep valleys and lofty mountains by snowy heights and over falls of water, through living rock and along the edges of furious torrents. . . . Oh, what greater things can be said of Alexander or of any of the powerful kings who had ruled in the world, than that they have made such a road as this and conceived the works which were required for it!"

CULVERT in Cusco shows how the Incas built these structures. Although the Incas did not possess the wheel, their highways were paved with fitted stones.

III

TIME-SPACE SYSTEMATICS: GAPSMANSHIP

TIME-SPACE SYSTEMATICS: GAPSMANSHIP III

INTRODUCTION

Having examined the romantic element in archaeological research, we can look at the systematic attempts to develop regional chronologies. As a result of romanticism, numerous sites in many areas of North and South America had been found, explored, excavated, and interpreted according to the best standards at the time. They were the mysterious, the exciting, the largest, and the earliest sites. The results of an archaeological age of discovery had come into the hands of the scholars through the professional journals, into the hands of the educated public through such magazines as *National Geographic* and the *London Illustrated News*. The old geographical voyages of discovery had become time voyages. Great explorations had been made into Mayan Mexico, Incan Peru, the Anasazi Southwest, as well as other parts of the New World.

The problem with all great exploratory voyages, geographical or temporal, has been that the destination or goal could not be chosen before the explorers embark—for the goal was precisely what lay in the unknown. The result was a patchwork quilt of knowledge and ignorance. The vast majority of the archaeological maps of time and space could still have been decorated with hippogryphs, unicorns, and mermaids, but at least the very rough outline of culture history could be perceived and the major problems could be recognized.

OBJECTIVES

A generation of archaeologists, recognizing the limitations of a romantic approach, realized that no synthetic histories, no reconstructions of cultures, and no scientific generalizations could be made until the gaps in the archaeological record were systematically filled in. They wanted to answer the questions "When?" and "Where?" Later there would be time to answer questions about how and why cultural events had taken place. Gapsmanship was the prerequisite to culture history. It was time to forego the romantic, exploratory voyages into the totally unknown, time for the careful natural historian to fill in the areas which were known to be unknown. Thus, Mayer-Oakes' article concerns the examination of a site which is thought to be the missing link between North and South American populations. Anderson's examination of Onion Portage is to document human occupation in the Arctic prior to 10,000 B.C., by which time there is clearcut evidence of human activity in Arizona and Mexico, for otherwise there would be a temporal and spatial gap.

The objectives then were:

1. To examine the archaeological record holistically, as a chronological

history of an area (not just examine a single site, a single set of buildings, or a set of beautiful artifacts).

2. To classify the archaeological sites and artifacts and the total record into meaningful units in order to develop chronologies.

3. To determine criteria for developing chronologies based on radiocarbon dating, stratigraphy, dendrochronology, seriation, and other dating techniques.

4. To order all the available data into a logical (and hopefully real) time and space framework.

All the articles in this section meet these objectives, though some (for example, Lanning and Patterson) do so more explicitly than others.

THE THEORETICAL PERSPECTIVE

The theoretical perspective under which this generation practiced was never explicitly formulated. There was never a school, although there were spokesmen to whose implicit assumptions the profession generally adhered. There was an unstated belief in the great chain of being, i.e., that the domain of cultural materials, like other domains, could be divided into "natural types." These types had a reality for the native manufacturer as well as for the archaeological analyst. They were cultural analogues to the divisions making up the Linnean classification, which reflected biological and analytical reality. The similarities do not end there. Both systems were hierarchically arranged, and the names, wares, types, and traditions were cultural corollaries to species, genera, and phyla. Furthermore, both systems were static; the "types" could not mutate from one category to another until the appropriate Darwins appeared much later upon their intellectual scenes. The categories were based on comparing specimens to an "ideal type" or first-recognized "type specimens." Since the latter were generally isomorphic with the former, the literature of this period is not only replete with missing cultures, links, and gaps, but filled with new types, links, and cultures which make the gaps intellectually significant to the analysts.

Mayer-Oakes' article, "Early Man in the Andes," is a good example. "What was needed was the discovery of a tool assemblage of sufficient size and richness to show relations among the various sites in South America and perhaps also a link to North American origins." The materials found at the El Inga site, the new link, are systematically compared to types found and defined at other sites in the New World. New El Inga types are defined where no previous type specimens from other sites are comparable to the El Inga material. Anderson's article demonstrates the hierarchy of categories. He defines a "tradition" as "a continuity of cultural traits that persist over a considerable length of time and often occupy a broad geographical area." Traditions are made up of groups of cultures whose "distinctive remains" he terms "complexes." From the base of the Onion Portage site, he classifies his materials into the American Paleo-Arctic Tradition, which is made up of the Kobuk and Akmak complexes.

RELEVANCE AND INTERPRETATIONS

The increasing systematic empiricism of this period was in many ways a reflection of the growing empirical bias of the other subdisciplines of anthropology. Ever since Boas had told his students to collect the ethnographic data with particular attention to cultural attributes, the discipline had become more and more data-oriented. The time-space systematists were applying Boasian empiricism to the past. What was critical was to find the archaeological data whose attributes would allow one to determine which types were present. One could then place the sites or cultures in their appropriate time-space position.

However, it would be unfair to these scholars to believe that their work was only substantive and chronological, and never interpretive. Interpretations were made, often as an afterthought, about the reality of cultural areas, cultural events, and cultural processes such as diffusion. Underlying these limited interpretations was the implicit acceptance of Wissler's and Kroeber's age-area concept; this concept is that the time needed for diffusion is directly related to the distance from the center of a cultural area, where innovation takes place, to the periphery of the area, where similar material objects are found. Cruxent and Rouse, however, provide a good example of a study in which the interpretation is not an afterthought. They explicitly attempt to find out from where and when man migrated into the Caribbean, and they effectively use time-space systematics to show that it was not a single or contemporaneous process.

METHODS

The methods that these archaeologists used were straightforward, pragmatic, and empirical. First, they determined that there was a gap in the record. This gap usually resulted from one of two causes. They found materials when excavating or surveying sites in known areas which did not fit into the already established classification and chronology of the area, and which therefore needed to be explained. Similarly inconsistent data were observed as archaeologists explored previously unexplored areas. These new data showed that new chronologies, cultural areas, and type classifications had to be formulated. The authors had to show both the reality and the greater efficacy of their classifications and chronologies. These were substantiated by new and more refined dates arrived at by such techniques as dendrochronology or radiocarbon dating. Finally, the entire chronology and cultural record had to be reformulated so that the old sites and materials could be reclassified into this new, more accurate scheme. All the articles in this section show this reclassification process.

Methodologically, there were three innovations for which these scholars were perhaps most responsible. They were (1) seriation, i.e., dating based on the style of cultural artifacts, (2) careful refinement of the nature of archaeological classification, and (3) the building of long-term chronologies based on the recognition that common units are needed to allow the work of many scholars to interdigitate.

SUMMARY: ADVANTAGES AND DISADVANTAGES

The major contribution of this group of scholars was that, by the time their work was completed, the major gaps in the time-space framework of New World archaeology were filled. A clear chronology had been developed, able to combine the work of many scholars. One need only note the large regional scope or the long time periods represented by the articles in this section (see Table IV) to recognize the wholistic approach which the authors are taking.

However, the greatest disadvantage of this work was that the means had become the ends. Originally, the development of time-space systematics had been a first step to solve problems and answer questions about the nature of cultural development and to help discover why and how people had lived. However, these questions not only took second place, but became for some scholars not even the appropriate domain for responsible research in archaeology. Some of the time-space systematists had come to feel that the original problems were problems of speculative history and speculative sociology. The result was that archaeology was tending to become a wasteland of trivial classificatory differences that musty scholars would argue over in trying to put each tiny piece of the jigsaw puzzle of where and when into its appropriate place. Needless to say, this was not the universal situation, and it was rapidly changed by the reconstructionists.

TABLE IV. Articles Employing the Perspective of Time-Space Systematics.

Author(s)	*Time*	*Area*	*Adaptive strategy*
Lanning and Patterson (1967)	10,000 ± 2000 years B.C.	South America	Hunting-gathering
Mayer-Oakes (1963)	6–8000 years B.C.	Ecuador	Hunting-gathering
Anderson (1968)	Pre-(?) 6500 B.C. (and to A.D. 1000)	Alaskan Arctic	Hunting-gathering
Cruxent and Rouse (1969)	5000 B.C. to A.D. 1500	West Indies	Hunting-gathering and agriculture

THE READINGS

Lanning and Patterson's "Early Man in South America" presents data from the Cerro Chivateros site in the lower Chillon Valley in Peru. Although several workers recognized the existence of early man in South America and the reality of three separate industries, there was no proof that any of the materials belonged to the late Pleistocene. A key radiocarbon date, and careful geological analysis of the stratigraphy of the Cerro Chivateros site, allow the authors to develop a relative chronology for the burin, biface, and chopper industries of Argentina, Chile, Peru, Ecuador, and Venezuela, and to relate these industries to the late Pleistocene climatic sequence of Peru, Chile and Colombia. They are then able to relate the stratigraphy of their site to the climatic sequences of the rest of South America and the classic sequence of Scandanavia.

"Early Man in the Andes" is William J. Mayer-Oakes' discussion of the implications of the excavation at the El Inga site in Andean Ecuador. The excavation and surface collection of more than 5,000 square feet during two field seasons revealed a rich obsidian assemblage. The material is systematically examined by stylistic and functional types. New types are invented for materials without precedent in other sites, and the assemblage is dated by examining the relative sequence of diagnostic types. Two sets of interpretations are made. First, the materials provide a link between cultures in North and South America. Second, the site is not merely a hunter's kill site, but a combination workshop and campsite.

Douglas Anderson's article, "A Stone Age Campsite At the Gateway to America," presents new data from the Onion Portage site on the Kobuk River in northwestern Alaska. The site, originally excavated by the late T. L. Giddings in 1941 and 1964 (see p. 92), continues to provide important chronological and cultural data under Anderson's direction. This article relates the stratigraphic and cultural sequences of the site. The earliest cultures, which Anderson defines as the Akmak and Kobuk complexes, provide data on early man near the suggested Beringian gateway to the New World. It partially fills the previous chronological gap that had appeared when there was clear evidence of early man in the Southwestern United States and Mexico by 10,000 B.C., but little Alaskan evidence of man prior to 3,000 B.C. Methodologically, it shows the importance of careful and complete stratigraphic analysis and the value of hierarchical archaeological classification for organizing complex cultural data into a series of meaningful traditions.

Cruxent and Rouse's "Early Man in the West Indies" uses time-space systematics to examine man's entrance into the West Indies. A series of alternative hypotheses are suggested for man's date of arrival, route, and method of transportation into the West Indies. After martialing the temporal and spatial evidence, and relating it to the new excavations of Casimira and Mordan in the Dominican Republic, each alternative is carefully considered. A Central American paleo-Indian migration is demonstrated to be the most likely alternative. Cruxent and Rouse clearly show that neither man's entrance nor the cultural development was a unified or contemporaneous process within the West Indies.

5 Early Man in South America

by Edward P. Lanning and Thomas C. Patterson
November 1967

Stone tools indicate that men lived in South America no less than 14,000 years ago. The oldest clearly dated tools in North America are 2,000 years younger, suggesting that other tools may be older

Archaeological investigations over the past 40 years have greatly extended the known span of man's presence in the New World. Once regarded as latecomers who scarcely predated 1000 B.C., the immigrant hunters from Asia who first populated both continents of the Western Hemisphere now appear to have arrived no less than 14,000 years ago, at a time when the last Pleistocene ice sheet still covered much of the land. Firm evidence pointing in this direction came to light in 1926, when expertly made flint projectile points were discovered near Folsom, N.M., in association with the bones of an extinct species of bison. Ten years later, when stone tools of equally fine workmanship were unearthed along with the dung of extinct ground sloths in caves near the southern tip of South America, it became increasingly clear that man not only had reached the New World earlier than had been thought but also had spread swiftly throughout the hemisphere. A little more than a decade later the development of carbon-14 dating proved that the South American cave discoveries were at least 8,000 years old and perhaps as much as 3,000 years older. Work at a variety of archaeological sites in South America since then strongly suggests an even greater antiquity for man in the New World.

Apart from specialists in South American archaeology, few have been aware of this trend. One reason is that the new findings contradict the accepted view of man as a post-Pleistocene newcomer to the Western Hemisphere. To understand how this view developed it is necessary to go back briefly to the mid-19th century. In 1842 the Danish naturalist Peter Wilhelm Lund found human bones mixed with the remains of both ancient and contemporary animals in a cave near the town of Lagoa Santa in Brazil. He concluded that men much like the Indians of historic times might have arrived in eastern South America while ground sloths, horses and camels—all later extinct—still roamed the area. Lund was cautious about his conclusion. He made it clear that the association of human and animal remains at Lagoa Santa might have been due to a mixing of bones of various ages by natural causes.

Lund's work went largely unnoticed until late in the 19th century, when the Argentine paleontologists Florentino and Carlos Ameghino called attention to South America by their claim of having found the remains of early man on the pampas. The Ameghinos reported site after site in Argentina at which human bones and man-made objects were discovered in apparent association with ground sloths and other extinct South American mammals such as glyptodonts and toxodonts. Obsessed with these finds, Florentino Ameghino went on to claim the Argentine pampas as the original birthplace of the human species.

In 1910 the American physical anthropologist Aleš Hrdlička and his colleague Bailey Willis went to South America to review Ameghino's evidence. They rejected his claims—and Lund's as well—on two grounds. The first was that the associations had not been well established. The second was that the human bones were all "modern" and hence could not be very old. Today the latter argument is known to be wrong; "modern" man has existed in the Old World for at least 30,000 years. Hrdlička and Willis' criticism of the field evidence, however, was generally sound. For example, human remains had been removed from their original location without any effort to determine whether they were genuinely contemporaneous with the remains of Pleistocene animals or whether they had come from graves dug at a later time.

Having done a service by showing that Lund's and Ameghino's claims were unsupported by the existing evidence, Hrdlička and Willis unfortunately did not leave well enough alone. They went on to reach the conclusion that man could not have arrived in South America until quite recently. Essentially their reasoning was that, because the evidence for great antiquity was not conclusive, the possibility of any antiquity had to be dismissed. This *non sequitur* was accepted as the final word and for nearly three decades thereafter no reputable archaeologist undertook to study early man in South America.

It was not until 1937 that Junius B. Bird of the American Museum of Natural History firmly established the contemporaneity of man and Pleistocene animals in South America. That year Bird excavated ancient refuse deposits near the Strait of Magellan. In two cave sites—Fell's Cave and Palli Aike—the deepest strata contained the bones of extinct mammals that had been killed and eaten by men. Fell's Cave was particularly important, because the animal bones, artifacts and human skeletons there had been sealed off by fallen rocks. This circumstance guaranteed that the association between animals and humans was not due to the later intrusion of human remains.

With the development of carbon-14 dating in the 1950's dates were obtained for the bottom strata of Bird's caves. These are respectively 6689 ± 450 B.C. for Palli Aike and 8760 ± 300 B.C. for Fell's Cave. The Fell's Cave date appears to us to be somewhat too early when it is compared with evidence secured elsewhere near the Strait of Magellan and also in the Andes. Taken together with the remains of extinct animals, however, the radiocarbon age of the caves is a good indication that man had reached the tip of South America toward the end of the last continental glaciation or at the latest in very early postglacial times.

Evidence that men lived in South America in early postglacial times has been found in many parts of the continent during the past decade. Numerous campsites of hunters and gatherers in this epoch have been identified, and they have been dated by stratigraphic and radiocarbon studies. It is now evident that soon after the end of the glacial period all South America, with the possible exception of the deep Amazon Basin and the Pacific coast of Colombia, was inhabited by men. The assemblages of stone tools belonging to these postglacial cultures are characterized by well-made projectile points, knife blades, scrapers and gravers flaked by pressure (as opposed to simple percussion). Some of the assemblages also include grinding stones and other tools for the preparation of plant foods [see "Early Man in Peru," by Edward P. Lanning; Scientific American, October, 1965].

Remains of a very different kind of culture have also been found throughout the Andes. They lack all the expertly made artifacts of the postglacial tool kit. These assemblages are characterized by elongated chopping tools and spearpoints coarsely flaked on both sides by percussion. The first such "bifacial" assemblage was discovered in 1956 by the Venezuelan archaeologist José M. Cruxent on the terraces of the Pedregal River in northwestern Venezuela. Soon thereafter the authors of this article found related tool assemblages on the central coast of Peru, as did Father Gustavo LePaige in the interior desert of northern Chile and Eduardo Cigliano in the Andes of northwestern Argentina. The similarity of the artifacts in all these assemblages made it apparent that they belong to a single widespread cultural stage for which we have proposed the name "Andean Biface Horizon." Among archaeologists working on these materials there was general agreement that the horizon was an early one, but for several years there has been no evidence to place it exactly in time.

Cruxent's work on the Pedregal River terraces yielded a sequence of ancient cultures, for the reason that the highest river terrace is always the first to be formed and the lowest the last. The oldest Pedregal assemblage was therefore the one found on the highest terrace. Called the Camare culture complex, it consisted almost exclusively of crude choppers and large flakes of quartzite, together with a few large, thick bifacial tools. The second culture complex, the Lagunas, was found on somewhat lower terraces. It is a typical member of the Andean Biface Horizon. Two even later complexes, characterized by pressure-flaked projectile points of the early postglacial type, were found on still lower terraces. Although his dating is only relative, Cruxent's work shows that the Camare complex is earlier than the Andean Biface Horizon. At several sites

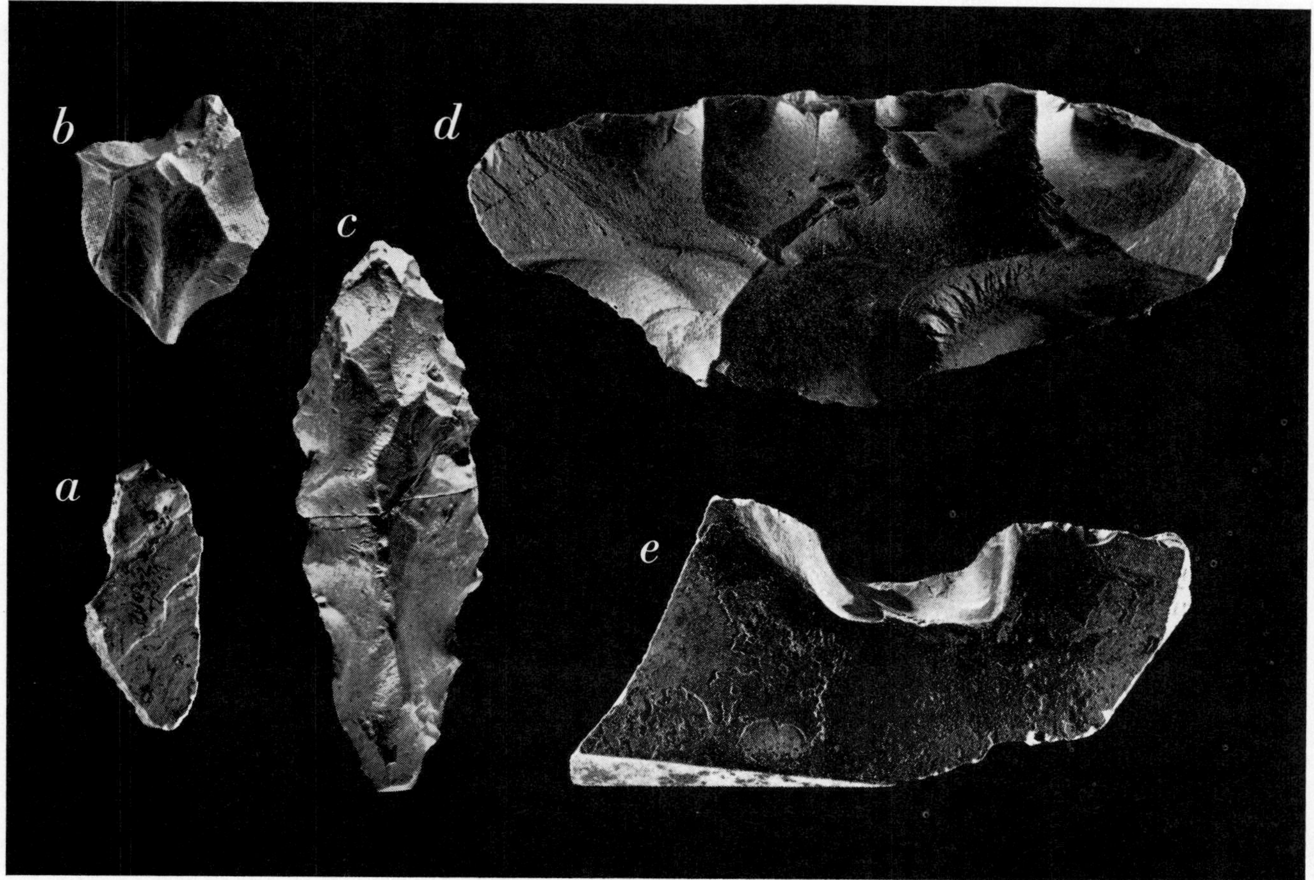

STONE TOOLS used by the early inhabitants of western South America were of different kinds at different times, as these representative implements show. At Cerro Chivateros in Peru, between 12,000 and 11,000 B.C., most were small tools made from flat pieces of quartzite (*a*). Elsewhere in coastal Peru, between 10,500 and 9500 B.C., the implements were also small but somewhat more advanced (*b*). Between 9500 and 7000 B.C. new kinds of tools were made at Cerro Chivateros. They included spearpoints (*c*) and choppers (*d*) flaked on both sides, and implements such as the simple one resembling a spokeshave (*e*) for making other tools out of wood or bone.

around Venezuela's Lake Maracaibo, Cruxent has also found rough choppers and a few large bifacial tools similar to those of the Camare complex but made of fossilized wood rather than quartzite. This fossil-wood assemblage he calls the Manzanillo complex.

At fossil-bearing sites of Pleistocene age at Muaco and Taima Taima on the Pedregal, Cruxent has found the bones of extinct animals, some of the bones scored by stone tools. This seems indisputable evidence that man was hunting such animals in northwestern Venezuela in late-Pleistocene times. Four radiocarbon dates from these sites (the samples include some of the scored bones) range from about 11,000 to 14,500 B.C. We do not know, of course, whether similar dates apply to either the Camare or the Lagunas complex or whether the hunters were still earlier inhabitants of the region. The situation is the same with a radiocarbon date of 11,970 ± 200 B.C. from Lake Maracaibo; this date could apply to the Manzanillo complex but is not clearly associated with Manzanillo artifacts.

While surveying the delta of the Chillón valley on the central coast of Peru in 1962 we located several sites containing the remains of another unusual stone tool industry. We named this culture complex Oquendo, after the hills in which the sites are located. Its assemblage of tools, mostly composed of small and simply made implements, is noteworthy for the lack of any artifact that could have been used as a spearpoint and for the abundance of the little cutting tools known as burins. A few burins are known from the postglacial site of El Inga in Ecuador, but the burins at the Oquendo sites number in the hundreds and are associated with a completely different kind of assemblage. Over the past five years one of us (Lanning) has come on similar burin industries on the coast of Ecuador and in the Atacama Desert of northern Chile, and the other (Patterson) has found two successive assemblages of the same kind in the Lurín valley of Peru. Neither the initial research in the Oquendo area nor studies of other related assemblages has produced any evidence for dating them.

Until very recently, then, there was no clear proof that man had lived in South America much before 8000 B.C., although the Fell's Cave radiocarbon measurement suggests a somewhat earlier date. The oldest Venezuelan radiocarbon date goes back even further, but it is not associated with any identifiable culture complex. Although several of us engaged in this work thought that the chopper, bifacial-tool and burin industries belonged to the Pleistocene, we had neither stratigraphy, radiocarbon dates nor associations with extinct animals to support our assumption.

Evidence of a late-glacial age for both the bifacial-tool and the burin industry is now available. It is provided by a stratified site in the lower Chillón valley, where one of us (Lanning) worked in 1963 and the other (Patterson) in 1966. The site, Cerro Chivateros, is about a mile from the sea in a range of steep hills composed of metamorphosed Cretaceous marine sediments, mostly sandstone and coarse-grained quartzite with outcrops of fine-grained quartzite here and there. Cerro Chivateros is the largest of the fine-grained quartzite outcrops, which were used by the makers of burins and bifacial tools as raw material. The slopes of the site are thickly covered with the debris of tool manufacture. The site seems to have been used as a quarry and workshop but not as a campsite. Nevertheless, a considerable depth of culture deposit accumulated during the time the outcrop was frequented by man.

Disregarding minor variations and subdivisions, our excavations at Cerro Chivateros revealed five major strata, each representing a different period of time and somewhat different climatic conditions. The lowest level, the "Red Zone," is a reddish silt that contains numerous chunks of unworked quartzite as well as a distinctive assemblage of artifacts. The assemblage of the Red Zone complex consists of little quartzite tools, the working edges of which had been made steeper by direct percussion with a cobblestone hammer. Prominent among these small tools are simple scrapers (straight-edged and notched), perfora-

MAN'S PRESENCE in South America during late Pleistocene times has been suggested by the discovery of distinctive stone tools at a number of sites. Until Cerro Chivateros, one of the sites in Peru excavated by the authors, provided a radiocarbon date of 8500 B.C., however, there was no concrete proof that the bifacially flaked tools discovered there were of great age. The finding suggests that other tool assemblages belonging to the same Andean Biface Horizon (*names in color*) are equally old and that tools of other kinds are even older.

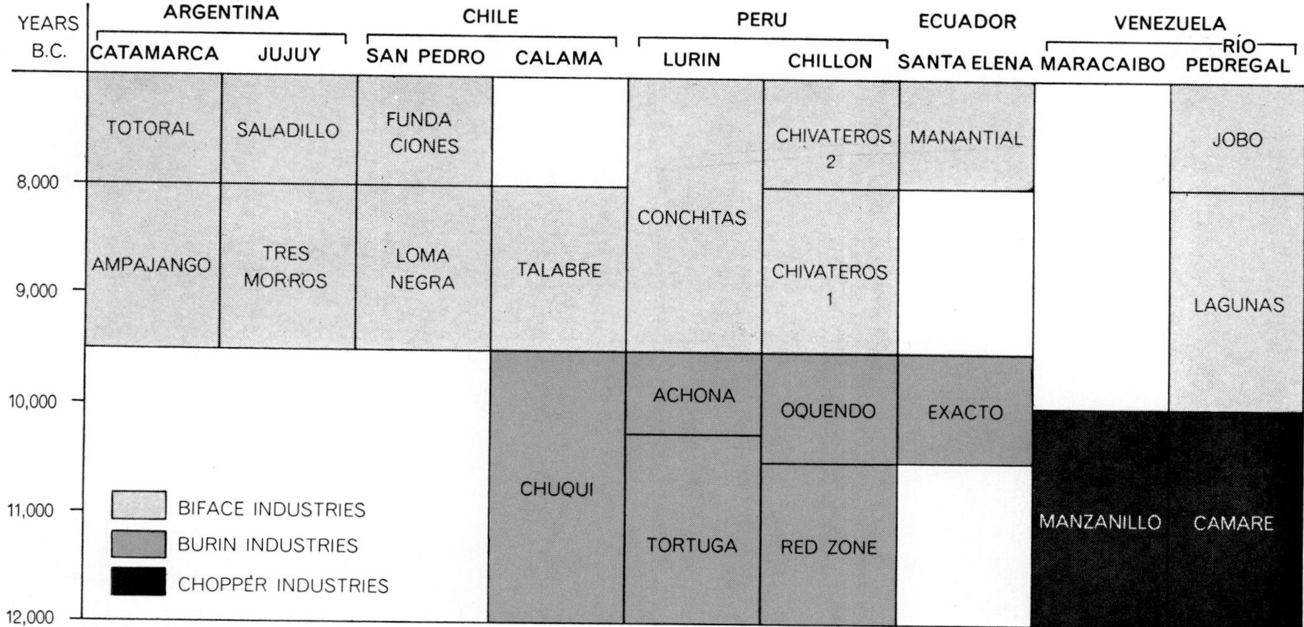

THREE STYLES OF TOOLS were used in various parts of South America. The stone implements used in Venezuela for 2,000 years or so after 12,000 B.C. included crude choppers and heavy tools flaked on both sides (*dark gray*). During the same period typical implements in Ecuador, Peru and Chile were much smaller (*color*). They included many chisel-like burins for working in wood and bone. Tools of the succeeding style, the Andean Biface Horizon (*light gray*), were larger and included a previously unknown artifact: the spearpoint. Perhaps evolved from Venezuelan choppers, bifaces spread widely between 10,000 and 9500 B.C. Except for the one firmly dated Andean biface stratum at Cerro Chivateros, the ages assigned to the various cultures listed here represent the authors' estimates.

tors pointed either at one end or both, and a few burins. How the silt that composes the Red Zone was formed has not yet been determined. It may have been laid down by the wind, and its color may be due to the oxidation of quartzite. If so, this would indicate that the area had a dry climate, similar to today's desert conditions, at the time of deposition.

A hard crust on the upper surface of the Red Zone constitutes the next stratum at Cerro Chivateros. Such formations, called *salitres,* are created on the surface when salty sediments are exposed to humid air; the salt crystals soak up moisture, expand and link up with one another. The process can be observed today on the Peruvian seashore where sea breezes provide the necessary moisture. Cerro Chivateros is too far from the sea for active salitrification today; the stratum we call the Lower Salitre could only have been formed at a time of increased humidity. In the Peruvian coastal desert such conditions would depend on a persistent belt of dense fog, perhaps coupled with a sequence of years in which some rain fell. Only a few artifacts of the Red Zone complex were found in the Lower Salitre.

The third stratum, another layer of silt, was deposited by the wind under very dry conditions. Wherever the silt is more than four inches thick the cultural material is confined to its upper portion. The assemblage of stone tools in this part of what we call the Lower Silt is typical of the Andean Biface Horizon; we have designated the complex Chivateros 1. The complex consists of many thick, pointed bifacial tools, large tools with serrated edges, and heavy unretouched flakes that were simply struck from a bigger piece. There are also a few large scrapers, notched stones and bifacially flaked spearpoints and knife blades.

The Upper Salitre, a salt-cemented deposit that overlies the Lower Silt, is the next stratum. It too contains Chivateros 1 artifacts. The evidence from these two levels therefore suggests that the manufacture of Andean Biface Horizon tools at Cerro Chivateros began partway through an extended dry period and continued during a humid one that followed.

The upper and most recent level at Cerro Chivateros—the Upper Silt—represents wind deposition during a dry period. The cultural content of this silt is two small workshops belonging to the complex we have designated Chivateros 2. The artifacts from these workshops are much the same as those of Chivateros 1, but they include many smaller double-point spearpoints and pointed tools with a rounded keel. The Chivateros 2 specimens, like those of the Red Zone, the Oquendo sites and Chivateros 1, were manufactured exclusively by cobblestone percussion.

No bones have been found in any of the strata at Cerro Chivateros. We attribute this partly to the fact that the site was not a camp and partly to the generally poor preservation of bones in the dry surface sediments of the Peruvian coast. We were fortunate enough, however, to find several pieces of wood in the Upper Salitre. From these samples the radiocarbon laboratory of the University of California at Los Angeles has obtained readings of 8420 ± 160 and 8440 ± 160 B.C. The dates apply to late Chivateros 1 and to the humid period that followed, during which the Upper Salitre was formed.

It is possible with the aid of these dates to correlate the alternating dry and humid cycles at Cerro Chivateros with the sequence of climatic changes elsewhere in the world during the late-glacial period. Long-term climatic changes associated with the late-glacial and postglacial periods have been documented in many parts of the Northern Hemisphere in the Old World and the New, and it has been shown that similar changes took place at about the same time in Europe and North America. The analysis of plant pollens in Colombia and Chile has shown that climatic changes in the New World's Southern Hemisphere are fairly well coordinated with those to the north. Glacial stages in the highlands of Peru are also correlated

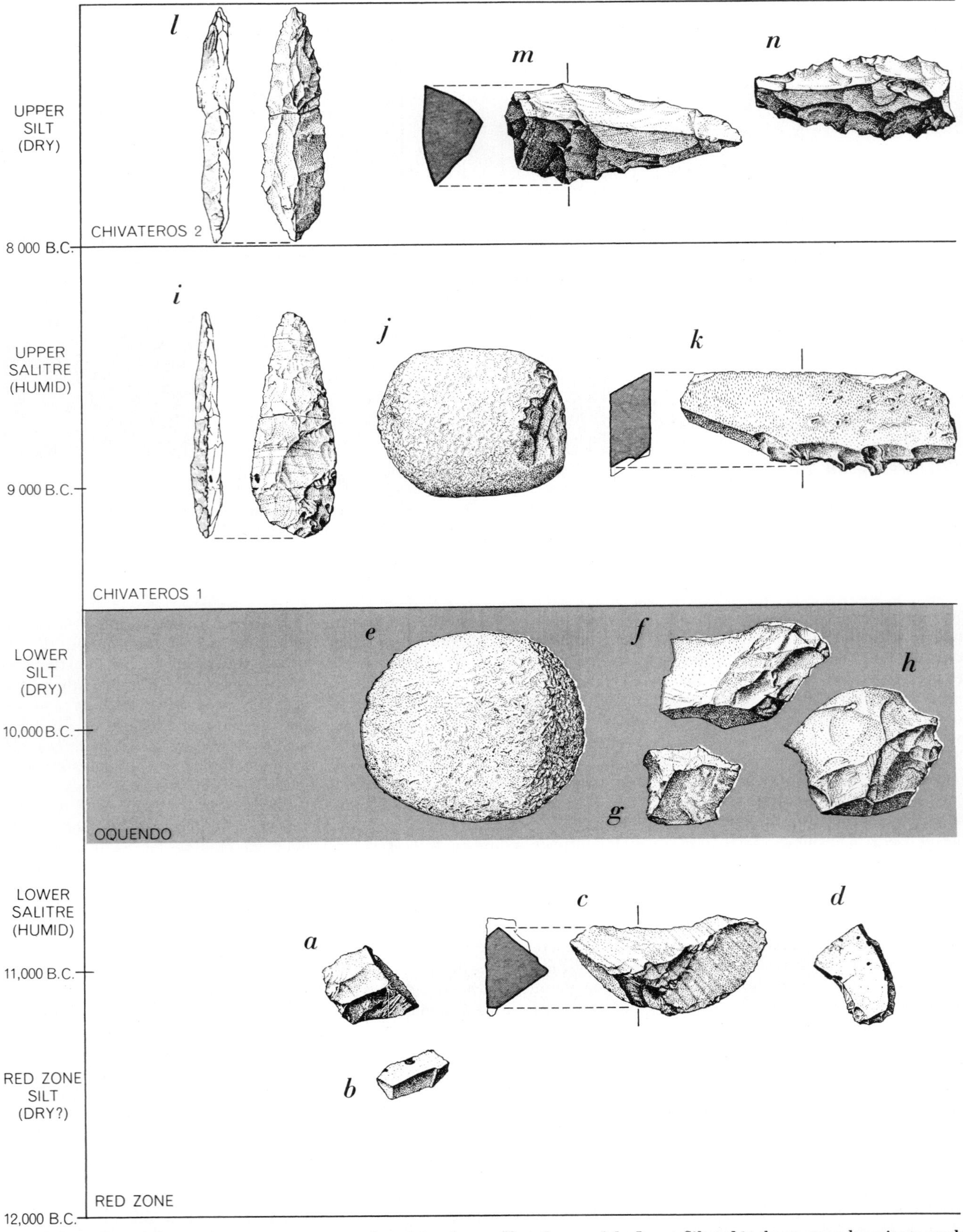

CULTURE SEQUENCE at Cerro Chivateros is evidenced by the artifacts typical of each. The lowest stratum, a red silt, and the saline-soil stratum above it contain cores (*a*), tiny burins (*b*, *d*) and knives (*c*; *note cross section*). The hammerstone (*e*) and burins (*f*, *g*, *h*) in the colored band are not from Cerro Chivateros; they are typical of the tools found in a similar stratum of silt at Oquendo. Near the top of the Lower Silt and in the stratum above it are much larger implements: spearpoints (*i*), hammerstones (*j*) and simple tools with toothed edges (*k*). Similar biface tools occupy the top stratum: coarser spearpoints (*l*) and implements with steeply "keeled" cross sections (*m*, *n*). Except for *e*, tools labeled *a* through *h* are shown half-size; *e* and *i* through *n* are shown one-third size.

with these worldwide climatic stages.

In general the evidence in South America indicates that in cool periods the mountain glaciers of the Andes reached their maximum extent. In these periods the altitudinal zones—the snow line, the tree line and the zone of regular annual precipitation—were depressed 3,000 feet or more, rainfall increased throughout the Andes, and the desert along the Pacific coast shrank in extent. Although the central Peruvian coast apparently remained arid, the velocity of winds blowing toward the shore was lower, dense fogs lay near sea level and years of irregular rainfall were more frequent. Although temperatures in the highlands were lower during these periods, temperatures along the coast may have been somewhat higher than they are today. The humid periods at Cerro Chivateros, represented by the *salitres,* should therefore be associated with times of worldwide low temperatures, and the dry periods, marked by the increased deposition of silt by the wind, should belong to times of high temperatures.

We have proposed a tentative correlation of the strata at Cerro Chivateros with the glacial stages of the Peruvian highlands, with the levels of pollen from various plants in Colombia and Chile, and with the more familiar climatic stages of the Northern Hemisphere [*see illustration on next page*]. In the highlands of Peru the Agrapa, Magapata and Antarragá stages were times of glacial advance, lowered altitudinal zones, decreased temperatures and increased rainfall. During intervening periods the climatic and altitudinal zones had approximately the same distribution as they have today.

If our correlations are correct, they allow us to suggest dates for the earlier strata at Cerro Chivateros and their contents. As far as the Upper Silt, Upper Salitre and Lower Silt are concerned, there are no significant problems. Each corresponds to a well-dated major fluctuation in world climate. Because the Chivateros 1 complex is found in the upper part of the Lower Silt but not in the lower part, for example, we estimate the beginning of the complex at about 9500 B.C.

For periods earlier than 10,000 B.C. we must rely on the Colombian pollen sequence alone; the Peruvian-highland glacial stages are not directly dated and the Chilean pollen sequence does not show any fluctuations. It is our view that the culturally impoverished Lower Salitre corresponds to the cool period of the Colombian pollen level designated *I a 3* and that the Red Zone below it corresponds to the warmer pollen level *I a 2*. Both of these stages in Colombia are somewhat earlier than their counterparts in Scandinavia (respectively the Older Dryas stage and the Bølling stage), probably because of Colombia's proximity to the Equator and because of the absence of a continental ice sheet in the region. If the Red Zone is indeed as old as pollen level *I a 2,* its cultural contents can tentatively be dated between 12,000 and 10,500 B.C.

The problem of dating the Oquendo culture complex, which is not represented at Cerro Chivateros, remains. One of us (Patterson) excavated a test pit in an Oquendo site in 1966 and found that the artifacts were concentrated in a 15-inch stratum of wind-deposited silt (like the Upper Silt and Lower Silt at Cerro Chivateros) overlying a culturally empty deposit of *salitre*. Oquendo artifacts are related to the artifacts of the Red Zone, but they show some tool forms and chipping patterns similar to those of Chivateros 1. We believe the Oquendo complex fits between the other two, and that the silt and *salitre* at the Oquendo site correspond to the lower half of the Lower Silt and the Lower Salitre at Cerro Chivateros. On this basis we tentatively date the Oquendo complex at 10,500 to 9500 B.C., the interval between the Red Zone and Chivateros 1.

It is not impossible that our proposed dates for both the Red Zone and the Oquendo complexes are too early. We believe, however, that the relative chronology of both complexes is soundly based on their stratum and tool relationships to Chivateros 1. Late Chivateros 1, in turn, has been dated by radiocarbon to the middle of the ninth millennium B.C. Even if our age estimate is somewhat too high, it is clear that the entire sequence belongs to late-glacial times and that it must have begun well before 10,000 B.C.

The remarkable homogeneity of artifacts belonging to the Andean Biface Horizon from Venezuela, Peru, Chile and Argentina suggests that they were roughly contemporaneous. Until further evidence is available we believe it is safe to apply the Chivateros 1 dates to the entire Andean Biface Horizon. As a result we can date the burin industries of South America, which are evidently related to the Oquendo complex and the Red Zone, as being older than 9500 B.C. We have prepared a chronology for the known burin and bifacial-tool industries of the Andes, aligned in time on this basis [*see illustration on page 47*]. Of course, no two of these industries are exactly alike; they differ not only in raw materials but also in the frequency with which various tool types occur and in the presence or absence of certain locally specialized forms or techniques. The burin industries are also more diversified than the bifacial-tool industries. Even so, they have in common many highly specialized types of artifacts not known in any later ancient Andean culture.

The early chopper-tool industries of northwestern Venezuela—the Camare and Manzanillo complexes—are quite different from the burin industries contemporaneous with them in Ecuador, Peru and Chile. Their relation to the Andean Biface Horizon is attested not only by the inclusion among these artifacts of a few large pointed bifacial tools but also by a fairly high frequency of other bifacially flaked forms and by the large size of both the complexes' artifacts and their unretouched flake tools. The present evidence suggests that these northern chopper industries were ancestral to the Andean Biface Horizon and that the bifacial-tool industries spread southward through the Andes from Venezuela (or perhaps Colombia), replacing the earlier burin industries in each region. For this reason we propose that the Lagunas culture complex started somewhat earlier than the other bifacial-tool industries. Without more evidence it is impossible to say whether this change involved an actual replacement of human populations or nothing more than the diffusion of a new economy—with its associated assemblage of tools—from one people to another.

We know almost nothing so far about how these earliest South Americans actually lived. Except for Cerro Chivateros, all the known early sites are either on the surface or extend only a few inches below it. Until sites are found that have deep layers containing animal bones, shells, plant debris, hearths and perhaps even human remains, culture reconstructions can be based only on the stone tools and the locations where they are found.

An inventory of the tools shows an overwhelming preponderance of artifacts evidently intended for working wood or bone. They include choppers, burins, toothed tools and bifacial tools. In the chopper and burin assemblages spearpoints are absent; they are also rare in all the bifacial-tool assemblages except those at the Loma Negra site in Chile. Smooth-edged scrapers, which are best suited for the preparation of skins, are rare too, although rougher scrapers (useful for extracting fibers from plants similar to maguey) are fairly abundant. This suggests that the Pleistocene human population placed little emphasis on hunting game of the kind that would be killed with spears or that would provide the hunter with both leather and meat. At the same time the majority of the stone tools show no particular specialization suggesting as a way of life either fishing or the gathering of plant foods. Instead most of the artifacts appear to have been secondary tools, that is, tools with which primary tools were made. They give us no information at all about what kinds of primary tool—made out of wood or bone—the earliest South Americans had.

Most of the known Pleistocene sites are stone quarries or workshops, although a few of them may also have served as camps. Their usual location is among steep hills near rivers or small streams, some of which have now disappeared. The Exacto sites in Ecuador, the Talabre sites in Chile and the Tres Morros sites in Argentina are exceptions. They are all in flat areas; a few Exacto sites are on or near the edge of sea cliffs and the Talabre sites are on the edge of a lake that has been dry since the end of Pleistocene times. Evidently the earliest South Americans preferred wooded valleys but exploited other areas when it was convenient.

From what we know of man's life elsewhere in the world in late-glacial times, we can make some guesses about Pleistocene life in South America. Presumably the people lived in small groups, probably including not more than a few families. Their economy must have been one of generalized hunting and gathering in which plant foods, and possibly in some cases seafood, predominated. Like most food-gatherers, they probably migrated seasonally from one part of their territory to another, taking advantage of the ripening of different food plants at different times of the year.

If man indeed lived in South America as early as 12,000 B.C., he must have been present in North America at a still earlier date. The oldest evidence of human occupation in North America is the tools of the specialists in big-game hunting belonging to the Clovis (or Llano) culture complex; the oldest such tools are dated about 9600 B.C. [see "Elephant-hunting in North America," by C. Vance Haynes, Jr. beginning on page 51]. Dates earlier than this have been proposed. Some are based on radiocarbon measurements of material that is not associated with identifiable assemblages of artifacts. Others involve assemblages for which direct evidence of age is not available. Some of the latter are quite similar to the artifacts of the Andean bifacial-tool industries and others include edge-retouched implements reminiscent of those in the Red Zone complex at Cerro Chivateros.

The interpretation of North American prehistory that is most widely accepted at present holds that the Clovis complex represents the continent's earliest human occupation. It seems to us that the new evidence from South America necessarily places man in North America well before Clovis times and perhaps even before the start of the late-glacial period. This conclusion does not, of course, prove that any of the current claims for earlier cultures in North America is correct, although it suggests that some of them may be. Primarily it shows that contemporary knowledge of early man in North America is far from complete and indicates that we should be busy searching for cultures older than the Clovis complex. We propose that some North American stone industries that include bifacial tools and edge-retouched artifacts may precede the Clovis complex. Our experience in South America certainly suggests that these industries merit further study.

YEARS B.C.	SCANDINAVIA	CERRO CHIVATEROS: STRATIGRAPHY	CERRO CHIVATEROS: CULTURES	PERU HIGHLANDS (GLACIAL STAGES)	CHILE (POLLEN ANALYSIS)	COLOMBIA (POLLEN ANALYSIS)
	PREBOREAL	UPPER SILT (DRY)	CHIVATEROS 2	INTERSTADIAL 4	IV WARMING	IV WARMING, DRY
8,000	YOUNGER DRYAS	UPPER SALITRE (HUMID)	CHIVATEROS I	ANTARRAGÁ ADVANCE	III COLD, WET	III COLD, DRY
9,000	ALLERØD	LOWER SILT (DRY)	(OQUENDO: NOT REPRESENTED AT CERRO CHIVATEROS)	INTERSTADIAL 3	II WARM, WET	II WARM, DRY
10,000	OLDER DRYAS			MAGAPATA ADVANCE	I COLD, WET	I b-c WARMER
		LOWER SALITRE (HUMID)				I a 3 COLD, WET
11,000	BØLLING	RED ZONE (DRY?)	RED ZONE	INTERSTADIAL 2		I a 2 WARMER, DRIER
12,000	OLDEST DRYAS			AGRAPA ADVANCE		I a 1 COLD, WET

RELATIVE AGES of undated strata excavated by the authors at Cerro Chivateros are estimated on the basis of changes in climate during late-Pleistocene times. The column at left presents the well-established sequence of climate changes in Scandinavia. The next two columns show the separate soil levels at the site and their culture content. The last three columns summarize the evidence for late-Pleistocene climate fluctuations in South America known from the study of mountain glaciers and analyses of ancient pollen.

Early Man in the Andes **6**

by William J. Mayer-Oakes
May 1963

A rich assemblage of obsidian tools has been discovered at El Inga, high in the mountains of Ecuador. It may provide a long-sought link between the prehistoric men of the U.S. and those of South America

In 1926 a distinctive kind of stone projectile point was found near Folsom, N.M., in unmistakable association with the bones of a long extinct species of bison. The discovery stimulated the search for further traces of the Paleo-Indians who had made the points and for evidence of the migrations of the men who first populated the New World. It is now fairly clear that the first Americans were nomadic hunters who crossed the Bering Strait from Asia on a land bridge that existed at the end of the last glacial period. As early as 10,000 years ago they had diffused across what is now Canada and the U.S. and down the spine of the Americas all the way to the Strait of Magellan. Filling in the details of this broad outline has proved to be difficult: the archaeological trail is faint. Investigators have found very few skeletal remains of the earliest men and hardly any artifacts made of perishable organic material that can be dated by the radioactive-carbon method. They have had to rely almost entirely on one kind of evidence: bits of worked flint and obsidian, the fragmentary weapons and tools of the ancient hunters, unearthed at sites from Alaska to the tip of South America.

By comparing the kinds of tools at various sites, their shapes and the precise chipping techniques by which they were fashioned, investigators are establishing relations among sites in the circumpolar region and reconstructing early man's movements across the U.S. in some detail. In recent years they have been able to find traces of North American tool industries as far south as Mexico and Central America. Below the Isthmus of Panama, however, the trail of these cultures seemed to end abruptly. Most sites in South America yielded quite different artifacts; their cultures seemed to be only obscurely related to one another and were not linked to the north. There was good evidence that men had camped in caves near the Strait of Magellan some 10,000 years ago but nothing to explain how quickly and by what route they had arrived there. What was needed was the discovery of a tool assemblage of sufficient size and richness to show relations among the various sites in South America and perhaps also a link to North American origins.

For the past three years Robert E. Bell of the University of Oklahoma and I have been investigating just such a site high in the Andes near Quito in Ecuador. El Inga, as we have named the place, appears to have been a workshop and campsite for some of the first South Americans. Its location confirms a current belief that the early migrants were a highland people who followed a mountain route, thus maintaining a fairly constant climatic and ecological environment as they moved through the equatorial regions to the sub-Antarctic.

El Inga was discovered by an American geologist, A. Allen Graffham, who worked in Ecuador from 1956 to 1959. Graffham is also an amateur archaeologist, and he often went on weekend outings with his family in search of sites and specimens. On one such excursion he came on a group of heavily eroded hummocks some 15 miles from Quito, near the gorge of the Rio Inga at an altitude of 9,100 feet. Scattered over the surface he noticed pieces of obsidian, a volcanic glass, that he quickly decided had been shaped by man and might represent a significant archaeological find. Graffham gathered some specimens; when he returned to the U.S. he took the collection to Bell, who agreed that his find was significant. The obsidian objects were projectile points and other tools that had been carefully worked by distinctive techniques, some of them reminiscent of the stoneworking methods of the Paleo-Indians in the North American Plains region.

Bell was particularly impressed by some of the fragments. They appeared to be the bases of lanceolate, or lance-shaped, spear or dart points and they were "fluted"; that is, "channel flakes" had been chipped from the bases parallel to the long axis of the points. Both shape and fluting resembled those of the Folsom points and the closely related Clovis points found in the western and southwestern U.S.

When Bell invited me to examine the find, I was struck by another aspect of the collection. For me the most distinctive items were several "fishtail"-stemmed points identical in shape with points unearthed nearly 30 years ago at the Strait of Magellan sites by Junius B. Bird of the American Museum of Natural History. Bird had found these points, sometimes associated with the bones of extinct sloth and horse species, in excavations at Palli Aike and Fell's Cave in a level he called Fell's Cave I.

It was apparent to us that excavations at El Inga might provide the link that had been lacking between the Paleo-Indians of the Plains region and the men of Fell's Cave and so tell much about the nature of the north-south migrations. The El Inga collection might also show us how the style characteristics of projectile points could serve in South America, as they had in North America, as significant markers for dating occupation levels and interrelating a number of sites.

In the fall of 1959 I joined Bell at the University of Oklahoma, and the next January we flew to Quito. Graffham had suggested that we go out to El Inga as he had—by taxi. This seemed a rather

OBSIDIAN BLADES were among the significant finds at El Inga. Blades, found here for the first time in South America, were long flakes struck from obsidian cones to serve as knives and as generalized blanks from which a wide variety of tools was fashioned.

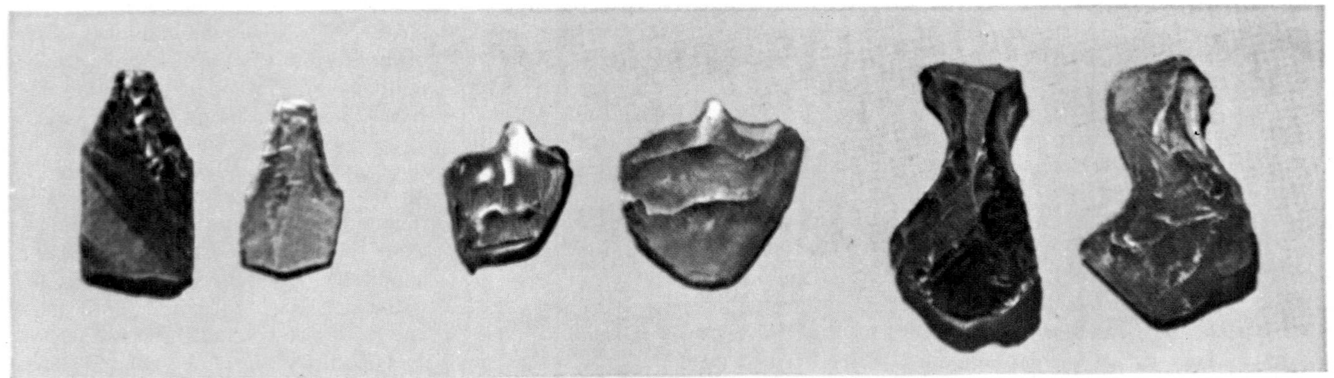

VARIOUS TOOLS made from blades are shown in this photograph made, like the others on this page, by Robert E. Bell of the University of Oklahoma. The two objects at the left are chisels. In the middle is a pair of gravers, pointed tools for cutting designs on stone or bone surfaces. At the right are two "strangulated," or notched, blades that served as spokeshaves for shaping round shafts.

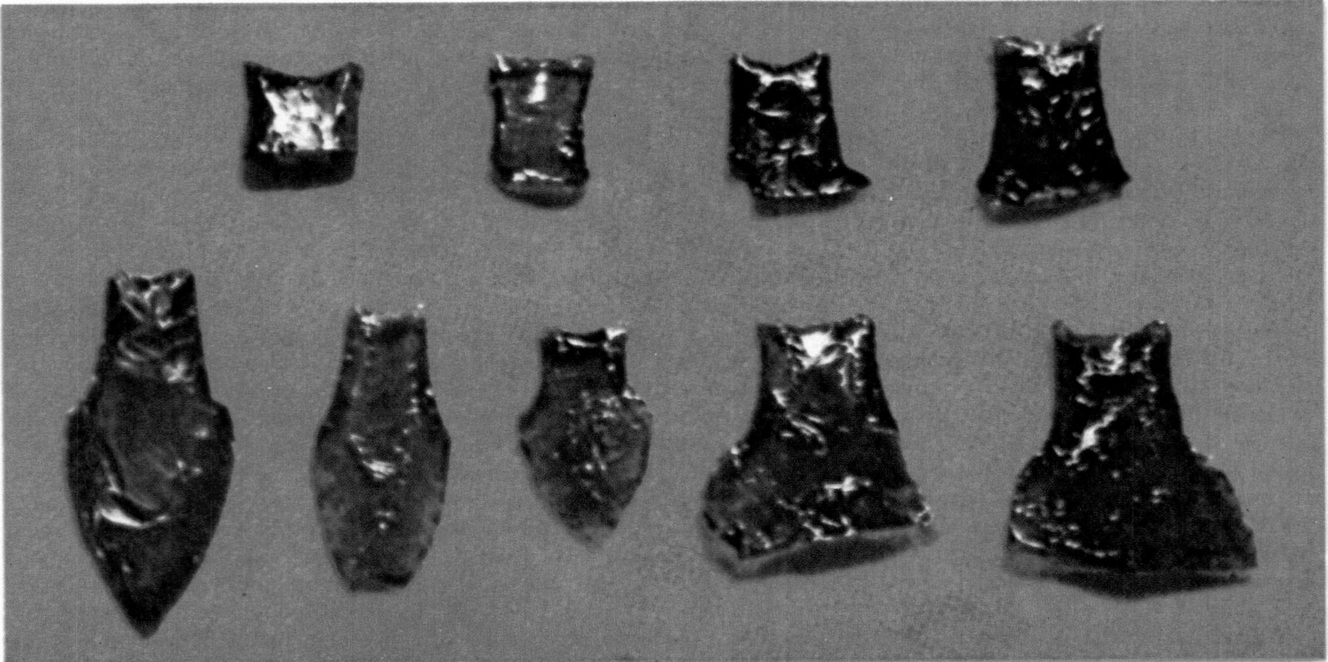

PROJECTILE POINTS and fragments at El Inga included these stemmed styles similar to points found at Level I of Fell's Cave at the tip of South America. Many of these points had "fluted" bases, as in the case of the two in the middle of the top row and the second, fourth and fifth from the left in the bottom row. All the tools shown on this page are reproduced at about their actual size.

MAJOR EXCAVATIONS got under way at El Inga in June, 1961, on the largest uneroded hummock from which rain had been washing the obsidian artifacts. The mountain ridge in the background, to the southeast, is the last one before the Amazon drainage basin.

mundane way of penetrating the high Andes to a newly discovered prehistoric site, but we found the driver he recommended and set out, armed with a sketch map of the site and the route to it from Quito. Beyond the little town of Tumbaco the dirt road forked and there were the landmarks indicated on the map: trail, bridge, mountain and, right next to the road, the eroded hummocks. But something else made us certain we had relocated El Inga. It was obsidian. The surface was littered with pieces of the shiny black glass.

Erosion had done the preliminary excavating here: rain water had cut into the hummocks, washing the artifacts of early man out of the topsoil onto exposed patches of the underlying hardpan, and they lay there in plain view. We spent the day scouting the area and picking up loose obsidian. For the next two weeks we commuted to the site daily, collecting artifacts from the surface and digging

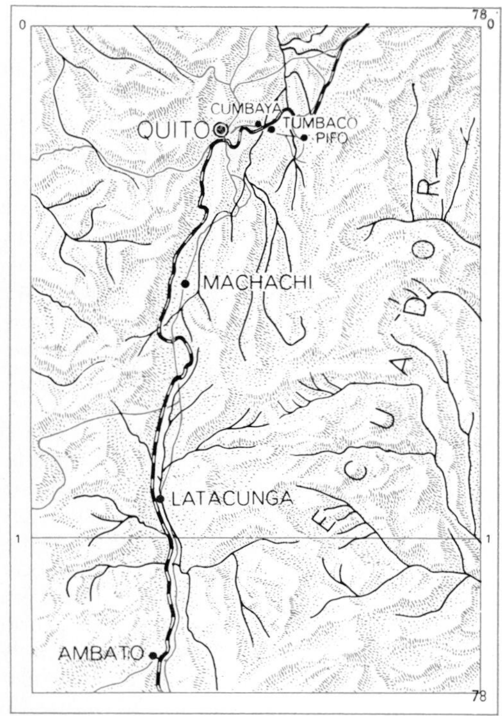

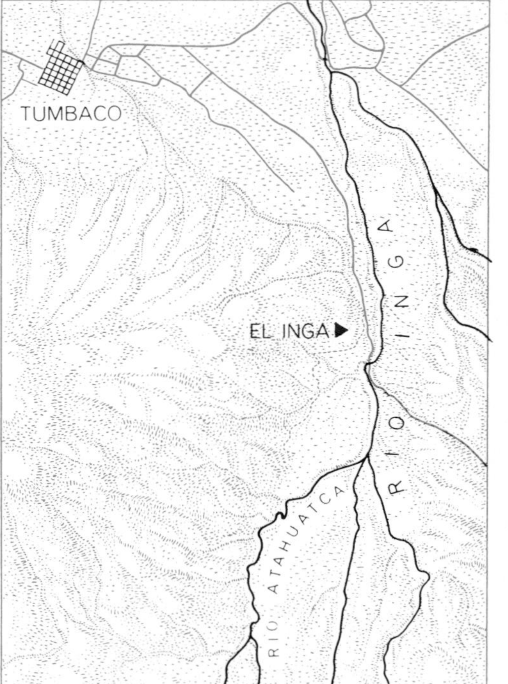

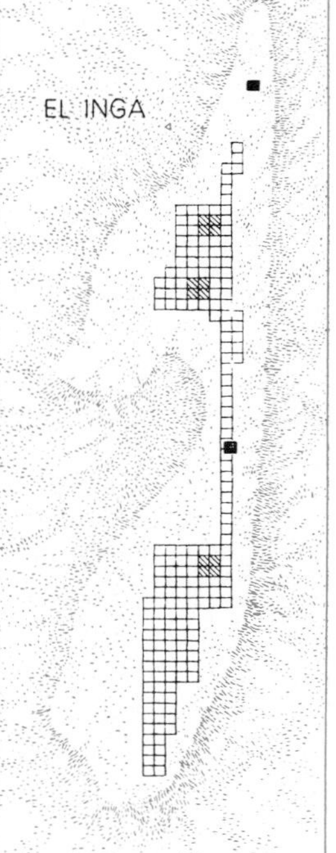

EL INGA is in northern Ecuador, east of Quito, between Tumbaco and Pifo on the map at the left. The center map shows the location of the site, on a trail that branches from the road along the Rio Inga gorge. The major excavation, laid out in five-foot squares, is shown at the right. The 10-foot squares (*hatched*) are the three "stratigraphic blocks" (*see text*); test pits are shown in black.

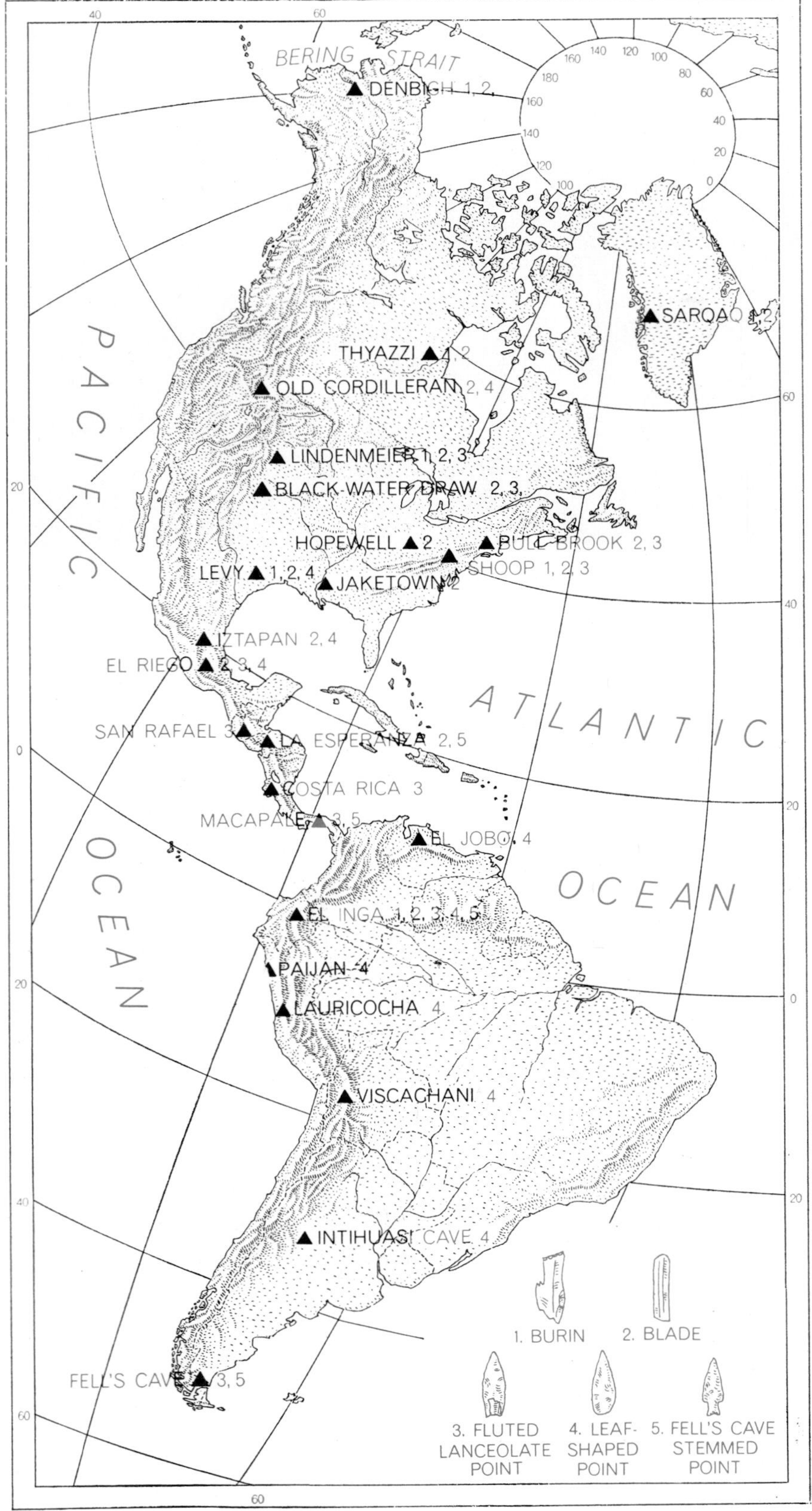

NEW-WORLD DISTRIBUTION of El Inga traits is shown on this map. Five significant El Inga artifacts are shown at the lower right and their occurrence at various sites is indicated by the numbers on the map. The importance of El Inga lies largely in the variety of its artifacts, suggesting relations to sites widely scattered in North and South America. The pattern of the sites on the map suggests how early men diffused through the Americas.

two five-foot-square test pits in an uneroded area. We found that there was a top level of soil, from eight to 10 inches deep, that had been periodically disturbed by plowing. Then came a darker band of unplowed soil, the "midden," in which most of the obsidian lay. This level extended to 18 or 20 inches below the surface and was underlain by a yellow hardpan, a consolidated volcanic tuff that contained no obsidian.

In two weeks we collected almost 600 pounds of obsidian, which we shipped back to Oklahoma. When we set to work sorting through the material and classifying it, the haul proved to be richer than we had expected. There was, first of all, a large sample of all the kinds of objects Graffham had brought back: points, scrapers, gravers and other tools. But we also found something new: a number of nicely fashioned parallel-sided flakes, smooth on one face and faceted with a few long surfaces on the other. These were "blades": flakes struck from specially prepared conical obsidian "cores" and subsequently used as knives or blanks from which many different specialized tools could be made. Flint or obsidian cores and blades are the hallmark of a number of rather advanced tool industries and are characteristic in particular of several Upper Paleolithic cultures in Europe and Asia. We knew that blades had been found at a few sites in North America and that they were typical of the pre-Columbian Mexican obsidian industries. But so far as we knew they had not yet been seen in South America.

In this preliminary search through the material we found one other significant detail. Among the numerous randomly shaped pieces, many of which were waste material from the toolmaking process, we noticed a number of peculiar flat-sided flakes of a distinctive shape. We suspected that they might have something to do with a burin industry, something so far unknown south of the U.S. Burins are special tools made by a special technique. They are chisel-pointed groovers or engraving tools fashioned by striking the end of a blade or a piece of a blade in such a way that slivers are split away to leave a cutting edge [*see top illustration on page 58*]. The peculiar flakes we saw appeared to be burin spalls, or slivers. Like most New World archaeologists, we were not closely acquainted with burin technology. But the indicated presence of burins at El Inga, combined with the presence of blades, suggested a strong connection with the northern cultures. El Inga deserved further investigation.

In the summer of 1961 Bell spent three months excavating the new Andean site. A large crew of local farmers and villagers cut a trench 200 feet long and five feet wide along the axis of the largest uneroded hummock. Then they expanded it where possible until some 5,000 square feet had been excavated in five-foot squares to an average depth of two feet—deep enough to penetrate the hardpan. We had noted from our 1960 test pits that there did not seem to be any correlation between the differences in the styles of the points and tools and the levels from which they had been recovered. But in such situations careful statistical classification of an excavated collection sometimes reveals changes in style and technology over a period of time. This kind of study requires that a large number of items be recovered and that they be kept separated according to the depth at which they were found. Bell had the workers dig carefully, slicing off the hard, dry soil in four-inch layers, screening each shovelful for pieces of obsidian and collecting the pieces from each four-inch level of each five-foot square separately. In a further effort to preserve whatever time sequence existed, Bell prepared three "stratigraphic blocks": 10-foot squares that were first isolated from the surrounding earth and then excavated only two inches at a time. By the end of the season he had a sample about as large as our first collection, but it came from throughout the mantle of soil as well as from the surface, and we knew precisely where each item had been found.

Unfortunately this major excavation failed to uncover any other explicit signs of occupation: no human burials or animal bones, no storage or garbage pits, no fireplaces. As a result we have no charcoal that can be subjected to radioactive-carbon dating. The fact that the undisturbed cultural deposit is between eight and 12 inches thick indicates that more than one occupation level may be represented. The variety of point styles and tool types also suggests that different cultures may be represented, perhaps covering as many as 4,000 or 5,000 years of intermittent occupation. The presence of different kinds of tools and quantities of waste material would seem to mean that El Inga was not merely a hunters' kill site but a combination workshop and campsite. Perhaps it was convenient to a good hunting area as well as to the extinct volcano Antisana, 21 miles to the southeast, where the

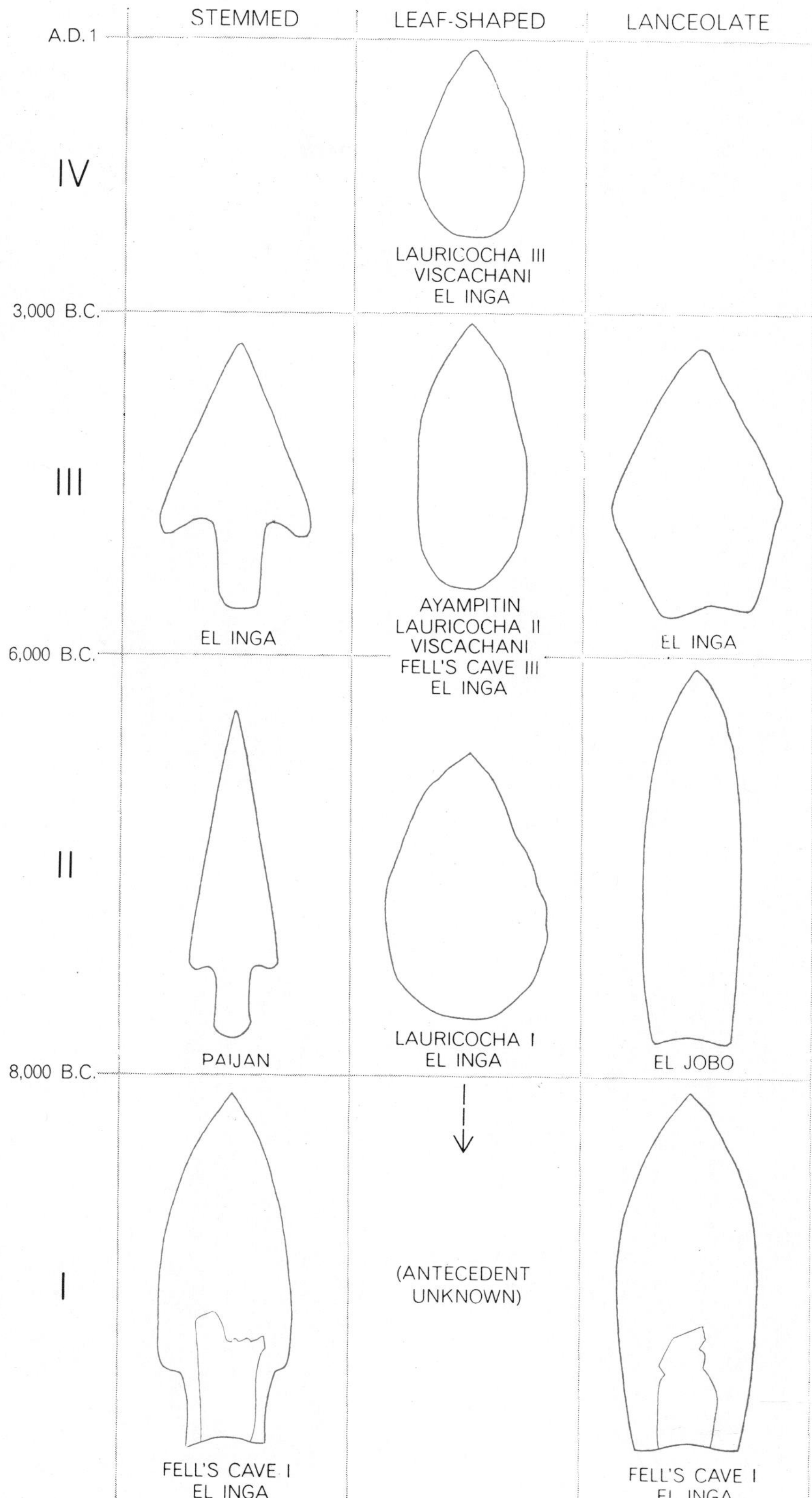

TIME SEQUENCE of three major early projectile-point styles in prehistoric South America is suggested here on the basis of the available evidence. Two of the El Inga points are judged to be very early because of their similarity to Fell's Cave Level I styles; others either look like or appear to be related to points from later levels at other sites. This tentative arrangement can be revised as firm dates are obtained for more of the early-man sites.

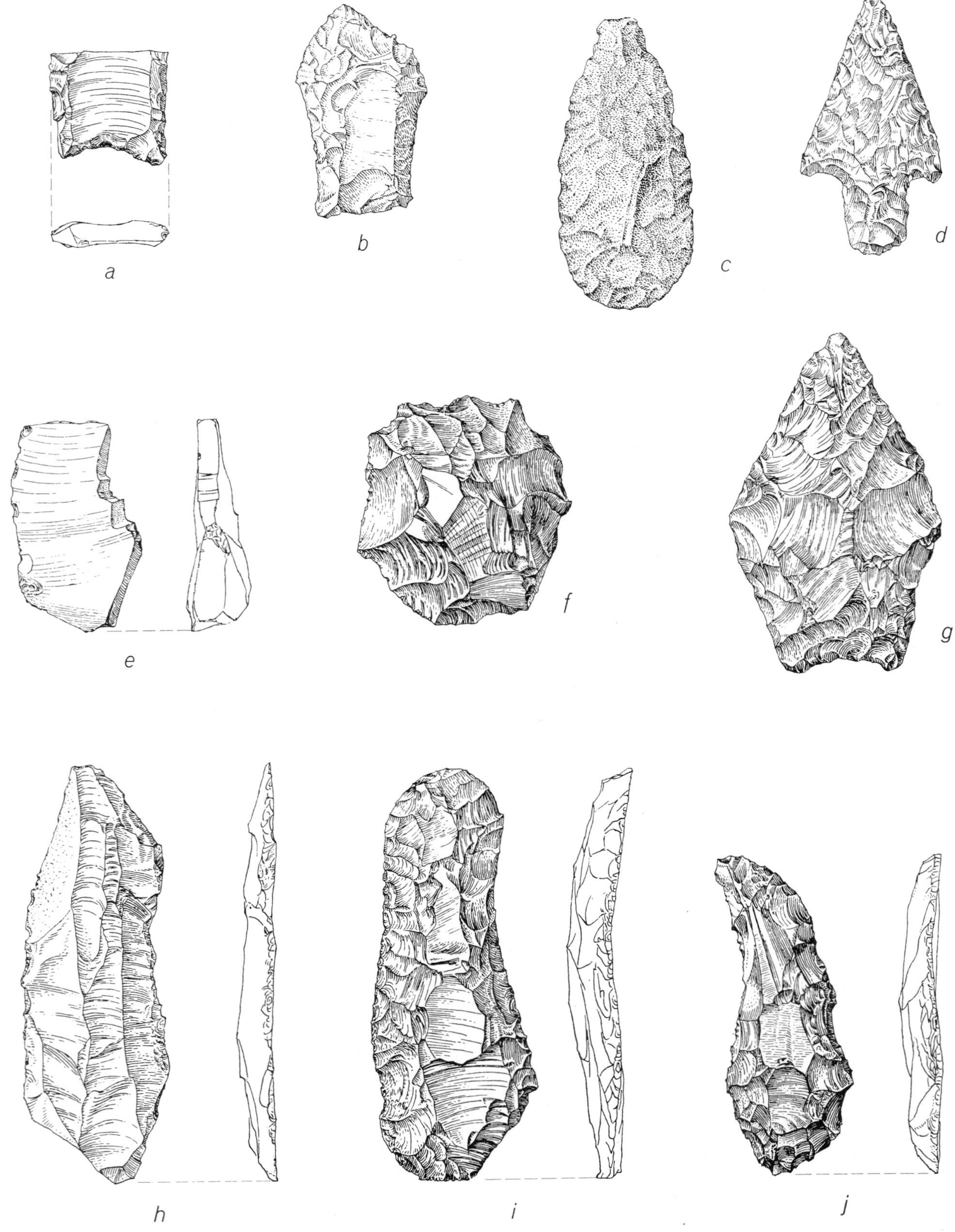

STYLES AND TECHNIQUES represented at El Inga are illustrated. Four different point styles are shown in the top row: the broken base of a Clovis-style point, fluted on both faces (*a*), a small Fell's Cave stemmed point (*b*), a leaf-shaped Ayampitín point (*c*) and a long-stemmed point peculiar to El Inga (*d*). The smooth, intricately chipped object (*e*) is an angle burin, a specialized grooving tool. The small hemispheric core (*f*) is seen from above. The large point (*g*) is in a modified lanceolate style. In the bottom row there are three unifacial tools, chipped only on one face: a blade (*h*), an end-and-side scraper (*i*) and a strangulated blade, or spokeshave (*j*). All tools are drawn at their actual sizes. The Ayampitín point (*c*) is basalt; all the other tools are obsidian.

hunters may have obtained their obsidian. All this is speculation. More definite conclusions must be based on detailed examination of the tools.

With Bell's return to Oklahoma in the fall of 1961 the detailed studies began in earnest. From the more than 15,000 pieces collected from the surface we selected for study 6,500 specimens that obviously were fashioned, functional tools. I have been analyzing this collection at the University of Manitoba while Bell works at Oklahoma with the 1961 excavation finds. The El Inga assemblage as a whole is characterized primarily by a wide variety of "unifacial" tools —tools made by chipping away at the upper, or faceted, surface of a blade. In the surface collection I have counted some 200 small hemispheric cores from which the blades were struck. The size of the cores suggests that they must have been worked down to become tools (of unknown function) in themselves after having yielded as many blades as possible. There are more than 500 blades and many hundreds of scrapers, gravers, chisels and other tools made on blades. So far I have found about 50 burins and several hundred burin spalls. Another group consists of bifacial tools—tools chipped on both faces. These include crude choppers, cleavers and food grinders made of basalt as well as knives and scrapers made of obsidian, and of course the points. The 23 complete projectile points and 204 fragments are in a number of different styles: they are stemmed in the Fell's Cave style; lanceolate, leaf-shaped and long-stemmed. Many of the Fell's Cave and lanceolate points are fluted. (It is possible that some of these merely appear to have been fluted. Having been fashioned from blades, they may still retain the original chipping pattern of the blade surface, which might account for their fluted appearance.)

The discovery of this diverse stone-tool technology, the like of which had not been seen before in the New World, comes at a time when a number of workers are turning their attention to the early hunting cultures of South America. Excavations in Venezuela, Peru, Bolivia and Argentina have yielded a variety of projectile points and other tools, and investigators are just beginning to see the outlines of an early highland culture pattern. South American archaeology, in other words, is about at the stage of North American early-man investigations in the late 1920's and early 1930's, when the Folsom points were being sought as the distinctive feature of the Paleo-Indian culture. The first discoveries have been made and are leading to others, and the task of synthesis is under way.

Ten years ago fluted points were found for the first time south of the U.S. border in Costa Rica. By now these points have also been identified in Mexico, Guatemala and Panama. Interestingly enough, the points from Costa

INITIAL TRENCH was laid out along the major axis of the hummock. It was 200 feet long and five feet wide. The crew excavated slowly, digging down four inches in a five-foot square, screening the earth for obsidian and then repeating the process.

STRATIGRAPHIC BLOCKS, prepared so that obsidian objects could not fall to a spurious level from the walls of the trench, were excavated two inches at a time to assure precise vertical control. Here the top level of a block is being cut away.

Rica and Panama are much like the El Inga fluted lanceolate points: they were struck from blades and are somewhat modified versions of the typical northern points. A different kind of evidence comes from Venezuela. The El Jobo assemblage there is quite unlike the Central American industries but is markedly similar to the Angostura industries that followed the fluted-point era in North America. All this evidence of relations between the Americas is tentative and suggestive; it may well be reinforced by the presence of lanceolate points at El Inga.

The implications of El Inga's leaf-shaped and stemmed points are less clear. Various versions of the leaf-shaped point have been found at sites in South America. One style takes its name from the Ayampitín level at Intihuasi Cave in Argentina, where it was found in a context carbon-dated at 6000 B.C. El Inga has yielded points in this style and others, some apparently earlier and some later than Ayampitín. As for the stemmed point, its typical style, from the very old Fell's Cave level, has now been entered in the record from El Inga. A long-stemmed variety that may have developed from it is also represented at the Ecuadorian site and, in slightly different form, at Paiján in Peru. And just recently Ripley P. Bullen of the Florida State Museum and William Plowden, Jr., reported finding fluted, stemmed points far to the north, at La Esperanza in the highlands of Honduras.

What is not yet determined is just how characteristic these various point styles are of specific peoples and times. If more firm dates are established for certain styles, and if it can be shown that they are good "horizon," or time, markers, tracing their occurrence across the continent should eventually reconstruct the pattern of early man's nomadic wanderings. The lack of dates at El Inga and many other sites is a handicap in this effort. But the fact that the leaf-shaped and stemmed varieties both occur at El Inga may yet lead to an insight that will make the whole jigsaw puzzle complete. La Esperanza may be a valuable additional source of information; Bullen and Plowden found blades—a sign of northern influence—in association with stemmed points there just as we have at El Inga.

Point styles and point technology aside, El Inga has a fascination that makes it unique among South American sites, and perhaps among all New World sites. This special quality stems from the sheer size and variety of the complex and the fact that it is a core-blade industry that includes burins. We were so intrigued by the burins that we asked Jeremiah F. Epstein of the University of Texas, who had studied burin technology in detail, to examine a portion of our collection. He too was surprised at the number and variety of burins and burin spalls. Having just spent the summer excavating an Upper Paleolithic site in southern France, he was struck by the similarities between this Ecuadorian tool industry and the French material. We borrowed a French Upper Paleolithic collection from the University of Minnesota and saw that both the French flint and the Ecuadorian obsidian industries were based on blades struck from cores and included burins and bifacial tools. Many of the tools in the two collections were almost identical; the only real differences seemed to be that the obsidian items were smaller than the flints and had finer and more complex chipping patterns. We are not proposing that there was a direct connection of any sort between the Old World culture and El Inga. No such link need be postulated. Most New World archaeologists would probably say that the first men who crossed the Bering Strait from Asia were an Upper Paleolithic people. "Upper Paleolithic" covers a long time span—perhaps 35,000 to 40,000 years—and Stone Age cultures persisted almost unchanged for many thousands of years. It is quite reasonable to expect that re-

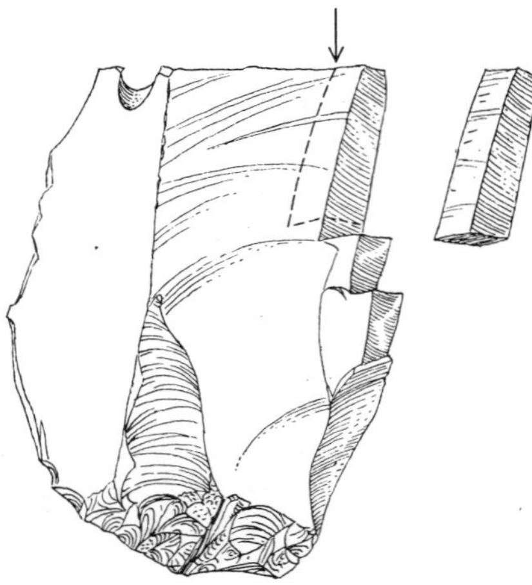

BURIN was fashioned by striking successive spalls, or slivers (*right*), from a blade. The next burin blow (*at the arrow*) would split away a spall outlined by the broken line. Striking successive spalls may have been the means of sharpening a dull burin.

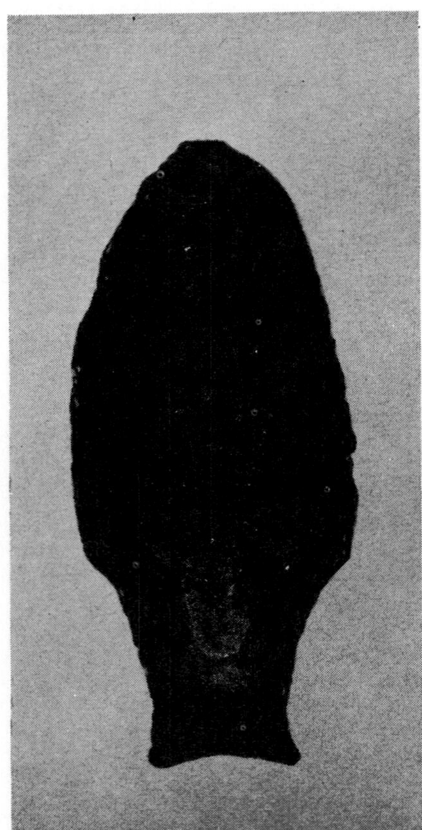

STEMMED POINT from Fell's Cave Level I is in the collection of the American Museum of Natural History in New York City. Made of basalt, it is 2.17 inches long.

CLOVIS POINT from Black-Water Draw in New Mexico is made of chalcedony and is 3.07 inches long. It is in the University Museum of the University of Pennsylvania.

lated Upper Paleolithic cultures and peoples existed in Europe and Asia, and that somewhere in China or Asiatic Russia someone will one day find tools that suggest the direct source of the earliest New World cultures. Recent work in Siberia and Japan has yielded tantalizing hints of such Asiatic sources but no unequivocal evidence.

In a way the correspondence between the Ecuadorian and the French tools is unfortunate. It is easy to make sweeping comparisons between New World and Old World cultures and to apply the terminology of the Old World Paleolithic without much reason or precision in South America. What really counts is not broad comparisons but specific relations among sites within reasonable distances of one another. As the analysis of the El Inga finds proceeds and as other finds of core-blade industries in the New World and in Asia are reported, it should be possible to establish relations between El Inga and more geographically appropriate sites than one in southern France.

TERRAIN AT EL INGA is examined by Robert E. Bell of the University of Oklahoma, with whom the author has collaborated in the investigations reported in this article. Bell is pointing to the contact between the obsidian-bearing "midden" and the light-colored subsoil exposed by erosion. This photograph was made during a preliminary field trip in 1960.

In this effort we shall not be making comparisons based on gross categories such as "hand axes," a practice that has often led to glib conclusions in the past. We shall be comparing very specific tool types: a "strangulated" blade (a blade notched to form a concave edge with which to shape arrow or spear shafts) or an "angle burin on a break" (a burin made on the broken end of a blade). We shall be looking at details of style and technique. This microanalytic approach gives promise of dredging up far more information from a site or indeed a single piece of stone than has previously been possible. Perhaps there are, in tool collections long considered safely described, typed and filed away, bits of evidence that can be reassessed in the light of the El Inga discoveries. Already Epstein has found burins at west Texas sites and in other New World complexes where they had been overlooked simply because they are hard to identify.

In addition to pressing ahead with our analytical study of the El Inga material and comparing it with other tool complexes, we are anxious to make an intensive survey of the Ecuadorian highlands. There are many indications that El Inga does not stand alone. With luck we may find at other sites in the area additional evidence that is lacking at El Inga, including even some skeletal remains of the early men. At least we should obtain some good organic samples for radioactive-carbon dating, and animal bones that will tell us what these early hunters hunted and provide information on their environment. New field work is also needed elsewhere in South America, and this too should be stimulated by El Inga. In the long run we expect that the Ecuadorian workshop and campsite will be significant not only for its rich collection of points and tools but also as a fertile source of research leads for investigators of early man in the New World.

A Stone Age Campsite at the Gateway to America

7

by Douglas D. Anderson
June 1968

Onion Portage in Alaska is an unusual Arctic archaeological site. It provides a record of human habitation going back at least 8,500 years, when its occupants were not far removed from their forebears in Asia

It seems virtually certain that men first migrated to the New World from Asia by way of the Arctic, yet for some time this fact has presented archaeology with a problem. By 10,000 B.C. Stone Age hunters were killing mammoths on the Great Plains. There is evidence suggesting that man was present in Mexico even earlier, perhaps as early as 20,000 B.C. Until 1961, however, the Arctic gateway region had yielded few traces of man before 3000 B.C. In that year excavations were begun at a site in Alaska where the remains of human occupation are buried in distinct strata, affording the investigators a unique opportunity for reliable dating.

The site is Onion Portage, on the bank of the Kobuk River in northwestern Alaska. It has been intensively excavated from 1964 through 1967. The findings may eventually demonstrate that man was present in Alaska as long ago as 13,000 B.C. Already they show that men with strong Asian affinities were there by 6500 B.C.

Why is the stratified site of Onion Portage so unusual? Archaeological evidence concerning the hunters of sea mammals who lived on the shores of Alaska and northwestern Canada is quite abundant. North of the Aleutian Islands, however, no coastal site has been discovered that is more than 5,000 years old. The reason is that the sea, rising as the last great continental glaciers melted, reached a point close to its present level some 5,000 years ago, thereby drowning the former coastline together with whatever evidence of human habitation it harbored.

The change in sea level would not, of course, have affected early sites in the interior. Such sites are scarce and usually unrewarding for other reasons. One is that the environment of tundra and taiga (treeless barren land and northern forest) could not support as many hunting groups as the game-rich shore. Another reason is that campsites on interior rivers were likely to be washed away or buried as the river shifted its course. In fact, throughout the interior only places where the ground is elevated and dry offer much archaeological promise.

The remains of numerous hunting camps have in fact been found on elevations in the Alaskan interior. These camps were apparently established to enable the hunters to catch sight of caribou on the tundra. As the hunters waited they made or repaired weapons and other implements; the campsites are littered with broken stone projectile points and tools and with the waste chips of their manufacture.

Herein lies another problem. At a rocky site where little or no soil is forming a 6,000-year-old spearpoint may lie beside one discarded only a century ago. It is nearly impossible to prove which is the older or exactly how old either one is. Even where soil has developed and the artifacts have been buried, the Arctic environment plays tricks. The upper layers of soil, soaked with water and lying on top of permanently frozen lower layers, tend to flow and disarrange buried objects. As a result both absolute and relative dating of archaeological material from sites in the Arctic interior was rarely possible before the discovery at Onion Portage.

Some 125 miles upstream from where the Kobuk River enters the Chukchi Sea the course of the river is a lazy meander five miles long. Situated at the upper end of the meander, Onion Portage is bounded by steeply cut banks on the upstream side and by a long natural levee downstream. The terrain has not been radically altered by stream erosion for at least 8,000 years. The name Onion Portage comes from the wild onions that grow profusely along the gravelly shore and from the overland haul across the base of the point, which saves five miles of upstream paddling. Today the boundary between trees and tundra is only a few hundred yards north of Onion Portage. Beyond the trees the open tundra continues all the way to the Arctic Ocean, 270 miles farther north. To the south the terrain is open taiga, dotted with patches of spruce, willow and (in sheltered places) birch.

A sandy knoll dominates the wooded landscape at the site. Hunters both ancient and modern have used this vantage as a lookout for the thousands of caribou that cross the river at Onion Portage, moving north in the spring and south in the fall. From the knoll the approaching animals can be seen soon enough for men to be stationed for the kill at points where the herd is likely to cross the river. The fishing at Onion Portage is also good; several species of salmon migrate upstream during the summer. The prized sheefish, which is scarce in other Alaskan rivers, is also caught by the local Eskimos.

Over thousands of years the lower and flatter parts of Onion Portage have been buried several times under sand eroded from gullies in the knoll. In places the alluvial fans that spread out from the gullies have built up layers of sand as

much as three feet thick. Unusually high spring floods have also engulfed the site from time to time, leaving thin deposits of silt. Windstorms too have spread thin sheets of drifted sand across the site. Each such covering killed the turf buried under it; the new turf that formed on the fresh surface was separated from the dead turf below by a sterile layer of sand or silt. All the deposits combined make up the sequence of strata at Onion Portage. In places the sequence is 20 feet thick. More than 70 of the surfaces show evidence of human occupation. The layers of turf are concentrated in bands, each of which contains from three to 14 occupation levels. The bands have been given consecutive numbers, starting with Band 1 just below the surface and ending with Band 8, the deepest dated series of occupation levels at the site.

The Onion Portage site was discovered in 1941 by the late J. L. Giddings, Jr., of Brown University, who was traveling down the Kobuk on a raft. He stopped and excavated several 500-year-old Eskimo house pits to gather material for an Arctic tree-ring chronology he was then establishing. He returned to the site 20 years later; test digging that year revealed the stratified layers. Giddings began a full-scale excavation in 1964, with the support of Brown University and the National Science Foundation. In the same year he died. Recognizing the uniqueness of the site, both institutions urged that the work be continued the following season. Froelich G. Rainey, director of the University Museum at the University of Pennsylvania, an Arctic specialist and a longtime colleague of Giddings', and I, one of Giddings' former students, were invited to take over the excavation. In the 1966 and 1967 seasons the work at Onion Portage has continued with the same support under my direction.

Our study is by no means complete. Soil samples from various levels at the site, for instance, are still being analyzed at the University of Uppsala, the University of Alaska and the University of Arizona for their chemical constituents, pollen content and even for microscopic diatoms. Samples of charcoal from each of the eight bands have already yielded carbon-14 dates that will enable us to fit the expected biological and geological information into a sensitive chronology. The chronology now spans a minimum of 8,500 years and may eventually go back another 6,500. Even now a preliminary correlation of the carbon-14 dates with the stone tools, weapons and other remains unearthed at Onion Portage has produced some surprising results. One finding substantially alters assumptions about cultural developments in the New World Arctic.

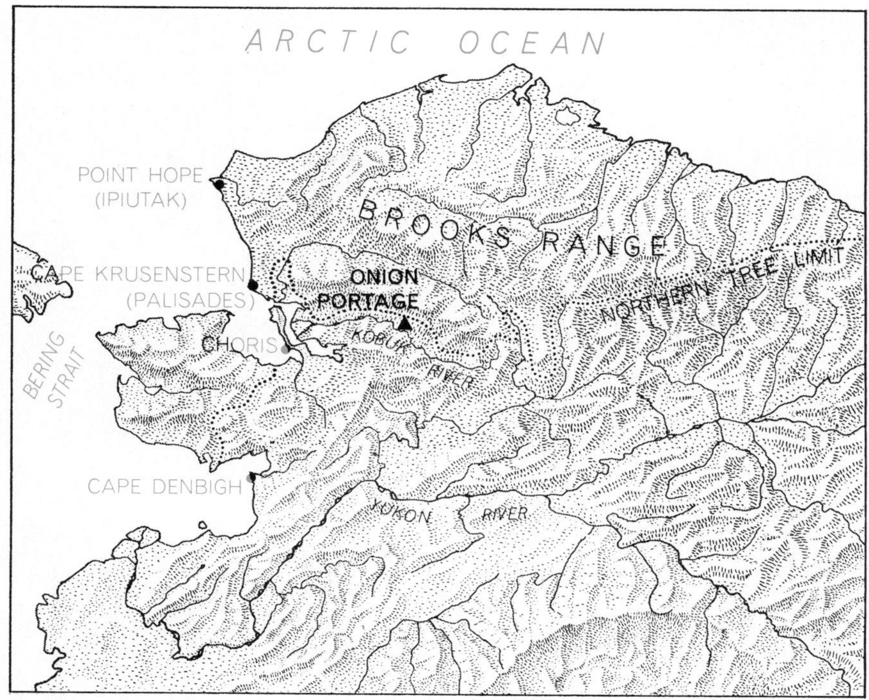

ALASKAN SITES at which artifacts have been found that resemble those unearthed at Onion Portage include the four located on this map. Onion Portage, the first known stratified site in the New World's Arctic interior, was discovered by J. L. Giddings, Jr., in 1941.

In presenting our preliminary results I shall start with the earliest of the three main cultural traditions we have found at Onion Portage. American archaeologists use the word "tradition" to describe a continuity of cultural traits that persist over a considerable length of time and often occupy a broad geographical area. A single unifying tradition may be shared by several distinct cultures. The word "complex" is used to describe the distinctive remains of a culture. A tradition usually includes more than one culture complex. It is with the earliest culture complex of the earliest tradition at Onion Portage that I shall begin.

The complex has been named Akmak, after the northern-Alaskan Eskimo word for chert, the flintlike stone that the hunting people of this complex most commonly employed to make tools and weapons. Most of the Akmak implements have been found on the sandy knoll at the site, between six inches and two feet below the surface. Some have been uncovered along the side of one of the gullies that cuts into the knoll and at the bottom of the gully's ancient channel, which is 10 feet below the bottom of the present channel. Others have been found below Band 8, where, having been carried down the gully, they had lain since before the first levels of Band 8 were formed. The fact that some of the material comes from below Band 8 indicates that the Akmak artifacts are at least 8,500 years old. They may be as much as 15,000 years old. Two fragments of excavated bone are being dated by carbon-14 analysis, but the sample is unfortunately too small to produce a reliable carbon-14 reading. We hope that future work at the site will produce material to settle the matter.

Most Akmak implements are of two classes. Comprising one class are large, wide "blades," the term for parallel-edged flakes of stone that were struck from a prepared "core." The other class consists of "bifaces," so named because the stone from which they were made was shaped by flaking surplus stone from both sides. From the blades the Akmak artisans produced a variety of tools. They include long end scrapers, curved implements with a sharp pro-

DEEP PIT at Onion Portage shows the characteristic layering of soil at the site. Each thin, dark horizontal band was formed when charcoal from hunters' fires or other material was buried under sand or silt. Artifacts found below the lowest band may be as much as 15,000 years old. The measuring stick at right center is three meters long.

ONION PORTAGE SITE is located by the white triangle (*top center*) in this aerial photograph. The site lies on the upstream bank of a point of land enclosed by a wide meander of the Kobuk River, 125 miles from the sea in the interior of northwestern Alaska.

tuberance resembling a bird's beak and knives shaped by flaking one or both faces of a blade. The bifaces, which have the general form of a disk, were usually made by first striking the side of a slab-like core; the detached flakes left scars that end at the center of the disk. Numerous smaller flakes were then removed around the margin of the disk to give it a sharp edge. Nothing like these implements has been found in Alaska before. Indeed, the tools that most resemble Akmak disk bifaces come from the area around Lake Baikal in Siberia, where they are found at sites that are between 12,000 and 15,000 years old.

Using a technique similar to the one for producing large blades, Akmak artisans also made "microblades." Most microblades are about an inch long and quarter of an inch wide. They were struck from a small core prepared in a way that is characteristic of "campus-type microcores," so named because the first to be discovered in America were found at a site on the campus of the University of Alaska. Campus-type microcores have been found in many other parts of Alaska and also in Siberia, Mongolia and Japan. The oldest ones come from the island of Hokkaido in Japan and the Kamchatka Peninsula in the U.S.S.R.

Many Akmak microblades were made into rectangular chips by breaking off both ends of the blade. Prehistoric hunters set such chips in a groove cut in the side of a pointed shaft of wood, bone or antler. The razor-sharp bits of stone gave the pointed weapon a wicked cutting edge. Grooved shafts of antler associated with rectangular microblades have been found both in Siberia and in the Trail Creek caves in western Alaska. Although grooved shafts have not been found at Onion Portage, it is reasonable to assume that the Akmak rectangles were intended for mounting in them.

The Akmak artisans also made burins: specialized stone tools with a sharp corner particularly useful for making grooves in antler and bone. The Akmak technique for producing burins was to strike a blow that left a chisel-like point at the corner of a flake [*see illustration on page 67*]. Akmak burins show signs of wear both at the tip and along the edge,

TRADITION	CULTURE	DATES	STRATIGRAPHIC LOCATION
ESKIMO	ARCTIC WOODLAND ESKIMO	A.D. 1000–1700	BAND 1
	?		
?	NORTHERN INDIAN?	A.D. 400–800	BAND 2
ARCTIC SMALL-TOOL TRADITION	NORTON/IPIUTAK		
?	CHORIS COMPLEX	1500–500 B.C.	BAND 3
ARCTIC SMALL-TOOL TRADITION	DENBIGH FLINT COMPLEX	2200–1800 B.C.	BAND 4
NORTHERN ARCHAIC TRADITION	PORTAGE COMPLEX	2600–2200 B.C.	BAND 5
	PALISADES II COMPLEX	3900–2600 B.C.	BAND 6
		4000–3900 B.C.	BAND 7
	HIATUS		
AMERICAN PALEO-ARCTIC TRADITION	KOBUK COMPLEX	6200–6000 B.C.	BAND 8
	AKMAK COMPLEX	? 13,000–6500 B.C.	BELOW BAND 8

FEET BELOW SURFACE: 0 1 2 3 4 5 6 7 8 9 10 11 12

EIGHT MAIN BANDS in the stratigraphic column uncovered at Onion Portage are related in this chart to the evidence of human occupation they contain. Starting before 6500 B.C., and probably much earlier, three major cultural "traditions" succeed one another. The third tradition, interrupted about 1800 B.C., was initially represented at the site by the culture named the Denbigh Flint complex. It was evidently ancestral to the Eskimo tradition that appeared at Onion Portage about A.D. 1000 and continued thereafter.

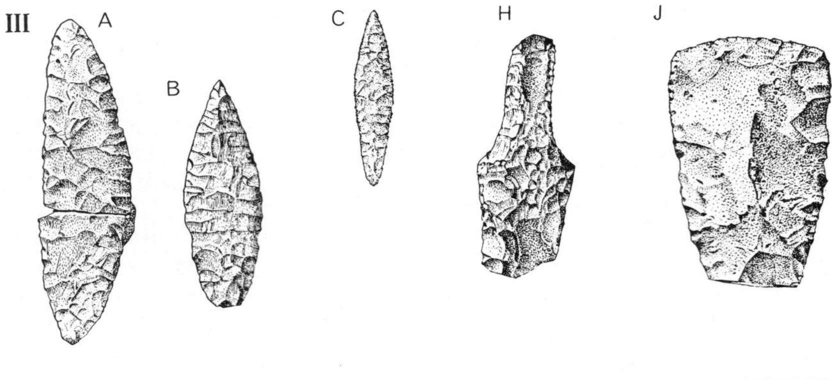

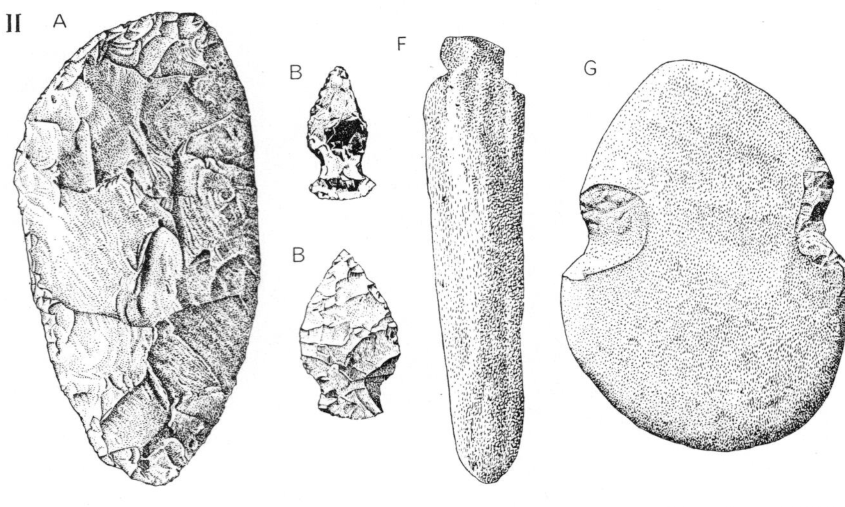

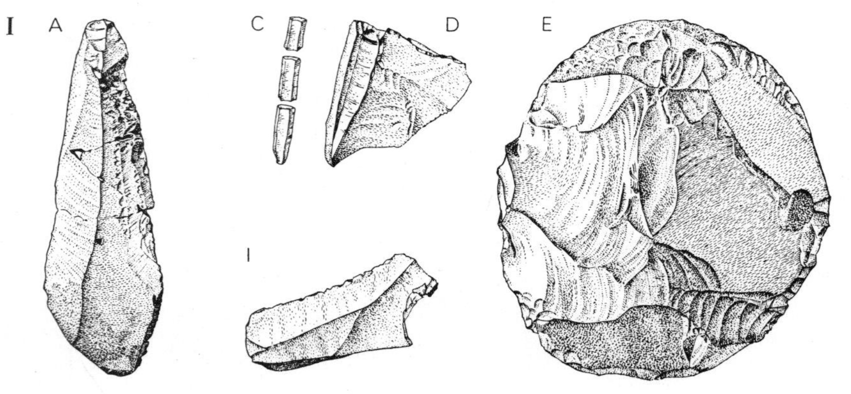

A — KNIFE
B — PROJECTILE POINT
C — EDGE INSET
D — CAMPUS-TYPE MICROCORE
E — DISCOID BIFACE
F — NEEDLE SHARPENER
G — PEBBLE SINKER
H — BEAKED TOOL
I — BURIN
J — ADZE BLADE

ARTIFACTS OF THREE PERIODS at Onion Portage reveal the presence of three separate cultural traditions: the American Paleo-Arctic (I), the Northern Archaic (II) and the Arctic Small-Tool tradition (III). Knives (*A*) are present in all three traditions and stone projectile points (*B*) in the last two. Hunters of all three traditions had projectiles, but the two Arctic traditions favored points made from antler or ivory and inset with tiny stone blades (*C*). Unique to the earliest tradition are "campus-type microcores" (*D*) and disk-shaped bifaces (*E*). Characteristic of the non-Arctic Archaic tradition are stones for sharpening needles (*F*) and sinkers for nets (*G*). Burins appear in both of the Arctic traditions; the one shown (*I*) is Akmak. Unique to the later Arctic tradition are peculiar beaked tools (*H*) and small adze blades (*J*). All the implements are reproduced at one-half natural size.

indicating that they were used not only for grooving but also for cutting.

The Akmak tools suggest relationships between Onion Portage and Asia. Considering the changes in Arctic geography during the past 30,000 years, this is scarcely surprising. At the height of the last continental glaciation Asia and North America were connected across what is now the Bering Strait. The land area that the lowered sea level had exposed was more than a mere isthmus. At its maximum extent between 20,000 and 18,000 years ago it was virtually a subcontinent, a tundra-covered plain 1,300 miles wide that must have been populated by herds of game and hunters pursuing them. The great plain, which has been named Beringia, made Alaska an extension of northern Asia. At the same time two continental glaciers in North America effectively cut ice-free Alaska off from the rest of the New World. The isolation of Alaska did not end until sometime between 14,000 and 10,000 years ago, when the glaciers began to melt rapidly. By then Beringia had already been twice drowned and reexposed by fluctuations in the level of the sea. Then, about 10,000 years ago, Beringia began its final submergence, a process that was not completed until some 5,000 years ago.

To repeat, the Akmak period at Onion Portage ended about 6500 B.C. and may have begun as early as 13,000 B.C. Between these dates dry land connected ice-free Alaska with Siberia while glaciers forbade or at least inhibited contact with the rest of North America. The resemblances between the Akmak culture and Siberian cultures, and the lack of resemblances between the Akmak culture and Paleo-Indian cultures to the south, reflect this geographic history. At the same time there are significant differences between the Akmak culture and the Siberian cultures, suggesting that the Akmak complex resulted from a long period of isolated regional development. Because the tradition of which the Akmak complex is the earliest appears to have been an indigenous development, arising from earlier Arctic-adapted cultures, I have named it the American Paleo-Arctic tradition.

The next evidence of human habitation found at Onion Portage is in two levels of Band 8. Carbon-14 analysis of material from the higher level suggests that the people who camped there did so sometime between 6200 and 6000 B.C. I have termed the remains from Band 8 the Kobuk complex.

The limited variety of Kobuk-complex

artifacts suggests that the material found at Onion Portage represents only a part of a larger assemblage of stone tools. Fewer than 100 worked pieces of stone have been recovered from the two levels. Most of them are rectangles made from microblades. There are also two burins made from flakes, a few remnants of campus-type microcores, a single obsidian scraper and several flakes, some of which have notched edges. All the implements were found adjacent to hearths on deposits of silt. The silt suggests that Onion Portage was a wet and uncomfortable place when the Kobuk hunters camped there. The hearths are probably those of small groups that stayed only briefly.

At a number of surface sites in the Brooks Range I have collected stone implements that are almost identical with those of the Kobuk complex. The only major difference is that the Brooks Range tool assemblage includes biface knives, which are missing from the Kobuk levels at Onion Portage. I suspect that the difference is more apparent than real; if we had unearthed a larger Kobuk inventory at Onion Portage, it probably would have included biface knives. In any case, the presence in both the Akmak and the Kobuk assemblages of microblade rectangles and campus-type microcores suggests that, although the Kobuk complex represents a later period, it is nonetheless a part of the American Paleo-Arctic tradition.

Quite the opposite is true of the material we have unearthed in Band 7, Band 6 and Band 5. After a hiatus of some 2,000 years an entirely new cultural tradition arrived at Onion Portage. Its lowest levels are dated by carbon-14 analysis at around 4000 B.C. There are no microblades among its tools. Instead of using weapons with microblades inserted in them the newcomers hunted with projectiles tipped with crude stone points that had notched bases and were bifacially flaked. The new assemblage also includes large, irregular knives made from flakes, thin scrapers, notched stone sinkers and large crescent-shaped or oval bifaces. We also unearthed two heavy cobblestone choppers.

The tools from Band 7 and Band 6, which contain the early and middle phases of the new tradition, are nearly identical with a group of tools from a cliff site overlooking Cape Krusenstern on the Alaskan coast 115 miles west of Onion Portage. The cliff site is known as Palisades; the name "Palisades II complex" has been given to these phases of the new tradition at Onion Portage. The tools of the Palisades II complex reflect an uninterrupted continuity, marked only by gradual stylistic changes, for 1,400 years. One such change affected the hunters' projectile points. The notched base characteristic of the early phase gave way in the middle phase to a base with a projecting stem.

The contents of Band 5 indicate that around 2600 B.C. a period of rapid change began at Onion Portage and continued for 300 years. Several new types of tools appear; projectile points, for example, are neither notched nor stemmed but have a straight base. These and other differences in the assemblage indicate that the occupation levels in Band 5 belong to later phases of the new tradition. They warrant a label of their own, and I have named them collectively the Portage complex.

How is the arrival of the new tradition at Onion Portage to be explained? It is noteworthy that the duration of the new tradition coincides almost exactly with a major alteration in the climate of Alaska. About 10,000 years ago, as the region's last glacial period drew to a close, the Alaskan climate entered a warming phase that reached its maximum between 4000 and 2000 B.C. Throughout the period of milder weather the forest margin moved northward, steadily encroaching on the tundra. By the time of the maximum the boundary between tundra and taiga had probably advanced well beyond the position it occupies today. During the 2,000 years of the maximum it seems likely that Onion Portage lay well within the northern forest zone.

Far to the southeast, in the forests of the eastern U.S., an Indian population had pursued a woodland-oriented way of life beginning as early as 6000 B.C. Its weapons and tools reflect a forest adaptation; they belong to what is known as the Archaic tradition, as op-

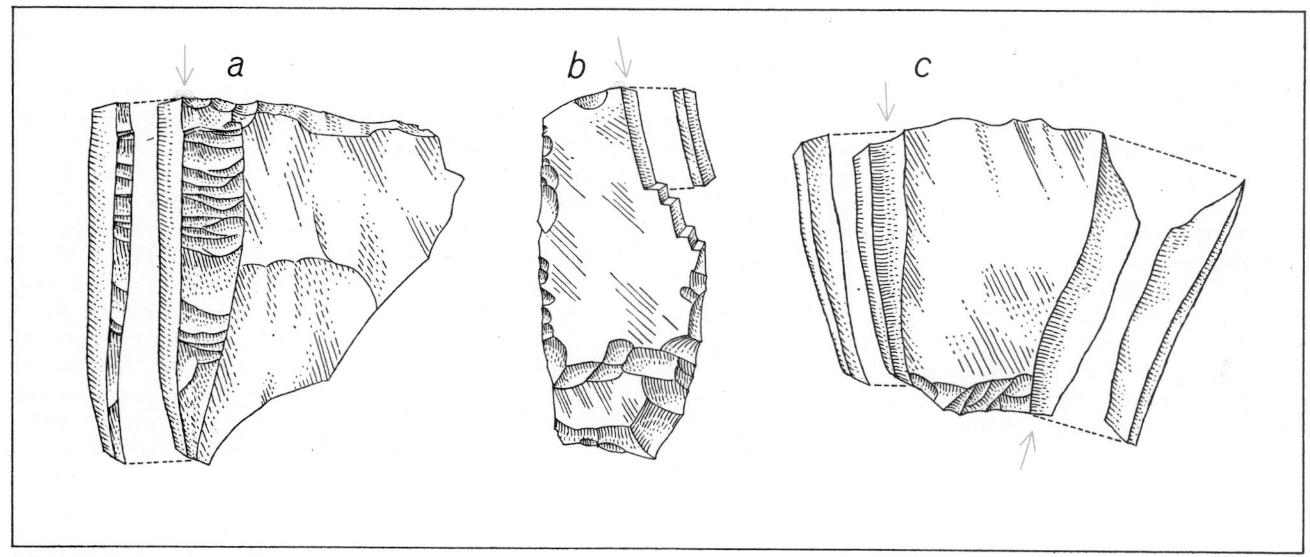

GROOVE-CUTTING TOOLS, or burins, were made by Akmak (*a*) and Denbigh (*b*) knappers at Onion Portage. The Akmak knappers chipped a notch into the edge of a prepared flake before striking a blow (*arrow*) that knocked off a long, narrow spall, giving the flake a sharp, chisel-like corner (*color*). The Denbigh knappers, using the same burin blow (*arrow*), knocked much smaller spalls off flakes carefully prepared in advance. They used the tiny spalls as tools for engraving. Choris knappers (*c*) used the burin blow to strike fine, regular spalls from flakes of irregular shape. This produced no burins; the knappers made tools from the spalls instead.

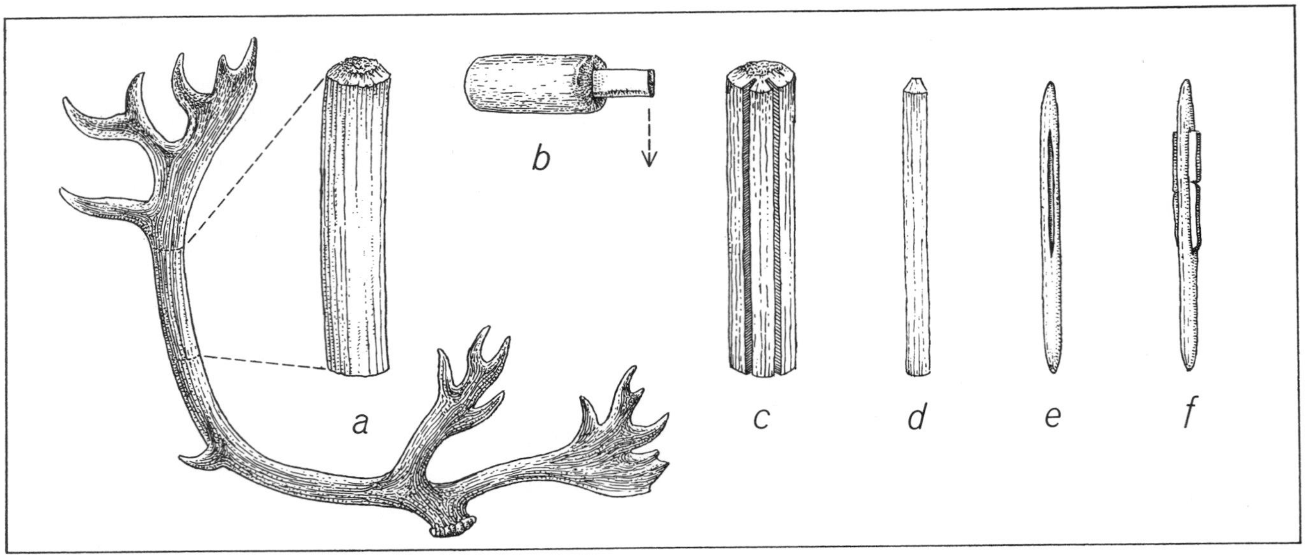

PROJECTILE POINTS can be made from antler and microblades as shown here. A length of antler (*a*) is deeply grooved (*c*) with a burin (*b*) mounted in a handle for easy use. The triangular antler segments (*d*) are then rounded and pointed, and grooves are made in one or both sides (*e*). Razor-edged bits of microblade are then set in the grooves (*f*) to form a cutting edge. The Akmak, Kobuk and Denbigh levels at Onion Portage contain edge insets. Akmak and Kobuk insets are rectangles; Denbigh insets are crescents.

posed to the older Paleo-Indian tradition. I find it significant that, during a time when the forest had shifted northward, an assemblage of tools with many resemblances to the Archaic tradition should appear at Onion Portage. Crescent-shaped bifaces, projectile points with notched and stemmed bases, heavy choppers and notched stones that the Indians of the Archaic tradition used as sinkers for nets are among the elements common to the two assemblages.

Up to now evidence for the early diffusion of the Archaic tradition northward and westward from the woodlands of the eastern U.S. does not go much beyond the Great Lakes region. Artifacts that resemble Archaic-tradition tools have been found in central and northwestern Canada and in central Alaska, but their age is undetermined. The fact that the tools are distributed throughout this area nonetheless suggests the possibility that Archaic peoples, or at least the art of making tools in the Archaic tradition, moved northward into the Arctic along with the advancing forest. The findings at Onion Portage seem to support this suggestion. I have therefore named the Palisades II complex and the Portage complex together the Northern Archaic tradition. The differences between the second tradition at Onion Portage and the American Paleo-Arctic tradition that preceded it seem great enough to suggest that they were the products of two different populations. They may have been respectively early Northern Indians and proto-Eskimos.

Almost immediately after 2300 B.C. there was a resurgence of Arctic culture at Onion Portage. The evidence in Band 4 marks the arrival of hunters representing the Arctic Small-Tool tradition. This tradition is well known from other Arctic sites. It is the culture of the earliest people in the New World Arctic who were equally at home on the coast and in the interior. The element of the tradition that is present at Onion Portage is the Denbigh Flint complex, first recognized at an Alaskan coastal site on Cape Denbigh [see "Early Man in the Arctic," by J. L. Giddings, Jr., beginning on page 92].

The characteristic implements of the Denbigh people are burins and edge insets—the sharp stones shaped for insertion into grooved weapons. Some Denbigh edge insets were made from microblades, but all of them differ from the rectangular Akmak and Kobuk insets in that they are delicately flaked into half-moon shapes. The Denbigh people produced microblades for a variety of other uses. For greater efficiency they devised a new form of microcore. It is wider than the campus-type core, and it allowed them to strike off wider and more easily worked blades.

The people of the Denbigh Flint complex flourished widely in the Arctic between 2500 and 2000 B.C. Many students of Arctic archaeology consider them to be the direct ancestors of today's Eskimos, pointing out that the geographic distribution of Denbigh sites almost exactly coincides with the distribution of Eskimos in historic times. Parallels between the Denbigh Flint complex and the American Paleo-Arctic tradition, including the use of microblades and edge-inset weapons, suggest that the Denbigh culture may well have descended from the Akmak and Kobuk cultures.

After 2000 B.C. the New World Arctic and coastal subarctic area supported a number of Eskimo regional groups, none of which developed along exactly the same lines. Choris is the name given to one regional people that inhabited the Alaskan coast near the mouth of the Kobuk River, hunting caribou and living in large oval houses. The Choris-complex people have an involved history that spans 1,000 years from 1500 to 500 B.C. At Onion Portage, Choris artifacts are found in Band 3.

The earliest known pottery in the New World Arctic comes from Choris sites. The pottery was well made, was decorated by stamping patterns on the surface and was fired at a reasonably high temperature. In the earliest phases of the Choris complex, evidence for which is found at sites on the coast but not at Onion Portage, the pots were decorated by striking the wet clay with a cord-wrapped paddle. The pots are too skillfully made for it to be likely that the Choris people were experimenting with clay for the first time. Instead a fully developed industry must have been introduced from the outside. Exact counterparts have not yet been found abroad, but the basic Choris pottery patterns suggest a source in Asia. This is apparently not the case for Choris-complex tools such as knife blades and skin scrapers. Some of the Choris edge insets for weapons resemble Denbigh types, but the other tools do not. If anything, they resemble Northern Archaic artifacts.

The Choris tool assemblage presents a puzzle in the form of large, regularly flaked projectile points that look very much like the Scottsbluff, Plainview and Angostura points made by the Paleo-Indian hunters of the Great Plains. The nearest Paleo-Indian sites, however, are removed from the Choris complex by some 2,500 miles and 3,000 years. What this likeness means in terms of a possible cultural relation between the Arctic and the Great Plains is a question to which I shall return.

From 500 B.C. to A.D. 500 the hunters who camped at Onion Portage left a record of steady Eskimo cultural evolution that includes evidence of increasing communication between the coast and the interior. Some of the artifacts recovered from the middle levels of Band 2, for example, are typical of those found at the seacoast site of Ipiutak, some 200 miles away on Point Hope. Regional variations nonetheless persist. Tools ground out of slabs of slate are found along with Ipiutak-complex tools at Onion Portage, but ground slate is unknown in the Ipiutak assemblage on Point Hope.

One final break in the continuity of Arctic-oriented cultures is apparent at Onion Portage. It is found in the upper occupation levels of Band 2, which were inhabited around A.D. 500 or 600. The artifacts in these levels are totally unlike those of contemporaneous Eskimo cultures along the coast. It seems logical to assume that forest Indians moving up from the south were responsible for the new cultural inventory. Whatever the identity of the newcomers, they did not stay long. Around A.D. 1000 Onion Portage was again in Eskimo hands.

Measured in terms of the number of artifacts and wealth of information, the modern period recorded in Band 1 is the best-known in the Onion Portage sequence. Our current studies, combined with Giddings' earlier ones, give a remarkably detailed picture of the Kobuk River Eskimos' gradual change from a part-time coastal economy to a full-time way of life adapted to tundra and taiga conditions, in which networks of trade maintained communication with the Eskimos of the coast.

Taken as a whole, the stratigraphic record at Onion Portage has cast much

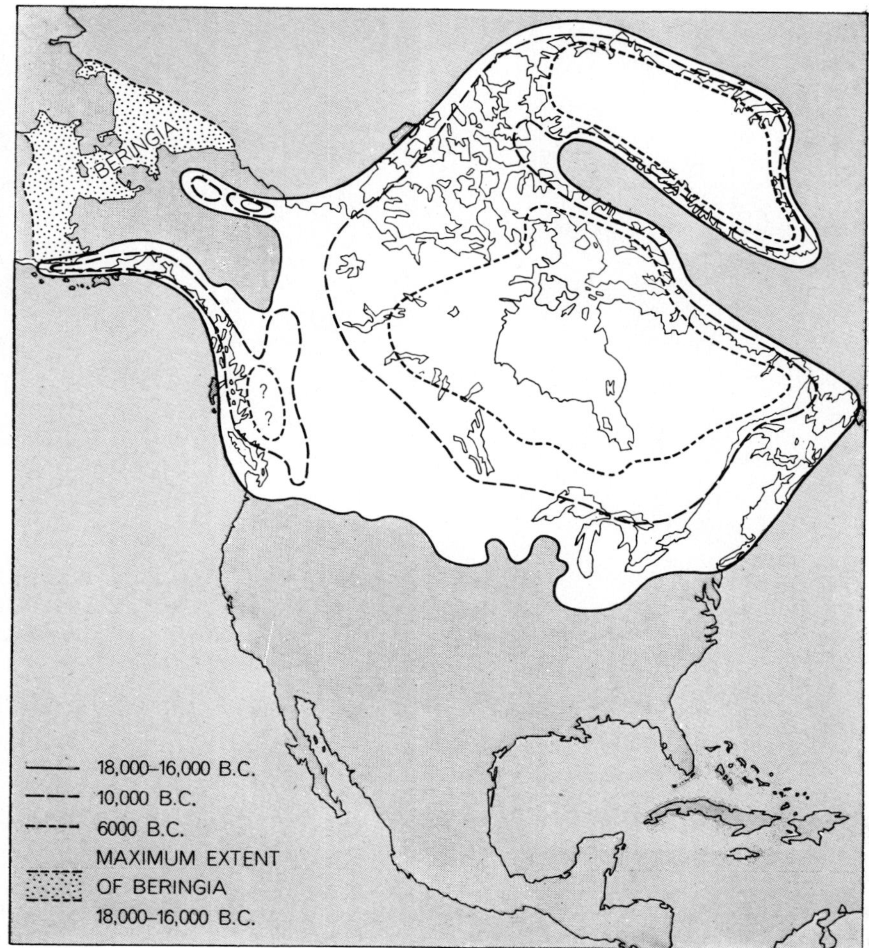

ICE BARRIER, formed by union of two continental glaciers, cut off Alaska from the rest of North America for perhaps 8,000 years. The era's lowered seas exposed Beringia, a vast area that made Alaska into an extension of Siberia. Arctic and Temperate North America were not reunited until the final withdrawal of the two ice sheets had begun (*broken lines*).

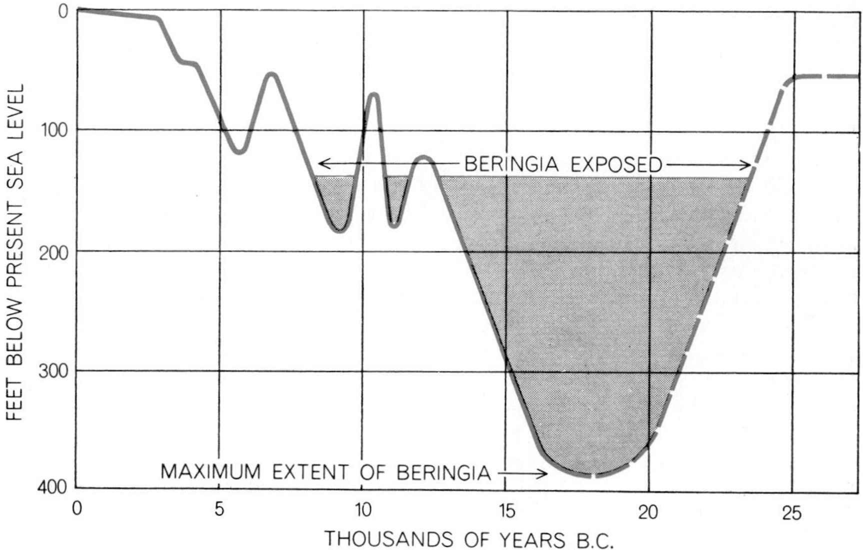

CHANGING SEA LEVEL in late Pleistocene times drowned Beringia 8,000 years ago. The link between Alaska and Siberia had been exposed earlier for two short periods and one long period when it was quite large. The graph is based on one by D. M. Hopkins of the U.S. Geological Survey; dating of sea-level changes before 18,000 B.C. is conjectural.

WORK CREW on the flats below the hill at Onion Portage slowly exposes one of the site's more than 70 levels with traces of human occupation. Silt carried by floodwaters and sand eroded from the hillside had accumulated in the flats to a depth of 20 feet in places.

new light on the relations between various poorly dated or undated Arctic archaeological assemblages. At the start we see Arctic peoples with cultural roots in Siberia adapting themselves to a life of hunting on the treeless tundra of interior Alaska, and later to hunting along the treeless coast. As we can infer from the abundance of microblade edge insets found at Onion Portage, a part of this adaptation involved the efficient use of materials other than wood for weapons, among them antler (and later ivory) spearpoints edged with stone. This indigenous tradition, based on Asian origins, had an uninterrupted development from perhaps as early as 13,000 B.C. until about 6000 B.C.

Sometime before 4000 B.C. we see the arrival at Onion Portage of a forest-adapted tradition that had its origins in the eastern woodlands of the U.S. The advance of the Archaic tradition into Arctic terrain coincided with the post-glacial shift in climate that allowed the forests to invade the northern tundra. With the reexpansion of the tundra at the end of the warm period Arctic cultures once again dominated the Kobuk River region. At the same time they spread rapidly across the entire Arctic area occupied by Eskimos today.

Until Onion Portage was excavated the archaeological record in the Arctic favored the view that early cultural developments there were somehow connected with the Paleo-Indians of the Great Plains. Many scholars suggested that the Arctic and Paleo-Indian cultures shared essentially the same cultural tradition, perhaps originating in the north or perhaps in the Great Plains but in either case occupying northwestern Alaska and Canada sometime between 7000 and 3000 B.C. The suggestion derived its strength primarily from the presence of projectile points almost identical with Paleo-Indian ones at several sites in Alaska and Canada. The projectile points found in the Arctic could not be dated, but it was speculated that they were as much as 7,000 or 8,000 years old. Such antiquity, of course, added strength to the Paleo-Indian hypothesis.

Even before the Onion Portage excavations some contrary evidence had come to light. For example, the Choris complex is rich in projectile points that are Paleo-Indian in appearance. Yet the Choris complex is firmly dated between 1500 and 1000 B.C.—scarcely half of the minimum age suggested by the Paleo-Indian hypothesis.

The findings at Onion Portage, in my opinion, cast even more doubt on the hypothesis. During the millenniums between 7000 and 3000 B.C.—nearly the entire interval of the postulated contact between (or identity of) the Arctic and the Paleo-Indian cultures—nothing from any occupation level at Onion Portage shows any hint of Paleo-Indian influence. On the contrary, the influence in the earlier part of the interval is Siberian and in the later part Archaic.

We hope that future work at Onion Portage will push the firmly dated record of Arctic prehistory back to even earlier times. We should also like to learn what cultures were developing along the Kobuk River between 6000 and 4000 B.C.—the period for which we have no record at Onion Portage. Meanwhile what we have already learned substantially clarifies the sequence of events at the gateway to the New World.

Early Man in the West Indies

8

by José M. Cruxent and Irving Rouse
November 1969

Until recently it seemed that the islands of the Caribbean were uninhabited up to about the time of Christ. Now it appears that men may have arrived 5,000 years earlier. How did they get there?

When and by whom the islands of the West Indies were first settled is a matter of debate among archaeologists. The debate may soon be intensified: evidence recently discovered suggests that people of the Paleo-Indian age, the earliest period in New World prehistory, reached one of the main islands 7,000 years ago. If this is so, it means that New World hunters managed to cross the Caribbean when their level of culture was no more advanced than that of the Paleolithic age in the Old World.

It is our intention in this article to present the new evidence and to relate it to older knowledge and conjecture about the aboriginal settling of the West Indies. Let us first briefly review the geography of the area, with special reference to the various island chains that provide natural migration routes outward from the mainland.

The West Indies consist of two major island chains and three minor ones. The southernmost major chain, the Lesser Antilles, consists of many small islands forming an arc along the eastern side of the Caribbean and separating it from the Atlantic. Starting near the mouth of the Orinoco River in Venezuela, the chain extends northward and then curves around to the northwest, so that its last members (the Virgin Islands) almost touch the first of the Greater Antilles.

The island next to the Virgin Islands is Puerto Rico. Starting there, the Greater Antilles extend westward along the north side of the Caribbean. The next islands in the chain are Hispaniola (politically divided between Haiti and the Dominican Republic) and Jamaica, which lies somewhat to the south. The chain ends with Cuba, whose western tip nearly fills the gap between the peninsulas of Yucatán and Florida at the mouth of the Gulf of Mexico. The Greater Antilles are much larger and better endowed with natural resources than the other islands of the West Indies, and today they are also much more populous.

Of the three lesser chains the southernmost stretches along the coast of Venezuela from the mouth of the Orinoco on the east to Lake Maracaibo on the west. Its main islands are Trinidad, which is the easternmost, and two smaller clusters: the Venezuelan islands of Margarita, Coche and Cubagua in the middle and the Dutch islands of Bonaire, Curaçao and Aruba in the west. The chain does not have a generally accepted name. In Spanish it is called the Leeward Islands, but the same name is used in English for a group of former British possessions in the Lesser Antilles. Here we shall call the chain the South Caribbean islands.

The next of the lesser chains crosses the Caribbean from Central America almost to Jamaica, following a submerged mountain ridge. Today this chain consists mainly of banks, reefs and cays, but two of its islands (Providencia and San Andrés, which are part of Colombia) are of fair size. When the sea level was lower a few thousand years ago, the chain formed a nearly continuous series of stepping-stones leading to the Greater Antilles. This group also lacks a generally accepted name; here we shall call them the Mid-Caribbean islands.

The last of the lesser chains consists of the Bahamas, which lie to the north and east of Hispaniola and Cuba and extend northward for some distance along the east coast of Florida. A series of small coral islets, they provide the best stepping-stone route between the mainland to the north and eastern Cuba and Hispaniola to the south.

Prevailing winds and currents in the Caribbean strongly favor some directions of travel over others. The trade winds blow from the northeast, making voyages in a westerly direction easy in both the Greater Antilles and the South Caribbean chain. The currents favor movement to the west and also movement from South America north to the major island chains. The South Equatorial Current flows across the Atlantic to the coast of Guiana and is deflected northwestward through the South Caribbean chain and the southernmost Lesser Antilles. The North Equatorial Current follows a similar course through the northern Lesser Antilles to the Greater Antilles. Still farther north, the Canaries Current skirts the north coast of Hispaniola and flows through the Bahamas. The effect of the currents is reinforced by the flow of the two major rivers of northern South America: the Orinoco and the Magdalena. Both discharge into the sea with such force that debris is carried offshore for miles to be picked up by the South Equatorial Current and, in the case of the Orinoco, carried some distance into the Lesser Antilles.

Given these conditions, one would expect that the West Indies were populated from South America. This was true at the time of the first European voyages to America. When the Spaniards reached the area, they found that both the Lesser and the Greater Antilles were inhabited by Indians who spoke Cariban and Arawakan, languages that are widespread in eastern South America. The inhabitants' material culture belonged to the final pre-Columbian age, or period of development, in the Caribbean area; that age is known as the Neo-Indian. This means that the Caribs and Arawaks made pottery. Coincidentally they also knew the art of farming and were skilled mariners, so that it is easy to understand their successful expansion through most of the West Indies.

The Neo-Indians, however, were relative newcomers to the islands. We now know that they migrated from South America at about the time of Christ, entered the Greater Antilles about A.D. 250 and did not populate their most northerly territory, the Bahamas, until A.D. 1000. As they moved along they overran an earlier West Indian population. When the Spaniards arrived, the earlier people existed only as remnants in western Cuba, in a few small Cuban offshore islands and in southwestern Hispaniola.

The earlier inhabitants' material culture belonged to the preceding Meso-Indian age. They knew nothing of pottery; they made their distinctive artifacts by grinding stone and by chipping flakes of flint. They did not know farming and fed themselves instead by fishing and gathering shellfish and wild vegetable foods. After a few decades under Spanish administration the remnant Meso-Indians, together with nearly all the Neo-Indians, had become extinct.

Perhaps because the Meso-Indians

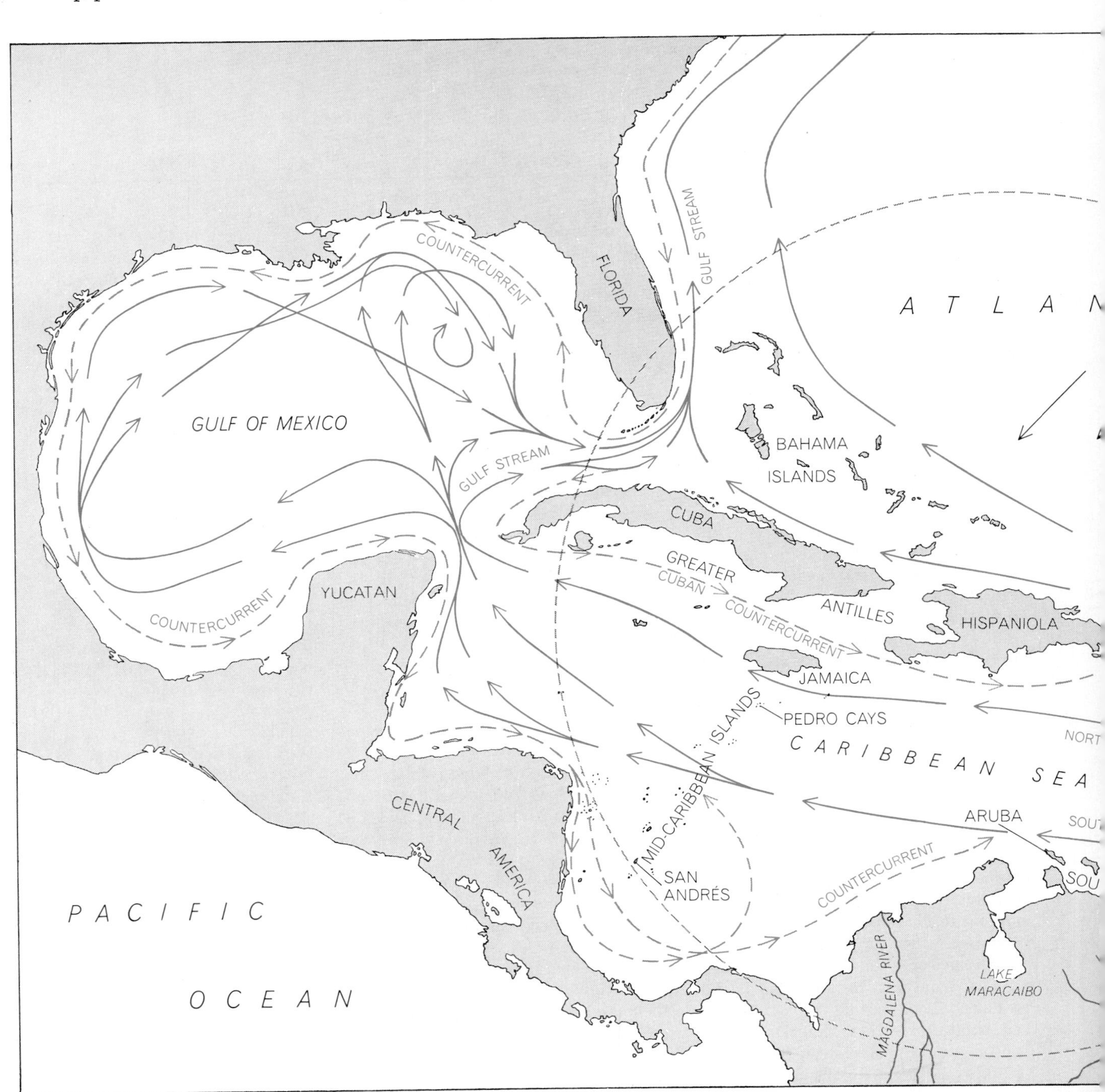

ISLAND CHAINS of the West Indies include the Greater Antilles (consisting of Cuba, Jamaica, Hispaniola and Puerto Rico), the Lesser Antilles (beginning with the Virgin Islands and ending with Grenada), the South Caribbean islands (from Trinidad, the most easterly, to Aruba, the most westerly), the Mid-Caribbean islands (extending from San Andrés to Pedro Cays) and the Bahama Islands (extending from Hispaniola to Florida). Hispaniola is geographically central (*broken circle*). The route to it from Vene-

were fishermen and presumably at home on the water the question of how and when they reached their island homes remained of limited interest to scholars until evidence of an even earlier West Indian population was discovered in recent years. These discoveries, both in the islands and on the adjacent mainland, now make it clear that, no matter how early the Meso-Indian occupation of the West Indies may have been, even earlier Paleo-Indian occupations preceded it. The sites—in Florida, Cuba and Hispaniola—were identified as Paleo-Indian by the absence of ground-stone artifacts; the only stone implements were made of flaked flint. How and when these primitive hunting peoples reached the islands are questions that have also stimulated increased interest in Meso-Indian origins.

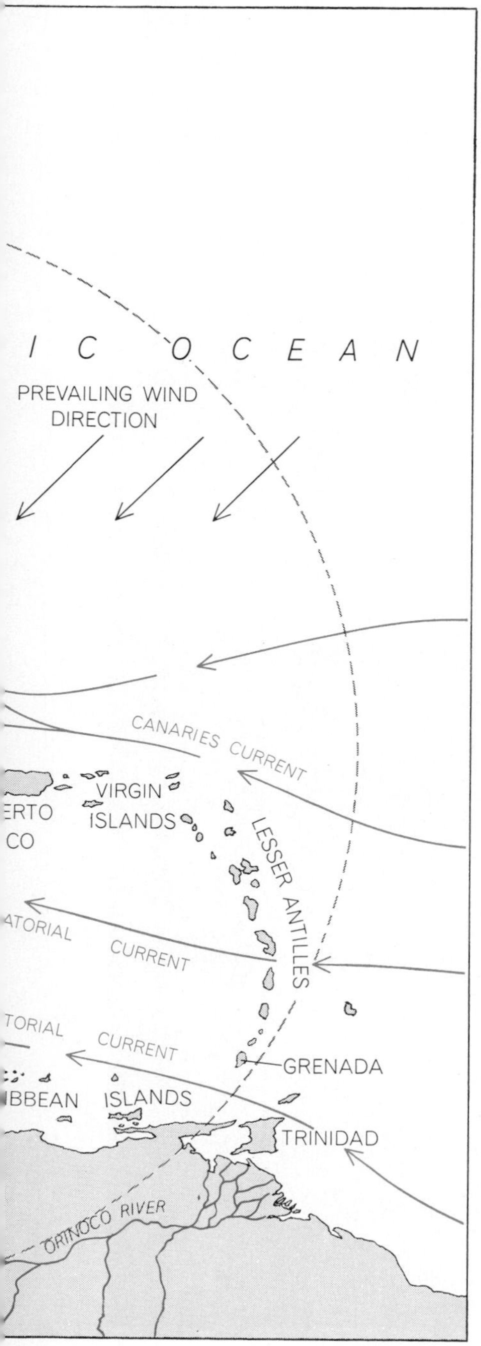

Meso-Indian sites are found in both the Greater Antilles and the islands of the South Caribbean chain. They are not known anywhere in the Lesser Antilles, with the exception of a site on St. Thomas, the member of the Virgin Islands group that is closest to Puerto Rico. How, then, did the Meso-Indians reach the Greater Antilles? The Meso-Indians who settled in the South Caribbean chain must have come from the Venezuelan mainland. There is no convincing evidence, however, that the Meso-Indians who settled in the Greater Antilles had moved to their final destination through the Lesser Antilles, as the Caribs and Arawaks had. Nor is there any conclusive evidence that the Meso-Indians followed either of the alternative routes: from Florida by way of the Bahamas or from Central America by way of the Mid-Caribbean chain.

There is still another alternative. The Meso-Indians in the Greater Antilles may simply have been descendants of the Paleo-Indians, and their more advanced material culture may have evolved on the spot. If that is the case, there are two further possibilities. The ancestral Paleo-Indians may have reached the islands during their initial period of development: the Early Paleo-Indian age, when their artifacts consisted of simple, unhafted flint flakes and crude flint pounders and choppers. Or they may have arrived during the subsequent period: the Late Paleo-Indian age, when some artifacts (particularly projectile points, which were unknown in the Early Paleo-Indian age) were made in shapes suitable for hafting.

Hispaniola lies near the geographic center of the West Indies; it is nearly equidistant from the other three islands in its chain. It is also roughly equidistant from Venezuela and Colombia to the south, Central America and Yucatán to the west and Florida to the north. This pivotal position made Hispaniola preeminent in West Indian cultural development during the Neo-Indian age. Was it also preeminent in the preceding ages? As we shall see, the answer appears to be yes.

The first evidence that Hispaniola harbored any archaeological remains earlier than Neo-Indian ones was unearthed a century ago, but it was not until 1933 that an unquestioned Meso-Indian site was excavated. The digging was done for the Museum of the American Indian by Godfrey J. Olsen at Île à Vache, an island near the southwest tip of Haiti. The site was a large mound of discarded shells from which Olsen excavated single-bitted and double-bitted ground-stone axes ground-stone mortars and pestles and a number of other objects. Some of the stones, evidently ceremonial, were engraved with elaborate designs. The designs are reminiscent of motifs seen on Hispaniolan pottery of the Neo-Indian age. It is quite possible, in fact, that the Île à Vache culture complex was contemporaneous with the Neo-Indian occupation of Hispaniola. The site is in a part of the island where Meso-Indians managed to survive until historical times.

Two years after Olsen's work five pre-pottery sites were excavated near Fort Liberté in northeastern Haiti by Froelich G. Rainey, then at Yale University's Peabody Museum, and one of us (Rouse). All five sites represented a single Meso-Indian complex that was given the name Couri. The Couri complex is clearly earlier than the Île à Vache one. Its ground-stone artifacts include vessels, milling stones, balls, pegs and double-bitted axes, but the decoration is unsophisticated [*see illustration on page 77*]. Only one stone vessel and a pendant made of shell bore simple rectilinear designs. The Couri people also made some tools out of flint, including large knives, scrapers and projectile points that have central stems for hafting. There are even some "backed blades," with one edge blunted by chipping, as in the Upper Paleolithic age of the Old World.

The Yale excavations stimulated Haitian archaeologists in their own search for pre-pottery sites. In 1940 Edward Mangonès of the Haitian Bureau of Ethnology found two deposits of flint tools in an area north of Port-au-Prince. Other investigators subsequently located six more sites in the same general area. All of them can apparently be grouped in the same complex, named Cabaret after the best-known of the eight localities. The absence of ground-stone artifacts means that the Cabaret complex belongs to one of the Paleo-Indian ages. Included among its flint artifacts are projectile points, showing that the Cabaret people were of the Late Paleo-Indian age; the points have stems for hafting. Among

zuela is by way of the Lesser Antilles, from Florida by way of the Bahamas, from Yucatán by way of Cuba and from Central America via the islands of the Mid-Caribbean chain.

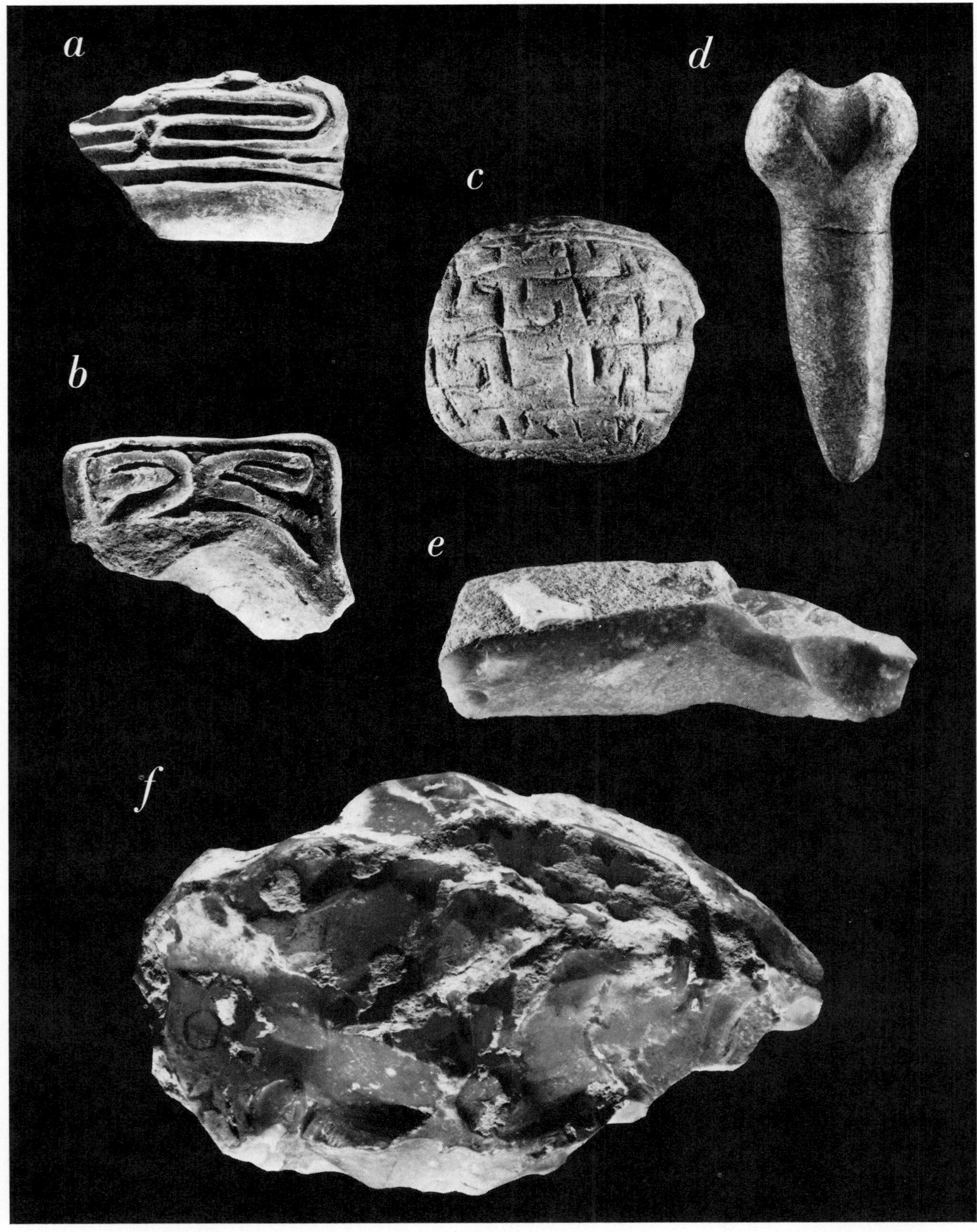

FOUR SUCCESSIVE AGES of prehistory on Hispaniola, a major island of the West Indies, are represented by these artifacts. They are (*a*, *b*) two fragments of Arawak pottery, typical of the most recent, Neo-Indian age; (*c*) an engraved stone bowl from Île à Vache and (*d*) a stone "pin" from a Couri culture site, both shaped by grinding and representative of the Meso-Indian age, whose people preceded and later coexisted with the Neo-Indians; (*e*) a flint projectile point from a Cabaret culture site, typical of the preceding Late Paleo-Indian age, and finally (*f*) a flint chopper of the more ancient Early Paleo-Indian age discovered at Rancho Casimira.

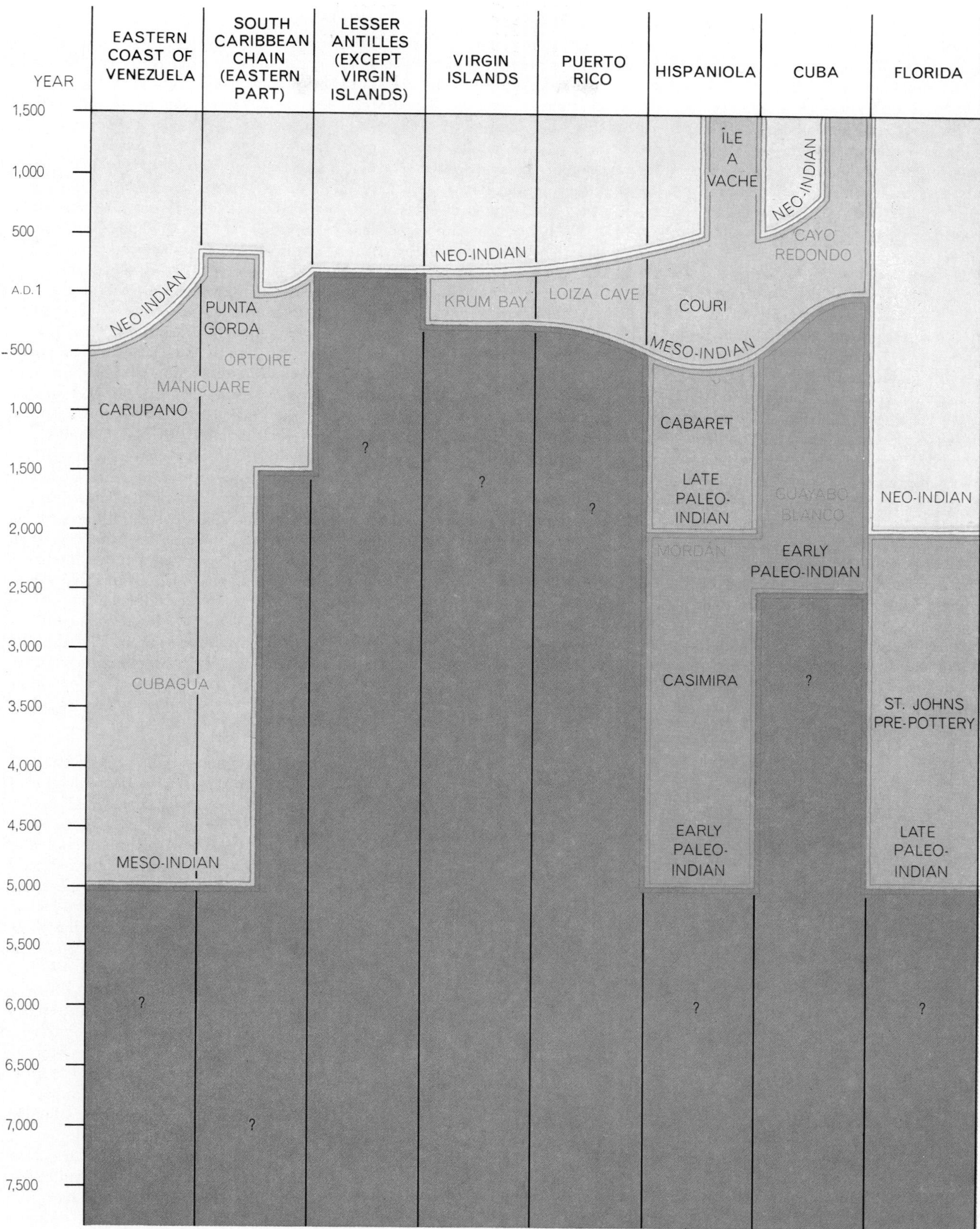

PREHISTORIC AGES were entered at different times in different parts of the West Indies. The Neo-Indian age, characterized by a knowledge of pottery, began in Florida, for example, about 2000 B.C. and in Venezuela late in the first millennium B.C. It had not yet begun in parts of Cuba and Hispaniola, however, at the time of the first European contact. On Hispaniola the Early Paleo-Indian age may have been introduced by migrants as long ago as 5000 B.C. By that time the inhabitants of Florida were representative of the Late Paleo-Indian age and the inhabitants of Venezuela had entered the subsequent prehistoric period, the Meso-Indian age. Many West Indian complexes are of uncertain age, but the dates indicated for the names shown in color are based on carbon-14 findings.

the other artifacts are long, narrow flakes of flint with ends that have been retouched [*see illustration on page 78*]. In their retouching the Cabaret workers took pains to reduce or eliminate the "bulbs of percussion" or the "striking platforms" that are present on the long flakes because of the way they are made. This presumably facilitated setting the flakes in hafts for use as scrapers or as knives.

The most recently discovered pre-pottery sites on Hispaniola also appear to be the island's oldest. They are located some 50 miles west of Santo Domingo on the island's south coast and were excavated in 1963 by the Dominican archaeologist Luis Chanlatte and one of us (Cruxent). In the 1920's the Danish archaeologist Gudmund Hatt had collected flint artifacts there, near the village of Barreras, and had reported that the region was rich in flint. At Mordán, a village near Barreras, Chanlatte and Cruxent excavated the first of their sites, a thick deposit of prehistoric refuse, primarily marine shells that had been brought from the seashore less than a mile away.

A trench two meters wide and four meters long was dug in the Mordán refuse deposit to a depth of one meter. In the top 25 centimeters of the trench fragments of pottery were common, but they became scarcer in the next 25 centimeters and were absent in the two lowest 25-centimeter sections. The lowest sections contained a number of flint artifacts; no projectile points were among them. All four sections contained small fragments of animal bone; none of the bones could be identified by species, but some were fishbones. In the bottom section a hearth yielded charcoal samples for carbon-14 analysis.

For a distance of at least three miles in all directions from Mordán the ground is littered with flint boulders and angular flint fragments embedded in the soil and half-exposed by erosion. These provided the raw material from which the Mordán workers fashioned their tools. The long flakes were apparently struck from cores with prismatic cross sections; we say "apparently" because no cores were recovered. The flakes, however, show the bulbs of percussion and prepared striking platforms characteristic of flints struck from such cores.

The Mordán workers did not follow the Cabaret practice of retouching their flakes to facilitate hafting. The absence of hafting and of projectile points shows that the complex belongs to the Early Paleo-Indian age. A few of the flakes show crude retouching on the edges, but most of them were apparently used just as they came from the core. The only secondary flaking visible on them is due to wear. They seem to have served as knives and scrapers, possibly for the manufacture of baskets.

Two other sites were found a short distance inland from Mordán. Both contained flint artifacts but no shell refuse or pottery. At one of them, Rancho Casimira, a two-by-two-meter trench was dug to a depth of 50 centimeters. No charcoal or hearths were found; the contents consisted exclusively of crudely made artifacts and waste flint of poorer quality than the Mordán flint. The upper 25-centimeter section at Casimira bore flint of a quality slightly superior to that in the lower section, as if the Casimira workers had used any flint at hand in the beginning but had later succeeded in finding a source of better material. Nonetheless, only a few of the flakes seem to be from prismatic cores, all the artifacts are strikingly larger and heavier than their Mordán counterparts and the flakes have thick, unretouched ends that would certainly have precluded hafting. None of the implements show evidence of retouching. Signs of wear indicate that the blades were used as scrapers and some of the heavier pieces served as pounders and choppers [*see illustration on pages 79 and 80*].

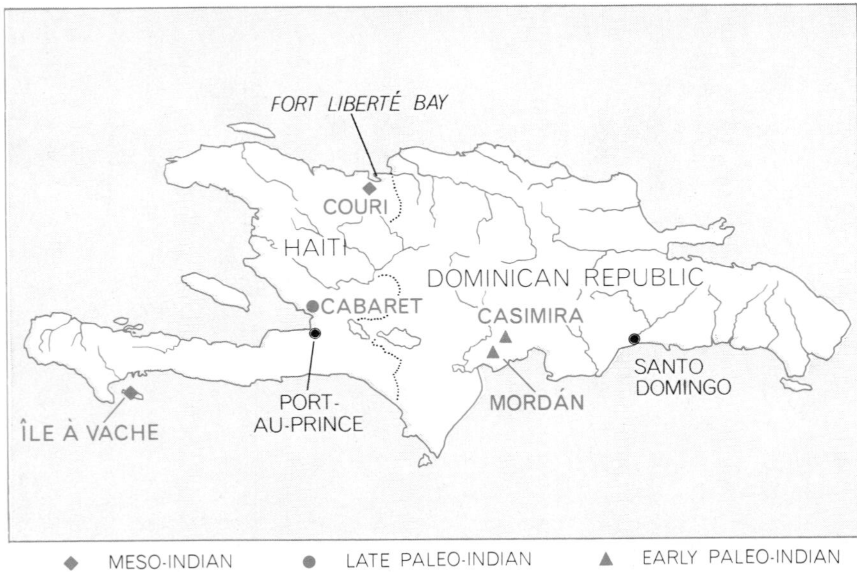

HISPANIOLA, politically divided between Haiti and the Dominican Republic, has a number of archaeological sites representative of the Meso-Indian and Paleo-Indian ages of New World prehistory. The artifacts unearthed at Île à Vache and Couri in Haiti are made out of stone that was shaped by grinding; they are therefore representative of the Meso-Indian age. At sites near Cabaret, also in Haiti, the artifacts are made from chipped flint. They include projectile points and thus belong to the preceding Late Paleo-Indian age. The sites at Mordán and Rancho Casimira in the Dominican Republic yielded Early Paleo-Indian artifacts. Carbon-14 dates show that the Mordán site is at least 4,000 years old. The Casimira site is apparently even older; it may have been first occupied as long as 7,000 years ago.

With the exception of Mordán and Casimira, all the Hispaniola sites described here were excavated before carbon-14 dating had been developed. In recent years work at a number of sites in the West Indies and on the mainland has produced a substantial list of carbon-14 dates. In the case of the Meso-Indian complexes of the Greater Antilles these dates have tended to cluster around the beginning of the Christian era. We had assumed that the same was probably true of the Cabaret complex in Hispaniola. The absence of projectile points and hafting preparations from the Mordán and Casimira complexes placed them in the Early Paleo-Indian age, however, and we eagerly awaited the carbon-14 analysis of the Mordán charcoal.

The samples yielded three dates: 2190 (±130) B.C., 2450 (±170) B.C. and 2610 (±80) B.C. This meant that we had been at least 2,000 years off in our estimate of when man first reached Hispaniola. Indeed, in view of the virtual certainty that the Casimira complex substantially predates the Mordán, the Casimira complex could date back as far as 5000 B.C. In any case the unexpected antiquity of the Mordán complex has made us revise our views concerning the chronology of the Paleo- and Meso-Indian complexes throughout the West Indies [*see illustration on page 75*].

Where do these new findings lead us? Let us put forward the hypothesis that the Casimira complex did appear on Hispaniola about 5000 B.C. What are the implications of this early date? One implication stems from the improbability that lower material cultures are derived from higher ones. For this reason the Casimira people are not likely to have been emigrants from either the northern or the southern mainland; they could scarcely have come from Florida because Florida's inhabitants were then in the Late Paleo-Indian age, and they could scarcely have come from Venezuela because by that time Venezuela's inhabitants were Meso-Indians.

If, on the other hand, Casimira is only slightly older than Mordán, there would seem to be no obstacle to attributing the complex to migrants from Cuba, where the Early Paleo-Indian age did not end until the time of Christ. The assumption of a later date for the Casimira complex would therefore appear to be fatal to our hypothesis, and the reader may view with suspicion our selection of the date that appears to serve the hypothesis best. Nonetheless, we can offer considerable evidence in support of this choice.

Let us first dispose of the weakest alternative: a migration from the south. One would have to assign Casimira a date hundreds and perhaps thousands of years earlier than 5000 B.C. before one could find a well-substantiated Early Paleo-Indian population available to emigrate from either Venezuela or the South Caribbean islands. The carbon-14 dates for the Meso-Indian culture sequence in that region run from 750 B.C. back to 3800 B.C., and it appears that a safe initial date for the Meso-Indian age there would be about 5000 B.C. We have no secure carbon-14 dates for the two Paleo-Indian ages in Venezuela, but we have reason to believe the transition from the Early to the Late Paleo-Indian age in that region took place about 12,000 years ago.

What about the possible migration from Florida? We know that the Neo-Indian age began in Florida about 2000 B.C. Near the headwaters of the St. Johns River a number of sites of an earlier age have been excavated. One of the principal artifacts, unearthed in large numbers, is a kind of gouge made by breaking a triangular section from the outer whorl of a conch shell and grinding one edge of it. These gouges are found in association with pins made of bone and with flint projectile points that are flaked on both sides. There are no carbon-14 dates for the sites, but the absence of ground-stone artifacts and the presence of projectile points suggest that St. Johns is a complex of the Late Paleo-Indian age. This complex is dated between 5000 and 2000 B.C. If Casimira is somewhat more recent than 5000 B.C., one could envision a migration from Florida as its source, except for two facts: neither the shell gouge, the characteristic St. Johns artifact, nor the St. Johns type of projectile point has ever been found on Hispaniola.

There remains the possibility of migration from Cuba. If the date of Casimira is closer to 2500 B.C. than to 5000 B.C., some of the Early Paleo-Indians of a complex known as Guayabo Blanco might have migrated to Casimira. Carbon-14 analysis indicates that the Guayabo Blanco complex was in existence as early as 2050 B.C., and it is our opinion that the complex or something quite like it existed in Cuba at least a few hundred years earlier. Could this complex be the source of Casimira? We think not: the artifacts of the Guayabo Blanco complex are made chiefly of shell and not of flint. They include shell vessels and, as in the St. Johns complex, the principal tool is the shell gouge. Objects made of flint are rare, which suggests that they may have been trade items. Unlike the flint artifacts of the St. Johns complex, none are projectile points.

The nearly contemporary age of the Mordán and Guayabo Blanco complexes and the absence of projectile points at both sites point to the closeness of the Hispaniolan and Cuban complexes of the Early Paleo-Indian age. Still, two facts—the paucity of flint tools at the Cuban site and the total absence of shell gouges on Hispaniola—seem to rule out intimate cultural ties between the two complexes. It seems more likely that Cuba's Early Paleo-Indian complex was

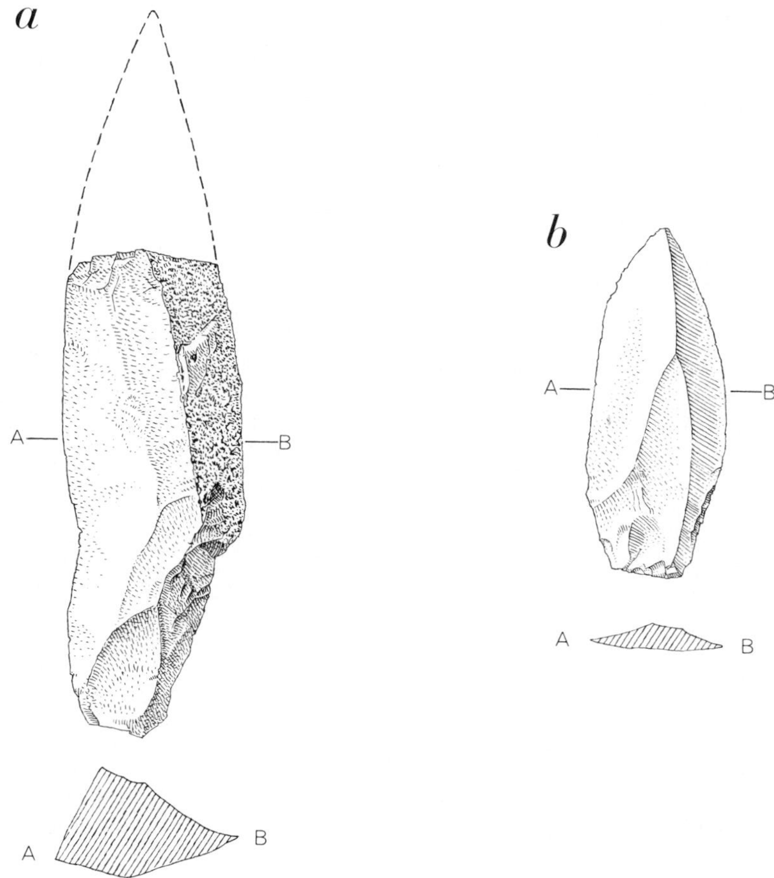

FLINT TOOLS of Paleo-Indian workmanship are from sites of the Cabaret complex in Haiti. The projectile point (*a*) has been given a lateral stem to allow hafting. Its tip is missing; the broken line suggests its original appearance. The flake (*b*) has also been reworked at one end for hafting; it was probably a scraper. Both belong to the Late Paleo-Indian age.

derived from Florida, although we know too little about the pre-pottery cultures of Florida to state this as a certainty.

With Venezuela, Florida and Cuba evidently ruled out as sources of the Casimira complex, only one mainland area remains: Central America. It is a further part of our hypothesis that the Casimira people pushed out from Central America into the Caribbean, traveling by way of the Mid-Caribbean island chain first to Jamaica and then to Hispaniola. This part of our hypothesis has weaknesses, at least for the present. For example, although a flint-working tradition like that at Casimira and Mordán is known in Central America, the mainland version is considerably more developed and its artifacts have been found only in a Neo-Indian context. We suggest

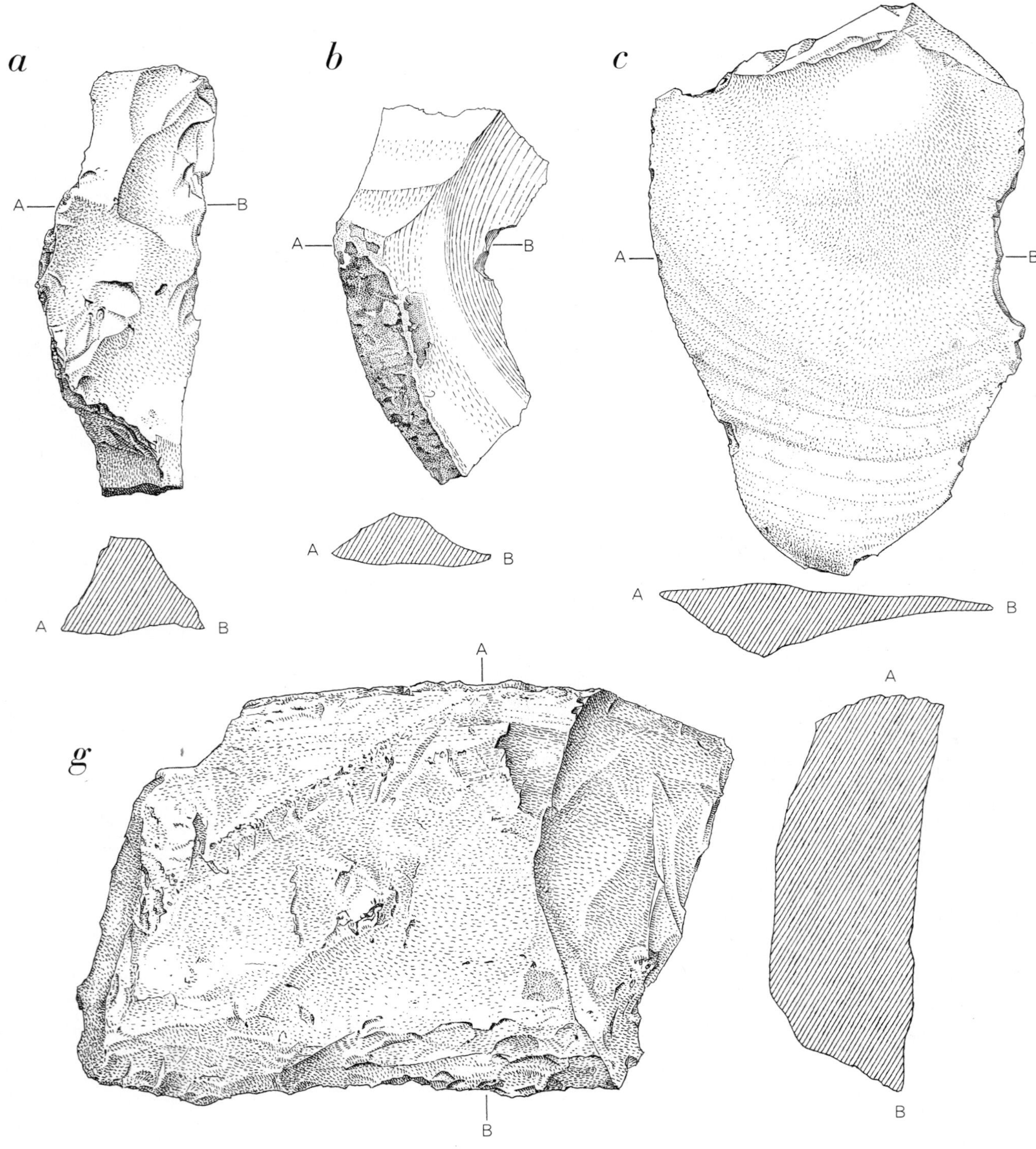

OLDEST-KNOWN TOOLS on Hispaniola, made from an inferior grade of flint, were excavated at Rancho Casimira in the Dominican Republic. Among them are narrow scrapers that are often quite long (*a*, *b*, *d*, *e*), broad scrapers, both large (*c*) and small (*h*),

that the Central American tradition has Paleo- and Meso-Indian antecedents that remain to be discovered. Another weakness is that no prehistoric habitation sites of any kind have been reported on the Mid-Caribbean islands and no Paleo- and Meso-Indian ones have been found on Jamaica. No one has systematically looked for such sites, however, and the absence of reports does not necessarily mean an absence of sites.

Two further questions remain to be answered with respect to our hypothesis: Why did the Casimira people leave the mainland and how? We believe the answer to both questions is implicit in the nature of the flint implements at Casimira. The scrapers, pounders and choppers are typical of the tools made by the big-game hunters of the Late Paleo-Indian age on the mainland, who used

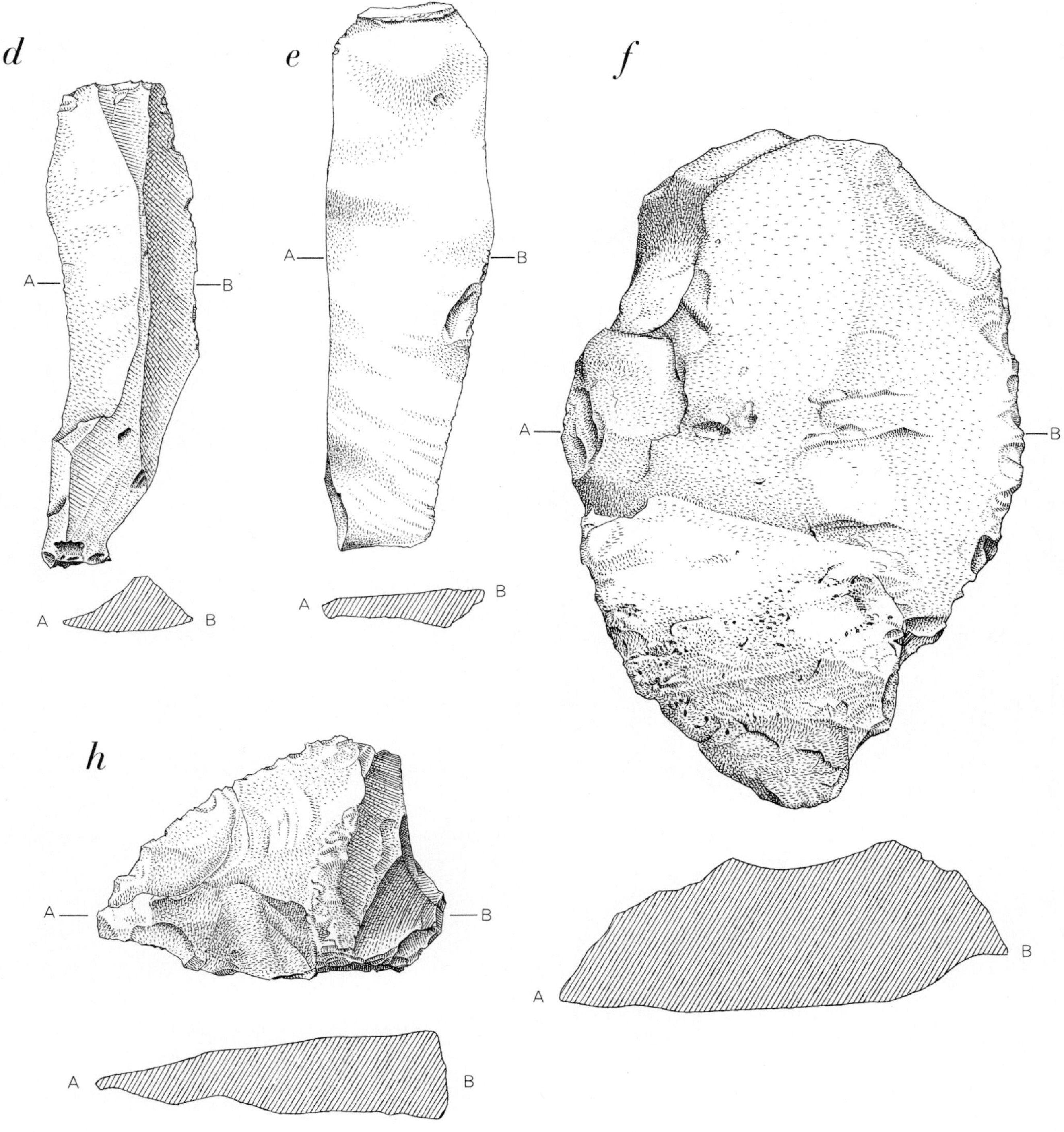

and massive chopping tools (*f, g*). Lacking projectile points, the Casimira people lived in the Early Paleo-Indian age. Their tools are nevertheless typical of mainland big-game hunters; they may have hunted large sea mammals such as the seal and the manatee.

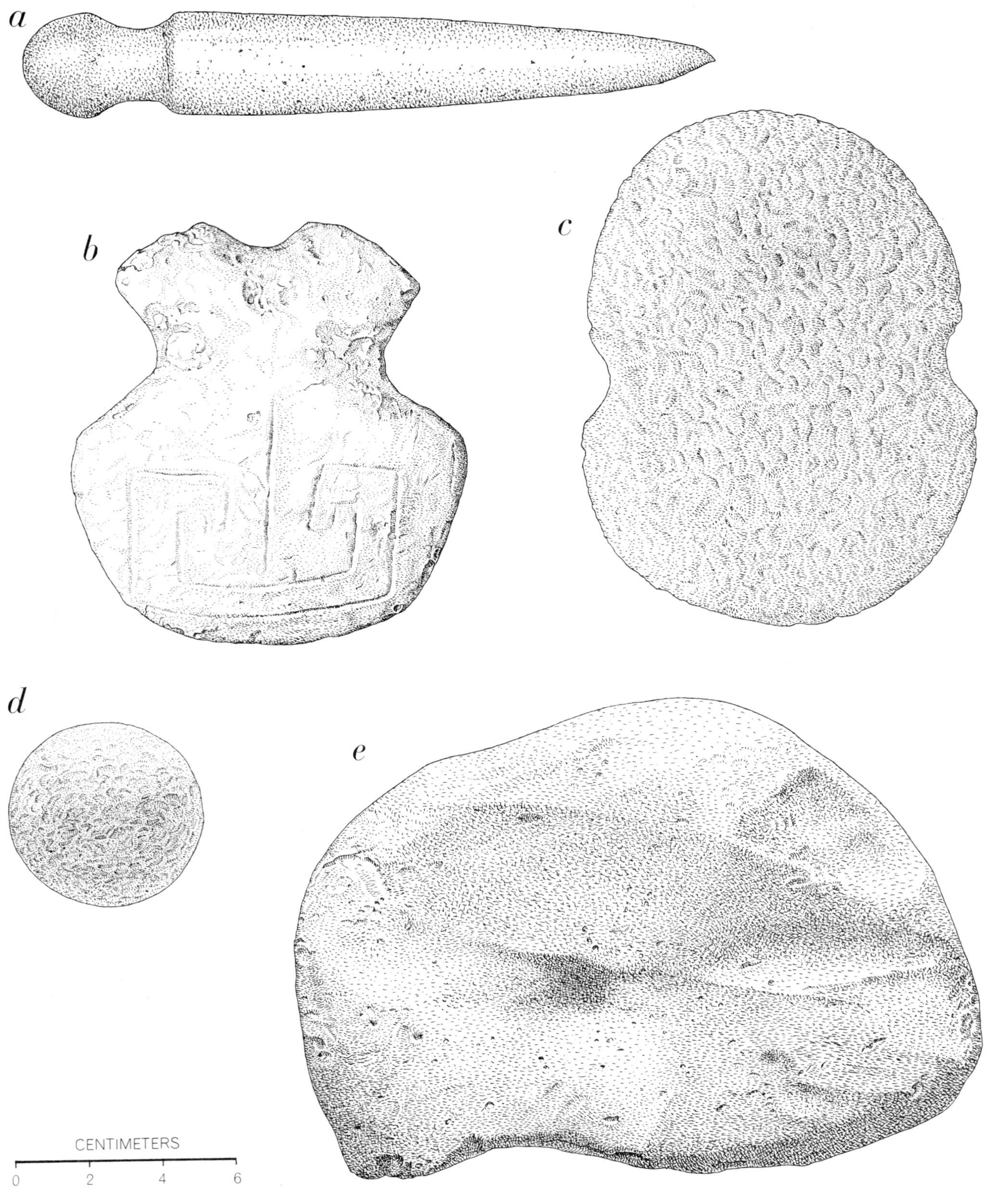

MESO-INDIAN ARTIFACTS from two sites in Haiti were made by grinding the desired shapes out of stone. The uses of the stone pin (*a*) and the engraved stone (*b*) from Île à Vache are not known; the Meso-Indians who made them may have been contemporaneous with the pottery-making Neo-Indians who reached Hispaniola about A.D. 500. The other artifacts are from sites of the Couri complex. They are a double-bitted axe (*c*), a stone sphere of unknown function (*d*) and a large stone with a shallow depression (*e*), possibly used as a kind of mortar for preparing wild vegetables. All but the large stone are shown two-thirds actual size. The Couri sites also belong to the Meso-Indian age but are clearly earlier in date than the more sophisticated complex unearthed at Île à Vache.

them to butcher and process their quarry. The implication that the Casimira people were hunters of big game does not mean that they did not also kill smaller animals and collect various vegetable foods, but large mammals would have been their main prey. Furthermore, we must assume that the Casimira people were at home on the water; wherever they came from, they did, after all, reach Hispaniola. Therefore their principal prey could easily have been large sea mammals. If we may judge by early Spanish accounts, manatees and seals once ranged among the islands in large numbers. Finally, we can logically expect that the Casimira people used rafts in pursuit of their quarry. So much for the "why"; we would assume that a mainland people followed sea mammals out to Hispaniola.

The "how" is far more conjectural. Rafts are largely at the mercy of winds and currents. Even assuming that the Casimira people could have equipped their rafts with mat sails, they would still have only been able to travel before the wind, and the prevailing winds are from the northeast. One can always conjure up a chance storm to drive a hunting party far out to sea, thus making at least the first migration accidental. The assembly of a viable breeding population on a remote island through pure chance, however, seems quite unlikely. We prefer to think of the Casimira people's moving purposefully out along the Mid-Caribbean chain (which, because of the lower sea level at the time, must have consisted of many more islands). Presumably they took advantage of winds and currents that would be in their favor at certain times of the year.

SCREEN SIFTER, suspended by ropes, was used to separate the seashell debris at the Mordán site from the animal bones, flint tools and other artifacts that the deposit contained.

Arriving on Hispaniola, the hunters would have found a supply of the flint from which they were accustomed to making their tools. There would have been sea mammals along the shore and quantities of vegetable food and fresh water, which were probably scarce on many of the Mid-Caribbean islets. All in all, it is easy to see why the Casimira people would have settled down once they reached Hispaniola.

Our hypothesis runs counter to an assumption common among New World prehistorians that Paleo-Indians could only travel overland. We suggest that this assumption be reexamined. It seems entirely possible to us that various Paleo-Indians were using rafts both for river crossings and for coastwise travel in very early times. The first Americans need not have been restricted to overland routes for their movements, as many have supposed.

IV

RECONSTRUCTIONS

RECONSTRUCTIONS IV

INTRODUCTION

Equipped with time and space sequences, or even just with methods for positioning a site in time and space, many archaeologists became increasingly interested in reconstructing prehistoric lifeways. The methods of time-space systematics, such as seriation (see Meggers and Evans, page 97), pottery typology (see Ford, page 164), and reliance on carbon-14 dates (see MacNeish, 1971, page 143), often form the basis for the reconstruction. The articles in this section are all examples of the reconstructionist perspective, which is basically historical. To reconstruct is to write culture history. Once a site has been excavated, the artifacts classified, the features notated, and other descriptions prepared, the archaeologist is in a position to reconstruct past activities. Many of the articles in the previous section, on Time-Space Systematics, exemplify some initial attempts at reconstruction, often in just the last paragraph or two. The articles here suggest what might have happened in prehistory.

OBJECTIVES

The over-all objective is to put back together something that was broken. The archaeological record constitutes the pieces, and it is the past that is being pieced together again. Of course, in order to put it back together again, one must have more than the pieces; there must be the "glue." The final reconstruction is more than the sum of the parts; those who reconstruct must add something, and gaps that have been destroyed or that are unknown are often filled in. Some reconstructions, based on the same pieces, the same archaeological record, are clearly more successful than others, depending on what has been added and how.

Reconstruction can be of at least three different kinds: of an event or period, of an historical sequence or set of events, or of an adaptive strategy. Each of these is discussed in this section, and readings have been selected as examples of the different modes of reconstruction.

METHODS

For the "glue" needed to do a reconstruction of the past, archaeologists often draw on resources other than the archaeological record. It is these sources, and how they are used, that may determine the success of a reconstruction. A primary resource employed by archaeologists is their knowledge of other cultures in the ethnographic present. If there are similarities in environment, material culture, or other conditions between a known culture and the archaeological findings, interpretations of the past can be based on analogy with the known culture. This method of ethnographic analogy, although valuable, must be used with caution, and archaeologists often discuss its validity. Too often, when used without due caution, it leads to a simplistic and poorly verified reconstruction. We know that a wide range of variables, for cultural and natural events and for processes and behaviors, could account for the archaeological record. In most reconstructions, the archaeologist selects the events or behaviors that seem most plausible. His judgment of this plausibility is often based on the ethnographic record. When available, ethnohistorical accounts of a more or less continuous cultural group, such as the Maya (see Borhegyi, page 176) or Iroquois (see Tuck, page 190), support the reconstruction of the antecedent archaeological population.

Many reconstructions are brought to life by the author's creative imagination and literary style. Although not all reconstructionists believe we can know everything about the past, most will agree that to do any reconstruction we must have more than just the prized items, the ideal types, the pretty pieces, the spectacular sites. To reconstruct prehistoric lifeways, archaeologists need other pieces of the past, and especially need the contextual evidence: the evidence of the context in which an artifact was recovered. Attempts to understand settlement patterns, and the associations between artifacts and other features of material culture, have been important in contributing to plausible reconstructions. Some reconstructionists have emphasized the economic aspects of prehistoric life as the most knowable, whereas others have taken a much more wholistic approach in trying to know and reconstruct a little about everything—from daily baths to the religious calendar and cult dances. This latter archaeological perspective often finds the archaeologist as a jack-of-all-trades, and master of none.

Attempts to formalize the methods of prehistoric reconstruction have been proposed. Although reconstruction is an essentially *ad hoc* method of elucidating the archaeological record, the more the reconstructionist knows about the variables or behaviors that could have led to the archaeological record, the more rigorous or credible the reconstruction could become. Judgments of the success of a reconstruction are then based more on the skill and knowledge of the archaeologist than on how much the archaeological record supports the purported or hypothesized reconstruction.

THEORETICAL FRAMEWORK

Theoretically, the reconstructionist perspective assumes that if we can put a culture back together again, it was together to begin with. Thus, it is a wholistic approach which assumes that culture consists of different parts that fit or function together, which is concerned about more than the distribution of artifacts or assemblages in time and space. Both ideological factors (such as ideas, norms and values) and ecological factors (such as rainfall and demography) are considered to have contributed to the manufacture of such artifacts. However, discovering exactly how these factors interacted within the cultural system to produce such material culture or archaeological patterning is outside the scope of the reconstructionist's aims.

WIDER RELEVANCE, ADVANTAGES AND DISADVANTAGES OF THE PERSPECTIVE

Reconstructions have a wide relevance and a great deal of public appeal, since one can identify more with a picture of daily life than with reports of artifacts that have been found at different times and places. The high degree of generalization and even ambiguity that the archaeologist must employ in reconstruction are essential for a successful job, for they allow the projection of one's self into the prehistoric picture. Some of the more popular reconstructions of prehistoric lifeways now being prepared for the public are being done not by archaeologists, but by skilled writers, editors, and artists, for whom these reconstructions are expressions of their creative literary and artistic skills. They do not feel constrained professionally by a lack of archaeological data or training when painting the complete picture that the public enjoys and can relate to. Of course, they depend on the continuing work of archaeologists of all perspectives for their ideas.

A weakness of many reconstructions is that they are often idiosyncratic and individualistic attempts to present us with a glimpse into the past. What aspects are chosen for reconstruction, how much adherence there is to the known archaeological record, varies from one reconstruction to the next. Since there are no common units, comparison is difficult, if not impossible. The use of ethnographic analogy, which so often makes the reconstruction more credible and brings "life" to the past, also tends to restrict the possible explanations and to delimit the search for the most testable hypotheses. The "verification" of a reconstruction often depends on its plausibility—"Can we believe the Aztecs did that?"—rather than on the archaeological record—"Are there several lines of evidence that support the hypothesis that the Aztecs did that?" Lastly, we know that human behavior today is diverse; this is an example of spatial diversity at one point in time. When we apply some of this spatial variability to the past, adding the temporal dimension, as is done in ethnographic analogy, it is often difficult to determine if the variation is due to temporal or spatial factors, or both.

There are certainly other advantages to doing reconstructions besides the appeal they have for the public. Clearly, archaeologists who reconstruct prehistoric lifeways have a closer bond with anthropology than do those who follow other archaeological perspectives. Reconstructionists draw on the pool of anthropological knowledge to find possible analogies to or models for prehistoric life, and, in the long run, actively contribute to that pool. Archaeologists are challenged by doing reconstructions, for the work demands creativity and an ability to bring together diverse kinds of evidence into a plausible picture of human behavior in the past. Since the reconstruction of any event or period brings into question all that happened before or after it, reconstructions ask questions about sequences of events, and implicitly, at least, about change and processes of change. Questions about change and its processes, it is often said, may well constitute one of archaeology's greatest potential contributions to our understanding of humanity. Reconstructionists have contributed substantially to our abilities to ask such questions.

RECONSTRUCTIONS OF EVENTS OR PERIODS

It is easy to see how an interest in reconstructing an event or period developed out of the time-space systematics perspective. This kind of reconstruction involves recreating something that happened in time and space. An event is selected to be reconstructed because it is deemed important; this involves some criteria as to *what* is important, and *why*. Many prehistoric events for which reconstructions have been attempted are considered important because they were events of origin (see Meggers and Evans, page 97) or of decline (see Proskouriakoff, page 127), or they were events that led to an impressive and visible archaeological record (see Millon, page 115), or they were events for which we have little or no archaeological evidence, i.e., a "gap." Often the aspects of prehistory that cry out for reconstruction are those inconsistencies or unexpected finds which do not quite fit into our current understandings and reconstructions. And, of course, the previously unknown and the "unique" as well as the "enigmatic" are frequently chosen as events worthy of reconstruction (see Tuck 1971, Proskouriakoff, Martin, and Schwartz).

The objective in reconstructing an event or period is not wholistic, in the sense that the wider context in which an event took place is not usually part of the reconstruction. These reconstructions are usually relatively synchronic in scope, being concerned with a particular short-term period or event: where and when pottery originated in the New World; the urban period of Teotihucán; the decline of the Maya as evidenced by one particular site; the period of social distance between two Southwestern Indian groups. From such reconstructions we can generate further research questions, dealing, for example, with how this event or period came into existence, or into what wider environmental or cultural context it fits.

TABLE V. Articles Employing the Perspective of Reconstruction of an Event or Period.

Author(s)	*Time*	*Area*	*Strategy*
Giddings (1954)	15,000–10,000 B.C.	Arctic	Hunting-gathering
Meggers and Evans (1966)	3000 B.C.	Coastal South America	Hunting-gathering
Tuck (1970)	2000 B.C.	Arctic Newfoundland	Hunting-gathering
Millon (1967)	A.D. 1–1000	Mesoamerica	Agricultural civilization
Proskouriakoff (1955)	A.D. 1168–1263	Mesoamerica	Agricultural civilization
Dozier (1957)	A.D. 1500–1950	Southwest	Agricultural

THE READINGS

Note that Giddings' article, "Early Man in the Arctic," was written twenty years ago, when inconsistencies and unexpected finds began to challenge the then current picture of the earliest culture history of the New World. Giddings suggests several possible "explanations" for the new finds, chooses the reconstruction most plausible to him, and explains why he favors this interpretation. Part of the plausibility argument rests on his knowledge of the enthnographic record and on notions of what hunters do, especially in northern forest areas. This understanding, when added to the archaeological record of similar microliths from site to site, and the occurrence of interdigitating layers, forms the basis for his reconstruction. The resulting reconstruction is of an archaelogical "tradition," known as the Denbigh flint complex, and the picture of the people's lifeways that Giddings presents is focused on their pattern of occupation and economics. It does not involve reconstruction of other aspects of the cultural system. We have certainly gone a long way in filling in the spatial and temporal gaps of the archaeological record since Giddings' article (see Anderson's 1968 article on the Onion Portage site in the previous section). Haag's 1962 article (in the next section) should be compared with this one by Giddings, for it broadens our understanding of the processes which brought early human populations to the New World, and how representative their remains (such as the Denbigh flint complex) might be of their total adaptation.

"A Transpacific Contact in 3000 B.C.," by Betty J. Meggers and Clifford Evans, is an example of one of the more controversial kinds of archaeological reconstruction. Although the authors adhere to the widespread theory that the original peopling of the New World took place over the Bering Land bridge, this article attempts to reconstruct how some traits of later New World groups may have been introduced from sources external to the continent, long after the land bridge was submerged (see their map, page 102). In conformity with more traditional ideas concerning the diffusion of cultural traits (see discussion of the age-area concept, page 102), many archaeologists seek the sources of "borrowed" traits within a limited proximity. More recently, they have sought sources in similar adaptive contexts within areas of plausible interaction. Meggers and Evans here attempt to "hazard a reconstruction of the way in which Jomon-like pottery (from Japan) came to be introduced to Ecuador." Since they are attempting to understand and reconstruct the processes of cultural development as these are reflected in material culture, the authors are implicitly systemic in their perspective, for they assume that there is an interrelationship between material culture and the social context of production and use (see next section). But their interpretations are based on assumptions about material culture and processes of change which may not be held by all archaeologists. These include assumptions about the development of variety and of "realism" and "complexity" in material culture; they view these as being late developments in cultural evolution. The reasons why their interpretation of transpacific contacts is most plausible to the authors are carefully developed, and this affords an excellent example for the study of the logic of an archaeological reconstruction. Because the interpretation offered here is one that the biologist G. G. Simpson would refer to as "sweepstakes evolution," it is even more important for the authors to document the probability of such an event, and to consider the degree of impact that a lost boatload of fishermen could have had on the local population.

The article by James Tuck, "An Archaic Indian Cemetery in Newfoundland," is an excellent example of a reconstruction of a period based on the identification of an archaeological "tradition." The description of the way of life of archaic Indian populations in western Newfoundland about 4,000 years ago is based on meticulous excavations (see his photographs), on classification of artifacts and faunal remains, on analyses of both the contexts of the finds and the patterns of association among them, and on some admitted speculation. This "unique site," because of its excellent state of preservation and large size, yielded a good sample of artifacts and skeletal remains on which to base a reconstruction for a time period which was known previously only from small ceremonial sites. Tuck shows how characteristics of a skeletal population can be used to infer their health and even some activities, such as from tooth wear caused by chewing hides. There is also a good analysis of how the associations among the archaeological remains can be used for the reconstruction. Tuck notes that amulets depicting certain animals are often in graves containing bones of the very same animal species. This implies totemism as known among ethnographic groups with similar adaptive strategies. In drawing his conclusions, following a detailed discussion of the material culture, Tuck elucidates the ecological approach (see Steward's article, page 9). He notes that some cultural similarities between the Maritime Archaic Tradition and other Newfoundland and Canadian Arctic groups are due more to ecological convergence than to direct contacts or racial relationships. And when compared with Giddings' reconstruction of the economic aspects of an archaeological tradition (page 92), it is clear how Tuck's reconstruction of a tradition takes advantage of the rich data derived from a ceremonial mortuary site to offer "tantalizing" speculations about the magico-religious activities of prehistoric peoples.

René Millon's article "Teotihuacán," is a reconstruction of the period known as the "urban revolution" in Middle America, particularly as evidenced by the recent and systematic investigations at Teotihuacán. To place the origin and evolution of Teotihuacán in the wider perspective of this world-wide "urban revolution" that took place at different times and in a variety of locales, one should refer to Sjoberg's article (page 271). The city of Teotihuacán, although never a "lost" one to archaeologists, has not been as well-known to most people despite its visible remains, size, early date, and importance in all spheres of pre-Columbian life. Millon's reconstruction touches on many aspects of that life, from the foreign relations and influence of Teotihuacán to changes in population size, density, and social organization within the city. Although Millon draws on the contemporary ethnographic record to support the reconstruction, the hypothetical continuity from Teotihuacán to Aztec times, coupled with what is known about Aztec lifeways, provides many clues for his interpretation of the archaeological record. His reconstruction also shows many ways in which the archaeological record itself can be interpreted. Architectural features at Teotihuacán suggest different kinds of spatial, and hence social, relations; patterns of artifact distribution suggest the organization of crafts; and sources of raw materials suggest trading relations. Other articles that add to the general outlines of Teotihuacán life and history as presented here include MacNeish's article on the evolutionary antecedents to Teotihuacán (page 155), Coe's article on the chinampa-irrigation system which may have developed during Teotihuacán times (p. 231), and Proskouriakoff's article on the decline of the related Maya civilization (p. 127). Since Millon derives much of his reconstruction from his knowledge of the city plan, comparison with Hammond's article (p. 281) on the planning of a Maya ceremonial center will indicate differences and similarities between the two civilizations.

Like the article by Millon on Teotihuacán, Tatiana Proskouriakoff's "The Death of a Civilization" places New World civilizations in perspective by relating them to the classic unfolding of the civilizational process as known in the Old World. Since the heritage of the Western world is oriented toward the Greco-Roman and earlier civilizations of the Mediterranean, an introduction to the aboriginal civilizations of the Americas is often carried out by comparison to the Old World pyramids, cities and other achievements and

agonies. But unlike the Millon reconstruction, which is concerned with the general outlines of life at Teotihuacán at its peak, Proskouriakoff focuses her reconstruction on "an important and neglected phenomenon for study—the death of a civilization"; and a well-known one, the Mayan. Since this article first appeared (in 1955) there has been continued attraction to the problem of the "Mayan collapse." There may well be as many hypotheses for its fall as there are for the origins of agriculture, another well-studied prehistoric process. As with the Teotihuacán mapping project, the Mayapan city plan (page 128) has produced a transformation of general notions about the cities into suggestive and detailed documents as sources for more complete interpretations. Proskouriakoff's own work on the Maya furthermore shows how the informational aspects of a cultural system—the art, calendrics, and scripts—can be used for reconstruction. Most archaeological reconstructions are based on ecological and economic evidences. A civilization is clearly a more complex cultural system, which needs more information to integrate and maintain its hierarchical structure. It is for civilizations that we have not only the most data, but the most data about these informational aspects of culture, and these should also be a source for reconstructions, whatever the level of cultural evolution.

Edward P. Dozier's article "The Hopi and the Tewa," is not concerned with archaeological reconstruction. Rather it is an ethonographic reconstruction of social relations between two Southwestern Indian groups. This article is included here because it is an example of the ethnographic record which is the source for the ethnographic analogies offered by reconstructionists in building plausibility. The article suggests that interpretations of social relations between different groups, or the archaeological reconstruction of cultural units, may involve variables not always considered by archaeologists. In this case study, a legend, language, marriage and descent patterns, psychological temperaments, and world views about man's ability to transform the environment are all factors that served as cultural isolating mechanisms between the Hopi and the Tewa. However, an archaeologist concerned only with house styles as indicators of social relations might reconstruct the two groups as one. This stresses the importance of the many lines of evidence that are necessary to build a plausible reconstruction, or to test a hypothesis about cultural affiliations. The different religious beliefs and practices described by Dozier, for example, are reflected in different "kiva" structures and associated paraphernalia. And with different agricultural traditions and beliefs, one would expect differing patterns of land use. In addition, the article points out that the eventual cooperation and affiliation between the Hopi and the Tewa were due to changes in the external social environment—the arrival of the white man—which allowed both groups to maintain a degree of ethnic differentiation from the newcomers.

9 Early Man in the Arctic

by J. L. Giddings, Jr.
June 1954

The similarity of stone tools found at many locations around the North Pole suggests that a well-defined culture existed in the Arctic long before man migrated southward in America

On a windswept trail in the far north near Hudson Bay there was discovered last summer a deposit of prehistoric hunters' flints which has radically disturbed long-accepted notions about the original peopling of America. Archaeologists had built up, from the little evidence they had, what seemed a plausible picture: About 10,000 to 15,000 years ago roving bands of hunters from Asia, either following herds of animals or seeking a virgin "promised land," crossed from Asia to Alaska over a Bering Strait land bridge [see "How Man Came to North America," by Ralph Solecki, SCIENTIFIC AMERICAN January 1951]. Most of the immigrants, supposedly a simple, comparatively unresourceful people, then pushed south down the North American continent to less rigorous climates, while a few tribes remained in the Arctic, surviving as the Eskimos of today. What is disturbing about the new find is that it forms a connecting link in an unexpected chain of early human habitation stretching around the Arctic Circle all the way from northern Europe across Asia and North America—a chain of able, resourceful peoples with a relatively advanced hunters' culture!

The idea of a Bering Strait gateway for Americans gained credence long before archaeology began in the far north. Some natural historians of the early 1800s thought the Indian mound builders of the Mississippi basin could be traced back along this trail to the areas of stone monuments in the Middle East and Europe. Later the ethnologists postulated the migrations over a "land bridge" between the continents and along valleys between Alaskan and Canadian glaciers. Speculations on this score, and on the relationship of early migrants to Eskimos, could be made without fear of contradiction because discoveries of very old artifacts were so few as to lie comfortably in almost any theoretical bed. The Folsom flints unearthed in our western deserts and plains appeared to confirm the picture of moving bands of hunters.

But during the last few years the new chain of sites found in the far north has raised puzzling questions. The sites around the Arctic Circle seem more closely related to one another culturally than do the sites along the trail from north to south. It is disturbing to students of "migrating" New World men to find that not only Eskimo culture but earlier cultures within the same area may have been mainly Arctic phenomena. If the far north has for thousands of years supported cultures well fitted to the region, how shall we explain the original peopling of the Americas?

The beginning of the dilemma goes back to discoveries on the campus of the University of Alaska near Fairbanks in the early 1930s. A student watching the freshman bonfire on the brow of College Hill one autumn evening scuffed

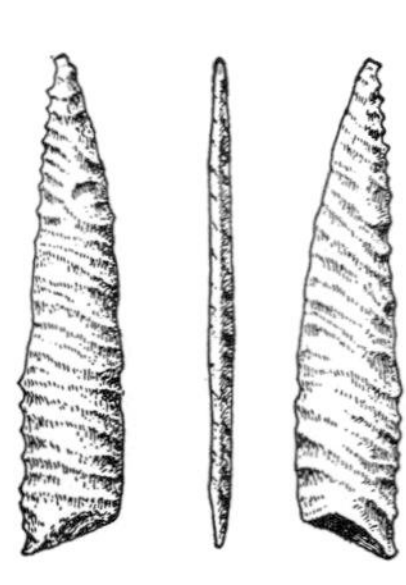
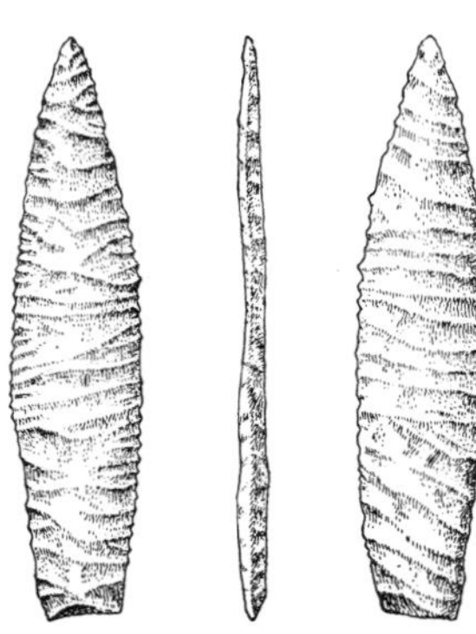
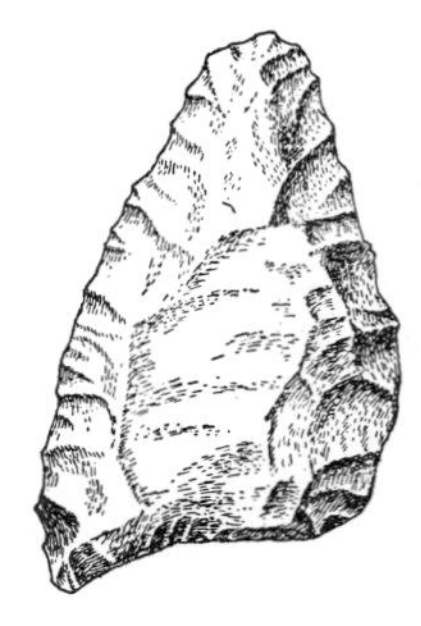

FLINTS used by Stone Age hunters were found at Cape Denbigh, Alaska (*see map on page 94*). Six of the finely worked specimens are shown in three views at slightly less than actual size. The side blade (*far left*) was designed to be fitted into an arrow along the

up a flint point which led to a series of excavations by the anthropology department. These brought to light a stone industry which the experienced archaeologist N. C. Nelson found similar to artifacts unearthed in Mesolithic sites in the Gobi Desert of Mongolia. The most characteristic feature of this work was a certain peculiar type of parallel-edged "microblade"—a thin sliver chipped delicately from a prepared flint core [*see photograph on page 95*]. The microblades involve a precise technique which can hardly have been learned independently in different places by chance.

For a time the Alaska campus site stood in an anomalous place—an almost unwelcome proof of connections between Asia and America because it held neither the earliest nor the later forms of the flints of the western plains. But it soon became part of a developing new picture in the Arctic. Similar microblade industries were discovered in the Brooks Range in northern Alaska, in early stratigraphic levels at Kluane Lake in Canada's Yukon Territory, and at Pointed Mountain and elsewhere in the Mackenzie River basin. The microblade and core, in other associations, are being recognized at various sites across northern Siberia and throughout the American Arctic.

In 1948 we made a field trip to Cape Denbigh, on the northern shore of Bering Sea, with the usual objective of digging under an Eskimo midden in the hope of finding an older culture. At a coastal spot known to the Eskimos as Iyatayet, on top of an ancient 40-foot terrace, we slowly exposed the floor and lower walls of a pit house several centuries old. It was a house of the "neo-Eskimo" period, and its culture was so nearly like that of the people now living in the area that our native helpers had no trouble in explaining details of use in the articles and structures uncovered.

Beneath the splinters of old flooring a test cut at the back of the house unexpectedly revealed that the dwelling had been originally set in soil containing the cultural deposits of some earlier people. Bits of well-fired pottery, thin side blades and arrow points of basalt and flintlike gray chert marked this as a deposit of the "paleo-Eskimo" culture, previously discovered only at a site at Point Hope far to the north.

The real surprise lay still deeper. On troweling through a sterile layer below the early Eskimo, we came to a dense clay, on the top of which lay quantities of small chips of chert and obsidian—and microblades in profusion! The artifacts in this level, now known as the Denbigh flint complex, continued to amaze us during the field seasons of 1949, 1950 and 1952. The microblades are like those of the University site, but there the resemblance ends. There are many tiny blades carefully shaped by diagonal flaking into thin and delicate side and end blades, the precision of which appears to be without equal elsewhere in the world. Other small blades were made into various tools by simply retouching parts of their edges.

Of the few large blades found in the complex, nearly all resemble ancient weapons unearthed in the plains and southwest areas of the U. S., where they are linked with early Americans' hunting of now extinct animals. They include a fluted point in the Folsom tradition and about a dozen fragments of the long, diagonally-flaked points known as the "Yuma oblique." With this distant tie to early Americans as incentive, I looked farther afield for comparisons in Old World literature, and to my surprise I found the Denbigh flint complex closely related to artifacts in the caves of Europe and the forests of Siberia.

The least expected find in the Denbigh flint complex was a number of forms of the burin—a grooving instrument which we deduced was used for sectioning antler, ivory and other hard organic material. At the time of its discovery at Cape Denbigh, this implement had not previously been recognized in America, though it was well known as a basic tool of the Upper Paleolithic and the Mesolithic periods in European prehistory. The Denbigh burin is a thin implement with teeth formed by chipping out one or more needle-like slivers. The slivers themselves also were used, probably as hafted engraving tools. Enlargement of one of these slivers, less than an inch in length, shows that its tip is a chisel.

As to the geological background of the Iyatayet site, D. M. Hopkins of the U. S. Geological Survey has joined with me to show that the deeper soil layers have been subject to movements and soil-forming processes no longer active. These layers record a sequence of climatic changes similar to known sequences in other parts of Alaska. Converging lines of evidence lead us to believe that the earliest dwellers at Iyatayet lived during a warm period more than 8,000 years ago. Unfortunately it has been impossible to date the level accurately by the radiocarbon method. The paleo-Eskimo level at this site, according to dating of its charcoal, is about 2,000 to 1,500 years old, and the neo-Eskimo occupation seems to have lasted from about 1200 to 1600 A.D.

While the story of Cape Denbigh and its Old World connections slowly un-

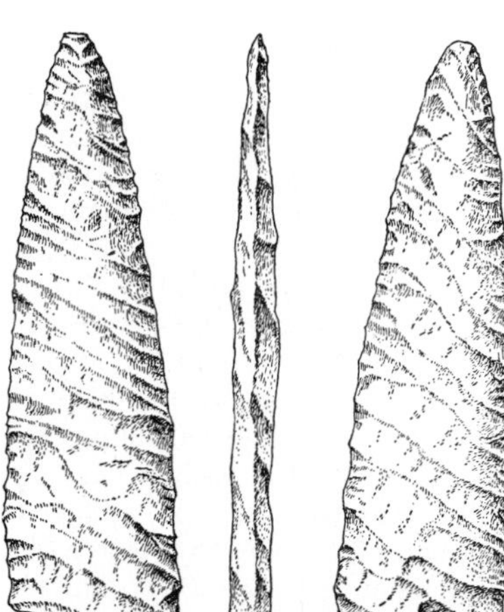
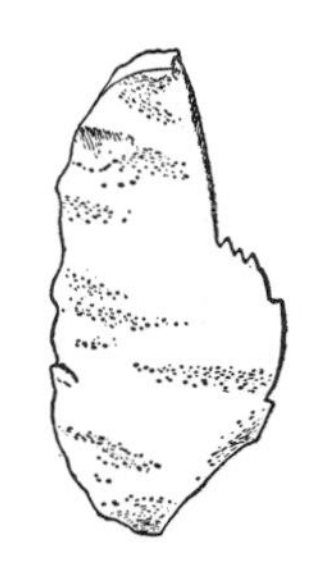
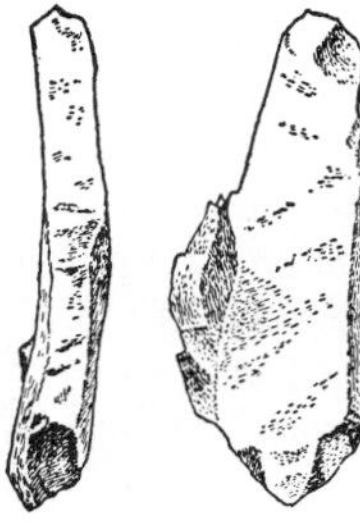
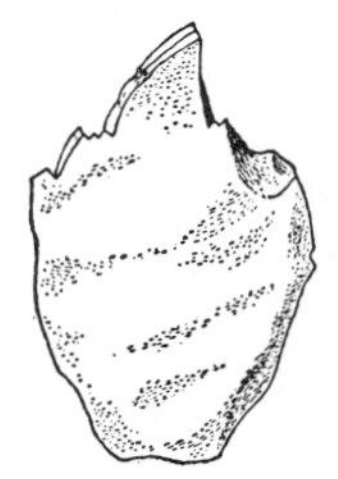
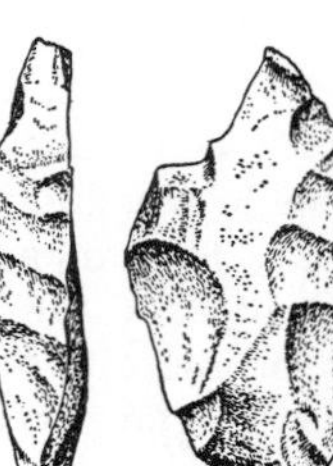

shaft behind an end point (*second from left*). The fluted point (*third*) resembles those of the Folsom type found in the U.S. Southwest, while tne large point (*fourth*) is of the type termed "Yuma oblique." Burins (*fifth and sixth*) were used as grooving tools.

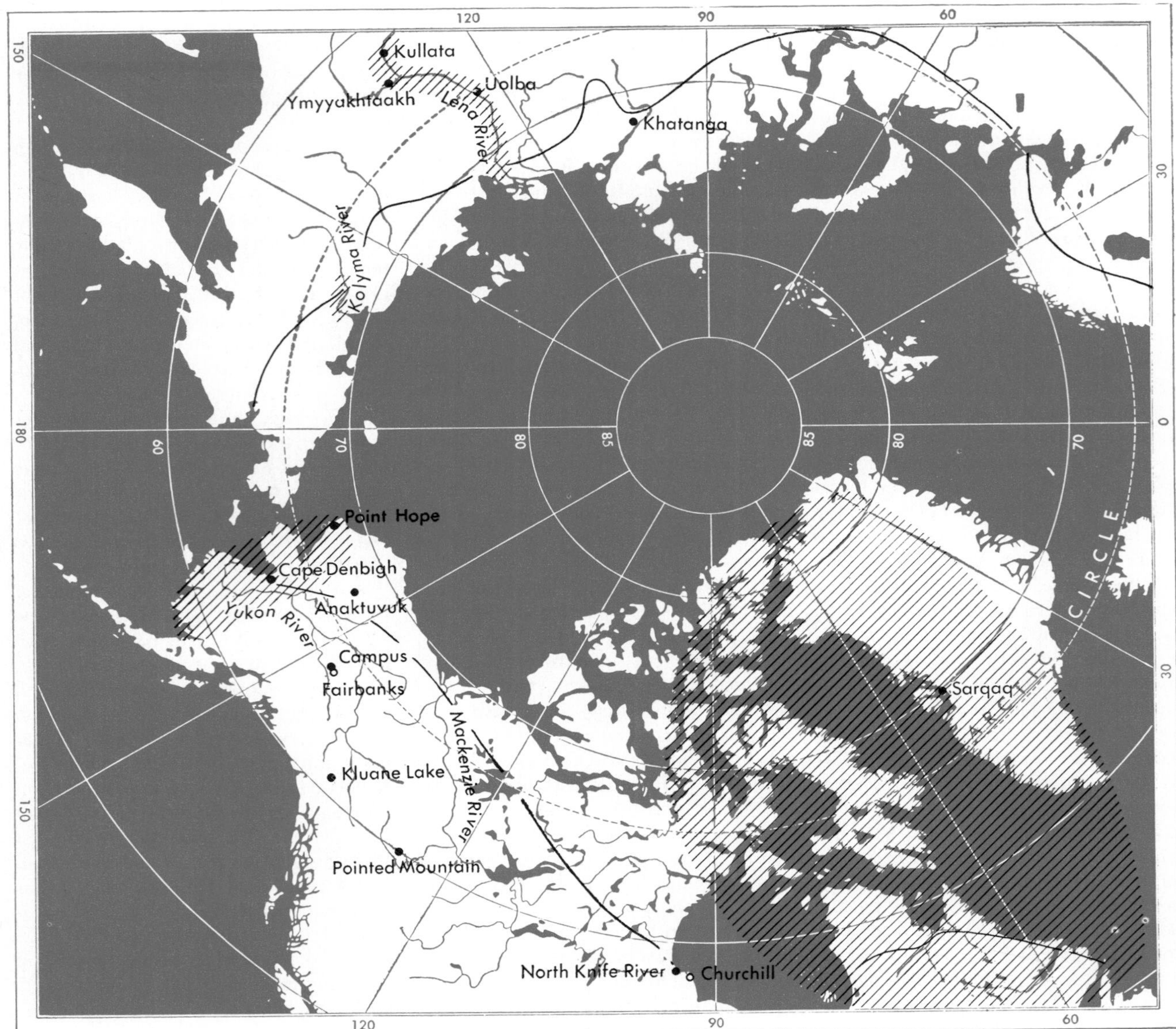

PRINCIPAL SITES at which tools were found are indicated by the black dots on this polar projection of the Arctic. The hatching at the top indicates the main region of such finds in Siberia. The hatching at the left outlines the known area of the paleo-Eskimo culture. The hatching at right shows the general extent of the Dorset culture. The black line indicates the northern limit of trees.

folded, a colleague exposed surprisingly similar cultural veins in neighboring areas. In 1949 Helge Larsen, of the National Museum of Denmark, discovered in mountain caves on the north side of Seward Peninsula a stratigraphic sequence in which microblades lay at the bottom. The following year his party again attacked the caves and came up with an interesting sequence. Near the bottom of the caves they found, along with material like the Denbigh flint complex, some unique artifacts which have not yet been described in print. Among them are slender antler shafts with side grooves into which microblades fit—a characteristic of certain Mesolithic sites of northern Europe and Asia. We cannot yet say whether these finds are older or younger than the Denbigh flint complex.

As microblades have turned up at other sites along the Arctic Circle, the idea has grown upon me that the people of the early flint complexes flourished on the forest edge—near the northern limit of spruce. Denbigh and some of the other sites are at the tree line today; there is evidence that forests extended, within the last few thousand years, even farther north than they do now. A hunting group living near the forest edge can retreat to it for tent poles and fuel, for moose and bear and for shelter from wind and cold. The barren lands beyond the forests are the highroads of caribou, as they must have been in earlier times for horses and bison, and it is here that hunters find it easiest to outwit large numbers of animals at the times of their annual crossings. Those who live at the tree line are doubly insured.

Last July I went to a settlement on the tree line far east of Alaska—the village of Churchill on the western shore of Hudson Bay. My main mission had to do with studying climate in tree rings, but I talked with the inhabitants about flint chips and arrowheads, in hopes of evoking the memory of some half-forgotten site. Just before leaving for a trip north into the barren lands inhabited by Caribou Eskimos, I had the good fortune to be shown a handful of flints which a Chipewyan Indian had shortly before given to a prominent resident of Churchill. In this collection of a dozen delicate objects of white chalcedony and agate were end blades, fragments of side blades and burins!

I thought at first these remains might belong to the so-called Dorset culture—an early Eskimo people who occupied Greenland and eastern Canada more than a thousand years ago. But under scrutiny the objects looked unlike those of the Dorset culture. In August the man who had found the flints and an Indian companion guided me to the site. It was some distance up the swift North Knife River, a stream that flows into Hudson Bay northwest of Churchill. We traveled by canoe about 25 miles up the river and then hiked a mile or more upland. The site lay on a strip of windblown sand and moss-covered ground between an old terrace and a long, shallow lake. In blown-out pits, where the milling of caribou had broken the sod and exposed the underlying sand to the wind, we found hundreds of chips of flinty material left by some early people, and a number of whole or broken artifacts. My companions explained that they had often hunted caribou at this place, but they professed to have no knowledge, legendary or otherwise, of the people who had left the flints.

The exciting fact soon emerged that this was indeed a site of burins and side blades, in addition to many of the sharpening spalls of burins, end blades and various scrapers. In all of the artifacts and raw chips, however, we found not a single microblade. This could not be Dorset culture. I remembered that a Danish archaeologist, Jorgen Meldgaard, had recently discovered at Sarqaq in Greenland side blades and burins which he thought were not Dorset either.

When I returned to Philadelphia from Hudson Bay, I wrote at once to Larsen in Copenhagen, telling him of my discovery. Again coincidence had worked! He wrote that his party had just returned from Disko Bay on the Greenland west coast. They had found a three-stratum site, containing the remains of neo-Eskimos on top, artifacts of the Dorset culture below, and at the bottom, beneath sterile soil, a layer containing only objects like those at Sarqaq. The Sarqaq and the Knife River finds, though mostly unlike in their precise form and style of workmanship, are remarkably alike in their broader types and frequency. And so the picture continues to emerge.

CAPE DENBIGH SITE at which artifacts were found is photographed from the air. In the foreground is an arm of the Bering Sea. The spot is called Iyatayet by the Eskimos.

The clues that we have so far are only bits and patches, but two possible alternate patterns are beginning to take form. We may reason, on one hand, that the sterile layers between the deposits of artifacts represent periods when the population had moved away from the whole region, and that the successive occupations were by new migrations. An extreme proponent of the migration theory might say that the Denbigh flint people came from Asia and then journeyed south, that much later the paleo-Eskimos came out of Asia and settled for a time in Alaska before moving to the eastern Arctic, and that finally the Eskimos of today arrived and remained.

In the opposite view, we can assume that the village sites that have been unearthed were merely abandoned for other habitations nearby. A hunting people move about in search of game but seldom venture far from the familiar hills, streams and meeting places that they know as home. We may suppose that our discoveries of flint collections are rare glimpses of a hunting people at

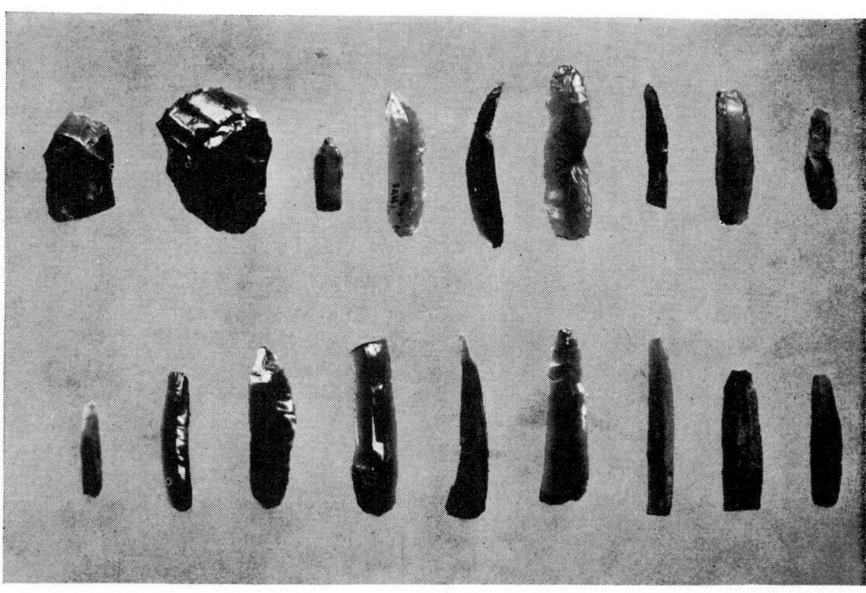

MICROBLADES were found in profusion at the Cape Denbigh site. They were struck from a larger stone, or core, with one blow. The large black stone at the upper left is such a core.

rest. I am inclined to this second view. The movement of a northern hunting family in the course of a year from its spring hunting grounds to its summer fishing banks to its autumn caribou crossings does not lessen its feelings of attachment to any of these places. "Home" for such people is often the area within which customary social and economic contacts are made, rather than any fixed village.

I am most skeptical of the idea that people from Asia picked up and deliberately undertook a long migration. Rather, I favor the theory that a very sparse Arctic population slowly spread over the belt of northern climate, neither pursuing nor evading pursuit, but simply existing and adjusting at random to the environment, the sons sometimes hunting beyond the range of their fathers but never really leaving home. Once established in the Bering Strait region, a population can hardly ever have drifted away completely, for the area had the resources of the predictable sea plus those of the rivers and nearby forests.

The flint work of the Denbigh flint complex, the oldest cultural horizon yet identified in the Bering Strait region, is not only unique but possibly the world's most sophisticated. It shows no signs of having been brought there *in toto* from elsewhere. The Bering Strait region was already a "culture center" at the time of deposit of the Denbigh flint layer. Its emanations were being felt both to the east and to the west. Since the culture at Bering Strait was more complicated than those nearby, there cannot have been a strictly one-way diffusion of ideas to either continent. People at Bering Strait could have passed along ideas received from either direction, but they would also have originated and disseminated ideas of their own.

One is struck by the fact that most of the early flint techniques were distributed primarily in a broad band centering at the Arctic Circle; they seldom strayed south. Proponents of a "circumpolar" culture have shown repeatedly that a high degree of identity exists in specific forms of objects across all of the Arctic—including hair combs, knife blades, skin boats, side blades and many other examples. To these may be added, for very early times and with emphasis, microblades and burins.

Shall we, then, regard the Arctic as a broad region where thin populations long ago spread themselves into all of the parts where meat was available—enjoying slowly changing cultures that have surmounted and actually taken advantage of the environment? Such a view leaves little room for migrating hordes. It suggests instead that America was first settled by people slowly filtering down from the Arctic population, reassorting their genes variously in the New World down through the millennia and drawing at first for their changing culture on circumpolar ideas.

A Transpacific Contact in 3000 B.C.

10

by Betty J. Meggers and Clifford Evans
January 1966

Archaeological evidence strongly indicates that pottery found in Ecuador, the oldest known in the New World, was introduced there by fishermen who had drifted from Japan

Although the time of man's first arrival in the New World from the Old World is still uncertain, authorities agree that the principal route was across the Bering Strait from Siberia to Alaska. Perhaps as early as 40,000 years ago, and surely by 13,000 B.C., groups of hunters and gatherers began to populate North America. As the millenniums passed, they spread throughout the hemisphere and gradually developed different ways of life. In some places, such as Mexico and Peru, the process of cultural evolution and differentiation culminated in civilizations that rivaled—and in the view of some Spaniards were superior to—the civilization of 16th-century Europe.

As these New World civilizations have become better known archaeologically, striking parallels have been observed with the architecture, religious practices and art styles of Asia. It has been suggested that these parallels are evidence of unrecorded "discoveries" of America long before Columbus. Most professional archaeologists have remained unconvinced because the possibility of an independent origin of the parallel traits could not be eliminated. Recent archaeological investigations on the coast of Ecuador, however, have brought to light facts that can lead to only one conclusion: a boatload of inadvertent voyagers from Japan strayed ashore in the New World some 4,500 years before Cortes reached Mexico.

There are two principal ways in which similar culture traits can come into existence in widely separated parts of the world. One is convergence, a process by which traits that were initially different come to resemble one another independently. The other is diffusion, or "borrowing," a process by which a trait is passed from a donor culture to a recipient one. Since borrowed traits are often modified during their transfer, it may be difficult to tell which of the two processes is responsible for any particular similarity.

Borrowing rather than convergence becomes the preferable explanation only if three criteria can be met. First, the trait or complex of traits in question must be shown to be older in the donor culture than in the recipient culture, or at least as old. Second, the antecedents of the trait or complex of traits should be traceable in the donor culture; conversely, the parallel item in the recipient culture should appear full-blown, with no observable antecedents. Third, the physical form of the trait should be unrelated to its function; this operates to rule out parallels that arise because of limitations set by the material from which an object is made or by the use to which it is put.

The first two criteria have not been satisfied for most of the culture traits that have been cited as evidence for contacts across the Pacific. Even though the areas of high culture in Mexico and South America are among the best-known parts of the New World, large sections remain almost untouched by archaeologists; the situation in most of Asia and the adjacent Pacific islands is no better. When more work has been done, other conclusions may be as surprising as the one we propose here: The knowledge of how to make pottery was first brought to Ecuador—where the earliest pottery so far discovered in the

FIRST CLUE to cultural contact between Asia and the New World 5,000 years ago was provided by fragments of a pottery vessel from the lowest level of a Valdivia culture site in Ecuador. They display a rim decorated with a "castellation," or peak; this decoration was uncommon elsewhere in the world at that time except on the Jomon pottery of Japan.

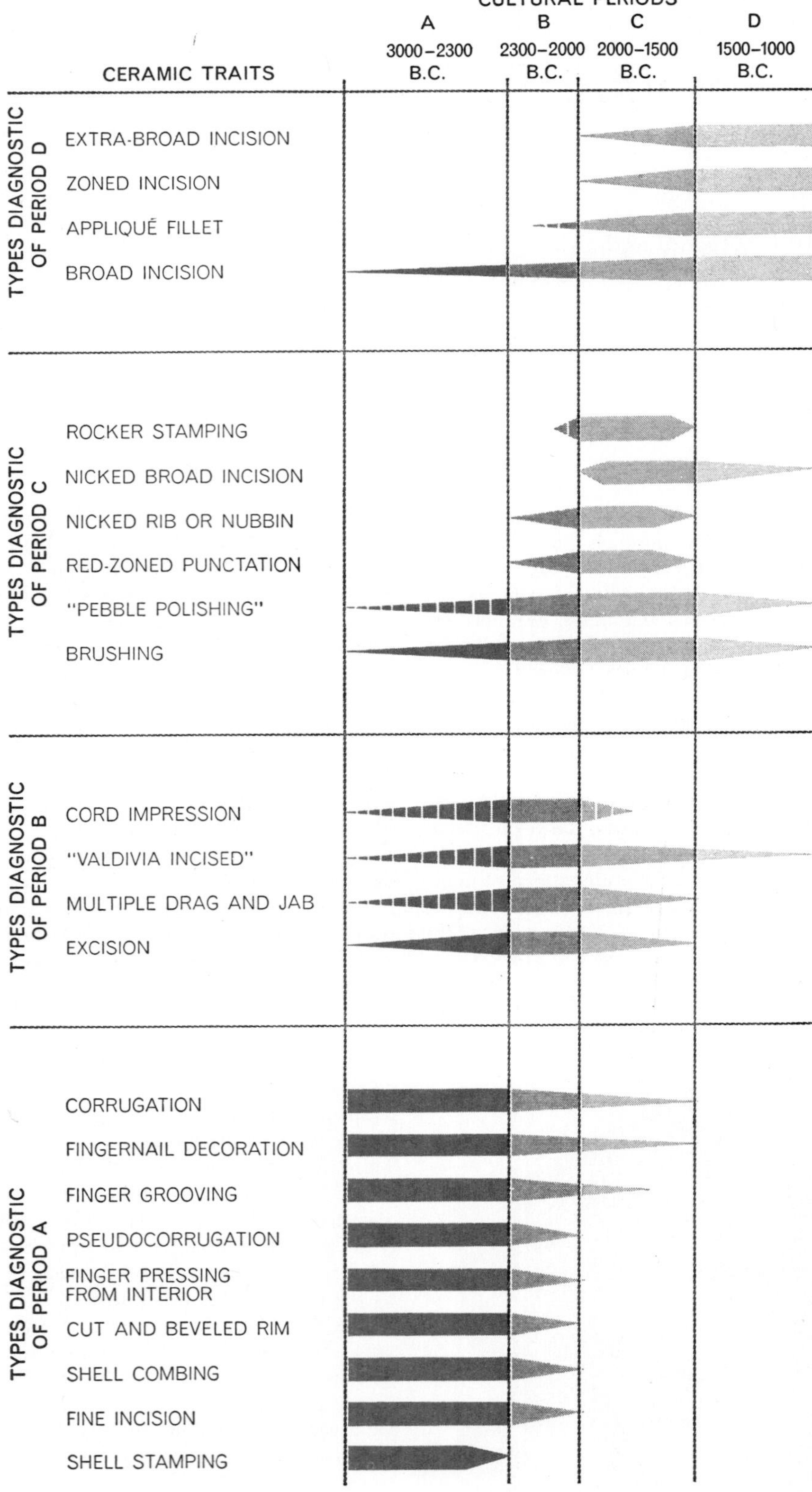

VARIETY OF TECHNIQUES used to decorate the earliest Valdivia pottery suggests that the craft was imported rather than invented locally. Each bar's length shows the duration of the ceramic trait it represents; tapering at the left indicates a trait's inception, at right its extinction. Broken tone implies uncertainty. Nine traits are typical of Period *A* pottery, and three of the four traits typical of Period *B* may first have appeared in Period *A*. Some of the parallels between this pottery and Jomon ware are illustrated on the opposite page.

New World has been found—by fishermen who had drifted there from Japan, more than 8,000 nautical miles away.

This conclusion was drawn only after a long period of fieldwork, classification and analysis. Rather than merely summarize the evidence on which the conclusion is based, we should like to review the chain of events that led to it. The starting point was the discovery of a series of seashell deposits along the coast of the Ecuadorian province of Guayas. An astute amateur archaeologist, Emilio Estrada, excavated one of these middens in the fall of 1956 and found that it contained heavily eroded fragments of pottery. He immediately recognized that the techniques of decoration resembled those used to ornament Guañape pottery—the earliest known on the coast of Peru—which dates back to about 2000 B.C. On the basis of this similarity Estrada proposed that the newly discovered Ecuadorian pottery belonged to the same early period as its Peruvian counterpart.

Estrada went on to investigate similar middens and found one with a deeper refuse deposit and better-preserved pottery near the modern fishing village of Valdivia. This name he gave to the culture that produced the pottery. Excavations at the Valdivia site since 1956 have provided material for carbon-14 analysis that extends the date of origin for the Valdivia culture back to about 3000 B.C., which makes it even older than Estrada had originally thought.

The antiquity of the Valdivia sites is reflected in their location on the margins of ocean inlets, which today are barren salt flats. Between 3000 and 1500 B.C. these flats were probably covered with, or ringed by, mangrove trees and were submerged by the sea either permanently or at high tide; such mangrove swamps still persist farther to the south along the Ecuadorian coast. The margins of these inlets were favored places of residence for the Valdivians because mollusks, crustaceans and fish, which were among their principal foodstuffs, were at hand. The people also ate deepwater species of fish, a fact that implies a knowledge of boating. The presence of deer bones in the refuse indicates that the Valdivians also practiced hunting.

No plant remains have been found in Valdivia sites, but both the habits of modern hunting-and-gathering peoples and archaeological evidence from Peru, where the dry climate helps to preserve perishable materials, make it a safe guess that the Valdivians did not neglect the edible wild plants of their region. They may even have taken some of the initial steps toward the domestication of plants, as did their contemporaries in Mexico and Peru. In general, however, their adaptation to a shore environment was so complete that it may have been their undoing. About 1500 B.C. the inlets began to dry up and the food supply to which the Valdivians were accustomed began to dwindle. The people retreated south and east toward the mouth of the Guayas River, but the new environment was less favorable and the Valdivia culture appears to have gradually become extinct.

A typical site of the Valdivia culture contains an abundance of mollusk shells, fair quantities of broken pottery and smaller amounts of bone and stone. There is little direct evidence of house construction, but fragments of burnt clay bearing the impression of twigs suggest that the Valdivians built huts with wattle-and-daub walls.

Although stone projectile points were manufactured by earlier peoples and are found frequently in the highlands of Ecuador, the Valdivians did not employ them. Stone tools for cutting, chopping and scraping were shaped only to the extent necessary to produce a working edge. Pebbles were converted into sinkers by cutting shallow notches at the sides to prevent the line from slipping off. Shell fishhooks were made with the aid of small sandstone saws and reamers. The fishhooks are small and almost circular, with a narrow gap separating the point from the shank. Tools made of bone are the scarcest of all; they consist chiefly of awls made of fishbone and punches fashioned from deer antler. In short, the surviving components of the Valdivians' tool kit are far from distinctive.

Quite the opposite is true of the pottery, which displays a variety of decorative techniques and vessel shapes that seems incongruous in the oldest pottery of the New World. For all its elaboration in shape and decoration, Valdivia pottery exhibits its primitive character by the thickness of the vessel walls and the imperfect symmetry of rim and body contours. The vessels were built up from coils of clay that sometimes were left visible on jar necks as an ornamental effect. The surface of most of the vessels was smoothed and often polished to a high gloss; about a fifth of them were given a red "slip."

PARALLELS between Jomon and Valdivia decoration techniques and design motifs are evident in these matching pottery fragments. In each example the Japanese pottery is at left and the Ecuadorian at right. At *a* the technique is excision and the motif is a "dog bone." At *b* the vessel rims are incised with parallel lines and the necks are decorated with zigzag incising. At *c* a multiple-edged tool has been alternately dragged and jabbed. At *d* fingers were used to form grooves. At *e* a tool has left fine lines at the bottom of each incision.

Numerous methods of decoration were employed, including incision, punctation, scraping, grooving, rocker-stamping, excision and appliqué. Decorative variety was increased by combining these methods with different kinds of surface finish; for example, incised designs were added to unpolished, polished or red-slipped surfaces. In addition, two kinds of decoration, such as incision and punctation, were sometimes applied to the same vessel. These combinations gave rise to a wide range of decorative effects.

One of the tasks facing the archaeologist is to reduce such variations to general categories that can be used to study change over a period of time and to compare one pottery complex with another. When Valdivia pottery is classified in this way, differences in the popularity of several of the decorated types become evident [*see illustration on page 98*].

Such differences provide a basis for dividing the history of the Valdivia culture into four periods. Most important for investigation of the origin of Valdivia pottery are the nine types of decoration characteristic of Period *A*. Typical early shapes include large, shallow, thick-walled bowls with slightly constricted mouths and round jars with thickened rims that were often ornamented by pressing the fingers on the lower edge of the rim. Other features characteristic of Period *A* are vessels with four small, closely spaced "feet," and others with rims that are undulating or "castellated" (formed into several peaks).

Figurines are another distinctive element of the Valdivia culture. Those of Period *A* were made of stone, but about the beginning of Period *B* pottery became the preferred material. The earliest figurines were nothing more than thin slabs of soft stone either selected for the symmetry of their natural form or worked into a rectangular outline; they are identifiable as figurines because of their early position in an evolutionary continuum that culminates in figurines with recognizable human characteristics.

The style changes completely with the introduction of pottery figurines at the beginning of Period *B*. The earliest of these, known as the Valdivia type, is realistic and often carefully made [*see illustration below*]. During Period *C* the realism gradually disappears, although the types known as San Pablo and Buena Vista retain traces of their ancestry. By Period *D* figurines have lost their popularity; the few examples of the type that is known as Punta Arenas are a far cry from the careful creations of Period *B*.

The abundance of fragments of figurines in the Valdivia sites suggests that the figurines were put to some common use. Two facts are relevant to inferences on this point. First, although many of the figurines represent females, the lack of emphasis on pregnancy or genitals makes it unlikely that they were fertility images. Second, the seemingly casual manner in which they were discarded suggests that their value was transitory. Today Indians in northern Colombia and Panama make for healing ceremonies wooden figurines that are similarly short-lived and unemphatic with respect to sex; new ones are carved for each ceremony and are then thrown away. Since they are made of wood, they soon disappear. The Valdivia figurines, made of durable materials, simply broke into fragments.

A survey of the characteristics of other early New World archaeological

POTTERY FIGURINES are first found at the end of Period *A* in Valdivia sites, or about 2350 B.C. They are more realistic than the stone figurines that precede them or the other pottery figurines that come after them (*see illustration at top of opposite page*). The majority are female and show great variability in the way the hair is dressed. Four of the figurines are shown from front and rear

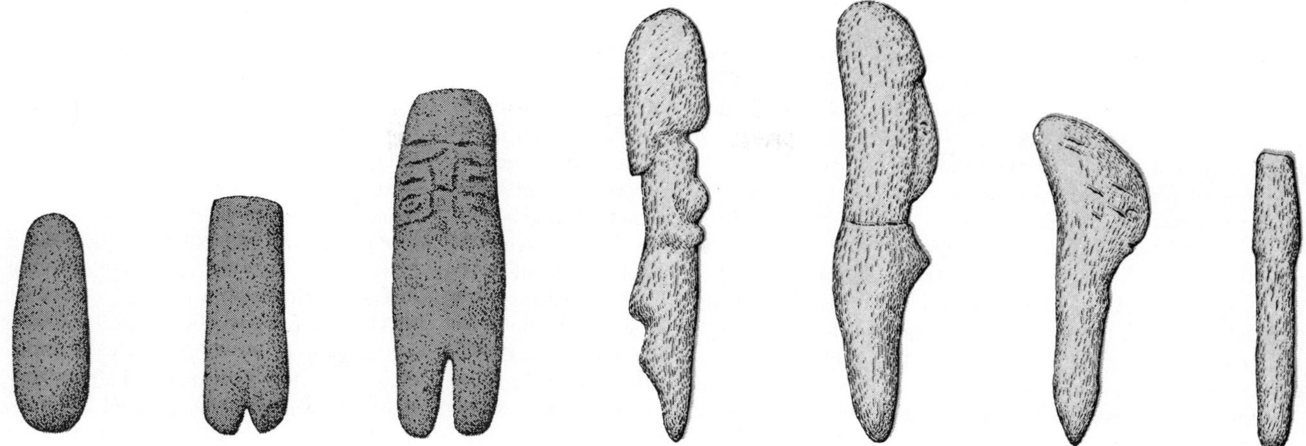

RISE AND DECLINE of realism in the style of the figurines unearthed at Valdivia cover a span of almost 2,000 years. Stone figurines of Period *A* began as flat slabs, then developed a basal notch to represent legs and next included anthropomorphic facial features on one side of the top (*front views at left*). The figurines of pottery that followed were, first, the realistic Valdivia type (*center and illustration at bottom of these two pages*). Next came the increasingly stylized San Pablo and Buena Vista types. During the last 400 years of Valdivia culture the pottery figurines degenerated into the featureless Punta Arenas type (*shown in profile view at far right*).

complexes serves to highlight the uniqueness of Valdivia pottery. Complexes such as the Monagrillo in Panama (2100 B.C.), the Puerto Hormiga in Colombia (3000 to 2500 B.C.) and the Guañape in Peru (2000 to 1000 B.C.) all have pottery characterized by a limited number of vessel shapes and fewer techniques of decoration. Furthermore, the carbon-14 dates for these complexes (with the possible exception of the Puerto Hormiga complex) are later than the earliest Valdivia dates, which means that none of these cultures could have been the source from which pottery-making was introduced to the coast of Ecuador. Still another alternative—the possibility that Valdivia pottery was a local invention—appears improbable because of the variety this pottery exhibits from the very start; such variety is understandable only as the culmination of a long period of development.

The clue that finally led to the most

alternately. They exhibit a grooved parting of the hair (*far left*), a braid front and back, with the crown of the head half-bare (*left*), a long bob with the sides tucked under a straight center hank at the back of the head (*right*) and a long bob with cross-bindings at front and rear that look like a hairnet (*far right*). Other variations are buns on each side of the head and purely geometric incisions.

probable origin of Valdivia pottery did not come to light until 1961, when the last shovelfuls of debris were being removed from the deepest part of the large stratified deposit Estrada had excavated at the Valdivia site. This clue was a fragment of a red-slipped and incised vessel with a unique type of rim: when the vessel was whole, the rim rose in a series of castellations [*see illustration on page 97*]. At a time as early as Valdivia Period *A* this form of rim is rare anywhere in the world except Japan. There it commonly occurs on pottery of the prehistoric Jomon period.

When we followed this clue by examining other characteristics of Jomon pottery, we discovered a large number of other similarities with Valdivia pottery, both in decorative technique and motif and in vessel shape. In fact, almost all the initial Valdivia characteristics could be identified in the Early Jomon and Middle Jomon pottery of Japan. Not only are techniques of decoration duplicated; the design elements and patterns are often nearly identical [*see illustration on page 99*].

In making a comparison of this kind it is desirable to demonstrate, if possible, that the traits in question not only occur together in the recipient culture but also form a complex in the donor culture. Often the facts are not available, either because not enough work has been done or because the approaches to classification in the two regions are so different that the materials cannot easily be compared. Until archaeology reaches the level of standardized concepts and procedures attained by the physical and biological sciences, this lack of comparability between results of investigations in different parts of the world will continue to be a problem. Here the difficulty was partly overcome by a National Science Foundation grant that enabled us to visit Japan and examine pottery from a number of Jomon sites on the islands of Honshu and Kyushu. This examination proved that a majority of the decorative techniques and motifs characterizing early Valdivia pottery are also present in pottery from sites in Kyushu dating from the period of transition between Early Jomon and Middle Jomon, or about 3000 B.C.

Three sites are outstanding in possessing almost all the relevant Valdivia traits: Ataka and Sobata near the modern town of Kumamoto in central Kyushu and Izumi on the western coast of Kyushu. Like the Valdivia sites, they consist of shell, bone and stone refuse mingled with fragments of pottery. The evidence suggests that the Jomon people of 3000 B.C. lived a life similar in many respects to the life of the coastal inhabitants of Ecuador and Peru in the same period. Much of their food came from the sea; it included mollusks and crustaceans gathered from tidal flats and deepwater fish caught with hooks by fishermen in canoes offshore. The stone, bone and shell implements are generally equivalent in function to those found in the Valdivia sites, although some of them are different in form.

The context in which pottery is found on Kyushu about 3000 B.C. is thus very similar to the context in which it suddenly appears on the coast of Ecuador at about the same time. An important difference is apparent, however, when the antecedents of the Jomon complex are considered. Valdivia pottery is the oldest so far discovered in South America; the Early Middle Jomon pottery of Japan, on the other hand, is indicated by carbon-14 dates to be the product of several millenniums of evolution in pottery-making. The earliest known pottery in Japan, which is more than 9,000 years old, is simple both in decoration and in vessel shape. The contents of a long series of progressively more recent sites serve to document the changes in decoration and vessel form that culminate in the Jomon pottery complex that

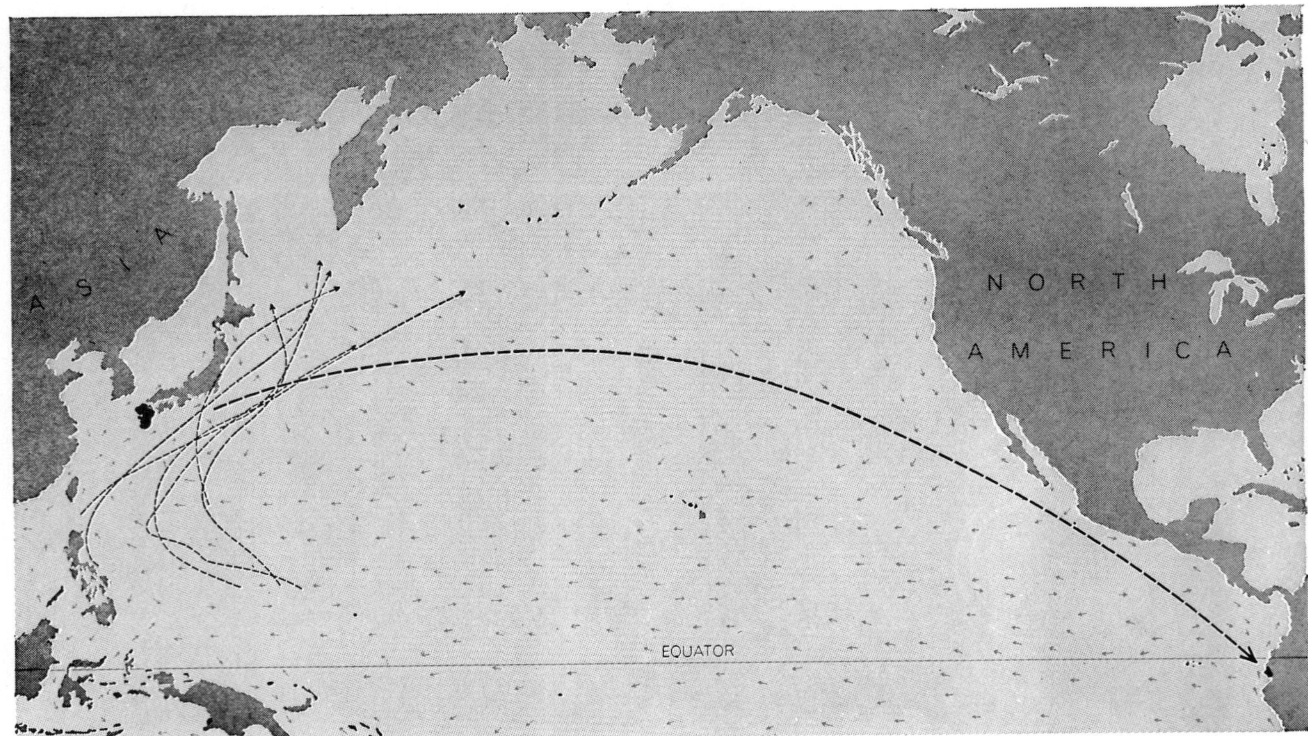

PROBABLE ROUTE from Kyushu to Ecuador is a product of the pattern of prevailing currents (*colored arrows*) and the assumption that a typhoon carried a party of Jomon fishermen so far to the northeast (*black arrows show sample storm tracks*) that a return to Japan was impossible. Thereafter the winds and currents favored continued drifting eastward along a great-circle course to Ecuador.

DEPTH OF DEPOSIT at a site near Valdivia, a village on the coast of Ecuador, is evident in this stratigraphic section that reached sterile soil at the bottom of the cut. Pairs of workers with wire screens are sifting pottery fragments and other bits of human handiwork from the accumulated debris of the earliest level of the Valdivia culture, in which Jomon-like pottery was unearthed.

flourished about 3000 B.C. and possessed the elements that make their sudden appearance on the coast of Ecuador at that time. Hence the Jomon sites on Kyushu satisfy two contextual criteria: equal or greater antiquity and well-established antecedents. The third criterion—absence of functional limitation—is also fulfilled, since the techniques of decoration and variations in rim and base form of these vessels are not dictated by the use to which they were put.

Enough is known about the pattern of subsistence during the Jomon period to hazard a reconstruction of the way in which Jomon-like pottery came to be introduced to Ecuador. Since the Jomon people engaged in deep-sea fishing, we may suppose that a group set out on what was meant to be a routine fishing trip. As they moved away from the southern shore of Kyushu they would have entered waters with some of the strongest currents in the entire Pacific Ocean. These currents move northeastward along the coast of Japan at 24 to 32 nautical miles per day—a speed that under normal circumstances would not have made it impossible for the fishermen to get home. South of Japan, however, is the region where typhoons develop, and the path of these storms often follows the northeast direction of the strong ocean currents.

Such a storm could have caught a boatload of fishermen and swept them far to the northeast. After the wind had died down the force of the current could have been so strong that the fishermen would not have been able to return to Japan. In such circumstances the fishermen would probably have settled down to await whatever end might be in store for them.

Those of us who belong to land-oriented cultures may find it difficult to believe that such involuntary voyagers could survive a few weeks at sea, let alone the months required to reach Ecuador. In possessing this attitude we reflect a background of several millenniums of civilized life, during which we have lost our ability to survive when thrown on our own resources in an unfamiliar environment. In contrast, the peoples of Micronesia are brought up even today to regard the sea as a source of food and an avenue of communication; they are not afraid to set out on long voyages, nor do they become panic-stricken if they lose their way. Although they do not always survive, their chances of doing so are relatively good. It seems likely that the prehistoric Jomon fishermen, like the modern Micronesians, knew how to keep themselves provided with food and water and were accustomed to spending days at sea exposed to sun, wind and rain.

Currents that move five to 10 nautical miles per day prevail along the Jomon fishermen's probable transpacific route, which curves far to the north of Hawaii and then southeastward along the coast of North America until it reaches the latitude of Baja California. There some currents bear to the west, out into the Pacific [*see illustration on page 102*]. Here chance could have turned a drifting boat away from land, but evidently the Jomon fishermen continued southward.

From a geographical standpoint Ecuador is a predictable landfall: its coast projects farther to the west than any other part of South America except the adjacent coast of Peru. It is also the point where ocean currents from north and south meet, join forces and form the equatorial current moving west. This pattern of currents would carry a drifting craft westward if it did not first reach the coast of Ecuador. Such may well have been the fate of similar voyagers in earlier or later times. The Jomon fishermen who introduced pottery to the coastal Ecuadorians were more fortunate. At landfall they had traveled more than 8,000 nautical miles. As a great-circle route this is the shortest distance between Kyushu and Ecuador, but it is still an epic voyage.

There may have been a physical resemblance between the Jomon fishermen and the people they met ashore. The modern Japanese, whose appearance is quite different from that of South American Indians, are comparatively recent arrivals from the Asiatic mainland and do not represent the physical type prevalent among the islands' inhabitants during Jomon times. Communication between the newcomers and the local people must have been restricted at first by the absence of a common language; patterns of social behavior and religious belief doubtless differed in general or in detail. More important than these differences was the fact that the Jomon people and the indigenous population represented an approximately equal level of cultural development; adjustment should not have been difficult.

One further difference that must have struck the newcomers was the absence of pottery in Ecuador. They began to instruct the Valdivians, who were such apt students that their pottery soon equaled and perhaps surpassed that of distant Kyushu. The newcomers may have brought about modifications in other aspects of the Valdivia culture. If so, the traces have been obliterated by the destructive action of nature and man during succeeding millenniums.

COAST OF ECUADOR, from Cabo San Lorenzo to La Puntilla, is the most westerly part of South America except for the portion of Peru between the Gulf of Guayaquil and Punta Negra. This position makes the region a logical transpacific landfall.

If our reconstruction of the origin of Valdivia pottery is correct, the question remains of whether or not this transpacific contact—and others that may later have resulted in the introduction of different technologies, art styles and patterns of behavior—significantly modified the direction of indigenous cultural development in the New World. Were transpacific influences from the high cultures of Asia fundamentally responsible for the development of civilization in the New World, or were their effects superficial, like the frosting on a cake? Two decades ago most archaeologists accepted the idea that civilization followed a parallel but independent course of development in the Old World and the New. Now we are not so sure. The origins of many major features of New World culture—for example metallurgy, mathematics and writing—are still unknown. Until it can be shown that these arts have local antecedents or that, like Valdivia pottery, they are transplants from the Old World cultural stream, no final answer can be given.

An Archaic Indian Cemetery in Newfoundland

11

by James A. Tuck
June 1970

Little has been known about the hunters and gatherers who roamed northeastern North America 4,000 years and more ago. The richness of their culture is now disclosed by work at a beach burial ground

A remarkable accident of preservation has helped to resolve a problem that first began to trouble New World archaeologists early in this century. At that time the first in a series of enigmatic archaeological sites, best described as great boneless cemeteries, was discovered in northeastern North America. Plainly locales where many persons had been ceremonially buried, the sites—which now number in the dozens—showed only traces of human bone and of artifacts made of perishable materials.

Because red ocher was almost always present in the graves the cemetery-makers were given the name (among others) "Red Paint People." Various objects made of stone, found along with the ocher, provided the small amount of information about the Red Paint People that was available. The cemeteries were found from Maine to Newfoundland, but few dwelling sites were unearthed. Indeed, until 1967 archaeologists had little beyond the evidence of mortuary ceremonialism provided by the cemeteries themselves to help reconstruct how the Red Paint People lived. The lack of organic remains in the graves made the burials almost impossible to date with precision. It was safe to say only that the stone artifacts were typical of the New World Archaic (or intensive hunting-gathering) period. The material resources of the Archaic Indians, although they were more sophisticated than those of the earlier, big-game-hunting Paleo-Indians, did not include a knowledge of agriculture or the art of pottery-making. In spite of this handicap and the pressures of a sometimes precarious existence based on hunting and gathering, the Archaic Indians managed to live a full life.

Just how full this life was, both technologically and ceremonially, is now revealed by the contents of a unique Archaic Indian cemetery discovered three years ago on the island of Newfoundland. Unlike the boneless cemeteries unearthed earlier, this site proved to contain the well-preserved skeletons of more than 100 individuals, together with a vast wealth of objects made of perishable materials that, like the skeletons, had been safely preserved for thousands of years. The Newfoundland cemetery was a preferred Archaic Indian burial ground over a span of nearly 1,000 years, from sometime late in the third millennium B.C. down to the final centuries of the second millennium.

The site is located at Port au Choix, a small fishing village on a point of land on the west coast of Newfoundland's Great Northern Peninsula [*see illustration on page 109*]. The village overlooks a stretch of water known as the Back Arm, a sheltered embayment that opens into the Gulf of St. Lawrence. In the past the water level was higher and the Back Arm extended farther inland; several raised beaches remain as evidence of the earlier encroachment.

One of the raised beaches, which lies about 19 feet above high water today, is almost a mile long and varies from 30 to 70 feet in width; a good part of Port au Choix is built on this natural terrace. The fine sand of the ancient beach is easily dug with the simplest of tools, which may partly account for its selection as a burial ground by the Archaic Indians. The beach has been kind to archaeologists in another way: it is extremely alkaline, with a pH that averages close to 8.0. This condition and the excellent natural drainage of the beach account for the burials' remarkable state of preservation.

Soon after the initial find was made the Memorial University of Newfoundland sent a group under my direction to Port au Choix to excavate the site with the sponsorship of the Department of Provincial Affairs and the National Museum of Canada. We discovered that there were three distinct sets of burials. The first, which we called Locus I, had been exposed in the fall of 1967 as the foundations for a new building were being prepared. The second and largest set of burials, which we called Locus II, was still mainly undisturbed. We also found two infants' graves that were evidently not associated with the other burials; this set we called Locus IV. (A settlement site that belonged to a later Dorset Eskimo group had already been named Locus III.)

Most of the material from Locus I had been removed at the time of discovery. The foundation builder and other observers reported that the eight skeletons then unearthed had their legs drawn up in a "flexed" position rather than stretched out in an "extended" one. The graves may have been arranged in a rough circle; at least one of the eight skeletons, later identified as male, had a bundle of grave goods cradled in its arms. Red ocher was present in most if not all of the graves.

Our group was able to locate one additional burial at Locus I. It contained the skeletons of two females in a grave pit lined with red ocher. One skeleton rested on its back, its lower legs doubled backward. The other lay in a tightly flexed position, probably because the body was partially decomposed at the time of burial and had been bound up in a shroud or a blanket. Our discovery of the additional grave at Locus I brings the total of individuals buried there to 10. Only two were males.

The second cemetery at Port au Choix is the most extensive Archaic Indian burial site known in Newfoundland and

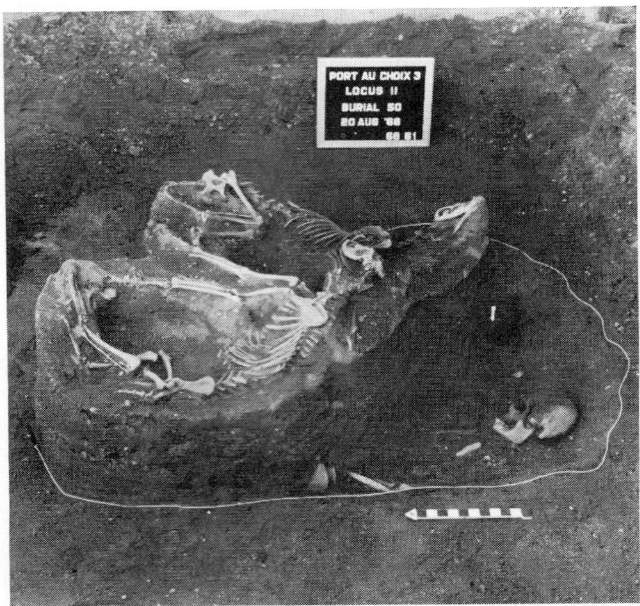

MOST ELABORATE BURIAL at Locus II contained the remains of two large dogs that had been placed above a grave containing an adult man and woman. No cause of death was evident for the dog in the foreground; the skull of the other had been crushed by a blow.

LOWER LEVEL OF SAME BURIAL contains a number of grave offerings in addition to the woman (*left*) and the man (*right*). The white arrows, placed in the grave by the excavators, point to some of the less visible objects. The posture of both skeletons is flexed.

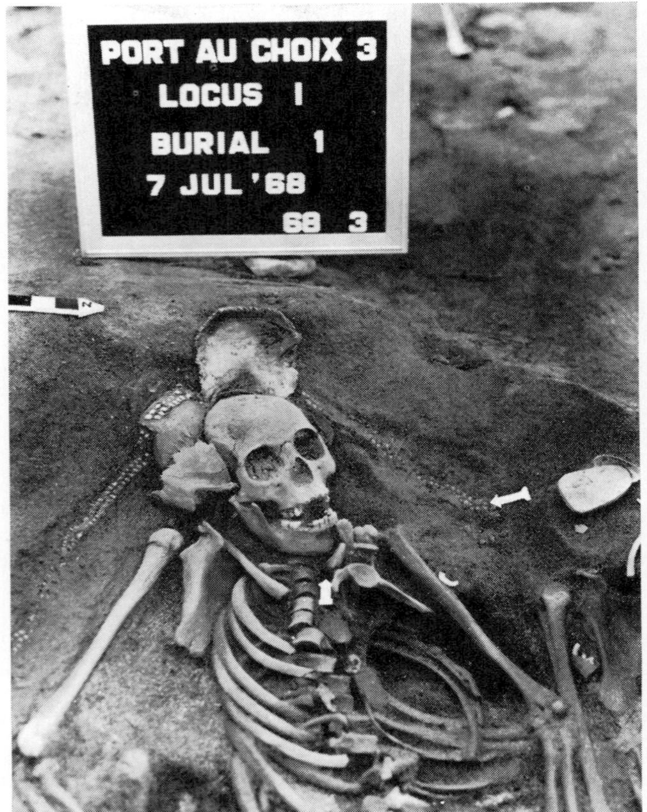

DECORATION OF CLOTHING is evidenced by the double row of beads that forms an inverted "*V*" with its apex at the skull of a young woman whose burial was unearthed at Locus I. The beads, made from the shells of small marine snails, were probably sewn to the edge of a hooded skin garment that was interred with the body. No garments survived millenniums of burial at the site.

TIGHTLY FLEXED BURIAL of a woman, unearthed at Locus II, was accompanied by three large stone axes. The degree of flexing suggests that the body was quite decomposed. Those Archaic Indians who died during the winter months evidently did not receive burial until after the ground thawed in spring or early summer. Sometimes only the skull and a bundle of bones were finally buried.

one of the largest in all of northeastern North America. It consists of 53 separate burials, arranged in three relatively compact groups. The burials contain a total of nearly 100 complete or incomplete skeletons and literally thousands of hunting implements, tools and other grave goods. Boulders or slabs of rock were placed over many of the burials, either to act as markers or to prevent disturbance by wild animals. Many of the graves nonetheless showed signs of intrusion. Usually the intrusions were the result of natural events, such as tree-root growth or the shifting of soil by the fall of a tree. Some of the intrusions, however, were evidently the result of visits to the site by later Archaic Indians.

After the last of these visits the site was covered with forest for perhaps 3,000 years, as we can tell by the accumulation of a stratum of dense, peaty humus as much as a foot thick on top of the beach sand. Where the sand and the humus meet, a thick calcareous crust was formed by the interaction of the alkaline sand and the acid humates percolating downward. The crust was undisturbed above all the burials found in Locus II.

The methods of burial at Port au Choix varied in both the posture of the dead and the condition of the individual. Infants and young children were generally buried in an extended position. Older children and adults who had been buried soon after death were usually interred in a flexed position. A practice known as secondary burial, which involves preliminary decomposition of the body and the later interment of the skull and a bundle of bones, was also known at Port au Choix. It is clear, however, that no rigid line separated the two practices. Skeletons were found reflecting all stages of decomposition, which suggests that people who had died during the winter were not buried until the ground thawed in spring or early summer.

Most of the articulated skeletons we unearthed at Locus II had been buried resting on their left side, but we could detect no particular orientation of the dead with respect either to the water of the Back Arm or to the points of the compass. The entire cemetery area, however, occupies an east-facing slope that overlooks the water; Archaic Indian burial grounds in similar locations are found elsewhere along the northeastern seaboard.

James E. Anderson of McMaster University is analyzing the skeletal material from Port au Choix. Some preliminary findings, particularly concerning the sex and age of the sample, are available. For example, it is apparent that the dead at Port au Choix were interred without regard to sex or age. The sex of each skeleton cannot always be determined, but of the burials at Locus II, 23 can be established as male and 18 as female. Adding to these the two males and eight females at Locus I, it appears that the ratio of the sexes buried at Port au Choix is almost equal.

As for the ages of the individuals at Port au Choix, the large sample from Locus II provides a good average distribution. Almost exactly half of the skeletons—a total of 44—are those of adults. Only seven of these individuals were more than 50 years of age; one was

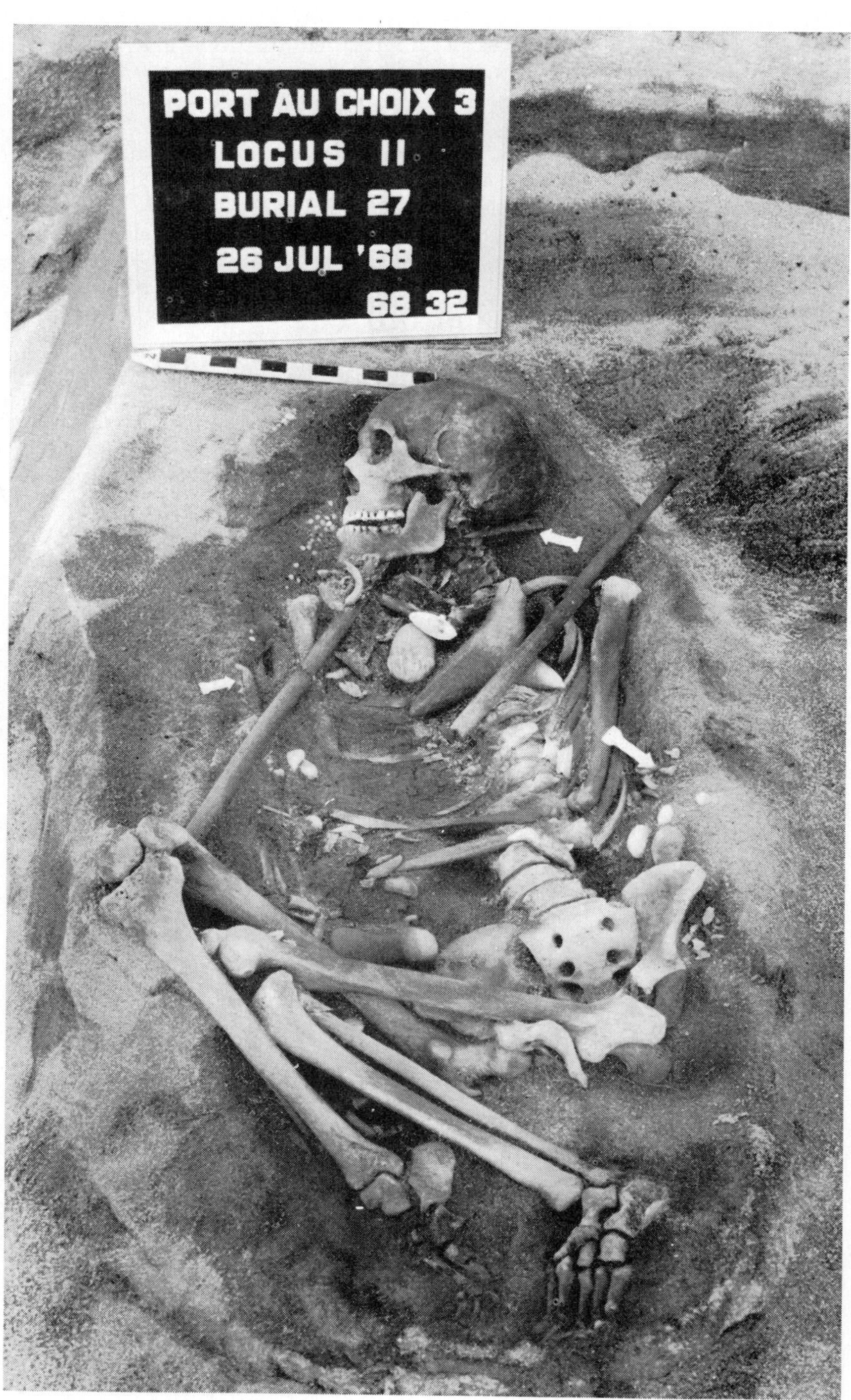

IMPORTANT YOUNG MAN, perhaps a shaman, was buried with grave goods of both ceremonial and utilitarian type. The latter include a barbed harpoon head near the skull (*uppermost arrow*) and two harpoon foreshafts that lie across the man's chest. The chief ceremonial object is the large killer-whale effigy near lower jaw (*see illustration on next page*).

between 18 and 21. The remaining adults can be called "middle-aged." Fifteen of the individuals at Locus II were between six and 18 years old and two between two and six years old. Infant mortality was high among these Archaic Indians: 15 of the dead were less than two years old and 12 were newborn.

The causes of death among the people buried at Port au Choix are obscure. The condition of the skeletons suggests that most individuals were healthy and robust. Tooth wear—perhaps partly due to softening hides by chewing—frequently exposed the adults' pulp cavities and even caused the loss of some teeth, but tooth decay was virtually absent. Some adults suffered from a mild arthritis of the spine, and an unusual manifestation of arthritis also affected the finger joints of several others. A perforating bone abscess, possibly the result of the bone-marrow malignancy known as multiple myeloma, appears on one skull. The principal evidence of trauma consists of broken ribs and several well-knit fractures of the arm and the leg.

The Port au Choix people are clearly unrelated to the Eskimos who have occasionally inhabited Newfoundland in both ancient and modern times. Comparison with other prehistoric New World skeletons is now in progress. So far the most significant finding is a close relationship between the Port au Choix population and a small but important series of Archaic Indian skulls discovered in the early 1960's on Morrison Island in the Ottawa River valley of Ontario. Carbon-14 dating shows that the Morrison Island skulls are about 4,400 years old: the dates fall between 2500 and 2300 B.C. This is in good agreement with the carbon-14 determinations recently obtained for the Port au Choix material. Locus II has proved to be the oldest of the three sites; its earliest date is 2340 ± 110 B.C. Other material from Locus II graves is dated from 1880 to 1740 B.C. Locus I is younger than Locus II. The single carbon-14 date so far available from Locus I is 1460 B.C. The site of the two infant burials, Locus IV, is the most recent of all, with a carbon-14 date of 1280 ± 220 B.C.

When one considers that the grave goods at Port au Choix were produced over a span of 1,000 years, it is not surprising that the artifacts show some differences in style. Nonetheless, they clearly belong to a single tradition. In the following reconstruction of this Archaic Indian tradition I have concentrated on the material from Locus II, which is the most abundant. The reconstruction nonetheless applies equally well to the Archaic Indians who left their dead at the other two loci in later years. It seems hardly necessary to warn the reader that, as with all such extrapolations, my reconstruction incorporates many speculative elements.

How did the Archaic Indians wrest a livelihood from this forested northern coast? We can begin to answer this question by making an inventory of the hunting gear found among the grave goods at Port au Choix. We uncovered a number of "bayonet" points (probably the heads of lances) fashioned by grinding pieces of slate to the desired shape. Several spear points with stemmed bases were also made of ground slate [*see top illustration on page 113*]. Stone was not the only material used to make objects of this kind; we found four stemmed spear points, three of them at Locus II and one at Locus I, that had been made by grinding pieces of bone instead of slate. There were also several "bayonet" points fashioned from bone and marked with deep barblike slashes near the tip [*see illustration on page 114*].

Presumably both lance points and spear points had once been mounted on wooden shafts and had been used as thrusting weapons to kill various kinds of game, particularly migrating caribou. A ceremonial aspect to the inclusion of these points in the burials at Port au Choix is evident in the fact that some of them were "killed," that is, purposely broken, before interment. It is noteworthy that, of all the stone points found at Port au Choix, only one was fashioned by chipping rather than grinding; it is a side-notched point made from gray quartzite.

In addition to thrusting weapons, the Archaic Indians were equipped with daggers, which were presumably useful for dispatching wounded game. We found one such dagger made from walrus ivory, another made from antler and several made from the leg bones of caribou. The walrus-ivory dagger may once have been carried in a sheath that combined pieces of antler with some perishable substance; only the antler portion remained intact.

Both the thrusting lances and the spears may have been used for hunting at sea as well as on land. The grave goods also include artifacts specifically designed for hunting sea mammals. These are harpoon heads of both the barbed and the toggling type, made from bone and antler and perforated for attaching a line. The toggling harpoon heads had an open socket to receive a foreshaft [*see illustration on page 112*]. Only two such foreshafts, however, were found in the graves. The barbed harpoon heads are equipped with from one to three barbs, and the base of the head is tapered, presumably for socketing in a wooden handle.

The graves also contained a number of unusual foreshafts made of whalebone. All of them have a slotted base, apparently for "tongue and groove" at-

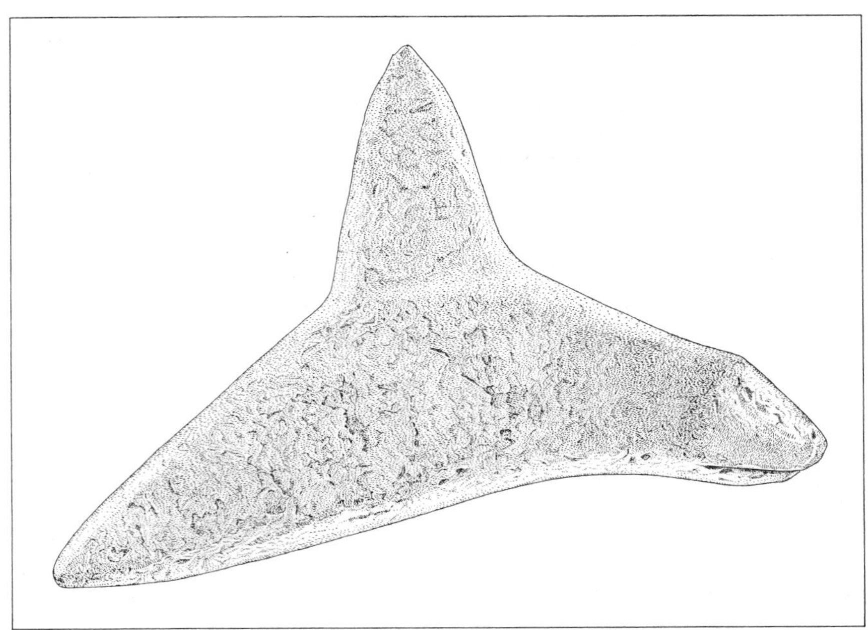

KILLER-WHALE EFFIGY represents the animal in motion; its head, mouth closed, is at right and its distinctive high dorsal fin dominates the sculpture. Two killer-whale effigies were found at Port au Choix; one is shown *in situ* in the illustration on the preceding page.

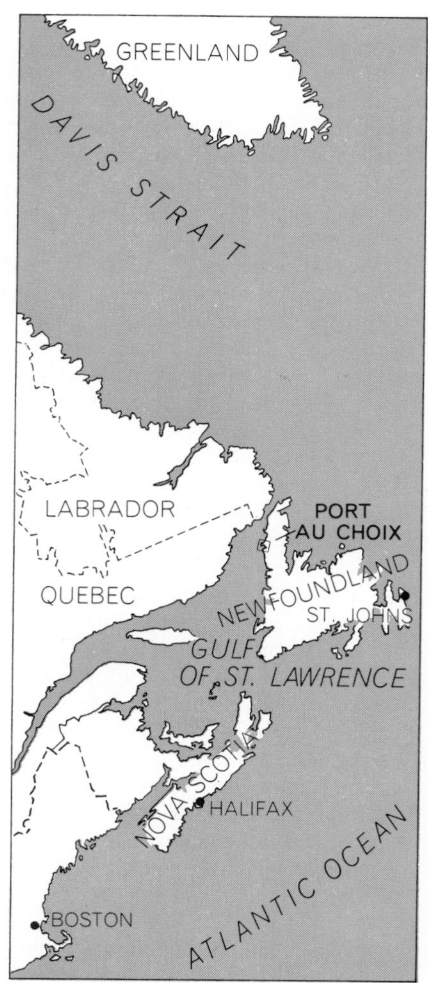

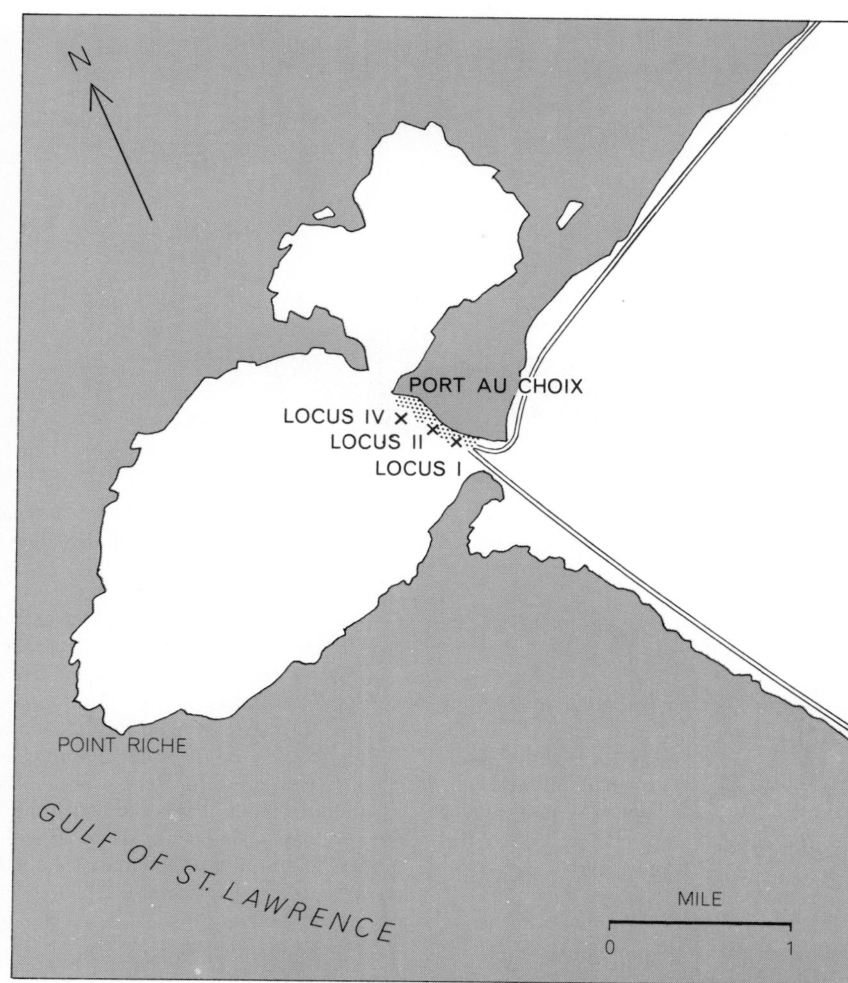

CEMETERY SITE lies on a promontory of the west coast of Newfoundland's Great Northern Peninsula (*left*), now occupied by a fishing village. The embayment where the village stands opens northeastward and the three sets of burials (*right*) face the sunrise.

tachment to a wooden handle. The tips of the foreshafts exhibit a variety of shapes. Some are slotted and have lugs or small holes that would aid in lashing a harpoon head into place. Others merely have a broad "V" or are bluntly tapered. Curiously, none of the harpoon heads from the graves nor any of the lance points we unearthed would fit the whalebone foreshafts. Perhaps the foreshafts had originally been fitted with heads of chipped stone that for some reason were not included in the burials. The one chipped-stone point unearthed at Port au Choix was not found in association with the whalebone foreshafts.

A slender foreshaft helps a hunter to drive the tip of his weapon deep into his prey, and a harpoon enables him to hold the animal at the end of a line. It thus seems logical to suppose that the Archaic Indians used both tipped foreshafts and harpoons in the pursuit of free-swimming animals whose vital organs are not easy to penetrate: seals, walruses and perhaps even small whales. This, in turn, supposes that the hunters were also sailors. The key evidence that the Archaic Indians were familiar with overwater travel is the fact that they reached the island of Newfoundland in the first place. The nearest point on the mainland is the coast of Labrador to the north, a minimum of 10 miles away across the often treacherous Strait of Belle Isle; to reach Newfoundland from Nova Scotia to the south calls for a 60-mile voyage.

The evidence for marine hunting from the graves at Port au Choix suggests that the Archaic Indians of Newfoundland knew more than just how to cross water; they must have been skillful boatbuilders and competent seamen. No boats or boat fragments have been found in the graves. Tools suitable for the construction of dugouts or skin boats were available, however, as were the raw materials for both kinds of craft.

Unless lance points and spear points also served the Archaic Indians as knives, there is a curious absence of implements for the dressing of game and the preparation of other food at Port au Choix. The easiest explanation would be that such work was done with knives made of chipped stone, and that these were not considered a necessary accompaniment for the dead. In contrast, the various tools used to prepare animal skins are well represented among the grave goods. They include scrapers made from the shoulder blade of caribou and two-handed "beaming" tools made from the split long bones of various mammals. Bone awls and a number of extremely fine bone needles attest to the use of sewn garments. Eight of the needles were found in a decorated needlecase that had been made from a caribou limb bone.

With the exception of a few whetstones, tools for working stone also appear not to have been considered necessary grave furnishings. We know, however, that the Port au Choix people used hammer stones for chipping and peck-

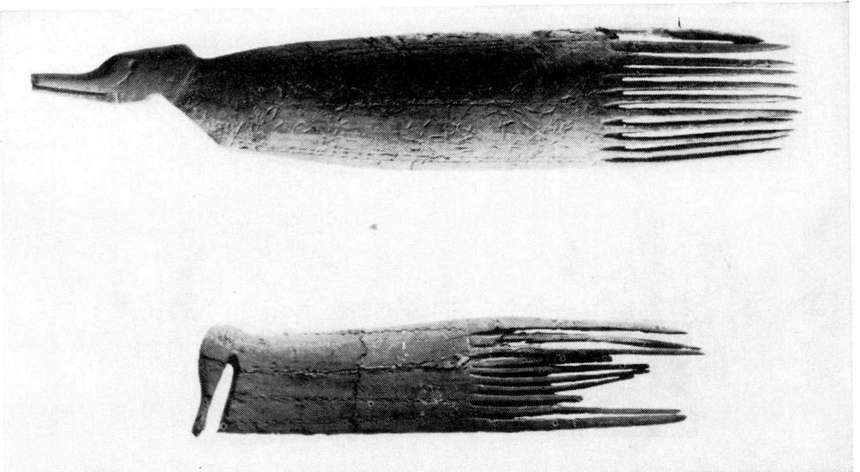

TWO COMBS made from caribou antler have been carved to represent birds' heads. The top comb decoration represents a merganser, the bottom a swan, goose or broad-billed duck.

ing. Unfinished stone tools in the graves clearly bear the marks of these implements.

The accident of preservation that enabled us to recover so many artifacts made of bone, ivory and antler from the graves of Port au Choix unfortunately did not protect objects made of wood and bark. Of the numerous artifacts the Archaic Indians must have fashioned from these materials only a few scraps of birch bark survive. Woodworking tools, however, are found in abundance. These include axes, adzes and gouges of several sizes, styles and materials. Most of the axes and adzes were made of slate, but some adzes were fashioned from ivory [*see illustration on page 112*]. The incisor teeth of beavers were also among the grave goods. They had been modified into woodworking tools by beveling and pointing their working edge or by shaping them into miniature gouges. A handle made of antler, with a beaver incisor hafted at each end, might even be regarded as foreshadowing the modern multipurpose implement of the subarctic: the "northern crooked knife." Some of the stouter bone awls among the grave goods may have been used in the manufacture of bark vessels for storage and cooking as well as for working with leather. The number and variety of such implements suggest a major woodworking industry among the Archaic Indians of Newfoundland.

A large proportion of the material unearthed at Port au Choix is nonutilitarian and may be classified as being either decorative or—with more caution—magico-religious. In the first category are thousands of beads, made from the shells of small marine snails, that were presumably used to decorate clothing and skin pouches and perhaps were sewn onto strips of hide. Strips decorated in this way were described by the first European visitors to Newfoundland. Another animal product used for beads by the Archaic Indians was the teeth of a species of skate common in Newfoundland waters; these distinctive objects may also have been used as hair ornaments.

A number of bone and antler pendants and pins, together with three bone combs, are objects that, although they are certainly decorative, must also reflect the religious beliefs of their makers. Some of the pendants depict birds such as ducks and loons; others are human figures, geometric forms and objects that have spearlike and swordlike shapes. Some are of slate and soapstone and one is formed from native copper. The pins display a variety of decorations; perhaps the most striking is one that ends with a bird's head, probably meant to represent the now extinct great auk [*see bottom illustration on this page*]. Of the three combs, two are decorated with a bird's head. One of them evidently represents a merganser; the other could be a swan, a goose or a broad-billed duck.

The grave goods also include collections of "exotic" stones, such as crystals of quartz, amethyst and calcite, and pebbles of quartz and iron pyrite. The pyrite pebbles may have belonged to fire-making kits, although the striking stones needed to complete the kits are rare and in only one case was a "striker" found in direct association with a pyrite. Other stones, either left unmodified or shaped to a greater or lesser extent, apparently represent different animal species and could have served as amulets. This seems indisputable in the case of two large, three-lobed sculptures that apparently represent killer whales [*see illustration on page 108*]. They invite speculation about parallels with the killer-whale cults found among the hunters of sea mammals in many parts of the world.

In addition to the snail shells and skate teeth used for decoration, other remains of animals are present in the burials. Some of them, such as seal claws and the teeth and jaws of caribou, bear, dog, wolf, fox, marten, seal and otter, may once have been sewn on clothing. The heads, bills and feet of gulls, mergansers and great auks may also have been sewn on clothing, but many of these objects seem instead to be the components of medicine bundles. Some of the objects still have specific significance as charms and amulets among the living aboriginal inhabitants of the subarctic and Arctic. The likelihood that

THREE DECORATIVE OBJECTS found among the grave goods at Port au Choix are a human figurine, made from antler, and two bone pins. The carving on the longer pin represents a great auk; the carving on the second may have been meant to represent a spear.

DOUBLE BURIAL at the Port au Choix cemetery area designated Locus II includes the well-preserved skeleton of a young woman who was interred resting on her left side and cradling a small child in her arms. Grave goods accompanying the burial include a number of quartz pebbles (*small white spheres*) and a barbed point made of caribou antler (*below lower jaw*), perhaps used as a spearhead.

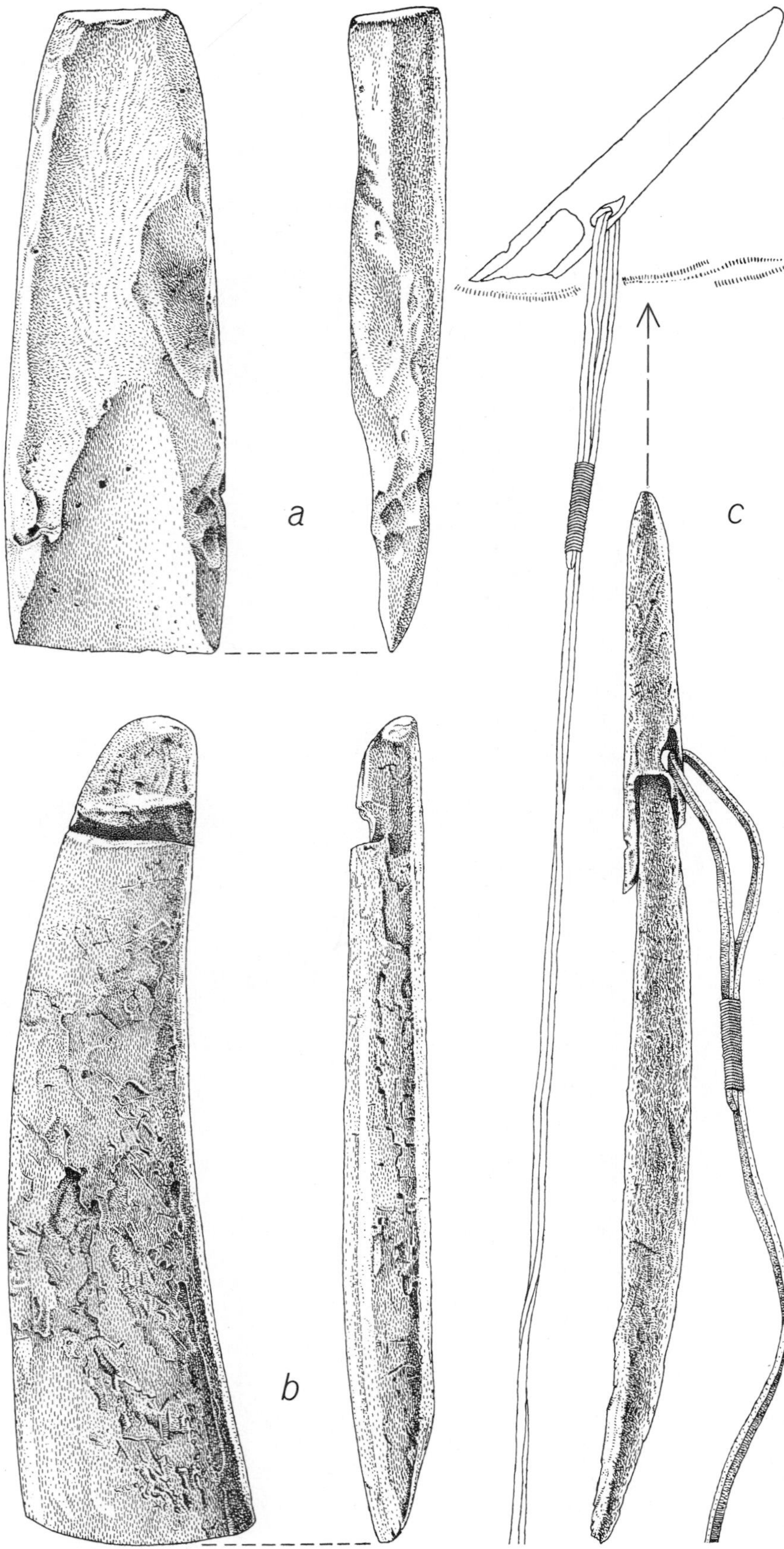

GOUGES FOR WOODWORKING were made from stone (*a*). Adzes were occasionally made from ivory (*b*). The number and variety of woodworking tools at Port au Choix suggest that the Archaic Indians were skilled in the use of wood. The principle of the toggling harpoon head is illustrated at right (*c*): the head, fitted over its foreshaft, is driven deep into the quarry. Tension on the harpoon line then twists the head, setting it sideways in the wound.

such beliefs also existed among the Archaic Indians is strengthened by our observation that items of possible ritual significance are not distributed randomly among the burials. For example, when a comb, a pin or a pendant that represents a particular species of bird is found in a grave, the heads, bills or feet in the grave frequently belong to the same species of bird.

So far we have completed only preliminary correlations between the age and sex of an individual and the kinds and quantity of goods in the grave. It appears, however, that adult males were accorded the most grave goods. Although some children's graves were richly accoutered, others held nothing but a few beads and ornaments. Women's graves frequently contained charms and amulets of the kind that modern tradition associates with male activities such as hunting.

What conclusions about Archaic Indian life can be drawn from the material unearthed at Port au Choix? We know that much of the durable contents of the graves resembles material found from Maine to as far north as Labrador (where Archaic Indian living sites have recently been discovered). It is thus apparent that a specialized type of culture existed in this part of northeastern North America during the latter part of the third millennium B.C. and most of the second millennium. I have named this culture the Maritime Archaic Tradition. The area where it flourished includes three separate biotic provinces—the Eskimoan, Hudsonian and Canadian—each with a distinctive flora and fauna. All three have enough in common ecologically, particularly in terms of the animal species most exploited by man, to have allowed a relatively uniform type of culture to flourish throughout the region.

At the time of the first European contacts the sea mammals of the region that were important to man included the harp seal, the harbor seal, other seal species and the walrus. It was probably much the same 4,000 years earlier. The land animals of greatest importance were the woodland caribou, the black bear and the beaver, and the birds included the great auk, the murre, the eider duck and the Eskimo curlew (whose flights once darkened the sky). Every summer spawning salmon filled the coastal rivers of the northeast. In the more southerly parts of the region there were the elk, the moose and perhaps the Virginia deer in addition to the caribou. This bountiful animal life, supplemented

POINTS FOR WEAPONS were skillfully formed from slate slabs that were shaped by grinding. Points of both sizes were probably hafted to wooden shafts to make spears and lances and both kinds of weapon used in hunting caribou ashore and sea mammals afloat.

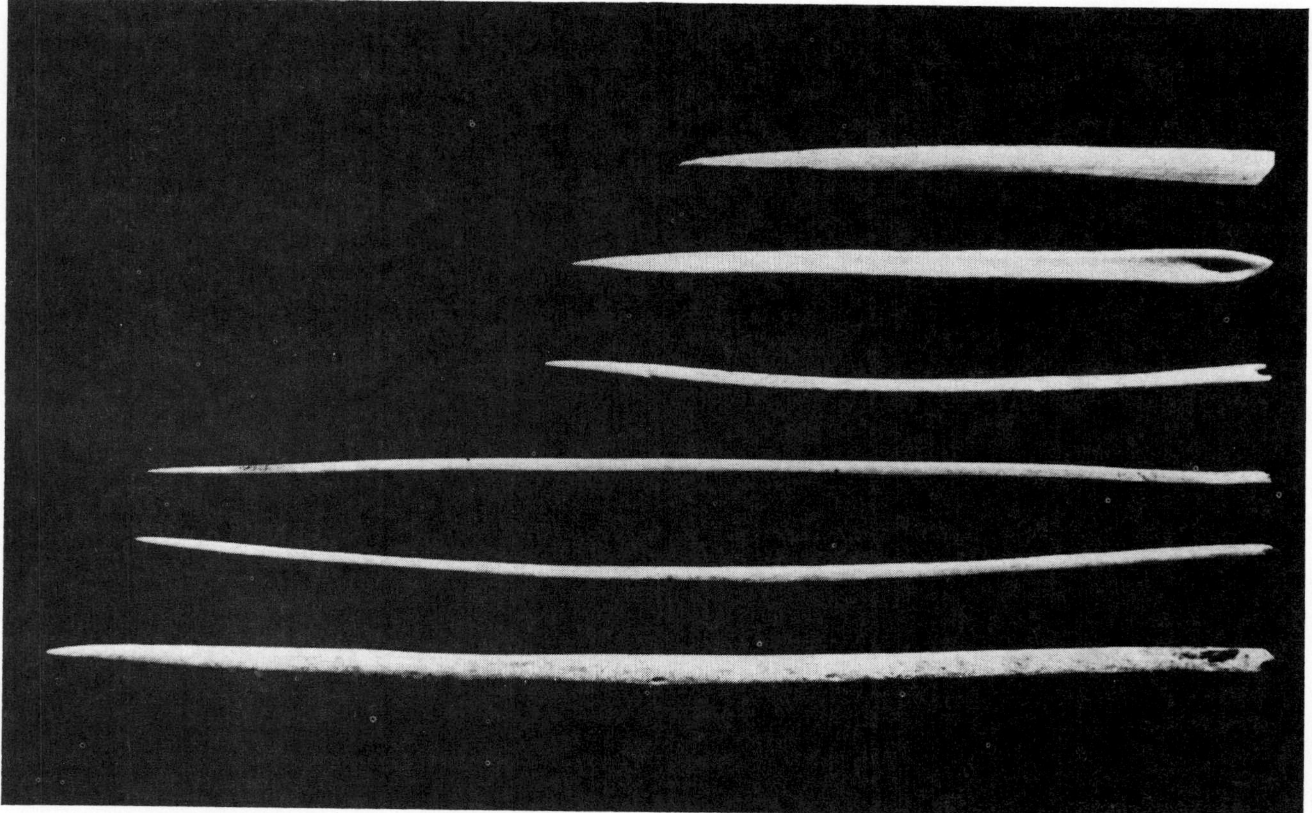

FINE NEEDLES, some made from the bones of birds, were formed by carving and grinding. The abundance of needles in the graves at Port au Choix, along with tools for dressing animal skins, suggests that the Archaic Indians dressed in tailored skin garments.

with certain wild vegetable foodstuffs, provided the economic basis of the Maritime Archaic Tradition.

The Archaic Indians, presumably organized in small bands, would have followed a more or less fixed seasonal round in exploiting the region's food resources. In the late fall each year, when the caribou congregate after the first snow to move from summer to winter grazing, the migrating herds were a prime target. It is not difficult to kill caribou as they migrate: the animals can be diverted into dead-end runways or speared as they swim across or ford rivers and lakes. The caribou meat can then be dried or, if the temperature allows, preserved by freezing. A few days of caribou-hunting might furnish enough meat for the winter months, and this basic winter ration could be supplemented with fresh kills of beaver, hare or larger mammals such as bear.

During the winter months the Indians of the Maritime Archaic Tradition probably stayed close to the inland sites where the caribou were killed. As spring approached and the caribou meat dwindled, the bands probably moved to the coast to hunt the harp seals and their young as they drifted southward with the pack ice. After the seal harvest there might be another inland caribou hunt to take advantage of the migrating herds' return to summer pasture. The caribou meat from these kills that was not eaten on the spot could be dried for later consumption.

The Indians of the Maritime Archaic Tradition would then have returned to the coast to spend the summer fishing for the migrating salmon, preying on molting aquatic fowl and their nestlings and venturing offshore in pursuit of sea mammals. In the same season a harvest of such wild vegetable foods as gooseberries, blueberries, squashberries and bakeapples was available to be eaten when picked or to be stored for future consumption. With the first snow the time came for the bands to travel inland again for the late-fall caribou hunt.

The detailed evidence of technological versatility provided by the grave goods at Port au Choix, including the artifacts of stone, bone, antler and ivory and the tools for working wood, bark and skin, is clear testimony to the material success of the Maritime Archaic Tradition in adapting to life in northeastern North America. The grave goods also offer us tantalizing glimpses of the tradition's magico-religious beliefs. In contemporary Indian and Eskimo practice, for example, a row or two of caribou incisors stitched to one's clothing ensures success in hunting these animals. Bear teeth bring strength and strike fear into the heart of an enemy. Dog teeth make the wearer a good fighter. Seal teeth bring success in sealing; seal claws give one strong arms. The heads or feet of gulls, mergansers and other diving birds bring luck in fishing for salmon.

One could cite a dozen more such beliefs of today, and it is tempting to see the charms and amulets of Port au Choix in a similar light. Moreover, if the presence in a single grave of both the image and the physical remains of a single animal species is more than a matter of chance, the use of amulets may have gone beyond hunting magic to embrace the concept of a personal guardian spirit or totem animal. Possibly the guardian was believed to be instrumental in conveying the dead individual and his buried goods to another world. Although the precise imagery must always remain obscure, the red ocher in the graves, and perhaps the crystals and pebbles too, may have been additional symbols of existence in an afterlife. The east-facing burial ground may be related to symbolism involving the rising sun. Lavish grave goods, including "killed" items, ocher, east-facing cemeteries—all this may be the first manifestation in the northeast of what William A. Ritchie of the New York State Museum calls the "basic core of religiosity" noted at many North American prehistoric sites of the following millenniums.

How did the Maritime Archaic Tradition evolve? Its artifacts resemble those of several Eskimo cultures that existed in Newfoundland and the Canadian Arctic at a somewhat later date. The similarities, however, are only the product of the tendency toward convergence in the face of the same environmental conditions; they are not the result of a racial relationship. Nor is there any direct relationship between the Maritime Archaic Tradition and the now extinct Beothuk ("Red Indians"), the aboriginal people of Newfoundland at the time the Europeans arrived. On the other hand, when comparisons are made with the Archaic Indian cultures in the forested belt of the Great Lakes region, significant similarities emerge.

These cultures to the west are the ones that Ritchie places in the Laurentian Archaic Tradition. Their relationship to the Maritime Archaic Tradition is unmistakable. The Morrison Island skulls, which closely resemble those from Port au Choix, were associated with artifacts of the Laurentian Tradition. A number of basic tools, including gouges and points made by grinding slate, are also common both to the Laurentian and to the Maritime Archaic. It appears likely that a forest-adapted population of hunters with a Laurentian-related material culture moved from the Great Lakes region along the St. Lawrence valley to the sea, where they quickly learned to exploit the animal resources of a new domain. Thereafter, with a culture economically, technologically and socially adapted to the maritime environment, the Archaic Indian hunters flourished along the coast from Maine to Labrador for at least 1,000 years.

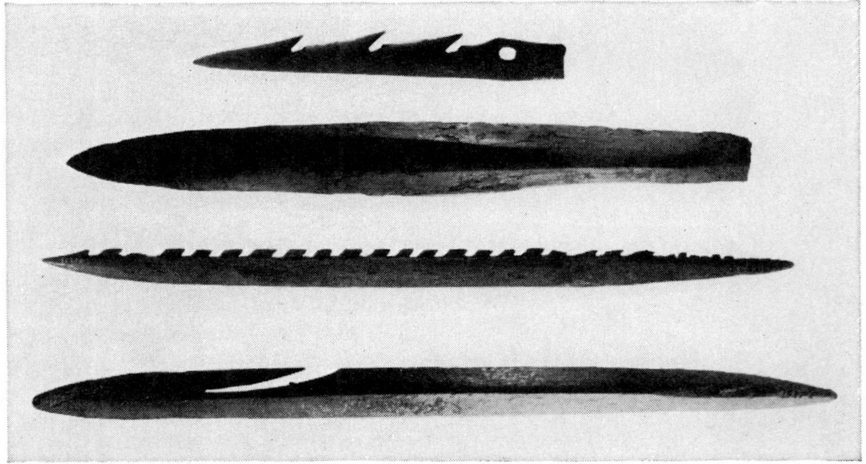

LAND AND SEA WEAPONS used by the Indians of the Archaic Maritime Tradition include, in addition to toggling harpoon heads, simple barbed ones (*top*). The ornamented bone "dagger" (*second from top*) could have served on land or at sea and may have been attached to a wooden shaft rather than being held in the hand. The square-barbed leister point (*third from top*) is made of bone and evidently formed part of a fish spear. Why the bone "bayonet" point (*bottom*) was made with an exaggerated single barb is not known.

Teotihuacán

12

by René Millon
June 1967

The first and largest city of the pre-Columbian New World arose in the Valley of Mexico during the first millenium A.D. At its height the metropolis covered a larger area than imperial Rome

When the Spaniards conquered Mexico, they described Montezuma's capital Tenochtitlán in such vivid terms that for centuries it seemed that the Aztec stronghold must have been the greatest city of pre-Columbian America. Yet only 25 miles to the north of Tenochtitlán was the site of a city that had once been even more impressive. Known as Teotihuacán, it had risen, flourished and fallen hundreds of years before the conquistadors entered Mexico. At the height of its power, around A.D. 500, Teotihuacán was larger than imperial Rome. For more than half a millennium it was to Middle America what Rome, Benares or Mecca have been to the Old World: at once a religious and cultural capital and a major economic and political center.

Unlike many of the Maya settlements to the south, in both Mexico and Guatemala, Teotihuacán was never a "lost" city. The Aztecs were still worshiping at its sacred monuments at the time of the Spanish Conquest, and scholarly studies of its ruins have been made since the middle of the 19th century. Over the past five years, however, a concerted program of investigation has yielded much new information about this early American urban center.

In the Old World the first civilizations were associated with the first cities, but both in Middle America and in Peru the rise of civilization does not seem to have occurred in an urban setting. As far as we can tell today, the foundation for the earliest civilization in Middle America was laid in the first millennium B.C. by a people we know as the Olmecs. None of the major Olmec centers discovered so far is a city. Instead these centers—the most important of which are located in the forested lowlands along the Gulf of Mexico on the narrow Isthmus of Tehuantepec—were of a ceremonial character, with small permanent populations probably consisting of priests and their attendants.

The Olmecs and those who followed them left to many other peoples of Middle America, among them the builders of Teotihuacán, a heritage of religious beliefs, artistic symbolism and other cultural traditions. Only the Teotihuacanos, however, created an urban civilization of such vigor that it significantly influenced the subsequent development of most other Middle American civilizations—urban and nonurban—down to the time of the Aztecs. It is hard to say exactly why this happened, but at least some of the contributing factors are evident. The archaeological record suggests the following sequence of events.

A settlement of moderate size existed at Teotihuacán fairly early in the first century B.C. At about the same time a number of neighboring religious centers were flourishing. One was Cuicuilco, to the southwest of Teotihuacán in the Valley of Mexico; another was Cholula, to the east in the Valley of Puebla. The most important influences shaping the "Teotihuacán way" probably stemmed from centers such as these. Around the time of Christ, Teotihuacán began to grow rapidly, and between A.D. 100 and 200 its largest religious monument was raised on the site of an earlier shrine. Known today as the Pyramid of the Sun, it was as large at the base as the great pyramid of Cheops in Egypt [*see bottom illustration on page 122*].

The powerful attraction of a famous holy place is not enough, of course, to explain Teotihuacán's early growth or later importance. The city's strategic location was one of a number of material factors that contributed to its rise. Teotihuacán lies astride the narrow waist of a valley that is the best route between the Valley of Mexico and the Valley of Puebla. The Valley of Puebla, in turn, is the gateway to the lowlands along the Gulf of Mexico.

The lower part of Teotihuacán's valley is a rich alluvial plain, watered by permanent springs and thus independent of the uncertainties of highland rainfall. The inhabitants of the valley seem early to have dug channels to create an irrigation system and to provide their growing city with water. Even today a formerly swampy section at the edge of the ancient city is carved by channels into "chinampas": small artificial islands that are intensively farmed. Indeed, it is possible that this form of agriculture, which is much better known as it was practiced in Aztec times near Tenochtitlán, was invented centuries earlier by the people of Teotihuacán.

The valley had major deposits of obsidian, the volcanic glass used all over ancient Middle America to make cutting and scraping tools and projectile points. Obsidian mining in the valley was apparently most intensive during the city's early years. Later the Teotihuacanos appear to have gained control of deposits of obsidian north of the Valley of Mexico that were better suited than the local material to the mass production of blade implements. Trade in raw obsidian and obsidian implements became increasingly important to the economy of Teotihuacán, reaching a peak toward the middle of the first millennium A.D.

The recent investigation of Teotihuacán has been carried forward by specialists working on three independent but related projects. One project was a monumental program of excavation and reconstruction undertaken by Mexico's National Institute of Anthropology, headed by Eusebio Dávalos. From 1962 to 1964 archaeologists under the direction of Ignacio Bernal, director of the

National Museum of Anthropology, unearthed and rebuilt a number of the structures that lie along the city's principal avenue ("the Street of the Dead"); they have also restored Teotihuacán's second main pyramid ("the Pyramid of the Moon"), which lies at the avenue's northern end. Two of the city's four largest structures, the Pyramid of the Sun and the Citadel, within which stands the Temple of Quetzalcoatl, had been cleared and restored in the 1900's and the 1920's respectively. Among other notable achievements, the National Institute's work brought to light some of the city's finest mural paintings.

As the Mexican archaeologists were at work a group under the direction of William T. Sanders of Pennsylvania State University conducted an intensive study of the ecology and the rural-settlement patterns of the valley. Another group, from the University of Rochester, initiated a mapping project under my direction. This last effort, which is still under way, involves preparing a detailed topographic map on which all the city's several thousand structures will be located. The necessary information is being secured by the examination of surface remains, supplemented by small-scale excavations. One result of our work has been to demonstrate how radically different Teotihuacán was from all other settlements of its time in Middle America. It was here that the New World's urban revolution exploded into being.

It had long been clear that the center of Teotihuacán was planned, but it soon became apparent to us that the extent and magnitude of the planning went far beyond the center. Our mapping revealed that the city's streets and the large majority of its buildings had been laid out along the lines of a precise grid aligned with the city center. The grid was established in Teotihuacán's formative days, but it may have been more intensively exploited later, perhaps in relation to "urban renewal" projects undertaken when the city had become rich and powerful.

The prime direction of the grid is slightly east of north (15.5 degrees). The basic modular unit of the plan is close to 57 meters. A number of residential structures are squares of this size. The plan of many of the streets seems to repeat various multiples of the 57-meter unit. The city's major avenues, which run parallel to the north-south axis, are spaced at regular intervals. Even the river running through the center of the city was canalized to conform to the grid. Miles from the city center the remains of buildings are oriented to the grid, even when they were built on slopes that ran counter to it. A small design composed of concentric circles divided into quadrants may have served as a standard surveyor's mark; it is sometimes pecked into the floors of buildings and sometimes into bare bedrock. One such pair of marks two miles apart forms a line exactly perpendicular to the city's north-south axis. The achievement of this kind of order obviously calls for an initial vision that is both audacious and self-confident.

A city planner's description of Teotihuacán would begin not with the monumental Pyramid of the Sun but with the two complexes of structures that form the city center. These are the Citadel and the Great Compound, lying respectively to the east and west of the city's main north-south avenue, the Street of the Dead. The names given the various structures and features of Teotihuacán are not, incidentally, the names by which the Teotihuacanos knew them. Some come from Spanish translations of Aztec names; others were bestowed by earlier archaeologists or by our mappers and are often the place names used by the local people.

The Street of the Dead forms the main axis of the city. At its northern end it stops at the Pyramid of the Moon, and

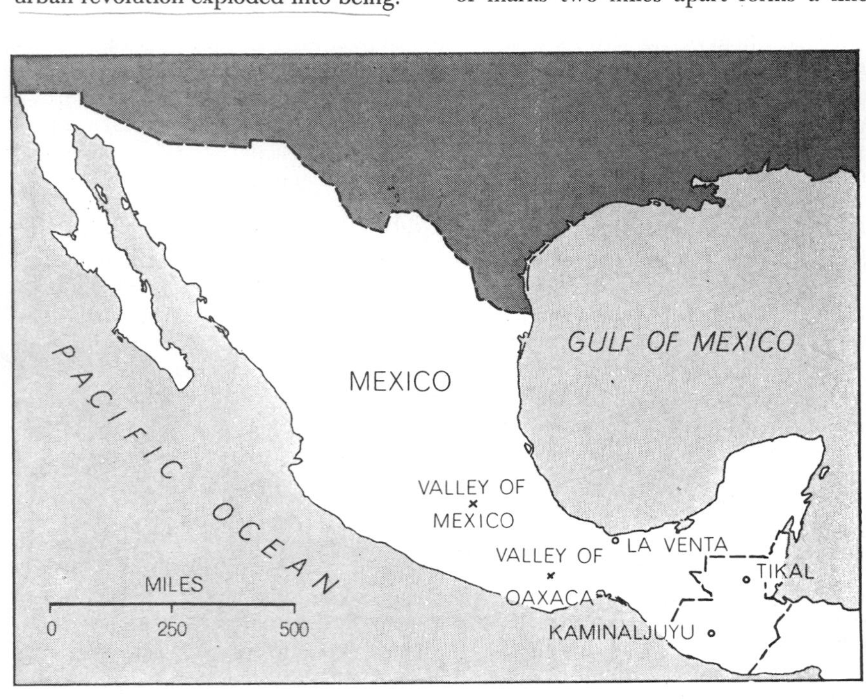

EARLY CIVILIZATION in Middle America appeared first in the lowlands along the Gulf of Mexico at such major centers of Olmec culture as La Venta. Soon thereafter a number of ceremonial centers appeared in the highlands, particularly in the valleys of Oaxaca, Puebla and Mexico. Kaminaljuyu and Tikal, Maya centers respectively in highlands and lowlands of what is now Guatemala, came under Teotihuacán's influence at the height of its power.

CEREMONIAL HEART of Teotihuacán is seen in an aerial photograph looking southeast toward Cerro Patlachique, one of a pair of mountains that flank the narrow valley dominated by the city. The large pyramid in

we have found that to the south it extends for two miles beyond the Citadel-Compound complex. The existence of a subordinate axis running east and west had not been suspected until our mappers discovered one broad avenue running more than two miles to the east of the Citadel and a matching avenue extending the same distance westward from the Compound.

To make it easier to locate buildings over so large an area we imposed our own 500-meter grid on the city, orienting it to the Street of the Dead and using the center of the city as the zero point of the system [*see bottom illustration,* p. 121]. The heavy line defining the limits of the city was determined by walking around the perimeter of the city and examining evidence on the surface to establish where its outermost remains end. The line traces a zone free of such remains that is at least 300 meters wide and that sharply separates the city from the countryside. The Street of the Dead, East Avenue and West Avenue divide Teotihuacán into quadrants centered on the Citadel-Compound complex. We do not know if these were formally recognized as administrative quarters of the city, as they were in Tenochtitlán. It is nonetheless possible that they may have been, since there are a number of other similarities between the two cities.

Indeed, during the past 25 years Mexican scholars have argued for a high degree of continuity in customs and beliefs from the Aztecs back to the Teotihuacanos, based partly on an assumed continuity in language. This hypothetical continuity, which extends through the intervening Toltec times, provides valuable clues in interpreting archaeological evidence. For example, the unity of religion and politics that archaeologists postulate at Teotihuacán is reinforced by what is known of Aztec society.

The public entrance of the Citadel is a monumental staircase on the Street of the Dead. Inside the Citadel a plaza opens onto the Temple of Quetzalcoatl, the principal sacred building in this area. The temple's façade represents the most successful integration of architecture and sculpture so far discovered at Teotihuacán [*see bottom illustration on page 124*].

The Great Compound, across the street from the Citadel, had gone unrecognized as a major structure until our survey. We found that it differs from all other known structures at Teotihuacán and that in area it is the city's largest. Its main components are two great raised platforms. These form a north and a south wing and are separated by broad entrances at the level of the street on the east and west. The two wings thus flank a plaza somewhat larger than the one within the Citadel. Few of the structures on the platforms seem to have been temples or other religious buildings. Most of them face away from the Street of the Dead, whereas almost all the other known structures along the avenue face toward it.

the foreground is the Pyramid of the Moon. The larger one beyond it is the Pyramid of the Sun. Many of the more than 100 smaller religious structures that line the city's central avenue, the Street of the Dead, are visible in the photograph. South of the Pyramid of the Sun and east of the central avenue is the large enclosure known as the Citadel. It and the Great Compound, a matching structure not visible in the photograph, formed the city's center. More than 4,000 additional buildings, most no longer visible, spread for miles beyond the center. At the peak of Teotihuacán's power, around A.D. 500, the population of the city was more than 50,000.

One therefore has the impression that the Compound was not devoted to religious affairs. In the Citadel there are clusters of rooms to the north and south of the Temple of Quetzalcoatl, but the overall effect conveyed by the temples and the other buildings that surround the Citadel's plaza is one of a political center in a sacred setting. Perhaps some of its rooms housed the high priests of Teotihuacán.

The plaza of the Compound is a strategically located open space that could have been the city's largest marketplace. The buildings that overlook this plaza could have been at least partly devoted to the administration of the economic affairs of the city. Whatever their functions were, the Citadel and the Compound are the heart of the city. Together they form a majestic spatial unit,

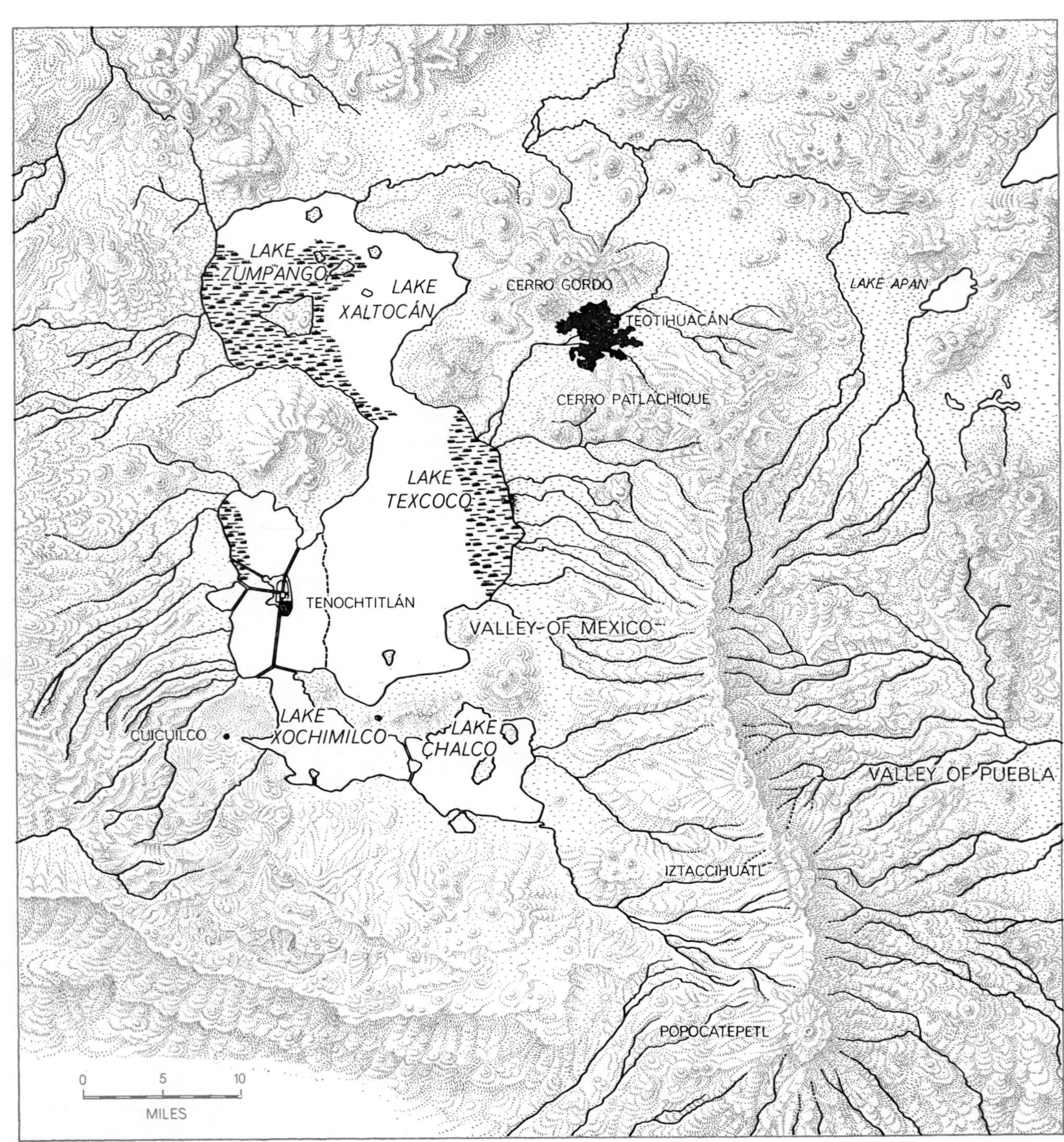

VALLEY OF MEXICO was dominated by shallow lakes in late pre-Hispanic times; in the rainy season they coalesced into a single body of water. Teotihuacán was strategically located; it commanded a narrow valley a few miles northeast of the lakes that provided the best route between the Valley of Mexico and the Valley of Puebla, which leads to the lowlands along the Gulf of Mexico (*see map at bottom of page 116*). It was an important center of trade and worship from 100 B.C. until about A.D. 750. Centuries after its fall the Aztec capital of Tenochtitlán grew up in the western shallows of Lake Texcoco, 25 miles from the earlier metropolis.

a central island surrounded by more open ground than is found in any other part of Teotihuacán.

The total area of the city was eight square miles. Not counting ritual structures, more than 4,000 buildings, most of them apartment houses, were built to shelter the population. At the height of Teotihuacán's power, in the middle of the first millennium A.D., the population certainly exceeded 50,000 and was probably closer to 100,000. This is not a particularly high figure compared with Old World religious-political centers; today the population of Mecca is some 130,000 and that of Benares more than 250,000 (to which is added an annual influx of a million pilgrims). One reason Teotihuacán did not have a larger population was that its gleaming lime-plastered residential structures were only

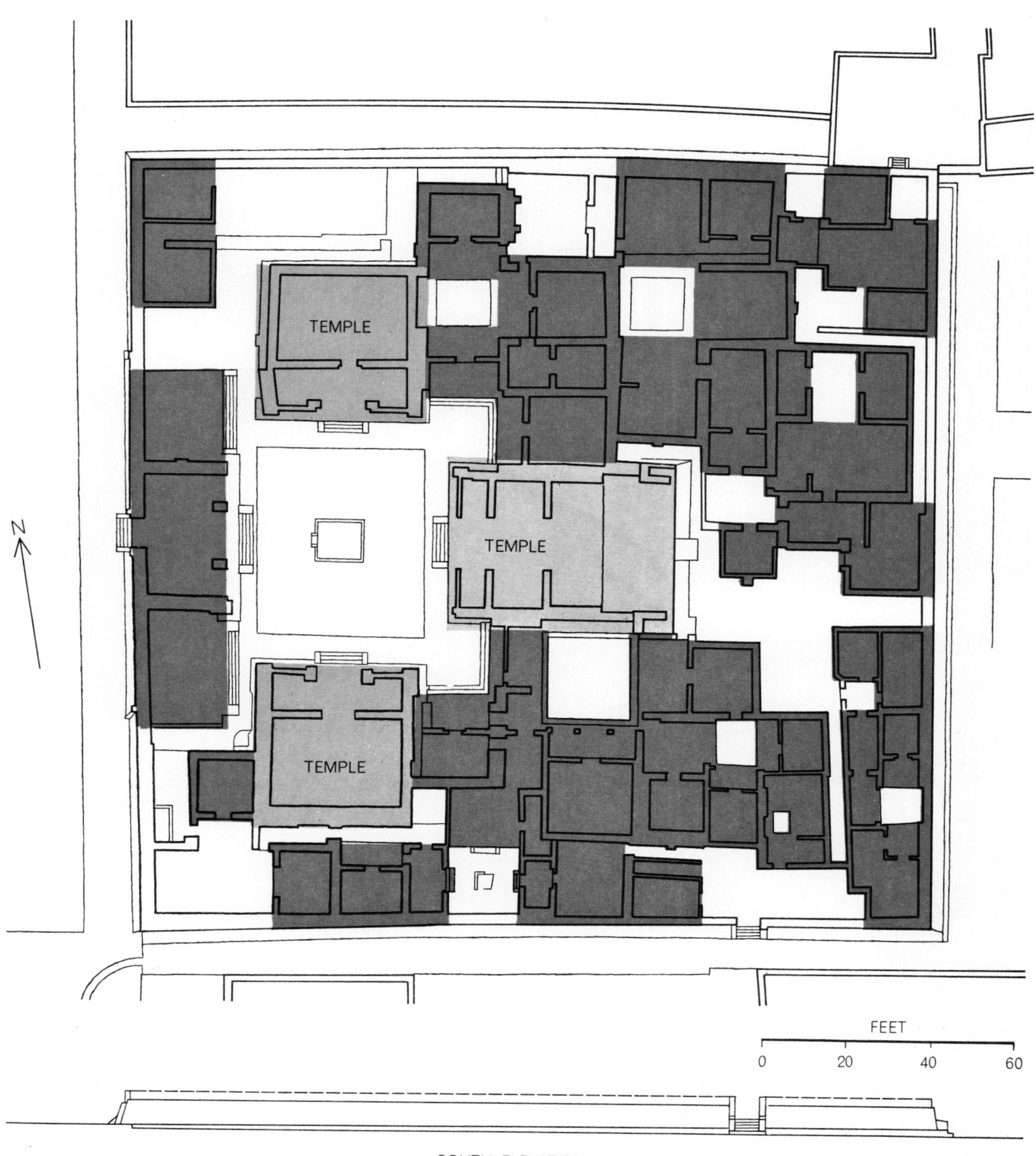

APARTMENT HOUSE typical of the city's many multiroomed dwellings was excavated in 1961 by Laurette Séjourné. The outer walls of the compound conform with the 57-meter module favored by the city's planners. Within its forbidding exterior (*see south façade at bottom of illustration*) individual apartments comprised several rooms grouped around unroofed patios (*smaller white areas*).

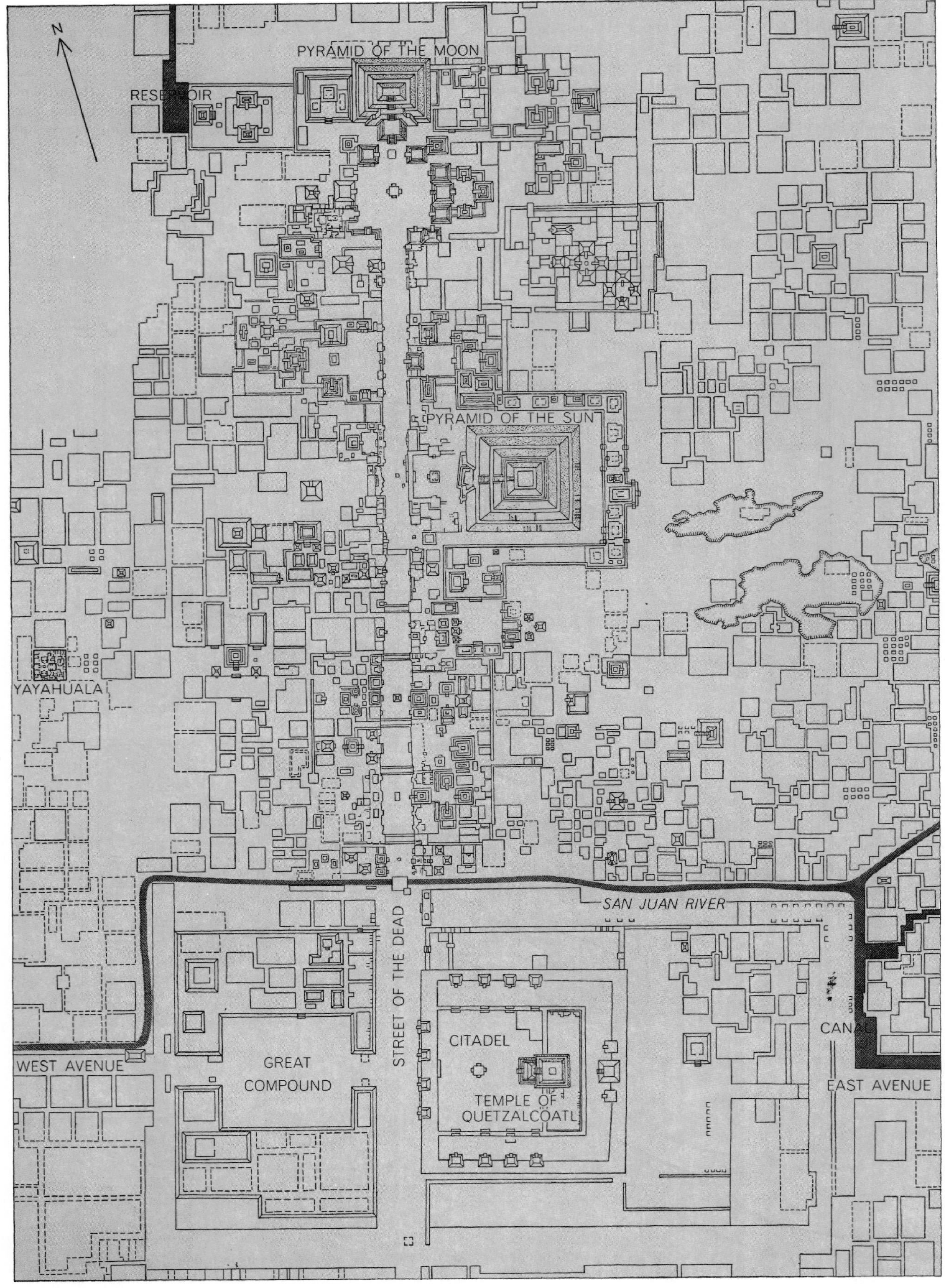
N
PYRAMID OF THE MOON
RESERVOIR
PYRAMID OF THE SUN
YAYAHUALA
SAN JUAN RIVER
STREET OF THE DEAD
CITADEL
CANAL
WEST AVENUE
GREAT
COMPOUND
TEMPLE OF
QUETZALCOATL
EAST AVENUE

one story high. Although most of the inhabitants lived in apartments, the buildings were "ranch-style" rather than "high-rise."

The architects of Teotihuacán designed apartments to offer a maximum of privacy within the crowded city, using a concept similar to the Old World's classical atrium house [*see illustration on page 119*]. The rooms of each apartment surrounded a central patio; each building consisted of a series of rooms, patios, porticoes and passageways, all secluded from the street. This pattern was also characteristic of the city's palaces. The residential areas of Teotihuacán must have presented a somewhat forbidding aspect from the outside: high windowless walls facing on narrow streets. Within the buildings, however, the occupants were assured of privacy. Each patio had its own drainage system; each admitted light and air to the surrounding apartments; each made it possible for the inhabitants to be out of doors yet alone. It may be that this architectural style contributed to Teotihuacán's permanence as a focus of urban life for more than 500 years.

The basic building materials of Teotihuacán were of local origin. Outcrops of porous volcanic rock in the valley were quarried and the stone was crushed and mixed with lime and earth to provide a kind of moisture-resistant concrete that was used as the foundation for floors and walls. The same material was used for roofing; wooden posts spaced at intervals bore much of the weight of the roof. Walls were made of stone and mortar or of sunbaked adobe brick. Floors and wall surfaces were then usually finished with highly polished plaster.

What kinds of people lived in Teotihuacán? Religious potentates, priestly bureaucrats and military leaders presumably occupied the top strata of the city's society, but their number could not have been large. Many of the inhabitants tilled lands outside the city and many others must have been artisans: potters, workers in obsidian and stone and craftsmen dealing with more perishable materials such as cloth, leather, feathers and wood (traces of which are occasionally preserved). Well-defined concentrations of surface remains suggest that craft groups such as potters and workers in stone and obsidian tended to live together in their own neighborhoods. This lends weight to the hypothesis that each apartment building was solely occupied by a "corporate" group, its families related on the basis of occupation, kinship or both. An arrangement of this kind, linking the apartment dwellers to one another by webs of joint interest and activity, would have promoted social stability.

If groups with joint interests lived not only in the same apartment building but also in the same general neighborhood, the problem of governing the city would have been substantially simplified. Such organization of neighborhood groups could have provided an intermediate level between the individual and the state. Ties of cooperation, competition or even conflict between people in different neighborhoods could have created the kind of social network that is favorable to cohesion.

The marketplace would similarly have made an important contribution to the integration of Teotihuacán society. If the greater part of the exchange of goods and services in the city took place in one or more major markets (such as the one that may have occupied the plaza of the Great Compound), then not only the Teotihuacanos but also the outsiders who used the markets would have felt a vested interest in maintaining "the peace of the market." Moreover, the religion of Teotihuacán would have imbued the city's economic institutions with a sacred quality.

The various social groups in the city left some evidence of their identity. For example, we located a walled area, associated with the west side of the Pyramid of the Moon, where large quantities of waste obsidian suggest that obsidian workers may have formed part of a larger temple community. We also found what looks like a foreign neighborhood. Occupied by people who apparently came to Teotihuacán from the Valley of Oaxaca, the area lies in the western part of the city. It is currently under study by

CITY CENTER is composed of two sets of structures, the Great Compound and the Citadel (*bottom of illustration on opposite page*). They stand on either side of the Street of the Dead, the main north-south axis of the city. A pair of avenues approaching the center of the city from east and west form the secondary axis. The city's largest religious monuments were the Pyramid of the Sun, the Pyramid of the Moon and the Temple of Quetzalcoatl, which lies inside the Citadel. Yayahuala (*left of center*) was one of many residential compounds. Its architecture is shown in detail on page 119.

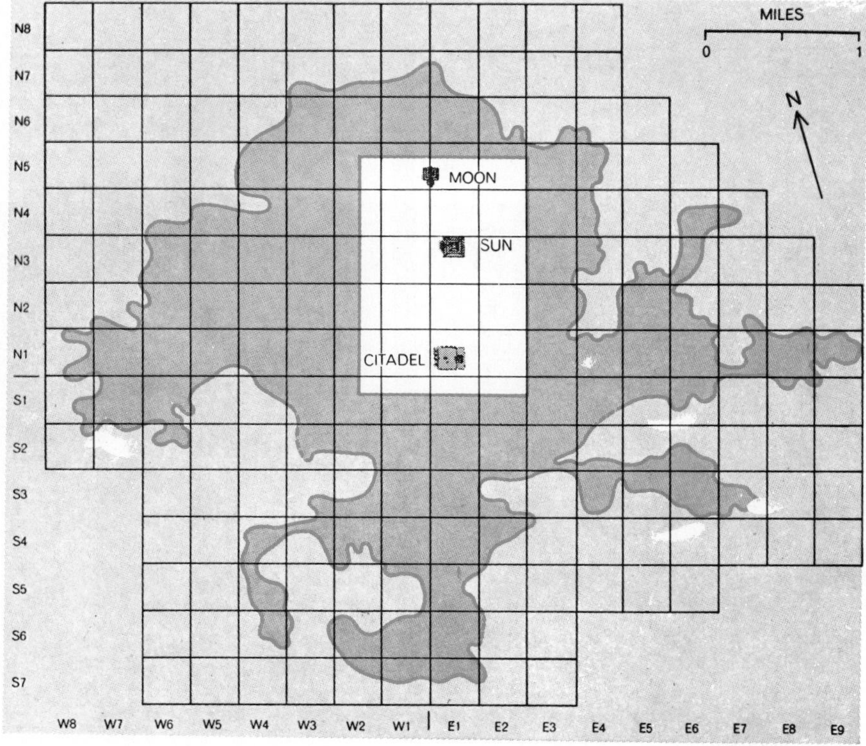

IRREGULAR BOUNDARY of Teotihuacán is shown as a solid line that approaches the edges of a grid, composed of 500-meter squares, surveyed by the author's team. The grid parallels the north-south direction of the Street of the Dead, the city's main avenue. One extension of the city in its early period, which is only partly known, has been omitted. A map of Teotihuacán's north-central zone (*light color*) is reproduced on page 120.

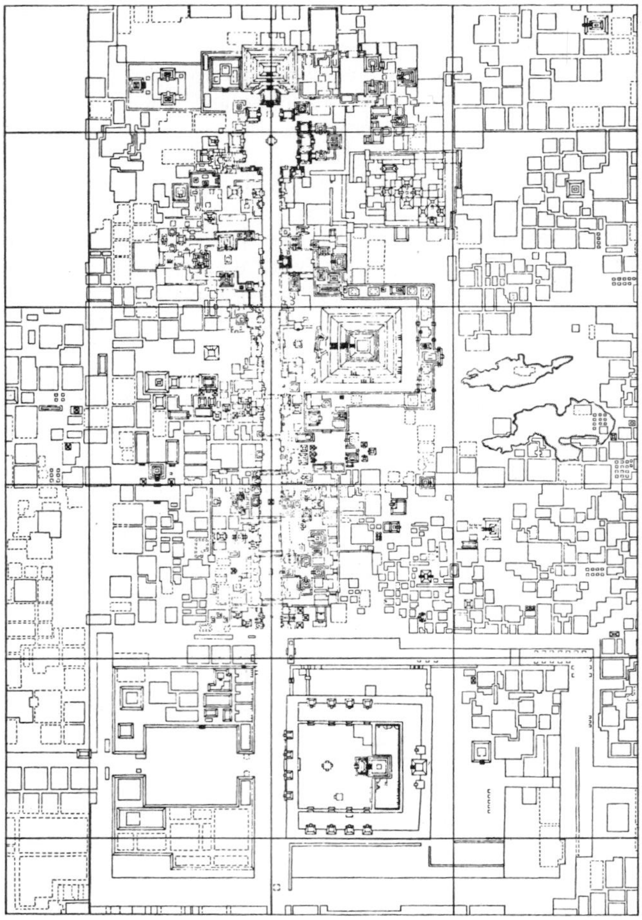

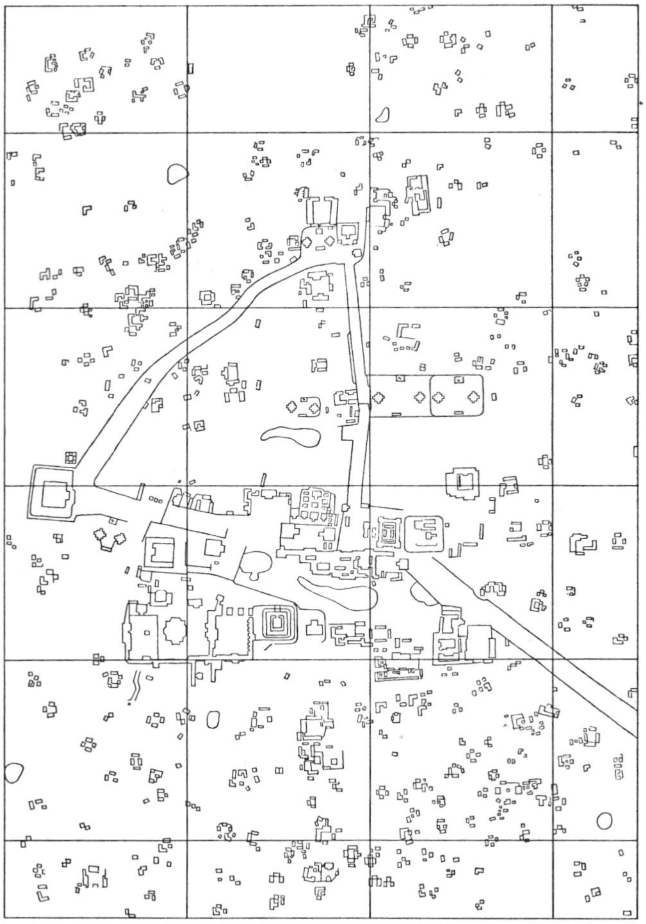

DENSITY OF SETTLEMENT at Teotihuacán is compared with that at Tikal, largest of the lowland Maya ceremonial centers in Middle America. The maps show the central area of each settlement at the same scale. The data for Teotihuacán (*left*) are from surveys by the author and the Mexican government. Those for Tikal (*right*) are from a survey by the University of Pennsylvania. Even though its center included many public structures, Teotihuacán's concentrated residential pattern shows its urban character.

PYRAMID OF THE SUN is as broad at the base as the great pyramid of Cheops in Egypt, although it is only half as high. It was built over the site of an earlier shrine during Teotihuacán's first major period of growth, in the early centuries of the Christian era.

John Paddock of the University of the Americas, a specialist in the prehistory of Oaxaca. Near the eastern edge of the city quantities of potsherds have been found that are characteristic of Maya areas and the Veracruz region along the Gulf of Mexico. These fragments suggest that the neighborhood was inhabited either by people from those areas or by local merchants who specialized in such wares.

We have found evidence that as the centuries passed two of the city's important crafts—the making of pottery and obsidian tools—became increasingly specialized. From the third century A.D. on some obsidian workshops contain a high proportion of tools made by striking blades from a "core" of obsidian; others have a high proportion of tools made by chipping a piece of obsidian until the desired shape was obtained. Similar evidence of specialization among potters is found in the southwestern part of the city. There during Teotihuacán's period of greatest expansion one group of potters concentrated on the mass production of the most common type of cooking ware.

The crafts of Teotihuacán must have helped to enrich the city. So also, no doubt, did the pilgrim traffic. In addition to the three major religious structures more than 100 other temples and shrines line the Street of the Dead. Those who visited the city's sacred buildings must have included not only peasants and townspeople from the entire Valley of Mexico but also pilgrims from as far away as Guatemala. When one adds to these worshipers the visiting merchants, traders and peddlers attracted by the markets of Teotihuacán, it seems likely that many people would have been occupied catering to the needs of those who were merely visiting the city.

Radical social transformations took place during the growth of the city. As Teotihuacán increased in size there was first a relative and then an absolute decline in the surrounding rural population. This is indicated by both our data from the city and Sanders' from the countryside. Apparently many rural populations left their villages and were concentrated in the city. The process seems to have accelerated around A.D. 500, when the population of the city approached its peak. Yet the marked increase in density within the city was accompanied by a reduction in the city's size. It was at this time, during the sixth century, that urban renewal programs may have been undertaken in areas

HUMAN FIGURE, wearing a feather headdress, face paint and sandals, decorates the side of a vase dating from the sixth century A.D. Similar figures often appear in the city's murals.

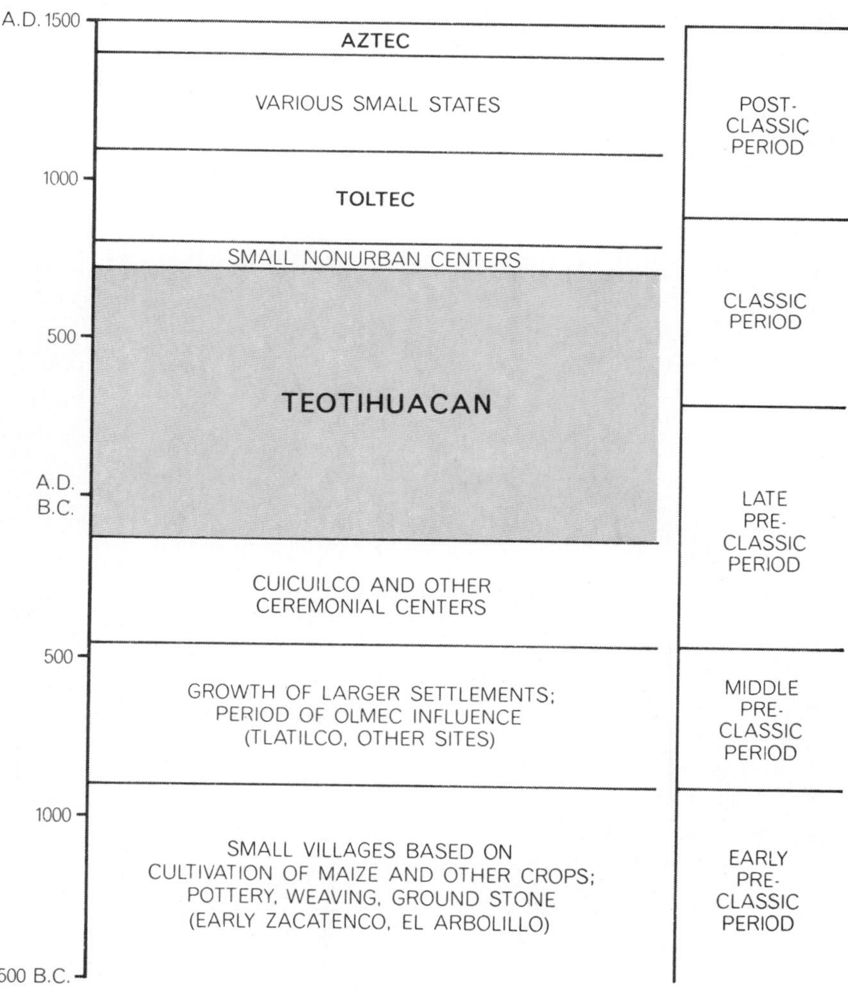

CITY'S BIRTH took place during the late pre-Classic Period in the Valley of Mexico, about a century before the beginning of the Christian era. Other highland ceremonial centers such as Cuicuilco in the Valley of Mexico and Cholula in the Valley of Puebla were influential at that time. Although Teotihuacán fell in about A.D. 750, near the end of the Classic Period, its religious monuments were deemed sacred by the Aztecs until Hispanic times.

PYRAMID OF THE MOON, excavated in the early 1960's by a Mexican government group under the direction of Ignacio Bernal, stands at the northern end of the Street of the Dead. The façade presented to the avenue (*above*) consists of several interlocking, truncated pyramids thrusting toward the sky. The structure, 150 feet high and 490 feet wide at the base, is smaller than the Pyramid of the Sun but is architecturally more sophisticated.

TEMPLE OF QUETZALCOATL is the major religious structure within the Citadel, the eastern half of Teotihuacán's city center. The building is believed to represent the most successful integration of sculpture and architecture to be achieved throughout the city's long history. A covering layer of later construction protected the ornate facade from damage.

where density was on the rise.

Such movements of rural and urban populations must have conflicted with local interests. That they were carried out successfully demonstrates the prestige and power of the hierarchy in Teotihuacán. Traditional loyalties to the religion of Teotihuacán were doubtless invoked. Nevertheless, one wonders if the power of the military would not have been increasingly involved. There is evidence both in Teotihuacán and beyond its borders that its soldiers became more and more important from the fifth century on. It may well be that at the peak of its power and influence Teotihuacán itself was becoming an increasingly oppressive place in which to live.

The best evidence of the power and influence that the leaders of Teotihuacán exercised elsewhere in Middle America comes from Maya areas. One ancient religious center in the Maya highlands—Kaminaljuyu, the site of modern Guatemala City—appears to have been occupied at one time by priests and soldiers from Teotihuacán. Highland Guatemala received a massive infusion of Teotihuacán cultural influences, with Teotihuacán temple architecture replacing older styles. This has been recognized for some time, but only recently has it become clear that Teotihuacán also influenced the Maya lowlands. The people of Tikal in Guatemala, largest of the lowland Maya centers, are now known to have been under strong influence from Teotihuacán. The people of Tikal adopted some of Teotihuacán's artistic traditions and erected a massive stone monument to Teotihuacán's rain god. William R. Coe of the University of Pennsylvania and his colleagues, who are working at Tikal, are in the midst of evaluating the nature and significance of this influence.

Tikal provides an instructive measure of the difference in the density of construction in Maya population centers and those in central Mexico. It was estimated recently that Tikal supported a population of about 10,000. As the illustration at the top of page 122 shows, the density of Teotihuacán's central area is strikingly different from that of Tikal's. Not only was Teotihuacán's population at least five times larger than Tikal's but also it was far less dispersed. In such a crowded urban center problems of integration, cohesion and social control must have been of a totally different order of magnitude than those of a less populous and less compact ceremonial center such as Tikal.

What were the circumstances of Teotihuacán's decline and fall? Almost certainly both environmental and social factors were involved. The climate of the region is semiarid today, and there is evidence that a long-term decline in annual rainfall brought the city to a similar condition in the latter half of the first millennium A.D. Even before then deforestation of the surrounding hills may have begun a process of erosion that caused a decrease in the soil moisture available for crops. Although persistent drought would have presented increasingly serious problems for those who fed the city, this might have been the lesser of its consequences. More ominous would have been the effect of increasing aridity on the cultivators of marginal lands and the semisedentary tribesmen in the highlands north of the Valley of Mexico. As worsening conditions forced these peoples to move, the Teotihuacanos might have found themselves not only short of food but also under military pressure along their northern frontier.

Whether or not climatic change was a factor, some signs of decline—such as the lowering of standards of construction and pottery-making—are evident during the last century of Teotihuacán's existence. Both a reduction in population and a tendency toward dispersion suggest that the fabric of society was suffering from strains and weaknesses. Once such a process of deterioration passed a critical point the city would have become vulnerable to attack.

No evidence has been found that Teotihuacán as a whole had formal defenses. Nonetheless, the valley's drainage pattern provides some natural barriers, large parts of the city were surrounded by walls or massive platforms and its buildings were formidable ready-made fortresses. Perhaps the metropolis was comparatively unprotected because it had for so long had an unchallenged supremacy.

In any case, archaeological evidence indicates that around A.D. 750 much of central Teotihuacán was looted and burned, possibly with the help of the city's own people. The repercussions of Teotihuacán's fall seem to have been felt throughout civilized Middle America. The subsequent fall of Monte Alban, the capital of the Oaxaca region, and of many Maya ceremonial centers in Guatemala and the surrounding area may reasonably be associated with dislocations set in motion by the fall of Teotihuacán. Indeed, the appropriate epitaph for the New World's first major metropolis may be that it was as influential in its collapse as in its long and brilliant flowering.

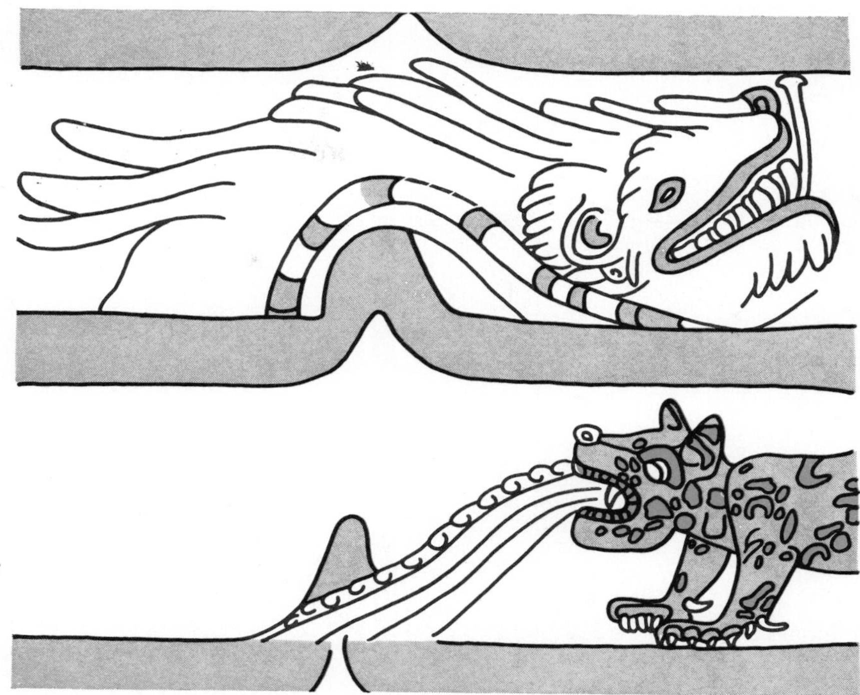

FEATHERED SERPENT, from one of the earlier murals found at Teotihuacán, has a free, flowing appearance. The animal below the serpent is a jaguar; the entire mural, which is not shown, was probably painted around A.D. 400. It may portray a cyclical myth of creation and destruction. The city's principal gods were often represented in the form of animals.

LATER SERPENT GOD, with a rattlesnake tail, is from a mural probably painted less than a century before the fall of Teotihuacán. The figure is rendered in a highly formal manner. A trend toward formalism is apparent in the paintings produced during the city's final years.

The Death of a Civilization

by Tatiana Proskouriakoff
May 1955

Toward the end of their history the Maya built Mayapan, a pale reflection of earlier glories. In its ruins archaeologists now reconstruct the forces that destroyed this remarkable culture

At the darkest time in European history, when the Vandals and Huns were destroying the last vestiges of the Greco-Roman civilization, two younger civilizations on the opposite side of the world were enjoying an era of extraordinary prosperity. One of these was the colorful culture of the Andes and the west coast of South America, which later was to be incorporated in the empire of the Incas. The other was the Middle American civilization whose best-known expression is the Maya culture. Here, in the subtropical jungle, was the birthplace of literacy in America. We do not know whether the Maya people originated this writing, the first in aboriginal America, but it was they who developed it most fully and who led the subsequent intellectual advance. What we have deciphered of their complex hieroglyphics shows that they had a wondrously intricate calendar, based on concurrent cycles merging into greater cycles as their multiples coincided in time. Some Maya calendrical computations span millions of years, and this grandiose concept of the vast dimension of time is all the more impressive if we recall how recently in Europe the creation of the world was placed at 4004 B.C.

The earliest flowering of the Maya culture was in a rainy forest region of northern Guatemala, now virtually uninhabited. Ecologists have repeatedly claimed that a tropical jungle could not give rise to a high civilization, and indeed the Maya region must have offered formidable obstacles to cultivation by a people who knew nothing of metals, who had no draft animals and whose experience of mechanics did not include even the simple device of the wheel. Nevertheless, with only primitive stone-age tools the Maya built large stone temples and erected beautifully carved monuments on which they inscribed a record of celestial and mundane events. They constructed many centers of artistic and intellectual activity, of which the greatest, and probably the oldest, was the city of Tikal [*see map on page 129*].

Surrounded by other civilized peoples who, like themselves, had more interest in trade than in war, the lowland Maya were in a good position to develop their arts and sciences. Yet their great early cities did not last. Why they were abandoned, and what happened to their inhabitants, remains a mystery. Little by little, however, the general pattern of the Maya's history is becoming apparent, and it presents a curious parallel to the fate of the Greco-Roman civilization in Europe about a thousand years earlier. The rise of intellectualism among the lowland Maya can be compared to the similar but more advanced rise of rationalism in ancient Greece; later the civilization of Middle America passed through phases that correspond to the ascendancy of the Roman Empire and the final fall of Rome to barbarian invaders. In Middle America the "Romans" were the Toltec people of Mexico, and their barbaric conquerors were the Aztec people, who created an empire with a capital at Tenochtitlan.

The Toltec capital, Tollan, which stood near the present town of Tula, north of Mexico City, never actually formed an empire or exercised such strict control over its colonies as did Rome, but like Rome it generated a proud tradition that survived even barbaric conquest. To be a Toltec in Mexico was to be an exponent of civilization. The Toltec tribe, a militant people who had drifted down from the north after the fall of the city of Teotihuacan, absorbed the older culture of the Valley of Mexico and eventually claimed for themselves the credit for all its intellectual accomplishments. Toltec warriors seized the provincial Maya city of Chichen Itza in northern Yucatan and for a time made it the center of Maya culture. They learned Maya techniques of building and even improved on them, making their buildings larger and more spacious. The columns of their temples were carved in the form of the feathered serpent, their principal deity, but most of their art was devoted to the portrayal of warriors and their exploits; it gives us a vivid picture of battles and processions and of the dramatic rite of human sacrifice. It was an art less intricate and less refined than the art of the Maya, striving for monumental effect rather than for precision of form.

In the year 1168 the Toltec capital at Tula fell to other warrior tribes. The subjugated Maya inhabitants of Chichen Itza seized the opportunity to rise against their Toltec masters. Tradition tells us that they killed the Toltec lords for their bad conduct, and that a time of troubles followed.

While the Toltec rule was being broken by successive waves of invasion by tribes from the north, culminating in the supremacy of the Aztec, there arose in Yucatan a Maya hero by the name of Kukulcan. (The name was the Maya version of Quetzalcoatl, the title of the chief Toltec deity; derived from the name of the colorful quetzal bird and the word for serpent, it means "feathered serpent.") Whatever his lineage or his pretension, this Kukulcan unified the Maya once more and founded a new capital at Mayapan [*see map, page 129*], about 25 miles south of the modern city of Merida. Here he brought together the native lords of the various provinces

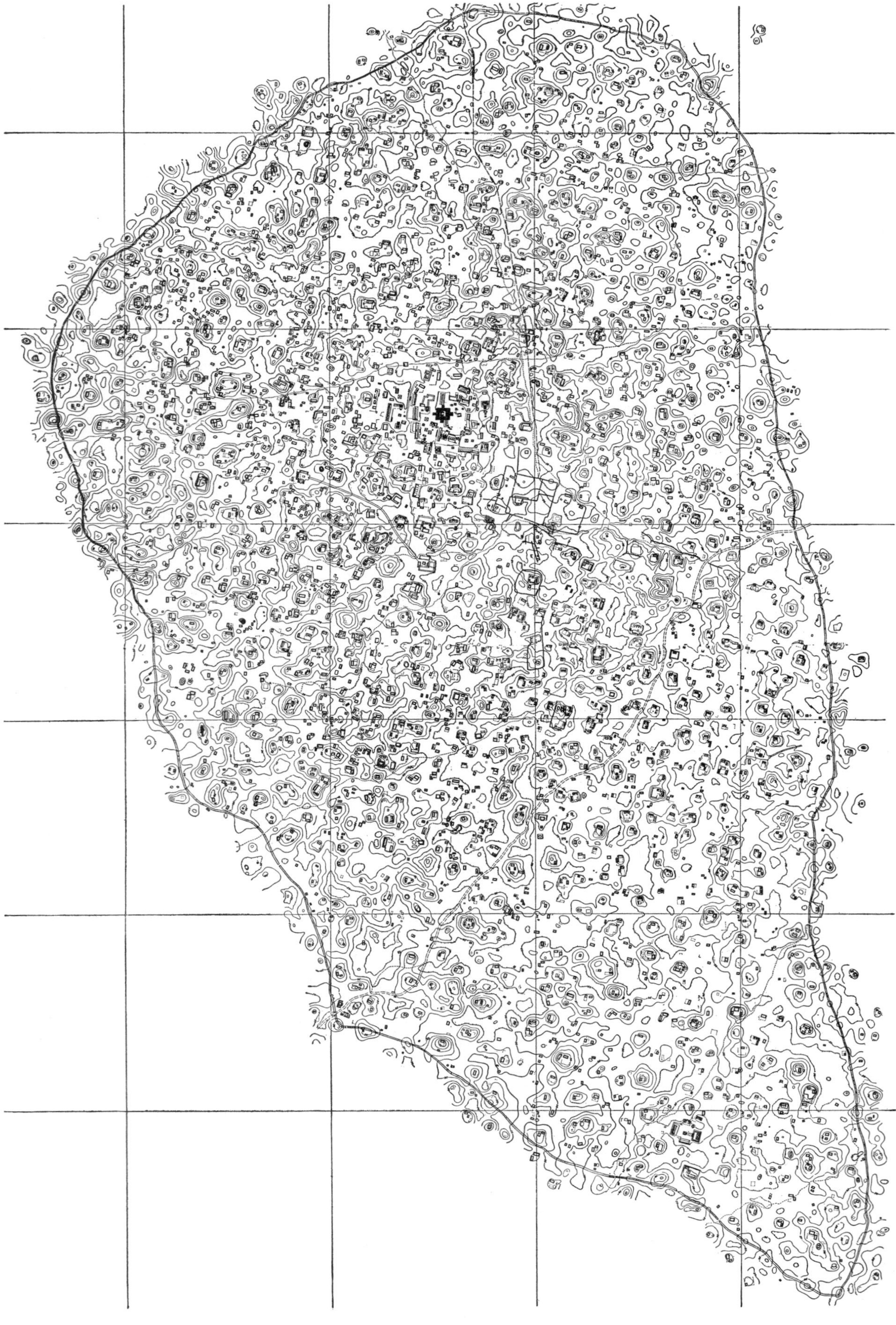

CITIES of Maya times are located on this map of part of Mexico and of Central America. Mayapan is at upper right in what is now the Mexican state of Yucatan. Tula is a modern town near the site of Tollan, capital of the Toltecs. Tenochtitlan was the Aztec capital.

(centered in Chichen Itza, Uxmal and Mayapan), who henceforth ruled their lands from the capital, appointing governors to look after their interests at home.

If tradition is to be believed, the hegemony of Mayapan lasted for almost two centuries. However, the Maya could not resurrect their formerly brilliant culture. The government proved unable to cope with internal conflicts between the rival lords, though it hired Mexican troops to suppress them.

When the Spaniards conquered Yucatan early in the 16th century, they were so intent on religious conversion of the people that they felt impelled to destroy the local written records as subversive documents. Later some of the more curious friars attempted to learn something about Yucatan's past, but by then the memories of the natives had dimmed, and those who might have served as informants were none too eager to display their knowledge. So we are left today only with scraps of contradictory, inadequate accounts of the Maya, some gathered by the friars from conversations with the natives, others compiled by 17th- and 18-century scribes from fragmentary and corrupt older texts. The result is a history that is at the mercy of its interpreters, who seldom seem to agree on even its outlines.

It is a challenge to archaeology to try to straighten out the conflicting versions of Maya history. With this purpose, in part, the Carnegie Institution of Washington in 1951 undertook to excavate and explore ancient Mayapan. The site had been visited by archaeologists before What they had seen did not encourage us to expect sensational finds. Mayapan is not the place to see the richness of the Maya culture in full flower, but it offered an important, and neglected, phenomenon for study—the death of a civilization, paralleling in a small way the decline and fall of Rome.

The first step in the archaeological project was to obtain a detailed and accurate map of the site. This was not easy, for Mayapan was matted over by an incredibly thick tangle of vicious thorns and brambles. Morris Jones, a young engineer of the U. S. Geological Survey, undertook to cut through that impenetrable bush to map the ruins. Fortunately he had the enthusiastic help of the local people, who are accustomed to chopping their way through the jungle with machetes. They liked the young American, who cheerfully shared their noon "posole," an unsavory porridge of ground corn mixed with water which is a staple of their diet. Jones spent two seasons at the hot, humid site, and he

COMPLETE MAP of Mayapan was made in two seasons by Morris Jones of the U. S. Geological Survey. The city had from 10,000 to 20,000 inhabitants and some 3,500 houses. It was surrounded by a wall. The large building above the center is the principal temple of the city. Grid lines are 500 meters apart.

produced a map of unusual accuracy and completeness. At a glance it showed us more about the city plan of Mayapan than we know about any other Maya site.

Mayapan had been known as a collection of ruins of shoddily built temples and colonnaded halls, surrounded by a thick masonry wall. The impression had developed that the Maya town was little more than a ceremonial center and perhaps a market in which people assembled from the countryside on special occasions. Jones's map showed for the first time that Mayapan was actually a residential metropolis of considerable size, covering about two and a half square miles and housing from 10,000 to 20,000 inhabitants. It had some 3,500 houses and a water supply consisting of a number of natural wells in the limestone rock. The houses were in closely packed groups, each surrounded by a rough masonry wall. The walls formed a maze of winding, irregular alleys.

How did the people live, and what were their chief activities and preoccupations? The Carnegie Institution staff began intensive excavation of the city in 1952 under the direction of H. E. D. Pollock. A. Ledyard Smith and Karl Ruppert were assigned to study the houses and the burials, which in Mayapan were usually placed in buildings, because the soil of Yucatan is too shallow for cemeteries. Robert E. Smith explored the refuse heaps and sinkholes in the rock for pottery, with the object of establishing sequences and dating the excavated remains. Edwin M. Shook investigated the pottery styles, the formal architecture of Mayapan and the ritual and commercial activities of the center of the town. Gustav Strömsvik had charge of restoring (in part) some of the typical buildings for the benefit of interested visitors; he also built us comfortable working and living quarters in a village near the site. My own task was to study all small artifacts other than pottery and to map the construction of the ceremonial center in detail.

Three seasons' work has amassed a huge body of data that awaits study and publication. Already we can discern a few clues that help to clarify the story of Mayapan. Our excavations confirm the legend which says that Kukulcan founded Mayapan "after the death of the lords," probably somewhere between A.D. 1263 and 1283. The construction of Mayapan's ceremonial plaza was started at a time when Chichen Itza had fallen into decay. The builders of Mayapan began their city on the same plan as that of the older capital: its principal temple is very nearly a replica of the great Castillo at Chichen Itza. Another structure, with serpent columns and a deep shaft filled with the bones of sacrificed victims, is very like a Chichen Itza building known as the "High Priest's Grave," and a massive round structure is comparable to the Caracol, which some believe to be an astronomical observatory. Both cities had long colonnaded halls, probably used as training quarters for warriors and priests. All the structures at Mayapan, however, were more shoddily built than those of Chichen Itza: they used plaster instead of skillfully worked stone, wooden roofs instead of masonry vaults and grotesque motifs instead of the classic serpent.

Late in the history of Mayapan new religious practices were introduced. They are reflected in the building of numerous small shrines that crowd the courts of the ceremonial center, and in the use of gaudily painted pottery censers made in the images of gods. The blackened interiors of these censers show that they were used for the burning of copal, an aromatic resin still used in religious rites by some Middle American Indians. From the censer images we get a clear impression of the credulous, inartistic and militant character of this age, which contrasts sharply with the scope and serenity of earlier Maya traditions. During the "classic" period (about A.D. 300 to 900) the Maya had made symbolic sculptures which suggest a highly organized, mystic mythology in which a sky serpent bearing celestial symbols played the central role. In the Chichen Itza period, the Toltec portrayed a feathered serpent as the dominant god. Mayapan, in contrast, had numerous gods. Some appear to be derived from Maya mythology; others can be linked with the gods of the valley of Mexico; still others probably were patrons of vocations and private ancestral gods.

Figures of some of the gods, excavated at Mayapan, appear below and on the next page. The man with the conch-shell on his breast is almost certainly Quetzalcoatl. He has the headdress of an animal, probably the jaguar, representing one of the Toltec military orders. He holds in his hand a ball of copal. The wide face, straight nose and narrow lips of Quetzalcoatl and some other gods identify them as Mexican—foreigners in the Maya country. More native in aspect is Chac, the Maya rain-god, with a pendulous nose. He wears a headdress representing the sky serpent, and his body is painted half red, half blue, possibly symbolizing the dry and the rainy seasons. An old man with a big Roman nose and a toothless mouth is thought to be the sky-god Itzamna. Very curious and unexpected at Mayapan are numerous representations of turtles. Some are of stone, others of pottery in the form

ITZAMNA, the sky-god of the Maya, is represented as a toothless old man with his head emerging from the mouth of a turtle. Such turtles were an unexpected find at Mayapan.

QUETZALCOATL found at Mayapan has the wide face, straight nose and narrow lips of Mexicans who were foreign to the Maya.

of a bowl. Usually the turtle holds the head of a god in its beak, but in one amusing piece a man or god with two immense front teeth is riding on the turtle's carapace.

With the proliferation of cults came a tendency to worship privately without the intercession of priests. In Mayapan every private house had some sort of shrine. Yet it is clear that the Maya descendants were not merely making excuses when they told Spanish priests that their ancestors had not been idol-worshipers before Kukulcan came. Certainly the hierarchic religion of the Maya in classic times had been very different from that in the time of Mayapan. Probably many of the new features were brought in by Mexican soldiers.

The same soldiers, said to have been stationed as a garrison in Mayapan, may have introduced the bow and arrow, for in no earlier Yucatan site have we found the tiny flint and obsidian arrowheads that turn up here. Previously warfare had been carried on with spears. The Mayapan walled fortification also was an innovation. With military progress there came a toughening of sensibilities, as evidenced at Mayapan by a barbarous flaying ceremony and by wholesale human sacrifices.

Yet somehow through all this a tenuous thread of the classic tradition survived. We hear a murky echo of its deep and powerful poetry and its grandiose scheme of time in a Maya script, written long after the fall of Mayapan, mourning the death of the city: "This is the pronouncement of 8 Ahau. This it was when occurred the depopulation of Mayapan. Evil is the pronouncement of the Katun in its great power. Thus it shall always come to pass, its pronouncement in Lord 8 Ahau. Then it shall return again to where our writing began according to the prophecy of the Great Priest Chilam Balam when he painted the aspect of the Katun in 8 Ahau, when he painted the glyph of the face of Katun 8 Ahau."

An ahau was a period on the Maya calendar, amounting to 7,200 days (about 20 years). There were 13 such periods, and 8 Ahau ran from A.D. 1441 to 1460. It was about this time that Mayapan was destroyed by an internal conspiracy of its lords. The records mention "fighting with stones in the fortress" and the breaking down of the city wall. The Maya country thereafter suffered recurrent local wars and disasters until its final subjugation by the Spaniards.

CHAC was the rain-god of the Maya. His face, with its drooping Roman nose, is more characteristic of the inhabitants of Mayapan.

In the light of historical perspective, the fall of Mayapan appears as a dramatic culmination of a long process of cultural decay. The causes of the decline of the brilliant Maya culture remain obscure, but to those who perceive the danger signals of esthetic decline and rising militarism in our own civilization, the story of Mayapan should have a vital and timely interest.

FIRST MESA in Arizona, the site of the coexistence of the Hopi and the Tewa Pueblo Indians, is shown in this aerial photograph. In the foreground is Tewa Village. At the center and far tip of the mesa, respectively, are the Hopi villages of Sichomovi and Walpi.

The Hopi and the Tewa

by Edward P. Dozier
June 1957

A tale of two adjacent villages which maintained distinct cultures for two centuries. Then a change in social environment brought them together, demonstrating one way in which minorities are assimilated

The problem of the relations between a dominant population and a minority—Negroes, Jews or an immigrant group—is one of the most interesting, as well as one of the most important, in the realm of social science. Sociologists and anthropologists have carried out many and varied studies in efforts to understand the factors that make for assimilation, on the one hand, or separation, on the other [see "The Jewish Community of Rome," by Leslie C. and Stephen P. Dunn; SCIENTIFIC AMERICAN, March]. This article will report a case study of an altogether unique situation. It concerns two groups of Pueblo Indians living side by side in the mesa country of Arizona. Ethnically and in many other ways they are very alike. Yet for more than 200 years they remained aliens in practically the same village. Then, through what might be considered a historical accident, the two groups were rapidly brought together, barriers fell and they began to live in happy harmony.

The groups are the Hopi and a small colony of families descended from Tewa Indians of the Santa Fe area. In 1949-50, as a graduate student in anthropology, I spent a year living with these people, and since then I have been able to revisit them several times, following up the study on foundation grants. To learn anything about their history and culture it was necessary to establish trustful relations with them and assure them that information was sought only to advance scientific knowledge. Unfortunately the sacred and colorful ceremonies of the Pueblo Indians have in the past been made to appear ludicrous in sensational magazine articles; the Indians now prohibit photographs of these events and have closed many of them to white observers.

Our story begins with the Spanish occupation of the Southwest in the 16th century. The coming of the Spaniards fell as a catastrophe upon the peaceful Pueblo Indians in the Santa Fe area. The white man's diseases and fanatical attempts to Christianize and "civilize" the Indians took a great toll of the Pueblos' lives. Finally in 1680 the Indians rebelled and drove the Spaniards from Santa Fe.

Among the leaders of the rebellion were a Tewa group who lived in five "pueblos" (towns of mud-walled

POLACCA VILLAGE at the foot of First Mesa is named for its Tewa founder, Tom Polacca. Modeled on the pattern of the whites' villages, it helped gain Hopi respect for the Tewa.

houses) south and east of Santa Fe. They had numbered some 4,000; now they were reduced to less than 1,000. When the Spaniards were driven out, these people moved into Santa Fe. But 13 years later Don Diego de Vargas returned with a well-armed Spanish force and quickly subdued them. Most of the Tewa in the town were taken as slaves; a few hundred resettled in a village north of Santa Fe. Three years later these Tewa, still rebellious and suffering repeated Spanish punitive expeditions, made a final raid on the city, killed their Catholic missionary and fled 400 miles west to the mesa country of the Hopi Indians.

The 200 men, women and children who made the journey did not find the bounteous welcome they had expected. According to a legend which their de-

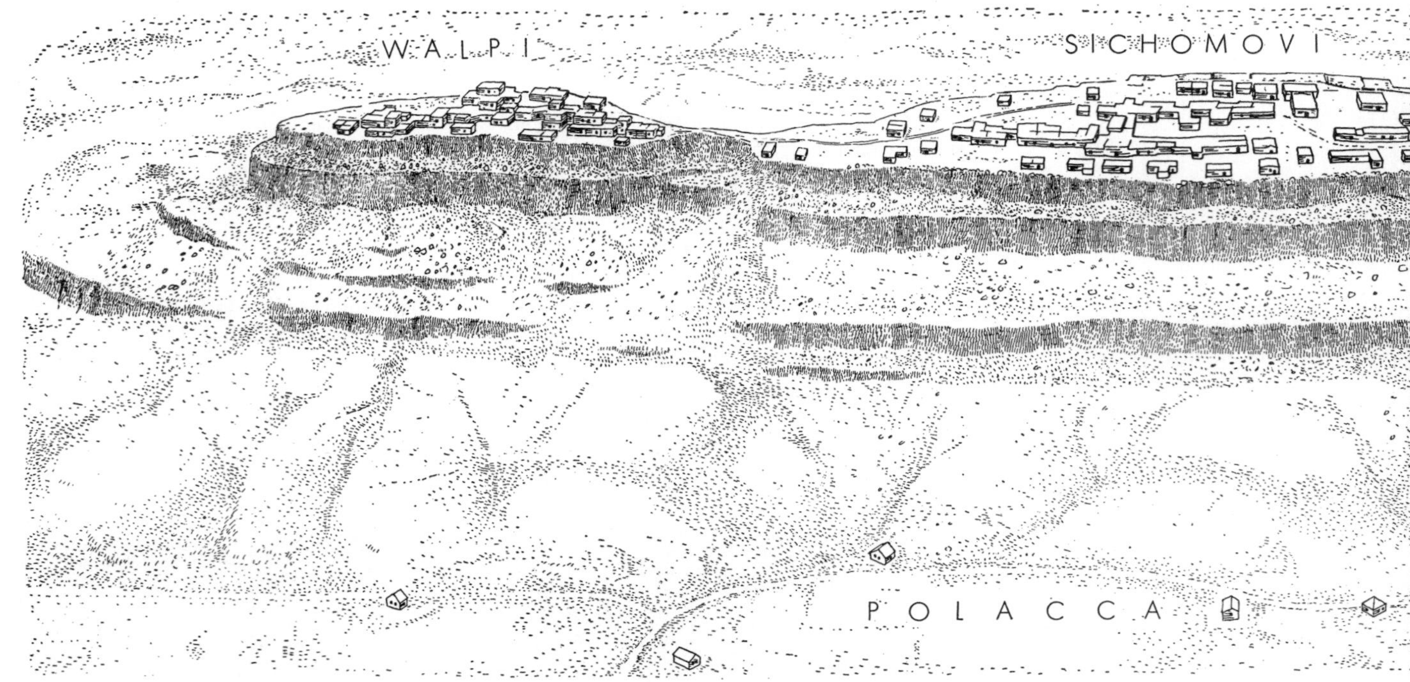

FIRST MESA COMMUNITIES are represented here as they are seen from the east. Though Sichomovi and Tewa Village are architecturally identical, and to all appearances are joined on the mesa, the unmarked border between the villages was well established in

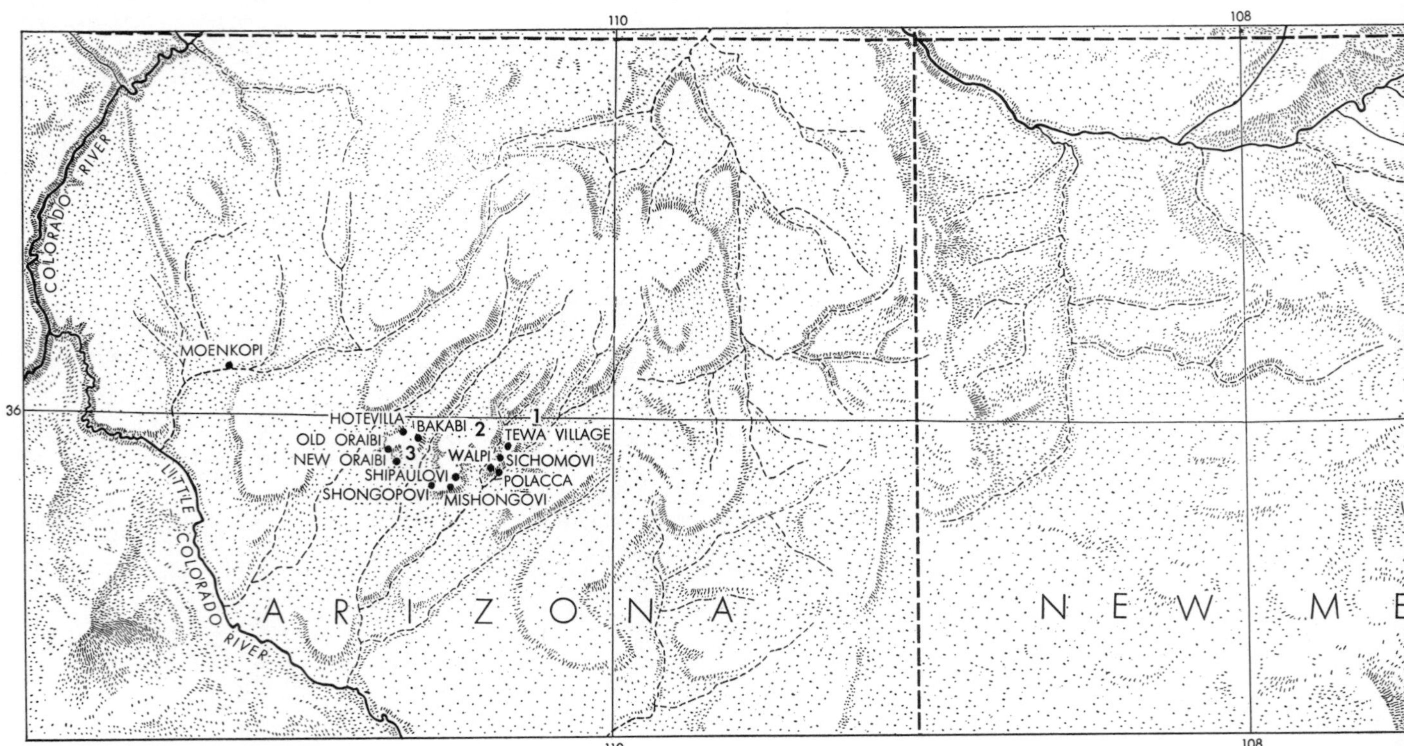

LAND OF THE PUEBLO INDIANS is shown in this map. South of Santa Fe (*right*) is the original home of the Tewa who migrated to Hopi territory (*left*). These people are now called the Southern Tewa. The area north of Santa Fe is still inhabited by a Tewa

scendants have kept alive from generation to generation, Hopi chiefs had repeatedly invited the Tewa to come, promising them land, food, sexual privileges with the Hopi women and assistance in settling in a permanent home. These inducements were offered because the Hopi needed the doughty Tewa as warriors to drive off their enemies. But after the Tewa had performed this service, says the legend, the Hopi failed to make good their promises, and the Tewa received only a meager village site at the end of a mesa (a flat-topped finger of land bordered by ravines). The Tewa responded by putting a "curse" upon the Hopi. They dug a pit between their village and the neighboring Hopi one, made the Hopi spit into the pit, then spat upon the spittle of the Hopi and filled the pit with earth. This action was intended to seal the Tewa culture forever from appropriation by the Hopi.

the minds of the two Indian groups during the 200-year period of mutual hostility.

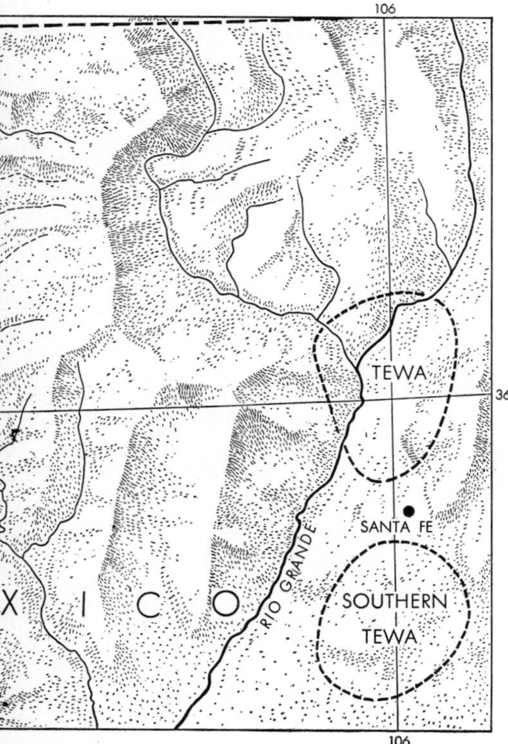

group. The numbers 1, 2 and 3 at left represent the First, Second and Third mesas.

Whether or not this legend is literally true, it has been effective in keeping the two peoples separate for hundreds of years. It has reinforced basic psychological and social factors which operated against assimilation.

First, and perhaps most important, the Tewa were a small but proud minority—only about 200 against several thousand Hopi. They refused to be assimilated; the passive Hopi, on the other hand, made no effort to impose their language or customs on the handful of militarily useful newcomers.

Secondly, while the two peoples were alike in many respects—both of them Pueblo Indian tribes of farmers at about the same technological level and with much the same ceremonial forms—they were temperamentally very different. The Tewa had come from a border region where they had constantly had to defend themselves against the Plains Indians and later against the Spaniards. They had lived in a country of rivers—the Rio Grande and its tributaries—in which it was possible to work with nature to irrigate their crops. They had been exposed to a century of Spanish example in asserting control over the environment. As a result the Tewa had developed a high measure of active self-reliance.

The Hopi, in contrast, lived in a region where men easily persuaded themselves that there was little they could do about the environment. In the mesa country there were no streams, and agriculture was at the mercy of the weather. They planted maize, beans and melons in the flat washes below their mesas—a series of finger-like projections at the southern end of the great Black Mesa which runs north almost into Utah. When too little rain fell, their plants withered and died in the hot sun; when it poured, raging floods uprooted the plants and washed them away. Thus weather was the most important concern of the Hopi, and it shaped their attitude toward nature and human existence.

The contrasting attitudes of the Tewa and the Hopi are expressed in their religious beliefs and practices. The Tewa religion has its share of magical concepts, but they fortify their appeals to magic with practical steps. Their medicine men not only perform magical rites but also administer medicinal herbs, massage and treatments for the injured: they are expert in setting broken bones. Their songs and dances exalt warrior prowess. When enemies threatened in the past, they formed war parties to meet them. In any crisis the Tewa offer prayers and then take action.

In the Hopi religion the dominant theme is reliance on the mystical forces which are believed to control the weather and natural environment. Elaborate ceremonies have been developed to coax these powers to favor the petitioners with bountiful harvests. The Hopi believe that if their rites and ceremonies are properly and regularly performed with a "good heart," there will always be enough to eat and everyone will be healthy. They depend upon the magical powers not only to provide rain for their crops but also to thwart sickness and ward off their enemies; rather than take up arms against attackers they appeal to the deities to deflect or immobilize the enemy. The deities believed to control the destinies of men are a group of vaguely conceived ancestral gods called the *katcina*. In the Hopi ceremonies men dressed in elaborate masked costumes represent these gods. The Hopi also carve dolls in the likeness of the deities and give them to young girls as fertility symbols. At regular intervals during the year the members of secret fraternal organizations go into retreats and emerge to perform rites to propitiate the gods. One of these ceremonies is the annual Snake Dance performed by the Hopi Snake Society.

The religious differences between the Tewa and the Hopi clearly illustrate the nature of the two peoples—the one aggressive and self-reliant, the other passive and mystical. From the start their incompatibility of outlook, together with the Tewa's resentment as an unhonored minority, made them hostile neighbors. The Hopi feared and disliked their protectors; the Tewa responded with aloofness and contempt.

The Tewa took up residence on what is known as the First Mesa. Their village, which the Tewa call Tewa and the Hopi call Hano, adjoins a Hopi vil-

TEWA WOMAN clad in traditional garments stands before a *kiva*, the meeting place of secret religious societies, in Tewa Village. Such clothes are worn only on festive occasions.

lage named Sichomovi. Thus the Tewa live literally next door to the Hopi. Their houses are indistinguishable; Tewa Village has all the appearances of a typical Hopi town. But for more than 250 years both groups have been keenly aware of a sharp boundary separating the two villages.

The sharpest division is in language. With constant invocation of the curse against transmission of their culture and secrets to the Hopi, the Tewa have restricted their language to their own group. Even when a Hopi marries a Tewa, the Hopi spouse does not learn the Tewa language. The Tewa, on the other hand, do speak Hopi: to maintain necessary communication they have become bilingual. Yet they have succeeded in defending their own language so well that only a single Hopi term has crept into the Tewa language in two and a half centuries. And this word has gained only a partial entry. It is the expression for "thank you": the Tewa men now use the Hopi term for "thank you," but the Tewa women still use the Tewa term.

The Tewa have borrowed a major social institution from the Hopi; it is, however, an institution which serves to preserve their exclusiveness. This acquisition is the Hopi system of maternal descent. In the Tewa village, as among the Hopi, women are the important members of the family. They own the land and houses, dispense the food and make the important decisions. The men perform religious rites, exercise disciplinary powers, support the family and teach the children how to "make a living," but they have little authority in the home. Residence and the family allegiance belong strictly to the mother. When a man marries, he goes to live in his wife's house, but he frequently visits his mother's house and considers that his home.

It is clear that this system supports the Tewa determination to maintain their own culture. A Tewa household is impervious to Hopi influence, even in cases of intermarriage. The Hopi husband would find it extremely difficult to impose Hopi values and customs on his children, even if he were disposed to do so. Any attempt at such subversion would be countered by the mother's authority and by reminders of the curse.

The Tewa have maintained an important difference in social organization from their neighbors. A Hopi village is a loose aggregation of clans. The maternal clans are virtually autonomous units. Once a year the clan heads meet to discuss the welfare of the village, but by and large ceremonial and political activities are controlled by the individual clans. The Tewa village, on the other hand, has a centralized organization. It is divided into two general units. The members of one group are called "winter people," of the other, "summer people." Every child is initiated into one of the two groups between the ages of six and 10. Each group has its own *kiva* (ceremonial house) and its own chief. The two chiefs cooperate in conducting the village's ceremonial and governmental activities, and each has certain special responsibilities for one half of the year. The general form of this organization is characteristic of all Tewa pueblos in New Mexico, and the Tewa who came to live on the First Mesa in Arizona have retained its major outlines.

For two centuries the Tewa and Hopi villages, despite their physical proximity, remained separate social islands. Intermarriage was discouraged or forbidden. The Tewa population continued to be a small minority: it still numbered only 200. The Hopi tolerated this independent group as mercenaries who performed useful functions as protectors and go-betweens in their relations with outsiders. They turned over to the Tewa the handling of all their relations with other Indian tribes and with the white authorities, but the Hopi looked down upon these functions as work suitable only for inferiors.

This state of arm's-length separation might have continued indefinitely if whites had not begun to move into the mesa country of the Hopis toward the end of the last century. The new white settlers had no intention of introducing social changes among the Indians; indeed, they were probably unaware of the differences between the Hopi and the Tewa. But their coming brought a change in cultural climate which had a subtle and powerful effect upon the Indian community.

The Tewa suddenly found themselves in a situation in which their qualities were highly valued. The white scheme of values favored the practical and aggressive spirit over the mystical. The practical Tewa readily and enthusiastically took to stock-raising, wagework and the white man's schools. Their children, already trained in two languages, learned English more quickly than the Hopi's. Moreover, their higher ardor as a minority spurred them to excel in the classroom. They became models for the Hopi children.

The Hopi began to develop a new respect for the Tewa. The Tewa's role as emissaries and interpreters to the white people grew in importance and prestige. Their value orientation, remarkably like that of the new white residents, no longer had to take a back seat. The Hopi saw that "it paid to be like the whites." They were greatly impressed by the achievements of some of the Tewa in this new climate. One of these was Tom Polacca, an interpreter who spoke five languages (Tewa, Hopi, Navaho, Spanish and English) and had been a leader in contacts with the U. S. Indian Service and other outsiders. He became a prosperous livestock raiser, built a large house below the First Mesa and started a new community which is now named Polacca Village. Equally impressive were the accomplishments of a Tewa woman named Nampeyo. She revived the art of pottery-making, copying old designs exacavated from Indian ruins in the area, and this quickly became an important industry, not only among the Tewa but also among the Hopi villagers.

With remarkable speed the antagonism and distinctions between the Hopi and Tewa began to disappear. The Tewa were accepted as "equals" and shed their onus as a minority. Their population grew: it has doubled in the past half-century. Intermarriage became common. The Hopi and Tewa worked together in pottery manufacture, in cattle cooperatives and even in religious rituals and ceremonies. The ancient legend that had divided the groups faded in influence, and social differences began to disappear. Curiously the Tewa have remained clannish about their language, but since they are equally fluent in Hopi, there are no barriers to communication.

Today hostility between the two groups has virtually disappeared. Only the old men try to keep alive the ancient Hopi "injustices," but the young people tend to laugh off their admonitions and bury the memory of the "curse."

The history of this little episode in human relations may hold some useful lessons. Social scientists differ on the possibility of manipulating human societies to desired ends, but one may hope that case studies such as this one will help mankind to find cures for groups in conflict and trouble.

RECONSTRUCTIONS OF HISTORICAL SEQUENCES

Often a sequence of events, each one involving a small, quantitative change, culminates in a culture's reaching a stage that seems qualitatively different from the culture's stage at the point where the sequence began. Reconstructions of such sequences are often concerned with tracing one or more of the evolutionary levels (see Steward, page 9) that a culture, an aspect of a culture, or a group of cultures may pass through during the course of such sequences. Archaeologists have often proposed models for describing sequences that result in different cultural adaptations or new kinds of cultural systems, the "step" and the "ramp" being two such models.

The articles in this subsection are all examples of reconstruction of an historical sequence. Many of these reconstructions focus on a major transformation in the subsistence base of the society, namely, the agricultural transformation, which has been a major research concern of archaeologists for decades. The articles here vary greatly in the amount of time that is being reconstructed. MacNeish's article on Mesoamerica, for example, deals with developments during thousands of years. Tuck's article reconstructs a 700-year span in the northeastern United States. The articles also vary in their concerns with the different evolutionary levels. MacNeish's reconstruction of the Mesoamerican sequence ranges from the simplest to the most complex evolutionary level in the regional culture history. Tuck's, on the other hand, is concerned only with the developments leading to the Iroquois confederacy.

TABLE VI. Articles Employing the Perspective of Reconstruction of a Historical Sequence.

Author	*Time*	*Area*	*Strategy*
MacNeish (1971)	20,000 to 1 B.C.	Peru	Hunting-gathering/agricultural
MacNeish (1964)	10,000 B.C. to A.D. 1500	Mesoamerica	Hunting-gathering/agricultural
Ford (1954)	2500 B.C. to A.D. 1200	Peru	Hunting-gathering/agricultural
Martin (1951)	2500 B.C. to A.D. 1300	Southwest	Hunting-gathering/agricultural
Borhegyi (1959)	1000 B.C. to A.D. 1500	Mesoamerica	Agricultural/hunting-gathering
Schwartz (1958)	A.D. 600–1800	Southwest	Agricultural
Tuck (1971)	A.D. 1100–1800	Northeast	Agricultural/hunting-gathering

It is easy to see how archaeologists developed an interest in reconstructing series of events, given that human activities take place within space and time, and given the preceding reconstructions of single events. These sequential reconstructions are more diachronic than synchronic, being clearly concerned with cultural developments through time, with the chronicling of one stage after another.

THE READINGS

In "Early Man in the Andes," Richard S. MacNeish reports on his reconstruction of a Peruvian regional sequence, which he undertook in order to have a basis for comparison with the Mesoamerican sequence he had just completed reconstructing (see the next article, page 155). Such "functional comparisons" are viewed as a potential source for generalizations about the rise of civilizations. His excavations and analysis, however, yielded results which were clearly unexpected, and if his interpretations are plausible, a new scheme of culture history of the New World should follow. In reporting on the excavations, he shows how soils, fauna, and artifact assemblages are used to develop a sequence of climate, another of technological adaptations. He interprets these sequences as being inconsistent with current notions of glacial oscillations and of the development of New World archaeological traditions. In claiming dramatic new finds that may upset current culture-historical sequences, the archaeologist needs to document carefully the basis for such interpretations; he needs to build credibility. Isotopic dating techniques (in this case, carbon-14 dating, mostly on bone) are used to establish the temporal basis for the new interpretations, and the identification of the volcanic rocks as stone tools is attributed to the "skilled eye" of the archaeologist. The credibility of the archaeologist's analysis therefore rests here on the reliability of the dating techniques and on the training of the archaeologist. In interpreting these stone tools and their evolutionary antecedents, MacNeish is careful to point out that he is engaging in speculation. He hopes that his hypothetical reconstruction of the sequence and of the plausible interrelationships between the different traditions in the New World will generate new research designs and problems for analysis.

"The Origins of New World Civilization," MacNeish's reconstruction of the 12,000-year occupation of the Tehuacan valley in Mexico, contains two stories. The first is an "archaeological detective story": how and why a site is located. In this case, paleobotany provided the "clues," in the form of theories of the domestication of corn, and in identification of fossil pollen as domesticated or wild. The origins of agriculture have always been a focus for archaeological research. From the romantic perspective, they are a "first"; from the time-space systematics perspective, they constitute a spatial and temporal reference point for the writing of culture history. From the reconstructionist perspective, they were a sequence of events that culminated in a qualitatively different way of life—civilization. From the systemic perspective, they were part of a long-term process of systemic change that involved the deviation and readjustment of certain variables; in some contexts the process led to civilization and cities, but in other contexts it did not. MacNeish points out that many disciplines are involved in the reconstruction of agricultural origins. Although it was current paleobotanical opinion that directed MacNeish's research toward wild corn as the probable ancestor for domesticated corn, botanical concepts change, as do archaeological ones; work during the past decade, since that of Mangelsdorf, has suggested a different ancestor for corn. Despite such shifts of opinion, the second story in this article still stands: that of life in the Tehuacan Valley. MacNeish describes the different phases in terms of clusters of traits: population size and mobility, foodstuffs and how they were obtained, artifact assemblages, treatment of the dead. When these clusters are considered in the context of ecological changes and cultural developments in Oaxaca or elsewhere, one can hypothesize what interrelated patterns of change led to the evolutionary sequence from hunter-gatherers to urban life. From this perspective the Tehuacan valley is exciting not just because the earliest corn, earliest pottery, and earliest skeletons are found there. It is the sequence of developments that is reconstructed from all the finds that has challenged previous notions of the rise of civilization in the New World. That archaeologists must remain flexible in their reconstructions in order to incorporate frequent revisions should be apparent from both this article and the preceding one on Peruvian archaeological traditions (page 143).

Two decades ago, when Ford's article, "The History of a Peruvian Valley," was written, team, rather than individual, investigations into prehistory were just developing. Today interdisciplinary research in archaeology is the standard mode of research. Ford and his colleagues were not so much an interdisciplinary team as a group of cooperating archaeologists and ethnographers who each contributed his specialized analyses of the "pieces" of the archaeological and ethnographic record. Ford here integrates these pieces into a single generalized reconstruction of the occupation of the Viru valley. The picture he gives is drawn quite directly from the archaeological record: they made pottery, wove fabrics, built fortlike structures, settled near or away from the rivers. The "glue" for his reconstruction is drawn from generalized ideas of the organization of complex societies, such as priest-craftsmen who made ceremonial types of pottery. The outlines of the civilizational process as known in the Old World also serve as a reference point and analogy for the general process that seems to have taken place in the Viru valley. The chart on page 169 is an elegant example of the way in which archaeologists may use ceramic sequences as indicators of changes in population composition or in sociocultural units. The past decades have evidenced increasing sophistication in understanding the relationship between types of material culture and the nature of the social groups producing them.

Although "The Peoples of Pine Lawn Valley" was written decades ago, it clearly displays one of the pervasive themes underlying and directing the research of Paul S. Martin. This theme is the need to understand the general processes of sociocultural change that all human groups experience to one degree or another. By reconstructing a long-term perspective on changing cultural systems, the archaeologist is in a position to discern these processes and explain them. Martin's reconstruction of almost 4,000 years of Mogollon culture history suggests that both the origins and the decline of this group came about under conditions that demanded readaptation. Human environments were threatened many times in prehistory, and understanding the ways in which such threats were met—for example, by means of new philosophies, changed subsistence bases, new organizational patterns, or all of these—is a major contribution of archaeology. Martin's reconstruction is direct; the story he tells depends on few speculative leaps, although it does depend on many then-standard assumptions about the evolution and "progress" of culture (see Steward's article, page 9). More importantly, Martin's article makes clear an important perspective that arose with increasing interest in archaeological reconstruction. For Martin, the importance of a "dig," and of understanding, reconstructing, and explaining the past, is practical rather than romantic. The romantic and spectacular may lure one into archaeology, but understanding the practical adaptive strategies of prehistoric groups is more realistic and contributes much more to the social sciences.

In "Underwater Archaeology of the Maya Highlands," Stephan F. Borhegyi reports how the chance discoveries of underwater divers in the Guatamalan

Lake Amititlan led to a more systematic recovery of Mayan artifacts under the direction of a professional archaeologist. Borhegyi presents the background history of the finds and the confirmation of their association with shoreline sites that resulted from reinvestigation of the latter. The resulting archaeological record was then pieced together to form a reconstruction of the 3,000 years of Mayan occupation along the lakeshore. In order to do this, Borhegyi accepted current anthropological assumptions; for example, he assumed the conditions of leisure and food surplus in which crafts are thought to develop. He suggests that an "awe" of the volcano, geysers, and springs may have provoked the tossing of ceremonial items into the waters as offerings or in appeasement. He employs knowledge of the wider Mayan culture, in which human sacrifice, for example, was practiced, to account for ochre-stained crania found in the lake. He makes use of knowledge of the area from ethnohistorical accounts, and he also uses art styles as indicators of the influence or even the presence of external or foreign groups. That beliefs about the lake still circulate today, despite the general conversion to Christianity in the seventeenth century, is additional support for Borhegyi's reconstruction of continued involvement with the lake and its associated natural and supernatural powers. The resulting reconstruction employs many kinds of "glue," and these suggest the many ways in which archaeological techniques (diving, aerial photographs) and anthropological knowledge are complementary in the building of an archaeological reconstruction.

Schwartz's article "Prehistoric Man in the Grand Canyon," reconstructs the previously unknown way of life and occupational patterns at the bottom of the Grand Canyon and on the plateau adjacent to it. The cultural origins and generalized patterns of cultural evolution are outlined in terms of the archaeological record. From short-term sites with remains of hunting gear and animal bones to larger, increasingly more permanent sites with increasingly complex architecture, agricultural practices and the use of irrigation and pottery attest to these broad outlines of changing adaptations. Schwartz's use of population curves in the two adjacent areas suggests a correlation that would be difficult to account for by chance alone. Rather, the fact that population grew in one locale as it shrank in the other locale is made plausible by the known raiding on the increasingly depopulated area. Schwartz explicitly views developments as adaptations to changing socioecological conditions. Examples are the changing patterns of mobility, especially the adoption of seasonal strategies of summer farming and winter hunting as the population increased and the plateau became more desiccated. The development of cliff houses is also viewed as an adaptive strategy for housing a burgeoning population within the circumscribed canyon floor, and for meeting increased defensive needs.

James Tuck's reconstruction of 700 years of culture history in upper New York state, "The Iroquois Confederacy," draws upon careful excavation (see the impressive photographs) and analysis in the context of the well-documented ethnohistory of the Iroquois during Colonial times. When viewed as probable antecedents of known customs, architecture, and ceramic styles, the earlier remains can be interpreted with more credibility. The cultural evolution toward the known Iroquois pattern of Colonial times and the probable origins of the strong (but difficult to account for) Iroquois alliances can be plausibly reconstructed, given the archaeological record, on the one hand, and the eventual form of sociopolitical organization, on the other. The reconstructionist's task is to bring these two lines of evidence into conformity. Tuck's results are convincing, for he has taken careful note of the chronological, spatial, and stylistic associations among sites that might provide information on Iroquois social relations. Tuck makes use of the general principles that underlie alliance-formation, and of the fact, as documented by ethnography, that spatially distinct units in a culture need integrating mechanisms, such as religious societies, marriage arrangements, and moieties.

These ethnographically known mechanisms support his hypothesis of the paired-village settlement pattern, which itself was reported in historical accounts. The strength of drawing on local ethnohistorical accounts as the "glue" for this reconstruction is based on the known cultural continuity of the area. That this alliance system is viewed by Tuck as a response to changing socioecological conditions suggests that what he is reconstructing is just as much an adaptive strategy as an historical sequence (see the next set of Reconstruction readings).

Early Man in the Andes

by Richard S. MacNeish
April 1971

Stone tools in highland Peru indicate that men lived there 22,000 years ago, almost twice the old estimate. They also imply that the first cultural traditions of the New World had their roots in Asia

Recent archaeological discoveries in the highlands of Peru have extended the prehistory of the New World in two significant respects. First, the finds themselves indicate that we must push back the date of man's earliest known appearance in South America from the currently accepted estimate of around 12,000 B.C. to perhaps as much as 20,000 B.C. Second and even more important is the implication, in the nature of the very early Andean hunting cultures now brought to light, that these cultures reflect Old World origins of even greater antiquity. If this is so, man may have first arrived in the Western Hemisphere between 40,000 and 100,000 years ago. The discoveries and the conclusions they suggest seem important enough to warrant this preliminary report in spite of the hazard that it may prove to be premature.

The new findings were made in 1969 and 1970 near Ayacucho, a town in the Peruvian province of the same name. All the sites lie within a mountain-ringed valley, most of it 6,500 feet above sea level, located some 200 miles southeast of Lima [*see top illustration on page 145*]. The valley is rich in prehistoric remains (we noted some 500 sites during our preliminary survey) and archaeological investigations have been conducted there since the 1930's. For me and my associates in the Ayacucho Archaeological-Botanical Project, however, the valley was interesting for other reasons as well.

A number of us had already been involved in a joint archaeological-botanical investigation at Tehuacán in the highlands of Mexico under the sponsorship of the Robert S. Peabody Foundation for Archaeology. Our prime target was early botanical evidence of the origin and development of agriculture in the area. This we sought by archaeological methods, while simultaneously recording the relation between agricultural advances and the material evidence of developing village life (and ultimately urban life) in Mexico before the Spanish conquest. By the time our fieldwork at Tehuacán had been completed in the mid-1960's we had gained some understanding of the changes that had come about in highland Mesoamerica between its initial occupation by preagricultural hunters and gatherers around 10,000 B.C. and the rise of pre-Columbian civilization [see the Origins of New World Civilization," by Richard S. MacNeish; SCIENTIFIC AMERICAN Offprint 625].

There was, however, at least one other major New World center that had been the site of a similar development from hunting bands to farmers and city folk. This is western South America. Its inhabitants had cultivated some plants that were unknown to the farmers of Mesoamerica, and they had domesticated animals that were similarly unique to the region. Mesoamerica certainly interacted with South America, but the earliest stages of this second regional development apparently took place in isolation. It seemed logical that the record of these isolated advances might provide the foundation for functional comparisons with the Tehuacán results and perhaps lead us to some generalizations about the rise of civilization in the New World.

This was the objective that brought several veterans of the Tehuacán investigation, myself included, to Peru. The work was again sponsored by the Peabody Foundation, where I now serve as director. Reconnaissance of a number of highland areas led us to select the Ayacucho valley as the scene of our investigations. Our decision was based primarily on ecological grounds: within a radius of 15 miles the varied highland environment includes areas of subtropical desert, thorn-forest grassland, dry thorn forest, humid scrub forest and subarctic tundra [*see bottom illustration on page 145*]. It is the consensus among botanists who have studied the question that many of the plants first domesticated in western South America were indigenous to the highlands and that their domestication had probably taken place in Peru. The Peruvian ecologist J. A. Tosi had concluded that the most probable locale for the event would be a highland valley that included a wide range of environments. An additional consideration was that the area where we worked should contain caves that could have served as shelters in the past and thus might prove to be the repositories of animal and plant remains. The Ayacucho valley met both requirements.

Two caves in the valley have in fact turned out to be particularly rich repositories. One of them, located about eight miles north of the town of Ayacucho, is known locally as Pikimachay, or Flea Cave. It lies some 9,000 feet above sea level on the eastern slope of a hill composed of volcanic rock; the mouth of the cave is 40 feet high in places and 175 feet wide, and the distance from the front of the cave to the deepest point inside it is 80 feet. Rocks that have fallen from the roof occupy the northern third of the interior of the cave and form a pile that reaches a height of 20 feet. In 1969 Flea Cave yielded the single most dramatic discovery of the season. During our last week of excavation a test trench, dug to a depth of six feet near the south end of the cave, revealed stone tools in association with bones of an extinct ground sloth of the same family as the fossil North American sloth *Megatherium*. One of the bones, a humerus, has

been shown by carbon-14 analysis to be 14,150 (±180) years old.

The other notable cave site, some 11 miles east of the town of Ayacucho, is known locally as Jayamachay, or Pepper Cave. Although Pepper Cave is as high and nearly as wide as Flea Cave, it is only 15 feet deep. Excavations were made at Pepper Cave with rewarding results in both the 1969 and the 1970 seasons. Because the significance of the findings at this site arises largely from a comparison of the material from both caves, I shall first describe the strata at Flea Cave.

What has been revealed in general by our work at all the cave and open-air sites in the Ayacucho valley (a total of 12 excavations) is a series of remains representative of successive cultures in an unbroken sequence that spans the millenniums from 20,000 B.C. to A.D. 1500. The archaeological sequence documents man's progression from an early hunter to an incipient agriculturist to a village farmer and finally to the role of a subject of imperial rule. The material of the most significance to the present discussion, however, is contained in the strata representing the earliest phases of this long prehistoric record. These strata have yielded a succession of stone-tool types that began some 20,000 years ago and continued until about 10,500 years ago. The earliest part of the record is found in the lowest levels at Flea Cave.

The oldest stratified deposit in the cave lies in a basin-like hollow in the lava flow that forms the cave floor. The stratum lies just above the bedrock of the basin. Labeled Zone k, the stratum consists of soils, transported into the cave by natural means, that are mixed with disintegrated volcanic tuffs from the rocks of the cave itself. Zone k is eight inches deep. Just before the deposition of the stratum ended, some animal vertebrae and a rib bone (possibly from an extinct ground sloth) were deposited in it. So were four crude tools fashioned from volcanic tuff and a few flakes that had been struck from tools. One of the flakes is of a green stone that could only have come from outside the cave.

DEEP CUT through part of an open-air archaeological site at Puente in highland Peru is seen in the photograph on the opposite page. The record preserved in the successive strata at Puente extends from the first appearance of pottery in the 16th century B.C. to about 7000 B.C., when the Andes were inhabited by hunters specializing in the pursuit of big game.

AYACUCHO VALLEY, between Lima and Cuzco, is undergoing joint botanical and archaeological investigation that will allow comparisons with a study of Tehuácan, in Mexico. The Robert S. Peabody Foundation for Archaeology is the sponsor of both studies.

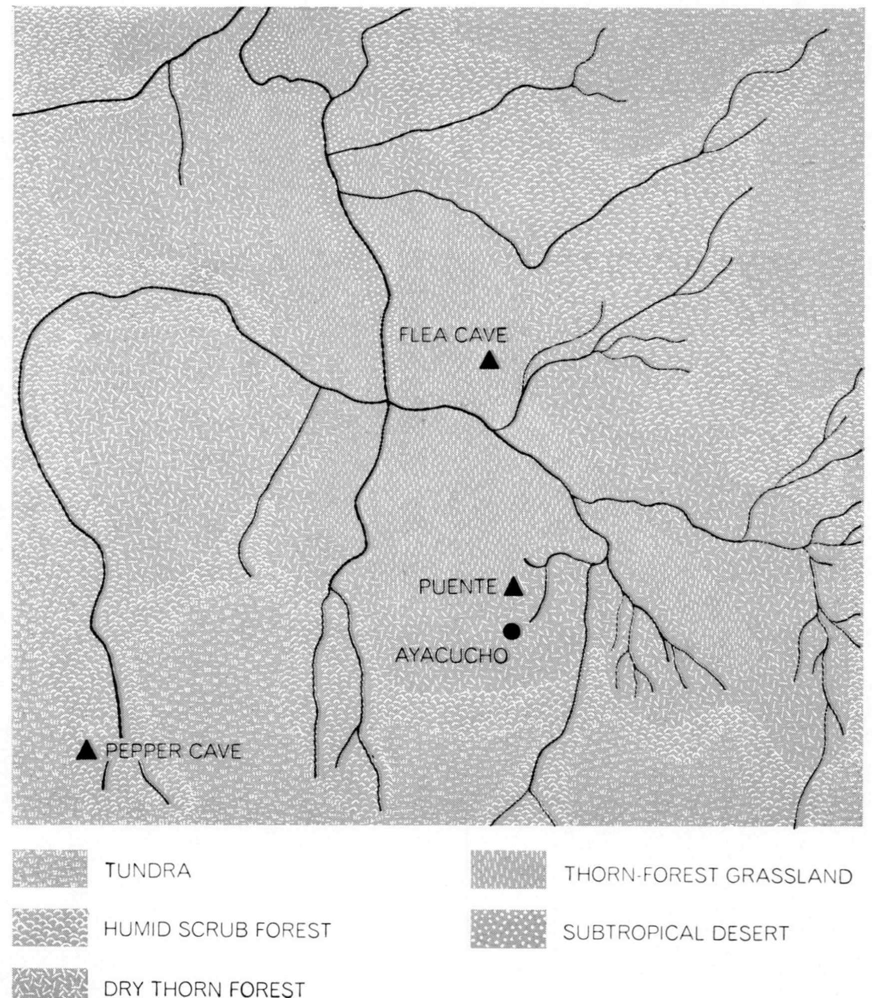

MAJOR SITES in the Ayacucho valley include Puente, near the town of Ayacucho, Flea Cave, a few miles north of Puente, and Pepper Cave, a few miles southwest. The existence of five distinct zones of vegetation in the valley (*key*) was a factor in its selection for study.

FLEA CAVE, the site that contains the oldest evidence of man's presence thus far unearthed in South America, lies at an altitude of 9,000 feet in an area of intermingled thorn forest and grassland. The mouth of the cave (*center*) is 175 feet wide and 40 feet high.

PEPPER CAVE, the other major cave site in the Ayacucho area, lies at an altitude of 11,000 feet on a hill where humid scrub forest gives way to upland tundra vegetation. The lowest strata excavated at Pepper Cave are evidently the product of local glacial outwashes.

The soils in Zone k are neutral in terms of acidity, which suggests that the vegetation outside the cave when the soils were formed was of the grassland variety, in contrast to the dry thorn-forest vegetation found today. The period of deposition that formed Zone k may have begun more than 23,000 years ago. It remains to be seen whether the climate at that time, as indicated by the neutral acidity of the soil, can be exactly correlated with any of the several known glacial fluctuations in the neighboring Andes.

Three later strata, all containing the bones of extinct animals and additional stone implements, overlie Zone k. They are labeled, in ascending order, zones j, i1 and i. Zone j is a brown soil deposit 12 inches thick. In various parts of this stratum we unearthed three vertebrae and two rib fragments of an extinct ground sloth and the leg bone of a smaller mammal, perhaps an ancestral species of horse or camel. Zone j yielded 14 stone tools; like those in Zone k, they are crudely made from volcanic tuff. There are in addition some 40 stone flakes, evidently the waste from toolmaking. Carbon-14 analysis of one of the ground-sloth vertebrae shows it to be 19,600 (±3,000) years old.

Zone i1, above Zone j, is a deposit of a more orange-colored soil; it is 15 inches thick, and it contains tools and both fossilized and burned animal bone. Carbon-14 analysis of one of the bones, a fragment of sloth scapula, indicates that it is 16,050 (±1,200) years old. The soils of zones j and i1 are both quite acid, suggesting that they were formed when the climate was less arid and the vegetation outside Flea Cave included forest cover.

The uppermost of the four strata, Zone i, consists of 18 inches of a slightly browner soil. The soil approaches that of Zone k in neutral acidity, suggesting a return to drier climatic conditions. Distributed through the deposit are crude stone artifacts, waste flakes and the bones of sloth and horse. Carbon-14 analysis of one of the bones shows it to be 14,700 (±1,400) years old.

The stone tools from all four of the lowest Flea Cave strata are much alike. There are 50 of them in all, uniformly large and crude in workmanship. The tool types include sidescrapers, choppers, cleavers, "spokeshaves" and denticulate (sawtoothed) forms. Most of them were made from volcanic tuff, which does not flake well, and it takes a skilled eye to distinguish many of them from unworked tuff detached from the

YEARS BEFORE PRESENT (ESTIMATED)	ASSOCIATED C-14 DATES (YEARS BEFORE PRESENT): FLEA CAVE	PEPPER CAVE	TOOL COMPLEX	CLIMATE AND VEGETATION	POSSIBLE GLACIATION STAGE
8,000	f1	C 8,250 (±125)	JAYWA	MODERN CLIMATE AND VEGETATION	ICE IN HIGH ANDES ONLY
		D 8,360 (±135)			
	8,860 (±125)	E			
	f2	F	PUENTE		
		G			
		H 8,980 (±140)			
		I			
	ROCKFALL	J	HUANTA	COOL	FINAL ICE RETREAT
		J1 9,460 (±145)			
		J2			
		J3			
		K			
		L			
		M			
12,000	g	N		COLD	FINAL ICE ADVANCE
	h	GRAVEL	BLADE, BURIN, LEAF-POINT?		
	h 14,150 (±180)		AYA-CUCHO	WARM FOREST	INTERSTADIAL
	h1			COLD	ICE
16,000	i 14,700 (±1,400)		PACCAI-CASA	GRASSLAND	ADVANCE
	i1 16,050 (±1,200)			WARM FOREST	INTERSTADIAL?
	j 19,600 (±3,000)				
20,000	k	ROCK FLOOR		COLD GRASSLAND	EARLY ICE ADVANCE ?

SEQUENCE OF STRATA at the major Ayacucho cave sites is correlated in this chart with the five earliest tool complexes that have been identified thus far. Carbon-14 determinations of the age of certain strata are shown in relation to estimates of the overall temporal sequence. The climate and vegetation are linked to probable stages of glaciation.

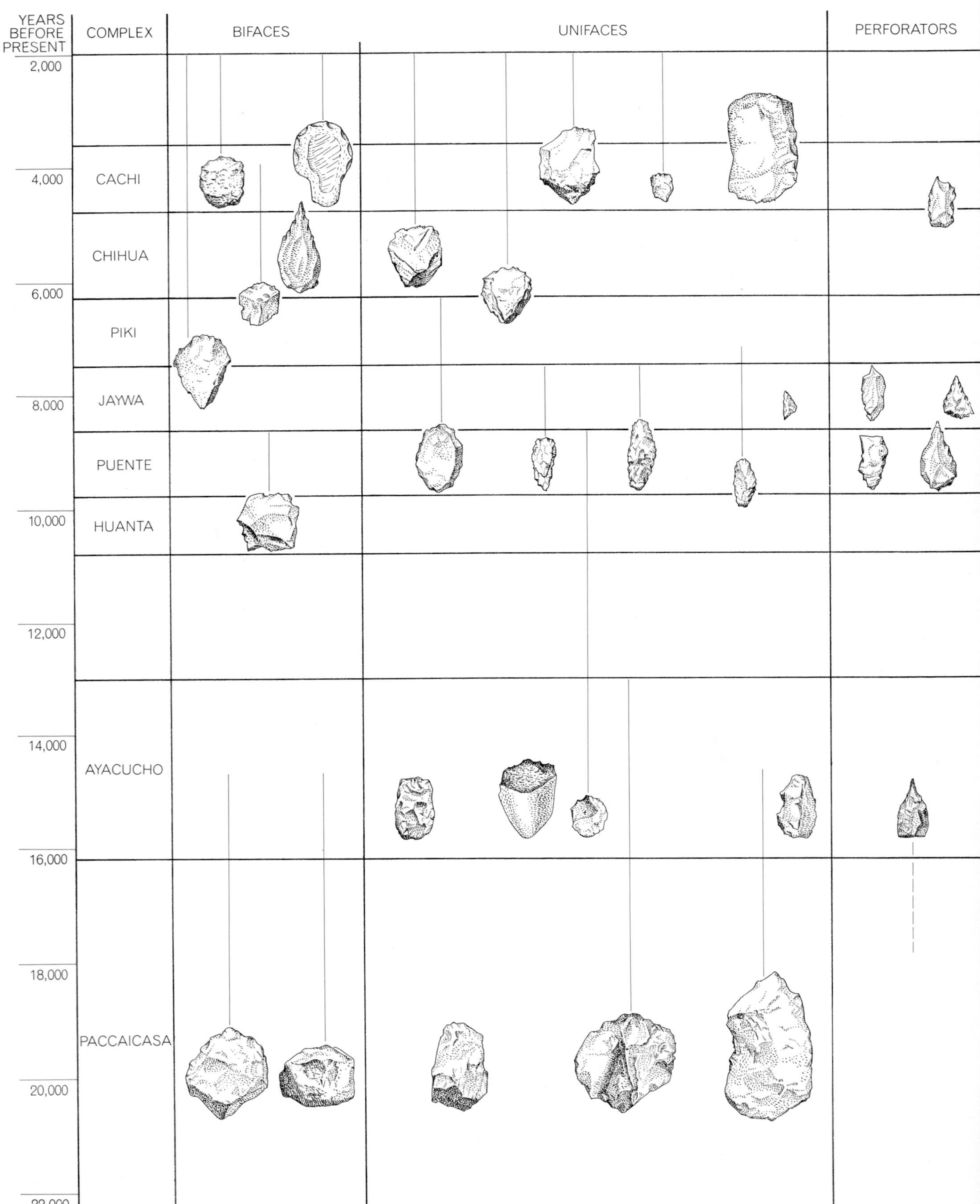

KINDS OF TOOLS discovered at 12 excavations in the Ayacucho valley appear in this chart in association with the complex (*names at left*) that first includes them. No complex more recent than the Puente, some 9,000 years old, is relevant to man's earliest arrival

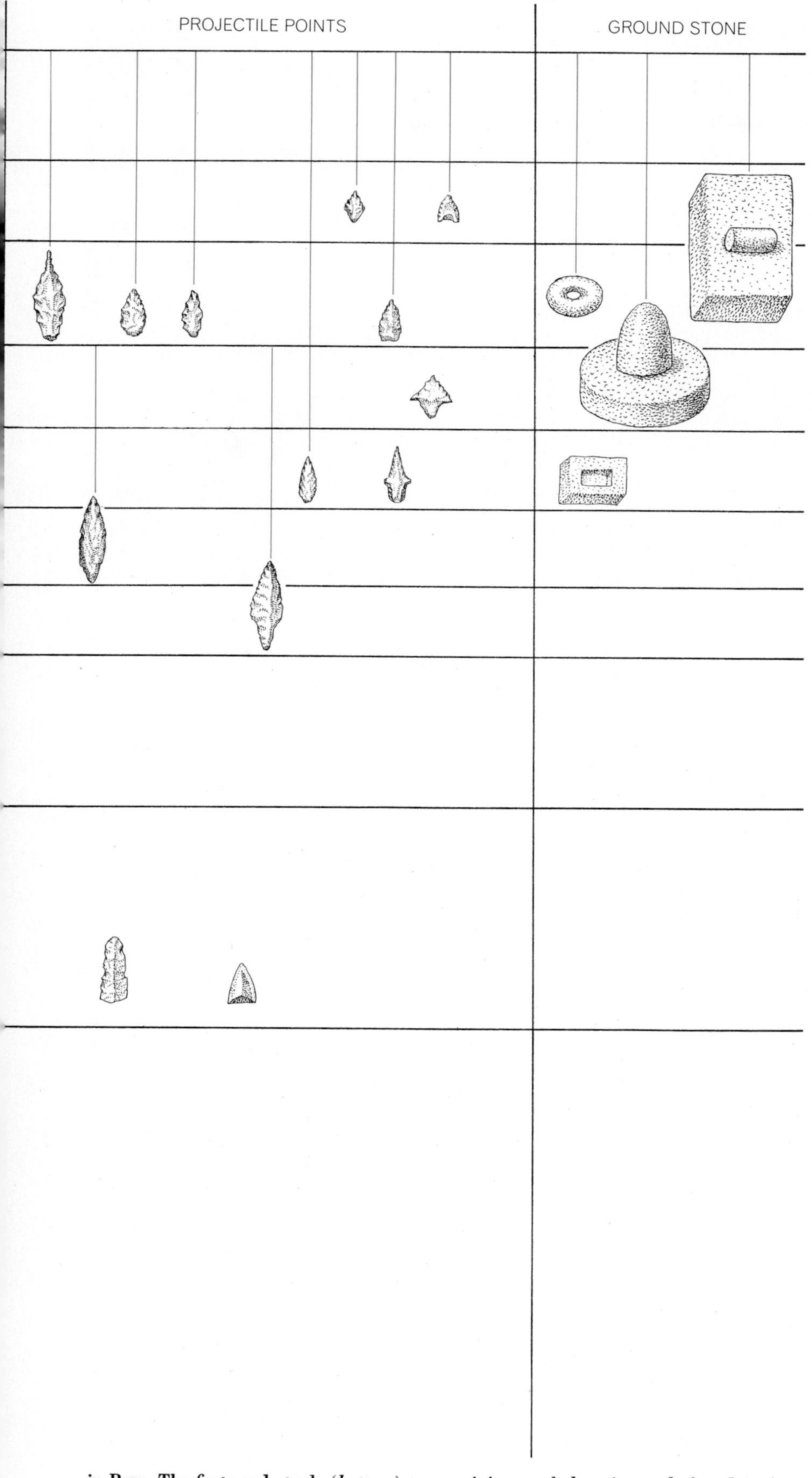

in Peru. The first crude tools (*bottom*) are reminiscent of chopping tools found in Asia. In the next complex projectile points first appear; some were made out of bone (*far right*).

cave walls by natural processes. A few of the tools, however, were made from other materials, such as rounded pebbles and pieces of basalt, that were collected outside the cave and carried back to be fashioned into implements. The tools in these four levels represent the earliest assemblage of tools, or tool complex, unearthed so far at a stratified site anywhere in South America. We call it the Paccaicasa complex, after a nearby village. The men who fashioned its distinctive tools occupied the Ayacucho valley from as much as 22,000 years ago to about 13,000 years ago.

The strata at Flea Cave that contain the Paccaicasa complex were excavated during the 1970 season. The previous year we thought we had already reached bedrock when we reached the top of the stratum just above Zone i: it was a very hard, yellowish layer of soil that included numerous small flakes of volcanic tuff. With the season nearly at an end we proceeded no farther. The yellow layer, now known as Zone h1, actually turned out to lie just above bedrock over an area of some 150 square yards of cave floor except for the natural basin near the south end of the cave. Digging into this stratum with some difficulty at the start of the 1970 season, we found that its 20-inch depth contained not only the bones of sloth, horse and possibly saber-toothed tiger but also numerous flakes of waste stone and some 70 tools, most of them quite different from the crude tuff artifacts of the strata below. A few tools of the older kind were present in Zone h1, but the majority are made from such materials as basalt, chalcedony, chert and pebbles of quartzite.

The use of new tool materials is also characteristic of Zone h, a 12-inch stratum of softer, light orange soil that overlies Zone h1. Here, however, the animal remains include many not found in the older strata. A kind of ancestral camel appears to be represented in addition to the sloth and the horse. There are also the remains of the puma, the hog-nosed skunk, an extinct species of deer and several unidentified species, possibly including the mastodon. This larger faunal assemblage suggests a return of the countryside around Flea Cave to forest cover. Indeed, the soil of Zone h is strongly acid, unlike the neutral soils of Zone i and Zone h1.

The tools in Zone h are abundant; in addition to more than 1,000 fragments of waste stone there are some 250 finished artifacts. Some of these artifacts are in the "core" tradition of tool manufacture: they were made by removing

LIMB BONE of an extinct ground sloth (*center*) was found at Flea Cave in a stratum that also contained stone and bone tools representative of the Ayacucho complex. Carbon-14 analysis of the bone shows that the stratum was deposited at least 14,000 years ago.

flakes from a stone to produce the desired shape. Among them are both the choppers and spokeshaves typical of the lower strata and new varieties of tool such as split-pebble scrapers and fluted wedges. The core tools are outnumbered, however, by tools consisting of flakes: burins, gravers, sidescrapers, flake spokeshaves, denticulate flakes and unifacial projectile points (points flaked only on one side). The unifacial points are the oldest projectile points found at Ayacucho.

At this stage the inhabitants of Flea Cave were also fashioning tools out of bone: triangular projectile points, polishers, punches made out of antler and "fleshers" formed out of rib bones. There is even one polished animal toe bone that may have been an ornament.

Zone h is the rich stratum that yielded the 14,000-year-old sloth humerus in 1969. The change in tool materials apparent in Zone h1 and the proliferation of new tool types in Zone h suggest that at Flea Cave a second tool complex had taken the place of the earlier Paccaicasa complex. We have named the distinctive assemblage from these two strata the Ayacucho complex.

The stratum immediately overlying Zone h is found in only a few parts of the excavation. It consists of a fine, powdery yellow soil that is neutral in acidity. This sparse formation, labeled Zone *h*, has so far yielded only three stone artifacts: a blade, a sidescraper and a large denticulate scraper. The lack of soil acidity suggests that the interval represented by Zone *h* was characterized by dry grassland vegetation. Further investigation may yield enough artifacts to indicate whether or not the stratum contains a distinctive tool complex suited to the changed environment. For the time being we know too little about Zone *h* to come to any conclusions.

For the purposes of this discussion the Flea Cave story ends here. Above Zone *h* at the time our work began was a three-foot layer of fallen rock, including some individual stones that weighed more than three tons. This rock was apparently associated with the much heavier fall in the northern half of the cave. A small stratum above the rock debris, labeled Zone f1, contained charcoal, the bones of modern deer and llamas, and a few well-made bifacial tools (stone tools flaked on both sides). These tools closely resemble tools of known age at Puente, an open-air site near Ayacucho where only the remains of modern animals have been found. On this basis one can conclude that the time of the rockfall at Flea Cave was no later than 10,000 years ago. It is worth mentioning that before any of the strata below the rock layer could be excavated, the rocks had to be broken up by pickax and carried out of the cave. The three-foot rock stratum was labeled Zone g.

The strata that tell the rest of our story are in a deep deposit in the southeast corner of Pepper Cave. Situated at an altitude of nearly 11,000 feet, this cave is surrounded today by humid scrub forest. It is adjacent to a tributary of the Cachi River, whose bed lies 150 feet below the level of the cave. The bottom stratum of the deep deposit at Pepper Cave consists of stratified sands and gravels close to the top of a high water-built terrace. This fluvial deposit is labeled Zone N. It is overlain by a three-foot layer of rocks that have fallen from the roof of the cave, mixed with stratified sands that indicate a continuation of fluvial terrace building. The mixed stratum comprises zones M and L. Preliminary geological studies suggest that the terrace was formed by outwash from the final advance of the Andean glaciers. There is no evidence of human activity in the three lowest strata at Pepper Cave.

Overlying these sterile layers is a 28-inch stratum of windblown sand and disintegrated volcanic tuff that has been labeled Zone K. Artifacts were found in the upper four inches of the deposit, and a few were also unearthed in one reddish area near the bottom of it. The artifacts represent a new complex of tools that was also found in the next three strata:

floors of human habitation that are labeled in ascending order zones J3, J2 and J1. No animal remains have been recovered from Zone K, but the three J zones contain the bones of horses, of extinct species of deer and possibly of llamas.

The characteristic artifacts of the new tool complex, which we have named Huanta after another town in the valley, include bifacially flaked projectile points with a "fishtail" base, gravers, burins, blades, half-moon-shaped sidescrapers and teardrop-shaped end scrapers. A carbon-14 analysis of one of the animal bones from the uppermost stratum, Zone J1, indicates that the Huanta complex flourished until about 9,500 years ago.

The five strata overlying the Huanta complex at Pepper Cave, like the single layer above the rockfall at Flea Cave, hold remains typical of the Puente complex. These strata have been designated zones J through F. One stratum near the middle, Zone H, is shown by a carbon-14 analysis of charcoal to have been laid down about 9,000 years ago. This date is in good agreement with the known age of material excavated at the Puente site. The contents of the strata above the Puente complex zones at Pepper Cave (zones E through A), like the contents of zones f1 through a at Flea Cave, will not concern us here.

Having reviewed the facts revealed at Ayacucho, let us consider their broader implications. What follows is not only interpretive but also somewhat speculative; it goes well beyond the direct evidence now at our disposal. Stating the implications straightforwardly, however, may serve two useful purposes. First, in doing so we are in effect putting forward hypotheses to be proved or disproved by future findings. Second, in being explicit we help to define the problems that remain to be solved.

Let us first consider the implications of our evidence concerning changes in vegetation and climate. Remains of the Puente complex overlie the sequences of earlier strata at both caves: they are on top of the material of uncertain character at Flea Cave and on top of the Huanta complex at Pepper Cave. To judge from carbon-14 measurements, the earliest appearance of the Puente complex, with its advanced tools and remains of modern animal species, may have been around 9,700 years ago. At about that time, then, the association of early man and extinct animals in this highland area evidently came to an end.

We have not yet completed the soil studies and the analyses of pollens in the soil that will add many details to the record of climate and vegetation. For the time being, however, I tentatively propose that the last of the pre-Puente strata at Flea Cave (Zone *h*) and the sterile zones N through L at Pepper Cave coincide with the last Andean glacial advance. Zone h at Flea Cave, with its acid soil and remains of forest animals, appears to represent an earlier "interstadial" period in the glacial record—a breathing spell rather than a full-scale retreat. Zones h1 and i, below Zone h, are characterized by the remains of different animals and by soil of neutral acidity, suggesting a colder climate and a glacial advance. Evidence from the still earlier zones i1 and j suggests a second interstadial period of relative warmth. Zone k, the lowest in the Flea Cave excavation, apparently represents another period of advancing ice. If the Ayacucho evidence holds true for Andean glacial activity in general, the South American glacial advances and retreats do not coincide with those of the Wisconsin glaciation in North America [*see illustration on this page*]. This apparent lack of correlation presents interesting problems. If glaciation is caused by worldwide climatic change, why are the South American oscillations so unlike the North American ones? If, on the other hand, widespread climatic change is not the cause of glaciation, what is? The precise sequence of Andean glacial advances and retreats obviously calls for further study.

What are the implications of the Ayacucho findings with respect to early man, not only in South America but also elsewhere in the New World? The results of local studies of the earliest phases of prehistory in South America are all too seldom published, so that the comments that follow are particularly speculative. Having warned the reader, let me suggest that the Paccaicasa complex in the Peruvian central highlands may well represent the earliest stage of man's appearance in South America.

To generalize from Ayacucho material, this earliest stage seems to be characterized by a tool assemblage consisting of large corelike choppers, large sidescrapers and spokeshaves and heavy denticulate implements. This I shall call the Core Tool Tradition; it is certainly represented by the Paccaicasa assemblage in South America and may just possibly be represented in North America by the controversial finds at the Calico site in the Mojave Desert north of Barstow, Calif. In South America the Core Tool Tradition appears to have flourished from about 25,000 years ago to 15,000 years ago.

Man's next stage in South America I call the Flake and Bone Tool Tradition. The only adequate definition of this tradition so far is found in the Ayacucho tool complex. That complex is characterized by a reduction in the proportion of core tools and a sudden abundance of tools made out of flakes: projectile points, knives, sidescrapers, gravers, burins, spokeshaves and denticulate tools.

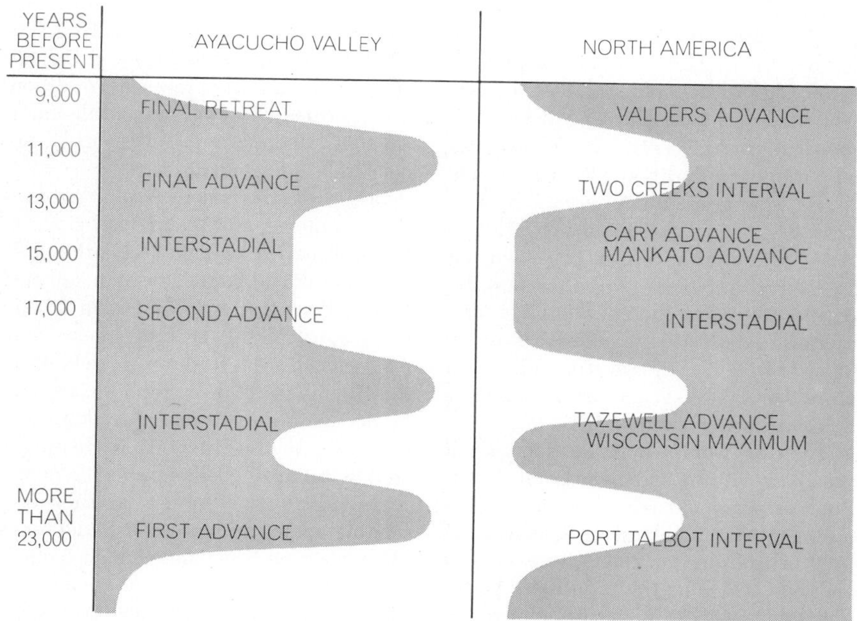

PHASE REVERSAL with respect to the glacial advances and retreats in the Northern Hemisphere during the final period of Pleistocene glaciation appears to characterize the record of fluctuations preserved at Ayacucho. The graph compares estimated Andean advances, retreats and interstadial phases with the phases of the Wisconsin glaciation.

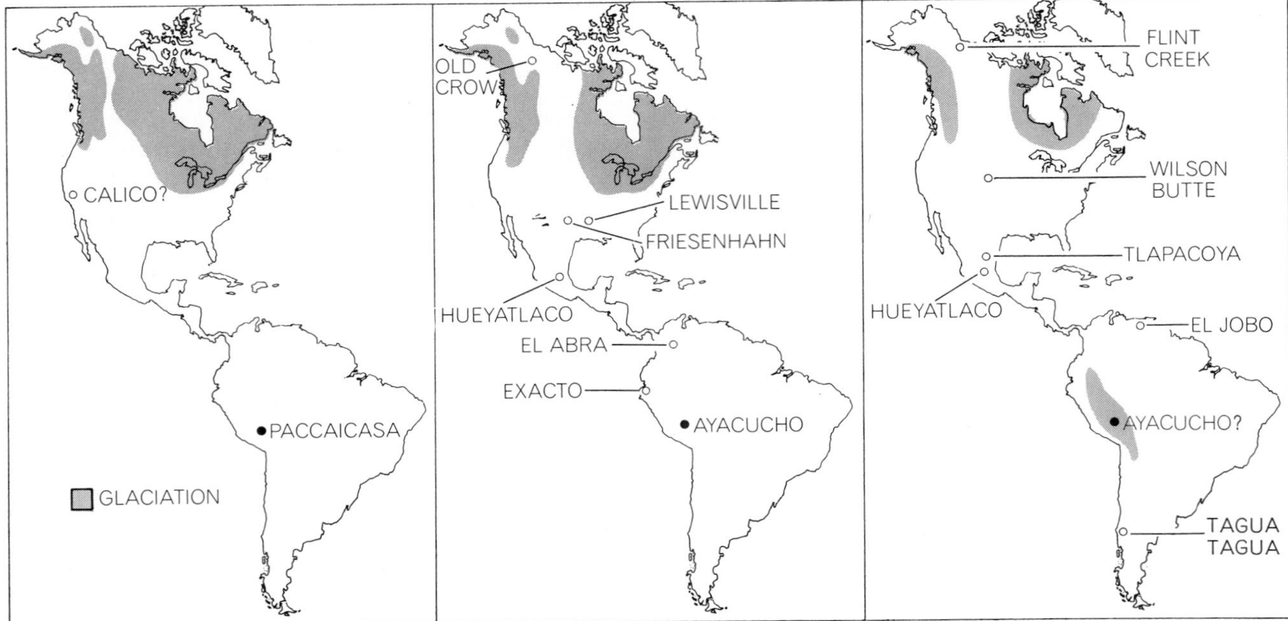

THREE TRADITIONS in New World prehistory are the Core Tool Tradition (*left*), the Flake and Bone Tool Tradition (*center*) and the Blade, Burin and Leaf-Point Tradition (*right*). The age of each tradition in North America, in cases where the age of a representative site is known, is substantially greater than it is in South America, suggesting that they stem from earlier Old World roots.

An important element in the tradition is the presence of bone implements, including projectile points, awls and scrapers. The Flake and Bone Tool Tradition apparently flourished from about 15,000 years ago to 13,000 or 12,000 years ago. Elsewhere in South America, although the evidence is scanty, the tradition may be reflected in surface finds attributed to the Exacto complex of coastal Ecuador and in flake tools from the El Abra cave site in highland Colombia; the El Abra material is estimated to be 12,500 years old. Some of the rare worked flakes from the Chivateros "red zone" of coastal central Peru may also represent this tradition [see the article "Early Man in South America," by Edward P. Lanning and Thomas C. Patterson, beginning on page 62]. Not all the North American sites that may be representative of the tradition are adequately dated. Where dates are available, however, they are from 10,000 to more than 20,000 years earlier than their South American counterparts.

The third South American stage I call the Blade, Burin and Leaf-Point Tradition. At present it is very poorly represented at our highland sites, consisting only of the three artifacts from Zone *h* at Flea Cave. The tradition is far better defined, however, in the El Jobo phase of Venezuela, where double-ended points, blades, burins and corelike scrapers have been unearthed in association with the bones of extinct animals. The El Jobo phase is not adequately dated, but estimates suggest that its tool industry flourished roughly between 10,000 and 14,000 years ago. A small amount of material found at Laguna de Tagua Tagua in central Chile may also belong to this third tradition; carbon-14 analysis indicates that the Chilean material is about 11,300 years old. The precise duration of the Blade, Burin and Leaf-Point Tradition is not yet known. My guess is that it flourished from 13,000 or 12,000 years ago until 11,000 or 10,000 years ago. Like the preceding tradition, it is represented at sites in North America that, where age estimates exist, appear to be somewhat older.

Seen from the perspective of the Ayacucho valley, early man's final stage in South America, which I call the Specialized Bifacial Point Tradition, appears to have flourished from 11,000 or 10,000 years ago to 9,000 or 8,000 years ago. At Ayacucho the tradition is defined in the Huanta complex at Pepper Cave and in the later Puente complex there and elsewhere in the valley. It is characterized by bifacially flaked projectile points that evidently represent a specialization for big-game hunting. The tradition's other characteristic implements include specialized end scrapers and knives suited to skinning and butchering. Elsewhere in South America the tradition is represented at Fell's Cave in southern Chile, where a number of carbon-14 determinations suggest ages clustering around 11,000 years ago. Other artifacts probably in this tradition are those from a stratum overlying the red zone at Chivateros (which are evidently some 10,000 years old), from Toquepala Cave in southernmost Peru (which are about 9,500 years old) and from a number of other South American sites. Sites representative of the Specialized Bifacial Point Tradition in North America are almost too numerous to mention.

What might these four postulated traditions signify concerning man's arrival in the New World from Asia? Considering first the latest tradition—the Specialized Bifacial Point Tradition—we find a bewildering variety of complexes throughout North America at about the time when the late Paleo-Indian stage ends and the Archaic Indian stage begins. Nearly all the complexes have something in common, however: a specialization in bifacially flaked projectile points of extraordinary workmanship. I suggest that these specialized point industries all belong to a single tradition, that for the most part they represent local New World developments and that there is little use in trying to trace them to some ancestral assemblage on the far side of the Bering Strait. Carbon-14 analysis of charcoal from Fort Rock Cave in Oregon indicates that the earliest known specialized projectile points in the New World are some 13,200 years old. On the basis of this finding I propose that the Specialized Bifacial Point Tradition originated in the New World, beginning about 14,000 years ago in North America, and reached South America 3,000 to 4,000 years later.

North American artifacts related to the preceding tradition—the Blade, Burin and Leaf-Point Tradition—in South America include material from Tlapacoya and Hueyatlaco in Mexico, respectively some 23,000 and 22,000 years old, and material at least 15,000 years old from the lower levels of Wilson Butte Cave in Idaho. Some artifacts of the Cordilleran tradition in Canada and Alaska may also be related to the South American tradition. Again there apparently is a lag in cultural transmission from north to south that at its longest approaches 10,000 years. If there was a similar lag in transmission from Asia to North America, it is possible that the Blade, Burin and Leaf-Point Tradition originated with the Malt'a and Buret tool industries of the Lake Baikal region in eastern Siberia, which are between 15,000 and 30,000 years old.

As for the still older Flake and Bone Tool Tradition, adequately dated North American parallels are more difficult to find. Artifacts from Friesenhahn Cave in central Texas and some of the oldest material at Hueyatlaco show similarities to tools in the Ayacucho complex, but in spite of hints that these North American sites are very old the finds cannot be exactly dated. There are bone tools from a site near Old Crow in the Canadian Yukon that carbon-14 analysis shows to be from 23,000 to 28,000 years old. It is my guess that the Yukon artifacts belong to the Flake and Bone Tool Tradition, but many more arctic finds of the same kind are needed to change this guess into a strong presumption. A few flake tools from the site at Lewisville, Tex., may also be representative of the Ayacucho complex. Their estimated age of 38,000 years is appropriate. Figuring backward from the time the tradition appears to have arrived in South America, it would have flourished in North America between 25,000 and 40,000 years ago. Is it not possible that the Flake and Bone Tool Tradition is also an import from Asia? Perhaps it came from some Old World source such as the Shuitungkuo complex of northern China, reportedly between 40,000 and 60,000 years old.

We now come to the most difficult question, which concerns the oldest of the four traditions: the Core Tool Tradition. I wonder if any of my more conservative colleagues would care to venture the flat statement that no Core Tool Tradition parallel to the one in the Paccaicasa strata at Flea Cave will ever be unearthed in North America? If it is found, is it not likely that it will be from 40,000 to as much as 100,000 years old? To me it seems entirely possible that such a core-tool tradition in the New World, although one can only guess at it today, could be derived from the chopper and chopping-tool tradition of Asia, which is well over 50,000 years old. (An example of such a tradition is the Fenho industry of China.) I find there is much reason to believe that three of the four oldest cultural traditions in the New World can be derived from specific Old World predecessors. That seems to be the most significant implication of our findings at Ayacucho. However much this conclusion may be modified by future work, one thing is certain: our knowledge of early man in the New World is in its infancy. An almost untouched province of archaeology awaits exploration.

YEARS BEFORE PRESENT	SOUTH AMERICA	MEXICO CENTRAL AMERICA	U.S. AND CANADA	EASTERN ASIA	
9,000–16,000	PUENTE HUANTA; FELL'S CAVE (11,000); EL JOBO; TAGUA; TAGUA (11,30(; AYACUCHO; EL ABRA (12,500); AYACUCHO (14,150)	IZTAPAN LERMA; AJUREADO	PLAINVIEW; FOLSOM; CLOVIS; FORT ROCK CAVE (13,200); WILSON, BUTTE (15,000)		SPECIALIZED POINT TRADITION
16,000–30,000	PACCAICASA (19,600)	HUEYATLACO (21,850); TLAPACOYA (23,150); HUEYATLACO	FRIESENHAHN CAVE; OLD CROW (23,000-28,000)	MALT'A-BURET U.S.S.R.	BLADE, BURIN, LEAF-POINT TRADITION
30,000–60,000			LEWISVILLE (38,000); CALICO (?)	SHUITUNG-KUO, CHINA	FLAKE BONE TOOL TRADITION
60,000–75,000				FENHO, CHINA	CORE TOOL TRADITION

Scale: 9,000; 10,000; 11,000; 12,000; 13,000; 14,000; 15,000; 16,000; 20,000; 25,000; 30,000; 40,000; 50,000; 60,000; 75,000

OLD WORLD SOURCES of the three earliest prehistoric traditions in the New World are suggested in this chart. A fourth and more recent tradition, marked by the presence of finely made projectile points for big-game hunting, seems to have been indigenous rather than an Old World import. Although much work will be required to establish the validity of all three proposed relationships, the foremost weakness in the hypothesis at present is a lack in the Northern Hemisphere of well-dated examples of the core-tool tradition.

The Origins of New World Civilization

16

by Richard S. MacNeish
November 1964

In the Mexican valley of Tehuacán bands of hunters became urban craftsmen in the course of 12,000 years. Their achievement raises some new questions about the evolution of high cultures in general

Perhaps the most significant single occurrence in human history was the development of agriculture and animal husbandry. It has been assumed that this transition from food-gathering to food production took place between 10,000 and 16,000 years ago at a number of places in the highlands of the Middle East. In point of fact the archaeological evidence for the transition, particularly the evidence for domesticated plants, is extremely meager. It is nonetheless widely accepted that the transition represented a "Neolithic Revolution," in which abundant food, a sedentary way of life and an expanding population provided the foundations on which today's high civilizations are built.

The shift from food-gathering to food production did not, however, happen only once. Until comparatively recent times the Old World was for the most part isolated from the New World. Significant contact was confined to a largely one-way migration of culturally primitive Asiatic hunting bands across the Bering Strait. In spite of this almost total absence of traffic between the hemispheres the European adventurers who reached the New World in the 16th century encountered a series of cultures almost as advanced (except in metallurgy and pyrotechnics) and quite as barbarous as their own. Indeed, some of the civilizations from Mexico to Peru possessed a larger variety of domesticated plants than did their European conquerors and had made agricultural advances far beyond those of the Old World.

At some time, then, the transition from food-gathering to food production occurred in the New World as it had in the Old. In recent years one of the major problems for New World prehistorians has been to test the hypothesis of a Neolithic Revolution against native archaeological evidence and at the same time to document the American stage of man's initial domestication of plants (which remains almost unknown in both hemispheres).

The differences between the ways in which Old World and New World men achieved independence from the nomadic life of the hunter and gatherer are more striking than the similarities. The principal difference lies in the fact that the peoples of the Old World domesticated many animals and comparatively few plants, whereas in the New World the opposite was the case. The abundant and various herds that gave the peoples of Europe, Africa and Asia meat, milk, wool and beasts of burden were matched in the pre-Columbian New World only by a half-domesticated group of Andean cameloids: the llama, the alpaca and the vicuña. The Andean guinea pig can be considered an inferior equivalent of the Old World's domesticated rabbits and hares; elsewhere in the Americas the turkey was an equally inferior counterpart of the Eastern Hemisphere's many varieties of barnyard fowl. In both the Old World and the New, dogs presumably predated all other domestic animals; in both beekeepers harvested honey and wax. Beyond this the New World list of domestic animals dwindles to nothing. All the cultures of the Americas, high and low alike, depended on their hunters' skill for most of their animal produce: meat and hides, furs and feathers, teeth and claws.

In contrast, the American Indian domesticated a remarkable number of plants. Except for cotton, the "water bottle" gourd, the yam and possibly the coconut (which may have been domesticated independently in each hemisphere), the kinds of crops grown in the Old World and the New were quite different. Both the white and the sweet potato, cultivated in a number of varieties, were unique to the New World. For seasoning, in place of the pepper and mustard of the Old World, the peoples of the New World raised vanilla and at least two kinds of chili. For edible seeds they grew amaranth, chive, panic grass, sunflower, quinoa, apazote, chocolate, the peanut, the common bean and four other kinds of beans: lima, summer, tepary and jack.

In addition to potatoes the Indians cultivated other root crops, including manioc, oca and more than a dozen other South American plants. In place of the Old World melons, the related plants brought to domestication in the New World were the pumpkin, the

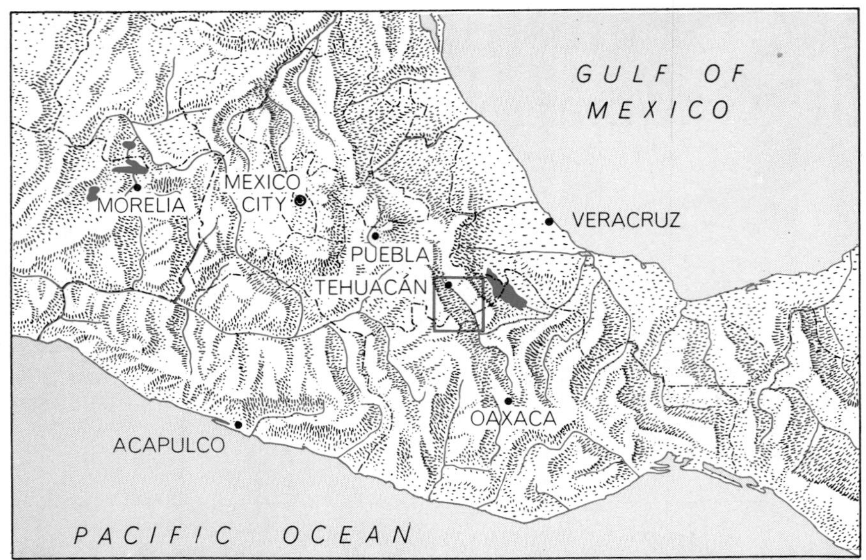

TEHUACÁN VALLEY is a narrow desert zone in the mountains on the boundary between the states of Puebla and Oaxaca. It is one of the three areas in southern Mexico selected during the search for early corn on the grounds of dryness (which helps to preserve ancient plant materials) and highland location (corn originally having been a wild highland grass).

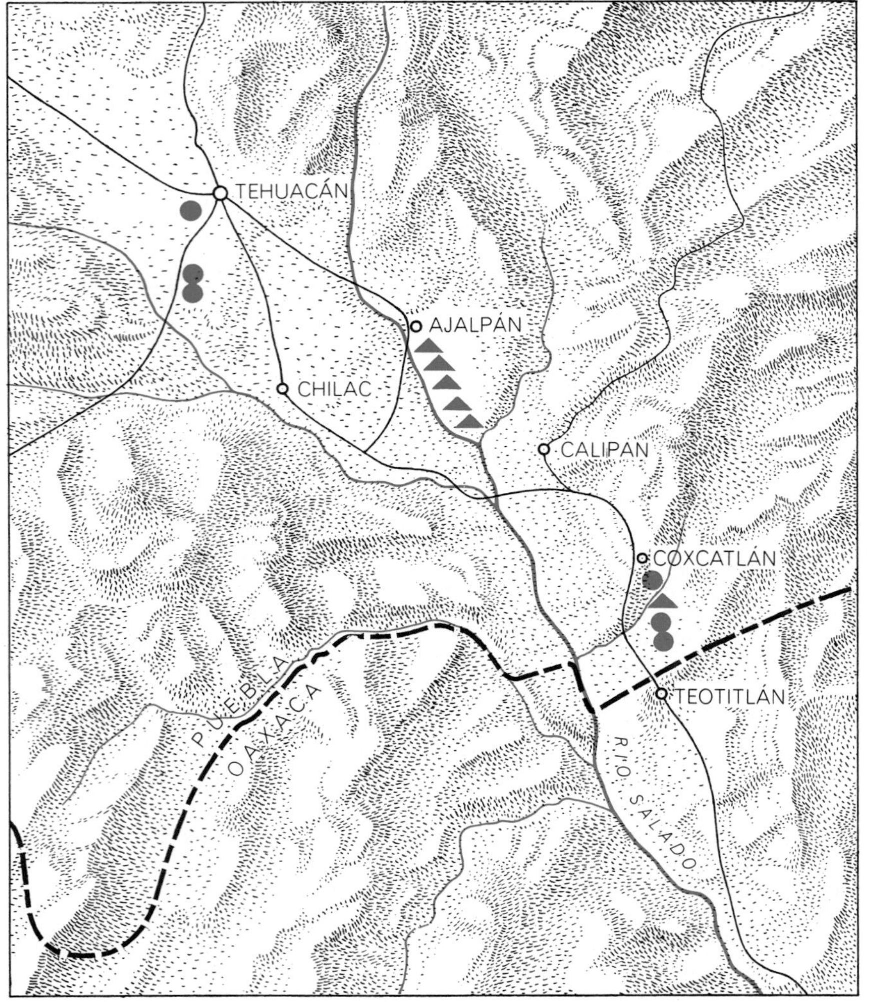

SIX CAVES (*dots*) and six open-air sites (*triangles*) have been investigated in detail by the author and his colleagues. Coxcatlán cave (*top dot at right*), where early corn was found in 1960, has the longest habitation record: from well before 7000 B.C. until A.D. 1500.

gourd, the chayote and three or four distinct species of what we call squash. Fruits brought under cultivation in the Americas included the tomato, avocado, pineapple, guava, elderberry and papaya. The pioneering use of tobacco—smoked in pipes, in the form of cigars and even in the form of cane cigarettes, some of which had one end stuffed with fibers to serve as a filter—must also be credited to the Indians.

Above all of these stood Indian corn, *Zea mays*, the only important wild grass in the New World to be transformed into a food grain as the peoples of the Old World had transformed their native grasses into wheat, barley, rye, oats and millet. From Chile to the valley of the St. Lawrence in Canada, one or another of 150 varieties of Indian corn was the staple diet of the pre-Columbian peoples. As a food grain or as fodder, corn remains the most important single crop in the Americas today (and the third largest in the world). Because of its dominant position in New World agriculture, prehistorians have long been confident that if they could find out when and where corn was first domesticated, they might also uncover the origins of New World civilization.

Until little more than a generation ago investigators of this question were beset by twin difficulties. First, research in both Central America and South America had failed to show that any New World high culture significantly predated the Christian era. Second, botanical studies of the varieties of corn and its wild relatives had led more to conflict than to clarity in regard to the domesticated plant's most probable wild predecessor [see "The Mystery of Corn," by Paul C. Mangelsdorf; SCIENTIFIC AMERICAN, July, 1950]. Today, thanks to close cooperation between botanists and archaeologists, both difficulties have almost vanished. At least one starting point for New World agricultural activity has been securely established as being between 5,000 and 9,000 years ago. At the same time botanical analysis of fossil corn ears, grains and pollen, together with plain dirt archaeology, have solved a number of the mysteries concerning the wild origin and domestic evolution of corn. What follows is a review of the recent developments that have done so much to increase our understanding of this key period in New World prehistory.

The interest of botanists in the history of corn is largely practical: they study the genetics of corn in order to produce improved hybrids. After the wild ancestors of corn had been sought for nearly a century the search had narrowed to two tassel-bearing New World grasses—teosinte and *Tripsacum*—that had features resembling the domesticated plant. On the basis of crossbreeding experiments and other genetic studies, however, Paul C. Mangelsdorf of Harvard University and other investigators concluded in the 1940's that neither of these plants could be the original ancestor of corn. Instead teosinte appeared to be the product of the accidental crossbreeding of true corn and *Tripsacum*. Mangelsdorf advanced the hypothesis that the wild progenitor of corn was none other than corn itself—probably a popcorn with its kernels encased in pods.

Between 1948 and 1960 a number of discoveries proved Mangelsdorf's contention to be correct. I shall present these discoveries not in their strict chronological order but rather in their order of importance. First in importance, then, were analyses of pollen found in "cores" obtained in 1953 by drilling into the lake beds on which Mexico City is built. At levels that were estimated to be about 80,000 years old—perhaps 50,000 years older than the earliest known human remains in the New World—were found grains of corn pollen. There could be no doubt that the pollen was from wild corn, and thus two aspects of the ancestry of corn were clarified. First, a form of wild corn has been in existence for 80,000 years, so that corn can indeed be descended from itself. Second, wild corn had flourished in the highlands of Mexico. As related archaeological discoveries will make plain, this geographical fact helped to narrow the potential range—from the southwestern U.S. to Peru—within which corn was probably first domesticated.

The rest of the key discoveries, involving the close cooperation of archaeologist and botanist, all belong to the realm of paleobotany. In the summer of 1948, for example, Herbert Dick, a graduate student in anthropology who had been working with Mangelsdorf, explored a dry rock-shelter in New Mexico called Bat Cave. Digging down through six feet of accumulated deposits, he and his colleagues found numerous remains of ancient corn, culminating in some tiny corncobs at the lowest level. Carbon-14 dating indicated that these cobs were between 4,000 and 5,000 years old. A few months later, exploring the La Perra cave in the state of Tamaulipas far to the north of Mexico City, I found similar corncobs that proved to be about 4,500 years old. The oldest cobs at both sites came close to fitting the description Mangelsdorf had given of a hypothetical ancestor of the pod-popcorn type. The cobs, however, were clearly those of domesticated corn.

These two finds provided the basis for intensified archaeological efforts to find sites where the first evidences of corn would be even older. The logic was simple: A site old enough should have a level of wild corn remains older than the most ancient domesticated cobs. I continued my explorations near the La Perra cave and excavated a number of other sites in northeastern Mexico. In them I found more samples of ancient corn, but they were no older than those that had already been discovered. Robert Lister, another of Mangelsdorf's coworkers, also found primitive corn in a cave called Swallow's Nest in the Mexican state of Chihuahua, northwest of where I was working, but his finds were no older than mine.

If nothing older than domesticated corn of about 3000 B.C. could be found to the north of Mexico City, it seemed logical to try to the south. In 1958 I went off to look for dry caves and early corn in Guatemala and Honduras. The 1958 diggings produced nothing useful, so in 1959 I moved northward into Chiapas, Mexico's southernmost state. There were no corncobs to be found,

EXCAVATION of Coxcatlán cave required the removal of one-meter squares of cave floor over an area 25 meters long by six meters wide until bedrock was reached at a depth of almost five meters. In this way 28 occupation levels, attributable to seven distinctive culture phases, were discovered. Inhabitants of the three lowest levels lived by hunting and by collecting wild-plant foods.

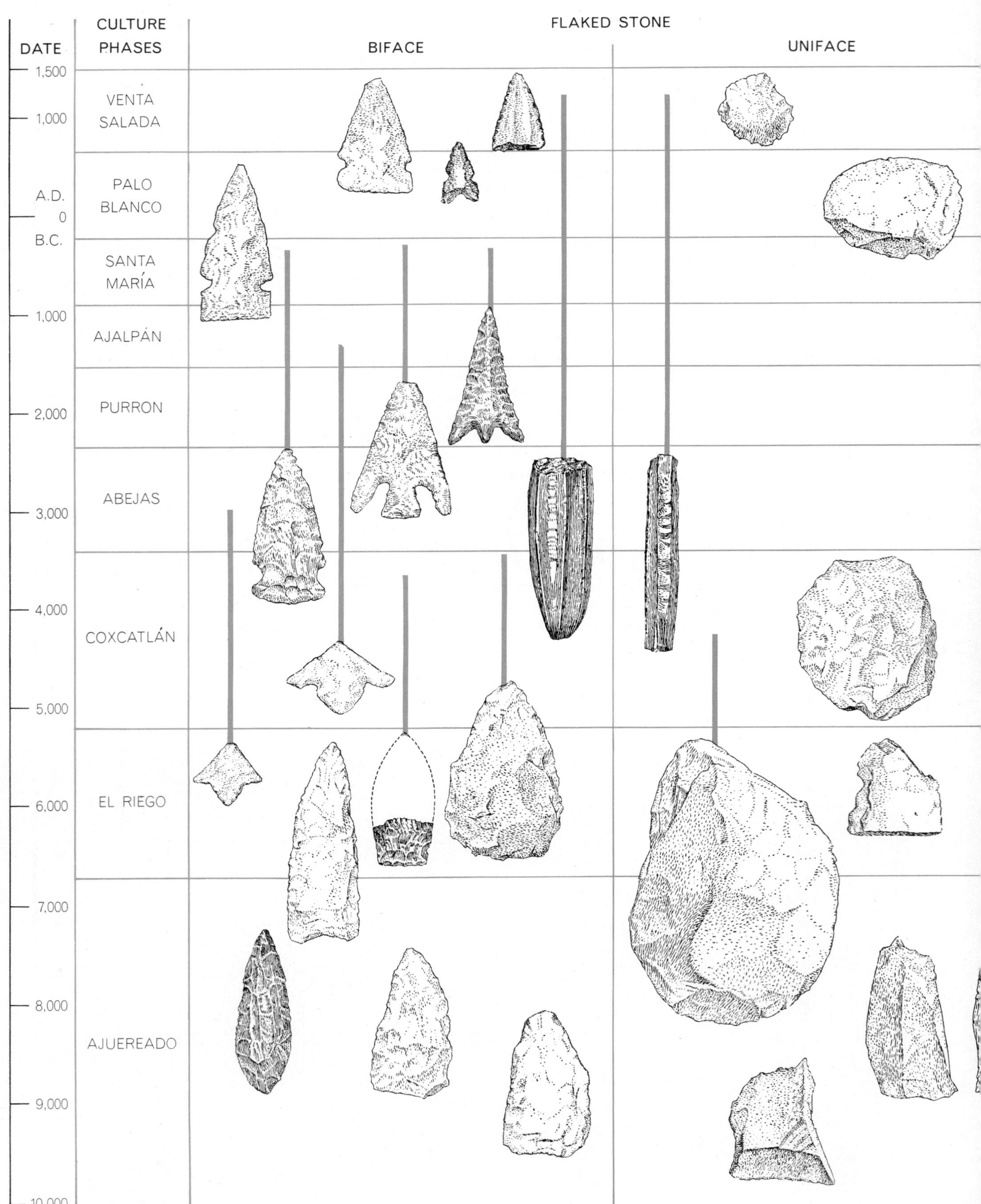

STONE ARTIFACTS from various Tehuacán sites are arrayed in two major categories: those shaped by chipping and flaking (*left*) and those shaped by grinding and pecking (*right*). Implements that have been chipped on one face only are separated from those that show bifacial workmanship; both groups are reproduced at half their natural size. The ground stone objects are not drawn to a common scale. The horizontal lines define the nine culture phases thus far distinguished in the valley. Vertical lines (*color*) indicate the extent to which the related artifact is known in cultures other than the one in which it is placed. At Tehuacán the evolution of civilization failed to follow the classic pattern established by the Neolithic Revolution in the Old World. For instance, the mortars,

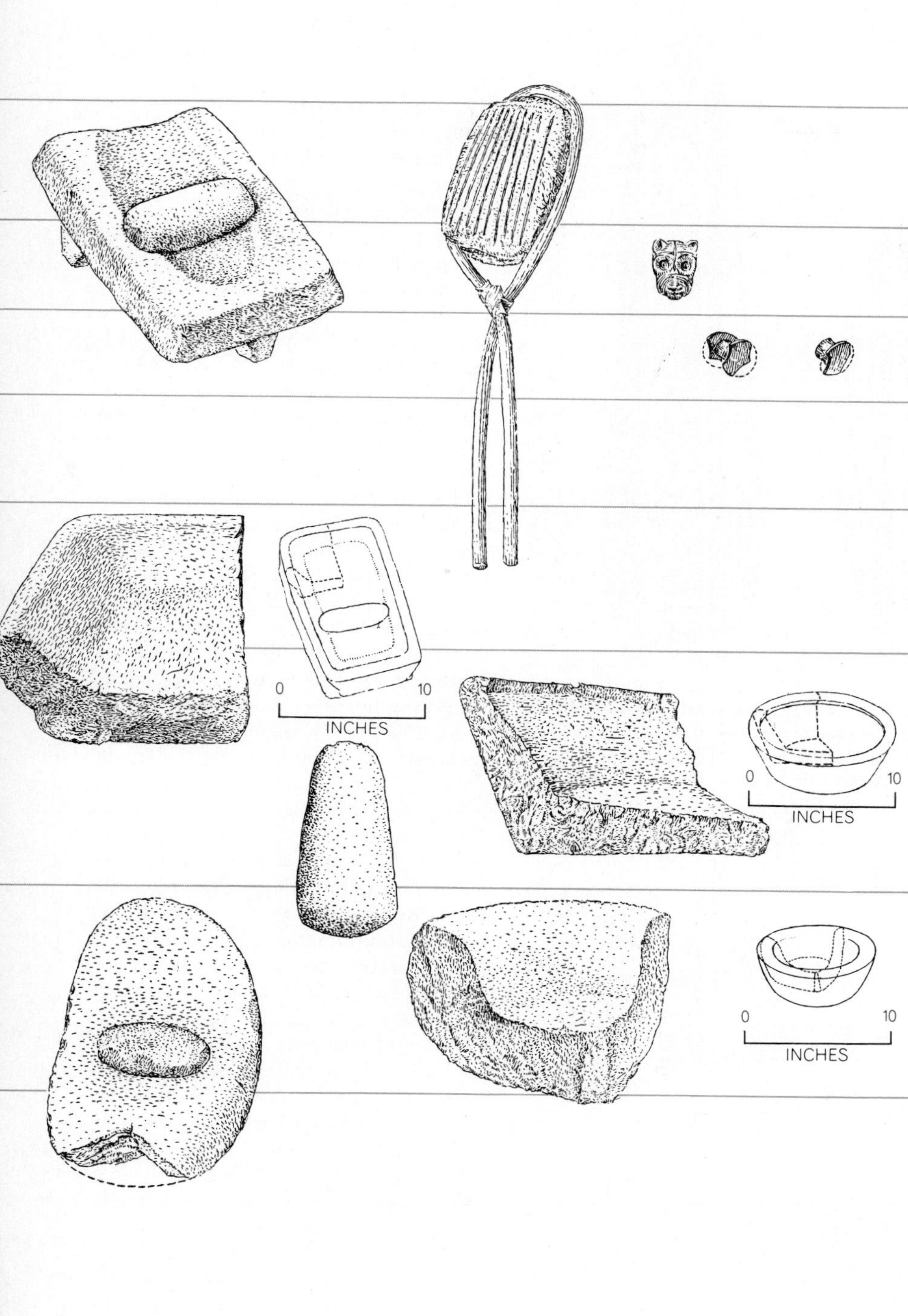

pestles and other ground stone implements that first appear in the El Riego culture phase antedate the first domestication of corn by 1,500 years or more. Not until the Abejas phase, nearly 2,000 years later (marked by sizable obsidian cores and blades and by grinding implements that closely resemble the modern mano and metate), do the earliest village sites appear. More than 1,000 years later, in the Ajalpán phase, earplugs for personal adornment occur. The grooved, withe-bound stone near the top is a pounder for making bark cloth.

but one cave yielded corn pollen that also dated only to about 3000 B.C. The clues provided by paleobotany now appeared plain. Both to the north of Mexico City and in Mexico City itself (as indicated by the pollen of domesticated corn in the upper levels of the drill cores) the oldest evidence of domesticated corn was no more ancient than about 3000 B.C. Well to the south of Mexico City the oldest date was the same. The area that called for further search should therefore lie south of Mexico City but north of Chiapas.

Two additional considerations enabled me to narrow the area of search even more. First, experience had shown that dry locations offered the best chance of finding preserved specimens of corn. Second, the genetic studies of Mangelsdorf and other investigators indicated that wild corn was originally a highland grass, very possibly able to survive the rigorous climate of highland desert areas. Poring over the map of southern Mexico, I singled out three large highland desert areas: one in the southern part of the state of Oaxaca, one in Guerrero and one in southern Puebla.

Oaxaca yielded nothing of interest, so I moved on to Puebla to explore a dry highland valley known as Tehuacán. My local guides and I scrambled in and out of 38 caves and finally struck pay dirt in the 39th. This was a small rock-shelter near the village of Coxcatlán in the southern part of the valley of Tehuacán. On February 21, 1960, we dug up six corncobs, three of which looked more primitive and older than any I had seen before. Analysis in the carbon-14 laboratory at the University of Michigan confirmed my guess by dating these cobs as 5,600 years old—a good 500 years older than any yet found in the New World.

With this find the time seemed ripe for a large-scale, systematic search. If we had indeed arrived at a place where corn had been domesticated and New World civilization had first stirred, the closing stages of the search would require the special knowledge of many experts. Our primary need was to obtain the sponsorship of an institution interested and experienced in such research, and we were fortunate enough to enlist exactly the right sponsor: the Robert S. Peabody Foundation for Archaeology of Andover, Mass. Funds for the project were supplied by the National Science Foundation and by the agricultural branch of the Rockefeller

EVOLUTION OF CORN at Tehuacán starts (*far left*) with a fragmentary cob of wild corn of 5000 B.C. date. Next (*left to right*) are an early domesticated cob of 4000 B.C., an early hybrid variety of 3000 B.C. and an early variety of modern corn of 1000 B.C. Last (*far right*) is an entirely modern cob of the time of Christ. All are shown four-fifths of natural size.

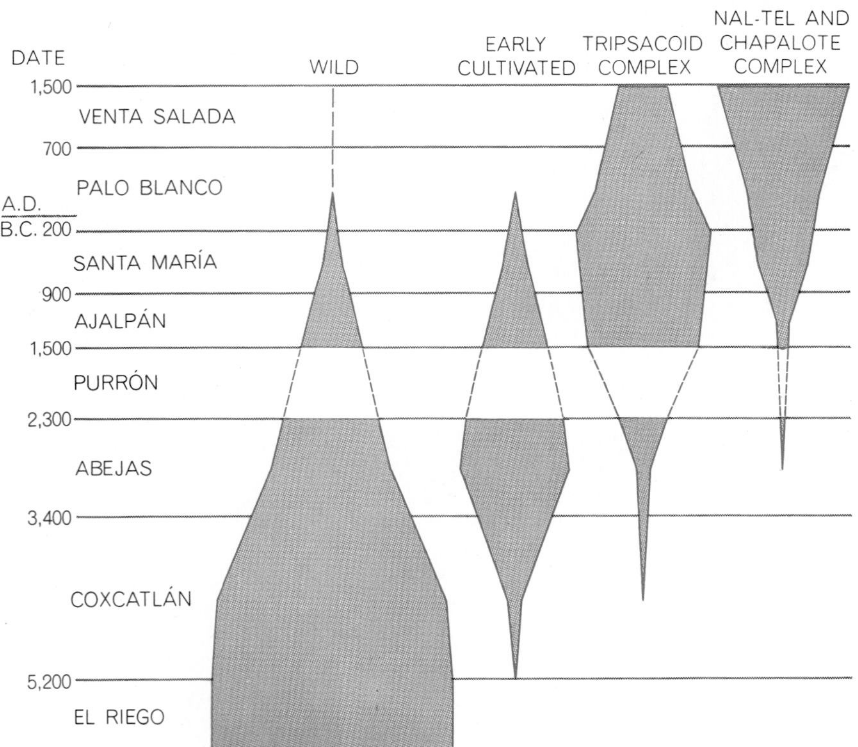

MAIN VARIETIES OF CORN changed in their relative abundance at Tehuacán between the time of initial cultivation during the Coxcatlán culture phase and the arrival of the conquistadors. Abundant at first, wild corn had become virtually extinct by the start of the Christian era, as had the early cultivated (but not hybridized) varieties. Thereafter the hybrids of the tripsacoid complex (produced by interbreeding wild corn with introduced varieties of corn-*Tripsacum* or corn-teosinte hybrids) were steadily replaced by two still extant types of corn, Nal-Tel and Chapalote. Minor varieties of late corn are not shown.

Foundation in Mexico, which is particularly interested in the origins of corn. The project eventually engaged nearly 50 experts in many specialties, not only archaeology and botany (including experts on many plants other than corn) but also zoology, geography, geology, ecology, genetics, ethnology and other disciplines.

The Coxcatlán cave, where the intensive new hunt had begun, turned out to be our richest dig. Working downward, we found that the cave had 28 separate occupation levels, the earliest of which may date to about 10,000 B.C. This remarkably long sequence has one major interruption: the period between 2300 B.C. and 900 B.C. The time from 900 B.C. to A.D. 1500, however, is represented by seven occupation levels. In combination with our findings in the Purrón cave, which contains 25 floors that date from about 7000 B.C. to 500 B.C., we have an almost continuous record (the longest interruption is less than 500 years) of nearly 12,000 years of prehistory. This is by far the longest record for any New World area.

All together we undertook major excavations at 12 sites in the valley of Tehuacán [*see bottom illustration on page 156*]. Of these only five caves—Coxcatlán, Purrón, San Marcos, Tecorral and El Riego East—contained remains of ancient corn. But these and the other stratified sites gave us a wealth of additional information about the people who inhabited the valley over a span of 12,000 years. In four seasons of digging, from 1961 through 1964, we reaped a vast archaeological harvest. This includes nearly a million individual remains of human activity, more than 1,000 animal bones (including those of extinct antelopes and horses), 80,000 individual wild-plant remains and some 25,000 specimens of corn. The artifacts arrange themselves into significant sequences of stone tools, textiles and pottery. They provide an almost continuous picture of the rise of civilization in the valley of Tehuacán. From the valley's geology, from the shells of its land snails, from the pollen and other remains of its plants and from a variety of other relics our group of specialists has traced the changes in climate, physical environment and plant and animal life that took place during the 12,000 years. They have even been able to tell (from the kinds of plant remains in various occupation levels) at what seasons of the year many of the floors in the caves were occupied.

Outstanding among our many finds was a collection of minuscule corncobs that we tenderly extracted from the lowest of five occupation levels at the San Marcos cave. They were only about 20 millimeters long, no bigger than the filter tip of a cigarette [*see top illustration on opposite page*], but under a magnifying lens one could see that they were indeed miniature ears of corn, with sockets that had once contained kernels enclosed in pods. These cobs proved to be some 7,000 years old. Mangelsdorf is convinced that this must be wild corn—the original parent from which modern corn is descended.

Cultivated corn, of course, cannot survive without man's intervention; the dozens of seeds on each cob are enveloped by a tough, thick husk that prevents them from scattering. Mangelsdorf has concluded that corn's wild progenitor probably consisted of a single seed spike on the stalk, with a few pod-covered ovules arrayed on the spike and a pollen-bearing tassel attached to the spike's end [*see bottom illustration at right*]. The most primitive cobs we unearthed in the valley of Tehuacán fulfilled these specifications. Each had the stump of a tassel at the end, each had borne kernels of the pod-popcorn type and each had been covered with only a light husk consisting of two leaves. These characteristics would have allowed the plant to disperse its seeds at maturity; the pods would then have protected the seeds until conditions were appropriate for germination.

The people of the valley of Tehuacán lived for thousands of years as collectors of wild vegetable and animal foods before they made their first timid efforts as agriculturists. It would therefore be foolhardy to suggest that the inhabitants of this arid highland pocket of Mexico were the first or the only people in the Western Hemisphere to bring wild corn under cultivation. On the contrary, the New World's invention of agriculture will probably prove to be geographically fragmented. What can be said for the people of Tehuacán is that they are the first whose evolution from primitive food collectors to civilized agriculturists has been traced in detail. As yet we have no such complete story either for the Old World or for other parts of the New World. This story is as follows.

From a hazy beginning some 12,000 years ago until about 7000 B.C. the people of Tehuacán were few in number. They wandered the valley from season to season in search of jackrabbits, rats, birds, turtles and other small animals, as well as such plant foods as be-

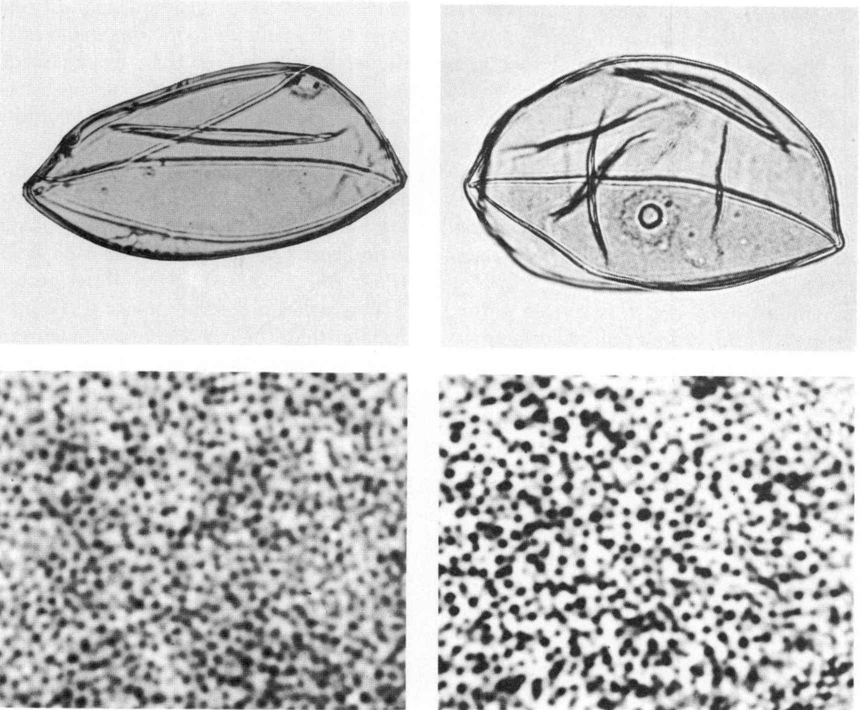

ANTIQUITY OF CORN in the New World was conclusively demonstrated when grains of pollen were found in drilling cores taken from Mexico City lake-bottom strata estimated to be 80,000 years old. Top two photographs (*magnification 435 diameters*) compare the ancient corn pollen (*left*) with modern pollen (*right*). Lower photographs (*magnification 4,500 diameters*) reveal similar ancient (*left*) and modern (*right*) pollen surface markings. The analysis and photographs are the work of Elso S. Barghoorn of Harvard University.

THREE NEW WORLD GRASSES are involved in the history of domesticated corn. Wild corn (*reconstruction at left*) was a pod-pop variety in which the male efflorescence grew from the end of the cob. Teosinte (*center*) and *Tripsacum* (*right*) are corn relatives that readily hybridized with wild and cultivated corn. Modern corn came from such crosses.

came available at different times of the year. Only occasionally did they manage to kill one of the now extinct species of horses and antelopes whose bones mark the lowest cave strata. These people used only a few simple implements of flaked stone: leaf-shaped projectile points, scrapers and engraving tools. We have named this earliest culture period the Ajuereado phase [*see illustration on pages 158 and 159*].

Around 6700 B.C. this simple pattern changed and a new phase—which we have named the El Riego culture from the cave where its first evidences appear—came into being. From then until about 5000 B.C. the people shifted from being predominantly trappers and hunters to being predominantly collectors of plant foods. Most of the plants they collected were wild, but they had domesticated squashes (starting with the species *Cucurbita mixta*) and avocados, and they also ate wild varieties of beans, amaranth and chili peppers. Among the flaked-stone implements, choppers appear. Entirely new kinds of stone tools—grinders, mortars, pestles and pounders of polished stone—are found in large numbers. During the growing season some families evidently gathered in temporary settlements, but these groups broke up into one-family bands during the leaner periods of the year. A number of burials dating from this culture phase hint at the possibility of part-time priests or witch doctors who directed the ceremonies involving the dead. The El Riego culture, however, had no corn.

By about 5000 B.C. a new phase, which we call the Coxcatlán culture, had evolved. In this period only 10 percent of the valley's foodstuffs came from domestication rather than from collecting, hunting or trapping, but the list of domesticated plants is long. It includes corn, the water-bottle gourd, two species of squash, the amaranth, black and white zapotes, the tepary bean (*Phaseolus acutifolius*), the jack bean (*Canavalia ensiformis*), probably the common bean (*Phaseolus vulgaris*) and chili peppers.

Coxcatlán projectile points tend to be smaller than their predecessors; scrapers and choppers, however, remain much the same. The polished stone implements include forerunners of the classic New World roller-and-stone device for grinding grain: the mano and metate. There was evidently enough surplus energy among the people to allow the laborious hollowing out of stone water jugs and bowls.

It was in the phase following the Coxcatlán that the people of Tehuacán made the fundamental shift. By about 3400 B.C. the food provided by agriculture rose to about 30 percent of the total, domesticated animals (starting with the dog) made their appearance, and the people formed their first fixed settlements—small pit-house villages. By this stage (which we call the Abejas culture) they lived at a subsistence level that can be regarded as a foundation for the beginning of civilization. In about 2300 B.C. this gave way to the Purrón culture, marked by the cultivation of more hybridized types of corn and the manufacture of pottery.

Thereafter the pace of civilization in the valley speeded up greatly. The descendants of the Purrón people developed a culture (called Ajalpán) that from about 1500 B.C. on involved a more complex village life, refinements of pottery and more elaborate ceremonialism, including the development of a figurine cult, perhaps representing family gods. This culture led in turn to an even more sophisticated one (which we call Santa María) that started about 850 B.C. Taking advantage of the valley's streams, the Santa María peoples of Tehuacán began to grow their hybrid corn in irrigated fields. Our surveys indicate a sharp rise in population. Temple mounds were built, and artifacts show signs of numerous contacts with cultures outside the valley. The Tehuacán culture in this period seems to have been strongly influenced by that of the Olmec people who lived to the southeast along the coast of Veracruz.

By about 200 B.C. the outside influence on Tehuacán affairs shifted from that of the Olmec of the east coast to that of Monte Alban to the south and west. The valley now had large irrigation projects and substantial hilltop ceremonial centers surrounded by villages. In this Palo Blanco phase some of the population proceeded to full-time specialization in various occupations, including the development of a salt industry. New domesticated food products appeared—the turkey, the tomato, the peanut and the guava. In the next period—Venta Salada, starting about A.D. 700—Monte Alban influences gave way to the influence of the Mixtecs. This period saw the rise of true

COXCATLÁN CAVE BURIAL, dating to about A.D. 100, contained the extended body of an adolescent American Indian, wrapped in a pair of cotton blankets with brightly colored stripes. This bundle in turn rested on sticks and the whole was wrapped in bark cloth.

cities in the valley, of an agricultural system that provided some 85 percent of the total food supply, of trade and commerce, a standing army, large-scale irrigation projects and a complex religion. Finally, just before the Spanish Conquest, the Aztecs took over from the Mixtecs.

Our archaeological study of the valley of Tehuacán, carried forward in collaboration with workers in so many other disciplines, has been gratifyingly productive. Not only have we documented one example of the origin of domesticated corn but also comparative studies of other domesticated plants have indicated that there were multiple centers of plant domestication in the Americas. At least for the moment we have at Tehuacán not only evidence of the earliest village life in the New World but also the first (and worst) pottery in Mexico and a fairly large sample of skeletons of some of the earliest Indians yet known.

Even more important is the fact that we at last have one New World example of the development of a culture from savagery to civilization. Preliminary analysis of the Tehuacán materials indicate that the traditional hypothesis about the evolution of high cultures may have to be reexamined and modified. In southern Mexico many of the characteristic elements of the Old World's Neolithic Revolution fail to appear suddenly in the form of a new culture complex or a revolutionized way of life. For example, tools of ground (rather than chipped) stone first occur at Tehuacán about 6700 B.C., and plant domestication begins at least by 5000 B.C. The other classic elements of the Old World Neolithic, however, are slow to appear. Villages are not found until around 3000 B.C., nor pottery until around 2300 B.C., and a sudden increase in population is delayed until 500 B.C. Reviewing this record, I think more in terms of Neolithic "evolution" than "revolution."

Our preliminary researches at Tehuacán suggest rich fields for further exploration. There is need not only for detailed investigations of the domestication and development of other New World food plants but also for attempts to obtain similar data for the Old World. Then—perhaps most challenging of all—there is the need for comparative studies of the similarities and differences between evolving cultures in the Old World and the New to determine the hows and whys of the rise of civilization itself.

SOPHISTICATED FIGURINE of painted pottery is one example of the artistic capacity of Tehuacán village craftsmen. This specimen, 2,900 years old, shows Olmec influences.

17

The History of a Peruvian Valley

by James A. Ford
August 1954

For 4,500 years the tides of civilization and conquest have flowed across the Virú Valley. An account of how its history was reconstructed by an intensive archaeological expedition

From the foothills of the high Andes facing the coast of northern Peru a river named Virú flows down a gently sloping valley into the Pacific Ocean. This little valley, some 20 miles long and nine miles wide at its broadest, where it fronts the sea, is typical of the many valleys that slice across the narrow coastal plain between the mountains and the sea in northern Peru. In that otherwise arid land, the small irrigated valleys have been oases of human settlement for thousands of years. Each valley has its own life and history—a history perhaps as old as the settlements where civilization began in the ancient Mediterranean world.

Today the Virú Valley is a rather conventional farming community of 8,000 people with a mixed Indian and Spanish culture, now beginning to be affected by the impact of the jeep and the juke box. Only some half-buried ruins suggest its more powerful and abundant past. The Virú Valley, indeed, was once as rich and fertile as the valley of the ancient Nile—a proud builder of great temples, fortifications and the wealth of empire.

Partly because of the glamor of the Incas, partly because of the gold buried in its prehistoric tombs, Peru has been a diggers' paradise ever since the Spanish adventurers discovered it. In our century serious archaeologists have collected and carefully studied Peruvian artifacts going back for thousands of

BRICK FORTIFICATION towers above the floor of the Virú Valley. Known as the Castillo de Tomaval, this imposing adobe structure was built during the Gallinazo period of about A.D. 100 to 800 and used during the Mochica period of about A.D. 800 to 1000.

years. But the finds were not systematically related to one another; some of the interpretations of them were clearly wrong. Several years ago the time seemed ripe to attempt an orderly retracing of Peru's prehistory. To organize and relate the known facts and to fill gaps in the history, a group of archaeologists decided to make a concentrated investigation of the history of a single valley, and they chose to study the Virú.

VIRU RIVER flows into the sea in northern Peru. Chan Chan was the Chimu capital; Wari, the Tiahuanaco; Cuzco, the Inca. The Mochica capital was probably in the Chicama Valley.

The day when the archaeologist, preferably equipped with beard and beautiful daughter, set off on solo expeditions has long passed. Nowadays archaeologists almost always work in teams, usually under the direction of an institution. Our group was a team of specialists from various institutions organized on a cooperative basis. We undertook to carry out in one season a program which would have taken a single investigator many years. Ten scientists made up our party—seven archaeologists, two ethnologists and a geographer. Coming together from eight different institutions, they formed an expedition under the auspices of the Institute of Andean Research, a scientists' "holding company" set up many years ago for just such cooperative projects.

The geographer was Webster McBryde of the Smithsonian Institution; the ethnologists were Allan R. Holmberg of Cornell University and Jorge C. Muelle of the Institute of Ethnology in Lima; and the archaeologists were Junius B. Bird of the American Museum of Natural History, William Duncan Strong of Columbia University, Clifford Evans, Jr. (now of the U. S. National Museum), Donald Collier of the Chicago Natural History Museum, Wendell C. Bennett of Yale University, Gordon R. Willey, then of the Smithsonian Institution, and the writer.

The group divided the investigation into a number of assignments—the geography of the valley and present use of the land, the culture of the present inhabitants, the various periods in the valley's history, the evolution of its pottery, the ancient building sites and so on. During its single season of field work (1946) the survey party systematically examined more than 300 sites.

The several investigators have already published separate reports on their work; this article will outline the integrated history of the valley as we were able to reconstruct it from the artifacts and the remains of ancient structures.

Irrigation by the river water is the dominant fact of life in the Virú Valley; it was responsible for the beginnings of social organization among the early peoples and still shapes the community pattern today. The upper part of the valley, which has first chance at the precious irrigation water, is occupied by a family-owned sugar plantation, Hacienda Tomaval. The central part is a community of small farms, centering in a village named Virú. The lower part near the sea, receiving the smallest share of irrigation water, is the property of a corporation-owned plantation, Hacienda Carmelo, which is worked by sharecroppers who raise corn and cattle.

Of the valley's earliest history little evidence remains. Near the sea were found three sites of human habitation which apparently belong to a period beginning about 2500 B.C. In the small mounds constituting these sites are curious underground houses with mud-plastered walls. The evidence suggests that no more than a few hundred people inhabited the valley at that time. Away from the shore the valley floor probably was covered with an almost impenetrable forest of thorn bush.

From finds in a well-preserved site of the same period in another valley north of the Virú, it was possible to learn more about these early Peruvians. They were already practicing agriculture, growing cotton, gourds, squash, beans and aji pepper. They wove cotton fabrics and made baskets; they caught fish and other food in the sea; they cooked with stones heated in the fire; they made crude stone hand axes and knives. But as yet they had no pottery.

Pottery first appears in the Virú Val-

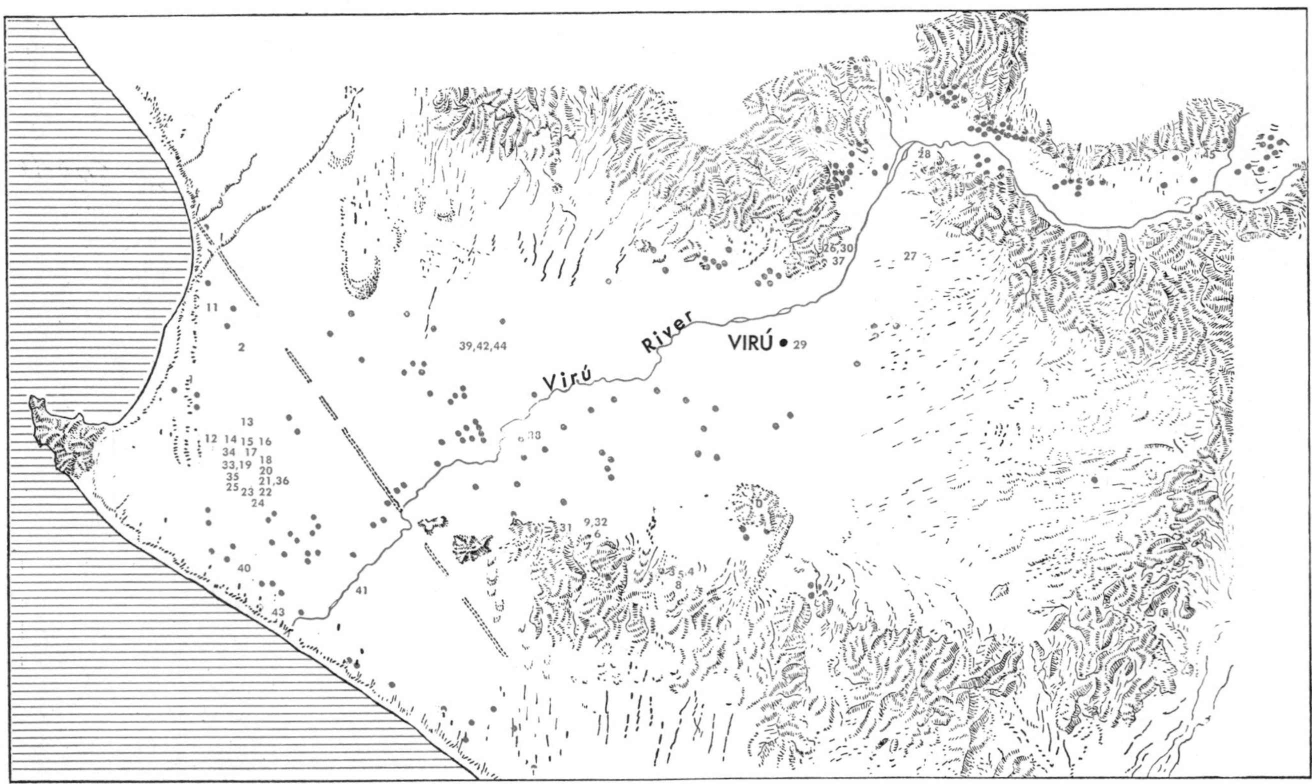

VIRU VALLEY is 20 miles long and nine miles wide at its broadest. The sites investigated by the expedition are indicated by colored dots. The principal sites are labeled with numbers. Number 1 is Huaca Prieta, a pre-ceramic refuse mound and cemetery. Numbers 2 to 7 are Guañape middens and rock-walled houses. Numbers 8 to 11 embrace a Puerto Moorin village, a midden with an adobe building and a midden with a cemetery. Number 10 is the Bitin hilltop fortress. Numbers 12 to 28 are the chief Gallinazo sites, including middens, dwelling construction mounds, pyramids, refuse mounds and cemeteries. Number 26 is the Castillo de Tomaval (*see page 164*). Number 28 is the Castillo de Sarraque, another vast adobe fortress complex. Numbers 29 to 33 are Mochica castillos and cemeteries. Number 30 denotes the Mochica habitation of the Castillo de Tomaval. Number 31 is the main Mochica complex called Castillo de Huancaco; it is a pyramid-dwelling-administrative center with fortifications. Number 32 denotes Mochica burials in Puerto Moorin structures. Number 33 indicates the Mochica habitation of a Gallinazo pyramid. Numbers 34 to 39 are Tiahuanaco middens, cemeteries and compounds. Numbers 38 and 39 are great rectangular enclosures. Numbers 40 to 42 are Chimu compounds. Number 42 indicates the Chimu phase at 39, a compound showing vestiges of all the ceramic periods of the valley. Numbers 43 to 45 are Inca compounds. Number 44 is the Inca phase at compound 39. The dotted lines mark the course of the Tiahuanaco highway.

ley about 1200 B.C. At first it was a plain, undecorated ware of simple shapes; later it took on the more definite character of a culture known as the Chavín complex, which was spreading over all of northern Peru, probably from Central America. The central element of the Chavín complex seems to have been a religious cult featuring a ferocious-looking cat-god with prominently displayed incisor teeth. This demon was to haunt the cosmology of the ancient Peruvians for the next 2,000 years; it is elaborately depicted on their ceramics and textiles over that whole period.

The Chavín influence introduced into the Virú Valley mirrors, finger rings, elaborately carved stone objects, gold-working techniques and the custom of placing rich offerings with the bodies of the dead. It also brought an important economic asset—corn. Doubtless it was this improved food supply that gave rise to the first villages in the valley by 500 B.C. They consisted of 20 to 30 single- or two-room houses, built of stone and handmade adobe. The rooms were small and frequently had rounded corners.

The fact that most of the dwellings and communities were on the flanks of the valley, several miles away from the river, strongly suggests that the people of Virú had already begun to establish an irrigation system. In the next period, ending about A.D. 1, the irrigation system was further developed and agriculture became the economic mainstay. This was a time of rapid increase in population, as is shown by the expansion in the number and size of dwellings. Consisting of small rectangular rooms, built adjacent to one another in an unplanned fashion, the new dwellings were probably occupied by extended families or kin groups. The communities spread over the wide floor of the lower valley.

Along with this marked increase in population came the first signs of broader social organization, at least for purposes of defense. Stone-walled forts were constructed on the crests of six prominent hills along the sides of the valley. A typical one stands atop a steep-sided hill some 800 feet above the valley floor. Within the stone wall encircling the hill's almost flat top, which is about 1,200 feet long and 300 feet wide, are three platform mounds that were the sites of pyramidal temples. They show that the organization of the community had a religious as well as a military basis. The dwellings in the valley during this period tended to cluster around the forts, suggesting that the inhabitants fled to these strong points in times of danger.

In the next period, from A.D. 1 to 800, the Virú culture reached its peak. Its irrigation system was fully developed; its population rose to at least 25,000; the entire valley was brought under the control of a central government. Four great "castillos" were built at strategic localities on rocky spurs in the upper part of the valley. Each castillo consisted of a large pyramidal mound with large adjoining rooms, the whole built of sun-dried bricks. In the lower part of the valley were about a dozen similar large brick pyramids. Along the edge of the cultivated lands were adobe and rock walls to aid in repelling invaders. The Virueños no longer had to flee to distant hilltop forts for protection.

The administrative and population center appears to have been in the open lower part of the valley. Around a great brick pyramid over 80 feet high are clustered the ruins of other pyramids and enormous apartment houses, honeycombed with small, brick-walled rooms. Apparently the rooms were entered from above, for few have doors. Evidently most of the citizens of this city did not live in luxury. There were many other settlements and individual houses scattered throughout the valley. Stone was employed for construction where it was readily available.

This time of the valley's heyday is known as the Gallinazo period, after the name given to its central city. Judging from the amazing amount of labor that was expended on public works, the valley must have been very strictly organized and its inhabitants had little leisure. It is hard to see how their religion could have been much consolation to these over-organized people, for it featured a particularly ferocious-looking version of the cat demon. But it apparently offered the promise of a pleasanter afterlife, for quantities of textiles, gold ornaments and pottery were buried with the dead in extensive cemeteries located outside the irrigated areas. The burial pottery was a fine, specially made ceremonial ware, much superior to the ordinary cooking and eating pots found in the houses. It probably was made by a corps of priest-craftsmen.

During the same period a development similar to that in the Virú Valley was also taking place in the more than 20 other parallel river valleys along the desert coast of Peru [see the article "The Lost Cities of Peru," by Richard P. Schaedel, beginning on page 26]. By A.D. 800 they constituted a series of valley states, insulated from one another by the intervening stretches of barren desert. There were local differences in their religions, pottery, architecture and textiles.

This situation of independent neighboring states is quite familiar to students of the history of Neolithic and Bronze Age cultures in the Old World. And, just as in the Mediterranean and in

BURIAL TREASURE of a Mochica dignitary is one of few such deposits which escaped looting. Among the objects are carved staffs and pottery adorned with the portraits of kings.

Mesopotamia, waves of conquest soon began to consolidate the separate communities on the Peruvian coast. From the Chicama Valley, 50 miles north of the Virú, a warrior tribe which has been named the Mochica conquered six of the valleys, among them Virú.

Mochica administrators moved into Virú and began to build a large building at the foot of a mountain mass on the southern edge of the valley. This structure, now called Huancaco, has a brick pyramid at one end and a series of large rooms bounded by massive brick walls extending for 800 feet along the mountain. While its architecture and the sun-dried bricks of which the building is constructed are of the Mochica type, there is a hint that the conquerors were not doing all the work. North of the building was an area about half a mile square, enclosed by high brick walls, which seems to have been a concentration camp housing a labor pool made up of the defeated Virueños. The continued prevalence of Virú houseware throughout the valley shows that the population was not replaced by immigrants.

There are indications that Huancaco was never completed. In any case, the Mochica domination of Virú was soon replaced by a new conquest by mountain people coming from south central Peru. Their culture was related to that of the famous site of Tiahuanaco in Bolivia. Perhaps these mountain people learned political and military organization from the states in the coastal valleys. If so, they learned well—as well as the Vandals learned warfare from the Romans—for about A.D. 1000 they conquered the entire Peruvian coast.

The conquest of the militaristic Mochica kingdom was probably a rather violent affair, and its effects can be seen in the history of Virú. Not only was there an abrupt change in the ceremonial pottery, but even the everyday household wares soon changed. This probably indicates that the conquerors were shifting and mixing populations. The new population elements brought to Virú black mold-made pottery of types that had been developing to the north.

The central city, Gallinazo, had already been abandoned under the Mochica occupation. Now the new conquerors gave up the castillos and other public buildings—though they did not go so far here as they did in Chicama Valley, where they destroyed great brick pyramids over 100 feet high. In Virú they built four high-walled, rectangular compounds, not far from the beach and near the river. These compounds measured as much as 400 by 750 feet, and in them rooms were arranged in an orderly fashion.

During this period, to which the name Tomaval has been assigned, the valley continued to be irrigated over nearly all its practical area; indeed, water appears to have been brought nearer the beach than before. Apparently the population did not decline. The conquerors introduced well-planned houses of a new type featuring several small rooms, perhaps bedrooms, and a large living room. Judging from the architecture, life became a little more comfortable in Virú.

The new rulers built what was evidently a through highway connecting the valleys; it runs straight across the Virú Valley but now loses itself under the sand dunes at the valley border. Adobe walls outline the 30-foot right of way. This is the coastal highway that the Inca later used so effectively to bind their empire together.

The mountain people had learned how to conquer, but their administrative apparatus must have been defective. Their rule lasted only 300 years. About A.D. 1300 the empire fell apart, and part of it, including Virú, was regrouped into a new political unit known as the Kingdom of Chimu. The capital of this kingdom was the great city of Chan Chan in Moche Valley, the next valley north of Virú.

In the period of Chimu domination, Virú did not prosper. Its population decreased markedly; large sections of the

CAT-GOD of terrifying mien was a principal deity worshiped in the Virú Valley, at least from Guañape into Chimu times. This example of a funerary vessel is approximately 10 inches high. It was found in a burial in the chief Gallinazo group (*see map on page 166*).

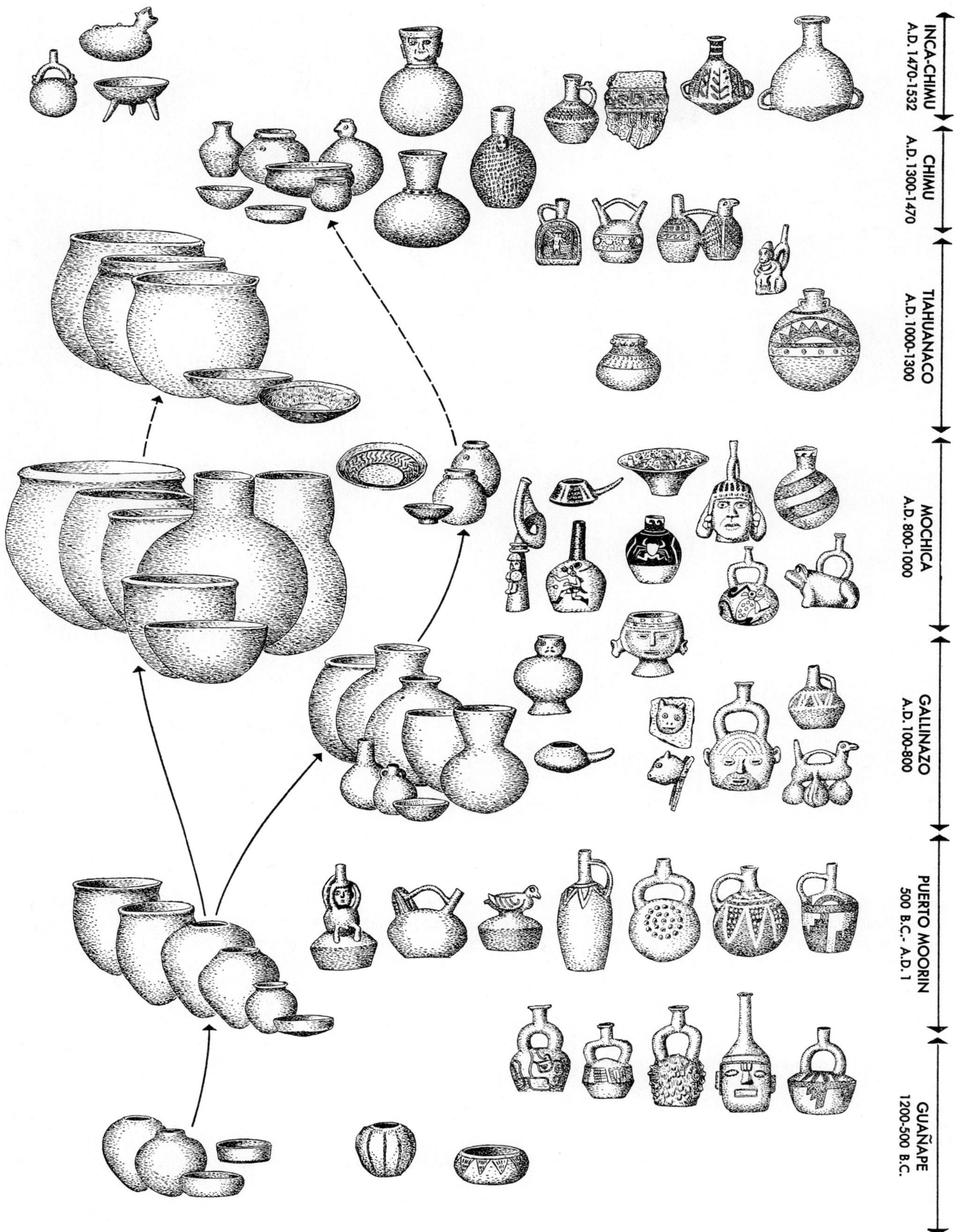

CERAMIC HISTORY of the Virú Valley is represented in this drawing. At the left is shown typical household pottery of successive periods, which are indicated on the vertical scale at right. Some wares tended to persist through several cultures. The more elaborate funerary pottery, shown at right, is actually smaller in scale than the plain ware. The arrows indicate patterns of development.

DWELLING of the Guañape period was excavated in the Chicama Valley. It consisted of a deep hole, faced with stones picked up on the beach and roofed over with any available material. In its shape and narrow entrance way it resembles the igloo of the Eskimo.

irrigation system were abandoned; and people lived mainly in the upper part of the valley, where they needed only short irrigation canals. There were, however, some settlements near the beach, and they adopted a new method of obtaining water for crops: the people laboriously removed the top three feet or more of soil, from areas as large as an acre, so that plant roots could reach the ground water flowing beneath the surface.

By this time technology had greatly advanced. Excellent and intricately carved wood objects of the Chimu period have been preserved. Weaving, which has a long history on this coast, was at an amazing peak of proficiency, probably unrivaled in any other pre-machine-age culture. Spectacular garments were made of the feathers of tropical birds brought from across the Andes. Gold, silver, copper and bronze were cast and hammered into a variety of ornaments and useful tools. Pottery was mostly mold-made, and apparently was turned out in job lots by specialists. The former distinction between the sacred and household pottery had almost disappeared.

The Virú Valley continued to be a pawn in the struggle for empire on the Peruvian coast. When the Inca tribe came down from the highlands in the 15th century to begin the conquests that were to set up an empire from Chile to Ecuador, its army found the Chimu kingdom its most formidable opponent, but the invaders overran Chimu and swallowed up Virú about A.D. 1470. The valley's population dwindled further. The Inca largely took over: their pottery replaced the existing types; they built at least two strongholds atop peaks in the upper valley. Beside the river and near the beach there is a rather elaborate Inca house, with a walled courtyard enclosing a large pool, which may have been the headquarters of the Inca administrator who ruled the sadly depopulated valley.

The conquest of Peru by Pizarro's army in 1532 marked the end of this remarkable American development. It is interesting to speculate on what might have happened had the Spaniards not come. So far as Peruvian history developed before this outside interference, it paralleled in general outline the development of the Neolithic and Bronze Age states and empires of Asia Minor and the Mediterranean.

The Peoples of Pine Lawn Valley

18

by Paul S. Martin
July 1951

For eight summers archaeologists have pieced together the cultural history of the Indians who lived in a small region of New Mexico while Greece and Rome rose and fell and northern Europe flowered

PEOPLE haven't changed much in the past two, five or 10 thousand years: witness the fact that in a prehistoric cave in New Mexico we found ropes tied in granny knots, square knots and slip knots; cradles, dice and mummies of ancient Indians with G.I. haircuts. We have devoted the past decade to reading the unwritten history of these Indians. Here is that history as we read it, layer by layer.

About 12,000 or 15,000 years ago the last great glaciers of the Ice Age had retreated into northern Canada, and wandering bands of Indians began to cross the Bering Strait from Asia into America. Some of these migrants settled in the southwestern part of the U. S.—Arizona, Colorado, New Mexico, Utah and Texas. In time, three important native "civilizations" developed: 1) Pueblo or Anasazi, 2) Hohokam, and 3) Cochise-Mogollon (pronounced Mog-ee-yoan). The first of these occupied mainly northern Arizona and New Mexico and southern Colorado and Utah. The second flourished mainly in southern Arizona. The third, the subject of our story, existed in a mountainous area in eastern Arizona and western New Mexico. I use the term "existed" because in many ways the Cochise-Mogollon Indians eked out a precarious life, and their culture was comparatively undeveloped, marginal and poor in material things.

We decided to investigate the Mogollon culture because it was much less well known than the Pueblo or Hohokam; indeed its existence had come to light only in 1934, when Emil W. Haury published the results of some excavations near Glenwood, N. M. We selected Pine Lawn Valley, near the town of Reserve in the west central part of New Mexico, as a promising theater of operations and laid out a comprehensive program of research. The Southwest Archaeological Expeditions of the Chicago Natural History Museum were organized and we began our work in 1939.

Now an archaeological expedition sounds romantic and exciting, and it is exciting; but I should like to point out that it also involves hard work, dust, heat and possibly illness—to mention only a few of our difficulties. Digging, of course, takes most of our time and money, but there are other matters that must be attended to so that digging may proceed smoothly. We must prepare carefully planned stocks of tools and other supplies, must order a three-months' supply of food and devise a way to store it, must arrange for a safe supply of milk and water (all of our water is hauled in a tank truck) and must make provision for laundry, delivery of mail, garbage disposal, and so on. We make friends with the people of the community and are prepared to render neighborly acts, to lend tools and supplies, to haul materials in case of truck breakdowns, to lecture to local clubs and schools, to stand by in case of sickness or death. All this is in addition to the main business of digging, washing, sorting and cataloguing the excavated objects, and shooting and developing movies and still pictures.

WE HAVE now worked eight summer seasons in the Pine Lawn Valley. During this time we have excavated the aforementioned cave and 76 rooms of houses at 10 different sites. They were probably inhabited over a time span of roughly 3,800 years—from about 2500 B.C. to A.D.1300. Pieced together, the small bits of information uncovered form a mosaic that reveals a fairly clear picture of what the American Indians were doing in Pine Lawn Valley during the rise and fall of Grecian and Roman civilizations and the rise of cultures in northern Europe.

We now know that this Mogollon culture grew directly out of an older subculture called the Cochise, so named for an Apache chief. Hence we shall start our story with the Cochise Indians.

The Cochise Indians settled in southeastern Arizona 10,000 years ago or somewhat later. Their history has been reconstructed by archaeologists and geologists from studies of old camp sites with hearthstones, charcoal, crude stone tools and the bones of extinct animals—all apparently lying exactly where the Indians had left them in the deposits of the Last Pluvial Age some 10,000 to 8,000 years ago. The climate of southern Arizona was then cool and moist. Hickory and other trees that like relatively moist places grew there, and the region abounded in lakes and streams that were frequented by beaver. In this place the Cochise Indians hunted several animals now extinct, such as the dire wolf, the American camel, the mammoth and the American horse. The people camped along the streams and lake shores, living on nuts, seeds, berries, roots and some animal food. We call such an economy a food-gathering one. Agriculture, architecture and pottery-making were unknown to them.

For about 8,000 years the Cochise Indians jogged along in the same old manner. There were changes and improvements in their tools, but food-gathering, plus some hunting, remained the subsistence pattern. In the meantime, however, the climate and environment had changed. The continental glaciers had receded, the very wet Pluvial Period was drawing to a close and the lakes and streams were drying up. Much of the lush country was fast becoming a desert. It became plain to the Cochise that their existence was threatened. It was a time of peril, unrest, insecurity. Life and conditions as they knew them were about to perish. The anguish of the Cochise people, three or four thousand years ago, must have been like our feelings in this age of uncertainty.

One thing was certain: some of the Cochise people had to move—and soon. Probably those in small, isolated camps farthest from water went first. Thus about 4,500 years ago, at the time when the Egyptian pyramids were being built, some Cochise migrants wandered into Pine Lawn Valley. Here, in this pleasant pine-covered valley, they found a

PIT DUG FOR A HOUSE is excavated in Pine Lawn Valley. In the large hole at the left side of the pit is a skeleton. The house was a beehive-shaped structure resting on posts that were sunk into the floor of the pit.

WOODEN HOUSE was built later than the pit house on page 172. Postholes and human bones have been dug out.

STONE HOUSE came still later. It was built on the surface of the ground and possessed several small rooms.

new homeland with sufficient food and water. Along the banks of a streamlet that issued from the mountain springs (and still does), they settled down and camped for centuries. They resumed their accustomed way of life—gathering seeds, nuts and roots, which they ground up on crude milling stones; cleaning skins with roughly formed scrapers; chopping poles and brush with heavy, ill-fashioned stone choppers; living in small tents. But in their new land they began to develop some worth-while new ideas.

By the year 1, the Cochise had progressed to the pit house, pottery-making and the practice of agriculture. The pit house, a shallow pit from 8 to 15 feet in diameter with a roof of poles and brush, may have been their own invention; more likely the Cochise borrowed the idea from a nearby people. Well before 1000 B.C. the Cochise people had begun to cultivate pod corn—a primitive type of maize.

ARCHAEOLOGISTS find it convenient to classify and name cultures, and we can say that roughly about the year 1, when pottery and houses were added to what the Cochise Indians had previously known and made, the primitive Cochise culture ended and the Mogollon culture (named after the Mogollon Mountains) began. There is no actual break in the story, only a transition from one stage of civilization to the next. When we speak of the Cochise "culture" or way of life we mean a food-gathering stage in which the people had certain types of stone tools but no pottery or agriculture. The term Mogollon means a continuation of the use of the Cochise stone tool types plus pottery, agriculture and houses.

Now the Cochise-Mogollon occupation of Pine Lawn Valley can be subdivided into seven periods, or phases, that mark changes in the evolution of this people's way of life. The first phase lasted from about 2500 B.C. to A.D. 1.

From this period we have recovered more than 70 stone tools of various kinds —milling stones, choppers, scrapers—that had been dropped or lost along the banks of the Wet Leggett arroyo. These artifacts were uncovered by a recent erosion cycle—a lucky accident for us, for they would otherwise have remained buried from three to 12 feet below the surface and no one would have dreamed of their existence. In addition, we have located several hearths and the floor of a shelter that was probably the site of a small skin tent.

During this period the people of Pine Lawn Valley began to accumulate possessions and found that they had to protect their homes and harvested crops from the rapacity of neighbors or enemies. In the second phase, lasting from about A.D. 1 to 500, they built villages containing from four to a dozen pit houses on high narrow mesas, one end of which was usually unscalable. Across this end was a wall behind which the people could retire in case of attack.

Each pit house was occupied by one or two families, related by blood or by marriage. The house was more or less round, with an average diameter of about 17 feet and an average depth in the ground of about three feet. It had a beehive-shaped roof of poles, branches and adobe, supported by one or more sturdy posts set in deep postholes. The occupants crawled into their house through a doorway consisting of a horizontal roofed-over tunnel or passage six feet long. A skin curtain or stone slab may have been used to shut out inclement weather. Food, skins and tools were stored in floor pits, some of which are six feet deep and four feet wide. Since each house was usually provided with several such "storerooms," they were probably covered by poles or planks; without such covers it would have been dangerous to walk about the house. We do not know what these people used for heat and light, for we have found neither fire pits nor hearths. Probably they did only a limited amount of cooking and carried it on outside the house. They ground corn meal and mashed nuts on milling stones or in stone mortars and pestles. Chairs and tables of course were unknown at this time. Rush or yucca mats and fur robes may have been used for bedding.

ALL THIS is reconstructed from the plain evidence of the remains. Where a pit house stood there is usually a shallow, saucer-shaped depression, with a collection of pottery fragments and broken stone tools. Excavation of such a depression discloses an outlining wall of earth that is harder than the deposited fill; postholes which sometimes

FOOD-GRINDING SLAB that was used by the inhabitants of Pine Lawn Valley some 4,500 years ago was laid bare by erosion in Wet Leggett arroyo.

still retain the stumps of posts that supported the roof; the lower part of the tunnel entrance, containing smaller postholes for the posts that held up the tunnel roof; pieces of adobe bearing the impressions of poles, branches, pine needles and the fingerprints of the builders; floor pits containing stone tools used for grinding, cutting and scraping; bone awls and needles, and fragments (in a burned house) of mats and baskets. The pottery of this period is all brown or red and lacks any decoration; we call such pottery "plain-ware." The stone tools, mainly made by grinding and pecking, include rubbing stones, milling stones, hammer stones, mauls and bowls. There are also some chipped implements: arrowheads, knives, scrapers, choppers and drills. For the most part, the types of stone tools found in this period are directly descended from the Cochise types.

The dead were frequently buried in a pit below the smoothed adobe floor, with the surviving members of the family continuing to occupy the house. Offerings to the dead are meager—a shell bracelet or two, perhaps a tubular tobacco pipe of stone, possibly a chopper or an arrowhead. Although burying the dead in the house may seem strange to us, perhaps the Mogollon Indians felt the same as the cowboy, who still pleads:

Oh, bury me not on the lone prairie,
Where the wild coyotes will howl o'er me . . .

We may assume that the Mogollon Indians, like all peoples, had religious convictions and dogmas. This assumption is strengthened by the fact that we have uncovered several "super" pit houses, perhaps temples of some kind, which measure some 33 feet in diameter and lack floor pits and other evidences of domestic usage.

The Mogollon culture of A.D. 100-500, in short, was undeveloped and unsophisticated, with no striking or dramatic features. Its people had few requirements and probably seldom sought contacts with other cultures. Yet it had made important advances over the more primitive Cochise culture and had started an upward trend.

IN the next three periods, extending from A.D. 500 to 1000, life slowly changed. Apparently unfriendly groups were conquered or dispersed, for we find that during this era pit houses were built in choice spots without necessarily being bunched together. They were made rectangular in shape instead of round and became markedly smaller—about 12 feet across. They also acquired fire pits or hearths and eliminated the floor storage pits; we do not know where food and tools were stored or where the dead were buried during this period. Corn was still ground indoors, but mortars and pestles were going out of fashion. Further internal evidence leads us to believe that agriculture (maize, beans, squash) and hunting had become the means of subsistence and that food-gathering was a thing of the past, although medicinal herbs may have been collected.

Perhaps the most striking changes took place in the pottery. Sometime between A.D. 500 and 650 the idea of painting designs on their pottery occurred to the Mogollon Indians. The earliest designs we have found were done in red on a brown background. They were geometric in layout and were applied with a steady hand. By the year A.D. 900 the designs and layouts had been so skillfully reworked, interwoven and varied that it takes an expert to perceive a relationship between this and the earlier work. By the time the Crusades were under way in the Old World the Mogollon potters had developed a painted ware that evokes the admiration of all who see it.

We assume that the density of the population had increased, for we find more rooms, or pit houses, at A. D. 900 than at A.D. 500. The individual pit houses of each village are smaller, from which we infer that only one family occupied a room and that perhaps an extended family (all members related by marriage or blood) occupied an entire village.

By the time William the Conqueror was invading England (A.D. 1066), a new period had been ushered in and profound changes had occurred in the Mogollon way of life in Pine Lawn Valley. Now we find that the Indians have suddenly changed their architecture; instead of pit houses they have multiroomed houses built entirely above the ground, with walls of stone masonry. As far as we can tell from our digging evidence, this change in type of dwelling did not develop out of any Mogollon tradition. It represents a borrowed idea, and was probably the result of Pueblo influence, perhaps an actual invasion of Pine Lawn Valley by Pueblo people. The Mogollon pottery also shows a sudden change; now it is white with black designs instead of red-on-brown—another indication of a fusion of Pueblo and Mogollon culture.

The Mogollon social structure, however, probably remained unchanged. We conjecture that the Mogollon Indians continued to reckon descent and inheritance through the female line, with several related families occupying a hamlet and the groom taking up residence at the home of the bride's mother.

Although our excavations have not proceeded beyond roughly A.D. 1150, we know from our reconnaissance of early village sites and of the ground in certain areas that the Mogollon culture continued to flourish for another hundred years or so. But about A.D. 1300 the Mogollon people suddenly abandoned this area. What was the reason? Disease, drought, displacement by Apaches? We do not know. Not until more than 400 years later was this region occupied again. This time it was settled by white men from Europe.

SOME SEASON soon we shall explore the villages of that last period of the Mogollon people in Pine Lawn Valley. But meanwhile a more pressing problem has arisen. All our digging up to the season of 1950 was in open sites in which only the durable and imperishable materials—bones, stone tools, pottery—remain. We had found no signs of the Mogollon Indians' clothing, objects of wood or leather or other perishable products of their culture. But by good luck—and a great deal of archaeology is luck—in the summer of 1949 we found several dry caves.

We decided to dig one of them, known as the Tularosa Cave, in 1950. In this work we have had unprecedented good fortune. Dry, well-preserved specimens have been turning up with such rapidity that we have scarcely had time to clean and catalogue them. Excavating in this cave is very arduous, because the dust has lain undisturbed for centuries. The slightest disturbance causes it to rise, and it remains in suspension for hours. We have therefore had to wear dust respirators and goggles in the cave.

We can only mention some of the more spectacular finds, because most of the materials still await careful analysis. The terrain near Tularosa Cave is covered with sharp volcanic rocks, thorns and a great deal of gravel. Consequently protection of the feet was of paramount importance to the Mogollon people who lived there, and they met this problem by making sandals. We have found about 200 sandals in various stages of wear. They were made of wild fibers—mostly of yucca—because skins and hence leather were scarce in this region.

The cave excavations also reveal that the Mogollon people resorted to ingenious methods to hunt meat. Of course they used spears and, in later times, bows and arrows, but they captured much of their game by means of snares. In one cache we found 11 large snares made of braided rope, each about six feet long. At one end of the snare was a tie for fastening it to a stake or a tree; at the other end, a large noose made with a slip knot. A noose such as this would easily snare a wild pig, a mountain sheep or a deer. We also learned that these early people knew all the knots we know, including the square knot, the granny, the slip, the half hitch and the sheet bend.

The ancient cave yielded a great treasure of other Mogollon artifacts: digging sticks for planting corn, rush mats, cradles, whistles or flutes, beads, fragments of cloth (some in colored designs), fur and feather blankets, string aprons, ornaments, bags, tobacco pipes, cigarettes, "Martini" sticks with juniper berries impaled like olives, wooden spoons (just like those sold in the 10-cent stores today), hair nets, cloth bags, religious fetishes or objects, a doctor's bag containing herbs and tools, baskets, and so on. But no hats of any kind.

Evidently the number one item in the Mogollon diet was corn. We have found in this cave the very early, primitive type of corn called pod corn. The interesting point about this is that whereas corn is supposed to have originated in South America, here in the North American Southwest we found a type of corn which may rank among the earliest and most primitive. The Mogollon Indians also grew popcorn, and popped it on the ear! Our corn may not settle the question as to the place in which corn originated, but it may greatly help botanists trace the history and development of this important cereal ("The Mystery of Corn," by Paul C. Mangelsdorf; SCIENTIFIC AMERICAN, July, 1950).

Besides corn these Indians raised beans, squash, pumpkins and gourds, and they ate walnuts, piñon nuts, grass seeds, sago-lily bulbs, yucca and cactus fruits.

The greatest of our finds in the Tularosa Cave last season were two mummies—the first to be surely identified with the Mogollon culture. They may date at about A.D. 700 or earlier. The mummies were those of two male Indians with hair trimmed in the G.I. style. One mummy wore a string apron and was wrapped in a fur robe. Each body had been laid on a soft bed of grass and had been carried to the grave on a large rush mat. A deerskin robe was placed over the body, then more soft grass and then dirt.

WE have traced here the story of a race of man from about 2500 B.C. to A.D. 1300—from a time before he had acquired the knowledge of agriculture, pottery and house-building to a time when he had become semicivilized. Why do we feel that this research is important? As far as we can tell, man has always suffered from economic and social ills, for which there has been no panacea. If we wish to seek alleviation for man's troubles, we must know as much as possible about the history of mankind, for only by studying the rise and fall of cultures can we hope to understand human societies and the way they function. By recovering all we can of the ancient Mogollon culture and by fitting it into its place in human history, we hope to contribute a mite to the knowledge and understanding of the causes of social disintegration.

19

Underwater Archaeology in the Maya Highlands

by Stephan F. Borhegyi
March 1959

At the bottom of a Guatemalan lake skin divers have found objects sacrificed to the lake spirits as early as 2,500 years ago. These finds help trace the history of a little-known branch of the Maya

When we hear the word "Maya," we usually think of the impressive flat-topped pyramids which archaeologists have cleared from the rain forest of Guatemala and southern Mexico. Or we may think of a second Maya area farther to the north on the plain of Yucatan, where the Spaniards pillaged the cities built by the ancestors of the present Indian inhabitants. Run your finger down the map from Yucatan southward across the rain forest and you come to a little-known third center of Maya civilization. This center lies in the Sierra Madre, which runs along the Pacific coast of Guatemala and of the Mexican province of Chiapas. Here in the cool highlands west of Guatemala City live nearly four million Maya Indians, cousins of the more familiar northern lowland tribes. In pre-Columbian times these highland Maya comprised one of the Western Hemisphere's great civilized states. Less advanced than the northerners (they made little use of the 365-day calendar, hieroglyphic writing and the corbelled arch), they nonetheless possessed a rich cultural tradition dating from about 1000 B.C. Today this tradition is yielding its history to an unusual kind of archaeology.

For the past few years the archaeology of the Maya highlands has proceeded on a modest scale. The ancient religious center of Kaminaljuyu and a number of other sites have been excavated, but for the most part the diggings have managed to stay out of the public eye. The reasons for this are twofold. First, the highland Maya rarely built in stone. Lacking the soft limestone of Yucatan, or metal tools with which to hew their own hard igneous rock, the highland architects resorted to sun-dried earth, adobe and plaster—materials that have crumbled with the passage of time and the tilling of the soil. Today every highland palace and temple has collapsed into a grassy mound, and smaller structures have almost vanished beneath the fields of Indian corn.

Second, there is none of that specious glamour that surrounds archaeological research in inaccessible places. Almost without exception the highland sites lie on the outskirts of modern towns, close to highways, railroads and all the comforts of civilization. No expeditions need be outfitted. There is none of the romantic austerity of camp life. The rainforest pyramids are another matter. Set in the deepest jungle, unseen for 1,000 years save by wandering chicle-gatherers and primitive Lacandon-Maya hunting bands, their appeal to the imagination is undeniable. Small wonder that the lowland Maya have eclipsed the fame of their highland relatives!

But every dog has its day, and the highland Maya have at last begun to attract attention. Curiously this has been brought about not by the archaeologist's spade but by modern techniques of free diving. By 1954 the new sport of aqualung diving had become an international pastime, and in that year a group of amateur divers began to probe the waters of Guatemala's Lake Amatitlan in search

SKIN DIVER in this photograph, wearing an aqualung, has just surfaced with two Maya incense burners from Lake Amatitlan in highland Guatemala. He is Jorge Samayoa, one of the lake's many amateur sportsmen-turned-archaeologists cooperating with the author.

LAKE AMATITLAN, set among volcanic peaks, is shown in this aerial photograph. From its western, or lower, basin (*upper left*) divers have recovered Maya offerings dating from about 500 B.C. Temple sites on the shore date from 1000 B.C. to 1500 A.D.

of fishing grounds. In April, 1955, one of these diving enthusiasts, Manfred Töpke, retrieved an interesting archaeological specimen from the bottom of the lake. It was the first of more than 600 intact pottery vessels, incense burners and stone sculptures discovered by the skin divers.

In the summer of 1957, when the news of these finds reached me, I was excavating in the highlands with a group of students from the summer school of San Carlos University. I wasted no time in getting in touch with the skin divers and examining their collections. With their help I mapped out a plan for a systematic survey of the lake bottom and shore. Jacques-Yves Cousteau, inventor of the aqualung, had initiated underwater archaeology five years before with his famous exploration of a Greek shipwreck near Marseilles. Since then much of the Mediterranean and Danish coast had been explored by skin divers, but this was to be one of the first such adventures in the Americas.

To be sure, the discovery of archaeological specimens in Lake Amatitlan came as no great surprise. As early as the mid-19th century travelers to Guatemala had made mention of apparently ancient pottery vessels found along the lake shore and in its shallow waters. Eduard Seler, a noted German archaeologist, visited the lake in 1896 and described "curious spiked vessels occasionally decorated with maguey-like leaf decorations." A later visitor, Marshall Saville of the Heye Foundation in New York, not only witnessed the recovery of pottery vessels from the lake by fishermen but also located two archaeological sites on the lake shore. During the 1940s members of the Carnegie Institution Guatemalan research team and I investigated and mapped these sites and others in the lake area. No one was aware, however, of the immense quantity and diversity of the underwater material.

Lake Amatitlan is a beautiful resort 17 miles south of Guatemala City on the highway from the capital to the Pacific seaport of San José. Its altitude is some 4,000 feet. Attractive week-end cottages belonging to the country's wealthier citizens line the shore, and in good weather the lake sees a good deal of swimming, boating and water-skiing. Two lakeside hotels feature thermal baths, said to be beneficial for arthritis and rheumatism. A short distance from the lake shore is the colonial town of San Juan Amatitlan, whose 6,000 permanent residents are mostly "Ladinos" of mixed Spanish and Pokomam-Maya ancestry. Spectacular lava hills surround the lake. In certain areas sulfurous water hot enough to boil an egg bubbles from the lake bottom or along the shore. Geysers appear and disappear erratically at various locations on the south side of the lake. The lake derives its name from the Amate tree (*Ficus moraceae*), which abounds on the southern shore.

The first task of our group was to prepare accurate maps of the lake. This we did with the aid of aerial photographs from the Guatemalan Bureau of Cartography plus some up-to-date bathymetric maps. We now tried to locate the exact sites of all underwater discoveries made by local skin divers since 1955. The upper basin of the lake is joined to the lower basin by a narrow channel only six feet in depth, crossed by a railroad

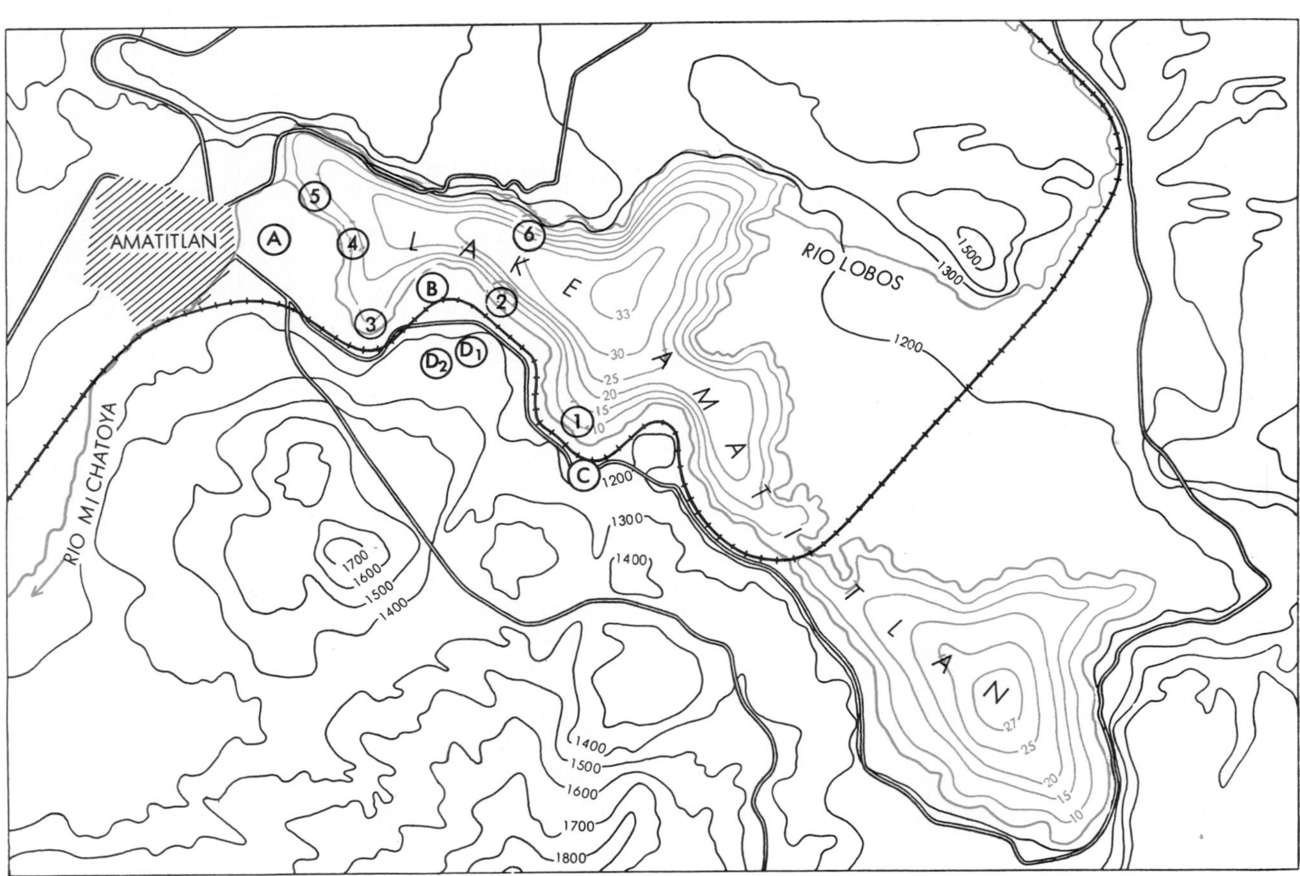

ARCHAEOLOGICAL SITES at Lake Amatitlan include lake-bottom deposits of offerings (*numbered 1 through 6*) and lake-shore sites of ancient groups of buildings (*lettered A through D2*). The colored contours indicate the depth of the lake in meters; the black contours, the height of the land above sea level in meters. In both map and plan views on page 179 and 180 north is at the top.

bridge [*see map on page 178*]. Since the Guatemalan divers reported that there was nothing to be found in the upper basin, we concentrated our efforts in the lower. The depth of this portion of the lake varies from 10 to 130 feet. Nearly 600 archaeological specimens in the divers' and other private collections were cleaned, photographed, described and measured. Each piece was catalogued according to its original location beneath the waters of the lake. We found that most of the material came from nine underwater deposits, seven of them near hot springs off the south shore and the other two in deeper water off the north shore. Fortunately for us the divers had made their collections with considerable care. They had carried depth gauges and taken accurate notes, numbering the specimens according to their original location. The specimens consisted of offering bowls, spiked vessels and incense burners. They ranged from a few inches to four and one-half feet in height. The incense burners were double-chambered or three-pronged; many bore unusual designs: cacao trees and pods, papaya fruits and flowers, quetzal birds, jaguar heads, spider monkeys, snakes, lizards, bats and even human skulls—motifs hitherto rare or unknown in the highland Maya area. Among the many Maya gods represented were the rain god, Chac or Tlaloc; the jaguar god; the sun god; Eecatl, the wind god (a form of Quetzalcoatl, the feathered serpent); Xipe Totec, a fertility god; and the death god. There were also beautifully executed human heads peering from the jaws of animals and monsters and the beaks of birds.

It soon became apparent that certain types of vessel and design motif were restricted to particular underwater localities. This raised the intriguing possibility that each underwater deposit might represent a different time period. The location of the deposits in relation to the shore line strongly suggested that the specimens had been thrown into the lake as offerings, probably to the lake or water gods. To confirm the time sequence of the sites it was necessary to reinvestigate all the archaeological sites on the shore. During the summers of 1957 and 1958, with the help of students from the San Carlos University summer school, the mapping and test excavations of all five archaeological sites on the southern shore were completed.

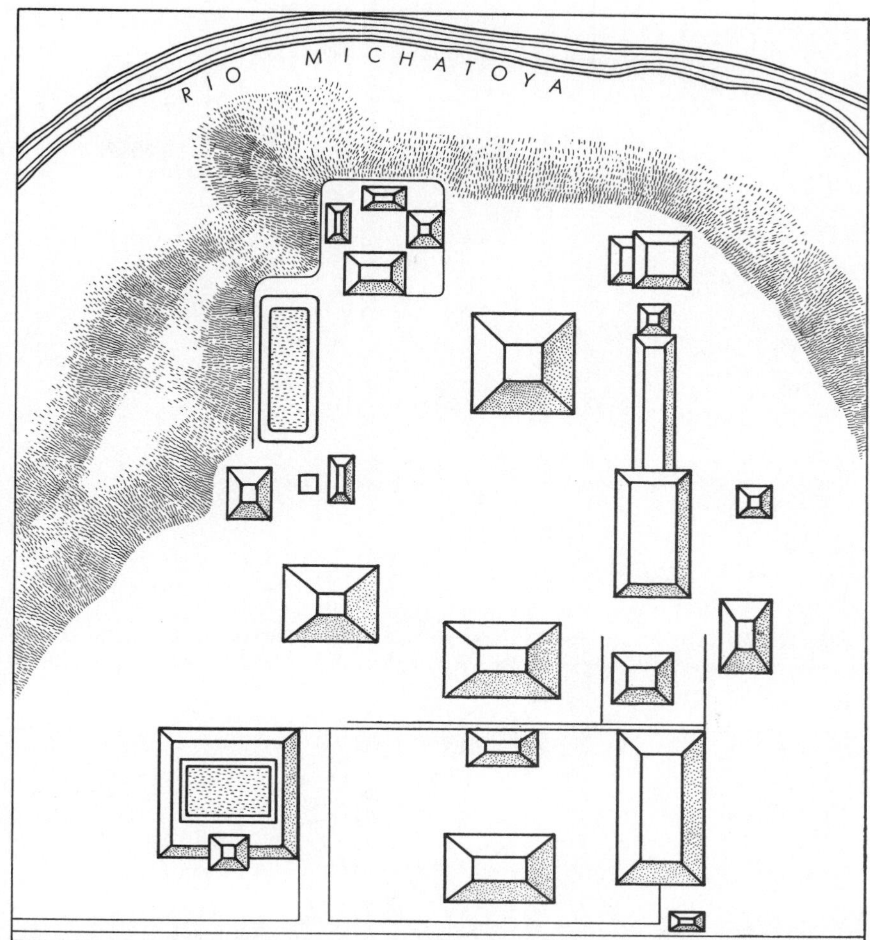

SITE A (AMATITLAN), the largest lake-shore site, dates from the Classic Period (200 to 1000 A.D.). The buildings reconstructed here include two ball courts (*stippled rectangles*).

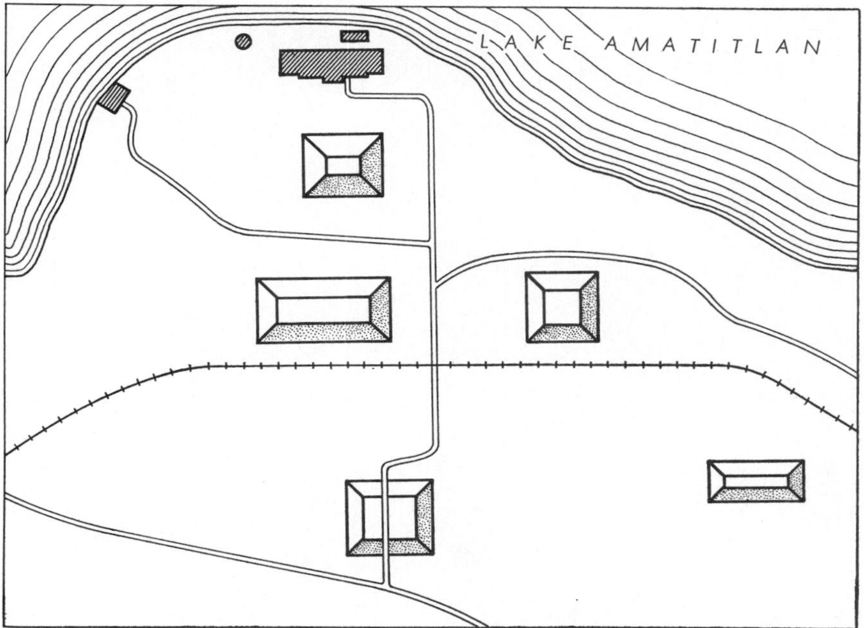

SITE B (CONTRERAS) is the oldest site, dating from the Pre-Classic Period (about 1000 B.C. to 200 A.D.). It stands near the south shore of Lake Amatitlan, 300 yards above the Contreras Yacht Club (*hatched buildings*). Modern roads and a railroad cross the area.

Site B (Contreras), the oldest lake-shore site, shows an occupation from the beginning to the end of the

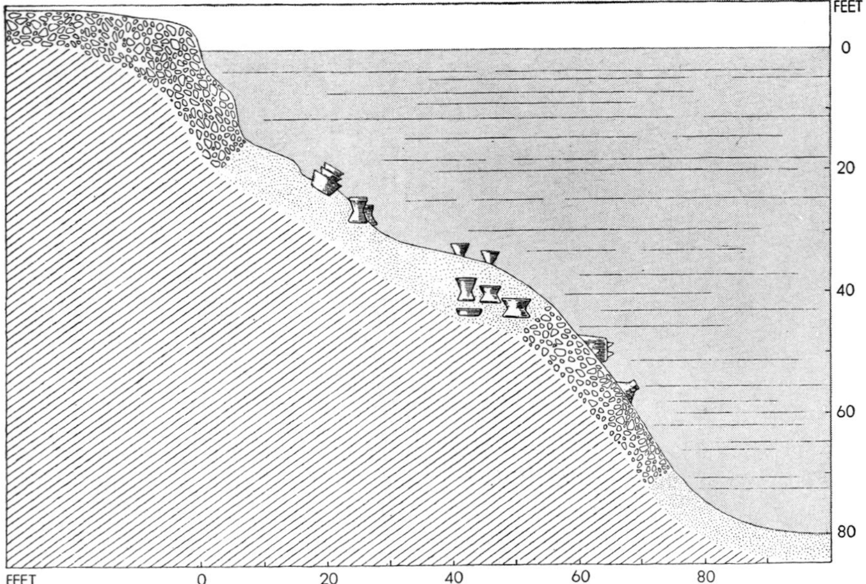

SITE C (MEJICANOS) belongs to the Early Classic Period (200 to 600 A.D.). Shown here are offerings from Site C carried under water by lava flow in which they were embedded.

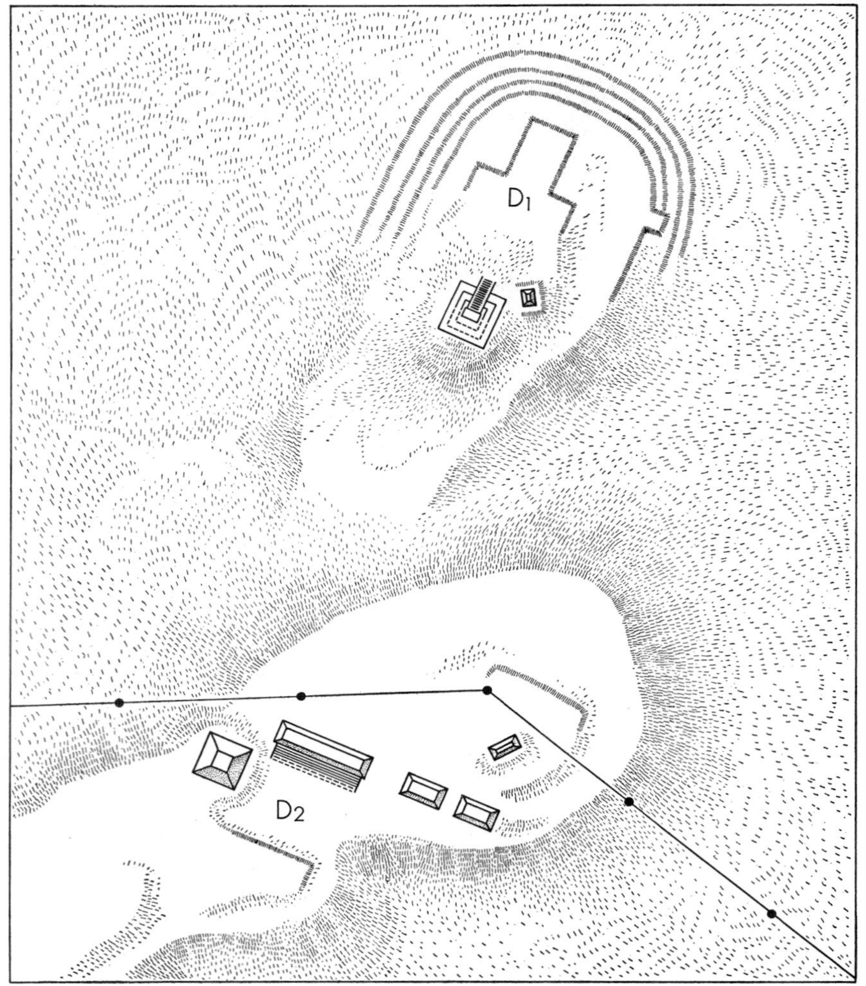

SITES D1 AND D2, referred to as Contreras Alto and Los Jicaques, are hillside settlements probably inhabited until the time of the Spanish conquest. One or both may be the "lost" city of Tzacualpal shown on an old colonial map. A modern power line crosses Site D2.

Maya Pre-Classic Period (about 1000 B.C. to 200 A.D.). It consists of five mounds located 300 yards from the shore behind the Contreras Yacht Club [*see bottom illustration on page 179*]. Since Contreras lies only a few feet above the level of the modern lake, we can assume that the water level has not risen for at least 2,000 years.

Site C (Mejicanos) consists of four mounds, also at or a little above lake level. The site occupies a small inlet valley, hemmed in on three sides by steep mountains which still show traces of pre-Columbian agricultural terracing. The mounds have been almost obliterated by modern corn cultivation and the use of their material for roads, but their remains are still distinguishable. They were constructed of stone and earth and were probably faced with adobe. Fragments of pottery collected from the site indicate that the major occupation of Mejicanos was during the Early Classic Period (200 to 600 A.D.).

Considerably larger is Site A (Amatitlan), located on higher ground overlooking the west end of the lake. Retreat to higher and more easily defensible positions characterized Maya behavior during periods of disturbance, so we need not infer a rise in the lake level. The site comprises buildings laid out in orderly fashion around aligned plazas. There are about 25 mounds of various sizes, two of them ancient ball courts. Extensive artificial terracing is still in evidence on the sides of the promontory. Many of the structures are faced with masonry of roughly cut stones and some with well-cut and dressed blocks. Several test pits and surface specimens indicate that the site was occupied during the entire Classic Period (200 to 1000 A.D.).

Two other sites, Contreras Alto (Site D1) and Los Jicaques (Site D2), were discovered on the slopes some 500 feet higher than Site B. Both of these sites must have been quite extensive, each with 10 to 15 large mounds and handsomely cut stone masonry. Although the majority of the pottery collected from the two sites dates back to the late Pre-Classic and Classic periods, enough Post-Classic pottery was found on the surface to indicate the possibility that this area was still inhabited at the time of the Spanish conquest in 1524 A.D. One, or both of the sites may represent the long-searched-for ruins of "Tzacualpal," indicated on a map made in 1690 by the Guatemalan historian Francisco de Fuentes y Guzmán.

Our excitement was great when our records of the specimens brought up by divers showed that there was a definite correlation between the type and age of the underwater specimens and those found at the nearest archaeological site on the shore. This correlation was confirmed by our student divers, who made many descents to each of the nine underwater deposits. The underwater specimens fall into an orderly sequence which corroborates our time-scale for the sites on the shore; we now have a record of the fact that the lake area had been continuously inhabited for nearly 3,000 years. Thus the region, though not comparable in architectural grandeur to Kaminaljuyu, the largest of the highland Maya sites, has a rich and full archaeological record. On the basis of this record I shall now attempt to reconstruct the history of the lake area.

While the archaeological record does not begin before about 1000 B.C., we can assume that prior to this time wandering Maya groups entered the highlands from the Pacific-coast area, and settled in more or less stable communities in the many fertile mountain valleys. Soon the domestication of corn and beans made it possible for these communities to set aside their food surplus for times of scarcity; this eased the tremendous pressure of keeping alive from one day to another. Increasing leisure made it possible and practical for members of the communities to manufacture objects of artistic and utilitarian value. Their various kinds of pottery and stone implements provide the first tangible chapter of prehistory. While archaeological data indicate a large population in the nearby Valley of Guatemala, no permanent structures remain to document this earliest period at the lake. However, utensils and figurines from the Contreras site suggest that a settlement of some sort must have existed. The main occupations of these first settlers, as in later times, were fishing, hunting and farming. Religious ideas from the ceremonial center of Kaminaljuyu reached this community around 1000 B.C., attested by the beginning of mound building. The gods became ever more important as men depended upon them to bless and protect their corn and bean plots. Gradually the ritual magic practiced by individuals gave way to organized religious offerings and ceremonies. Religion was probably the concern of the menfolk, who erected buildings and monuments and carved sculptures in honor of their gods or their dead. The religion at this time was unsophisticated in concept, being entirely animistic; every aspect of nature had its spiritual

OFFERINGS found at the bottom of the lake include censer covers shaped like a jaguar (*top*) and a Mexican god (*middle*), either the "Old Fire God" or Quetzalcoatl. At bottom is a young woman's ocher-stained cranium in a bowl, possible evidence of human sacrifice.

counterpart. It is easy to see why the sulfurous springs and geysers on the southern shore of Lake Amatitlan would be awe-inspiring to these pre-Columbians. This awe, combined with fear of the four-peaked active volcano Pacaya overlooking the lake, could easily have made men believe that particularly powerful spirits or gods dwelt in the area. By about 500 B.C. it was customary to cast offerings into the lake waters to appease the gods. But offerings at this time were neither as specialized nor as abundant as those in later periods.

Apparently the Contreras site was abandoned by the beginning of the Early Classic Period, sometime around 200 A.D. Two new ceremonial centers were then established, one at Mejicanos, adjacent to the hot springs, and the other at Contreras Alto on the nearby hill slopes. The latter site, of considerable size, may indicate a growing population that needed to build and cultivate the surrounding agricultural terraces. Mejicanos, with its four small mounds on the shore, must have served only as a shrine for pilgrims, who by now came in droves, bringing rich and varied offerings to the water gods. The number and variety of specimens from the underwater deposits of Lavaderes nearby suggest that by this time the lake had become a pilgrimage center for highlanders from far and near.

INCENSE BURNER found in the lake is of the "three-pronged" variety. The decoration depicts a finely molded Maya face looking out through the beak of an unidentified bird.

Periodic eruptions of the volcano Pacaya may also have prompted some offerings. Our divers found bowls in groups of four or five, standing erect and occasionally embedded in lava on the lake floor. This could only mean that to placate the angry gods residing in the volcano these objects had been placed in lava flows near the shore and were thus carried into the lake. Major eruptions, probably accompanied by earthquakes, may have prompted the more extravagant offerings, including human sacrifices. One of our divers recovered at Lavaderes a brown-black jar with a modeled Tlaloc face on the neck. It was unusually heavy and upon investigation turned out to contain liquid mercury. After further cleaning we found in it fragments of cinnabar and graphite and nearly 400 ceremonially smashed fragments of jade ear-spools, the most treasured jewelry of the Maya.

Another diver brought up an offering bowl containing a cranium, apparently of a woman somewhere between 16 and 25 years old. The cranium still showed faint traces of red ocher. Human sacrifice, or at least offerings of bodies of the dead, was probably not an uncommon practice among the pre-Columbian inhabitants of the Amatitlan region. Frequent representation of Xipe Totec, a god associated with human sacrifice, and many incense burners depicting jaguars and human skulls, strengthen the possibility that this unsavory practice had entered religious ritual by the Classic Period (200-1000 A.D.). Similar evidence of human sacrifice is abundant among the northern Maya. All of the specimens found from this period bespeak the religious and artistic influence of nearby Kaminaljuyu and even of Teotihuacan in central Mexico.

At the end of the Classic and during the following Post-Classic period (1000-1500 A.D.) two more large population centers had come into prominence, that of the hilltop sites Amatitlan (Site A) and Los Jicaques (Site D2). The number of buildings and ball courts at these sites suggests that they were not merely ceremonial centers but also permanent residences, at least for the governing classes. We have yet to determine whether they were cities in the true sense. We also question whether the inhabitants of these sites were completely Maya in origin, since this is the time when Nahuat-speaking Pipil and Toltec groups from Mexico began to infiltrate the highlands. According to the *Account Book of the Town of San Juan Amatitlan, 1559-1562,* an important document in the Smithsonian Institution, the town was inhabited shortly after the Spanish conquest both by people who spoke Pocomam-Maya and by others who spoke Nahuat. The Pipil and Toltec preference for spiked vessels and the representation of speech scrolls, jaguars, spider monkeys, human skulls and intricate vines and flowers can be seen in many late Classic and Post-Classic objects recovered from the lake bottom, indicating that these Mexican groups were present. Amatitlan and Los Jicaques must have been flourishing at the time of the Spanish conquest of Guatemala in 1524, for the historian Fuentes y Guzmán included them on his map made in 1690.

One matter not yet established is whether Pipil, Toltec and Maya inhabitants shared the same settlements or merely lived as friendly neighbors.

Unfortunately we do not know much of colonial times at the lake. Our best documents are the writings of an enterprising English Dominican friar, Thomas Gage, a parish priest of San Juan Amatitlan during the years 1635-36. According to Brother Thomas, Amatitlan was by then a prosperous commercial center surrounded by numerous large sugar plantations. Commoners and gentry from the capital still came there to bathe and take the waters, or to fish or row about the lake in boats or *canoas*.

Lake Amatitlan still plays a mystical role in the beliefs of present-day highland Maya Indians and Ladinos. The majestic stone church on the town plaza of San Juan Amatitlan is the home of an elaborately carved Spanish colonial wooden figure of the Santo Niño de Amatitlan, acclaimed for its miraculous healing powers. According to local legend, similar magical powers were once attributed to a carved stone idol called Jefe Dios which in pre-Columbian days stood on a cliff on the north shore of the lake. One night during the 17th century, the story goes, there was a great rumbling in the earth accompanied by a severe hailstorm, and the stone idol sank beneath the waters of the lake. The following morning devout visitors to the "pagan" shrine of Jefe Dios found in its place the charming wooden statue of the Santo Niño (Christ Child), and with elaborate ceremonies it was removed to the church on the town plaza.

Ever since then on May 3, the day of the Festival of the Cross, devout pilgrims from all parts of the Republic of Guatemala come to the Fiesta of Amatitlan. The little wooden figure of the Christ Child is borne from the church in a magnificent religious procession across the lake to the spot where legend places its miraculous appearance. Hundreds of gaily painted boats and canoes follow the statue on its journey; flowers and fruits are thrown into the lake by the pilgrims. It would seem that this modern Christian festival is a survival of ancient Maya lake rituals. In it we can see another example of the persistence of human ideas. The pre-Columbian belief that powerful spirits inhabited Lake Amatitlan, and with it the desire to placate these spirits, has survived virtually unchanged over a period of 3,000 years. It has managed to withstand or incorporate all foreign religious influences, including Christianity.

Prehistoric Man in the Grand Canyon

by Douglas W. Schwartz
February 1958

In an oasis at the bottom of the Canyon live the Havasupai Indians, who have now been linked to a vanished people who settled the surrounding plateau in the seventh century A.D.

The Grand Canyon in Arizona was discovered by Spanish explorers in 1540, but so far as is known no white man entered the Canyon itself until two and a half centuries later. In July of 1776 a Franciscan priest, Francisco Thomás Garcés, was traveling on a mission toward the Hopi country, and en route along the Colorado River he heard of an Indian tribe living deep in the Canyon. Since his mission was to convert Indians wherever he found them, Father Garcés asked to be led to the tribe so that he might take them the word of God. With the help of a guide the padre descended by steep trails to a valley almost a mile below the Colorado Plateau, in a small branch of the Colorado River called Cataract Creek. There he found a verdant oasis offering the pleasantest possible contrast to the desert country above. On the canyon bottom, between the bare, brown cliffs, ran a beautiful spring-fed stream,

CATARACT CREEK CANYON is a fork of the Grand Canyon. It is now the home of the Havasupai Indians. On the high ledges of the canyon wall, and atop the sloping rock debris at its base, are the granaries and shelters of an ancient people.

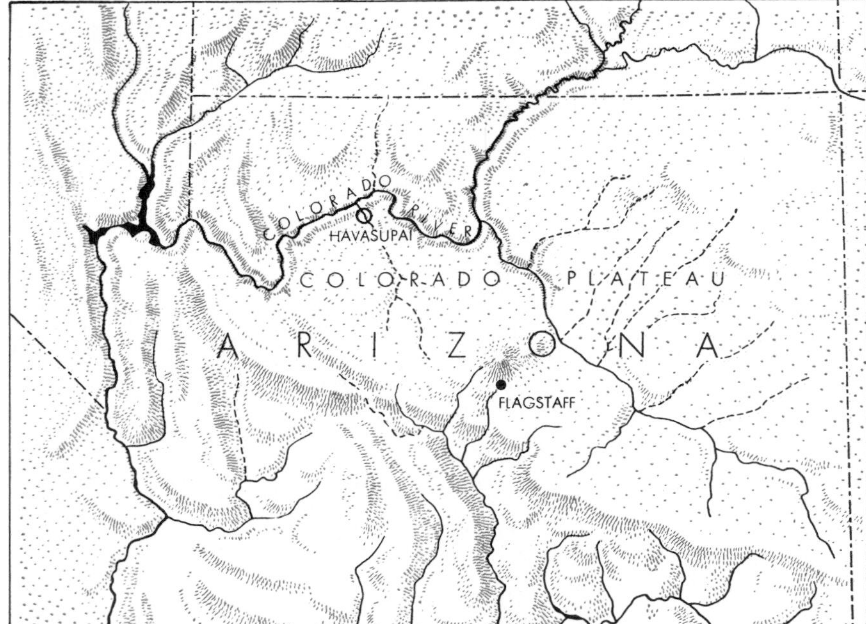

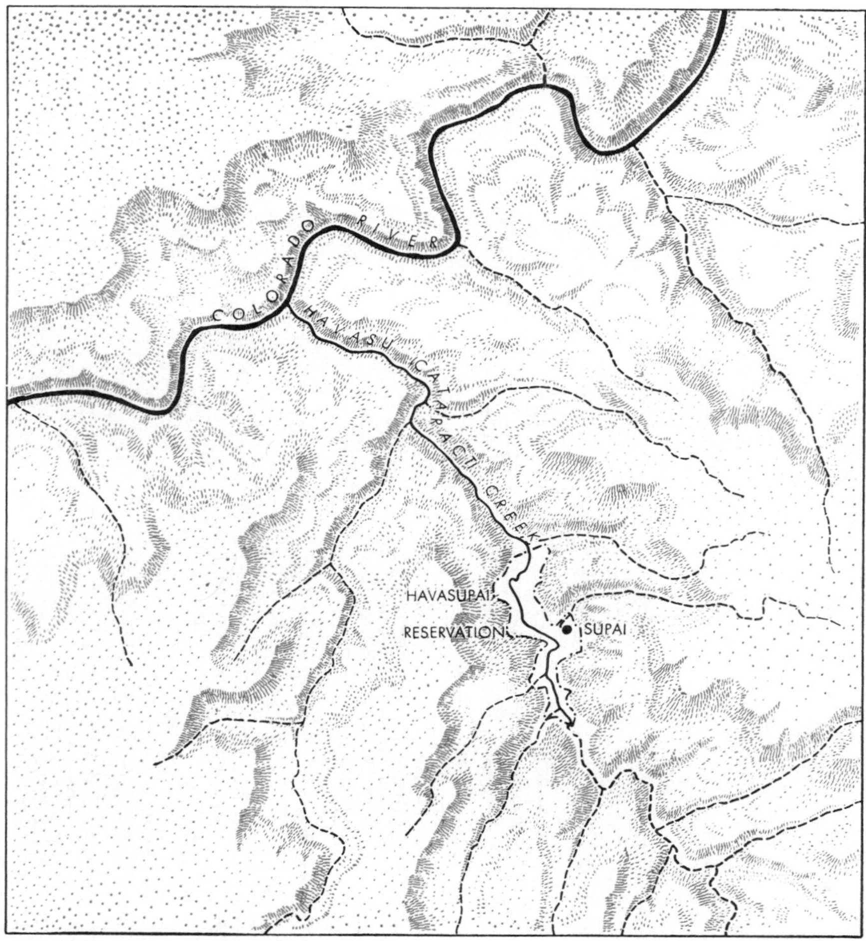

GRAND CANYON of the Colorado River cuts through the Colorado Plateau in northern Arizona. The relation of the Havasupai territory to the Grand Canyon is shown on the map at top. The map at bottom shows the exact location of the Havasupai Reservation in a widening of Cataract Creek Canyon. To the west, on the Coconino Plateau, are the ruins of houses built by the Cohonina people. The author believes they were ancestors of the Havasupai.

creating a green paradise of trees, flowers and luxuriant grass. It was occupied by a village of Indians called the Havasupai—"people of the blue-green water."

Garcés noted that the Havasupai made good use of the life-giving stream. They had developed a system of irrigation ditches to water their hundred or so arable acres, and in their small fields they were growing corn, beans, squash and a few European crop plants—apricots, figs, peaches, alfalfa—which they had obtained from other Indian tribes, who in turn had received them from the Spaniards. Father Garcés also observed a number of other things about the Havasupai's culture during his short stay of several days in the village. At dawn each family went out to work in the fields with digging sticks, hatchets and hoes. But as soon as the sun rose high enough to beat down in the Canyon, generating oven-like heat, everyone retreated from the fields to the huts and shades of the village. The men gossiped at the "sweatlodge," a counterpart of the village drugstore. The women indulged in their favorite sport—gambling with dice made of sticks. The children spent most of their afternoon hours swimming in the fast-flowing stream.

The peripatetic padre moved on, taking away only a momentary picture of these people and knowing little (since he had no interpreter) about their fascinating history and way of life. Not for well over a century was much more heard about the Havasupai. The waves of trappers, prospectors, soldiers, railroad scouting parties and scientific expeditions that overran the Southwest through the 19th century saw little of this shy tribe, which ventured less and less from its canyon retreat. But about 30 years ago Harold S. Colton, director of the Museum of Northern Arizona at Flagstaff, became interested in the history of Indians of the area, for remains going back some 1,200 years had been found on the plateau above the Canyon. He unearthed many old camp sites and houses of a people on the plateau who seemed to have disappeared around 1100 A.D. The mystery of their disappearance, as well as the peculiar isolation of the Havasupai, excited my curiosity when I began to work in the Grand Canyon area eight years ago. I became convinced that the key to the prehistory of the Colorado Plateau and Canyon Indians lay in the Havasupai home at the bottom of the Canyon.

In the winter of 1953-54 I lived with the Havasupai for six months in their canyon village. It was apparent that there was no hope of finding any ancient Havasupai remains in the village area. In early spring and in late summer floods as high as 40 feet often rush down the narrow canyon of Cataract Creek. The Havasupai villages have repeatedly been washed away by these floods. But at such times the Indians have taken refuge, as far back as they can remember, in rock shelters at the base of the cliff walls. We therefore excavated these shelter sites, hoping to find cultural remains of the Indians going back to the beginning of their occupation of the Canyon. The excavations were so successful that, combining information from the diggings in the Canyon and on the Plateau with our knowledge of the present descendants, and injecting a dash of poetic license (if my professional colleagues will not object), it is now possible to reconstruct the general history of the Havasupai for some 13 centuries.

Some time around 600 A.D. a few small family groups of Indians began to settle in the Colorado Plateau area above the Canyon [*see map on opposite page*]. They came from the west, possibly leaving an overcrowded region. (Colton named them the Cohonina, a Hopi word meaning "those who live to the west.") For a century they lived a frontier life, depending heavily on game and berries for food, searching for water sources, trying out the land for farming and settlement possibilities. After about 100 years they had learned to live off their new land so well that the population began to increase and settlements spread to all parts of the plateau. In the winter months they supplemented their farm crops by hunting near their plateau homes and in the great canyons that bordered them on two sides. It is possible that the Cataract Creek Canyon oasis was discovered during one of these early expeditions and thereafter served as a hunting base.

By 700 or 800 A.D. the plateau settlers had developed an efficient agriculture, were building some stone houses, and were making pottery with designs and decorations borrowed from their Indian neighbors in the Little Colorado and San Juan country to the north and east. In another century or so they had progressed to constructing granaries for their crops and were adopting a new style of house with what looks like a patio at one end. They also built a large, thick-walled structure which may have been a fort or a ceremonial building.

Meanwhile the population had overflowed into Cataract Creek Canyon. The canyon pioneers developed their own way of life, clearing the heavy brush, using the creek to irrigate their patches of land, and developing trails to the plateau a mile above. Possibly the tribe might eventually have split into two groups, one living primarily in the canyon, the other on the plateau. But as Colton observed, around 1100 A.D. the plateau population began to disappear, and within 100 years its settlements were deserted. Our excavations suggested a likely explanation. It seems that the plateau dwellers, as well as some Indians from other areas, were driven into the canyons by wandering tribes of raiders. The archaeological remains show that the Cataract Creek Canyon population increased greatly at this time. The valley floor became so overcrowded that people took up residence in the rock shelters at the base of the cliffs. Furthermore, they began to build cliff dwellings in the face of the cliffs, no doubt to defend themselves against the raiders. Every available ledge became a home, and on the large ledges the canyon people erected elaborate structures.

Apparently by the middle of the 13th century the raiding of the area by outside bands had subsided. The Canyon people abandoned their cliff dwellings. By this time they had evolved a new way of life. To find enough food for the large valley population they had had to organize frequent hunting parties

CLIFF SHELTER on a high ledge of the canyon wall is shown according to the author's reconstruction. Now a ruin, it was used as a refuge from floods or enemy raiding parties.

to go up on the plateau. Now these hunting and food-gathering expeditions to the top, particularly in winter, became a fixed feature of Havasupai life. The canyon refugees could not go back to living on the plateau again, even if they had wanted to. Conditions on the old plateau had changed, as the old men may have remarked. The annual rainfall had diminished. The vegetation was no longer as lush; the flowers were not as bright. Farming on the plateau had become impossible.

So the Havasupai developed a double life: summer in the canyon, winter on the plateau. All summer they led a sedentary existence in the valley, watching the crops grow. After the harvest, when the days grew cool, they moved up to the plateau and pitched camp in the cedar thickets. But they could not stay long in any one place: the winter life of hunting and gathering wild fruits and nuts kept them on the move over the great expanses of the plateau. Their rather precarious winter existence gained some security, however, from the crop reserves they were able to bring with them from the canyon. In the spring the Havasupai went back to the canyon village to take up their sedentary farming life again.

SHELTERS AND GRANARIES on high ledges illustrate the near-inaccessibility of the sites in which the author excavated early Havasupai remains. A stone house with a window can be seen (*upper right*) and, below it, a row of granaries on a narrow ledge (*bottom*).

For 300 years, until early in the 17th century, the Canyon Indians passed a tranquil existence. They had friendly relations with the Navaho, Hopi, Walapai and other neighboring tribes. Each August the Havasupai invited their neighbors to their annual harvest dance —a five-day feast of eating, dancing, trading and gambling which is still the highlight of Havasupai life today. The Havasupai culture changed little in the three centuries.

But this stability began to break down in the early 1700s. Long before Father Garcés arrived, the coming of the white man was heralded in Cataract Creek Canyon by new goods which filtered to the Havasupai from other tribes. The Spanish settlers themselves did not come near the canyon; the land of the Havasupai was of no use to them. The fact that the little canyon was well hidden from the plundering hands of the conquistadors saved the Havasupai from the fate that overtook many other Southwestern Indian tribes. They retained most of their aboriginal culture: their pottery, clay pipes, stone knives, fire drills, bone tools, bows and arrows, basketry and skin clothing. But through the Hopi they began to receive crockery, metal pans, guns, plants and cloth. When the first white man, Father Garcés, laid eyes on them, they already had horses, cattle and some Old World plants.

Although they have continued to have less contact with white people than almost any other Indian tribe, their culture has gone on adapting itself to the white man's ways. In the middle of the 19th century the unaggressive Havasupai accepted a reservation of only about 500 acres in the bottom of the Canyon. Secluded in their deep valley, the "people of the blue-green water" have nevertheless, by diffusion from the Hopi and other Indian neighbors and by deliberate education through Federal Government workers, moved rapidly toward immersion in American culture in recent decades. Each year several hundred tourists descend the Canyon to see their blue oasis, with beautiful waterfalls that tumble down the creek bed, and to see the gentle, cheerful Havasupai, now a small group of some 35 families. Their village, Supai, has a post office and a schoolhouse, and on occasion the villagers are treated to Hollywood movies of the "Wild West."

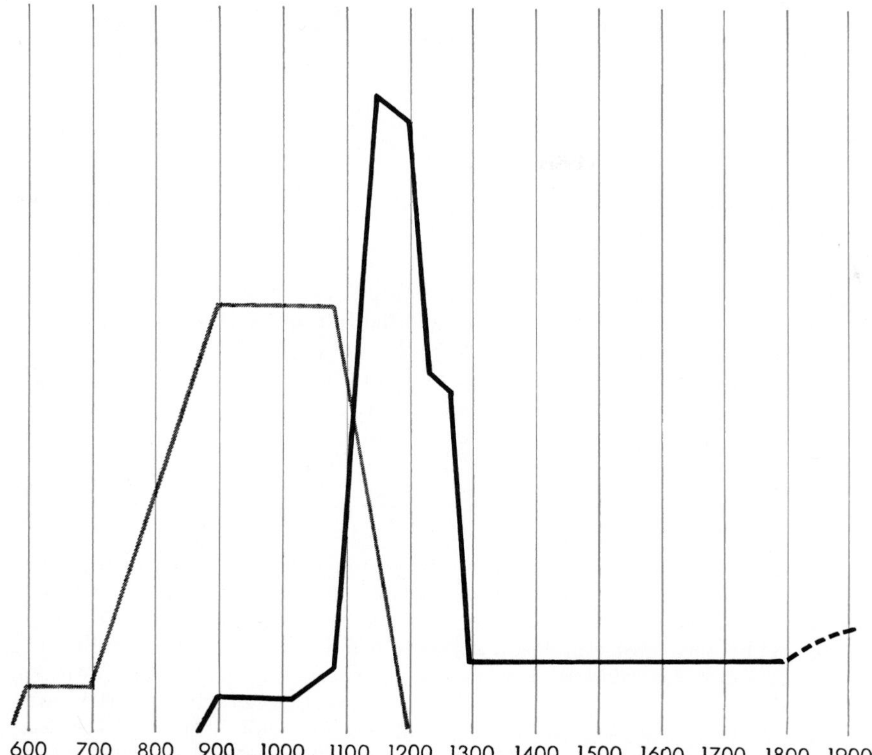

CHANGES OF POPULATION on the Coconino Plateau (*gray line*) and in Cataract Creek Canyon (*black line*) are shown schematically. The plateau population began to decrease in the 12th century, probably because of enemy raids followed by climatic change. The raids filled the canyon with refugees. When the raiders left, canyon population fell.

21 The Iroquois Confederacy

by James A. Tuck
February 1971

This alliance of Woodland Indian tribes played a significant role during the European colonization of North America. Excavations in New York now cast new light on their origins and social evolution

Among the Indians in the American Northeast none affected the lives of the European colonists more than the few thousand who lived near Lake Ontario and spoke the Iroquoian language. With firearms acquired in the 17th century, first from the Dutch and then the English, an alliance of five Iroquois tribes forayed east into the maritime provinces of Canada and west as far as the Illinois River. They crushed the nearest of their traditional Algonkian-speaking enemies and even destroyed Iroquois-speaking tribes that did not belong to their confederacy. Since the Algonkians were allies of the French, the Iroquois did much to help the English win control of Canada in the 18th century. Then they fought for both sides during the War of Independence.

The role played by these "Romans of the New World," as the historian Francis Parkman called them, seems out of all proportion to the slim resources at their disposal. How did the Iroquois manage to accomplish so much? The question has made Iroquois prehistory a controversial subject; a leading scholar in the field has remarked that more ink has been spilled over the Iroquois than over any other aboriginal American people. Yet the five tribes of the confederacy never had more than 12,000 members, and probably had considerably fewer. Their fighting men numbered only some 2,200.

Some scholars have maintained that the Iroquois came originally from Georgia and the Carolinas. That area was the home of the "civilized" Cherokees, who spoke an Iroquoian language and whose ready adoption of European ways was considered an indication of their superiority to other Indians. It has also been suggested that the Iroquois came from the north, moving down the valley of the St. Lawrence under pressure from the advancing Algonkians. One source even places the Iroquois homeland in the Pacific Northwest. Not until recently has it been realized that the Iroquois culture might simply have arisen in the area where the European colonists first encountered it.

Today it is clear that the actual origin is the last one. Archaeological evidence collected at more than a score of sites over the past two decades shows that the Onondagas—the key tribe in the confederacy—developed into full-fledged Iroquois from a preceding level of pre-Iroquois culture in the years after A.D. 1000 without ever leaving a 25-by-15-mile area in upper New York State near modern Syracuse. What is true of the Onondagas must surely hold for the other tribes in the confederacy: the Oneidas and Cayugas immediately to the east and the west, the Senecas of the Genesee valley farther to the west and the Mohawks of the Mohawk valley farther to the east.

What is known about the Iroquois in Colonial times is helpful in interpreting their prehistory. Like most of the other aboriginal inhabitants of the region, they were representatives of the Late Woodland period of Northeastern prehistory. Farmers and hunters, they lived in villages in forest clearings, protected from raiders by one or more palisades made of saplings. In the clearing beyond the palisade the women of the village raised corn, beans, squashes and tobacco. The women also collected wild plant foods and the men hunted and fished. Except for dogs, domestic animals were unknown. Inside the palisade stood several "longhouses," which were long indeed: typically they were 25 feet in width and 50 to 100 feet in length. This was the traditional Iroquois form of house, consisting of a framework of saplings covered with sheets of bark. It was divided into apartments that were usually occupied by closely related families. Running down the middle of the house was a corridor where the families living on each side shared fireplaces.

Each of the five tribes of the confederacy occupied two or more such villages, usually only a few miles apart. Village affairs were supervised by a local council. Above the local council was a tribal council, which generally met in the largest village. The tribes were banded together in a "Great League of Peace," the formal name for the confederacy, which was governed by a council of 50 sachems representing all the tribes. Iroquois religious observations marked both the events of the agricultural cycle (with such occasions as a "planting festival" and a "green corn festival") and the progress of the seasons (exemplified by an annual "wild strawberry festival" and similar events).

As a tribe whose leader was prominent in founding the Great League of Peace, the Onondagas were traditionally at the center of confederacy affairs. The tribe was "keeper of the central fire," and the name of their tribal leader, Atotarho, was adopted by an Onondaga when he rose to be sachem. Thus it seems likely that the trends and events of Onondaga

INDIAN VILLAGE on a hilltop near Syracuse, N.Y., is seen in the photograph on the opposite page during excavation. It is a 14th-century Iroquois site known as Furnace Brook. Stakes mark rotted saplings that formed walls and inner partitions. Dominating the scene is the outline of a structure that was 22 feet wide and 210 feet long: an Iroquois longhouse.

SAVAGE RITUAL at a 15th-century Iroquois village site known as Bloody Hill is evidenced by a bathtub-shaped pit discovered by a Syracuse University team in 1967. A fire burning under the stones transformed the pit into a platform suitable for roasting.

CLOSE-UP OF PIT during its excavation shows pieces of broken and cut human bone. Arrows point to knife marks. Part of a skull was also unearthed. Evidently an adult male had been cooked and eaten. The incident preceded the founding of the Onondaga tribe.

prehistory parallel those of the other tribes. All five tribes must have been subjected to much the same environmental and social pressures. Indeed, the career of the Onondagas probably reflects the events taking place among many of the Indians of the American Northeast in the era following the introduction of the cultivation of corn, beans and squashes around 1000 B.C.

The Late Woodland culture of the pre-Iroquois inhabitants of New York is named Owasco after a site at Owasco Lake near the center of the state. The earliest Owasco village that is pertinent to Onondaga prehistory lies some eight miles north of Skaneateles Lake and is known as the Maxon-Derby site. (This site and others, by the way, take their names from the local landowner or from local topographic features.) The Maxon-Derby site was excavated in 1959 and 1960 by William A. Ritchie of the New York State Museum in Albany. The site covers two acres and includes the floors of seven houses. Two separate carbon-14 analyses show that the village was occupied around A.D. 1100. Apparently it had no palisade of the kind that surrounded the villages of historical times.

The outlines of the seven houses can be traced partially or completely by rows of post molds: dark patches of humus in the subsoil that mark the position of the saplings that once formed the frame. Most of the houses were small, with parallel sides and rounded ends, but two of them appear to be precursors of the Iroquois longhouse: they were 25 feet wide and 60 feet long. The hearths in these larger houses, however, were along one wall rather than in a central corridor. The fact that the houses had several hearths suggests that they sheltered several related families.

The food remains at the Maxon-Derby site included the bones of mammals, birds and fish, the debris of wild plants and charred kernels of corn. Among the artifacts were triangular stone arrow points, bone tools and fired-clay tobacco pipes. All these objects in one way or another foreshadow Iroquois forms. The most abundant artifacts at the site were fragments of pottery; their rims had been decorated with impressions made by the edge of a paddle wrapped with cord.

A second Owasco village, known as the Chamberlin site, is some three miles southeast of the Maxon-Derby site. Early historical records indicate that it was once surrounded by a low ring of earth, which has now disappeared. A field party from Syracuse University excavated the site under my direction in the summer of 1967. Carbon-14 analysis indicates that the village was occupied around A.D. 1290, some two centuries later than the Maxon-Derby village. The pottery showed a corresponding degree of development, although it still clearly represented the late phase of Owasco culture.

The Chamberlin houses in particular show advances along Iroquois lines. Although the hearths are still next to one wall, the houses are more than 80 feet long. I suspect that the obliterated ring of earth once formed the base of a defensive palisade, which may mean that by the end of the 13th century village defense was becoming an important consideration.

Remains at still a third village site only a little east of the Chamberlin site show the transition from the Owasco culture to the nascent culture of the Iroquois. This is the Kelso site, excavated by Ritchie in 1963. The Kelso site actually consists not of one village but of two overlapping villages. Both were heavily fortified; the palisade of one consisted of three concentric rings of saplings. Some of the Kelso houses were small and oval, but the longhouses were nearly 130 feet in length and the hearths are along a central corridor with a door at each end. Although the overlapping outlines of the palisades show there had been two villages, only a single carbon-14 date was obtained. This is A.D. 1390, just a century later than the Chamberlin date. Not only the form of the Kelso longhouses but also the details of decoration on tobacco pipes and pottery allow the site to be assigned to the earliest phase of the full Iroquois culture.

On the basis of the available evidence the connection among the three sites is not entirely clear. It is nonetheless possible that the three villages, considering their closeness in time and space and the similarity of their artifacts, were occupied successively by a single community. Periodic relocations could have been motivated by the need for new supplies of firewood, for new hunting grounds and perhaps for new soil for horticulture.

Four village sites that are comparable in age to the first three and that also reflect the transition from the Owasco culture to the Iroquois are located among the tributaries to Lake Onondaga, some 15 miles farther east. The first of these sites, the Cabin site, was apparently a small, undefended hilltop village. A large trash heap on the steep slope next to the village yielded a wealth of artifacts. These are primarily fragments of pottery but also include triangular arrow points, tobacco pipes of late Owasco style, bone awls, pins, scrapers and fish-spear points, and a bangle fashioned from the toe bone of a deer [*see top illustration on pages 196 and 197*]. Another find was a tiny stylized clay effigy of a human face. This may foreshadow the later practice of wearing life-size effigy masks, which became an important feature of Iroquois religious ritual in historical times. No absolute date has been established for the Cabin site, but the inventory of artifacts suggests that it was occupied between A.D. 1250 and 1300.

Four miles to the north are the remains of a two-acre village known as the Furnace Brook site. It is not quite contemporaneous with the Kelso site to the west but, like the Kelso villages, it was completely surrounded by a palisade. Two carbon-14 determinations show that Furnace Brook was occupied between A.D. 1300 and 1370. Some of its houses are small and reminiscent of the ones at the Maxon-Derby site, but Furnace Brook has a longhouse that is of unusual dimensions for the period. It was 22 feet wide and 210 feet long; a door at each end opened on a central corridor where the hearths were located. The artifacts unearthed at Furnace Brook show that, like the Kelso site, it belongs to the earliest phase of the full Iroquois culture.

A third village site less than two miles away is Howlett Hill. It has the well-defined remains of three longhouses. The largest is also of unusual dimensions: it is 334 feet long [*see illustration on page 195*]. Analysis of charcoal from a post mold of this house yields a carbon-14 date of A.D. 1380, which suggests that the Howlett Hill village may have been a successor to the Furnace Brook one. The increase in longhouse size (the largest at Howlett Hill is a third longer than the largest at Furnace Brook) clearly reflects a similar increase in the number of occupants. In any case, the people of both villages had progressed beyond the Owasco culture to the Iroquois.

The last of the villages in the vicinity of Lake Onondaga is known as the Schoff site. It was partly excavated by our Syracuse University group in 1967, and it proved to have the longest of all the longhouses: it extended almost exactly 400 feet. A limited number of artifacts unearthed at the village include trumpet-shaped tobacco pipes and pottery with incised neck decorations. Both suggest that the villagers had attained the phase of Iroquois cultural development that follows the nascent phase. Analysis of material from the site has provided a carbon-14 date of A.D. 1410.

I have already suggested that the

FIVE TRIBES of the Iroquois confederacy were, from west to east, the Senecas, the Cayugas, the Onondagas, the Oneidas and the Mohawks. At the beginning of the 18th century their power extended from Maine to Illinois and from southern Ontario to Tennessee. The Tuscaroras became the sixth after being ousted by white settlers in the Carolinas.

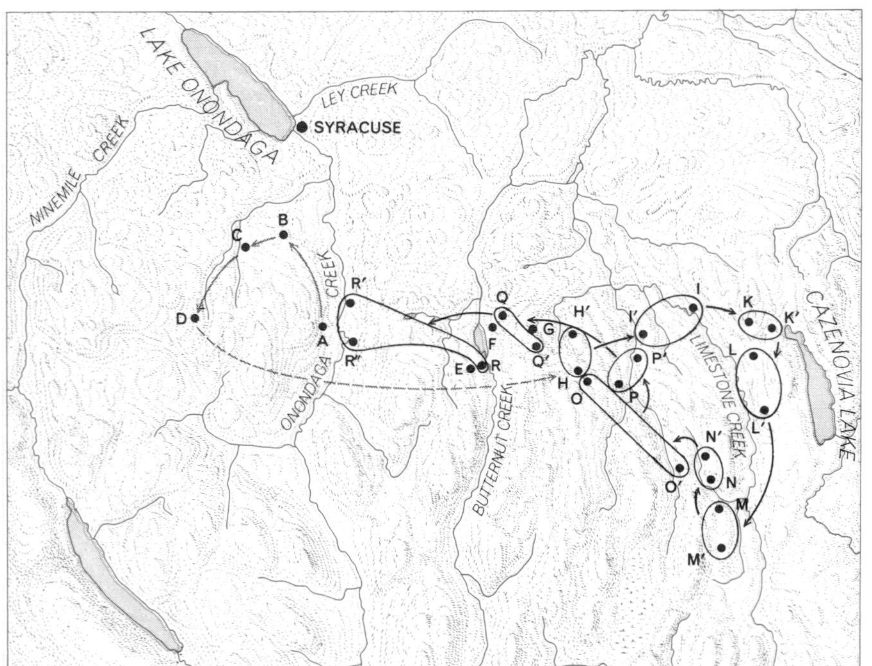

A	CABIN	L'	ATWELL
B	FURNACE BROOK	N	CHASE
C	HOWLETT HILL	N'	QUIRK
D	SCHOFF	M	SHELDON
E	COYE II	M'	DWYER
F	KEOUGH	O	CARLEY
G	BLOODY HILL	O'	POMPEY CENTER
H	BURKE	P	INDIAN HILL
H'	CHRISTOPHER	P'	INDIAN CASTLE
I	NURSERY	Q	JAMESVILLE PEN
I'	CEMETERY	Q'	WESTON
K	BARNES	R	TOYADASSO
K'	MCNAB	R'	UPPER VALLEY OAKS
L	TEMPERANCE HOUSE	R"	LOWER VALLEY OAKS

VILLAGE SITES occupied by the Indians who eventually founded the Onondaga tribe are identified by letters on this map. Arrows indicate successive occupations. The period runs from the end of the 13th century through the 18th. Establishment of two adjacent villages (*H–H'*) late in the 15th century marks the foundation of the tribe. Thereafter the tribe usually occupied pairs of villages.

three western sites could have been the successive residences of a single social group. The probability that another single group successively occupied the four central sites is stronger. The four villages are close to one another, and their successive occupation—if I am right—represents a series of moves into fresh territory first from south to north and then south again. Moreover, the three most recent villages are separated in time by no more than a century, and the progressive increase in the size of their longhouses might reflect the natural increase in the group's numbers. Lastly, certain aspects of the assemblage of artifacts at these sites, notably a high percentage of pottery vessels with incised neck decorations compared with the low percentage of this kind of decoration at other sites, suggest a degree of cultural continuity that may be characterized as a "microtradition."

The sequence of sites from Cabin to Schoff therefore appears to reflect the activities of a single group. The group's next move apparently was to abandon the Lake Onondaga watershed altogether. In spite of long and intensive reconnaissance and the excavation of test pits in a zone extending for miles in all directions from the Schoff site, no trace of a successor village has been found. The trail does not, however, grow completely cold.

The largest number of sites in the Onondaga region are found in the area east of Syracuse. The record preserved in these eastern sites extends from nascent Iroquois times through the period of European contact and up to the final decades of the 18th century. Three of the earliest sites in the eastern group are roughly contemporaneous with the Howlett Hill and Schoff sites in the cen-

LARGER LONGHOUSE, at the Howlett Hill site, is 334 feet in length. Closely set stakes outline the house wall. Other stakes within the house show where its inner structural supports stood. Numbered placards locate 16 hearths that lined a central corridor.

tral group; the earliest of them is known as Coye II. Like the Kelso site in the west and Howlett Hill in the central group, Coye II is a village that was occupied by people at the nascent phase of Iroquois cultural development. This is evidence that still a third social group in the Onondaga region participated in the transition from the Owasco to the Iroquois culture.

Two sites slightly later than Coye II are Keough and Bloody Hill. Both were small villages. No absolute date is available for Keough but a carbon-14 analysis of material from Bloody Hill places its time of occupation around A.D. 1420. The percentages of similar artifacts of various kinds from both sites are nearly identical, suggesting that the villages were occupied at about the same time.

Bloody Hill has also yielded evidence that ritual torture and cannibalism, which were familiar in historical times, were an established part of the Iroquois culture in the 15th century. In the summer of 1967 our digging exposed a large pit shaped somewhat like a bathtub: it was about eight feet long, four and a half feet wide and two and a half feet deep. The soil showed signs of having been subjected to intense heat. We found that the pit had been filled with firewood, some of it logs as much as six inches in diameter, which was then ignited. A layer of boulders and cobblestones had been placed on top of the burning logs, and the blaze soon transformed the cobble pavement into a roasting platform. A few scraps of refuse were present on the platform but the principal remains on it were fragments of an adult male's skull and long bones; the bones showed the marks of cutting tools. In the light of later Iroquois practices, it is not difficult to see in these human remains the ordeal and ultimate disposition of a captured enemy. The pit is testimony to the bellicose characteristics of early Iroquois society every bit as eloquent as the village fortifications.

About two miles east of Bloody Hill are two later sites I believe contain evidence of how the village groups of the time reacted to local strife. One of these areas is known as the Christopher site. It appears to cover two acres, and thus it represents a village much larger than either Keough or Bloody Hill. I suggest that the Christopher site in fact represents a merger of the two earlier communities, probably in the interests of improved security.

The second area, called the Burke site, is another extended village. It was occupied for a considerable time and, as the relocation of its palisade and one of its longhouses indicates, it was rebuilt at least once. The real surprise at the Burke site, however, is the presence of the same pottery-decorating microtradition that was characteristic of the Schoff site and its predecessors in the central area. At Burke we seem to have picked up the trail that had vanished earlier. Not only does the Schoff microtradition reappear at Burke but also one of the Burke longhouses is almost as generous in its proportions as the houses of the central area are. Although it has not yet been fully exposed, it already measures more than 240 feet. Moreover, the forms of the arrow points and tobacco pipes at Burke indicate a gradual evolution from the forms found at Howlett Hill and Schoff. That would be natural. The only available date for the Burke site, based on a carbon-14 study of material prob-

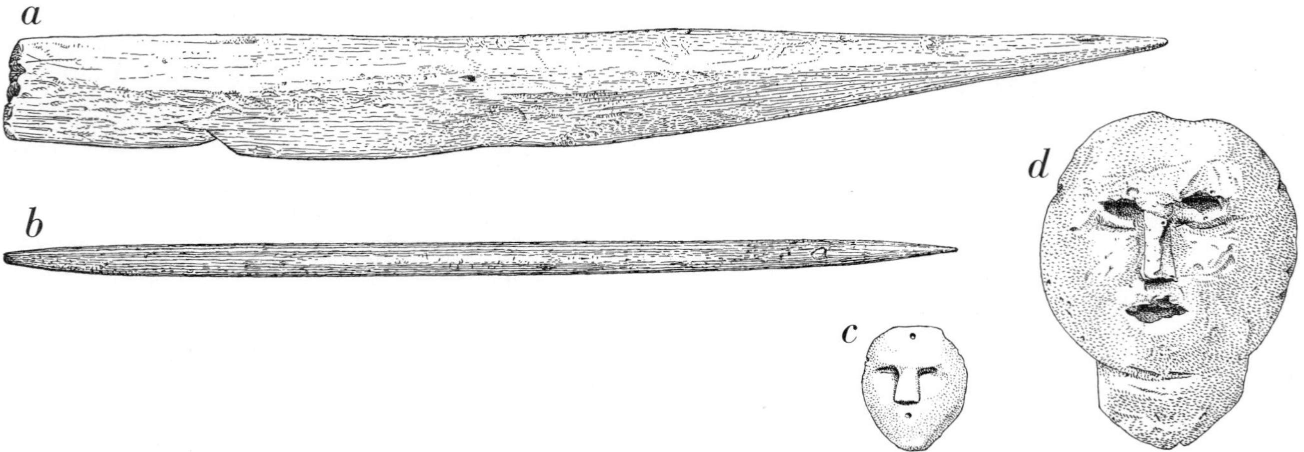

CHARACTERISTIC ARTIFACTS of the Owasco and Iroquois cultures include a bone awl (*a*), a bone point for a fish spear (*b*), an effigy of a human face modeled in clay (*d*) and a bangle fashioned from the toe bone of a deer (*e*). All are from the Cabin site,

ably deposited near the end of the village's occupation, is about A.D. 1480, or almost a century later than the Schoff village.

Why would a group intent on relocation choose to settle only two miles away from a large, well-defended and strange village? The choice has implications that bear on the eventual development of the Iroquois confederacy. It is hard to imagine that two potentially hostile communities could have existed so close together without an understanding, however informal, about mutual defense. At the very least some kind of nonaggression pact would have been needed to prevent clashes that could have been disastrous for one village if not both. I interpret the evidently peaceful coexistence of the inhabitants of the Christopher and Burke sites as an arrangement that marks the founding of the Onondaga tribe. The two groups probably became closely allied between A.D. 1425 and 1450, and it appears that an Iroquois two-village system and a subsequent pattern of intertribal nonaggression alliances may have begun here.

How soon after this time the two allied villages developed a sense of common identity and took a single name is impossible to say, but it should not have been long afterward. ("Onondaga" is an Iroquois word meaning "the people on the hills.") The merger would provide most of the advantages of combining military forces while at the same time avoiding the pressure that too large a concentration of people in a single village would exert on the environment. In this simple balancing of security require-

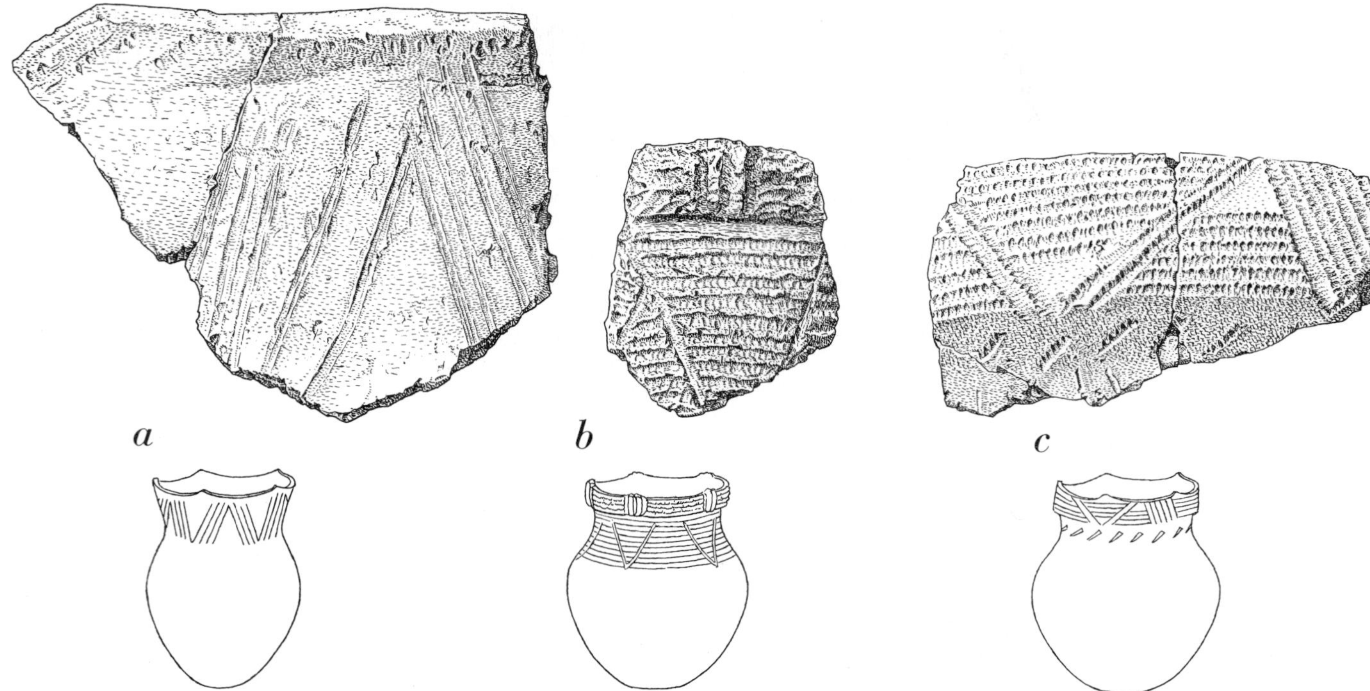

POTTERY DECORATION was applied principally to the neck of cooking vessels by incising lines in the clay or pressing it with a paddle wrapped with cord. The decorated fragments are illustrated two-thirds actual size; the form of the entire vessel is shown schematically below. The first examples are from village sites that may have been occupied successively by the same group: the

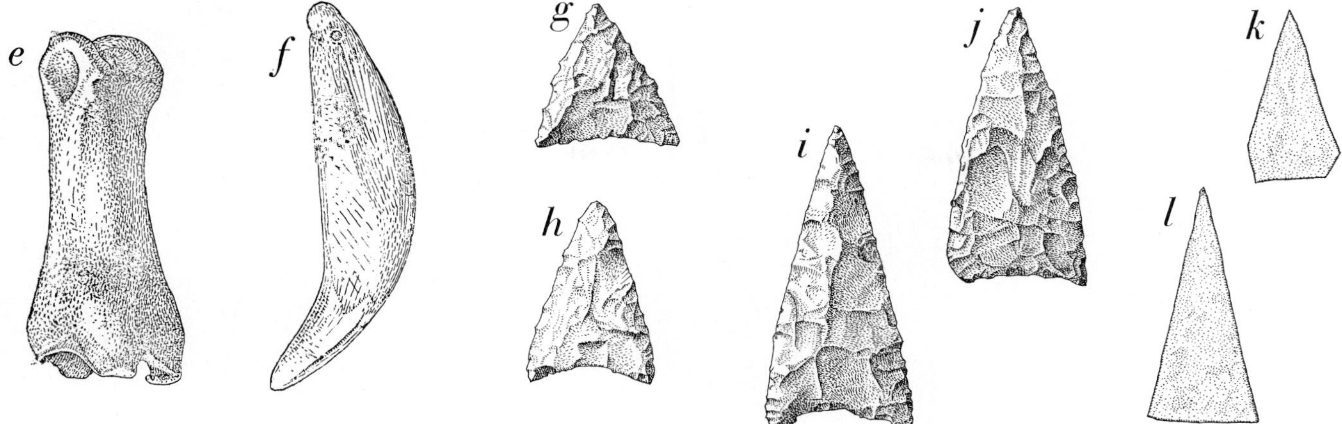

which was occupied around A.D. 1250 or 1300 by a group that was at the Owasco stage of cultural development. The smaller effigy (*c*), bear tooth (*f*) and arrow points (*g–j*) are from later Iroquois sites. Brass arrow points (*k, l*) mark the arrival of European trade goods.

ments with ecological imperatives, I believe, lies the basis of the later and larger political groupings that gave rise to the Great League of Peace.

For nearly three centuries, beginning with the first removal and resettlement of the twin villages late in the 15th century, the Onondaga tribe shifted its living sites a number of times. Although the removals were surely not simultaneous on each occasion, the general pattern consisted in occupying one smaller and one larger village that were never more than a few miles apart. Before the tribe's final post-Revolution move to the Onondaga reservation, it had occupied nine such pairs of villages. To describe the 18 sites in detail would be unnecessary; a short summary will suffice to complete the record of Onondaga cultural development.

The late prehistoric period of the Iroquois lasted until late in the 16th century. During that time the Onondaga villages were successively relocated in a northeasterly direction. The next, or protohistoric, period was marked by the introduction of European trade goods, although there was no direct contact between the Iroquois and Europeans. During this time the direction of relocation was southward, along the valley of Limestone Creek. Sites with steep approaches were favored, and the villages were usually well fortified. The houses were considerably smaller than the great longhouses of earlier days; the change may be indicative of social evolution that made the traditional house obsolete.

After a few southward removes the Onondagas reached the Allegheny Plateau and began to move northward again

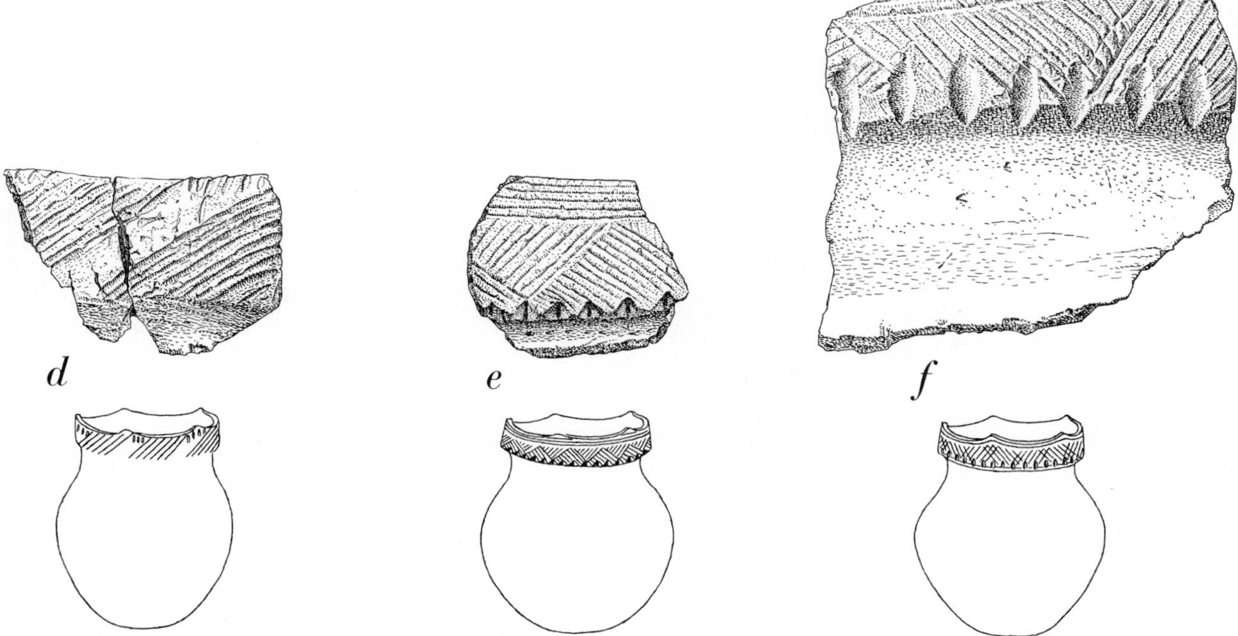

Cabin site (*a*), inhabited before A.D. 1300, and the Furnace Brook (*b*), Howlett Hill (*c*) and Schoff (*d*) sites, which were inhabited during the 14th century and the early 15th. The next sherd (*e*), from the Burke site, reveals its Owasco ancestry by its decoration with impressions of the edge of a cord-wrapped paddle. Finally, a fragment from the Cemetery site (*f*) exemplifies Onondaga ware.

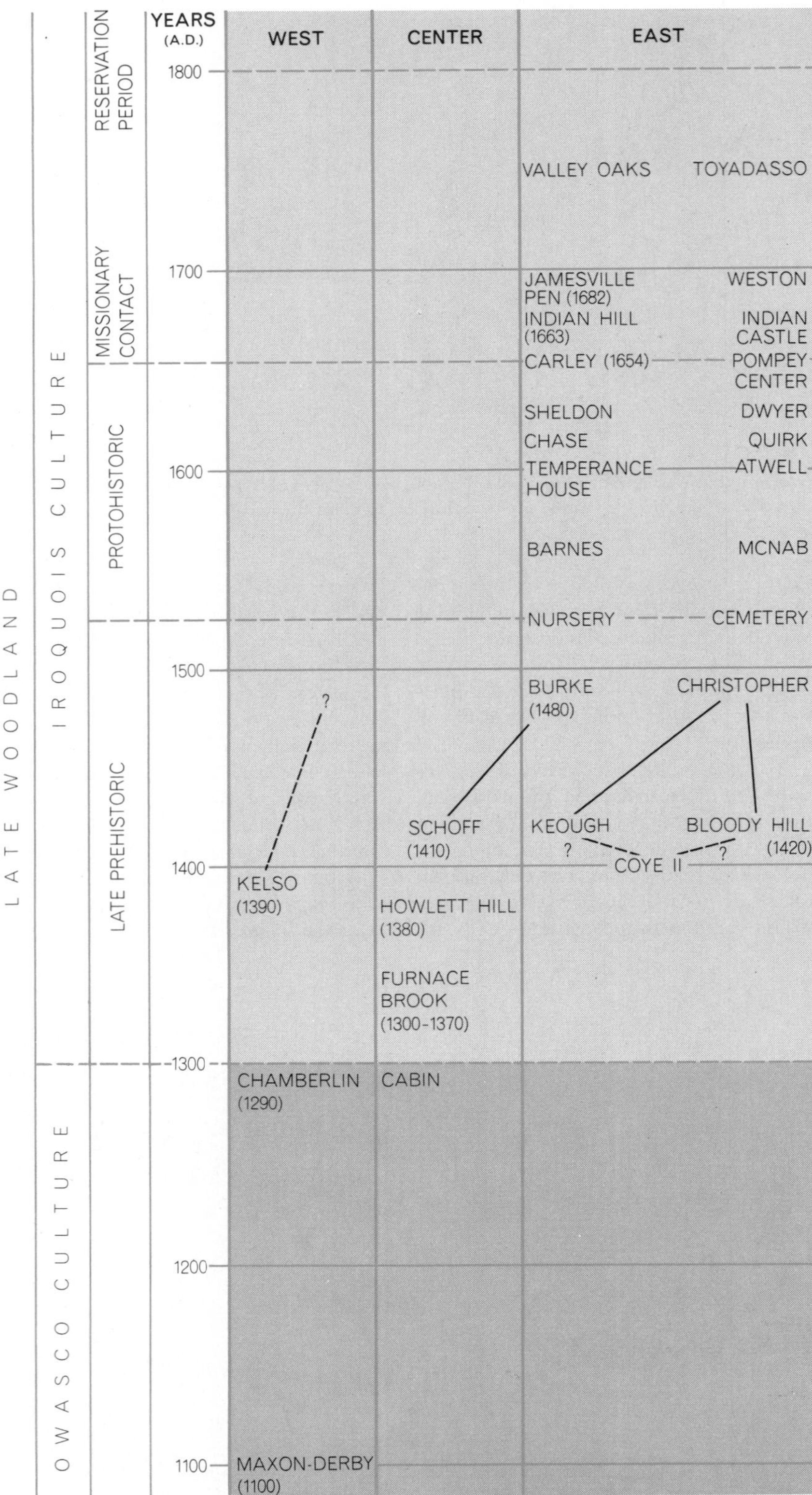

CHRONOLOGICAL CHART shows the relative ages of selected Late Woodland Indian sites in the Syracuse area. Three of the oldest lie north of Skaneateles Lake. The artifacts they contain demonstrate a transition from the preceding Owasco culture to nascent Iroquois. The three sites may have been occupied successively by the same group, but no trace of the group is found after A.D. 1390. The four more central sites also show the transition from Owasco culture to Iroquois. Development of a "microtradition" that favors incised decoration of pot necks suggests that they were occupied successively by the same group that subsequently occupied the eastern village represented by the Burke site, where the same microtradition is present. Coalition with a third group of Iroquois villagers is suggested by the proximity of the Burke and Christopher sites. Villages are usually paired thereafter.

along the valley of Butternut Creek. Villages were still located in defensible positions, but they were no longer necessarily protected by steep slopes. A steady decay in native arts and crafts provides a measure of the growing importance of European trade goods. Stone axes, knives and arrow points disappear and metal ones take their place. By the time of the first recorded contact between the Onondagas and Europeans the native manufacture of pottery had become virtually a lost art. We may surmise that many less tangible elements of Iroquois culture had been eroded at the same rate.

On August 5th, 1654, a French missionary, Father Simon LeMoyne, entered the leading Onondaga village. As he writes, he was "singing the ambassador's song and receiving addresses of welcome." The next year two more French priests arrived; they supervised the building of a small bark chapel and started the work of Christianizing the Onondagas. Tradition has it that they came to the village now known as the Indian Hill site. Jesuit records, however, indicate that Indian Hill was not settled until about 1663, so that it is more likely that Father LeMoyne entered an earlier Onondaga village, perhaps the Carley or the Pompey Center site.

A European who came to Indian Hill in 1677 left this eyewitness description: "The Onondagoes have butt one towne, butt it is very large, consisting of about 140 houses, nott fenced; it is situate upon a hill thatt is very large, the banke on each side extending it self att least two miles, all cleared land whereon the corne is planted. They have likewise a small village about two miles beyond thatt, consisting of about 24 houses." (The latter was apparently a village to the south of Indian Hill now called the Indian Castle site.)

The visitor's words attest to the Onondaga two-village settlement pattern and also to the extensive plantings that surrounded the settlements. It further allows us to deduce that the dwellings at Indian Hill were not the traditional Iroquois longhouses; the site is much too small to have accommodated 140 houses of any great size. That the settlement Indian Hill was "nott fenced" is surprising. Evidently by this time the Onondagas no longer built the customary village palisade.

The sites of historical Onondaga villages need further study, but the archaeological work that has been done at Indian Hill so far suggests that by the 1670's European trade goods were predominant. Virtually the only items of

VILLAGE DEFENSE depended primarily on a stout palisade made of timbers brought from the nearby forest and set upright in a ring around the village. The holes indicate where the timbers stood that formed the palisade surrounding the site at Furnace Brook.

native manufacture found there (or at Jamesville Pen, the successor village to Indian Hill) are tobacco pipes.

This was the period of the confederacy's greatest influence. The Iroquois conquered the Huron Indians in 1649, the Tobacco and "Neutral" tribes in 1650, the Eries in 1656 and other groups in succeeding years. By that time the confederacy held sway from the Illinois River in the west to the Kennebec in the east and from the Tennessee River north to the Ottawa. In 1711 the British settlements in North Carolina expelled the Iroquoian-speaking Tuscaroras from their lands. The Tuscaroras moved north and were formally adopted by the Oneidas, increasing the membership of the confederacy from five tribes to six.

The confederacy sided successfully with the British in the many bloody frontier campaigns of the French and Indian Wars, but the War of Independence that followed led to its destruction. Nominally the Great League of Peace remained neutral, but each tribe was left free to choose the side it preferred. Only the Oneidas favored the cause of the Revolution. The Senecas and the Mohawks actively supported the loyalists until Revolutionary punitive campaigns in 1779 defeated them, decimated the Onondagas and brought general destruction to the Iroquois homeland.

The surviving Onondagas took refuge first on a reservation near Buffalo and finally on a parcel of land near Syracuse part of which today constitutes the Onondaga Indian Reservation. Of the other tribes, the Oneidas chose a new home in Wisconsin, and many of the surviving Mohawks and Cayugas remained allied with the loyalists and moved to Canada.

In this summary of some 700 years we first find traces of the early and apparently successive activities of three small Late Woodland Indian groups in the upstate New York area where the Onondaga tribe eventually arose. Around A.D. 1400 we lose track of the westernmost group; its contributions to the Onondaga culture, if any, remain unknown. The villages successively occupied by the other two groups, however, are more easily traced. The movements of one group can be followed for a period of 200 years as it shifts from place to place in an area just west of modern Syracuse. As the group moves, its members acquire Iroquois ways and develop a concern about self-defense that may have arisen because of the increase in population pressure throughout the American Northeast that followed the introduction of agriculture.

Between A.D. 1425 and 1450 the western group leaves its ancestral domain, moves eastward and settles near a community of a similar kind that had inhabited a similar local territory for some generations. Although there is a tradition of warfare and human sacrifice, the strangers' incursion appears to have been peaceful. This strife-free event we take to mark the founding of the Onondaga tribe, the central group in the later Iroquois confederacy. From earlier mergers of small groups and from political unions such as this one, presumably aimed at nonaggression and mutual defense, there seem to have arisen such powerful Iroquois social institutions as the "medicine societies" and perhaps even the system of tribal organization in moieties, or dual groups. Both would have served a socially integrative function in newly formed communities. The medicine society gathers individuals from separate kinship groups into a single unified organization. The moiety system, in turn, ensures a system of complementary rituals and ceremonies, ranging from the exchange of marriage partners between the two halves of the tribe to burial rituals and the elevation of sachems.

The increase in nonhostile contacts between the Iroquois villages and tribes that led to the Great League of Peace can be seen in the archaeological evidence. It appears in the gradual transformation of local microtraditions into patterns that are more broadly homogeneous. This is particularly evident in certain styles of pottery among the Onondagas, the Oneidas and the Mohawks that eventually become almost identical.

The heyday of the confederacy in the 16th century must have been a relatively peaceful time. Although village fortifications testify to a continuing concern about defenses, raids from the outside could not have been nearly as disruptive as the earlier intertribal battles. Over the next two centuries, however, direct and indirect contacts with Europeans, and Iroquois involvement in European quarrels, proved fatal. These contacts brought about the collapse of the Great League of Peace, the steady erosion of the Iroquois way of life and the eventual transformation of the Romans of the New World into wards of a white man's society.

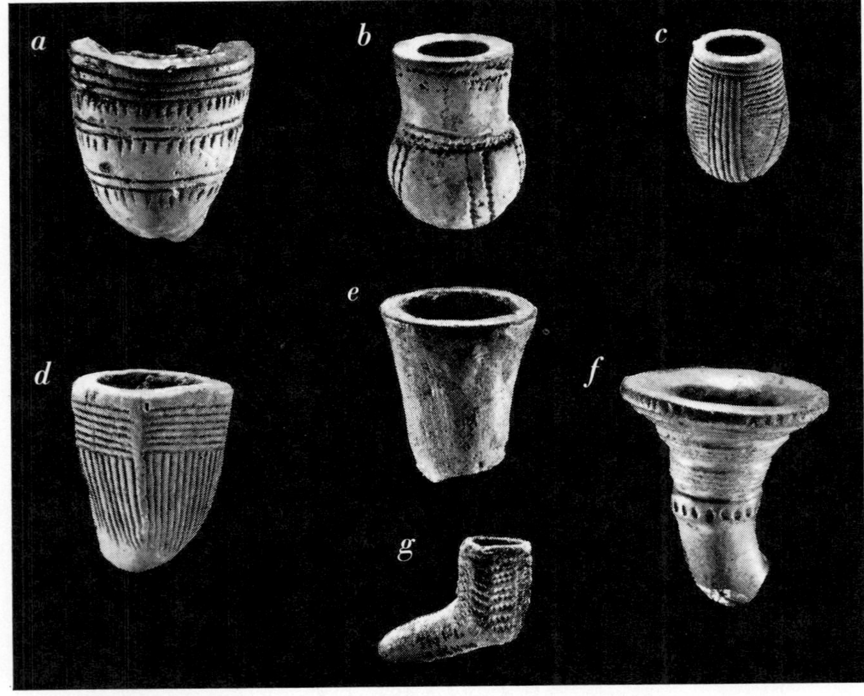

TOBACCO PIPES, a common Woodland Indian artifact, were made in a number of styles. A miniature model (*g*) shows the form of an intact pipe. The rest have lost their stems and are represented only by their bowls. The conical bowl, decorated with impressions from a cord-wrapped paddle (*a*), is from the Furnace Brook site and resembles the pipes of the preceding Owasco culture. The pot-shaped (*b*), barrel-shaped (*c*) and square bowls (*d*) are from the same site, an Iroquois village that was occupied between A.D. 1300 and 1370. A somewhat trumpet-shaped bowl (*e*) from the Bloody Hill site, which was occupied around 1420, presages the form of Iroquois trumpet pipe (*f*) popular in historical times.

RECONSTRUCTIONS OF STRATEGIES

The readings here are examples of reconstructions of just one component of a cultural system, often of a particular strategy that was undertaken by a cultural group in adapting to its environment. Strategies are purposeful activities, undertaken to meet the conditions in which the population lives. Most strategies are implicitly adaptive, in that they take place in a certain context of action, and are attempts to achieve an equilibrium with the environment, both cultural and natural.

Most of the strategies that archaeologists reconstruct are economic, partly because some archaeologists feel that the economic aspects of prehistoric life are the most knowable, partly because much of the archaeological record is most obviously related to subsistence strategies and technological adaptations, e.g., stone tools, ceramics, storage pits, irrigation canals, food remains. The articles here are concerned with elephant-hunting (Haynes, page 204), bison-hunting (Wheat, page 213), irrigation techniques of agricultural systems (Coe, page 231; Parsons and Denevan, page 241), metal-working (Easby, page 249), and ritual (Prufer, page 222).

These reconstructions are concerned both with the strategy itself (e.g., irrigation) and with the conditions that may have caused such behavior (e.g., population increase, environmental conditions). Thus many of them tend to focus on cause and effect relationships, and on how the particular strategy fits into the rest of the cultural system and natural environment. These strategies are viewed as having a certain function in the total system; hence reconstructions of strategies are often "functional reconstructions." These differ from the preceding reconstructions of events, which are not so explicitly

TABLE VII. Articles Employing the Perspective of Reconstruction of a Strategy.

Author	*Time*	*Area*	*Strategy*
Haynes (1966)	10,000 to 5000 B.C.	North America	Hunting-gathering
Wheat (1967)	6500 B.C.	Western U.S.	Hunting-gathering
Prufer (1964)	100 B.C. to A.D. 550	Eastern U.S.	Agricultural/ hunting-gathering
Coe (1964)	A.D. 500 (?)–present	Mesoamerica	Agricultural
Parsons and Denevan (1967)	Pre-Columbian	Tropical South America	Agricultural
Easby (1966)	Before A.D. 1400	New World	Hunting-gathering/ agricultural civilization

concerned with the context of human behavior. Thus, it is apparent that the reconstructions of strategies are closer to the goals, objectives, and theory of the systemic perspective than to those of the time-space perspective.

Recall that we can see how reconstructions of events followed from the well-developed spatio-temporal chronologies, and how reconstructions of events led to reconstructions of sequences of events. It is also easy to see how this kind of sequential reconstruction generated interest in reconstructing strategies, since so many sequences involved changing adaptive strategies. And it was from this last kind of reconstructionist perspective that research dealing with systems and processes could develop (see Section V).

THE READINGS

"Elephant Hunting in North America," by C. Vance Haynes, is the first of six articles that may be viewed as reconstructions of adaptive strategies. Because the precise chronology and pathways of the first Americans is not yet secure, Haynes' article brings the situation up to date (1966) for Paleo-Indian hunting groups that used projectile point tool kits (compare MacNeish 1971, page 143, and Haag, 1962, page 263). Haynes attempts to set the spatial and temporal parameters for this big-game hunting strategy, and to understand the precise technological and behavioral repertoire that enabled mammoth-hunters to succeed. He relates the widespread finds of a specialized hunting technology to preceding geological contexts and to demographic processes that allowed the radiation of these hunters across the United States. This contextual evidence contributes to the plausibility of his reconstruction.

"A Paleo-Indian Bison Kill" by Joe Ben Wheat is an amazingly detailed reconstruction of the bison kill at the Olsen-Chubbuck site in eastern Colorado and an impressive microadaptive statement. The analysis is only of the bison-kill activities at this single site. The reconstruction covers the hunting and butchering strategy and the estimates of how many people were involved and of how long they might have been fed by this kill. The detail with which this kill can be reconstructed derives from the geographical context and the clearly patterned deposition of the bones and other archaeological remains that were revealed by careful excavation. Observations were made of the orientation of skeletons and projectile points, of the clustering of artifacts, and of the patterns of bone deposition resulting from the butchering techniques. Wheat interprets the significance of the patterning by means of various kinds of knowledge: of historic buffalo trails; of recent Plains Indians; of the ecology and behavior of bison; of meat yields from bison; of the preservability of such meat; and of the probable amounts of fresh and/or dried meat that Plains Indian groups could transport. The detail of his reconstruction has recently been "brought to life" in the Time-Life book *The First Americans,* wherein artists' drawings recreate the story as told here by Wheat.

Olaf Prufer's reconstruction, "The Hopewell Cult," is rather unique, since his focus is on the components and operation of a ritual system or cult that is widely documented across the eastern United States, whereas most other reconstructions of strategies are concerned with economic and subsistence strategies. This cult is defined in terms of certain assemblages of artifacts, primarily grave goods, and types of earthworks that often housed burials. Prufer's demonstration that these characteristics, although widespread, are not necessarily indicative of the same cultural group is an important prelude to the systemic perspective, which would view the ritual subsystem among these groups as an adaptation which was participated in by different groups. These groups did not participate in or even share other modes of adaptation to their differing environments. This study is an important contribution to archaeological reconstruction and explanation in two respects. First, it points out the difficulties in identifying a cultural unit based on similarities in some of the material culture from different sites, especially those manifesting differences in settlement and subsistence strategies. Second, it deals with ritual as an adaptive strategy, which is a perspective often overlooked by archaeologists. It is enlightening to view this ritual system, with its corresponding trade network and integrative effects, as being just as necessary an adaptive strategy as was agriculture, for example.

In "The Chinampas of Mexico," Michael Coe has reconstructed the probable origin and, in particular, the operation of the chinampa-irrigation system, which is known to have supported the agriculture of the Aztec empire and, most likely, of the Teotihuacano civilization of earlier times (see Millon, page 115). This strategy performed at least two functions; it was both a land-reclamation system and an irrigation system that allowed for incredible continued productivity. Another benefit was the use of the chinampa canals as a transportation system, which brought trade and tribute to the major cities of a civilization that lacked both the wheel and well-developed roadways (see von Hagen on the Peruvian roads, page 33). The systemic perspective is implied in this reconstruction, in that one can see how feedback developed among the components of the total cultural system; these components, or subsystems, included land-reclamation activities, the irrigation system, agricultural productivity, population size and distribution, and management of the chinampas and their produce. These evolving subsystems soon grew to a point where innovations, such as aqueducts and dikes, were needed to keep them going. How the chinampas "work" can still be observed today in the remaining chinampas of Xochimilco. Understanding their antiquity and relation to the evolution and maintenance of civilization in highland Mexico is the concern of the reconstruction.

This reconstruction of "Pre-Columbian Ridged Fields," by James J. Parsons and William M. Denevan, is primarily a description of the form and locations of ridged agricultural fields found in at least four widely separated areas of tropical South America. It is also an attempt to understand the kinds of ecological adaptations that took place in order to support an increasingly larger and more complex social system. Understanding the agricultural basis of civilization is a common theme for reconstructionists (see MacNeish 1964, page 155; Millon, page 115; Coe, page 237). No archaeological excavations contribute to this reconstruction. Survey, aerial photography, and mapping of the earthworks form the basis for reconstructing how Pre-Columbian agriculturalists handled both drainage and irrigation. In the absence of extensive archaeological excavation, the known ecology of root crops is used to suggest that manioc, rather than maize, may have been the cultigen. In one instance (Surinam), sediment analysis suggests that it was an encroaching sea that led to the innovative ridged sites in order to continue the old way of life. Like Tuck's article (page 190), this reconstruction contributes to Steward's ecological approach (page 9) by elucidating the similar adaptive strategies that develop under similar socioecological conditions.

In "Early Metallurgy in the New World," Dudley Easby has reconstructed many of the diverse techniques and products of pre-Columbian metal workers in the New World. He had very little contextual data as a basis for understanding how metal objects were made. Most of the metal artifacts that we have do not come from archaeological excavations, but from private collections. Little mention is made in the ethnohistorical accounts of the techniques employed, and Easby's reconstruction is based on laboratory studies of the artifacts themselves. The spatio-temporal distribution of metal artifacts in the New World is wide-ranging, and the diversity of artifacts produced is impressive. The reconstruction of techniques presented here is only the first step toward investigation into sources of production, the use of the artifacts in social, ceremonial, economic, or other cultural subsystems, and the conditions under which the techniques were discovered, learned, and supported by the society.

22

Elephant-Hunting in North America

by C. Vance Haynes, Jr.
June 1966

Bones of elephants that vanished from the continent 10,000 years ago are found together with the projectile points early men used to kill them. Indeed, the hunters may have caused the elephants' extinction

Elephant-hunting today is a specialized activity confined to a handful of professionals in parts of Africa and Asia; 11,000 years or so ago it provided a living for one of the earliest groups of humans to inhabit the New World. At that time hunting bands whose craftsmen made a particular kind of stone projectile point by the thousands ranged across North America from the east coast to the west coast, as far north as Alaska and as far south as central Mexico. Two generations ago such a statement would have been hard to support. Since 1932, however, the excavation of no fewer than six stratified ancient sites of mammoth-hunting activity in the western U.S. and the discovery of scores of significant, if less firmly documented, sites elsewhere in North America have proved its validity beyond the possibility of challenge. It is the purpose of this article to present what we know of the lives of these mammoth-hunters and to suggest when they arrived in the New World.

The first evidence that man had been present in the New World much before 2000 B.C. touches only indirectly on the history of the mammoth-hunters. This was a discovery made near Folsom, N.M., by an expedition from the Denver Museum of Natural History in 1926. Careful excavation that year and during the next two seasons uncovered 19 flint projectile points of unusual shape and workmanship lying 10 feet below the surface among the bones of 23 bison. The bison were of a species that paleontologists had thought had been extinct for at least 10,000 years. The Denver Museum excavation at Folsom thus made it plain that as long ago as 8000 B.C. hunters armed with a distinctive type of flint point had inhabited what is now the western U.S. The association of the projectile points with the bison bones made it almost certain that the bison were the hunters' prey; any doubts on this score were settled when Frank H. H. Roberts of the Smithsonian Institution, digging at the Lindenmeyer site in Colorado, found a Folsom point firmly lodged in a bison vertebra.

In 1932 a cloudburst near Dent, Colo., hastened the erosion of a gully near the South Platte River and exposed a large concentration of mammoth bones. Investigators from the Denver Museum went to work at the site; the bones proved to represent 11 immature female mammoths and one adult male. Along with the animal remains they found three flint projectile points and a number of boulders that were evidently not native to the surrounding accumulation of silt. In the 1930's the carbon-14 technique of dating had not yet been invented, but the geologists in the party estimated that the Dent site was at least as old as the Folsom site and perhaps older. Certainly the projectile points found at Dent, although they bore a general resemblance to those found at Folsom, were cruder in work-

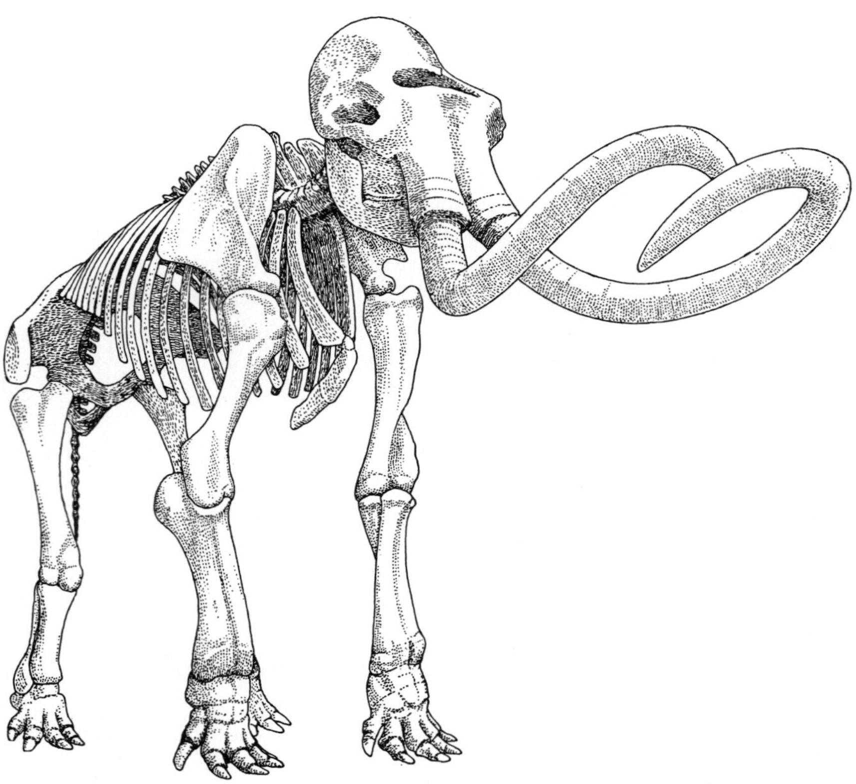

AMERICAN ELEPHANTS were all of the genus *Mammuthus*. They included the woolly mammoth, which also ranged the Old World, and the imperial, confined to North America. This skeleton of one imperial variety, the Columbian, is 12 feet at the shoulder.

manship. In any case, the excavation at Dent made it evident that early hunters in western North America had preyed not only on extinct bison but also on the mammoth.

Beginning in 1934 John L. Cotter of the Academy of Natural Sciences in Philadelphia excavated a site known as Blackwater Draw near Clovis, N.M., which proved to contain the answer to the relative antiquity of the Folsom and Dent finds. In the Clovis sediments projectile points like those from Folsom were found in the upper strata associated with bison bones. Below these strata, associated with the remains of two mammoths, were four of the cruder, Dent-style projectile points and several flint tools of a kind that could have been used for butchering. Also found at Clovis was an entirely new kind of artifact—a projectile point fashioned out of bone. At the completion of nearly two decades of work at the site by investigators from the Philadelphia Academy and other institutions, students of New World prehistory were generally agreed that two separate groups of hunters had once inhabited western North America. The earlier group, using flint projectile points of the type found in the lower Clovis strata, had been primarily mammoth-hunters; the later group, using Folsom points, had been primarily bison-hunters.

The most obvious characteristic that Clovis and Folsom points have in common is that they are "fluted." After the flint-knapper had roughed out the point's general shape he beveled its base; then, with a deft blow against the beveled base, he detached a long flake, leaving a channel that extended a third or more of the point's length [*see illustration at right.*] The fluting, on one or both sides of the point, gave the point a hollow-ground appearance. It has been suggested that the flute channels facilitated the bleeding of the prey, as do the blood-gutters of a modern hunting knife. A more plausible explanation is that the fluting made the point easier to fit into the split end of a wooden shaft. The assumption that the points were hafted in this manner is strengthened by the fact that their edges are generally dulled or ground smooth for a distance from the base about equal to the length of the flute channel. If a sinew lashing was used to mount the point in a split shaft, it would be mandatory to have dull edges where the lashing was wrapped; otherwise the flint would cut through the taut sinew.

To judge from the ease with which

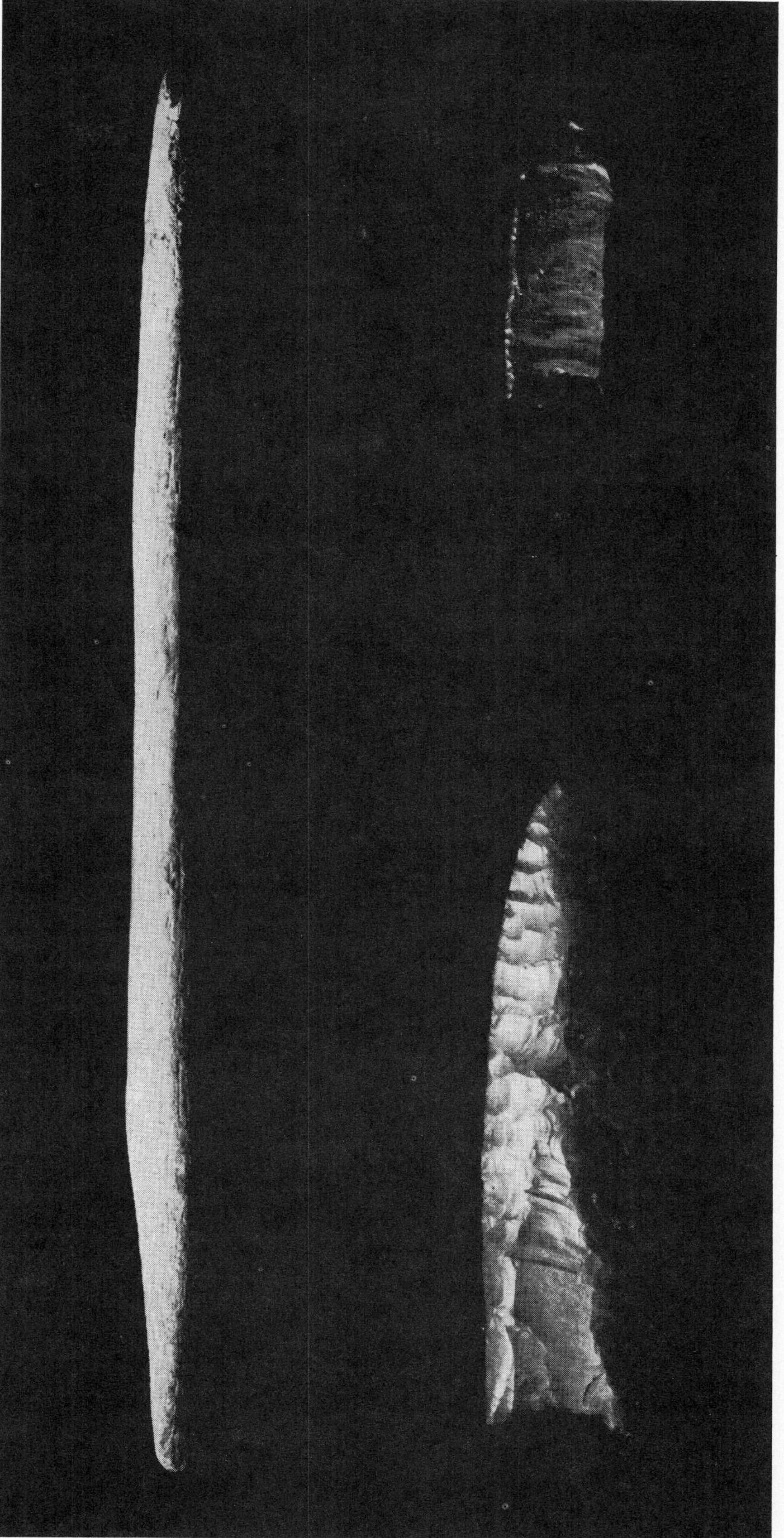

PROJECTILE POINTS used by early hunting groups in North America include one of bone (*left*) and one of flint (*lower right*) found near Clovis, N.M., in the mid-1930's. These artifacts were used to kill mammoths. The smaller flint point (*upper right*) was made by a later group that hunted bison. The first of these were found near Folsom, N.M., in 1926.

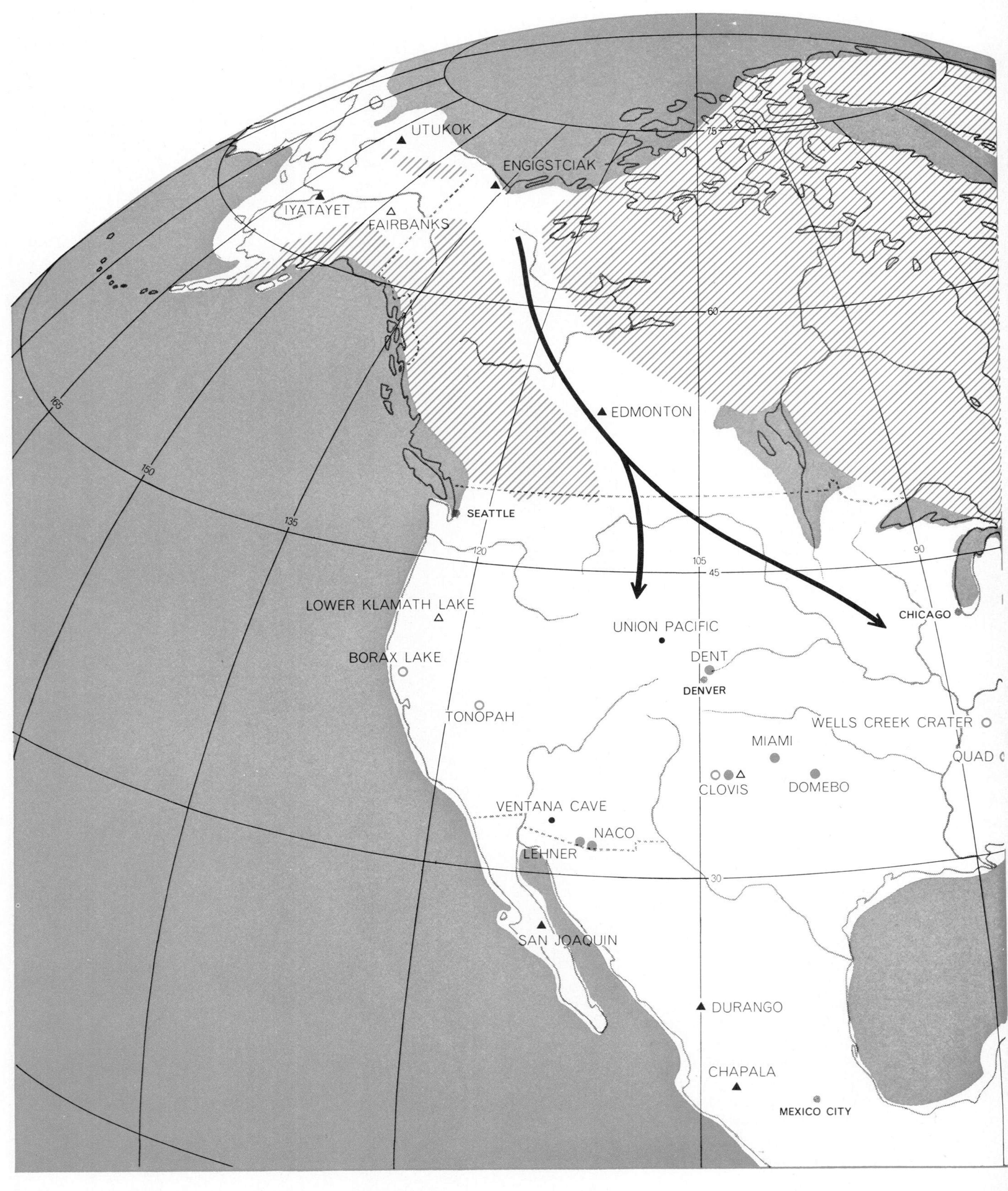

ICE-FREE CORRIDOR in western Canada may have opened some 12,000 years ago. The author suggests that the mammoth-hunters who made both the characteristically fluted flint projectile points and the needle-like bone ones left the Bering Strait area earlier than that and reached the unglaciated part of North America some 11,500 years ago. Symbols by the names distinguish among campsites, kill

a few self-taught flint-knappers today can turn out a classic Clovis or Folsom point in a matter of minutes by striking raw flint with a "baton" of deer antler or hardwood, it is reasonable to believe that the early hunters also used this technique of baton percussion, at least in roughing out their points. There are even indications that such roughed-out blanks were produced at various flint quarries and then carried back to campsites for the finishing touches. Detaching the channel flake or flakes was obviously the crucial step; once successfully fluted, the point was finished by sharpening the tip, trimming the edges either by rasping or by pressure-flaking, and dulling the lower edges where the lashing would be wrapped around. If the tip of a point broke off, the point might be sharpened again [*see top illustration on page 209*].

Although the points from any one site exhibit a considerable range in size and appearance, it is usually not difficult to distinguish between Folsom and Clovis points. The fluting of a Folsom point is typically a single channel that extends all the way to the tip of the point or nearly so, and the edges of the point are delicately chipped. A Clovis point is typically larger, with coarsely chipped edges; usually more than one flake has been removed to produce the flute channel and these have "broken out" less than halfway to the tip in what is called a "hinge" fracture. In some cases the hinge fracture broke inward rather than outward, snapping the unfinished point in half. If early man used profane language, such an incident must surely have inspired an epithet or two.

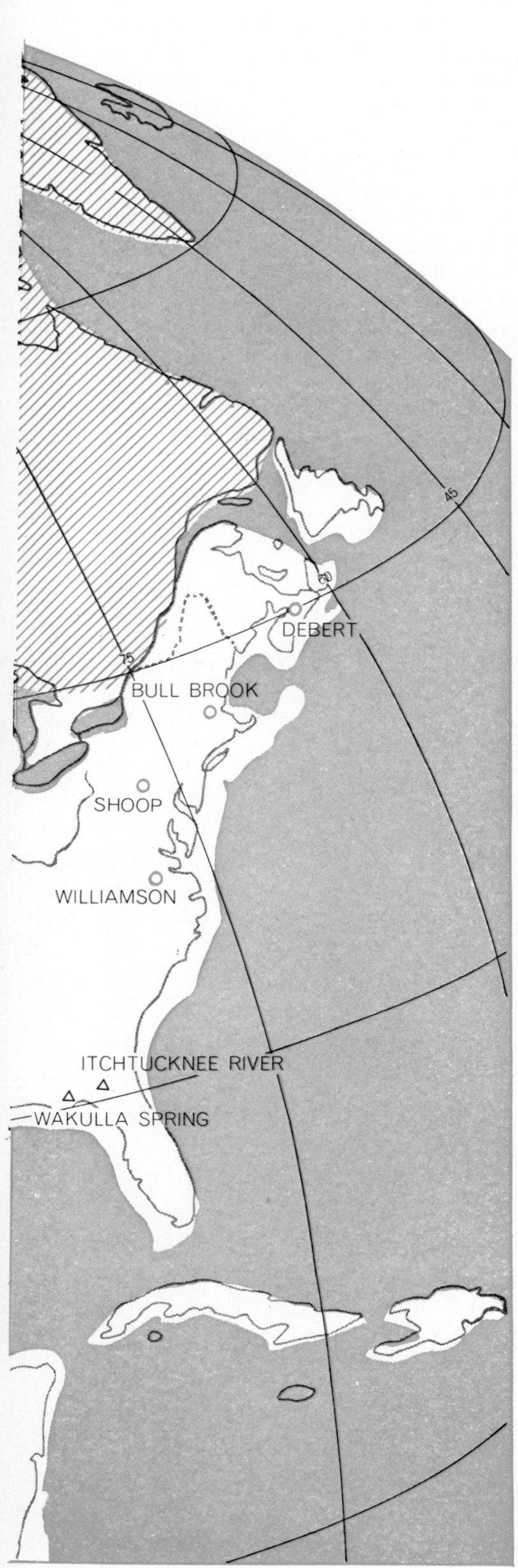

▲ ISOLATED FINDS OF FLUTED FLINT POINTS

sites and significant isolated finds. In the northeast Debert and Bull Brook probably include non-Clovis Paleo-Indian material.

Carbon-14 dating has now established the antiquity of four of the six sites in which mammoth bones are associated with Clovis points. Two of the sites are Clovis itself and Dent; the others are Domebo Canyon in Oklahoma, where a single mammoth was found together with three Clovis points and an assembly of flint butchering tools, and Lehner Ranch Arroyo in New Mexico, where among the bones of nine immature mammoths Emil Haury of the Arizona State Museum uncovered 13 Clovis points and eight butchering tools in 1955 and 1956. It was charcoal from a campfire hearth at the Lehner site that in 1959 yielded the first Clovis carbon-14 dates to be determined; they averaged 11,260 ± 360 years before the present, or a little earlier than 9000 B.C. The carbon-14 dates from Dent, Clovis and Domebo fall in this same time interval, as do the dates of two other early sites in the western U.S. that may or may not have Clovis connections. These are Union Pacific, Wyo., where mammoth bones and flint tools are found, and Ventana Cave in Arizona, which has no mammoth remains. The other two stratified Clovis sites that contain mammoth bones—Miami in the Texas Panhandle and Naco, Ariz., where Haury and his associates uncovered the bones of a single mammoth in 1951 with five out of eight Clovis points concentrated in its chest area—have not been dated by the carbon-14 method.

These and other carbon-14 determinations, together with geological analyses, have established a general framework for North American prehistory in the Rocky Mountains, the Great Plains and the Southwest. The earliest period ends about 10,000 B.C.; its fossil fauna include the mammoth and extinct species of camel, horse and bison, but there are no artifacts associated with their remains that positively indicate man's presence. There follows a gap of about 500 years for which information is lacking. In the next period, between 9500 and 9000 B.C., the early fauna is still present and Clovis projectile points are frequently found in association with mammoth remains. In the following period, between 9000 and 8000 B.C., mammoth, camel and horse have all disappeared; only the extinct bison species remains, and the artifacts found among the bison bones include Folsom projectile points rather than Clovis. The next cultural complexes overlap Folsom somewhat and are dated between 8500 and 7000 B.C. Several sites in this span of time are assigned to the Agate Basin complex. Finally, between 7000 and 6000 B.C., the Agate Basin complex is replaced by the Cody complex. These later "Paleo-Indian" cultures do not concern us. What is interesting is that, in spite of their wide geographical distribution, all the dated Clovis sites apparently belong to the same relatively narrow span of time.

Although the Clovis sites mentioned thus far are all in the western U.S., it would be a mistake to think that the mammoth-hunters were confined to that part of North America. Clovis points have been found in every one of the mainland states of the U.S. and there are more Clovis points at any one of three eastern sites than at all the stratified western sites combined. The trouble is that, with a very few exceptions, the eastern Clovis artifacts are found on the surface or only inches below the surface; it is impossible to assign dates to them with any degree of reliability. An example of the complexity of the problem is provided by the Williamson site near Dinwiddie, Va., where Clovis points and Civil War bullets are found side by side in the same plowed field.

In spite of the problem of dating the eastern discoveries, no grasp of the vigor and extent of the mammoth-hunters' culture is possible without consideration of its maximum range. In addition to the sites in the western U.S. already mentioned, Clovis points—flaked from obsidian rather than flint—have been unearthed at Borax Lake, a site north of San Francisco. Here, unfortunately, the stratigraphy is disturbed and artifacts of various ages are mixed together. Another western Clovis site is near Tonopah, Nev., where fluted points were found on the surface around a dry lake, together with flint scrapers, gravers and perforators. Neither the site nor the artifacts have been described in detail, however, and the Tonopah material is not available for study. (It is in a private collection.)

Projectile points made of bone and ivory, nearly identical with the ones found at Clovis, have also been found elsewhere in the West. Two come from deposits of muck in central Alaska that contain mammoth bones. Unfortunately the Alaskan muck is notorious for its mixed stratigraphy, and the relative ages of artifacts and animal remains in it are not easily determined. The other bone points have been found at Klamath Lake in California, in deposits as yet undated. These deposits also contain mammoth bones, but the artifacts and animal remains are not in direct association.

In the eastern U.S. large numbers of similar bone points have been found underwater at two locations in Florida: the Itchtucknee River and Wakula Spring. The latter site has also yielded mammoth remains. Something of the difficulty facing investigators who wish to assign dates to such underwater discoveries as the 600 bone points from Wakula Spring can be appreciated when one considers that the same six-foot stretch of sandy bottom may yield a bone point, a mammoth tooth and a

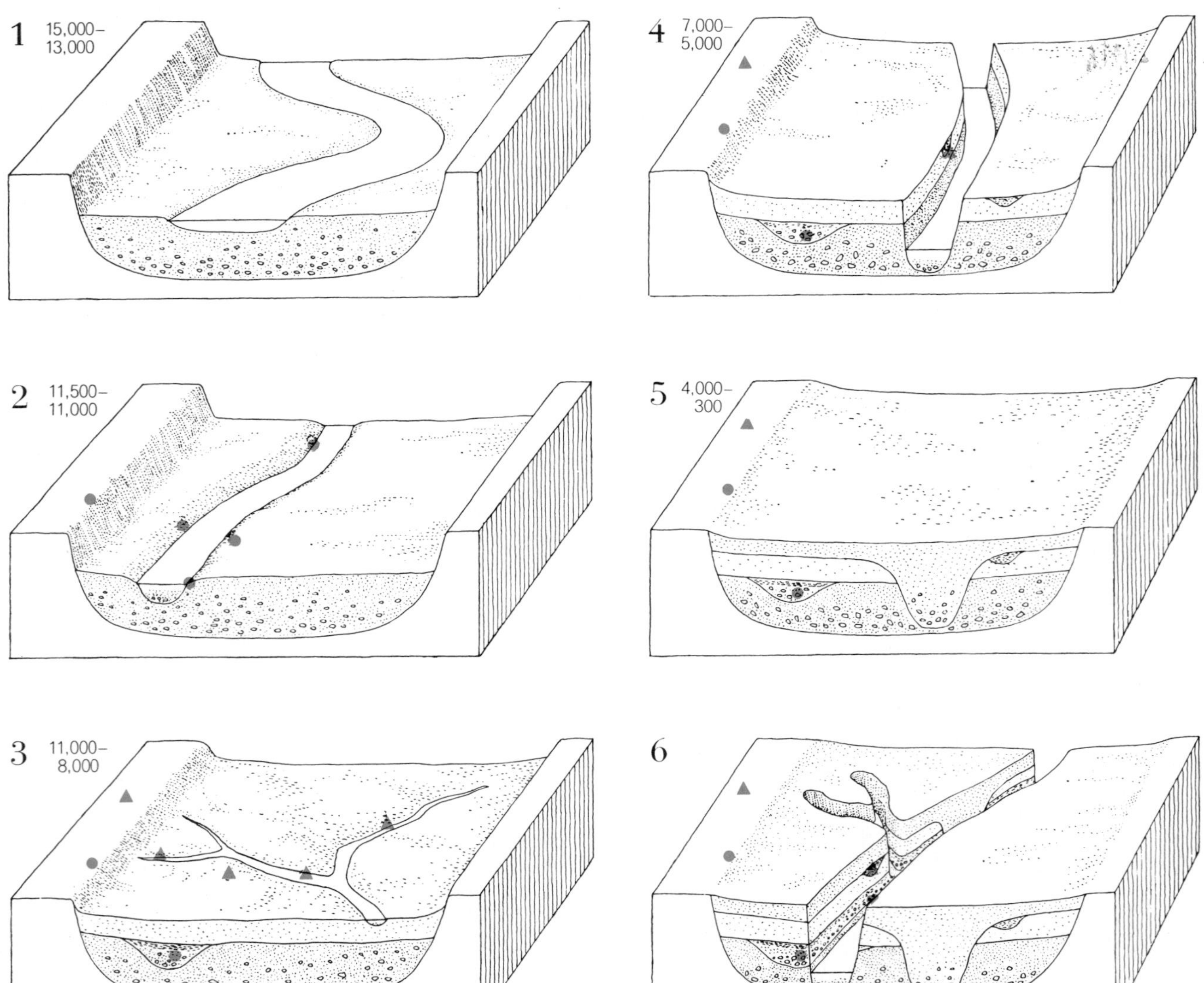

SEQUENCE OF DEPOSITS at a hypothetical valley site shows how a sediment-filled river valley (*1*) was inhabited by the Clovis mammoth-hunters (*2*). Dates are given in number of years before the present. Next (*3*) the Clovis valley sites are covered by fresh sediments on which the later Folsom bison-hunters camped. Both the Clovis and the Folsom campsites on the terrace above the valley escape burial; surface sites of this kind are difficult to date. Later cycles of erosion and deposit (*4 and 5*) leave the Clovis and Folsom valley sites deeply buried. Finally (*6*), today's situation is shown; erosion has now bared two superposed kill sites (*center*).

soft-drink bottle. The prospect of dating the abundant Clovis finds elsewhere in the East is in most instances not much brighter. Nevertheless, thanks to amateur archaeologists who have taken pains to report the exact location of their surface discoveries, it is now apparent that the greatest concentration of fluted projectile points is centered on Ohio, Kentucky and Tennessee. When the places in which Clovis points have been discovered are plotted on a map, the distribution of the points corresponds closely to that of mammoth fossils and those of the other New World proboscid, the mastodon.

The curious fact remains that, with one possible exception, no Clovis point in the eastern U.S. has ever been found in association with animal bones. The possible exception is a Clovis point found in 1898 at Big Bone Lick in Kentucky, where mammoth bones have also been uncovered. At the time, of course, the point was not recognized for what it was, and there is no evidence that the point was found in association with the mammoth bones.

The major surface discoveries of Clovis artifacts in eastern North America have been made at the Williamson site in Virginia, at the Shoop site near Harrisburg, Pa., at the Quad site in northern Alabama and at Wells Creek Crater in Tennessee [*see illustration on pages 206 and 207*]. To judge from the hundreds of Clovis points and thousands of other flint tools that have been picked up at these locations, each must represent a large campsite.

The same is probably true of Bull Brook near Ipswich, Mass.; hundreds of fluted points from this site have been analyzed by Douglas S. Byers of the R. S. Peabody Foundation in Andover, Mass. Unfortunately the stratigraphy at Bull Brook is disturbed. No campfire hearths or clear-cut levels of human habitation are known; four charcoal samples that may or may not be associated with the flint points yield carbon-14 dates that range from 4990 ± 800 B.C. to 7350 ± 400 B.C. It is evident that the Bull Brook deposits cover a considerable span of time.

The only other significant stratified site in eastern North America that has yielded carbon-14 dates is near Debert in the Canadian province of Nova Scotia. Debert is being studied by investigators from the R. S. Peabody Foundation and the National Museum of Canada. Here fluted projectile points have been found that are neither Clovis nor Folsom in style. The average of

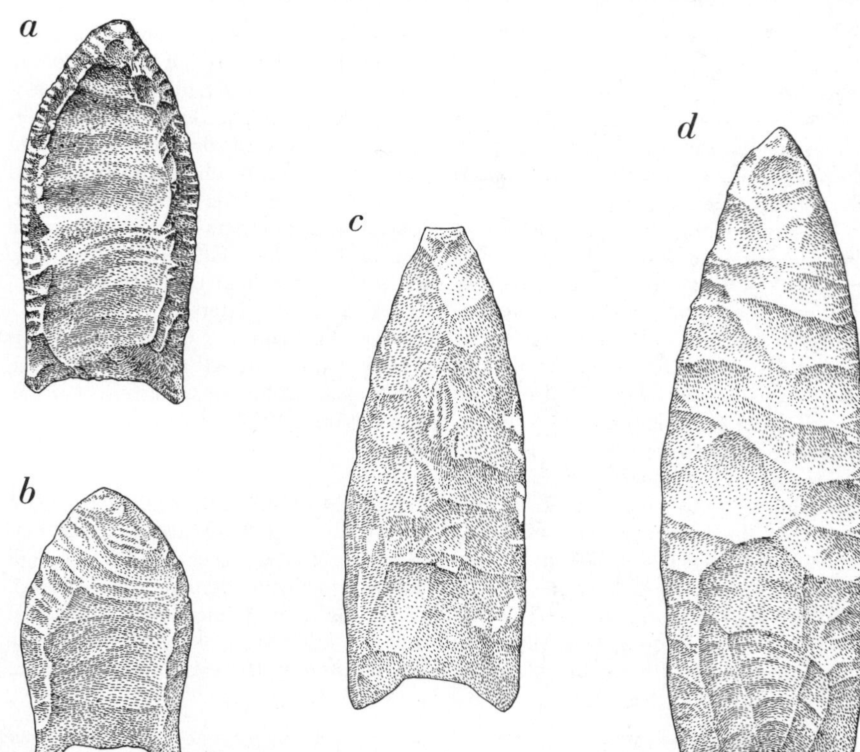

CHARACTERISTIC DIFFERENCES between Folsom ("*a*" *and* "*b*") and Clovis ("*c*" *and* "*d*") projectile points include the Folsom point's long neat flute scar, produced by the detachment of a single flake, and the delicate chipping of its cutting edges. Clovis points tend to be coarser and larger; flute scars are short and often show the detachment of more than one flake. The shorter of the Folsom points may have been repointed after its tip broke off.

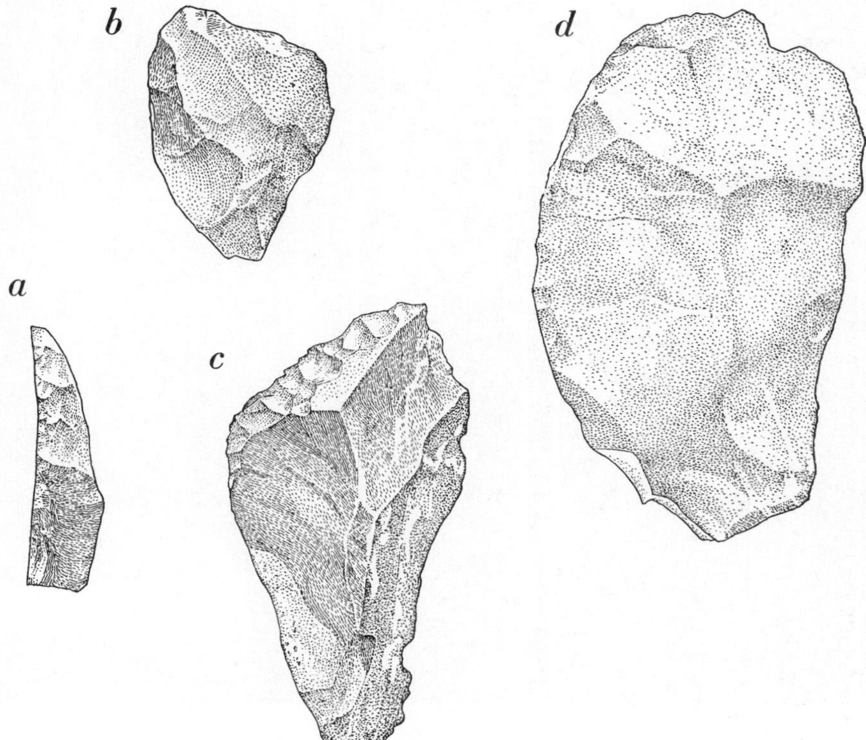

STONE TOOLS found at the Lehner site in New Mexico include keeled scrapers (*a*) and a variety of sidescrapers ("*b*," "*c*" *and* "*d*"). The latter were made from large flakes of flint knapped on one side. Choppers suitable for butchering were also found at this Clovis site.

carbon-14 dates at Debert is 8633 ± 470 B.C., or roughly 1,000 years later than the Clovis sites in the western U.S.

East or west, buried or exposed, most Clovis discoveries can be classified either as campsites or sites where animals were killed. A campsite is characterized by the presence of a wide variety of flint implements in addition to fluted points. A kill site is characterized by the presence of animal bones together with fluted points and a few flint butchering tools or no other tools at all. Recent excavations at Clovis itself indicate that the area around an extinct lake that attracted game to the site was used by the mammoth-hunters for both killing and camping. Not only butchering tools but also flint scrapers, gravers and knives have been discovered in the lower strata of the Clovis site. Apart from Clovis, however, the only other campsites in the western U.S. appear to be Tonopah, with its mixture of points and other artifacts, and Borax Lake.

Fortunately the major Clovis sites in the eastern U.S. provide abundant evidence of camp life. Some contain literally thousands of flint implements in addition to the characteristic fluted points; these include choppers, gravers, perforators, scrapers and knives made out of flint flakes. The locations of these sites show the kind of place the mammoth-hunters preferred as a camp. Shoop, Williamson, Quad and Wells Creek Crater are all on high ground, such as a stream-cut terrace or a ridge, overlooking the floodplain of a river or creek.

Analysis of the kill sites, in turn, reveals something about the Clovis people's hunting techniques, although many questions remain unanswered. The number of points found with each kill, for example, is inconsistent. At the Dent site only three Clovis points were found among the remains of a dozen mammoths. At Naco the skeleton of a single mammoth was associated with eight points. One interpretation of this seeming contradiction is that the Naco mammoth may have been one that got away, escaping its hunters to die alone some time after it was attacked. The 12 mammoths at Dent, according to the same interpretation, were butchered on the spot and the hunters recovered most of their weapons. One piece of negative evidence in support of this interpretation is that no butchering tools were found at Naco. Such tools, however, are also absent from Dent.

The Dent site affords a reasonably clear picture of one hunt. The mammoth bones were concentrated at the mouth of a small gully where an intermittent stream emerges from a sandstone bluff to join the South Platte River. It seems plausible that here the Clovis hunters had stampeded a mam-

STAMPEDED MAMMOTHS were unearthed near Dent, Colo., in 1932 by workers from the Denver Museum of Natural History. Among the bones of 11 immature female elephants and one adult male elephant they found several boulders and three typical Clovis projectile points. Photographed at the site were (*left to right*) Rev. Conrad Bilgery, S.J., an unidentified Regis College student, two Denver Museum trustees (W. C. Mead and C. H. Hanington) and Frederick Howarter of the museum's paleontology department.

moth herd over the edge of the bluff. Some of the animals may have been killed by the fall; others may have escaped. Those that were too badly hurt to fight free of the narrow gully may then have been stunned with boulders—an assumption that helps to explain the presence of these misplaced stones among the mammoth bones—and finally dispatched with spear thrusts. The bag of 11 cows and one bull would have constituted a highly successful day's work, but it may also have been the result of several hunts.

All six mammoths found at Clovis could also have been taken by stampeding a herd, in this case into shallow water where the footing was treacherous. Whether this actually happened, or whether the animals were simply surprised while watering, is impossible to determine. Clovis nonetheless affords a tantalizing glimpse into another of the mammoth-hunters' thought processes. One of the springs that fed the lake contains hundreds of flint flakes and a number of intact flint tools, including three Clovis points. Did the ancient hunters deliberately toss waste chips and usable artifacts into the spring? If not, how did these objects accumulate?

The concept of cutting a herd—separating the young and less dangerous animals from the more formidable adults—may be what is demonstrated by the remains at the Lehner site, where all nine mammoths were immature or even nurslings. At Lehner, as at Domebo (where only a single adult was killed), the animals apparently had been attacked while watering along a spring-fed stream.

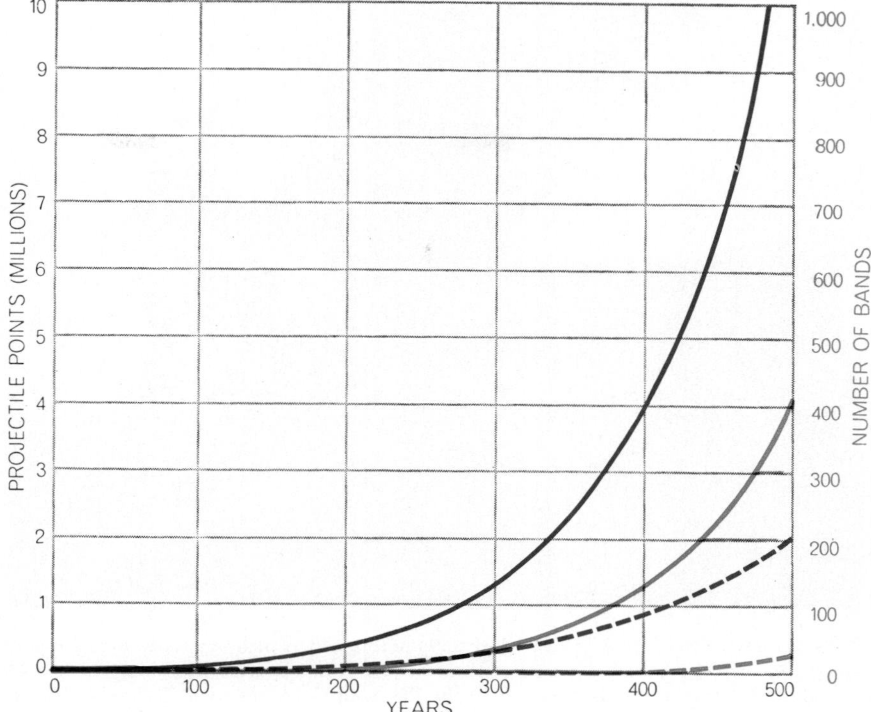

POPULATION INCREASE among the mammoth-hunters in the course of 500 years is calculated on the assumption that an original 30-member hunting band multiplied by a factor of 1.2 or 1.4 each 28-year generation (*color*). Black curves show the total number of Clovis points produced during 500 years, assuming that one person in four made five each month.

Although the way in which the hunters' fluted projectile points were mounted seems clear, the kind of haft on which they were mounted remains unknown. That the points were used as arrowheads seems unlikely; the bow reached the New World or was independently invented there at a much later date. The Clovis points must therefore have been mounted on spears or darts. Whether launched from the hand or propelled by a spear-thrower, neither may have been a weapon of much effectiveness against an infuriated mammoth. It seems possible that, when the prey showed fight, most of the hunters devoted their efforts to keeping the mammoth at bay while a daring individual or two rushed in to drive a spear home to its heart from behind the foreleg.

The analysis of kill sites provides one further fact about the Clovis hunters. Although they were evidently specialists in the pursuit of mammoths, they were not unwilling to take other kinds of quarry. At two of the sites—Clovis and Lehner—bison bones are also found.

The fluted projectile point is a highly specialized artifact that must have passed through a considerable period of development, yet no precursors are known in the New World or elsewhere. Obviously the archaeological record is incomplete, and perhaps it will remain so. For the time being, however, this absence of evident precursors suggests that the Clovis people arrived in the New World, already equipped with their specialized tool kit, between 12,000 and 13,000 years ago. Carbon-14 dates obtained during the past 15 years have built up a reasonably consistent picture of the way in which the New World was peopled during the final stages of the Pleistocene ice age. When the most recent glacial period was at its peak, 14,000 to 20,000 years ago, a large portion of the earth's water supply was stored in the Northern Hemisphere's ice sheets. The so-called land bridge between Alaska and Siberia in the area of the Bering Strait, exposed by the low level of the earth's oceans at that time, was no narrow isthmus but a broad land mass joining Asia and North America in a single continent.

The Bering land mass, however, was not a thoroughfare from the Old World to the whole of the New. The Cordilleran ice cap covered the Canadian Rockies from Vancouver to eastern Alaska, and the Laurentide ice cap covered most of the rest of Canada and much of the northern U.S. These two glacial formations merged at the foot of the Canadian Rockies, leaving central Alaska, the Bering land mass and eastern Siberia unglaciated but cut off from the more southerly Americas by an ice barrier.

A little more than 12,000 years ago there occurred a marked period of glacial retreat known as the Two Creeks interval. Carbon-14 dates indicate that the warm interval came to an end scarcely more than a century or two later, or about 9900 B.C.; another glacial advance began soon thereafter. As we have seen, Clovis points make their first appearance in western North America in 9500 B.C., or roughly half a millennium after the Two Creeks interval. A tenable hypothesis connecting the two events is that the Two Creeks glacial retreat opened a trans-Canadian corridor between the Cordilleran and

CLOVIS BONE POINT, partly cleared of surrounding matrix at lower right, lies in direct association with the bones of a mammoth foreleg. Unearthed at Clovis, this evidence of early man's hunting ability is displayed at the Philadelphia Academy of Natural Sciences.

the Laurentide ice caps. The progenitors of the Clovis people, confined until then to central Alaska but already specialists in big-game hunting, could thus make their way down an ice-free corridor into a world where big game abounded and had scarcely been hunted until that time.

This, of course, is no more than a hypothesis, but it is a useful one on two counts. First, it provides a logical explanation for the abrupt appearance of Clovis points in North America at about 9500 B.C. Second, it is easily tested. All that is needed to destroy the Two Creeks hypothesis, for example, is the discovery of a Clovis site more than 12,000 years old located south of the ice sheet. Thus far no such Clovis site has been found. Meanwhile the Two Creeks hypothesis can also be tested indirectly in demographic terms.

Assuming that the first Clovis people passed through northwestern Canada some 12,000 years ago, they would have had to travel at the rate of four miles a year to reach the most southerly of their western U.S. sites, 2,000 miles away, within 500 years. Is such a rate of human diffusion realistic? Edward S. Deevey, Jr., of Yale University has noted that, under conditions of maximal increase in an environment empty of competitors, mankind's best efforts produce a population increase by a factor of 1.4 in each 28-year generation [see "The Human Population," by Edward S. Deevey, Jr.; SCIENTIFIC AMERICAN Offprint 608]. James Fitting of the University of Michigan has recently investigated a prehistoric hunting camp in Michigan; he suggests that Paleo-Indian family hunting bands numbered between 30and 60 indiviuals.

Making conservative use of these findings, I have assumed that the first and only Clovis band to pass down the corridor opened by the Two Creeks interval numbered about 30, say five families averaging six persons each: two grandparents, two parents and two offspring. I have assumed further that one in four knew how to knap flint and produced Clovis points at the rate of five a month. In case Deevey's growth factor of 1.4 is too high, I have also made my calculation with a smaller factor—1.2—on the grounds that a plausible extrapolation probably lies somewhere between the two.

Applying these production rates, I find that in 500 years an original band of 30 mammoth-hunters evolves into a population numbering between 800 and 12,500, comprised of 26 to 425 hunting bands. In the same 500 years the bands' flint-knappers will have made—and left scattered across the land—between two million and 14 million Clovis points. Assuming that the demographic model is a reasonable one, the Clovis hunters could easily have spread across North America from coast to coast in the brief span of time allotted to them. Indeed, if the higher figure is in any way realistic, the rapid increase in the number of mammoth-hunters could easily be one of the main reasons why these animals became extinct in North America sometime around 9000 B.C., leaving the succeeding Folsom hunters with no larger prey than bison.

A Paleo-Indian Bison Kill

by Joe Ben Wheat
January 1967

Some 8,500 years ago a group of hunters on the Great Plains stampeded a herd of buffaloes into a gulch and butchered them. The bones of the animals reveal the event in remarkable detail

When one thinks of American Indians hunting buffaloes, one usually visualizes the hunters pursuing a herd of the animals on horseback and killing them with bow and arrow. Did the Indians hunt buffaloes before the introduction of the horse (by the Spanish conquistadors in the 16th century) and the much earlier introduction of the bow? Indeed they did. As early as 10,000 years ago Paleo-Indians hunted species of bison that are now extinct on foot and with spears. My colleagues and I at the University of Colorado Museum have recently excavated the site of one such Paleo-Indian bison kill dating back to about 6500 B.C. The site so remarkably preserves a moment in time that we know with reasonable certainty not only the month of the year the hunt took place but also such details as the way the wind blew on the day of the kill, the direction of the hunters' drive, the highly organized manner in which they butchered their quarry, their choice of cuts to be eaten on the spot and the probable number of hunters involved.

The bison was the most important game animal in North America for millenniums before its near extermination in the 19th century. When Europeans arrived on the continent, they found herds of bison ranging over vast areas, but the animals were first and foremost inhabitants of the Great Plains, the high, semiarid grassland extending eastward from the foothills of the Rocky Mountains and all the way from Canada to Mexico. Both in historic and in late prehistoric times the bison was the principal economic resource of the Indian tribes that occupied the Great Plains. Its meat, fat and bone marrow provided them with food; its hide furnished them with shelter and clothing; its brain was used to tan the hide; its horns were fashioned into containers. There was scarcely a part of the animal that was not utilized in some way.

This dependence on big-game hunting probably stretches back to the very beginning of human prehistory in the New World. We do not know when man first arrived in the Americas, nor do we know in detail what cultural baggage he brought with him. The evidence for the presence of man in the New World much before 12,000 years ago is scattered and controversial. It is quite clear, however, that from then on Paleo-Indian hunting groups, using distinctive kinds of stone projectile point, ranged widely throughout the New World. On the Great Plains the principal game animal of this early period was the Columbian mammoth [see the article "Elephant-hunting in North America," by C. Vance Haynes, Jr., beginning on page 204]. Mammoth remains have been found in association with projectile points that are usually large and leaf-shaped and have short, broad grooves on both sides of the base. These points are typical of the complex

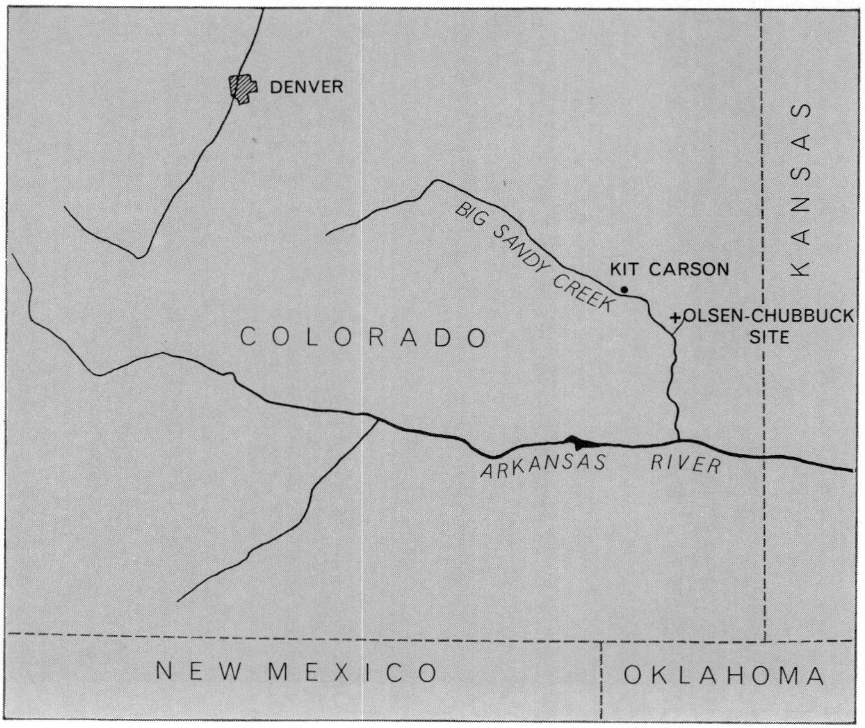

SITE OF THE KILL is 140 miles southeast of Denver. It is named the Olsen-Chubbuck site after its discoverers, the amateur archaeologists Sigurd Olsen and Gerald Chubbuck.

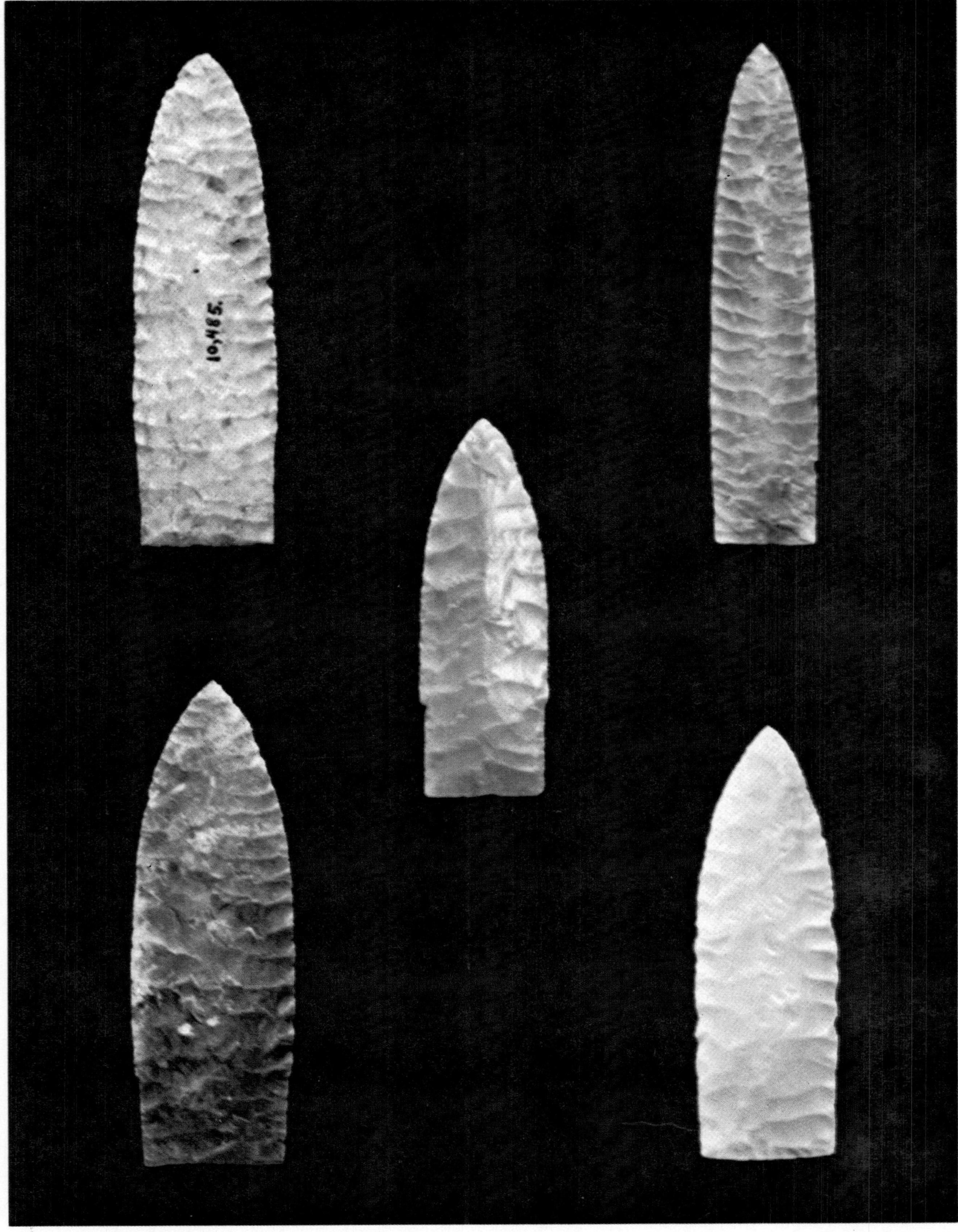

PROJECTILE POINTS found at the site show a surprising divergence of form in view of the fact that all of them were used simultaneously by a single group. In the center is a point of the Scottsbluff type. At top left is another Scottsbluff point that shows some of the characteristics of a point of the Eden type at top right. At bottom left is a third Scottsbluff point; it has characteristics in common with a point of the Milnesand type at bottom right. Regardless of form, all the points are equally excellent in flaking.

of cultural traits named the Clovis complex; the tool kit of this complex also included stone scrapers and knives and some artifacts made of ivory and bone.

The elephant may have been hunted out by 8000 B.C. In any case, its place as a game animal was taken by a large, straight-horned bison known as *Bison antiquus*. The first of the bison-hunters used projectile points of the Folsom culture complex; these are similar to Clovis points but are generally smaller and better made. Various stone scrapers and knives, bone needles and engraved bone ornaments have also been found in Folsom sites.

A millennium later, about 7000 B.C., *Bison antiquus* was supplanted on the Great Plains by the somewhat smaller *Bison occidentalis*. The projectile points found in association with this animal's remains are of several kinds. They differ in shape, size and details of flaking, but they have some characteristics in common. Chief among them is the technical excellence of the flaking. The flake scars meet at the center of the blade to form a ridge; sometimes they give the impression that a single flake has been detached across the entire width of the blade [*see illustration on opposite page*]. Some of the projectile points that belong to this tradition, which take their names from the sites where they were first found, are called Milnesand, Scottsbluff and Eden points. The last two kinds of point form part of what is called the Cody complex, for which there is a fairly reliable carbon-14 date of about 6500 B.C.

Paleo-Indian archaeological sites fall into two categories: habitations and kill sites. Much of our knowledge of the early inhabitants of the Great Plains comes from the kill sites, where are found not only the bones of the animals but also the projectile points used to kill them and the knives, scrapers and other tools used to butcher and otherwise process them. Such sites have yielded much information about the categories of projectile points and how these categories are related in time. Heretofore, however, they have contributed little to our understanding of how the early hunters actually lived. The kill site I shall describe is one of those rare archaeological sites where the evidence is so complete that the people who left it seem almost to come to life.

Sixteen miles southeast of the town of Kit Carson in southeastern Colorado, just below the northern edge of the broad valley of the Arkansas River, lies a small valley near the crest of a low divide. The climate here is semiarid; short bunchgrass is the main vegetation and drought conditions have prevailed since the mid-1950's. In late 1957 wind erosion exposed what appeared to be five separate piles of bones, aligned in an east-west direction. Gerald Chubbuck, a keen amateur archaeologist, came on the bones in December, 1957; among them he found several projectile points of the Scottsbluff type. Chubbuck notified the University of Colorado Museum of his find, and we made plans to visit the site at the first opportunity.

Meanwhile Chubbuck and another amateur archaeologist, Sigurd Olsen, continued to collect at the site and ultimately excavated nearly a third of it. In the late spring of 1958 the museum secured permission from the two discoverers and from Paul Forward, the owner of the land, to complete the excavation. We carried out this work on summer expeditions in 1958 and 1960.

The Olsen-Chubbuck site consists of a continuous bed of bones lying within the confines of a small arroyo, or dry gulch. The arroyo, which had long since been buried, originally rose near the southern end of the valley and followed a gently undulating course eastward through a ridge that forms the valley's eastern edge. The section of the arroyo that we excavated was some 200 feet long. Its narrow western end was only about a foot and a half in depth and the same in width, but it grew progressively deeper and wider to the east. Halfway down the arroyo its width was five feet and its depth six; at the point to the east where our excavation stopped it was some 12 feet wide and seven feet deep. At the bottom of the

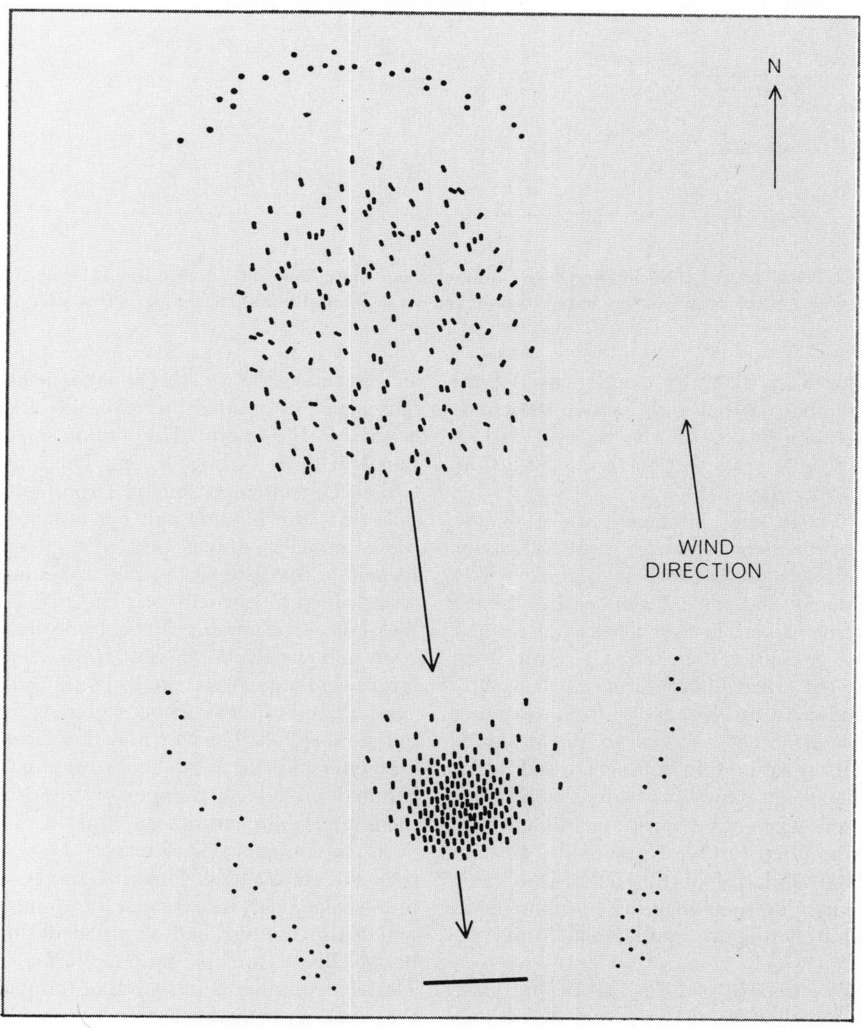

BISON STAMPEDE was probably set off by the Paleo-Indian hunters' close approach to the grazing herd from downwind. Projectile points found among the bones of the animals at the eastern end of the arroyo (*bottom*) suggest that some hunters kept the bison from veering eastward to escape. Other hunters probably did the same at the western end of the arroyo.

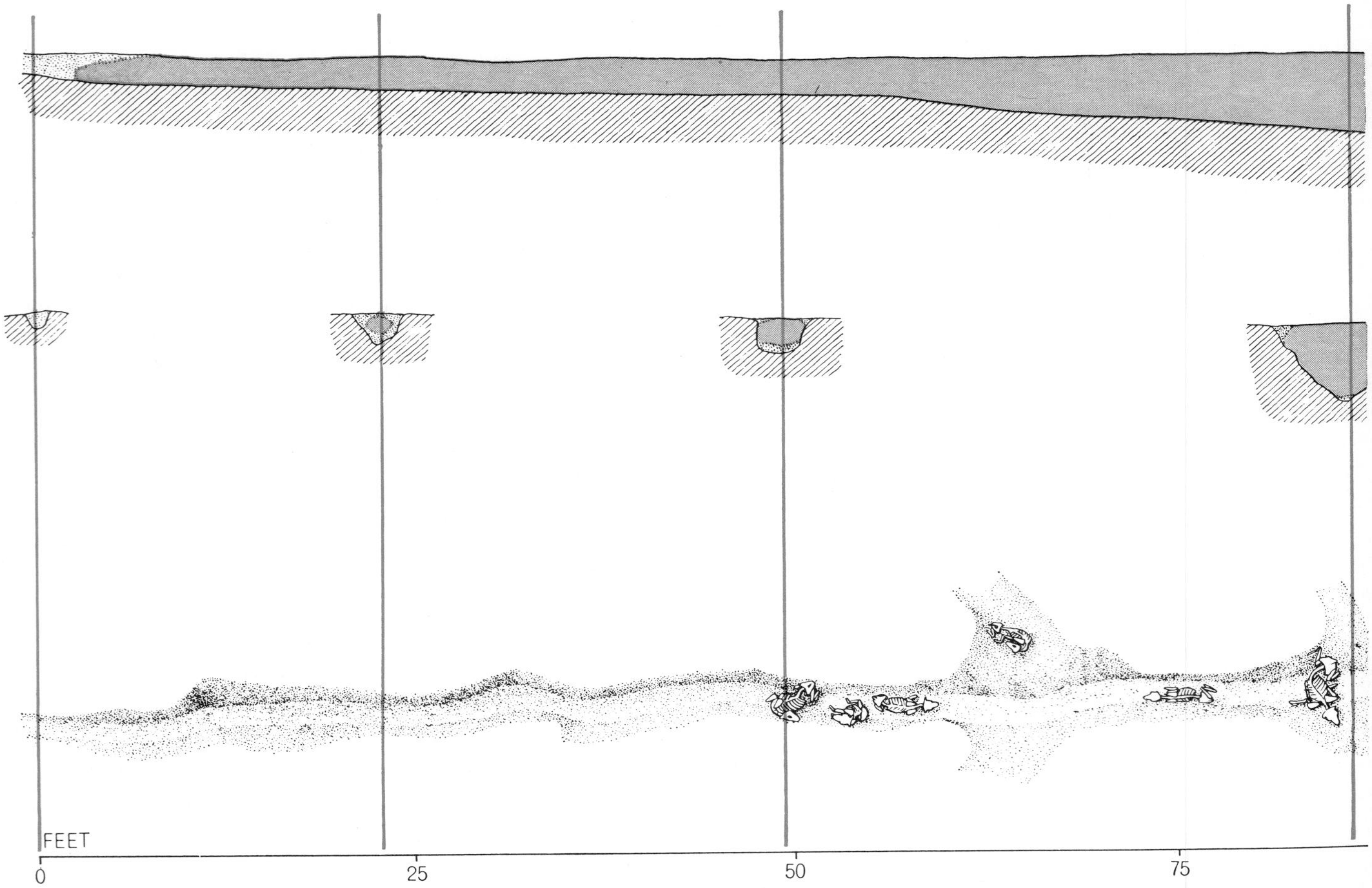

SECTION AND PLAN of the Olsen-Chubbuck site show how the remains of the dead and butchered bison formed a deposit of bones that lined the center of the arroyo for a distance of 170 feet (*color at top*). One part of the site had been excavated by its discoverers

arroyo for its entire length was a channel about a foot wide; above the channel the walls of the arroyo had a V-shaped cross section [*see top illustration on page 218*].

Today the drainage pattern of the site runs from north to south. This was probably the case when the arroyo was formed, and since it runs east and west it seems certain that it was not formed by stream action. Early frontiersmen on the Great Plains observed that many buffalo trails led away from watering places at right angles to the drainage pattern. Where such trails crossed ridges they were frequently quite deep; moreover, when they were abandoned they were often further deepened by erosion. The similarity of the Olsen-Chubbuck arroyo to such historical buffalo trails strongly suggests an identical origin.

The deposit of bison bones that filled the bottom of the arroyo was a little more than 170 feet long. It consisted of the remains of nearly 200 buffaloes of the species *Bison occidentalis*. Chubbuck and Olsen unearthed the bones of an estimated 50 of the animals; the museum's excavations uncovered the bones of 143 more. The bones were found in three distinct layers. The bottom layer contained some 13 complete skeletons; the hunters had not touched these animals. Above this layer were several essentially complete skeletons from which a leg or two, some ribs or the skull were missing; these bison had been only partly butchered. In the top layer were numerous single bones and also nearly 500 articulated segments of buffalo skeleton. The way in which these segments and the single bones were distributed provides a number of clues to the hunters' butchering techniques.

As the contents of the arroyo—particularly the complete skeletons at the bottom—make clear, it had been a trap into which the hunters had stampeded the bison. Bison are gregarious animals. They move in herds in search of forage; the usual grazing herd is between 50 and 300 animals. Bison have a keen sense of smell but relatively poor vision. Hunters can thus get very close to a herd as long as they stay downwind and largely out of sight. When the bison are frightened, the herd has a tendency to close ranks and stampede in a single mass. If the herd encounters an abrupt declivity such as the Olsen-Chubbuck arroyo, the animals in front cannot stop because they are pushed by those behind. They can only plunge into the arroyo, where they are immobilized, disabled or killed by the animals that fall on top of them.

The orientation of the skeletons in the middle and lower layers of the Olsen-Chubbuck site is evidence that the Paleo-Indian hunters had initiated such a stampede. Almost without exception the complete or nearly complete skeletons overlie or are overlain by the skeletons of one, two or even three other whole or nearly whole animals; the bones are massed and the skeletons are contorted. The first animals that fell into the arroyo had no chance to escape; those behind them wedged them tighter into the arroyo with their struggles. Many of the skeletons are sharply twisted around the axis of the spinal column. Three spanned the arroyo, deformed into

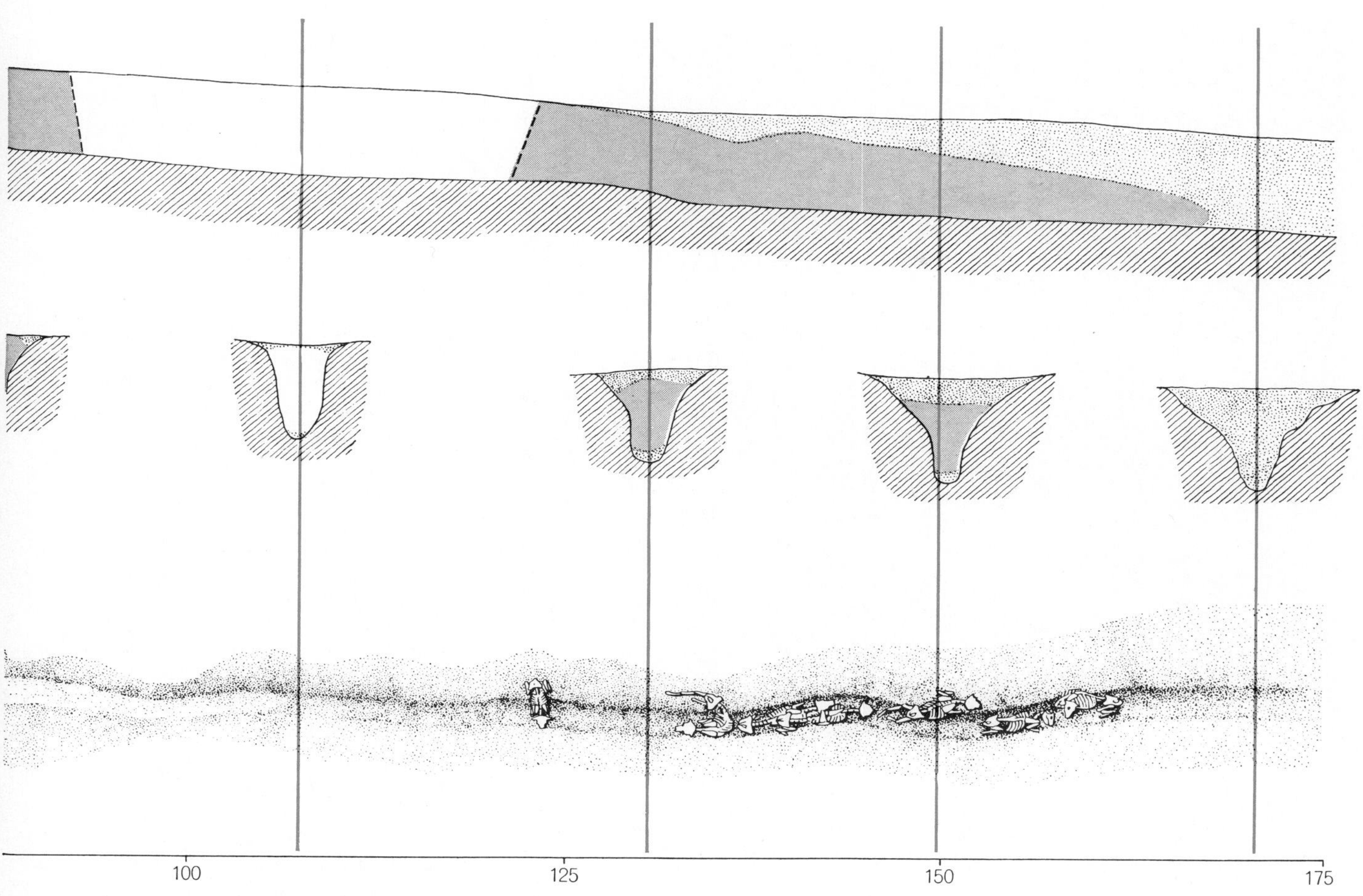

before the author and his associates began work in 1958; this area is represented by the 20-foot gap in the deposit. The shallow inner channel at the bottom of the arroyo can be seen in the plan view (*bottom*); outlines show the locations of 13 intact bison skeletons.

an unnatural U shape. Ten bison were pinned in position with their heads down and their hindquarters up; an equal number had landed with hindquarters down and heads up. At the bottom of the arroyo two skeletons lie on their backs.

The stampeding bison were almost certainly running in a north-south direction, at right angles to the arroyo. Of the 39 whole or nearly whole skeletons, which may be assumed to lie in the positions in which the animals died, not one faces north, northeast or northwest. A few skeletons, confined in the arroyo's narrow inner channel, face due east or west, but all 21 animals whose position at the time of death was not affected in this manner faced southeast, south or southwest. The direction in which the bison stampeded provides a strong clue to the way the wind was blowing on the day of the hunt. The hunters would surely have approached their quarry from downwind; thus the wind must have been from the south.

We have only meager evidence of the extent to which the stampede, once started, was directed and controlled by the hunters. The projectile points found with the bison skeletons in the deepest, most easterly part of the arroyo suggest that a flanking party of hunters was stationed there. It also seems a reasonable inference that, if no hunters had covered the stampede's western flank, the herd could have escaped unscathed around the head of the arroyo. If other hunters pursued the herd from the rear, there is no evidence of it.

Even if the hunters merely started the stampede and did not control it thereafter, it sufficed to kill almost 200 animals in a matter of minutes. The total was 46 adult bulls and 27 immature ones, 63 adult and 38 immature cows and 16 calves. From the fact that the bones include those of calves only a few days old, and from what we know about the breeding season of bison, we can confidently place the date of the kill as being late in May or early in June.

As we excavated the bone deposit we first uncovered the upper layer containing the single bones and articulated segments of skeleton. It was soon apparent that these bones were the end result of a standardized Paleo-Indian butchering procedure. We came to recognize certain "butchering units" such as forelegs, pelvic girdles, hind legs, spinal columns and skulls. Units of the same kind were usually found together in groups numbering from two or three to as many as 27. Similar units also formed distinct vertical sequences. As the hunters had removed the meat from the various units they had discarded the bones in separate piles, each of which contained the remains of a number of individual animals. In all we excavated nine such piles.

Where the order of deposition was clear, the bones at the bottom of each pile were foreleg units. Above these bones were those of pelvic-girdle units. Sometimes one or both hind legs were attached to the pelvic girdle, but by and large the hind-leg units lay separately among or above the pelvic units. The next level was usually composed of spinal-column units. The ribs had been removed from many of the chest vertebrae, but ribs were still attached to some of the other vertebrae. At the top

EXCAVATION at the eastern end of the arroyo reveals its V-shaped cross section and the layers of sand and silt that later filled it. The bone deposit ended at this point; a single bison shoulder blade remains in place at the level where it was unearthed (*lower center*).

BISON SKULL AND STONE POINT lie in close association at one level in the site. The projectile point (*lower left*) is of the Scottsbluff type. The bison skull, labeled *4-F* to record its position among the other bones, rests upside down where the hunters threw it.

of nearly every pile were skulls. The jawbones had been removed from most of them, but some still retained a few of the neck vertebrae. In some instances these vertebrae had been pulled forward over the top and down the front of the skull. When the skull still had its jawbone, the hyoid bone of the tongue was missing.

Like the various butchering units, the single bones were found in clusters of the same skeletal part: shoulder blades, upper-foreleg bones, upper-hind-leg bones or jawbones (all broken in two at the front). Nearly all the jawbones were found near the top of the bone deposit. The tongue bones, on the other hand, were distributed throughout the bed. About 75 percent of the single foreleg bones were found in the upper part of the deposit, as were nearly 70 percent of the single vertebrae. Only 60 percent of the shoulder blades and scarcely half of the single ribs were in the upper level.

The hunters' first task had evidently been to get the bison carcasses into a position where they could be cut up. This meant that the animals had to be lifted, pulled, rolled or otherwise moved out of the arroyo to some flat area. It seems to have been impossible to remove the bison that lay at the bottom of the arroyo; perhaps they were too tightly wedged together. Some of them had been left untouched and others had had only a few accessible parts removed. The way in which the butchering units were grouped suggests that several bison were moved into position and cut up simultaneously. Since foreleg units, sometimes in pairs, were found at the bottom of each pile of bones it seems reasonable to assume that the Paleo-Indians followed the same initial steps in butchering that the Plains Indians did in recent times. The first step was to arrange the legs of the animal so that it could be rolled onto its belly. The skin was then cut down the back and pulled down on both sides of the carcass to form a kind of mat on which the meat could be placed. Directly under the skin of the back was a layer of tender meat, the "blanket of flesh"; when this was stripped away, the bison's forelegs and shoulder blades could be cut free, exposing the highly prized "hump" meat, the rib cage and the body cavity.

Having stripped the front legs of meat, the hunters threw the still-articulated bones into the arroyo. If they followed the practice of later Indians, they would next have indulged themselves

BONES OF BISON unearthed at the Olsen-Chubbuck site lie in a long row down the center of the ancient arroyo the Paleo-Indian hunters utilized as a pitfall for the stampeding herd. The bones proved to be the remains of bulls, cows and calves of the extinct species *Bison occidentalis.* Separate piles made up of the same types of bones (for example sets of limb bones, pelvic girdles or skulls) showed that the hunters had butchered several bison at a time and had systematically dumped the bones into the arroyo in the same order in which they were removed from the carcasses. In the foreground is a pile of skulls that was built up in this way.

by cutting into the body cavity, removing some of the internal organs and eating them raw. This, of course, would have left no evidence among the bones. What is certain is that the hunters did remove and eat the tongues of a few bison at this stage of the butchering, presumably in the same way the Plains Indians did: by slitting the throat, pulling the tongue out through the slit and cutting it off. Our evidence for their having eaten the tongues as they went along is that the tongue bones are found throughout the deposit instead of in one layer or another.

The bison's rib cages were attacked as soon as they were exposed by the removal of the overlying meat. Many of the ribs were broken off near the spine. The Plains Indians used as a hammer for this purpose a bison leg bone with the hoof still attached; perhaps the Paleo-Indians did the same. In any case, the next step was to sever the spine at a point behind the rib cage and remove the hindquarters. The meat was cut away from the pelvis (and in some instances simultaneously from the hind legs) and the pelvic girdle was discarded. If the hind legs had been separated from the pelvis, it was now their turn to be stripped of meat and discarded.

After the bison's hindquarters had been butchered, the neck and skull were cut off as a unit—usually at a point just in front of the rib cage—and set aside. Then the spine was discarded, presumably after it had been completely stripped of meat and sinew. Next the hunters turned to the neck and skull and cut the neck meat away. This is evident from the skulls that had vertebrae draped over the front; this would not have been possible if the neck meat had been in place. The Plains Indians found bison neck meat too tough to eat in its original state. They dried it and made the dried strips into pemmican by pounding them to a powder. The fact that the Paleo-Indians cut off the neck meat strongly suggests that they too preserved some of their kill.

If the tongue had not already been removed, the jawbone was now cut away, broken at the front and the tongue cut out. The horns were broken from a few skulls, but there is little evidence that the Paleo-Indians broke open the skull as the Plains Indians did to take out the brain. Perhaps the most striking difference between the butchering practices of these earlier Indians and those of later ones, however, lies in the high degree of organization displayed by the Paleo-Indians. Historical accounts of butchering by Plains Indians indicate no such efficient system.

In all, 47 artifacts were found in association with the bones at the Olsen-Chubbuck site. Spherical hammerstones and knives give us some idea of what constituted the hunter's tool kit; stone scrapers suggest that the bison's skins were processed at the site. A bone pin and a piece of the brown rock limonite that shows signs of having been rubbed tell something about Paleo-Indian ornamentation.

The bulk of the artifacts at the site are projectile points. There are 27 of them, and they are particularly significant. Most of them are of the Scottsbluff type. When their range of variation is considered, however, they merge gradually at one end of the curve of variation into Eden points and at the other end into Milnesand points. Moreover, among the projectile points found at the site are one Eden point and a number of Milnesand points. The diversity of the points clearly demonstrates the range of variation that was possible among the weapons of a single hunting group. Their occurrence together at the site is conclusive proof that such divergent forms of weapon could exist contemporaneously.

How many Paleo-Indians were pres-

INTACT SKELETON of an immature bison cow, uncovered in the lowest level of the arroyo, is one of 13 animals the Paleo-Indian hunters left untouched. The direction in which many bison faced suggests that the stampede traveled from north to south.

ent at the kill? The answer to this question need not be completely conjectural. We can start with what we know about the consumption of bison meat by Plains Indians. During a feast a man could consume from 10 to 20 pounds of fresh meat a day; women and children obviously ate less. The Plains Indians also preserved bison meat by drying it; 100 pounds of fresh meat would provide 20 pounds of dried meat. A bison bull of today yields about 550 pounds of edible meat; cows average 400 pounds. For an immature bull one can allow 165 pounds of edible meat, for an immature cow 110 pounds and for a calf 50 pounds. About 75 percent of the bison killed at the Olsen-Chubbuck site were completely butchered; on this basis the total weight of bison meat would have been 45,300 pounds. The *Bison occidentalis* killed by the Paleo-Indian hunters, however, was considerably larger than the *Bison bison* of modern times. To compensate for the difference it seems reasonable to add 25 percent to the weight estimate, bringing it to a total of 56,640 pounds. To this total should be added some 4,000 pounds of edible internal organs and 5,400 pounds of fat.

A Plains Indian could completely butcher a bison in about an hour. If we allow one and a half hours for the dissection of the larger species, the butchering at the Olsen-Chubbuck site would have occupied about 210 man-hours. In other words, 100 people could easily have done the job in half a day.

To carry the analysis further additional assumptions are needed. How long does fresh buffalo meat last? The experience of the Plains Indians (depending, of course, on weather conditions) was that it could be eaten for about a month. Let us now assume that half of the total weight of the Olsen-Chubbuck kill was eaten fresh at an average rate of 10 pounds per person per day, and that the other half was preserved. Such a division would provide enough fresh meat and fat to feed 150 people for 23 days. It seems reasonable to assume that the Paleo-Indian band was about this size. One way to test this assumption is to calculate the load each person would have to carry when camp was broken.

The preserved meat and fat, together with the hides, would have weighed about 7,350 pounds, which represents a burden of 49 pounds for each man, woman and child in the group (in addition to the weight of whatever other necessities they carried). Plains Indians are known to have borne loads as great as 100 pounds. Taking into account the likelihood that small children and active hunters would have carried smaller loads, a 49-pound average appears to be just within the range of possibility.

A band of 150 people could, however, have eaten two-thirds of the kill fresh and preserved only one-third. In that case the fresh meat would have fed them for somewhat more than a month. At the end the meat would have been rather gamy, but the load of preserved meat per person would have been reduced to the more reasonable average of 31 pounds.

One possibility I have left out is that the Paleo-Indians had dogs. If there were dogs available to eat their share of fresh meat and to carry loads of preserved meat, the number of people in the group may have been somewhat less. In the absence of dogs, however, it seems improbable that any fewer than 150 people could have made use of the bison killed at the Olsen-Chubbuck site to the degree that has been revealed by our excavations. Whether or not the group had dogs, the remains of its stay at the site are unmistakable evidence that hunting bands of considerable size and impressive social organization were supporting themselves on the Great Plains some 8,500 years ago.

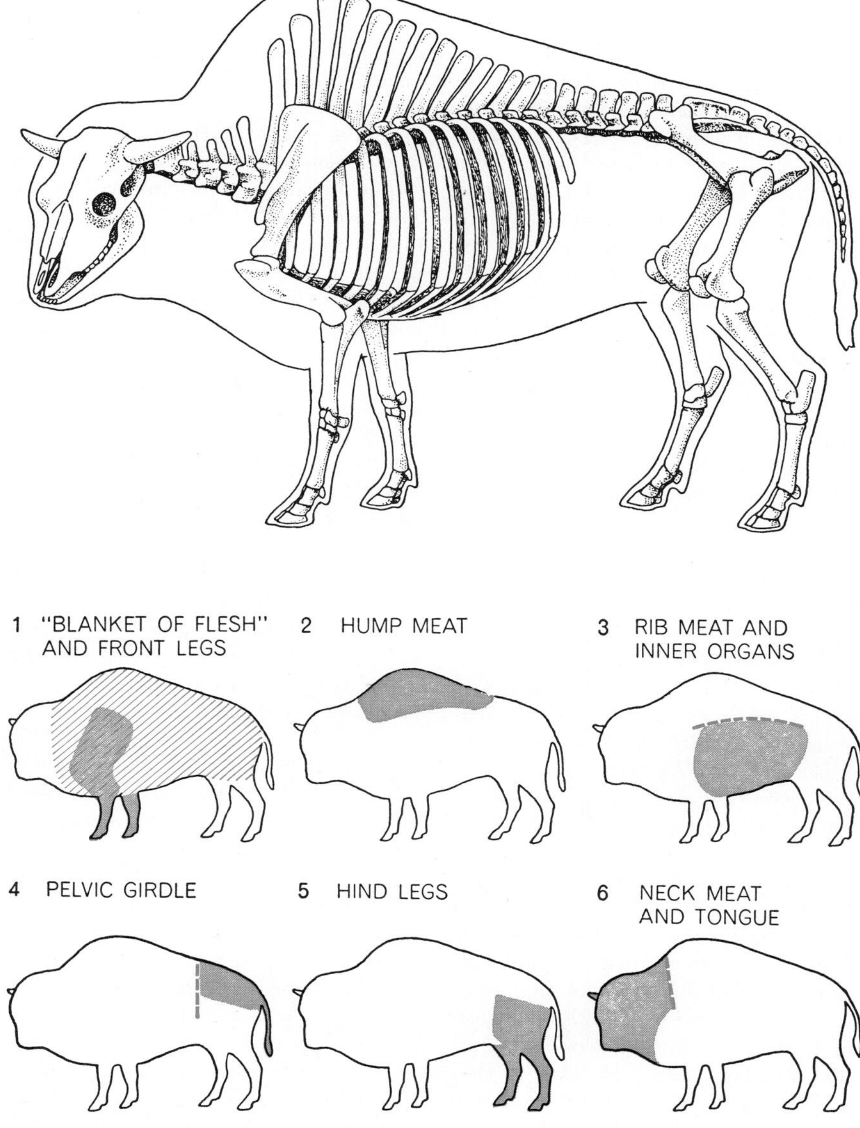

BUTCHERING METHODS used by the Paleo-Indians have been reconstructed on the dual basis of bone stratification at the Olsen-Chubbuck site and the practices of the Plains Indians in recent times. Once the carcass of the bison (*skeleton at top*) had been propped up and skinned down the back, a series of "butchering units" probably were removed in the order shown on the numbered outline figures. The hunters ate as they worked.

24 The Hopewell Cult

by Olaf H. Prufer
December 1964

A 1,500-year-old rubbish heap unearthed in southern Ohio holds the answers to some key questions about the ancient Indians who lived there and built huge funeral mounds filled with offerings

As Europeans explored North America, they found that many of the continent's river valleys were dotted with ancient earthworks. Scattered from western New York to North Dakota and south to Louisiana and the Florida Keys were uncounted thousands of burial mounds, temple mounds, hilltop ramparts surrounded by ditches, and earthen walls enclosing scores of acres. Some Colonial scholars were so impressed by these works that they thought they must have been built by an unknown civilized people that had been exterminated by the savage Indians. In due course it became clear that the earthworks had been put up by the Indians' own ancestors, and that they belonged not to one culture but to a series of separate cultural traditions spanning a period of 3,000 years.

Perhaps the most striking assemblage of these works is located in southern Ohio in the valleys of the Muskingum, Scioto and Miami rivers. It consists of clusters of large mounds surrounded by earthworks laid out in elaborate geometric patterns. As early as 1786 one such group of mounds at the confluence of the Muskingum and the Ohio (the present site of Marietta, Ohio) was excavated; it was found to be rich in graves and mortuary offerings. It was not until the 1890's, however, that the contents of the Ohio mounds attracted public attention. At that time many of them were excavated to provide an anthropological exhibit for the Chicago world's fair of 1893. One of the richest sites was on the farm of M. C. Hopewell, and the name Hopewell has been assigned to this particular type of mortuary complex ever since.

More recent excavations have shown that the Hopewell complex extends far beyond southern Ohio. Hopewell remains are found in Michigan and Wisconsin and throughout the Mississippi valley; there are Hopewell sites in Illinois that are probably older than any in Ohio. Typical Hopewell artifacts have been unearthed as far west as Minnesota and as far south as Florida. The mounds of southern Ohio are nonetheless the most numerous and the richest in mortuary offerings.

Thanks to carbon-14 dating it is known that the Hopewell complex first materialized in southern Ohio about 100 B.C. and that the last elaborate valley earthwork was constructed about A.D. 550. Until recently, however, there were other questions to which only conjectural answers could be given. Among them were the following: In what kinds of settlements did the people of southern Ohio live during this period? Where were their habitations located? On what foundation did their economy rest? Answers to these questions can now be given, but first it is necessary to say exactly what the Hopewell complex is.

What is known about the Hopewell complex of Ohio has been learned almost exclusively from the nature and contents of burial mounds. In many places these structures are found in groups enclosed by earthworks linked in a pattern of squares, circles, octagons and parallel lines [*see top illustration on page 224*]. The dimensions of some of the enclosures are immense: the largest known Hopewell earthworks in Ohio—the Newark Works in Licking County—covered four square miles. Many of the burial mounds are also large: the central mounds on the Hopewell farm and at the Seip and Harness sites, all of which are in Ross County, range from 160 to 470 feet in length and from 20 to 32 feet in height. Within the mounds are the remains of numerous human bodies, some of them alone and some in groups. If the bodies were simply interred, they rest on earthen platforms surrounded by log cribs; if they were cremated, the bones are found in shallow basins of baked earth.

The sequence of events in the construction of a major mound seems to have been as follows. Bare ground was first covered with a layer of sand; then a large wooden structure was raised on this prepared floor. Some of the structures were so extensive that it is doubtful that they had roofs; they were probably stockades open to the sky. Individual graves were prepared inside these enclosures; in many cases the burials were covered with low mounds of earth. When the enclosure was filled with graves, the wooden structure was set afire and burned to the ground. Then the entire burial area was covered with layer on layer of earth and stone, forming the final large mound.

The quantity and quality of the grave goods accompanying the burials indicate that the people of the period devoted a great deal of time and effort to making these articles. A marked preference for exotic raw materials is evident. Mica, frequently cut into geometric or animate shapes, was imported from the mountains of Virginia, North Carolina and Alabama [*see illustration on opposite page*]. Conch shells, used as ceremonial cups, came from the Gulf

SILHOUETTED HAND made from a sheet of mica (*opposite page*) is typical of the elaborate grave offerings found at the Hopewell site near Chillicothe, Ohio. Human, animal and geometric figures of mica are characteristic Hopewell funerary goods; they are particularly abundant in southern Ohio.

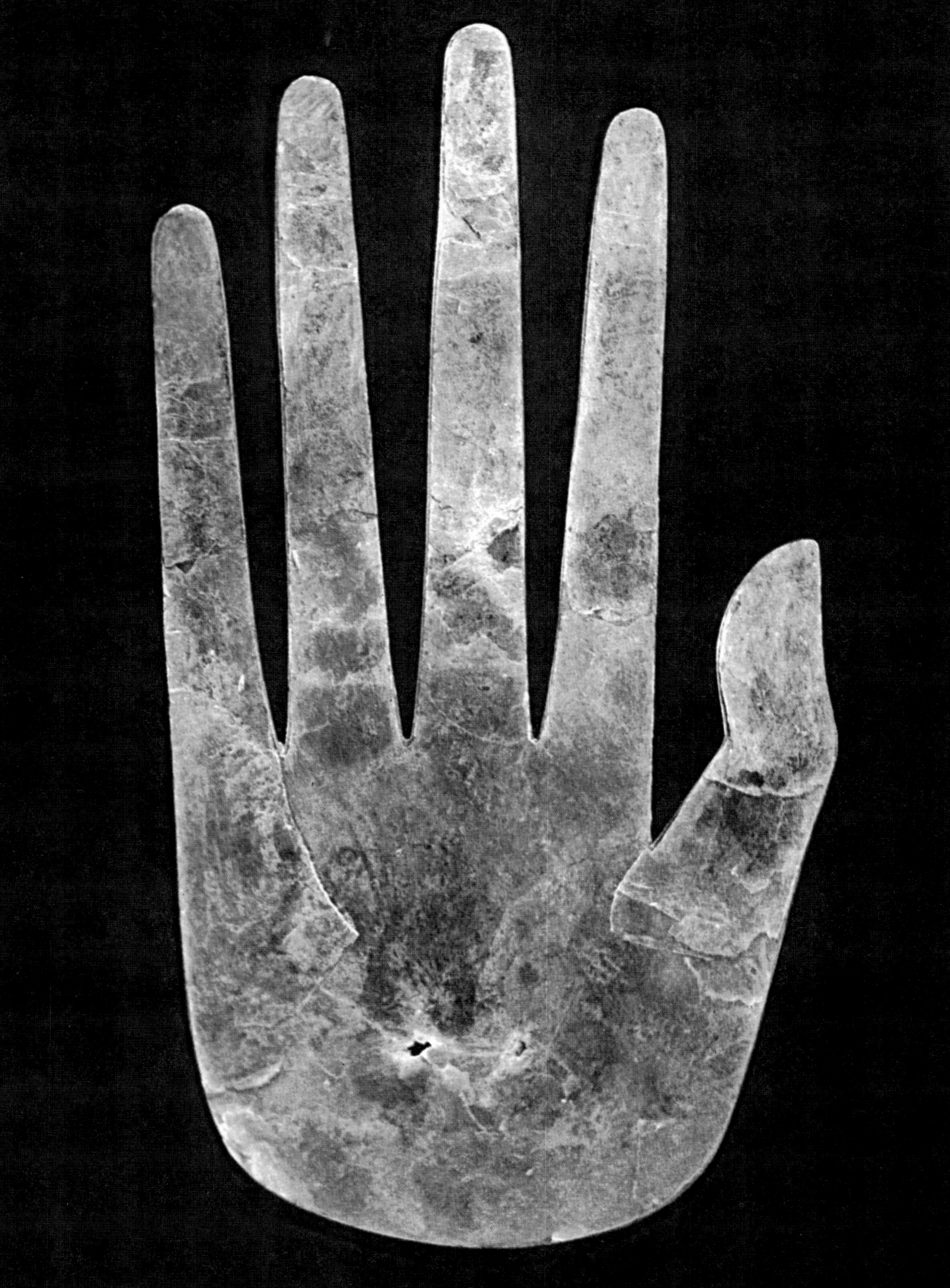

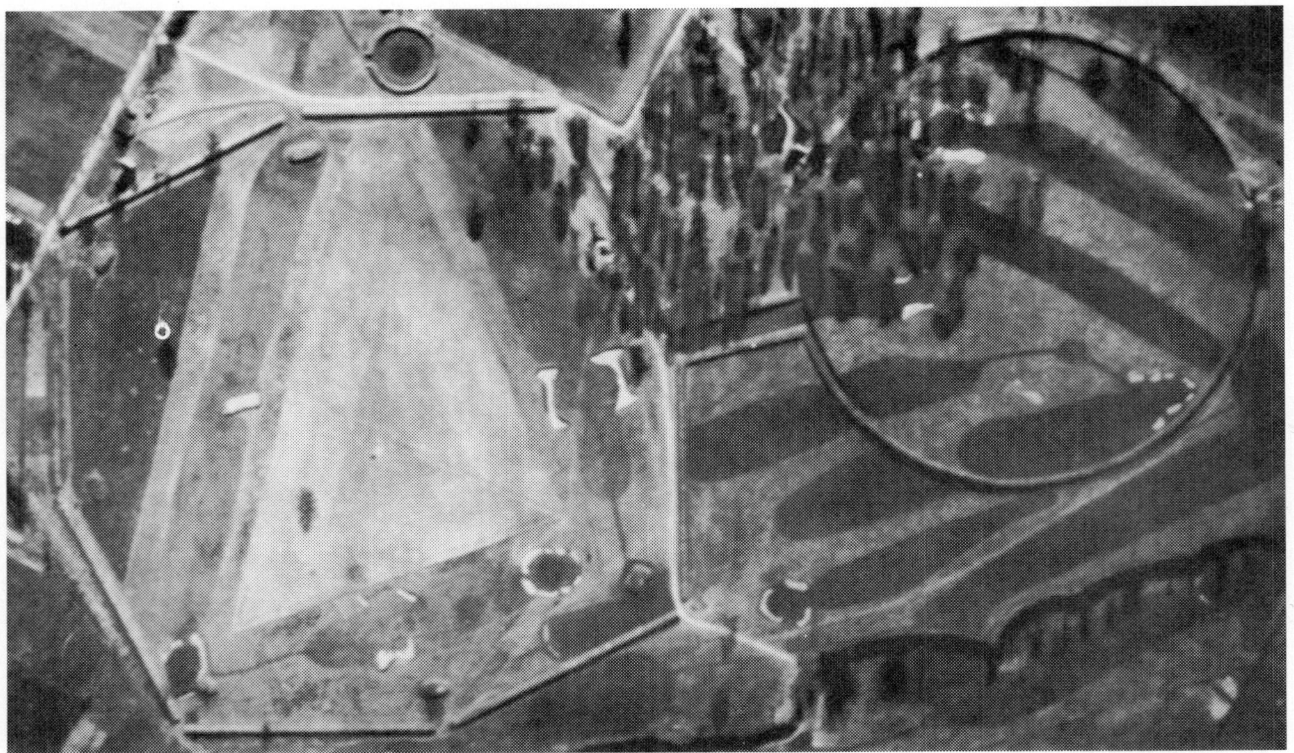

OCTAGON AND CIRCLE in this aerial photograph are a portion of the earthworks marking the most extensive known Hopewell construction: the site at Newark, Ohio. Most of the four-square-mile array (*see original plan below*) has now been obliterated by modern building. Only these figures (now part of a golf course) and another circle (used for years as a fairground) have been preserved.

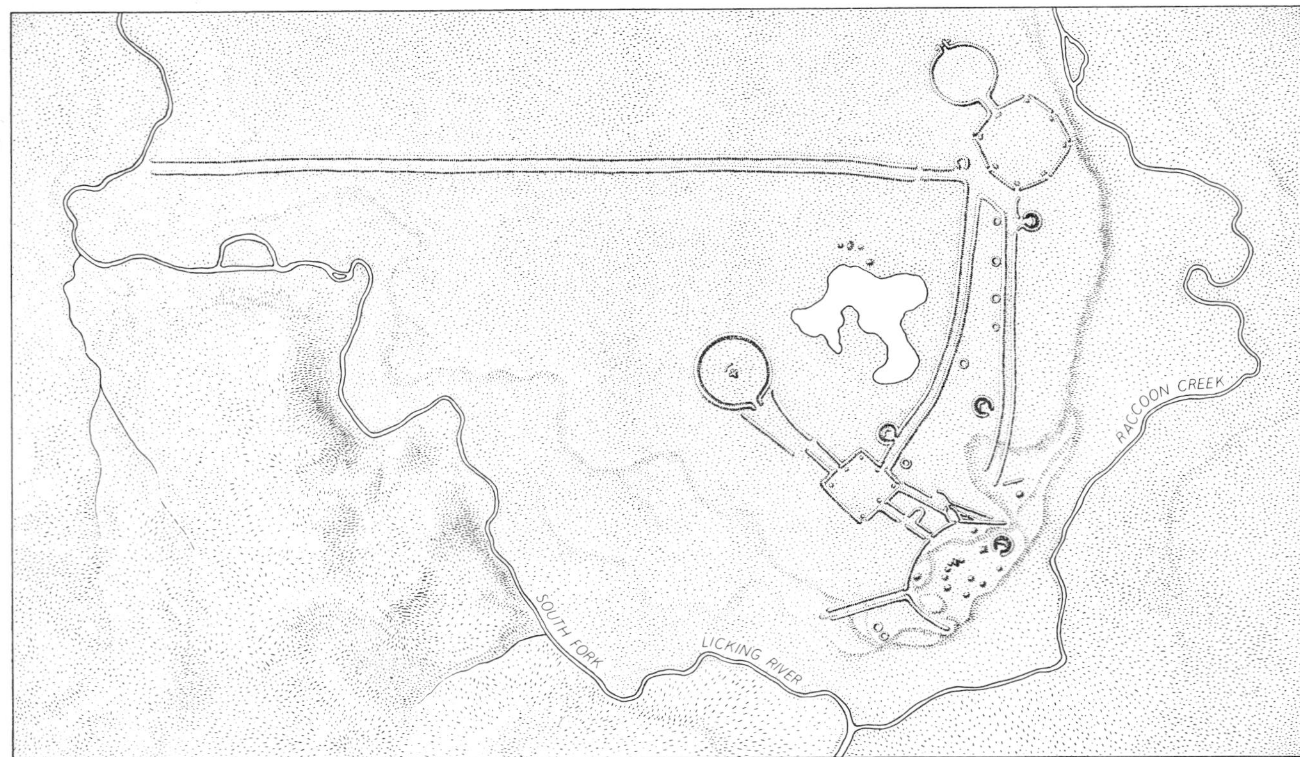

LONG AVENUES bounded by parallel earthen walls constitute the major parts of the Newark site. When first surveyed, the longest parallels (*top*) extended from the paired figures shown in the photograph at top of page to the Licking River, two and a half miles distant. Both circles are quite precise: the fairground circle (*center*) diverges at most 13 feet from a mean diameter of 1,175 feet, and the golf course circle only 4.5 feet from a mean diameter of 1,045 feet. The Newark site has never been systematically excavated.

Coast. Obsidian, exquisitely flaked into large ritual knives, was obtained either from what is now the U.S. Southwest or from the Yellowstone region of the Rocky Mountains. The canine teeth of grizzly bears, frequently inlaid with freshwater pearls, may also have been imported from the Rockies. Copper, artfully hammered into heavy ax blades and into ornaments such as ear spools, breastplates and geometric or animate silhouettes, was obtained from the upper Great Lakes.

Even in their choice of local raw materials the Hopewell craftsmen of Ohio favored the precious and the unusual. Much of their work in stone utilized the colorful varieties of flint available in the Flint Ridge deposits of Licking County. The freshwater pearls came from the shellfish of local rivers, and they were literally heaped into some of the burials. The tombs of the Hopewell site contained an estimated 100,000 pearls; a single deposit at the Turner site in Hamilton County has yielded more than 48,000.

Other typical Hopewell grave furnishings are "platform" pipes [*see lower illustration on page 228*], elaborately engraved bones of animals and men, clay figurines and highly distinctive kinds of decorated pottery. Projectile points of flint show characteristic forms; the flintworkers also struck delicate parallel-sided blades from prepared "cores."

For the most part these characteristic objects of the Hopewell complex are the same wherever they are found. In spite of this fact the Hopewell complex cannot be classed as a "culture" in the anthropological sense of the word, that is, as a distinct society together with its attendant material and spiritual manifestations. On the contrary, the Hopewell complex was only one segment of the cultural totality in each area where it is encountered. A reconstruction of life in eastern North America from 500 B.C. to A.D. 900 reveals the existence of distinct cultural traditions in separate regions, each rooted in its own past. During the Hopewell phase each of these regional traditions was independently influenced by the new and dynamic religious complex. The new funeral customs did not, however, take the place of the local culture; they were simply grafted onto it. Although the word "cult" has some unfortunate connotations in common usage, it is more appropriate to speak of a Hopewell cult than of a Hopewell culture.

The exact religious concepts that

EARTHWORKS characteristic of the burial cult are found throughout eastern North America. Major Hopewell centers, from the Gulf Coast to the Great Lakes, are named on the map.

SOUTHERN OHIO is the locale of the most abundant and richest Hopewell sites. The majority are found along the Miami, Scioto and Muskingum rivers and range in date from 100 B.C. to A.D. 550. After that no more lowland centers were built; instead hilltops were fortified (*colored dots locate three major examples*). The McGraw site was excavated by the author.

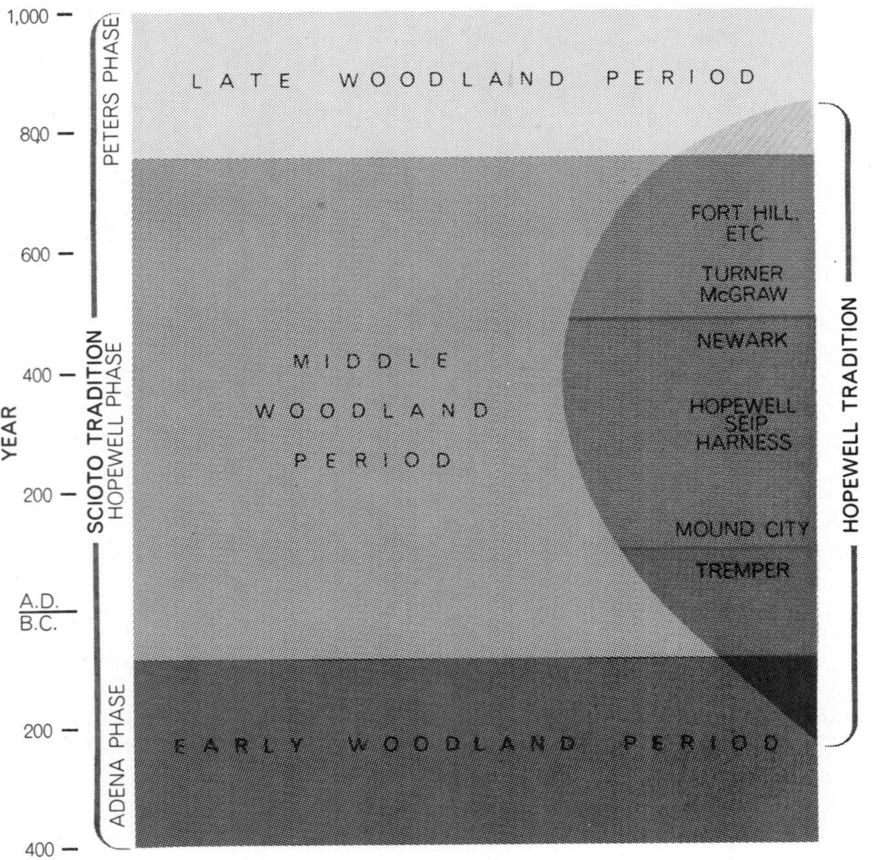

SEQUENCE OF CULTURES in southern Ohio during the rise and decline of the Hopewell funeral complex indicates that a local tradition of Woodland culture, called Scioto, was present in the area before the Hopewell cult appeared and continued both during and after it. The earliest of the Woodland culture periods began about 1200 B.C. in southern Ohio.

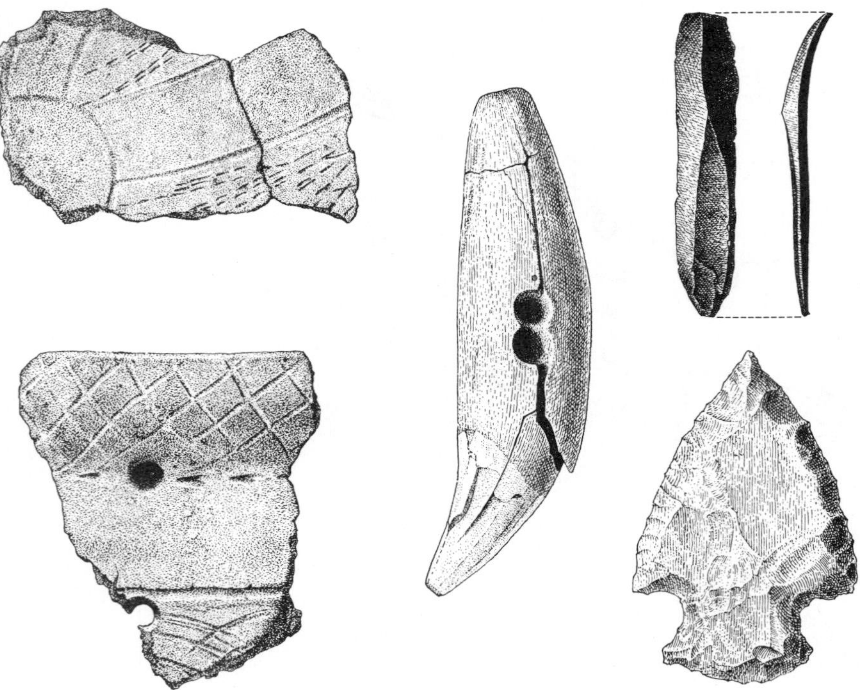

IDENTITY OF FARMSTEAD discovered at the McGraw site as the residence of Indians who participated in the burial cult is proved by the presence of characteristic Hopewell tools and ceremonial objects. The fine, parallel-sided flint blade is typically Hopewell, as is the "Snyders" projectile point. The bear canine and the pottery are standard burial finds.

permitted the successful diffusion of the Hopewell cult necessarily remain unknown. Curiously enough, however, the cult's consumption of exotic materials for grave goods may have provided a mechanism for its diffusion. Procurement of raw materials entailed an exchange system of almost continental proportions; many widely separated areas in North America must have been brought into contact as their natural resources were tapped by practitioners of the Hopewell rites.

Students of the Hopewell remains in southern Ohio have been disturbed for more than a century by the lack of evidence for any habitation sites linked to the great funerary centers. In other Hopewell areas, notably Illinois, large villages are clearly associated with the local ceremonial sites. Years of patient fieldwork in Ohio had failed to produce anything that could legitimately be called a settlement. The extensive enclosures and their associated clusters of burial mounds contain no evidence of habitation to speak of. The little that has been found seems to mark brief squatters' tenancies, probably associated with the construction of the final mounds or with ceremonies that may have been performed from time to time. Clearly the nature of Hopewell society and its settlement patterns in Ohio were markedly different from those in Illinois.

Still another puzzle was the fact that remains of corn have been found at only two Ohio Hopewell sites—Harness and Turner—and in both cases under doubtful circumstances. It was therefore supposed that the Hopewell phase in Ohio was one of simple hunting and collecting and no agriculture. Whether because of this supposition or because earlier investigators were looking for sizable villages, most of the search for Hopewell habitation sites has been confined to regions near the ceremonial centers, leaving the rich bottomlands along the rivers largely unexplored.

While reflecting on all these factors in 1962 I was struck by a possible parallel between the Ohio Hopewell sites and the classic ceremonial sites of certain areas in Middle America, where the religious center remained vacant except on ritual occasions and the population lived in scattered hamlets surrounding the center. To apply such an assumption to the Ohio Hopewell complex meant granting the people agriculture; it meant, furthermore, that the bottomlands were the very zones in which to look for small farming communities. Survey work along the floodplain of the middle and lower Scioto River during the past two years has amply demonstrated the validity of this assumption. Our survey teams from the Case Institute of Technology have turned up 37 small sites—the largest of them little more than 100 feet in diameter—marked by thinly scattered objects on the surface. These objects include sherds of cord-marked pottery, chips of flint, fragments of shell and bone and, most important, the fine, parallel-edged bladelets that are among the characteristic artifacts of the Hopewell complex.

It is certain that many such habitation sites are now lost forever under the accumulated silt of river floodplains and that others have been destroyed by river meandering. A perfect example of flood burial in the making is provided by the McGraw site, which is located on bottomland near an ancient meander of the Scioto River two miles south of Chillicothe. Alva McGraw, the owner of the land, brought the site to our attention in 1962. Surface indications were scanty; over an area 10 feet square we found only a few potsherds, some shell fragments, bits of flint and fire-cracked rocks. The site was on a nearly imperceptible rise of land, the remnant of a knoll that had been almost covered by river silts.

Under ordinary circumstances no archaeologist would have been attracted by such an impoverished find. It happened, however, that this site and similar ones on the McGraw farm were soon to be destroyed by road construction. We therefore decided without much enthusiasm to sound the area with a modest trench. Where the trench cut into the ancient knoll we found no remains at depths lower than the plow zone: eight inches below the surface. But where the trench extended beyond the knoll, proceeding down its slope to the adjacent silt-covered low ground, we struck a dense deposit of residential debris, evidently the refuse heap of an ancient farmstead.

This deposit, a foot thick and 95 by 140 feet in extent, was packed with material. There were more than 10,000 pottery fragments, some 6,000 animal bones, nearly 2,000 identifiable mollusk shells, abundant remains of wild plants and both an ear and individual kernels of corn. In fact, this single rubbish heap contained enough material to answer the questions posed at the beginning of this article.

First, in spite of the pattern of organized village life associated with the Hopewell cult 400 miles to the west in Illinois, the people of southern Ohio lived in small, scattered farm dwellings. This does not mean that the population was sparse; indeed, the size and complexity of the ceremonial earthworks in Ohio imply ample manpower. The significant fact is that the two groups shared a religion but lived quite different secular lives. In seeking parallels for this phenomenon one turns to the early, expansionist days of Christianity or of Islam, when a religion was shared by peoples with sharply contrasting cultures.

Second, the Ohio Hopewell people built their dwellings not near ceremonial centers but on the floodplains of the

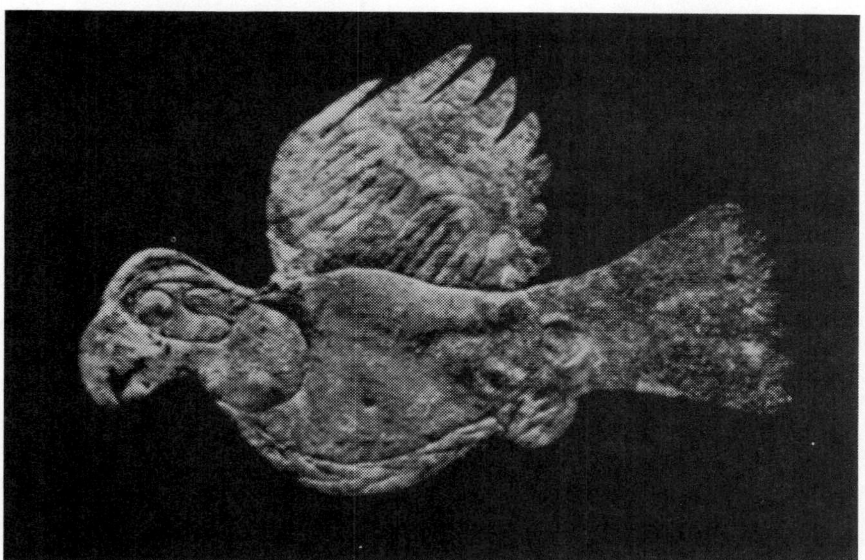

BIRD EFFIGY from Mound City combines cutout and repoussé techniques in copper work. The metal was imported from outcroppings at Isle Royale in Lake Superior. Hopewell funeral offerings of copper include rings, ear spools, breastplates and headdresses, many geometric forms, copper-plated wooden objects and large ax blades, evidently cold-forged.

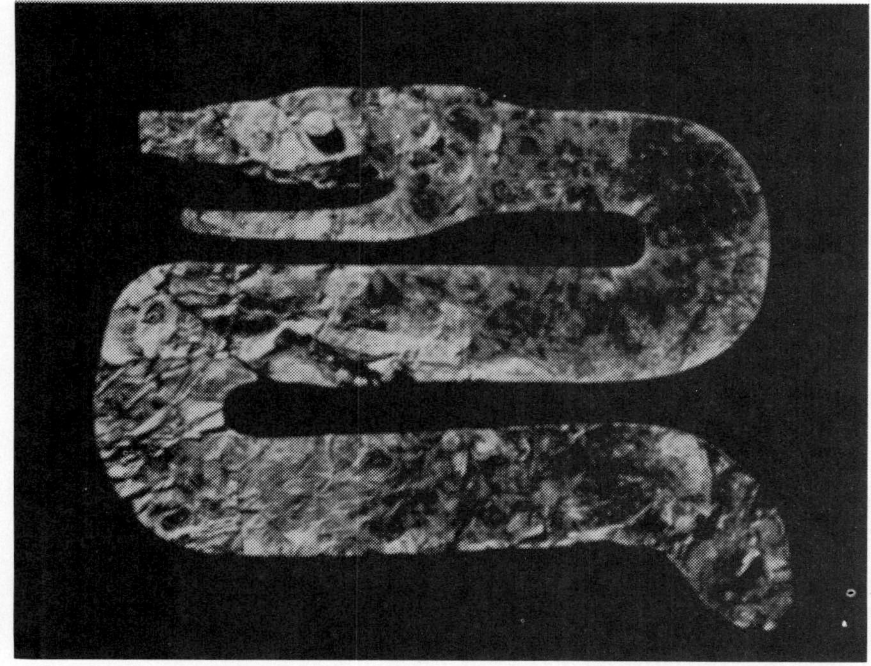

SNAKE EFFIGY from the Turner site is a foot-wide mica silhouette cut from a sheet imported from Virginia or North Carolina. Some Ohio burials were literally blanketed by mica.

HUMAN FIGURES representing a kneeling man and a standing woman are modeled in terra-cotta. Unearthed at the Turner site, they were ritually broken, or "killed," before burial.

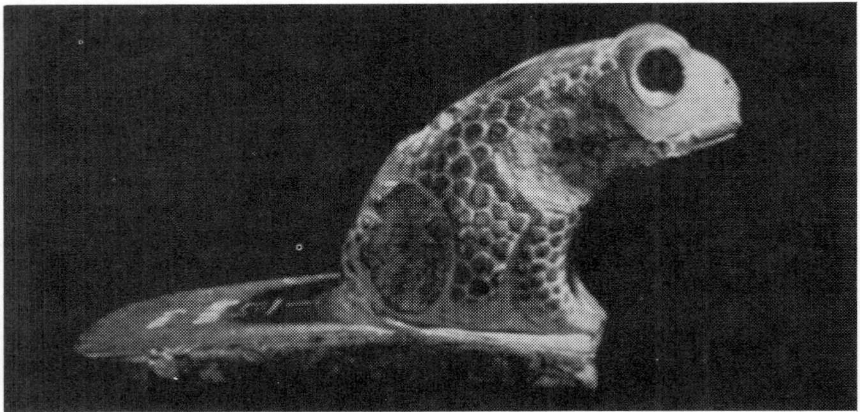

PLATFORM PIPE from the Mound City site has a bowl carved to represent a toad. Pipes showing birds, fishes, mammals and human figures were also made for Hopewell burials.

rivers, presumably because the bottomland was most suitable for agriculture. As for their economy in general, they raised corn, but a substantial part of their food came from hunting, fishing and collecting. Analysis of the animal bones in the McGraw deposit shows that the commonest source of meat was the white-tailed deer. Other game animals that have been identified in the deposit are the cottontail rabbit and the turkey. River produce was of equal or perhaps greater importance for the larder; we found the bones and shells of a variety of turtles, the bones of nine species of fish and the shells of 25 species of mollusk.

Among the wild-plant foods these people collected were nuts: the deposit contained charred remains of hickory nuts, walnuts and acorns. Other wild plants that have been identified are the hackberry and the wild plum. Apparently corn was the only plant the people cultivated, but the remains make it clear that their knowledge of corn-raising had not been recently acquired. The charred ear of corn from the McGraw site, still bearing a number of kernels, is of a 12-row variety. It appears to be of a type intermediate between the northern flint corn grown in Ohio in late pre-European times and the ancient flint corns and popcorns known from elsewhere in the Western Hemisphere. One of the isolated kernels from the deposit has been identified as belonging to an eight-row or 10-row variety of corn; it possibly represents a full-fledged, although small, member of the northern flint type. These relatively advanced types of corn imply a long period of agricultural activity before the site was first occupied.

The date of the McGraw site's occupation can be estimated both from the style of its artifacts and from carbon-14 determinations; it is roughly A.D. 450. The bulk of the artifacts could have come from any pre-Hopewell site in Ohio; for example, less than 4 percent of the pottery fragments found in the deposit are characteristic of the Hopewell complex. This reinforces the point made earlier: Whenever the influences of the Hopewell cult appear, they are imposed on an already existing culture that for the most part continues in its own ways.

The McGraw site is nevertheless clearly identified as belonging to the Hopewell complex not only by the few Hopewell potsherds but also by other characteristic Hopewell artifacts. Parallel-sided flint bladelets were found in large numbers, and the bulk of the projectile points were of the classic Hopewell type known as "Snyders," after the site of that name in Illinois. The inhabitants of the McGraw farmstead evidently included craftsmen engaged in the production of grave goods for the Hopewell cult: cut and uncut mica was found in abundance. One bear tooth turned up in the midden, with typical countersunk perforations but without any inlay of pearls. There were also two ornaments made of slate that, like the bear-tooth ornament, were unfinished. Perhaps all these objects were discards; this would help to explain their presence in a refuse heap.

The McGraw site therefore casts considerable light on life in southern Ohio

CEREMONIAL BLADES unearthed at the Hopewell site are of obsidian, probably from the Yellowstone area of the Rocky Mountains. The largest (*center*) is 13 inches in length.

during the latter days of the Hopewell phase. Skilled hunters and food-collectors, gifted artisans in a wide range of materials, the people who manufactured the rich grave goods for the ritual burials lived in small scattered farmsteads on the river bottoms.

But were the people who made the grave goods the same as those who were buried in the great Hopewell mounds? Curiously this appears to be unlikely, at least in southern Ohio. To explain why, it is necessary to sketch what is known about the rise and decline of the Hopewell complex against the general background of the various prehistoric cultures in eastern North America.

Of the four successive major culture stages in this part of the New World—Paleo-Indian, Archaic, Woodland and Mississippian—only the third is involved here. In southern Ohio the Woodland stage begins about 1200 B.C. and ends shortly before the arrival of the Europeans. In the entire eastern part of North America, southern Ohio included, the Woodland stage is divided into Early, Middle and Late periods.

MYTHICAL BEAST with four horns and feet with five talons decorates the surface of a narrow stone object 10 inches long. It was found at the Turner site. Its purpose is unknown.

In southern Ohio the people of the Early Woodland period were mound builders long before the Hopewell cult arose. They belonged to the Adena culture (which takes its name from a mound site near Chillicothe). The remains of the Adena people show that they were roundheaded rather than longheaded. They lived without contact with the Hopewell cult until about 100 B.C.; at that time, according to carbon-14 determinations, the Tremper mound of Scioto County was raised. This mound contained some 300 crematory burials. Many of the grave offerings are typical of the Adena culture, but some of them show Hopewell influences.

As skulls from later burials indicate, the arrival of the Hopewell cult in Ohio (presumably from Illinois) was accompanied by the arrival of a new population; these people were longheaded rather than roundheaded. How many immigrants arrived is an open question. The total number of individuals found in Ohio Hopewell mounds—an estimated 1,000—can represent only a fraction of the population of this region during the Middle Woodland period. It seems probable that most of the local inhabitants were the roundheaded Adena folk, many of whom may well have continued to live typical Adena lives untroubled by the neighboring Hopewell cultists. The fact that numerous Adena mounds continued to be built during Hopewell times is strong evidence for this.

To judge from their production of Hopewell ceremonial objects, the residents of the McGraw site would not have been undisturbed Adena folk. It is equally unlikely that they were immigrants from Illinois. It seems more probable that the immigrants were a privileged minority who in some way had come to dominate some of Ohio's Adena people, among whom were the farmers of the McGraw site.

Why did the Hopewell complex ultimately disappear? It may be that one part of the answer is plain to see. From their first arrival in southern Ohio until A.D. 550 these cultists evidently not only felt secure in themselves but also appear to have taken no steps to guard from raiders the treasures buried with their dead. After that time, however, no more ceremonial centers were built in open valleys. Instead it seems that every inaccessible hilltop in southern Ohio was suddenly crowned by earthworks that appear to have served a defensive function.

This does not mean that such sites as

Fort Hill, Fort Ancient and Fort Miami were permanently inhabited strongholds. Quite the contrary; at Fort Hill, for example, a survey of the land surrounding the foot of the hill has revealed several small farmsteads resembling the McGraw site. It is probable that the hilltop earthworks were places of refuge that were occupied only in time of danger. That there were such times is demonstrated by the evidence of fires and massacres at the Fort Hill, Fort Ancient and Fort Miami sites.

What was the nature of the danger? As yet there is no answer, but it is interesting to note that at about this same time the Indian population in more northerly areas first began to protect their villages with stockades. Unrest of some kind appears to have been afoot throughout eastern North America.

This being the case, it is not hard to envision the doom of the Hopewell cult. Whatever its basic religious tenets, the tangible elements of the ceremony were the celebrated grave goods, and the most notable of the goods were produced from imported raw materials. The grave goods were of course cherished for their part in the religious scheme; could the scheme itself be kept alive when the goods were no longer available? I suggest that the Hopewell cult could survive only as long as its trade network remained intact and, further, that the postulated current of unrest in eastern North America during the seventh and eighth centuries A.D. was sufficient to disrupt that network.

Whether or not this caused the collapse of the Hopewell cult, there is no question that it did collapse. By the beginning of the Late Woodland period, about A.D. 750, elaborate burial mounds containing rich funeral offerings were no longer built. For the very reason that Hopewell was only a cult and not an entire culture, however, the distinctive local traditions that had participated in the Hopewell ceremonies now reasserted themselves.

In Ohio this regional tradition is named Scioto [*see top illustration on page 226*]. Because of the alien nature of the Hopewell ceremonial complex, the phase of the Scioto tradition—called Hopewell—during which the funeral centers were built has a dual status. In terms of chronology the Hopewell phase was only one subdivision of the Scioto tradition. At the same time the Hopewell religious cult must be granted the status of a full-fledged tradition in its own right.

The Chinampas of Mexico

by Michael D. Coe
July 1964

They are highly productive farm plots surrounded on at least three sides by canals. Created in an ancient drainage project, they were the economic foundation of the Aztec empire

When the Spanish conquistadores entered Mexico in 1519, they found most of the peoples in the region unwillingly paying tribute to the emperor of the Aztecs, who ruled from a shimmering island capital in a lake on the site of modern Mexico City. Less than 200 years earlier the Aztecs had been a small, poor, semibarbaric tribe that had just settled in the area after centuries of wandering in search of a home. Shortly after their arrival they fought with their neighbors and were obliged to retreat to two small islands in the lake. There they adopted a unique form of land reclamation and agriculture known as the chinampa system. This system, which had long been practiced on the margins of the lake, was one of the most intensive and productive methods of farming that has ever been devised. It provided the Aztecs with land to live on and with the first surplus of food they had ever known. Their new wealth enabled them to create a standing army that soon subjugated nearby peoples. Driven by the demands of their sun-god for sacrificial captives, and supported by chinampa agriculture (which was also practiced by some of their vassals), the Aztecs quickly expanded their empire throughout Mexico.

The Spaniards toppled the Aztecs within two years and razed their magnificent pyramid temples, but the chinampa system has persisted to the present. Now, after enduring for perhaps 2,000 years, it too appears to be facing extinction.

Chinampas are long, narrow strips of land surrounded on at least three sides by water. Properly maintained, they can produce several crops a year and will remain fertile for centuries without having to lie fallow. The important role they have played in the long history of Mexico is probably unknown to the *chinamperos* who tend them and to the many tourists who visit the most famous chinampa center: the town of Xochimilco south of Mexico City.

In Xochimilco the guides relate the charming story that chinampas are, or once were, "floating gardens." This is a tall tale that goes back at least to 1590, when a Father Acosta included it in his *Natural and Moral History of the Indies:* "Those who have not seen the seed gardens that are constructed on the lake of Mexico, in the midst of the waters, will take what is described here as a fabulous story, or at best will believe it to be an enchantment of the devil, to whom these people paid worship. But in reality the matter is entirely feasible. Gardens that move on the water have been built by piling earth on sedges and reeds in such a manner that the water does not destroy them, and on these gardens they plant and cultivate, and plants grow and ripen, and they tow these gardens from one place to another."

Acosta may have been deceived by the rafts of water vegetation that even today are towed to the chinampas and dragged onto them as compost. The real interest of a chinampa town such as Xochimilco lies not in its fables and its tourist attractions—flower-garlanded boats plying canals, waterborne mariachi bands and floating soft-drink purveyors—but in the problem of the nature and origin of the chinampas and the relation of this form of agriculture to the rise of the pre-Columbian civilizations of central Mexico.

The chinampa zone is located in the Valley of Mexico, a landlocked basin entirely surrounded by mountains of volcanic origin. The valley, which is a mile and a half above sea level, has an extent of some 3,000 square miles. In pre-Spanish times a sheet of water, called by the Aztecs the Lake of the Moon, covered a fourth of the valley during the rainy summer season. In the dry winter season evaporation reduced this shallow body of water to five separate lakes: Zumpango on the north, Xaltocán and Texcoco in the center and Xochimilco and Chalco on the south [*see illustration on following page*]. The last two were really a single lake divided by an artificial causeway. Villages were established in the valley sometime late in the second millennium B.C.; since then the valley has supported dense populations of farmers. During the first or second century A.D. the populous city of Teotihuacán, which covered at least eight square miles at the northeastern edge of the valley, came to dominate the region. Although Teotihuacán was overthrown as long ago as A.D. 600, its enormous pyramid temples still stand. The last, most powerful and best known of the civilized states of the valley before the arrival of the Spanish was the empire of the Aztecs, centered on the island of Tenochtitlán-Tlatelolco in the western part of Lake Texcoco.

Since the Spanish conquest in 1521 man has drastically changed the valley. In the colonial era the water was partly drained in the course of reclaiming land for agriculture. Far more, however, was removed by a great tunnel bored through the mountains to the north in 1900, during the rule of Porfirio Díaz. The valley has been further dried out by the tapping of springs and digging of wells to provide water for the rapid growth of Mexico City. Of the estimated six billion cubic meters of water avail-

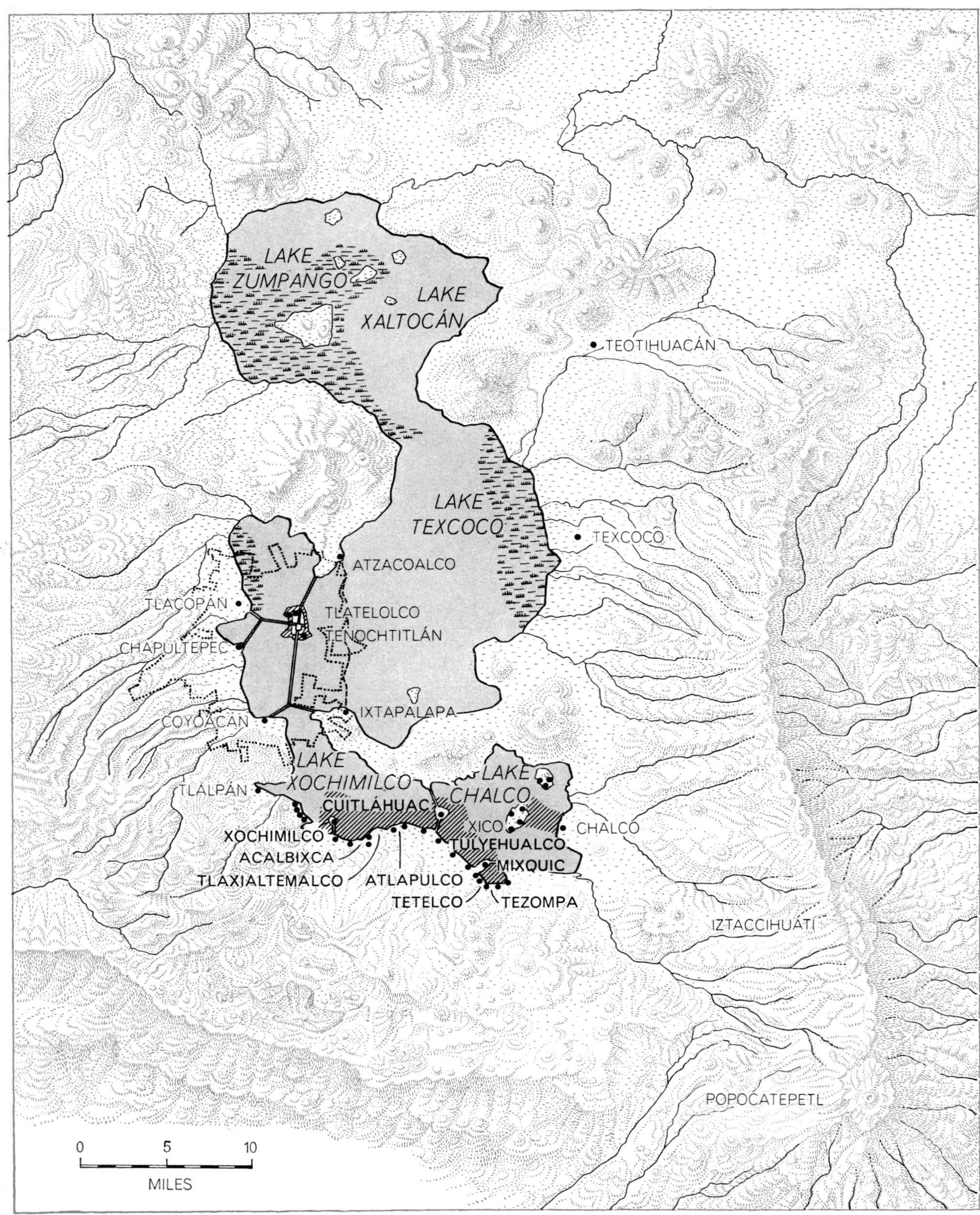

CHINAMPA AREAS (*hatched*) **and the Valley of Mexico are shown as they appeared in summer at the time of the Spanish conquest in 1521. In the rainy summer season the five lakes coalesced into one large lake: the Lake of the Moon. Tenochtitlán-Tlatelolco was the Aztec capital. The dotted line marks the limits of modern Mexico City. The broken line between Atzacoalco and Ixtapalapa shows the location of the great Aztec dike that sealed off and protected the chinampas from the salty water of Lake Texcoco. Causeways and aqueducts leading to the Aztec capital are also shown. The names of the nine chinampa towns that remain today are given in heavy type. The large black dots without names are the sites of the freshwater springs that fed the chinampa zones.**

able in the valley each year, 744 million cubic meters is consumed by the urban population. Most of the rest evaporates. As a result only isolated puddles of the Lake of the Moon remain, including parts of Lake Texcoco and Lake Xochimilco. Dehydration has so weakened the underlying sediments that the larger buildings of Mexico City are sinking at the rate of about a foot a year.

The removal of the water has also had a disastrous effect on the chinampas. From ancient times down to the past century or so many chinampa towns—small urban centers surrounded by the lovely canals and cultivated strips—existed on the western and southern margins of the old Lake of the Moon. Today only nine remain, and eight of them are probably doomed. Xochimilco alone may endure because of its importance as a tourist center.

In a masterly study of Xochimilco published in 1939 the German geographer Elizabeth Schilling established to the satisfaction of most interested scholars that the chinampa zone is an example of large-scale land reclamation through drainage. Recently detailed aerial photographs have confirmed her judgment. These show Xochimilco to be a network of canals of various widths laid out generally at right angles to one another to form a close approximation of a grid. This could not have been achieved by a random anchoring of "floating gardens." Departures from the pattern have probably come about through destruction and rebuilding of the chinampas, which are easily ruined by flooding and neglect.

To the trained observer the photographs reveal carefully planned canals that drained the swampy southern shore

CHINAMPA GARDENS and canals that surround each of them on at least three sides form a grid pattern in this vertical air view. The grid "tilts" about 16 degrees east of north. Many of the canals that appear to be silted up are simply covered with waterweeds. Part of the town of Xochimilco, south of Mexico City, is at lower left. First canals were dug 2,000 years ago to drain swampy areas.

ANCIENT AZTEC MAP of a portion of Tenochtitlán-Tlatelolco shows that it was a chinampa city. Six to eight plots are associated with each house. Profile of the householder and his name in hieroglyphs and in Spanish script appear above each house. Footprints indicate a path between plots or beside a canal. This is a copy of a small part of the damaged map, which is in the National Museum of Anthropology in Mexico City.

of Lake Xochimilco, where water flowing in from numerous springs had been held in the spongy soil. Here the water table was higher than the surface of the open lake to the north. The canals permitted the spring water to flow freely into Lake Xochimilco and thence into Lake Texcoco, which was deeper. The peaty sediments then released much of the trapped water. Mud dug out in making the canals was piled between them, adding height to the narrow islands and peninsulas that constitute the chinampas. The sides of the garden plots were held in place by posts and by vines and branches woven between them. Later living willow trees replaced many of these wattle walls. Until a few decades ago the water flowed out of Lake Xochimilco into Lake Texcoco through the willow-bordered Canal de la Viga, which carried native women to the market of Mexico City in canoes laden with the rich produce of Xochimilco. Now abandoned, the canal is largely silted up.

In many ways this remarkable drainage project resembled land-reclamation schemes elsewhere, such as those in the fens of eastern England or the polders of the Netherlands. It was unique, however, in the kind of farm plots that resulted, in the technique of their cultivation and in their enormous productivity. Each chinampa is about 300 feet long and between 15 and 30 feet wide. The surrounding canals serve as thoroughfares for the flat-bottomed canoes of the farmers. Ideally the surface of the garden plot is no more than a few feet above the water. Before each planting the *chinamperos,* using a canvas bag on the end of a long pole, scoop rich mud from the bottom and load it into their canoes. The mud is then spread on the surface of the chinampas. In the wet season (June through October) water held in the chinampa provides enough moisture for the crops; toward the end of the dry season, when the canals are lower, the plots must be watered. After a number of years the surface of a chinampa is raised too high by the repeated application of mud and must be lowered by excavation. The surplus soil is often removed to a new or rebuilt chinampa.

New chinampas are made, naturally enough, by cutting new canals, which today is accomplished with power dredges. Older plots that have fallen into disrepair are often reconditioned. In both operations rafts of water vegetation are cut from the surface of the canals, towed to the plot and dragged

DIGGING WITH A "COA," the cultivating stick of the ancient Mexicans, the rain-god tills magic maize. The drawing is copied from a late preconquest Mexican religious work. The *coa* is considerably broader near the digging end than it is toward the handle.

into place one on top of another until they reach the desired height. After that they are covered with the usual mud. Thus each plot has its own built-in compost heap.

An essential element in chinampa farming is the technique of the seed nursery, which has been thoroughly investigated by the anthropologist Pedro Armillas of Southern Illinois University and the geographer Robert West of Louisiana State University. The nursery, at one end of the chinampa near a canal, is made by spreading a thick layer of mud over a bed of waterweeds. After several days, when the mud is hard enough, it is cut into little rectangular blocks called *chapínes.* The *chinampero* makes a hole in each *chapín* with a finger, a stick or a small ball of rag, drops in the seed and covers it with manure, which now comes from cattle but in Aztec days came from humans. For protection against the occasional winter frosts the seedbed is covered with reeds or old newspapers. During dry weather the sprouting plants are watered by hand. Finally each seedling is transplanted in its own *chapín* to a place on the chinampa, which has been cultivated and leveled with a spade or hoe (the Aztecs employed a

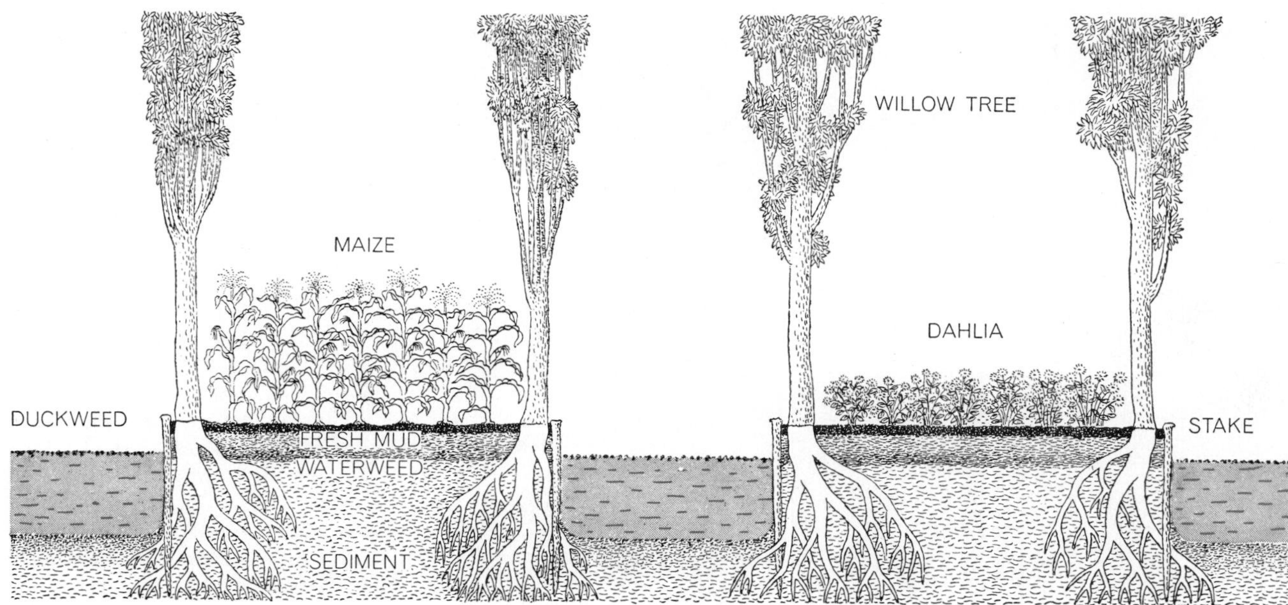

CROSS-SECTION DIAGRAM of chinampas and canals gives an idea of their construction. Fresh mud from bottom of canals and weeds for compost beneath the mud keep the chinampas fertile. Trees and stakes hold the sides of the chinampas firmly in place.

SEED NURSERY, made from small squares of rich mud, is an essential element of chinampa farming. Each square, or *chapín*, holds one seed and manure for it. When seedlings sprout, they will be transplanted in the *chapines* to places on the chinampa.

SCOOPING UP MUD from the bottom of the canal, the *chinamperos* load it into their canoe. They will spread the mud on the chinampa plot before setting out the new crop.

digging stick called a *coa*) and then covered with canal mud. The only crop for which the seedbed stage is not necessary is maize, which is planted directly in the chinampa.

The *chinamperos* report that they usually harvest seven different kinds of crop a year from each plot, of which two are maize. Crops raised today at Xochimilco include five varieties of maize, beans, chili peppers, tomatoes and two kinds of grain amaranth—all of which were cultivated before the Spanish arrived. Also grown are vegetables introduced from Europe, such as carrots, lettuce, cabbages, radishes, beets and onions. Xochimilco means "place of the flower gardens" in the Nahuatl language spoken by the Aztecs and still used today by the older people of the chinampa towns. The growing of flowers for sale goes back to the preconquest era, when flowers were offered on the altars of the pagan gods. Native species have imaginative Nahuatl names: *cempoaxóchitl* ("twenty flower," a marigold), *oceloxóchitl* ("jaguar flower"), *cacaloxóchitl* ("crow flower"). The gardens produce dozens of varieties of dahlia, the national flower of Mexico. European flowers include carnations, roses and lilies.

Carp and other fishes abound in the canals and are netted or speared by the *chinamperos*. Another inhabitant of the canals is the axolotl, a large salamander valued by zoologists as a laboratory animal and prized by the people of Xochimilco for its tender meat and lack of hard bones. Water birds were once caught in nets but are now scarce due to the indiscriminate use of firearms.

A basic question for the archaeologist and the historian is: How old are the chinampas? The traditional histories of the peoples of central Mexico list the Xochimilcas as one of eight tribes (the Aztecs were another) that came into the valley after a migration from a legendary home in the west. They were settled at Xochimilco by A.D. 1300 and were ruled by a succession of 17 lords. In 1352 and again in 1375 they were defeated by the Aztecs; finally, in the 15th century, they were incorporated into the Aztec state, which had absorbed the rest of the chinampa zone as well.

Some recent archaeological evidence makes it appear certain that Xochimilco, and by extension the other chinampa towns, existed long before the Xochimilcas arrived. A local newspaperman and booster of Xochimilco, José Farias

Galindo, has been collecting fragments of ancient pottery and clay figurines found by the *chinamperos* in the mud of the canals and in the garden plots. It is evident that such signs of human residence must postdate the initial digging of the canal system; until that had been done no one could have lived in the tangled marshes. Aztec bowls, dishes and figurines of gods and goddesses abound in Farias Galindo's collection, as might be expected from the many references to Xochimilco in Aztec documents. Of particular interest is the much older material that has been found. This includes a bowl of Coyotlatelco ware made between A.D. 600 and 900, heads broken from figurines of the Teotihuacán III culture, which flourished between A.D. 200 and 600, and Teotihuacán II figurine heads, which are as old as the beginnings of the great city of Teotihuacán in the first and second centuries A.D. Therefore it is likely that the chinampas of Xochimilco were planned and built almost 2,000 years ago.

Who was responsible? The only power in central Mexico at that time capable of such an undertaking was the growing Teotihuacán state, so that whoever built Teotihuacán also created the chinampas. Another piece of information points to the same conclusion. The grid of the Xochimilco canals is not oriented to the cardinal directions but to a point 15 to 17 degrees east of true north. So are the streets of the ruined city of Teotihuacán, and so are the grids of most of the other chinampa towns. We do not know why this is, but there were probably astrological reasons. It has been said that an urban civilization as advanced and as large as Teotihuacán must have been based on irrigation agriculture, but field archaeologists can find no trace of large-scale irrigation works. It seems far more likely that the growth of Teotihuacán was directly related to the establishment and perfection of the chinampas on the southern shore of the lake. Successive peoples and powers entered the valley and took advantage of the same system.

On the eve of the Spanish conquest Xochimilco was a flourishing island town under Aztec control, with at least 25,000 inhabitants—craftsmen as well as farmers. Cortes wrote of its "many towers of their idols, built of stone and mortar." The town, which was and still is on higher and drier ground than the chinampas, was approached from the south by a causeway crossing many canals. Its numerous wooden bridges could be raised to delay the approach of enemies. At the mainland end of the causeway was a large market; this is now the center of town. Xochimilco was divided into 18 *calpullis,* each with its own name. The Aztec institution of the *calpulli* is not well understood, but it seems to have been a local ward based on kinship. Their names survive today, and every *chinampero* knows to which ward he belongs. The *calpullis* were grouped into three larger units; the town as a whole was ruled by a native lord closely related to the Aztec emperor.

Wills, petitions and other documents filed early in the colonial period show that in Xochimilco land tenure, as well as the social system, was basically the same as that in the Aztec capital of Tenochtitlán-Tlatelolco. There were three categories of chinampa lands: (1) chinampas belonging to the *calpullis,* which could be used by a *calpulli* member to support himself and his family as long as he did not leave the land uncultivated for two years in succession; (2) office land, which belonged to the position filled by a noble official but not to him personally; (3) private land, which could be disposed of as the individual saw fit.

The island capital of the Aztecs was also surrounded by chinampas. The National Museum of Anthropology in Mexico City possesses a remarkable Aztec map on a large sheet of native paper made from the inner bark of a fig tree. This document, studied in recent years by Donald Robertson of Tulane University, shows a portion of the Aztec capital generally covering the section that is now buried under the railroad yards of Mexico City. In all likelihood it was drawn up as a tax record by Aztec scribes and used by bureaucrats into the period of Spanish domination. The similarity of the plan to that of modern Xochimilco is obvious. It shows a network of canals laid out in a grid, with the larger canals crossing the pattern diagonally. Roads

POTTERY FIGURINES of the types found in the chinampas and canals of Xochimilco were made in Aztec times, A.D. 1367 to 1521 (*top three*), during the Teotihuacán III period, A.D. 200 to 600 (*middle four*), and in the Teotihuacán II era, A.D. 1 to 200 (*bottom*). This ancient evidence of human occupation indicates that the chinampas are 2,000 years old.

and footpaths parallel the major canals, which the Spaniards said were crossed by wooden bridges.

The plan depicts some 400 houses, each with the owner's head in profile and his name in hieroglyphs. The Spanish later added Spanish transliterations of the names and also drawings of churches and other colonial structures. The property surrounding each house consists of six to eight chinampas. It was the cutting of canals and the construction of chinampas by the poor and hungry Aztecs who first came here in the 14th century A.D. that filled in the swampy land between the low rocky islands on which they had camped. The work eventually resulted in the coalescence and enlargement of the islands into the marvelous capital city that so impressed the conquistadores.

The more substantial houses of stone and mortar occupied the central sections of the capital, where the land was higher and firmer. In the very center were such large public buildings as the pyramid temples and the palaces of the emperor and his chief nobles. The bulk of the population was nonagricultural, consisting of priests, politicians, craftsmen, traders and soldiers. Nevertheless, Tenochtitlán-Tlatelolco was a chinampa city; the Spanish described it as another Venice. Thousands of canoes laden with people and produce daily plied the hundreds of canals, which were bright green with water vegetation. An Aztec poet has described the beauty of his native home:

The city is spread out in circles of jade,
Radiating flashes of light like quetzal plumes.
Beside it the lords are borne in boats:
Over them spreads a flowery mist.

The real basis of the native economy in the Valley of Mexico was the chinampa zone, which extended all the way from Tenochtitlán-Tlatelolco south to the shore of Lake Xochimilco and then east into Lake Chalco. The rest of the land in the valley, although it produced crops, was far less favorable to farming because of the arid climate. The chinampas, however, presented two difficult problems apart from those involved in their cultivation and day-to-day maintenance. One problem was to keep the water level high, the other was the prevention of floods.

The valley had no external outlet. Year after year over the millenniums nitrous salts had been swept down into

RUINS OF TEOTIHUACÁN, the large city that dominated much of Mexico from about A.D. 100 to 600, are still among the most impressive in Mexico. The rise of this great urban center may have been made possible by the development of the chinampas to the south.

the Lake of the Moon by the summer rains and had been concentrated by evaporation in the eastern part of Lake Texcoco. It was essential to keep the deadly salts away from the chinampas. For this reason the chinampas could only function properly if they were fed constantly by freshwater springs, which maintained the water level and held back the salt water. Such springs are found today in greatest abundance south of Lake Xochimilco, where chinampa towns still exist. Long ago there were adequate springs on the island of Tenochtitlán-Tlatelolco, but the rapid growth of the Aztec capital and its associated chinampas made the springs inadequate. The problem was solved by the construction of aqueducts to bring fresh water from mainland springs. It has sometimes been assumed that the sole purpose of the aqueducts was to carry drinking water to the inhabitants of the capital, but, as the ethnohistorian Angel Palerm of the Pan American Union has noted, their thirst must have been incredible.

These covered masonry watercourses were no mean structures. The first was completed in the reign of Montezuma I (1440–1468); it brought water over a causeway from the west into the city from a large spring at the foot of Chapultepec hill. Cortes wrote that the flow was "as thick as a man's body." A second aqueduct was built by the emperor Ahuítzotl (1486–1502). For this aqueduct a spring at Coyoacán, on a point of land separating Lakes Texcoco and Xochimilco, was enlarged; the aqueduct ran along the causeway that led north to Tenochtitlán-Tlatelolco. Ahuítzotl's effort was initially crowned with disaster: the volume of water was so great that violent floods resulted. The flow of the spring diminished, it was recorded by pious Aztec chroniclers, only when the emperor sacrificed some high officials and had their hearts thrown into it, along with various valuable objects.

The second major problem of the chinampas—periodic flooding by salty water—was also finally solved by construction works. The nitrous salts, which had already made the waters of the eastern part of Lake Texcoco unsuitable for chinampas, rose and moved into the chinampa zone during the summer rains, in spite of the flow from the springs. The problem apparently became acute only in the Aztec period, when, according to the pollen chronology worked out by Paul B. Sears of Yale University, the climate of the region seems to have been wetter than at any time since the end of the last ice age. The floods nearly destroyed the entire economy of the Valley of Mexico. In the 15th century Nezahualcóyotl, the poet-king of Texcoco, supervised for his relative Montezuma I the construction of an enormous dike of stones and earth enclosed by stockades interlaced with branches. The dike, on which 20,000 men from most of the towns of the valley labored, extended 10 miles across the Lake of the Moon from Atzacoalco on the north to Ixtapalapa on the south. It sealed off the Aztec capital and the other chinampa towns from the rest of Lake Texcoco, leaving them in a freshwater lagoon. The three stone causeways connecting the capital with the mainland were pierced in several places and floodgates were installed to provide partial control of the water level in the lagoon.

The entire chinampa zone, then, represented a gigantic hydraulic scheme based on land drainage and the manipulation of water resources. The Aztecs refined and exploited it to establish a vast empire for the glory of their gods and the profit of their rulers. Defeated peoples were quickly organized as tributaries under the watchful eye of a local Aztec garrison and military governor. Twice a year they had to render a huge tribute to Tenochtitlán-Tlatelolco. The Aztec tribute list records that every year the capital received 7,000 tons of maize, 4,000 tons of beans and other foods in like quantity, as well as two million cotton cloaks and large amounts of more precious materials such as gold, amber and quetzal feathers. In fact, in supporting the dense population of the capital, variously estimated at 100,000 to 700,000 (the latter figure is highly unlikely), tribute greatly outstripped local production in importance.

It would probably be no exaggeration to say that the chinampas gave the ancient peoples of the Valley of Mexico intermittent sway over most of the country for 1,500 years before the arrival of the Spaniards. For this reason a detailed study of all aspects of this unique system as it now operates should be made before the chinampas disappear altogether in the name of progress.

Pre-Columbian Ridged Fields

by James J. Parsons and William M. Denevan
July 1967

In four areas of tropical lowland in South America there are huge arrays of ancient earthworks. Many of them are ridges put up to farm land subject to seasonal flooding

In South America thousands of square miles of tropical lowlands are submerged in shallow floodwaters for weeks or months during the rainy season and are parched by drought during the dry season. Covered either with savanna grasses or with forest, these poorly drained river floodplains have generally been considered unfit for agriculture since the Spanish Conquest. When they are exploited at all, it is usually as cattle range. In the open savanna the grass is renewed by annual burning; in some wooded areas today the trees are being cleared to make way for planted pasture.

Recently the surprising discovery has been made that areas in several such regions were once intensively farmed. The pre-Columbian farmers had a specialized system of agriculture that physically reshaped large parts of the South American continent. Aerial reconnaissance and surface exploration have now located the intricate earthworks required by this system in the tropical lowlands of four widely separated regions: eastern Bolivia, western Ecuador, northern Colombia and coastal Surinam (Dutch Guiana). Similar earthworks are said to exist in other parts of the continent, but such reports have not yet been substantiated. Here we shall describe the earthworks in the four areas that have been identified and mapped thus far, review what is known about prehistoric earthmoving for agricultural purposes elsewhere in the Americas (both lowland and highland) and then examine the implications of these early works with respect to the rise of civilization in the New World.

Except for two brief references in early chronicles, the first mention of agricultural earthworks in South America was made in the 1900's by the Swedish ethnographer Erland Nordenskiöld, in connection with his studies in the Llanos de Mojos (Plains of Mojos) of northeastern Bolivia. Located in the heart of the South American continent, between the Andes and the Brazilian highlands, most of the Mojos plains area is less than 800 feet above sea level. Bounded by the Beni and Mamoré rivers, these broad lowlands are a sea of grass in which occasional islands of forest mark the higher, better-drained ground; indeed, the vegetation is locally known as *pampa-isla*. Here for as much as seven months of the year floods cover the grasslands with a sheet of water ranging in depth from a few inches to several feet.

Faced with a hostile environment of this kind people everywhere usually adapt their lives to the circumstances; a commonplace example in areas subject to flooding is the building of houses on stilts. The modern cattle ranchers of the Llanos de Mojos do much the same: they simply select high ground for building sites. The pre-Columbian inhabitants of the area chose instead to modify the landscape. They raised mounds, causeways and serried ridges for their crops, all of which stood high enough to surmount the floodwaters. To this day the wet savannas are crisscrossed with narrow causeways that connect the natural islands of high ground. The causeways are as much as seven miles long; their total length in the Llanos de Mojos, as measured on aerial photographs, exceeds 1,000 miles. Also visible in the area are many artificial mounds that served as sites for burials, for houses and even for small villages.

The agricultural earthworks in the area cover at least 50,000 acres. They are of three kinds. West of the town of Trinidad the prevailing pattern is narrow, closely spaced ridges. South of Lake Rogoaguado the ridges are much larger: as much as 80 feet wide and 1,000 feet long. In other areas there are rows of small circular mounds six to eight feet in diameter. Whatever their form, most of the earthworks are less than two feet high. Originally they were doubtless high enough to stand above the average flood level.

In 1908 and 1909 Nordenskiöld excavated several burial mounds east of the Mamoré River that were associated with some of the Mojos causeways. Within the mounds he found fragments of elaborately decorated pottery, which he attributed to the ancestors of the region's Arawak Indians. This work of half a century ago is the only serious archaeology that has been undertaken in the area. Early Jesuit accounts of the region imply that the socioeconomic development of the Indians was advanced enough to enable them to construct the kinds of earthworks found there, but such literature, some of which is quite detailed, makes no mention of any agricultural ridges. Indeed, the extent of the ridges was not realized until 1960, when swamp buggies engaged in petroleum exploration encountered seemingly endless ridges near the town of Trinidad. Thereafter the ridge system was examined on aerial photographs. Here in Bolivia, however, the lack of archaeological investigation

ANCIENT EARTHWORKS visible in the aerial photograph of the San Jorge River area in Colombia on the opposite page are evident where the forest still stands and where trees have been cleared for pasture (*upper left*). In pre-Columbian times the inhabitants of this seasonally flooded river lowland built such ridged fields over an area of some 80,000 acres.

makes it impossible to determine exactly when the ridges and other earthworks were raised.

Another ridged area is in northern Colombia some 150 miles inland from the Caribbean coast. There the waters of the San Jorge and Cauca rivers join with those of the Magdalena in a great interior basin that is less than 80 feet above sea level. Known as the Mompos Depression, this seasonally flooded alluvial plain is covered with a constantly changing complex of lakes and swamps. When it is not covered with water, it is a rich reserve of pasturage for Colombia's two leading beef-producing provinces, Córdoba and Bolívar.

Since the Spaniards entered the region in the 16th century the western part of the Mompos Depression has also been famous for its Indian mounds and their content of gold. Neither the early settlers nor today's *colonos,* however, seem to have been aware that some 80,000 acres along the San Jorge are covered by a pre-Columbian ridged-field system.

The San Jorge ridges, like those of the Llanos de Mojos, are not easily perceived on the ground. From a dugout canoe, a common means of travel in the area, they are virtually invisible. The local people are aware of the ridges but few recognize them as man-made features. From the air the ridges are clearly distinguishable [*see illustration on page 240*]. When the Mompos Depression is partly inundated, slight differences in relief are emphasized and the ridge pattern is sharply outlined by the floodwaters. Moreover, both before and after the rains the color of the grass reflects the difference between the dry ridge crests and the damp ditches between them; for several weeks the pattern is clearly painted in tan and green.

The San Jorge fields are of three kinds. In one type the ridges are on the natural levees of old stream channels and are perpendicular to the channels. In the second type short ridges are arrayed in a checkerboard pattern. In the third type the ridges are in clusters, generally parallel but unoriented with respect to the higher ground of the levees. Averaging about 20 feet in width, the ridges vary in length from a few feet to almost a mile; the ditches between them are in some places wider than the ridges and in some places narrower. The majority of the ridges are two to three feet high; a few are nearly five feet. Most of the San Jorge fields have been invaded by forest since they were abandoned. Where the trees have been cleared and the area has been planted with pasture grass the ancient ridge system gives the landscape a distinctive corrugated appearance.

A third ridged area is immediately north and east of the airport for Guayaquil in Ecuador. To the east of the Guayas River, opposite Guayaquil and just north of the town of Durán, an extensive system of parallel ridges is visible that looks almost exactly like the ones at San Jorge and Mojos. Another area of earthworks lies some 15 miles north of Guayaquil, in the lowlands between the Babahoyo and Daule rivers, where rectangular mounds predominate. These relics of pre-Columbian agriculture in Ecuador seem not to have been recognized for what they are until we observed them in 1966. We might not have noticed them ourselves if it had not been for our familiarity with the earthworks of Bolivia and Colombia.

The ridged fields of the Guayaquil area cover substantially less ground than those of San Jorge and Mojos; the floodplain and swampland they occupy probably total some 10,000 acres. The system of ridges near Durán is currently being cleared of second-growth forest and sharecroppers are planting it mainly with rice and maize. Rice seedlings are transplanted from seedbeds into the ditches, the soil of which is heavier than that of the better-drained ridges. The ridges, which are 30 to 40 feet wide and as much as two miles long, are being planted with maize, squash, beans, sugarcane and cotton.

As in Bolivia and Colombia, serious archaeological investigation that could identify the peoples who raised the Guayaquil earthworks has yet to be undertaken. The Guayas floodplains are known to have been occupied from about A.D. 500 to the time of the Spanish Conquest by a people of the Milagro culture, noted for its elaborate work in gold. The low-lying countryside is dot-

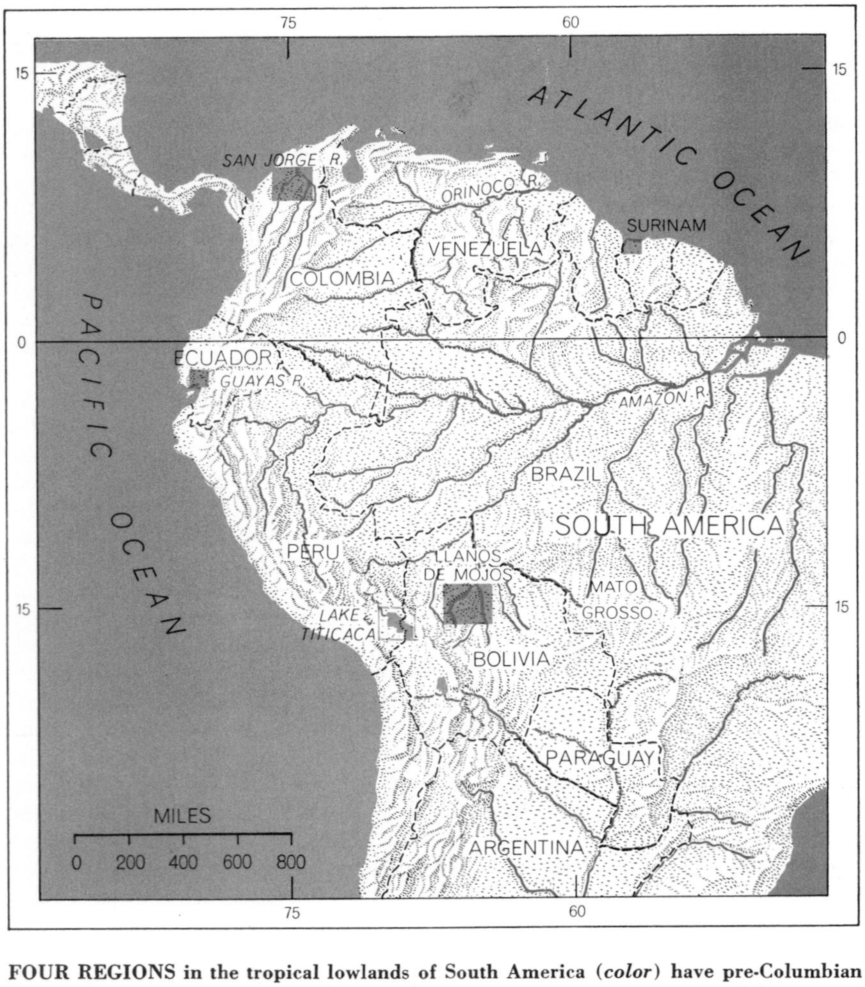

FOUR REGIONS in the tropical lowlands of South America (*color*) have pre-Columbian earthworks built so that lands subject to seasonal flood and drought could be utilized for farming. Similar earthworks were also built in the Andean highlands at Lake Titicaca.

RIDGED FIELDS in Colombia, built on the natural levees that adjoin abandoned stream channels, are usually oriented perpendicularly to the course of the stream. The height of the ridges seen in this aerial photograph is from two to five feet above the ground.

ted with thousands of *tolas,* or artificial mounds, built by the Milagro people for burial places and house sites. Some of the *tolas* appear to be associated with ridge systems and others with the rectangular earthworks. It is possible that the same culture made both. Only investigation can prove or disprove the association.

The coast of Surinam, the site of our fourth example of ridged-field agriculture, is a low-lying plain consisting of a series of ancient beaches running parallel to the present shoreline. Between these fossil beaches are swampy strips of clayey soil that support savanna vegetation. At a number of places along the coast ridged fields have been noted in these grassy swamps. The most extensive system of ridges is associated with an artificial mound known as Hertenrits, which is about 800 feet in diameter and rises six to seven feet above the level of the surrounding swamp. Hertenrits is three miles from the coast between Nieuw Nickerie and Caroní, in the middle of a long-uninhabited savanna belt that is now being reclaimed as part of a government rice-growing project. The mound is being investigated by the Dutch archaeologist D. C. Geyskes and the Dutch pollen analyst D. M. Laeyendecker-Roosenburg.

The Hertenrits ridges are short—perhaps three times as long as they are wide —and haphazardly arrayed. Some stand alone; others are clumped together like sausages in a pan. The aerial photographs indicate that the ridges rise two to three feet and that in many places they support vegetation distinctly different from that of the surrounding savanna.

Analysis of pollen contained in peat taken from the Hertenrits mound and from an adjacent swamp indicates that the mound was raised not long after A.D. 700. At that time the sea had encroached on the area; the evidence for the encroachment is a marked increase in the abundance of mangrove pollen in the samples. The Dutch investigators suggest that, in order to continue living in the area under these conditions, the local people were obliged to build the mound as a village site and presumably also to make ridges for their crops. They calculate that the mound was occupied until at least A.D. 900 and probably later.

The pollens identified at Hertenrits do not include those of any cultivated plants such as maize. Although the evidence is admittedly negative, this fact suggests that the ridges were devoted to growing manioc, a plant that rarely flowers and is propagated not by seed but by stem cuttings. Manioc was a staple crop in much of tropical South America at the time of the Spanish Conquest, and it is still widely grown today. The cuttings are usually planted at the start of the rainy season and require good drainage. More than most crops, manioc would call for artificially raised ground in areas subject to flooding. It is probable that not only here but also in Bolivia, Colombia and Ecuador the peoples who made mile after mile of ridges were growers of manioc. It seems possible, although it is by no means proved, that the oldest earthworks in some of these areas may date back to a period before maize had arrived from Middle America.

In the absence of archaeological investigation making possible carbon-14 dating or other age determinations, one can only speculate on the antiquity of most of these early agricultural works. The ridged-field system in the Mompos

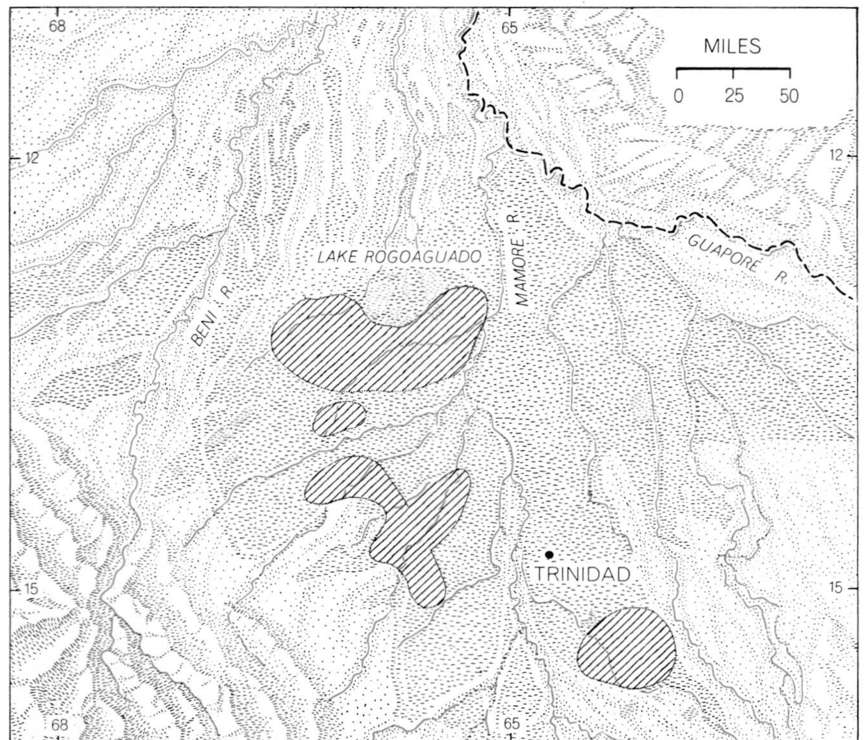

MOJOS GRASSLANDS of northeastern Bolivia have earthworks of several kinds in the indicated areas. These include causeways, settlement mounds and 50,000 acres of ridged fields.

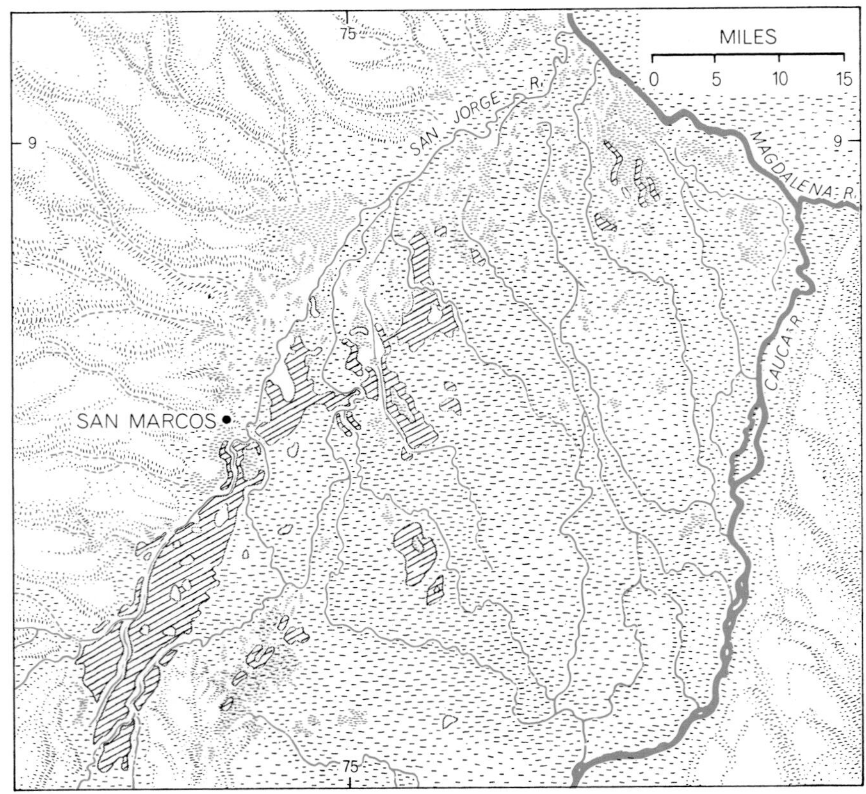

MOMPOS DEPRESSION is the alluvial plain in Colombia where seasonally flooded ridged fields are found. Fields near San Marcos are shown on the preceding page and on page 240.

Depression of Colombia appears to be associated with the Indian mounds there, and the mounds seem to have been more or less continuously occupied for a long time before the Spaniards arrived. A hundred miles or so to the north, near the Caribbean coast, there are mounds of shells that have been dated by the carbon-14 method. These dates range from 800 B.C. at Momil to about 3000 B.C. at Puerto Hormiga, making the latter the oldest-known site in the New World where pottery is found. There is no evidence that the San Jorge fields are equally old, but it is interesting that some of the shell mounds occupy a similar ecological niche, being located on the margin of seasonally flooded lands.

One possible means of determining the age of the San Jorge earthworks arises from the fact that there the ridge pattern is often oriented at right angles to old stream channels. A reconstruction of the district's history of sedimentation might provide a key to the question of age. Many of the ridges appear to be related to the oldest and longest-abandoned channels, which are now choked with water hyacinths when they contain any water at all.

Although many other lowland regions of tropical South America have terrain suited to ridged-field agriculture, our investigations up to now have produced concrete evidence of their existence only in the four areas described here. Nonetheless, promising conditions for the discovery of similar earthworks exist over huge areas: the Orinoco delta, Marajó Island at the mouth of the Amazon, the Pantanal region of the western Mato Grosso in Brazil and the broad llanos of Venezuela and Colombia.

South of the old colonial city of Barinas in the Venezuelan llanos a complex of man-made causeways as much as six feet high, 20 feet wide and three miles long has been described by the Venezuelan archaeologist J. M. Cruxent. Both in Bolivia and Surinam similar causeways, possibly used as footpaths during periods of flooding, are associated with ridged fields. Our inspection of the available aerial photographs of the grassy Venezuelan plains has failed to reveal any ancient agricultural earthworks, but the area deserves more intensive examination. The 16th-century Spanish chronicler Juan de Castellanos, writing of the plains country, mentions "old cultivation ridges" (*labranzas viejas camellones*), an indication that the agricultural areas of this kind he had seen or heard about had been abandoned at the time of his observations. Yet some 200 years later the author of *Orinoco Ilustrado*, Father José Gumilla, clearly described the continuing use of ridged fields. "In poorly drained sites," he wrote, the Indians "without burning the grass... lift the earth from ditches on either side, mixing the grass with the earth and then planting their maize, manioc and other root crops, along with pimento."

Father Gumilla does not say exactly where he observed this practice. It could have been anywhere in the llanos of Colombia or Venezuela, but visible remnants of this farming system must still persist. Bush pilots, if they are on the lookout for such ridges, may find them on the lower floodplains of such major tributaries of the Orinoco as the Apure, the Arauca and the Meta.

Several parallels to the ridged fields of the tropical lowlands are found in the highlands of South and Central America. It seems likely that the earth-moving practices in both environments were related in function, if not always in form. One of the closest approximations in both form and function are the ridged fields recently discovered along the western shore of Lake Titicaca, at an altitude of 12,000 feet in the Andes. These fields, covering some 200,000 acres, are found over a distance of more than 160 miles, from north of Lake Arapa in Peru to the Straits of Tiquina in Bolivia. Today the ditches are encrusted with alkali and the ridges are highly saline, so that cultivation is usually impossible. The fields still serve as grazing land, however, particularly during the dry season. At that time the upland pastures are parched and brown, but the high water table along the shore of the lake serves to keep the grass among the ancient earthworks green.

The Titicaca ridges are from 15 to 40 feet wide and range up to hundreds of feet in length. The height from ditch bottom to ridge crest is usually three to four feet. Most of the ridged fields are on the poorly drained margin of the lake plain and are subject to flooding in years of high water. The fields form checkerboard or ladder-like patterns or are irregular; their resemblance to the ridged fields in the Mojos area nearby in lowland Bolivia is striking.

Another form of agricultural earthworks in the Andean highlands consists of narrower parallel ridges, often built on sloping ground and running straight downhill rather than across the slope. Some of these ridge systems are old but others are new. Called *huachos*

CAUSEWAY in the level, seasonally flooded Mojos savanna of Bolivia runs among a series of ancient ridged fields made more prominent by the play of the late-afternoon shadows.

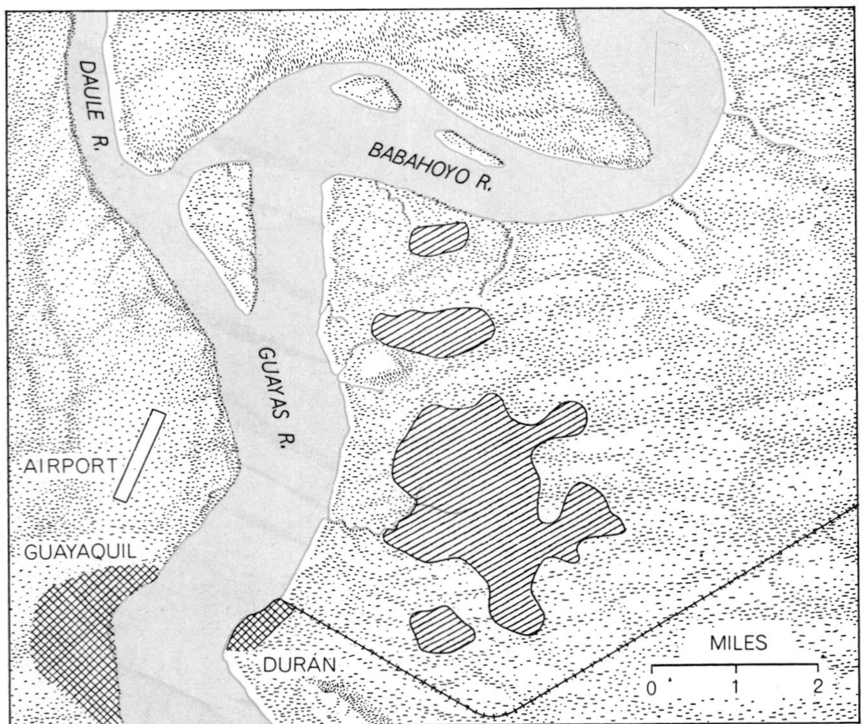

RIVER JUNCTURE near Guayaquil airport in Ecuador is area with ridged fields. To the north are found broader agricultural platforms (*see top illustration on opposite page*).

in Peru and Bolivia, they help to aerate heavy sod, to channel excess water from parts of a slope and to improve drainage on slopes so gentle that they are subject to waterlogging. In Colombia's central mountains, where old second-growth forest is being cleared to establish coffee plantations and pasture, the ancient ridge systems are so abundant that the hillsides in places give the appearance of having been combed. These pre-Columbian ridges are five to six feet wide, as much as twice the width of the *huachos* that are built today.

Huachos are usually confined to hillsides but are also found on level plains. Near Like Titicaca, for example, recently dug *huachos* can be found overlying the pre-Columbian ridge systems. Above 10,000 feet in the central Andes *huachos* are planted mainly with potatoes. To the north in the Colombian Andes, where the earthworks have been raised at much lower altitudes, they are used to grow maize, manioc and the white carrot-like root known as *arracacha*.

The well-known chinampas, or artificial islands, of the Valley of Mexico have some characteristics in common with the various drainage-promoting earthworks that are found in South America. Although many chinampas were built up in shallow lake waters, others served to convert swampy ground into useful fields. Still others were evidently formed on lake margins subject to seasonal flooding. At Xochimilco, the classic chinampas site [see the article "The Chinampas of Mexico," by Michael D. Coe, beginning on page 231], the planting areas are quite large. They are squares 100 yards or more on a side, surrounded by navigable canals edged with alders and willows. In the poorly drained basin at the headwaters of the Balsas River in the nearby state of Tlaxcala another example of artificial-island agriculture is found; it is apparently a variation on the Valley of Mexico pattern.

Raised fields built to avoid the hazards of floodplain agriculture are not confined to Latin America. Henry Schoolcraft, a pioneer ethnographer who worked in the U.S. Middle West in the middle of the 19th century, described agricultural earthworks or "planting beds" in valley bottoms extending from the vicinity of Fort Wayne, Ind., to the St. Joseph, Kalamazoo and Grand rivers in Michigan. Parallel ridges were laid out in rectangles with "paths" between them; some were as much as 300 acres in extent. Similar tracts existed in Illinois, Wisconsin and Missouri. Observing that the contemporary Indian inhabitants of the region cultivated maize only by "hilling," Schoolcraft concluded that the ridged fields were the work of an earlier culture, perhaps the then little-known Mound Builders. The possibility of some link between these garden farmers of the Mississippi valley and the ridged-field farmers of Latin America invites further study, particularly by those who are reluctant to accept the idea that similar environmental adaptations are independently invented again and again.

Putting together all our evidence concerning pre-Columbian agriculture in the seasonally flooded lowlands of tropical South America, we find that remarkably little is known other than what can be deduced from studying the ridged fields themselves. In the absence of any but the scantiest of early accounts, the means used to build the earthworks, the crops raised on them and the ways in which the crops were fertilized and rotated remain matters for speculation. It is especially difficult to attempt a projection of the number of people who could have supported themselves on the produce of the ridged fields, although some useful insights can be gained by examining the populations of areas where similar agricultural systems are used today.

Before considering this question it is only fair to mention several explanations of the earthworks that deny them any agricultural function, or at least rule out the role of improving drainage. Some observers have suggested that they might be fortifications, others that they might be the remnants of sluice-mining systems. They have been called fishponds, irrigation channels or enclosures for the culture of freshwater mussels. They have even been declared to be the result of natural sedimentation processes and not the works of man at all. The last is the easiest of the alternative claims to disprove. The evidence of the aerial photographs—in particular the variety of intermingled patterns they reveal—makes it clear that man is responsible for the raised ground. The tremendous extent of the works may seem to present a puzzle. What we know from the construction of contemporary chinampas in Mexico and from gardening practices in New Guinea indicates, however, that simple digging sticks and wooden spades are the only tools needed for similar earth-moving projects today.

What are the advantages that floodplain rivers and their associated swamps offer as a habitat for a settled people? For one thing, the rich protein resources of such an environment would have allowed a settled way of life even before the development of agriculture. In the tropical lowlands of South America the rivers, swamps and even the flooded grasslands harbor abundant

ANCIENT ECUADORIAN FIELDS are being cleared of trees and cultivated by local sharecroppers today. Between the 30-foot-wide platforms the damp ditches (*darker areas*) are used for rice. Maize and other staples are planted on the higher and drier platforms.

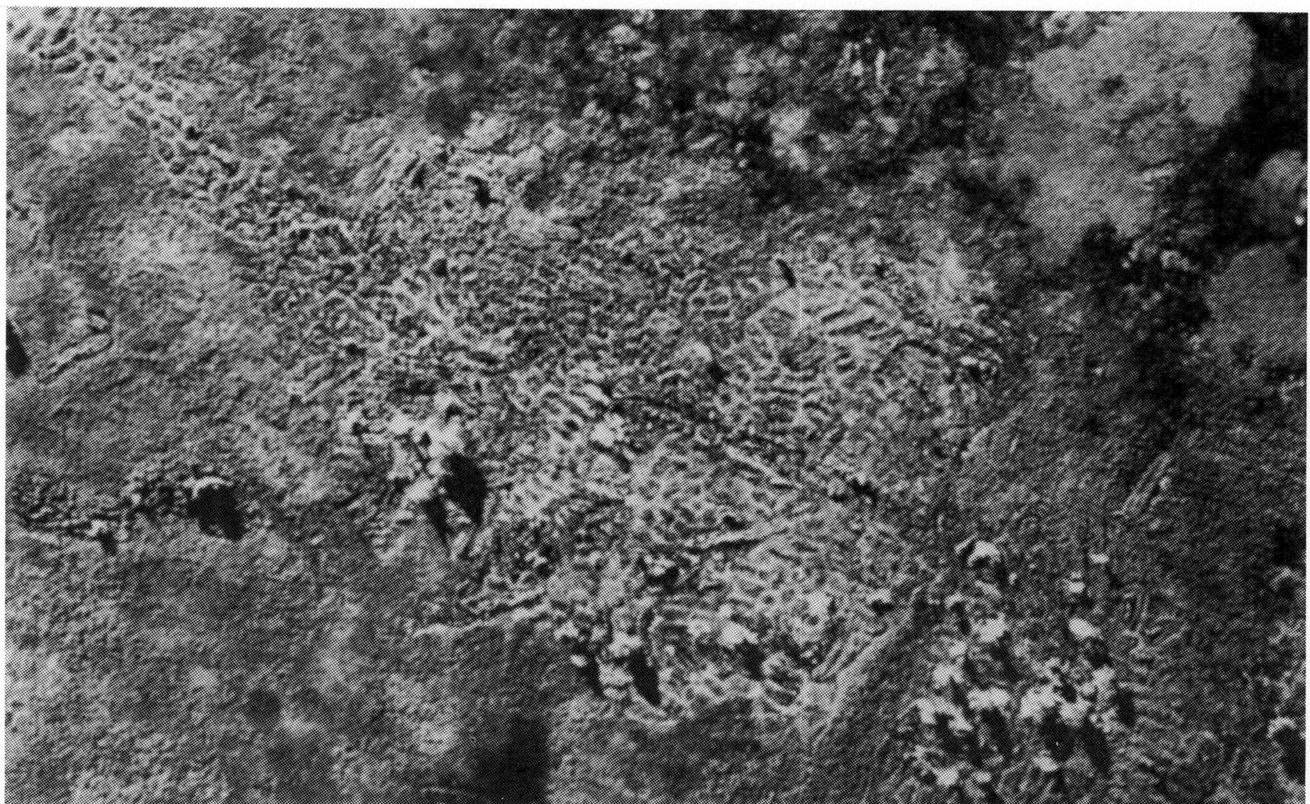

SWAMPY SAVANNA near the coast of Surinam has numerous examples of raised fields. The clusters of sausage-shaped ridges in the vertical aerial photograph are near a large, man-made earthwork, known as Hertenrits, that was put up soon after A.D. 700.

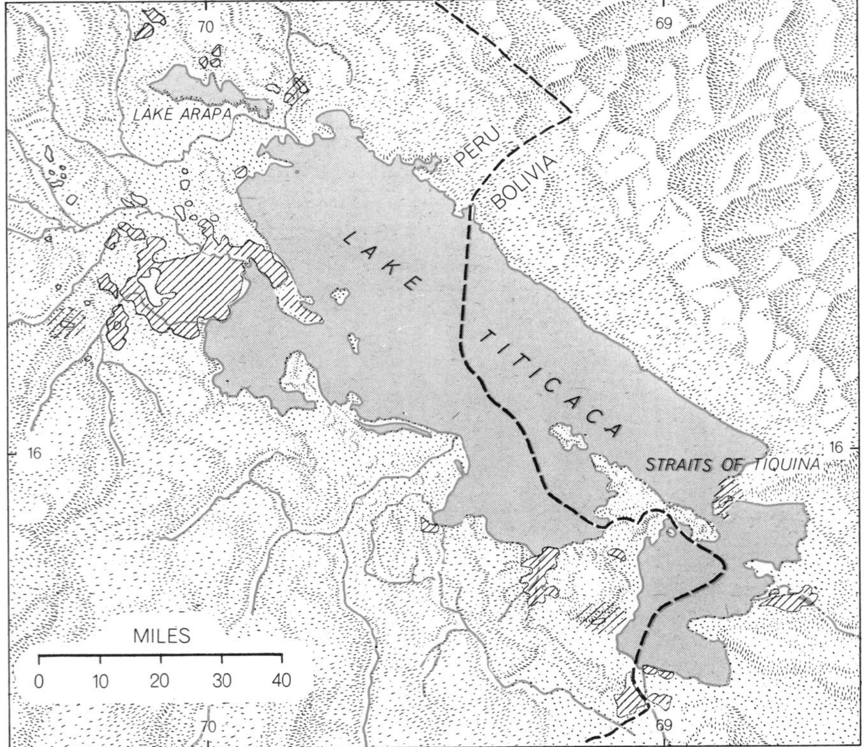

EXTENSIVE ARRAY of ridged fields lies in the Andean highlands on the poorly drained western shore of Lake Titicaca. Spread over 160 miles, the fields cover 200,000 acres.

TITICACA RIDGES, three to four feet high, are white with the accumulated salt that makes farming difficult today. When the photograph was made, the ditches were filled with water.

fishes, turtles (both land and water), iguanas, manatees and large rodents such as capybaras, pacas and agoutis. There is also a large and diverse population of waterfowl. Even after farming had become an established way of life, tropical agriculturists whose main food was a starchy root crop such as manioc would have valued the animal protein available in this environment.

A dual economy of this kind—ridged-field agriculture supplemented by hunting and fishing—should have been able to support far larger populations than the ones that scratch a living from the tropical forests today. Estimates of population density based on the extent of the ridged fields, however, are risky. For one thing, we do not know what fraction of the fields in a given area were under cultivation at any one time. The fields along the San Jorge River in Colombia, if they were all cultivated at the same time, could have supported as many as 400 people per square mile. In 1690 the Llanos de Mojos of Bolivia had a population of about 100,000 Indians. A century earlier, before the first contacts with Europeans resulted in deadly epidemics of Old World diseases, the population very likely numbered several hundred thousand. There is no reason to believe it was any smaller when the pre-Columbian ridged fields were under cultivation.

New archaeological evidence and new analyses of historical records attest to the existence of a surprisingly large aboriginal population in many parts of tropical South America. Both the extent of the seasonally flooded tropical farming areas and the evidence for a massive human effort that they provide suggest that the early lowland cultures had achieved a highly complex adjustment to their environment. The direction of flow of early cultural influences between the highlands and the lowlands of South America is a matter of continuing controversy. Those students of the question who contend that major cultural elements moved upstream from the lowlands of the Amazon, Orinoco and Magdalena regions into the Andean highlands in the past 2,000 or 3,000 years may find their arguments supported by the evidence for a complex, socially stratified lowland culture in pre-Columbian South America presented here. It is certain that future archaeological studies of South America's tropical lowlands and the complex ecological relations worked out by the region's early farmers should contribute much toward a more precise reconstruction of New World culture history.

Early Metallurgy in the New World

by Dudley T. Easby, Jr.
April 1966

In 4000 B.C. the people of the Great Lakes region were hammering tools out of native copper. By the time of Columbus the gold work of cultures from Peru to Mexico rivaled the best in the Old World

The practice of metallurgy in the New World before the time of Columbus is one of the most fascinating and, on occasion, infuriatingly enigmatic subjects in the history of technology. Early accounts by European eyewitnesses are rare. One outstanding exception is the description of "lost wax" casting in ancient Mexico recorded by the Franciscan friar Bernardino de Sahagún in the Florentine Codex, but even that account suffered from inept translations until 1959. A 16th-century Spanish chronicler, Pedro Cieza de León, gave a brief description of the *huaira*, or wind furnace, used in the Andes when the Spaniards first arrived in that region, and there are historical references to primitive methods of mining, such as placer mining for alluvial gold and platinum, shallow shaft mining and the strip mining of surface outcrops. A few references to metalcraftsmen, their favored position in society, their deities and ceremonies, and some vague allusions to metalworking centers also are known, but practically nothing has been preserved concerning technology. How, for example, were New World metalworkers able to make articulated metal figures and produce objects that were half silver and half gold? The tale persists that the egotistical Benvenuto Cellini spent months trying to ascertain how an ancient Mexican craftsman had fashioned a silver fish with gold scales and finally conceded that he was baffled.

Occasionally a crumb of contemporary technical information will turn up in an unlikely place. In an anonymous report to the president of the Council of the Indies in 1519 it is stated that a large gold solar disk presented to Cortes by Montezuma had been "worked, as when they work over pitch." This is obviously a description of the repoussé technique of decoration, in which a raised design is formed on a metal sheet by resting the sheet on pitch or leather and impressing a design from the back with a blunt tool. A similar reference to working sheet-gold masks "over pitch" is contained in one account of Columbus' second voyage.

Large-scale metal workshops are known to have flourished at Chan Chan in Peru, and others—called *patios de Indios*—are reported to have existed in Colombia. Azcapotzalco, near the Aztec capital of Mexico, was a great metalworking center, and there undoubtedly were other centers in those Mexican towns that are known from surviving records to have paid tribute to the Aztecs in the form of gold artifacts. Of none of these, however, is there any archaeological evidence; indeed, in the New World it is the exception rather than the rule that objects made of precious metal were discovered in the course of controlled excavations. Among the notable exceptions are the finds made at Monte Albán and Zaachila in Mexico, at Coclé in Panama and at Batan Grande and Lambayeque in Peru. The fact remains that most of the gold and silver objects in public and private collections today have been retrieved by means of clandestine graverobbing. Their archaeological origins are without documentation, and frequently their place of origin and age may be debatable.

Much information can nonetheless be gleaned from the artifacts themselves. Visual examination, for example, will reveal tool marks that at times even show whether the artisan was right-handed or left-handed. The appearance of a casting will indicate whether the original model was "faced" with an emulsion of powdered carbon in order to give the casting greater sharpness, and it will also indicate how the mold was vented to ensure a better flow of the molten metal. X-ray studies will disclose internal structures and hidden defects. Chemical and spectrographic analyses reveal the composition of the ancient alloys, from which their physical properties can be deduced. Examination of polished and etched sections of metal with the metallurgical microscope often reveals what steps were taken in the process of manufacture. In brief, laboratory investigation yields a surprising amount of information about the materials and techniques employed by these ancient craftsmen.

The earliest-known metal artifacts in the New World are those of the "Old Copper" culture that flourished in the upper Great Lakes region of North America beginning about 4000 B.C. The tools and weapons of this culture have been found in northern Michigan and Wisconsin and in southern Ontario; stratigraphic, geological and paleontological evidence, as well as carbon-14 dating, suggest that they were made during the course of the next 2,000 years, which was a warm, low-water period. The raw material was "native" copper, that is, copper occurring in nature as a relatively pure metal rather than copper that had to be extracted from an ore by smelting.

The Old Copper craftsmen probably looked on the metal as a new kind of stone that differed from flint in not needing to be chipped or ground to give it form. Native copper is sufficiently soft and malleable to be shaped by hammering. In common with other nonferrous metals, copper has an additional property of which the Old Copper artisans apparently took no advantage: it becomes increasingly hard the more it is hammered, until finally it is too hard

ANTHROPOMORPHIC FIGURE occupies the center of a bronze disk cast in South America by the "lost wax" method about the end of the first millennium A.D. Unearthed near Cobres, a pre-Columbian copper mining and smelting center in northwestern Argentina, the disk is six inches high. A pair of curly-tailed mammals are represented beside the figure's shoulders; the figure's feet rest on the beaks of a pair of birds portrayed upside down.

and brittle to be worked further. This phenomenon, known as work-hardening or strain-hardening, results from the breakdown of the metal's microscopic grains. Work-hardening can be reversed, and the metal softened to allow further working, by annealing, that is, heating the object to some temperature below the melting point. Annealing causes the work-distorted grains to recrystallize, forming new grains. Under the microscope parallel bands called annealing twins can often be seen in the new grains. Such bands may also appear in metal that has been forged while hot. Annealing twins have been detected in Old Copper implements, which has caused speculation whether these implements were cold-worked and then annealed or hot-worked.

The implements of the Old Copper culture include knives, chisels, axes, harpoon heads, awls and projectile points. The shapes of these artifacts were derived for the most part from prototypes made of stone, bone, horn or shell, although sockets in projectile points and the rolling of conical points represent innovations made possible by the plasticity of the metal.

The apogee of fine copper work in the region north of Mexico was reached long after the Old Copper culture had vanished. This high point was achieved by the craftsmen of the Hopewell culture. The most notable examples of their work come from Mound City and nearby sites in Ohio and were made sometime around A.D. 200. The Hopewell artisans did not know how to cast or solder, but they showed remarkable skill in hammering, in repoussé decoration, in cutting intricate designs out of sheet metal, in crimping, in riveting and in hammer-welding copper and silver or copper and meteoric iron to produce bimetallic objects. In hammer-welding the two pieces of metal were placed together and joined by repeated blows.

As for the other metals used north of Mexico, gold—the decorative metal par excellence in the Old World and in much of the New—apparently was restricted largely to Florida, where a few ornaments fashioned from sheet gold have been found. Thin flakes of gold, probably the remains of sheathing, have been reported on some Hopewell copper ornaments, and rudely shaped and perforated gold beads were reportedly found at the Etowah mound site in Georgia. Far to the north the Eskimos of the Dorset and Thule cultures in eastern arctic North America hammered and ground meteoric iron to make knives, which they often set in handles of walrus ivory.

In South America the oldest evidence of the use of metal, dating back to at least 2,000 years before the Spanish Conquest in 1532, has been found in northern Peru. Here, as in the Great Lakes area, the first metal to be used was in the native state. In Peru, however, the metal was not copper but gold. The earliest objects were ornaments cut out of sheet gold and given repoussé decoration in the Chavin style [*see illustration on page 255*]. This is a stage of development that was not attained in North America until Hopewell times.

Later metalworkers in the Andes were by no means limited to native metals in their choice of raw materials. Their efficient *huairas*—cylindrical furnaces of terra-cotta about three feet high with a series of openings along the sides—were capable of smelting a variety of ores. A charge of crushed ore and charcoal was placed inside the furnace and ignited. At the base of each opening along the wall of the cylinder was a small terra-cotta platform; piles of charcoal were kept burning on these platforms during the smelting process, sending a current of hot air and carbon monoxide through the furnace. Oxide and carbonate ores were reduced by the charcoal, the oxygen being driven off as carbon dioxide. The molten metal settled and was drained off through a tap at the base of the cylinder. These furnaces were usually placed on hillsides, where the prevailing winds provided a forced draft. There is evidence that in both Peru and Mexico copper was extracted from oxide and carbonate ores by this kind of charcoal reduction and from sulfide ores by a combination of roasting and charcoal reduction. Metallic tin was also smelted from cassiterite, and lead from galena. In spite of the rudimentary methods used, the metals recovered were surprisingly pure.

The tradition of making ornaments out of sheet gold continued in Peru down to the time of the Incas. Other techniques were also employed in this region. They included a method of "raising" beakers, cups and other vessels from flat disks of sheet metal by hammering them over a series of anvils and annealing them when necessary. (This is the same technique that was employed at the Mesopotamian site of Ur in the third millennium B.C.; it is still used by many handcraftsmen.) Large numbers of identical beads were formed by pressing thin sheets of gold or silver over carved replicas or into carved matrices of wood, stone or even metal. Artisans on the northern coast of Peru in the period from A.D. 200 to 700 occasionally decorated their masterpieces with elaborate mosaic inlays using as many as four different materials. In the same general area during Chimú times (A.D. 1200 to 1400) decorative techniques including painting with the red mercury ore cinnabar, encrusting with turquoise, and dividing the surface of a metal object with small partitions and then filling the spaces with cinnabar (a method resembling the cloisonné work of the Old World).

A further advance in technology—casting—probably first occurred in Colombia shortly before the birth of Christ. Decorative pins in the Calima style are topped with effigy figures that were cast by the lost-wax process, to which we shall return. Casting did not arise in Peru, however, until some-

AXE-BLADE CASTING as practiced in Mexico is depicted in Bernardino de Sahagún's study of pre-Columbian technology. Copper was brought to melting temperature with a blowpipe; the molten metal ran out of a furnace tap into a stone mold. On the ground is a finished axe blank; this will be given its final form by hammering (*see illustration below*).

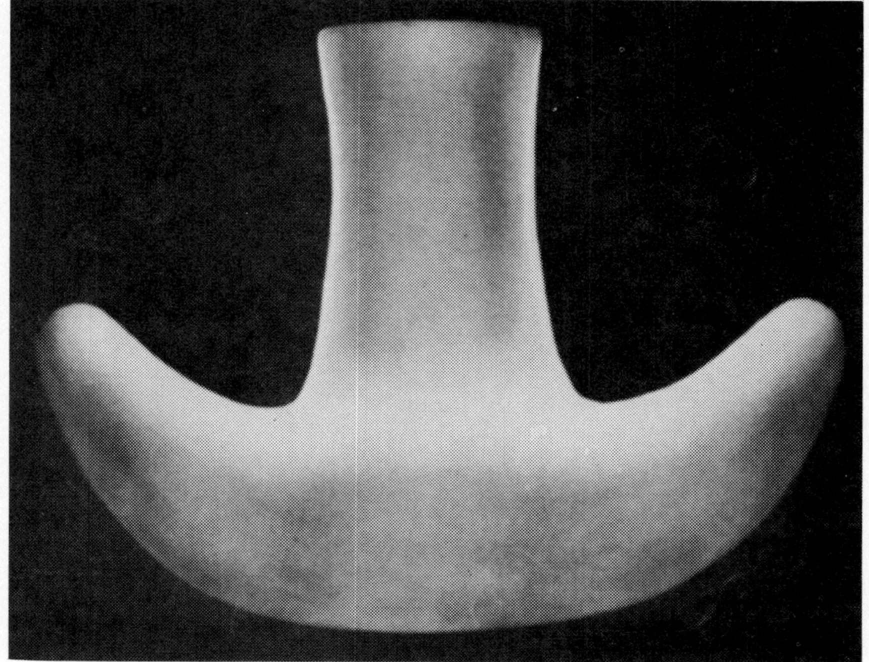

X-RAY PHOTOGRAPH of a copper axe blade from western Mexico reveals that the hammering process with which the blade was finally shaped has left it thickest (*lightest areas*) where blade and shank meet. Narrow raised flanges along both edges of the shank were also produced by hammering. Copper axe blades were a New World medium of exchange.

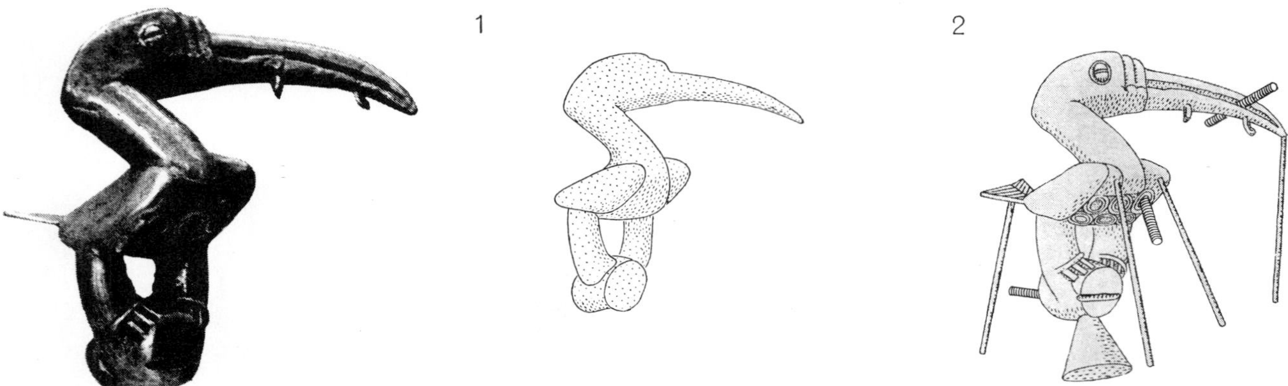

STEPS IN LOST-WAX CASTING are reconstructed, using a golden bird from Colombia that once formed the head of a staff (*photograph at far left*) as a hypothetical example. The first step is production of a core, made of clay and charcoal, that closely resembles the final figure (*1*). The core is then covered with a wax coating the thickness of which determines the thickness of metal in the casting. The metalworker models all the fine detail that he desires in this wax coating; he then adds wooden pegs to hold the core in place

time after the birth of Christ; the technique reached full flower there between A.D. 1200 and the arrival of the conquistadors.

Although most Peruvian metalwork was made to be worn as personal adornment or carried in ceremonies, copper weapons and tools also appeared when casting was introduced. Casting in copper is generally regarded as difficult, but impurities the early workers could not eliminate made a kind of alloy and thus facilitated the process. By the time the Spaniards had arrived Inca craftsmen were turning out weapons and tools of bronze. Analyses of these bronze artifacts indicate some appreciation and understanding of the effect of differing percentages of tin on such physical properties of the alloy as hardness and mold-filling ability.

Bronze objects have also been found in Bolivia, Chile and Argentina. Indeed, the first bronze in the New World was probably made about A.D. 700 in Bolivia, an area still famous for its tin deposits. In northwestern Argentina a few remarkable bronze castings have been discovered not far from Cobres, where early in this century a French scientific mission unearthed a pre-Columbian copper mining and smelting operation [*see illustration on page 250*].

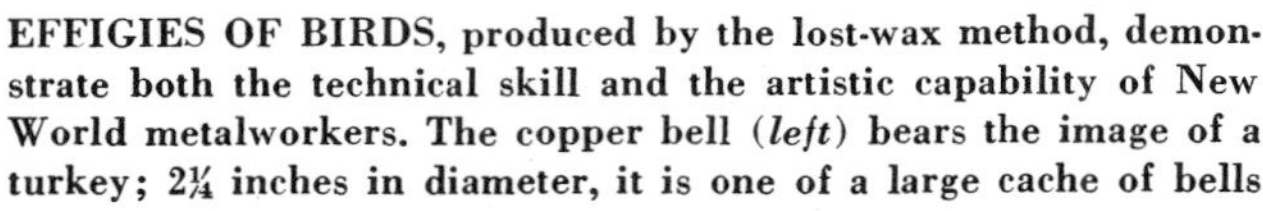

EFFIGIES OF BIRDS, produced by the lost-wax method, demonstrate both the technical skill and the artistic capability of New World metalworkers. The copper bell (*left*) bears the image of a turkey; 2¼ inches in diameter, it is one of a large cache of bells discovered in a cave in Honduras. Both the owl and the eagle heads are hollow gold castings little more than an inch wide. They are in the Mixtec style of western Mexico, where the art of lost-wax casting reached its highest state of development in the New World.

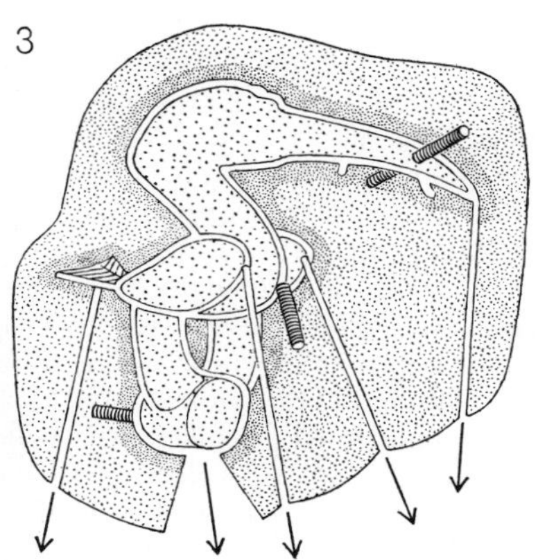

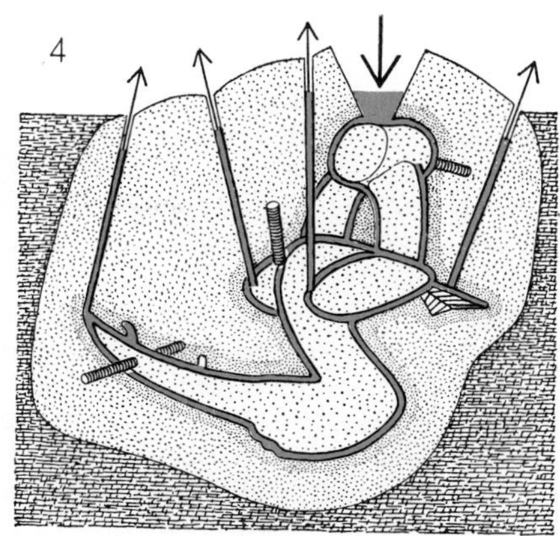

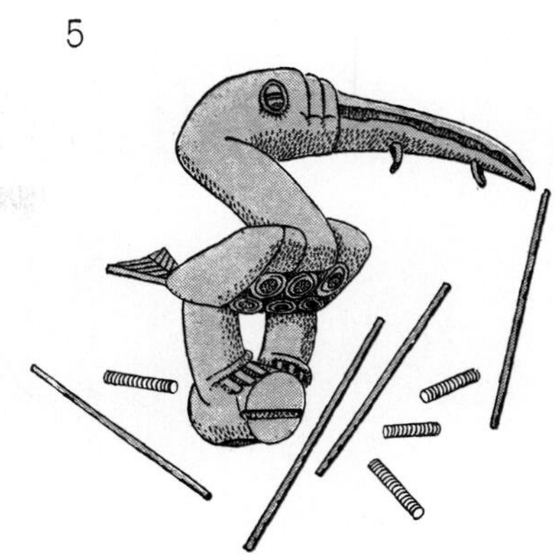

within the mold, wax rods to provide air vents and a wax cone to provide the casting funnel (*2*). The model is then invested in a mold of clay and charcoal that is dried and heated (*3*) so that the wax melts and runs out of the mold. The hot mold is then inverted (*4*) and the molten metal poured in through the funnel. When cold, the mold is broken away, the core supports and surplus metal are removed and the core is broken up and extracted through the various holes in the casting that were made by the core supports (*5*).

The pre-Columbian craftsmen of Ecuador have aroused the admiration of modern metallurgists by their manufacture of almost microscopic beads from an alloy of gold and platinum. Platinum has a very high melting point—more than 3,000 degrees Fahrenheit—but Ecuadorean smiths overcame the problem by mixing grains of platinum with gold dust. They repeatedly heated and hammered the mixture until the combination of temperature and pressure blended the two metals into a homogeneous mass without ever actually melting the platinum. The discovery of bits of this alloy in various stages of manufacture enabled the Danish metallurgist Paul Bergsøe to reconstruct the ancient practice, which is really an application of a basic principle of modern powder metallurgy, the sintering of refractory metals.

EFFIGY OF REPTILE, from the Coclé site in Panama, is a typical coreless lost-wax casting. The model was fashioned wholly of wax; as a result the cast figure is solid gold.

Although more an economic than a metallurgical matter, metallic money appeared in Ecuador and northern Peru about A.D. 1000 or slightly earlier. It consisted of small copper axe blades, too thin for any practical purpose, that were used as a medium of exchange. This concept of copper axe-money was transmitted, probably by maritime contacts, to western Mexico, where hoards of such axes numbering in the hundreds have been found in the state of Oaxaca.

In Colombia, Panama and Costa Rica gold was the principal metal, but a gold-copper alloy known as *tumbaga* was also widely used. Some ancient craftsman discovered that when an object made of this alloy was heated in the open air, a thin layer of copper oxide formed on the surface. If the heated object was then quenched in an acid bath of plant juices, some of the copper and copper oxide on the surface was dissolved; each time the process was repeated the proportion of gold at the surface increased.

In this process, known today as "pickling," the gold comes from the object itself; nothing is added, as it is in gold-plating. The extent to which true plating was practiced in the New World remains to be established. Gold foil was often applied as sheathing, and Bergsøe has shown that fusion-gilding, in which a molten gold-copper alloy is applied to preheated copper by flowing, was used on some Ecuadorean objects. Recent metallographic studies by the New York metallurgist Sidney B. Tuwiner have shown that metal disks from Vicús in Peru are sandwiches made up of copper between layers of gold applied by this same fusion-gilding process, which is a first cousin to the Old World technique known as Sheffield plating.

The outstanding achievement of the metalworkers of Colombia, Panama and Costa Rica was the perfection of lost-wax casting. In this process the artisan began by making an exact wax model of the object he wished to cast in metal, much as a sculptor works in clay. The wax, still called *cera de Campeche* in Mexico, came from the stingless bees of the rain forest; it was mixed with copal gum or some other resin to give it firmness and workability. Adding little pellets and threads of wax to his model as decorative details, the artisan next affixed a cone of wax, which later served as a funnel-shaped pouring channel for the molten metal, to the model's base. If the model had a complex form, with undercutting or other recesses where air might be trapped in the course of pouring the metal, wax rods were joined to these parts; the rods became air vents when the wax was burned out.

When the wax model was complete, it was usually faced with an emulsion of powdered charcoal in water to ensure a smooth surface and a clean, sharp casting. The Aztecs called this emulsion *teculatl,* literally "charcoal water"; its equivalent in modern precision casting

GOLD FIGURINE of a seated woman with flowers in her hands was made by the lost-wax method in Colombia. It was cast in separate sections that were soldered together.

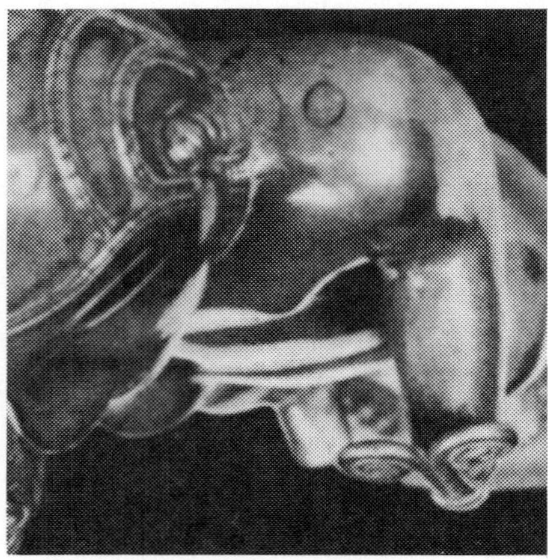

CLOSER VIEW of the figurine's shoulder reveals a circular plug of gold that fills a hole in the casting. This seeming flaw marks the point where a peg supported the core of the figurine during the casting process (*see top illustration on preceding two pages*).

is a mold wash made of water glass (sodium or potassium silicate) and graphite. Rough surfaces on the back of some Panamanian, Costa Rican and Mexican cast pieces and on both front and back of Chibcha votive figures from Colombia show that these areas were not faced.

The next step was to cover the model with an outer shell made of a mixture of moist clay and crushed charcoal. This, of course, had to be done without covering the pouring funnel or the tips of the wax rods that would form air vents. After the outer shell had dried, the entire assembly was fired. This strengthened the mold, burned out the wax and left a cavity of the same shape and volume as the now-lost wax model. The mold was then brought to red heat to facilitate the flow of molten metal, placed with the pouring channel uppermost, and the molten metal was poured in. When the metal had solidified, the mold was broken away, revealing a duplicate in metal of the wax original. The excess metal in the pouring channel (called a "casting button") and the rods that had formed in the air vents were cut off and the cuts were burnished down. The finished object was then given a final polish.

If the casting was to be hollow rather than solid, the process differed in two respects. The starting point was the preparation of a porous core made of clay and crushed charcoal. When the core had dried, it was carved to shape and covered with a layer of wax, the details of the model being completed as before. The thickness of the wax coating determined the thickness of the metal in the finished casting. Before the model was faced and covered by the outer shell of the mold the core had to be anchored to keep it from slipping out of place later when the wax was melted out. This was done by piercing the wax model at inconspicuous places with compact wooden pegs or cactus thorns that penetrated the core and projected above the surface of the wax. The projecting ends were embedded in the outer shell when it was applied and formed little bridges between the mold and the core, anchoring the core in place. These core supports of course left small holes in the finished casting. In some lost-wax castings from Colombia and Panama these tiny holes have been expertly plugged with the same metal or alloy used for the casting [*see bottom illustration at left*].

Both in Peru and in Mexico bimetallic objects made by multiple casting have been found. In this process a metal with a lower melting point, such as silver, is cast around a metal with a higher melting point, such as gold. A modern industrial counterpart is the "cladding" of one metal with another that has a lower melting point.

Lost-wax casting in the New World reached its highest development in the Oaxaca area of Mexico, where during the 15th and 16th centuries A.D. Mixtec master craftsmen produced little hollow castings that are unrivaled for delicacy, realism and precision. A favorite Mixtec decorative device was a fine cast filigree; the model for this cast wire presumably was made by extruding long strands of wax thread much as toothpaste is squeezed from a tube. A similar extrusion technique is still used in India. Drawn wire (as opposed to cast or rolled wire) has not been found in the New World so far.

Soldering, fairly common both in Peru and in Colombia, apparently was never fully mastered in Mexico. The solder customarily used for small work was a finely pulverized copper oxide or copper carbonate mixed with some organic binder. The mixture was applied to the metal parts to be joined and then reduced to metallic copper on the spot by means of flame and a blowpipe. According to the late Herbert Maryon of the British Museum, the same process was used by the Etruscans.

For a time it was believed that casting metal in molds might have been mastered by the Hohokam culture of Arizona in the period between A.D. 900 and 1100. This belief was based on a find of 28 cast copper bells at the Snaketown site. Large numbers of similar bells, however, have since been found in the states of Nayarit and Michoacan in western Mexico. In both the Snaketown and the western Mexico bells the copper had been extracted by the smelting of sulfide ores, and it is now generally accepted that the Hohokam bells were imported from this area of Mexico.

The question arises: Whence came the knowledge and skill of these talented New World metalworkers? It is not hard to imagine that the Old Copper people learned their techniques empirically, but what about the wide range of metallurgical practices and techniques employed later in other regions? Undoubtedly the craftsmen of Panama, Costa Rica and Mexico were the recipients of practices developed in and spread from the Andean

PRE-COLUMBIAN HAMMERED WORK ranged from simple to elaborate. The Peruvian ceremonial knife (*left*) has a blade of gold and silver segments, probably joined by the hammer-welding technique. It was probably made between A.D. 1200 and 1400. The Peruvian cutout jaguar figure (*top right*) is typical of the earliest-known New World work in gold, dating from about 500 B.C.; the design was raised by working from the reverse side with a blunt tool. The human head, raised on a sheet of copper by the same technique, is from the Spiro site in Oklahoma and is about 500 years old. Metalwork north of Mexico was rarely more complex than this.

region of South America, but how did these older skills evolve? In the traditional "parallelist" view there is no reason to assume, even in the absence of evidence for the local beginnings and evolution of such skills, that the ancient Indians were incapable of independently discovering them. Opposed to this view is the "diffusionist" position that the metallurgical processes are so complex that they must have been imported from across the Pacific. At present there is no concrete and persuasive evidence to support either contention.

EARLIEST METALWORKERS in the New World produced knives, projectile points and other kinds of tool from nearly pure native copper found in the Great Lakes area of North America. Artisans of the "Old Copper" culture, which flourished between 4000 and 2000 B.C., shaped their products primarily by hammering. Their manufacture of rolled points (*left*) and sockets (*center*) shows their appreciation of the plasticity of the new raw material.

KNIFE OF METEORIC IRON, with a handle of walrus ivory, was made by the Cape York Eskimos of Greenland. Meteoric iron was made into tools by hammering and grinding. Although the metal is far from abundant, it was used wherever chance made it available.

V

ANALYSIS OF SYSTEMS AND PROCESSES

V ANALYSIS OF SYSTEMS AND PROCESSES

INTRODUCTION

Until recently, specialization was the scientific strategy for the solution of the "insoluble" problems. This trend was exhibited in the proliferation of subdisciplines, such as biochemistry and geophysics, and even of subsubdisciplines, such as geochronology. Successful research required continually larger research teams and continually larger amounts of funding for studies that were focused on continually narrower fields. Although such specialization had led to a great increase in knowledge, it also led to a grave lack of communication among scientists in general, and even among scientists working within the same general discipline. Specialization brought solutions at the expense of communication.

Archaeology was no exception to this pattern. Both area and topical specialities had developed, and scholars were known for their studies in, for example, the South African Paleolithic or Mayan ceramics. Small regional or topical societies, with such names as the Friends of the Pleistocene or the Pecos Conference, provided forums for these subspecialists. Only the national meetings provided a true discipline-wide interchange.

Concomitant with the development of interdisciplinary research, the shortcomings of what had become overspecialization started to be recognized. For example, similar solutions to similar problems in different specialities were being ignored, not because they were not understood, but because they were not recognized to be specialized solutions to general problems. General systems theory was designed as an explicit attempt to reverse this process of specialization and to capitalize upon interdisciplinary research. Such a theory of systems serves as a bridge between the highly generalized constructions of pure mathematics and the numerous specific theories of the specific disciplines. It can be derived both inductively and deductively; it can also be applied both inductively and deductively. In addition, by having a similar theory for open systems, or for closed systems, one could transcend the boundaries between the biological, physical, and social sciences.

As the 1950's drew to a close, archaeologists found themselves faced by a multipronged dilemma. First, many disciplines, such as palynology, demography, ecology, zoology, and geology, were providing not only more, but more significant, information for archaeologists. Second, many younger archaeologists felt that they could no longer ask only when and where, but also had to explain how and why. One reason for this feeling was that, at many institutions in the United States, archaeology had come to be thought of as a theoretically bankrupt stepchild of the other subdisciplines of anthropology. Third, as the time-space systematists and the reconstructionists filled in the historical and cultural record, increasingly more data could not be fitted into the extant theoretical schemes. The inconsistencies were proving to be far more subtle than were at first expected. The few general explanatory principles, such as simplified social theory and multilineal evolutionary theory, were insufficient for the more sophisticated explanations that were now desired. In short, the archaeologists had begun to ask how and why, but did not have a viable theory on which to base answers. It was not surprising that some authors from a wide diversity of backgrounds turned to general systems theory, the reversal of specialization, in order to find a theory adequate for such explanations. However, because use of this theory forced one to focus on explicit a priori problems and a problem orientation, those who used it as a basis for their explanations were to find that it had both advantages and disadvantages.

THEORY AND PARATHEORY: ADVANTAGES AND DISAVANTAGES

Archaeologists have proposed two systemic definitions of culture, both of which define a system as being composed of inputs, outputs, components, and interrelationships. However, archaeological opinion about other systemic questions began to diverge rapidly. Binford saw culture as an ecologically based system in which energy is the important flow. Kemp's "The Flow of Energy in a Hunting Society" provides a clear systemic concept of culture and draws out some of the implications for prehistoric man. Hammond's "The Planning of a Maya Ceremonial Center" uses a systemic economic analysis, in which planning is examined in terms of investment in energy and materials. Clarke, on the other hand, argued that information is the critical unit of flow. Information is far more difficult to deal with than material culture, and very few archaeological articles have attempted this task. (One of the most interesting treatments is John Justeson's "Limitations of Archaeological Inference: An Information Theoretic Approach with Applications in Methodology" in the April 1973 issue of *American Antiquity*.) However, its importance is implied in Sjoberg's "The Origin and Evolution of Cities," in which he emphasizes the importance of information systems in written form as a prerequisite for complex administrative and legal systems.

These systemic definitions of culture provided archaeologists with multiple advantages. First, they allowed archaeologists to organize data from many disciplines under a single theoretical rubric. An example of this interdisciplinary approach is presented in Haag's "The Bering Strait Land Bridge."

Second, since general systems theory is universalistic, it can be applied to all cultures at all times. (Notice the wide range of times and areas covered by the articles here. See Table VIII.)

Third, the theory can be used at all levels of analysis, being infinitely additive or divisible. One can divide a culture into a wide variety of subsystems (for example, the standard economic, social, and ideological subsystems), and analyze each independently. Or one can focus on a certain cultural manifestation (such as cities or hunting sites) and examine it as a system. Complementarily, since the systemic models are additive, one can combine systemic analyses of a variety of cultures into a regional analysis, or combine a series of multitemporal analyses into a temporal synthesis. For example, Hammond's excellent article systemically examines the growth of a site in terms of economic planning and then places it into a regional economic system.

Fourth, since subsystems of a culture interdigitate, it is possible to postulate, predict, and test relationships even if the subsystem in question did not leave material evidence. This is particularly important to archaeologists, who face continual problems because the data are not uniformly preserved, and especially to those whose interests are specifically in the sociological and ideological areas.

Fifth, the formality of this type of analysis tends to make the problems more hypothetical and more predictable, the solutions more quantifiable and more testable. For example, Hammond's article shows that the costs for prehistoric city planning can be measured and compared to strict expediency. Not only is he able to show that considerable cost will be met in order to maintain planning, but, by developing quantifiable measures of traffic flow and accessibility, he can classify sites according to their functions and show that these classifications are significant. Similarly, Kemp's article is a classic in energy cost accounting.

Sixth, systems analysis seems to increase the researcher's sensitivity to the variety of potential relationships and the diversity of components that may be involved in a cultural system.

One disadvantage of the systemic approach is that its results demand both more technical knowledge and more sophistication on the part of the reader who wishes to understand the implications of systemic knowledge. As a result, articles based on the systemic approach tend to be highly technical, and do not appeal to as wide and variable an audience as do articles about "the earliest *x*" or "the largest *y*." A second disadvantage is that a systemic approach tends to degenerate into tautology and circular reasoning when it is poorly executed. Since all parts of a system can cause all other parts of the system to change, there may appear to be no priorities, no causal variables, and no prime movers—sometimes it has been asked whether there are any movers at all! A third is that systemic work tends to be descriptive, particularistic, and easily contradicted. Yet most authors of systemic descriptions tend to consider them to be sufficient explanations in themselves. A fourth is that, since the systemic approach tends to be descriptive and problem-specific, the systems arrived at tend to be noncomparable because they are based on different variables and different types of assumptions. Indeed, and this is a fifth disadvantage, the proliferation of assumptions in the systemic approach sometimes leads to Victorian models with detail in Swiss Rococo; that is, there seems to be delight in complication. It is thought that the greater the number of variables that are taken into account in a model, the more accurate the model's predictions will be. As a result, systemic analyses sometimes fail because they are overaccurate; that is, the model gives predictions that are so subtle they cannot be confirmed by observation. A sixth disadvantage is that systemic analyses tend to rely heavily on the optimization principle (the principle of homeostatic equilibrium), which is a first-rate assumption for *some* ecological and economic problems, but not all, and is clearly not relevant for all archaeological problems. A seventh and final disadvantage is that systemic research is fairly recent and innovative; relatively few such studies have been published, and thus there is no pool of studies upon which productive comparison may be based.

METHODOLOGY

The methodology needed for a systemic approach to research is different from that needed by romanticists, time-space systematists, or reconstructionists. The questions and the methodology of a systemic approach are problem specific; that is, there is no correct universal methodology. When you ask the question "why," you need to formulate the methodology in terms of what you are asking about. To explain why the Maya fell requires a methodology different from that needed to explain why all cities have similar characteristics. Having hypothesized a systemic answer to such a question, one must define, examine, and test the reality of its hypothesized components, relationships, and processes against the full variability of the real data.

Since systematists tend to use models and simulations more than other scholars, their research designs tend to be more explicit, programmed as well as programmable. Usually, they are divided into ten steps, which are:

1. problem formulation,
2. observation and analysis of real-world data,
3. mathematical formulation of the model,
4. systemic formulation of the model,
5. the development of parameters for operating characteristics of the model related to the real-world data,
6. model and parameter evaluation estimates based on the observed data,
7. optional formulation of the simulation design,
8. design of system or simulation experiments,
9. analysis of experimental data or simulation data,
10. validation of the system.

It is a clear, direct research strategy, but it also creates, according to some critics, uneasy constraints on interpretations. There is no place for artistic or literary insights with their breadth and visions of other societies. Man is limited to being rational or, if irrational, he must follow clear stochastic variables. Prehistoric cultures become operational analytical concepts to be manipulated with other sets of data, at the cost of man becoming Hobbes' machine. Although this paradigm probably provides the most successful set of archaeological tools we have yet developed, there is yet room for improvement.

In short, perhaps the uneasiness one feels with systemic analysis is a result of our psychological fears of too accurate an understanding. Hare's limerick expresses it well:

There once was a man who said, "Damn,
It is borne in upon me that I am
An engine that moves
In predestinate grooves;
I'm not even a bus, I'm a tram."

It is a most disquieting thought.

TABLE VIII. Articles Employing the Perspective of Analysis of Systems and Processes.

Author	*Time*	*Area*	*Strategy*
Haag (1962)	100,000 to 15,000 B.C.	Arctic	Hunting-gathering
Sjoberg (1965)	5500 B.C. to A.D. 1950	General	Agricultural/industrial
Hammond (1972)	A.D. 570–730	British Honduras	Agricultural
Kemp (1971)	ethnographic present	Arctic	Hunting-gathering/ industrial

THE READINGS

Haag's article, "The Bering Strait Land Bridge," shows the importance of interdisciplinary research for the future of archaeological reconstructions and interpretations. Haag contrasts the first archaeological concepts of a narrow Bering Land Bridge with the type of bridge necessary for the slow and large-scale diffusion of multiple species of plants and animals, including man, into the New World. Drawing upon biological, oceanographic, botanical, and geological theory and data, he asks what the requirements are for a valve that would allow this large migratory flow. His 1,300-mile-wide bridge implies that most early Beringian archaeological sites are now under 300 feet of water and 100 feet of sediment. One should also note his exceptionally clear presentation of a process model for the glacial advance and retreat as a homeostatic equilibrium system.

Sjoberg's article, "The Origin and Evolution of Cities," is not specifically a systemic article. In fact, it could have been included as a reconstruction of a sequence of events. However, it illustrates many attributes of the systemic approach. First, the article is strongly problem-oriented. It directly attempts to answer two questions: what factors brought about the origin of cities, and through what evolutionary stages did cities pass. Second, although the stages of urbanization are defined by attributes, these attributes are themselves processes. Sjoberg uses the supply of and demand for food, demographic growth, organizational principles, and administrative and other processes to help differentiate the development of cities. The importance of these processes varies with time and place. For example, Sjoberg effectively shows the positive reinforcement that exists between the spread of empires and the development of urban forms, as well as the significant differences between New and Old World urbanization. This article has the same general impact as V. Gordon Childe's work on urbanization, which it updates. Not only does it consider modern industrial urbanization in an historical context but it also suggests answers to a unique set of well-specified problems.

Hammond's article on a Mayan archaeological site in the British Honduras, "The Planning of a Maya Ceremonial Center," measures the costs for prehistoric city planning relative to strict expediency. By analyzing the traffic flow, the accessibility, and centrality of a variety of structures from a systemic perspective in combination with basal area and height measurements of the structures, he is able to answer questions about the functional purposes of various areas of the site. The site of Lubaátuun is shown, because of its ecological and trade relations, to be at the center of a regional market system. Kemp's "The Flow of Energy in a Hunting Society" is a detailed example of energy accounting for Eskimos on Baffin Island. Although it is not directly archaeological, it provides, by comparison of two households, one traditional and one modern, quantifiable data on traditional hunting and gathering economies, and demonstrates the effects that imported technology has had upon ecological adaptation. It thus clarifies one direction in which archaeological research is moving. The formal model he presents is a sophisticated example of a systemic definition and description of culture. It illustrates particularly well one advantage of a systemic approach, namely, the freedom to analyze many components separately and then integrate them into a meaningful whole. Although particularistic in being based on data specific to a 54)week period in the life of two households, the general characteristics of the model are relevant for all analyses of Arctic hunters and gatherers, and show similarities to reconstructions based on archaeological data.

The Bering Strait Land Bridge

by William G. Haag
January 1962

It is widely thought to have been a narrow neck of land over which man first came to America. Actually it was 1,300 miles wide and was traveled by large numbers of plants and animals

The New World was already an old world to the Indians who were in residence when Europeans took possession of it in the 16th century. But the life story of the human species goes back a million years, and there is no doubt that man came only recently to the Western Hemisphere. None of the thousands of sites of aboriginal habitation uncovered in North and South America has antiquity comparable to that of Old World sites. Man's occupation of the New World may date back several tens of thousands of years, but no one rationally argues that he has been here even 100,000 years.

Speculation as to how man found his way to America was lively at the outset, and the proposed routes boxed the compass. With one or two notable exceptions, however, students of American anthropology soon settled for the plausible idea that the first immigrants came by way of a land bridge that had connected the northeast corner of Asia to the northwest corner of North America across the Bering Strait. Mariners were able to supply the reassuring information that the strait is not only narrow—it is 56 miles wide—but also shallow: a lowering of the sea level there by 100 feet or so would transform the strait into an isthmus. With little else in the way of evidence to sustain the Bering Strait land bridge, anthropologists embraced the idea that man walked dry-shod from Asia to America.

Toward the end of the last century, however, it became apparent that the Western Hemisphere was the New World not only for man but also for a host of animals and plants. Zoologists and botanists showed that numerous subjects of their respective kingdoms must have originated in Asia and spread to America. (There was evidence also for some movement in the other direction.) These findings were neither astonishing nor wholly unexpected. Such spread of populations is not to be envisioned as an exodus or mass migration, even in the case of animals. It is, rather, a spilling into new territory that accompanies increase in numbers, with movement in the direction of least population pressure and most favorable ecological conditions. But the immense traffic in plant and animal forms placed a heavy burden on the Bering Strait land bridge as the anthropologists had envisioned it. Whereas purposeful men could make their way across a narrow bridge (in the absence of a bridge, Eskimos sometimes cross the strait in skin boats), the slow diffusion of plants and animals would require an avenue as broad as a continent and available for ages at a stretch.

The expansion of the Bering Strait land bridge to meet these demands is a task that has intrigued geologists for many years. Although their efforts have not completely satisfied zoologists and botanists, it is apparent that the Old and New worlds were once one world, joined by a land mass that now lies submerged beneath the seas on each side of the Bering Strait. The clues to the appearance and disappearance of this land mass are to be found both on the bottom of these waters and in such faraway places as the coral atolls of the South Pacific and the delta of the Mississippi River.

Today the maximum depth in the Bering Strait is about 180 feet. On a clear day from the heights at Cape Prince of Wales in Alaska one can look across the strait and see land at Cape Dezhnev in Siberia. St. Lawrence Island, Big Diomede Island, Little Diomede Island and smaller islands make steppingstones between. South of the strait is the Bering Sea. Its floor is one of the flattest and smoothest stretches of terrain on the entire globe. With a slope of no more than three or four inches to the mile, it reaches southward to a line that runs from Unimak Pass in the Aleutians to Cape Navarin on the Asiatic shore. Along this line—the edge of the continental shelf—the sea floor plunges steeply from a depth of about 450 feet down 15,000 feet to the bottom of the ocean. The floor of the Chukchi Sea, north of the Bering Strait, is not quite so smooth; the depth varies from 120 to 180 feet, and irregularities of the terrain bring shoals upward to depths of only 45 feet and lift the great granite outcrops of Wrangell and Herald islands above the surface of the sea. Along a line that runs several hundred miles north of the Bering Strait, from Point Barrow in Alaska to the Severnaya Zemlya off Siberia, the sea floor plunges over the northern edge of the continental shelf to the bottom of the Arctic Ocean.

Sounding of the Bering and Chukchi seas thus depicts a vast plain that is not deeply submerged. At its widest the plain reaches 1,300 miles north and south, 600 miles wider than the north-south distance across Alaska along the Canadian border. The granitic islands that rise above the water testify that the plain is made of the same rock as the continents.

David M. Hopkins of the U.S. Geological Survey has shown that this great plain sank beneath the seas somewhat more than a million years ago as a result of the down-warping of the crust in the Arctic region that began with the Pleistocene epoch. Before that, Hopkins calculates, most of the area was above sea level throughout most of the 50-million-year duration of the preceding Tertiary period.

The continuity of the land mass of Asia and North America during the Tertiary period helps to solve a major portion of the biologist's problem. The paleontological evidence indicates that numerous mammals, large and small, moved from Asia to America during that time. With the subsidence of the land, however, the flow must have stopped. Nor is there any chance that the land rose up again during the million-year Pleistocene period. It is true that the Pacific region along the Aleutian and Kurile island chains is geologically active. But by comparison the Bering Strait region is rather stable; studies of ancient beach terraces on the islands in the surrounding seas indicate that the vertical movement of the land could not have exceeded 30 feet in the course of the Pleistocene. The smoothness of the Bering Sea floor is another indication of prolonged submergence. Deep layers of marine sediment have smoothed out whatever hills and valleys it acquired when it was dry land and exposed to erosion.

Fossil evidence for the origin and geographic distribution of North Ameri-

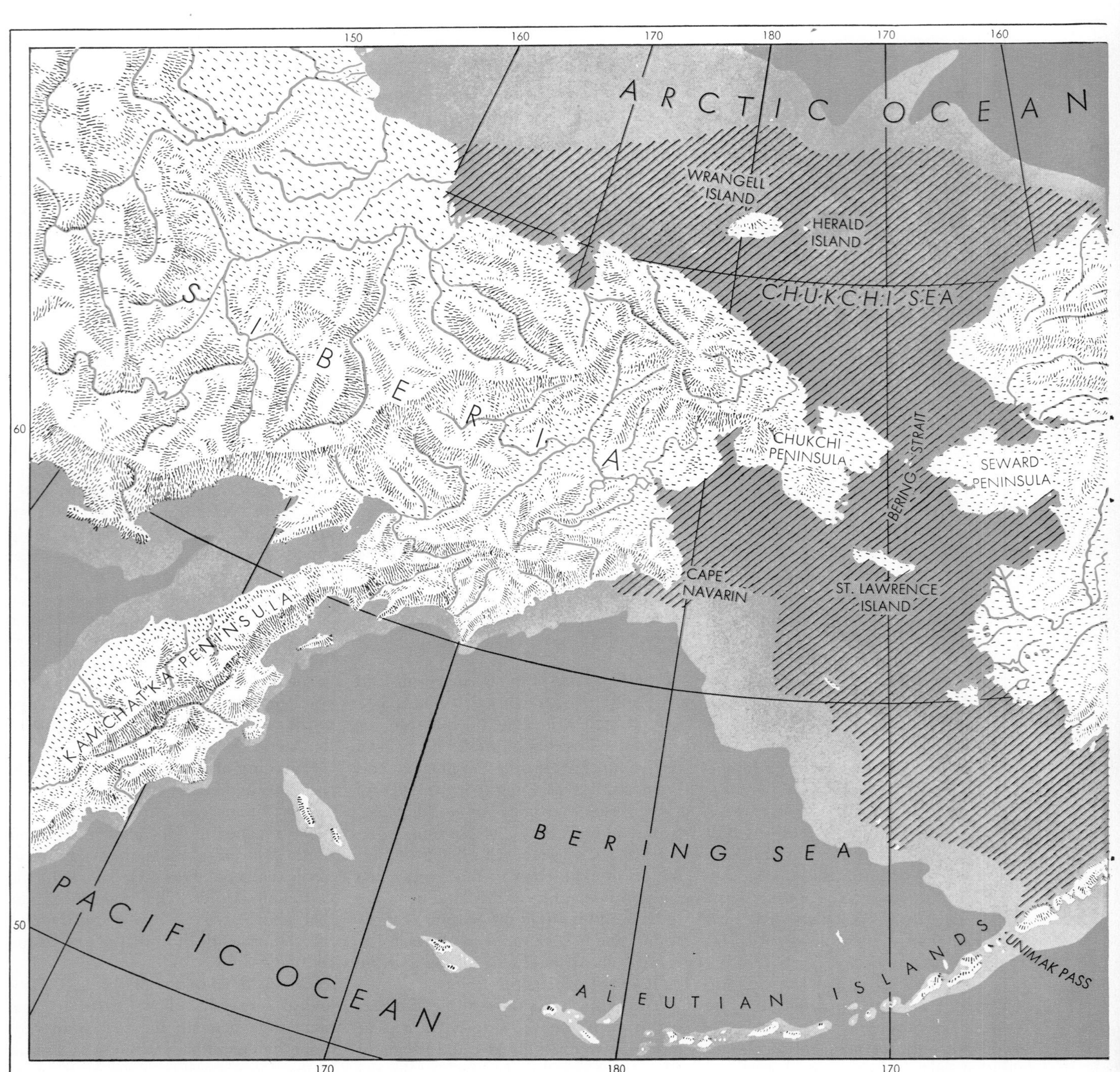

BERING STRAIT LAND BRIDGE during much of Wisconsin glaciation was at least as wide as hatched area, which marks present-day depths to 300 feet. The lighter color covers depths to 600 feet. The 600-foot contour roughly marks the margin of the continental

can mammals nonetheless shows that numerous animals, large and small, came from Asia during the Pleistocene. Beginning early in the Pleistocene, several genera of rodents arrived; such small mammals breed more rapidly than, say, elephants, and they spread far southward across North America, although not into South America. Later came the larger mammals: the mastodon and mammoth, musk oxen, bison, moose, elk,

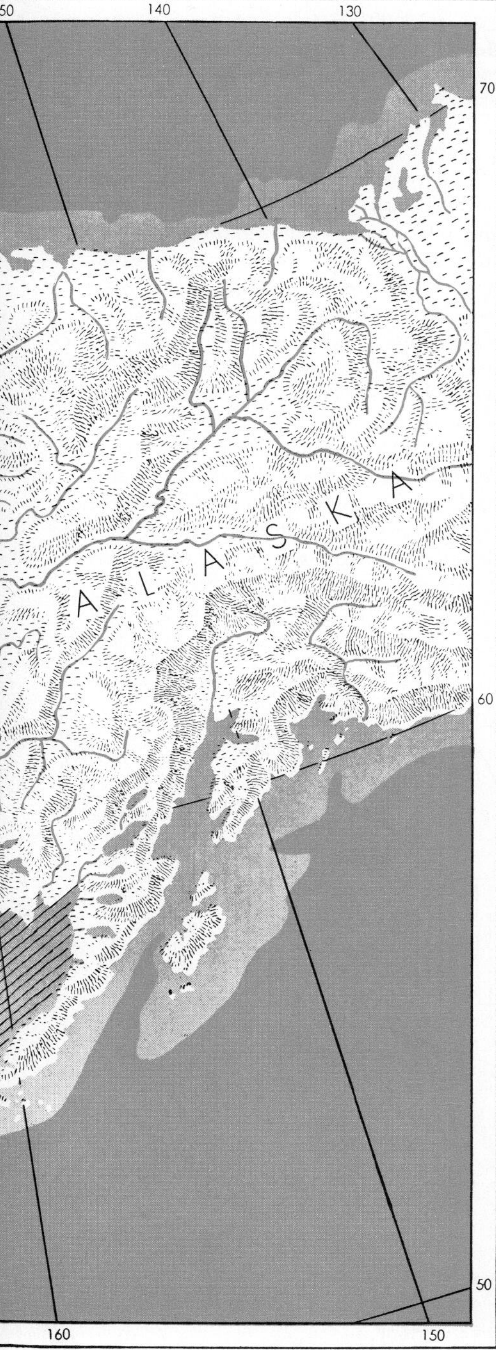

shelf, with its sharp drop to the bottom of the deep ocean, several thousand feet lower.

mountain sheep and goats, camels, foxes, bears, wolves and horses. (The horses flourished and then died out in North America; the genus was not seen again in the New World until the conquistadors brought their animals across the Atlantic.) Evidence from botany as well as from zoology requires a substantial dry-land connection between Asia and North America throughout the Pleistocene.

At this point it is well to remember that the sea level at any given place on the globe depends not only on the height of the land but also on the depth of the ocean. The depth of the ocean in this sense is a question of the volume of water in the ocean. With the Pleistocene began the ice age that has apparently not yet run its course. During this million-year period, for reasons subject to warm debate, at least four great ice sheets have built up, advanced and retreated on the Northern Hemisphere. That the ice can lock up considerable quantities of water on the land is evident even in the present interglacial period. The abrupt melting of the Greenland and Antarctic icecaps would, according to various estimates, raise the present world-wide sea level by as much as 300 feet.

To estimate the volume of water locked up on the land in the great continental glaciers of the Pleistocene one begins with the measurement of the land area covered by the glaciers. The great ice sheets gathered up sand, gravel and larger rubble and, when the ice proceeded to melt, deposited a mantle of this "till" on the exposed ground. From such evidence it is calculated that ice covered 30 per cent of the earth's land area during the glacial maxima of the Pleistocene.

To arrive at the volume of water in the glaciers, however, one must have some idea of the thickness of the ice as well as the area it covered. The Greenland icecap is more than a mile deep, and in Antarctica the rock lies as much as three miles below the surface of the ice. It is clear that the Pleistocene glaciers could have been thousands of feet thick. Multiplication of the area of the glaciers by thicknesses predicated on various assumptions has shown that the freezing of the water on the land may have reduced the ancient sea level by 125 to 800 feet. Such calculations are supported by evidence from coral atolls in tropical seas. Since the organisms that build these atolls do not live at depths greater than 300 feet, and since the limy structures of such islands go down several thousand feet, a lowering of the sea level by more than 300 feet is necessary to explain their existence.

By all odds the best evidence for the rise and fall of the ancient sea level is offered by the Mississippi Valley, its delta and the adjoining shores of the Gulf of Mexico. In Pleistocene times about a dozen major streams entered the Gulf. As ice accumulated in the north, lowering the level of the sea, the streams followed the retreating shore line downward. On the steeper gradient the water flowed faster, cutting deeper and straighter valleys. Then, as the ice retreated, the sea rose and again moved inland, reducing the velocity of the streams and making them deposit their burdens of gravel and silt at their mouths and farther inland. Consequently during the glacial minima the rivers built up great flood plains over which they wore meandering courses. Each glacial advance brought a withdrawal of the Gulf and quickened the rivers; each retreat raised the level of the Gulf and forced the rivers to build new flood plains.

Had the earth's crust in this region remained stable, all traces of the preceding flood plain would have been erased by the next cycle of cutting and building. But the rivers, particularly the Mississippi, deposited vast quantities of sediment in their lower valleys, building "crowfoot" deltas like that of the Mississippi today. (Many large rivers, such as the Amazon, have never built such deltas because coastwise currents distribute their sediments far and wide.) The accumulating burden of offshore sediments tilted the platform of the continent, pressing it downward under the Gulf and lifting it inland. In succeeding cycles, therefore, the build-up of the flood plain started farther downstream.

Evidence of the succession of flood plains remains today in the terraces that descend like a flight of steps down both flanks of the Mississippi Valley toward the river. Near Memphis, Tenn., the highest and oldest terrace lies about 350 feet above the plain of the present river and slopes toward the Gulf with a gradient of about eight feet per mile. The terrace below lies 200 feet above the plain and slopes about five feet per mile; the third terrace lies 100 feet above the plain, with a slope of about 18 inches; the fourth, only 40 feet above, with a slope of only six inches. The present flood plain has a gradient of about three inches per mile. Out in the Gulf, where the river has buried the older deposits

SUCCESSIVE TERRACES that formed in lower Mississippi Valley during the Pleistocene glaciations are shown in this highly schematic cross section. The terraces, with the oldest at the top, were flood plains laid down between glaciations. During each glacial period the river, rejuvenated by the fall in sea level and the consequent drop in its mouth, cut deeply into the preceding flood plain. The Prairie Terrace represents the flood plain that the river laid down between the early Wisconsin and the late Wisconsin glaciations.

under the younger, the successive slopes of the river bed are steeper.

In this setting geologists have been able to measure with great confidence the degree to which each of the glacial advances of the Pleistocene lowered the level of the sea. Borings along the axis of the old stream channels reveal the gradient of the bottom. The terraces show the slope of the alluvial plain associated with the successive streams. From these data the elevations of the earlier river mouths and consequently the sea level can be determined. The Rhine and Rhone rivers have yielded similar information, and on the Kamchatka Peninsula in Siberia it has been observed that the streams flowing into the Bering Sea are flanked by steeply sloping terraces.

The Mississippi-Gulf region has provided especially secure and precise information about the course of the last great Pleistocene glaciation, the so-called Wisconsin stage of the Pleistocene. In no other area of the globe have oil prospectors drilled so many test holes through the recent sediments into the Pleistocene; the number of holes runs into the thousands, and they dot the map 30 miles out into the Gulf. In accordance with the law, the records of these wells show the types of material brought up by the drills at fairly evenly spaced intervals. The undersea sediments that were uncovered by the retreat of the sea at the maximum advance of the Wisconsin glacier mark a horizon familiar to all well drillers. Where these sediments were exposed to the air long ago they became oxidized and show as a bright reddish-orange zone. From the examination of many well records one can tell where, geographically, these sediments were exposed to air and where

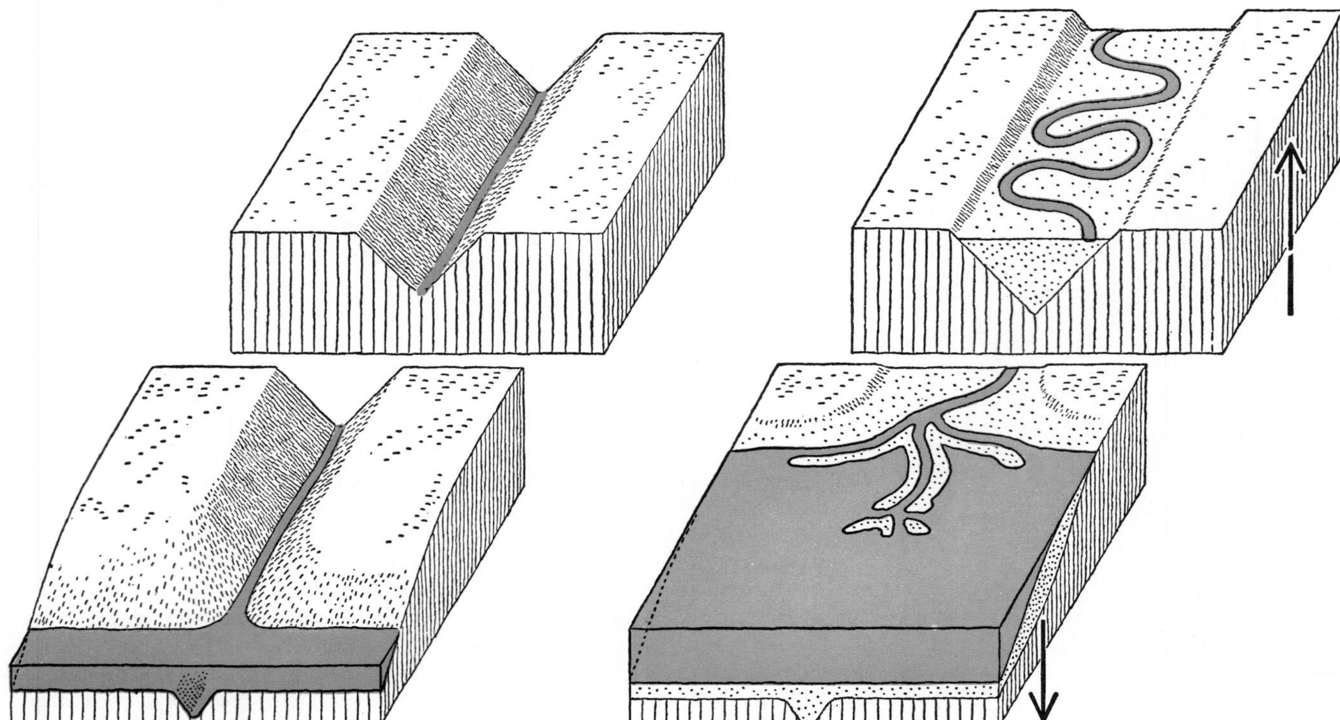

EFFECTS OF GLACIAL ADVANCE AND RETREAT on rivers entering Gulf of Mexico are shown in these diagrams. Upper block of each pair is river valley, lower block is mouth of river. At left, glaciers have lowered sea level. River flows faster and cuts a deep,

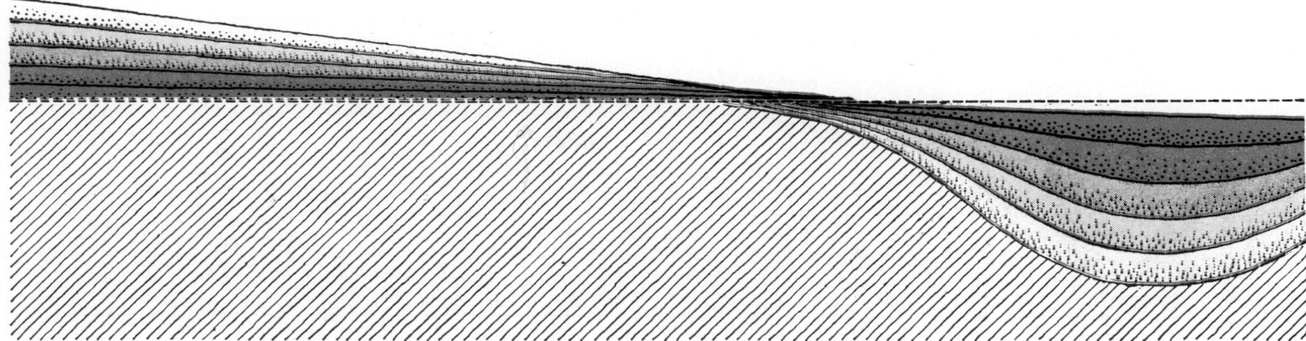

SLOPE OF TERRACES is illustrated in this schematic longitudinal section of lower Mississippi and Gulf region. The weight of the accumulated sediments (*right*), with the oldest deposit at the bottom, made the crustal rock sink and the adjacent land area rise like a great lever with the fulcrum near the coast. Because of this tilt the flood plains laid down during interglacial periods remained as terraces. The broken horizontal line marks present sea level. Hatched area is the older material of the continental crust.

they remained underwater, and so fix the coast line at the time the sea reached its lowest level. In addition, numerous samples of formerly living matter have been recovered from well borings at known depths and from archaeological sites. The dating of these by carbon-14 techniques permits accurate plotting of the course of events in time.

From this rich supply of evidence it has been determined that the Wisconsin glacier reached its maximum 40,000 years ago and lowered the sea level by as much as 460 feet. As the glacier grew and the oceans receded, an ever broader highway was revealed at the Bering Strait. With a sea-level fall of only 150 feet, the bridge connecting the two continents must have been nearly 200 miles wide. Because the slope of the sea floor is so gentle, a further fall in the sea level uncovered much larger regions. At 450 feet the entire width of the undersea plain from one edge of the continental shelf to the other must have been exposed, providing a corridor 1,300 miles wide for the flow of biological commerce between the no longer separate continents. During the peak periods of the earlier glaciations the Bering Strait land bridge would have presented much the same appearance.

Because the maximum exposure of the land bridge necessarily coincided with a maximum of glaciation, one might think the bridge would have been blocked by ice. Geological evidence shows, however, that neither the Chukchi Peninsula in Siberia nor the westward-reaching Seward Peninsula of Alaska were glaciated during the Wisconsin period. Even large areas of central Alaska remained ice-free throughout the period. As for the now submerged plain on the floor of the Bering Strait and

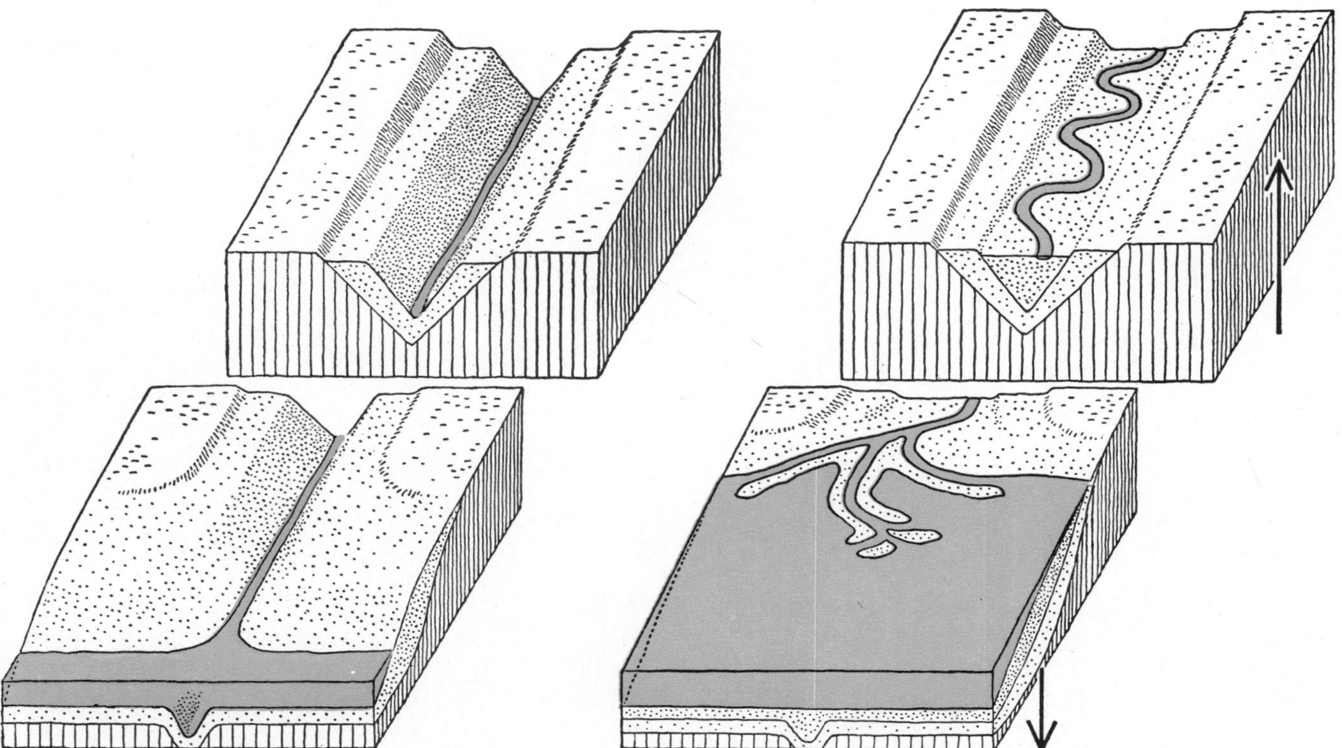

straight valley. Then glaciers melt, mouth of river rises and river deposits sediments to make flood plain in valley and delta at mouth. The crust under the Gulf sinks, raising the river valley (*second from left*). The cycle is repeated at next glaciation and interglacial.

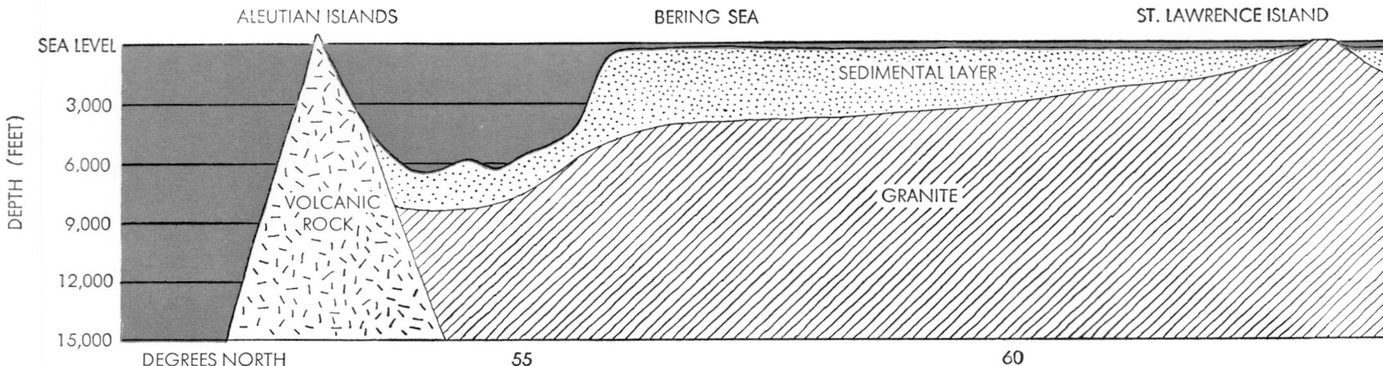

CROSS SECTION THROUGH BERING STRAIT along 169 degrees west latitude shows great breadth of shallow region. Earth's crust beneath strait is granitic and is part of continental shelf. Big Diomede Island lies in the narrowest part of the strait. The whole

the adjoining seas, it seems clear that the rocky rubble, found where currents clear away the silt, was "rafted" there by icebergs; no part of this accumulation is attributed to glacial till deposited by the melting of glacial ice on the surface.

Conditions are made the more propitious for life on the bridge by the latest theory on the causes of glaciation. Paradoxically, this demands a warm Arctic Ocean over which winds could become laden with moisture for subsequent precipitation as snow deep in the Hudson Bay area, where the glacier had its center of gravity. Western Alaska would have had little snowfall and no accumulation of ice. This deduction is supported by the finding of trees in the Pleistocene deposits on Seward Peninsula. It is not thought, however, that the land bridge was ever anything but tundra.

It must be admitted that the Bering Strait land bridge of the geologist, appearing only intermittently above sea

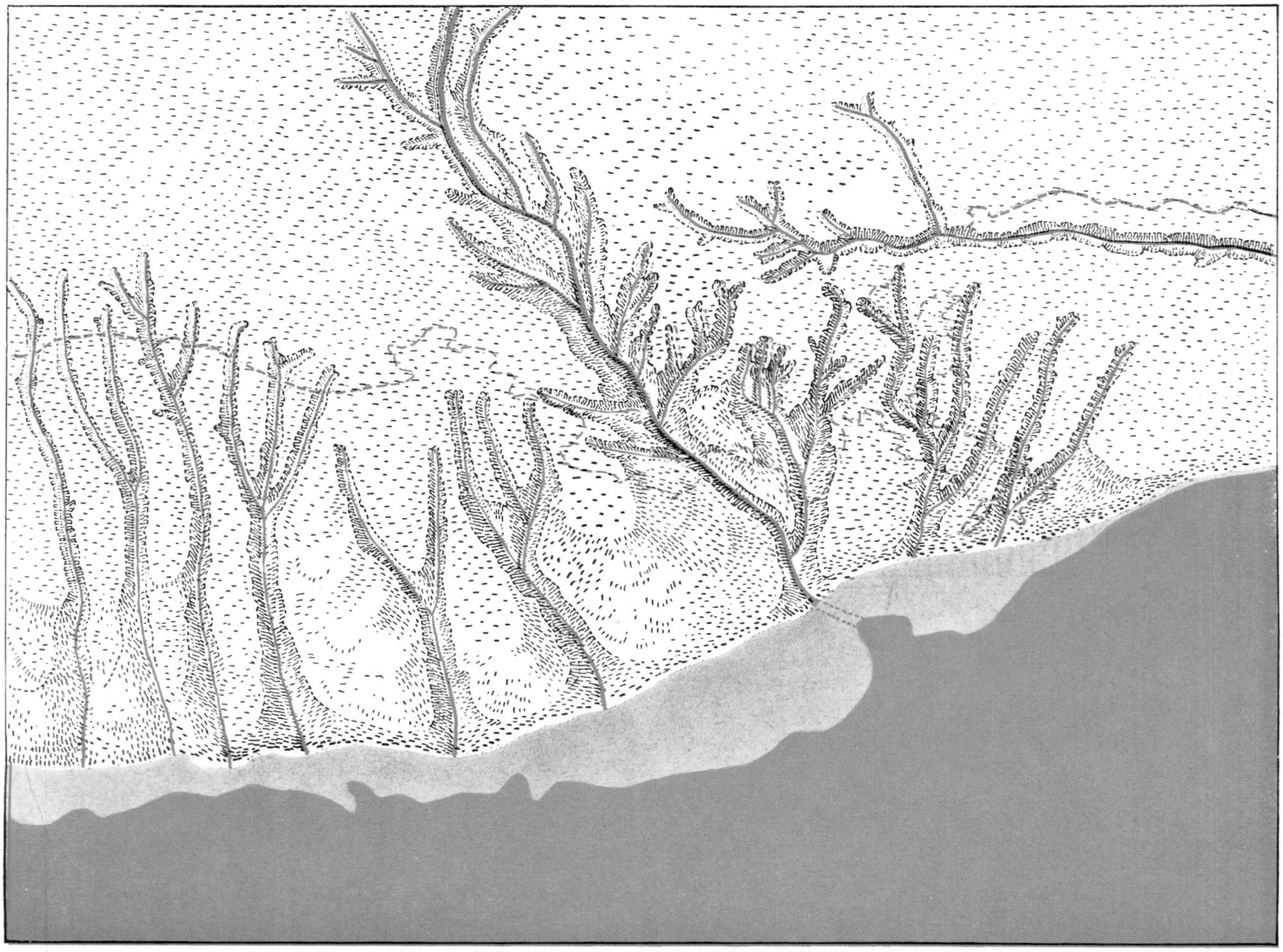

WITHDRAWAL OF WATER of the Gulf of Mexico at height of the Wisconsin glaciation exposed most of continental shelf. Edge of shelf is 600-foot-depth contour, where dark color starts. The rivers cut deep valleys and dumped their sediments in the deep water.

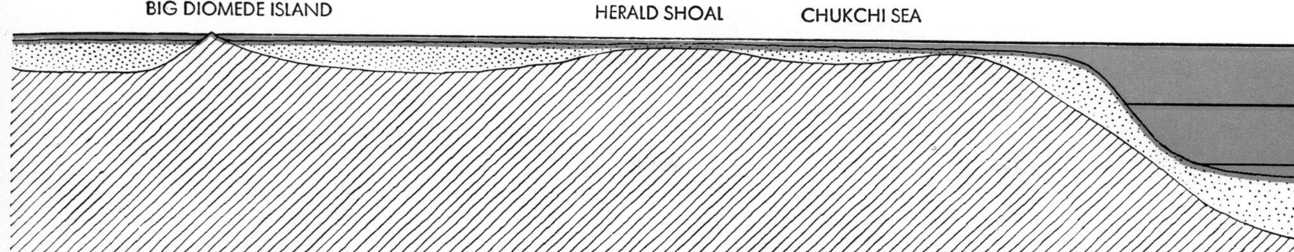

shallow area has been tectonically stable for the past million years. Glaciations rather than local uplift exposed its surface. The thickness of the sedimental layer is actually not definitely established for much of the region. Pacific Ocean is at left, Arctic Ocean is at right.

level, does not fully serve the purposes of the zoologist and botanist. Most zoologists find no evidence in the movement of animals that requires alternate opening and closing of the passage between the continents, and they argue for a broad bridge available throughout nearly all of the Pleistocene. What is more, the animals that came across the bridge were not typically cold-climate animals (none of the true cold-climate animals, such as the woolly rhinoceros, ever reached America). On the contrary, the animals were the ones that would prefer the warmer interglacial times for their spread. They may, of course, have made the crossing just as the climate was warming up and conditions on the American side were increasingly favorable to population increase and diffusion.

The botanists find even more compelling evidence for a broad land bridge throughout most of the Pleistocene. Eric Hultén of the University of Lund

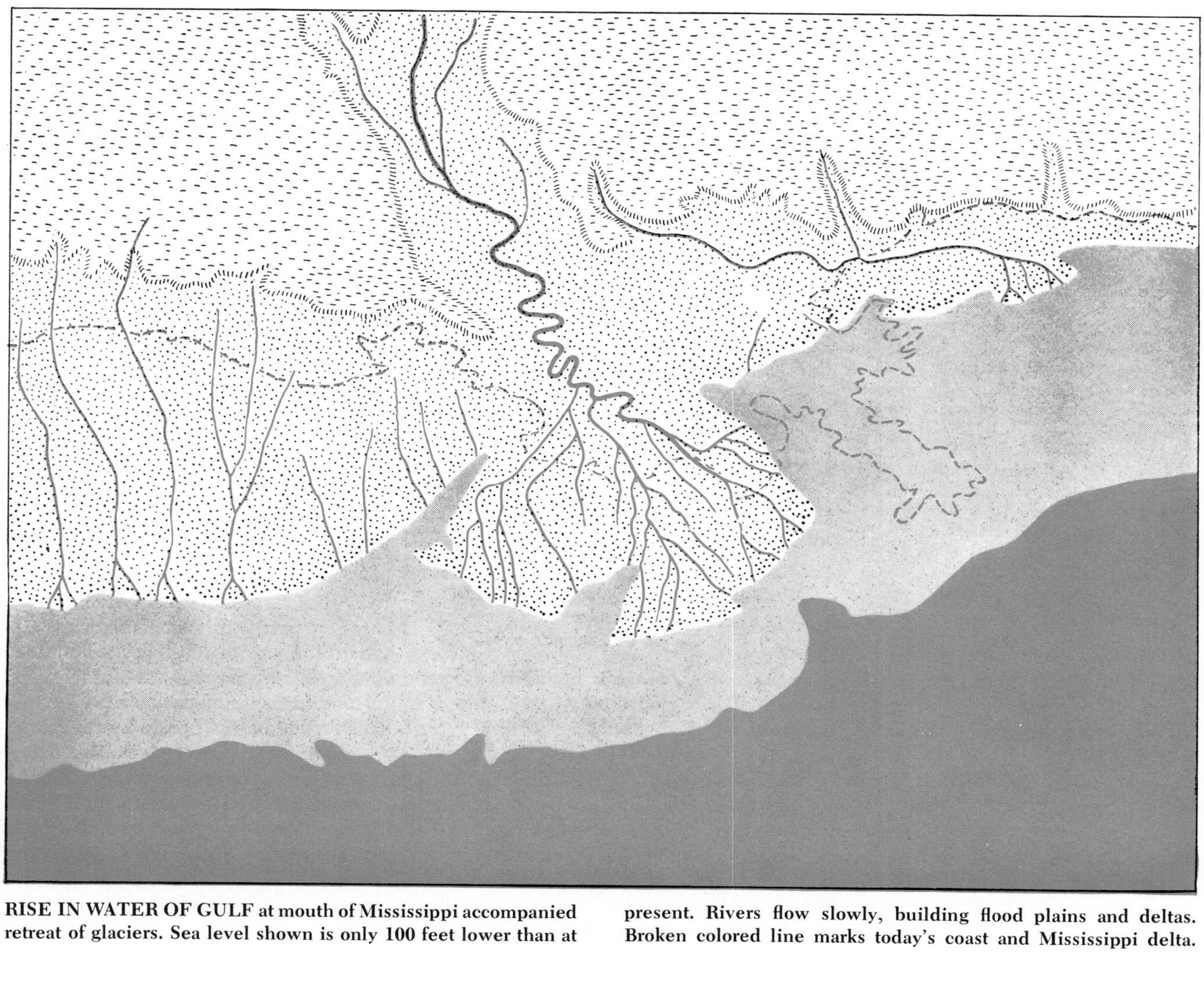

RISE IN WATER OF GULF **at mouth of Mississippi accompanied retreat of glaciers. Sea level shown is only 100 feet lower than at present. Rivers flow slowly, building flood plains and deltas. Broken colored line marks today's coast and Mississippi delta.**

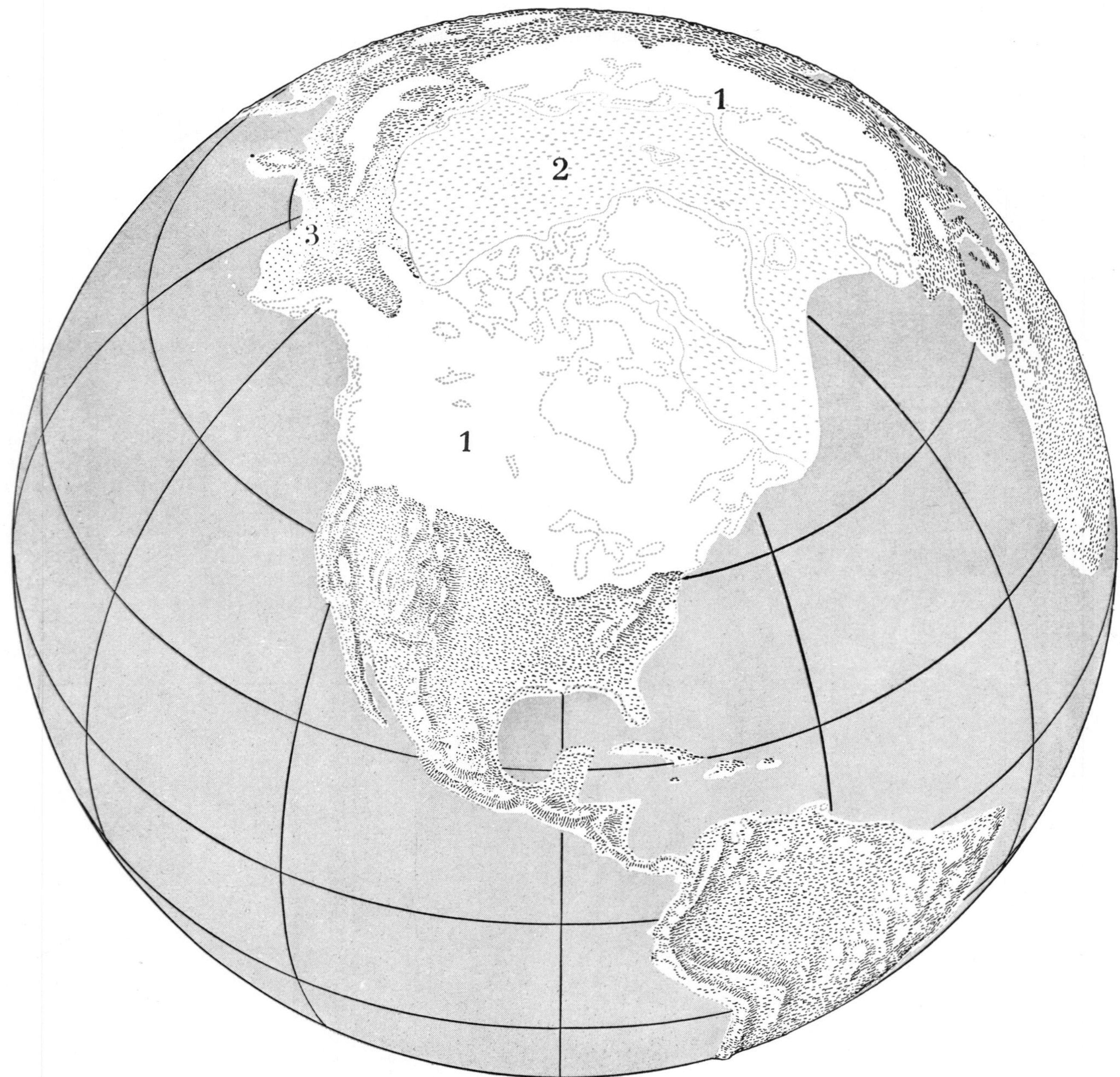

LAST GREAT GLACIATION, the Wisconsin, at its maximum covered about 30 per cent of the earth's land area. The glaciers (*1*) and accompanying pack ice (*2*) locked up vast quantities of sea water, lowering sea level by 460 feet and exposing a 1,300-mile-wide, ice-free land bridge in the region of Bering Strait (*3*). The broken colored line marks present-day seacoasts and lake shores.

in Sweden recently calculated that a bridge 700 miles wide is necessary to account for the distribution of plants in Alaska and northeastern Siberia.

Giving full weight to the biological evidence, it seems amply demonstrated that a bridge wider than present-day Alaska joined the Old and New worlds during a large part of the Pleistocene. There is much to suggest that the land surface of this bridge was smooth and unbroken. And it appears that large animals moved freely across it during the 80,000 years of the Wisconsin stage and probably throughout much of the preceding interglacial stage.

Before the end of the Wisconsin period the first men must have crossed the bridge. It seems almost a truism that Asiatic man would have followed the slow spread of Asiatic animals into the New World. The men would most likely have come along the coastal margins and not across the interior that lies under the present-day strait. Their remains are covered, therefore, not only by 300 feet or more of water but also by as much as 100 feet of sediment laid down in the Recent period as the sea encroached on the continental shelf. Archaeologists need not be surprised in the future to discover evidence of man here and there in North America 50,000 years old and even older.

The Origin and Evolution of Cities

by Gideon Sjoberg
September 1965

The first cities arose some 5,500 years ago; large-scale urbanization began only about 100 years ago. The intervening steps in the evolution of cities were nonetheless a prerequisite for modern urban societies

Men began to live in cities some 5,500 years ago. As the preceding article relates, however, the proportion of the human population concentrated in cities did not begin to increase significantly until about 100 years ago. These facts raise two questions that this article proposes to answer. First, what factors brought about the origin of cities? Second, through what evolutionary stages did cities pass before the modern epoch of urbanization? The answers to these questions are intimately related to three major levels of human organization, each of which is characterized by its own technological, economic, social and political patterns. The least complex of the three—the "folk society"—is preurban and even preliterate; it consists typically of small numbers of people, gathered in self-sufficient homogeneous groups, with their energies wholly (or almost wholly) absorbed by the quest for food. Under such conditions there is little or no surplus of food; consequently the folk society permits little or no specialization of labor or distinction of class.

Although some folk societies still exist today, similar human groups began the slow process of evolving into more complex societies millenniums ago, through settlement in villages and through advances in technology and organizational structure. This gave rise to the second level of organization: civilized preindustrial, or "feudal," society. Here there is a surplus of food because of the selective cultivation of grains—high in yield, rich in biological energy and suited to long-term storage—and often also because of the practice of animal husbandry. The food surplus permits both the specialization of labor and the kind of class structure that can, for instance, provide the leadership and command the manpower to develop and maintain extensive irrigation systems (which in turn make possible further increases in the food supply). Most preindustrial societies possess metallurgy, the plow and the wheel—devices, or the means of creating devices, that multiply both the production and the distribution of agricultural surpluses.

Two other elements of prime importance characterize the civilized preindustrial stage of organization. One is writing: not only the simple keeping of accounts but also the recording of historical events, law, literature and religious beliefs. Literacy, however, is usually confined to a leisured elite. The other element is that this stage of organization has only a few sources of energy other than the muscles of men and livestock; the later preindustrial societies harnessed the force of the wind to sail the seas and grind grain and also made use of water power.

It was in the context of this second type of society that the world's first cities developed. Although preindustrial cities still survive, the modern industrial city is associated with a third level of complexity in human organization, a level characterized by mass literacy, a fluid class system and, most important, the tremendous technological breakthrough to new sources of inanimate energy that produced and still sustains the industrial revolution. Viewed against the background of this three-tiered structure, the first emergence of cities at the level of civilized preindustrial society can be more easily understood.

Two factors in addition to technological advance beyond the folk-society level were needed for cities to emerge. One was a special type of social organization by means of which the agricultural surplus produced by technological advance could be collected, stored and distributed. The same apparatus could also organize the labor force needed for large-scale construction, such as public buildings, city walls and irrigation systems. A social organization of this kind requires a variety of full-time specialists directed by a ruling elite. The latter, although few in number, must command sufficient political power—reinforced by an ideology, usually religious in character—to ensure that the peasantry periodically relinquishes a substantial part of the agricultural yield in order to support the city dwellers. The second factor required was a favorable environment, providing not only fertile soil for the peasants but also a water supply adequate for both agriculture and urban consumption. Such conditions exist in geologically mature mid-latitude river valleys, and it was in such broad alluvial regions that the world's earliest cities arose.

What is a city? It is a community of substantial size and population den-

FAINT OUTLINES of a forgotten Persian city appear in the aerial photograph shown on page 278. The site is on the south bank of the Gurgan River, east of the Caspian Sea near the present border between Iran and the U.S.S.R. A natural frontier between Persia and the steppe country to the north, the Gurgan region served as a barrier to penetration by nomads at least since the Iron Age. The citadel on the opposite bank of the river (*top right*) defended the city from steppe raiders. The photograph is one of many made in Iran by Erich F. Schmidt for the Oriental Institute of the University of Chicago.

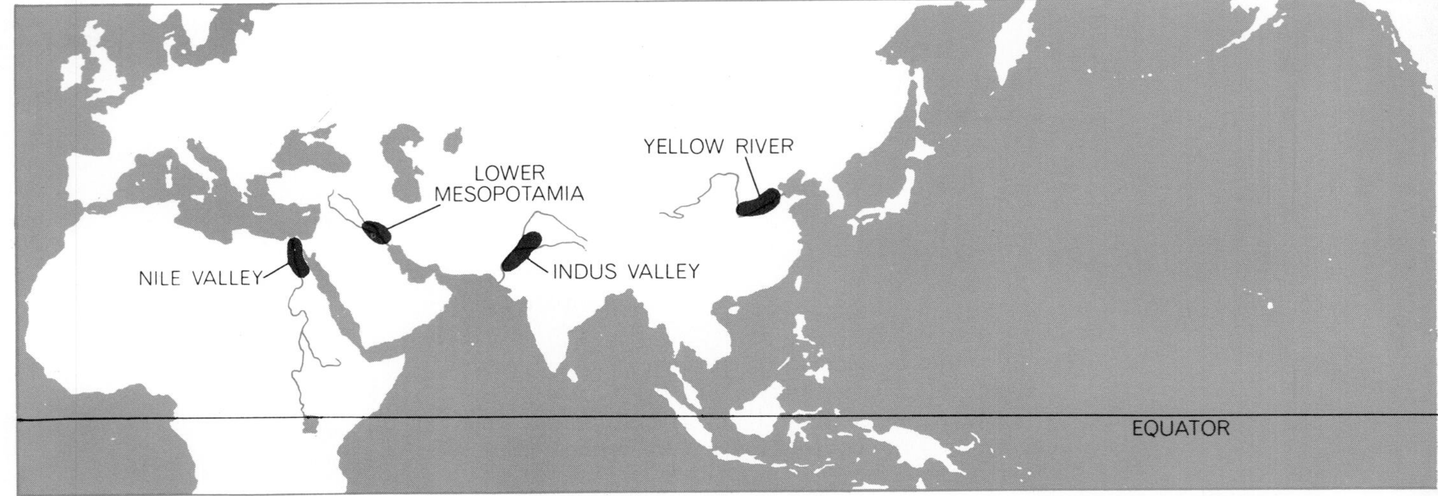

WORLD'S EARLIEST CITIES first evolved from villages in lower Mesopotamia and in the Nile valley (*left*). Soon thereafter cities also arose in similar alluvial regions to the east, first in the Indus valley and then along the Yellow River; Mesopotamian influences

sity that shelters a variety of nonagricultural specialists, including a literate elite. I emphasize the role of literacy as an ingredient of urban life for good reasons. Even though writing systems took centuries to evolve, their presence or absence serves as a convenient means for distinguishing between genuinely urban communities and others that in spite of their large size and dense population must be considered quasi-urban or nonurban. This is because once a community achieves or otherwise acquires the technological advance we call writing, a major transformation in the social order occurs; with a written tradition rather than an oral one it is possible to create more complex administrative and legal systems and more rigorous systems of thought. Writing is indispensable to the development of mathematics, astronomy and the other sciences; its existence thus implies the emergence of a number of significant specializations within the social order.

As far as is known, the world's first cities took shape around 3500 B.C. in the Fertile Crescent, the eastern segment of which includes Mesopotamia: the valleys of the Tigris and the Euphrates. Not only were the soil and water supply there suitable; the region was a crossroads that facilitated repeated contacts among peoples of divergent cultures for thousands of years. The resulting mixture of alien and indigenous crafts and skills must have made its own contribution to the evolution of the first true cities out of the village settlements in lower Mesopotamia. These were primarily in Sumer but also to some extent in Akkad, a little to the north. Some—such as Eridu, Erech, Lagash and Kish—are more familiar to archaeologists than to others; Ur, a later city, is more widely known.

These early cities were much alike; for one thing, they had a similar technological base. Wheat and barley were the cereal crops, bronze was the metal, oxen pulled plows and there were wheeled vehicles. Moreover, the city's leader was both king and high priest; the peasants' tribute to the city god was stored in the temple granaries. Luxury goods recovered from royal tombs and temples attest the existence of skilled artisans, and the importation of precious metals and gems from well beyond the borders of Mesopotamia bespeaks a class of merchant-traders. Population sizes can only be guessed in the face of such unknowns as the average number of residents per household and the extent of each city's zone of influence. The excavator of Ur, Sir Leonard Woolley, estimates that soon after 2000 B.C. the city proper housed 34,000 people; in my opinion, however, it seems unlikely that, at least in the earlier periods, even the larger of these cities contained more than 5,000 to 10,000 people, including part-time farmers on the cities' outskirts.

The valley of the Nile, not too far from Mesopotamia, was also a region of early urbanization. To judge from Egyptian writings of a later time, there may have been urban communities in the Nile delta by 3100 B.C. Whether the Egyptian concept of city living had "diffused" from Mesopotamia or was independently invented (and perhaps even earlier than in Mesopotamia) is a matter of scholarly debate; in any case the initial stages of Egyptian urban life may yet be discovered deep in the silt of the delta, where scientific excavation is only now being undertaken.

Urban communities—diffused or independently invented—spread widely during the third and second millenniums B.C. By about 2500 B.C. the cities of Mohenjo-Daro and Harappa were flourishing in the valley of the Indus River in what is now Pakistan. Within another 1,000 years at the most the mid-

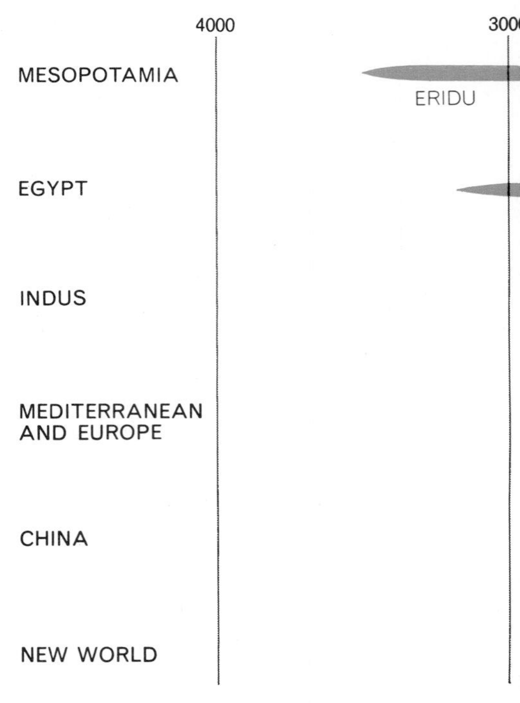

SEQUENCE of urban evolution begins with the first cities of Mesopotamia, makes its

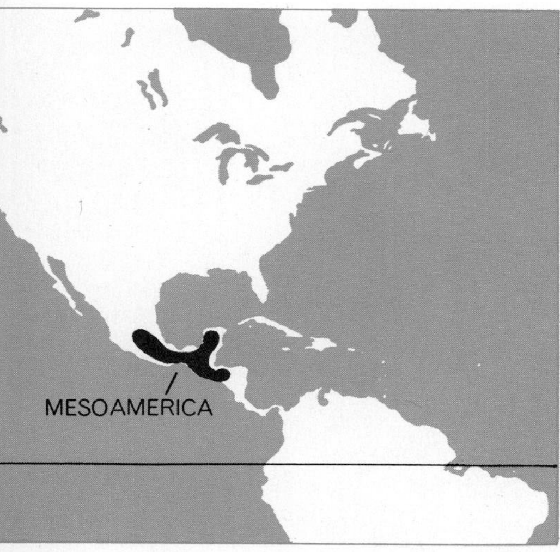

may have reached both areas. The cities of Mesoamerica (*right*) evolved independently.

dle reaches of the Yellow River in China supported urban settlements. A capital city of the Shang Dynasty (about 1500 B.C.) was uncovered near Anyang before World War II; current archaeological investigations by the Chinese may well prove that city life was actually established in ancient China several centuries earlier.

The probability that the first cities of Egypt were later than those of Sumer and the certainty that those of the Indus and Yellow rivers are later lends weight to the argument that the concept of urban living diffused to these areas from Mesopotamia. Be this as it may, none will deny that in each case the indigenous population contributed uniquely to the development of the cities in its own area.

In contrast to the situation in the Old World, it appears certain that diffusion played an insignificant role or none at all in the creation of the pre-Columbian cities of the New World. The peoples of Mesoamerica—notably the Maya, the Zapotecs, the Mixtecs and the Aztecs—evidently developed urban communities on a major scale, the exact extent of which is only now being revealed by current investigations. Until quite recently, for example, many New World archaeologists doubted that the Maya had ever possessed cities; it was the fashion to characterize their impressive ruins as ceremonial centers visited periodically by the members of a scattered rural population. It is now clear, however, that many such centers were genuine cities. At the Maya site of Tikal in Guatemala some 3,000 structures have been located in an area of 6.2 square miles; only 10 percent of them are major ceremonial buildings. Extrapolating on the basis of test excavations of more than 100 of these lesser structures, about two-thirds of them appear to have been dwellings. If only half the present-day average household figure for the region (5.6 members) is applied to Tikal, its population would have been more than 5,000. At another major Maya site—Dzibilchaltun in Yucatán—a survey of less than half of the total area has revealed more than 8,500 structures. Teotihuacán, the largest urban site in the region of modern Mexico City, may have had a population of 100,000 during the first millennium A.D. [*see illustration on next two pages*].

Although only a few examples of writing have been identified at Teotihuacán, it is reasonable to assume that writing was known; there were literate peoples elsewhere in Mesoamerica at the time. By the same token, the achievements of the Maya in such realms as mathematics and astronomy would have forced the conclusion that they were an urban people even in the absence of supporting archaeological evidence. Their invention of the concept of zero (evidently earlier than the Hindus' parallel feat) and their remarkably precise calculation of the length of the solar year would surely have been impossible if their literate elite had been scattered about the countryside in villages rather than concentrated in urban centers where a cross-fertilization of ideas could take place.

Mesoamerica was by no means the only area of large, dense communities in the New World; they also existed in the Andean region. A culture such as

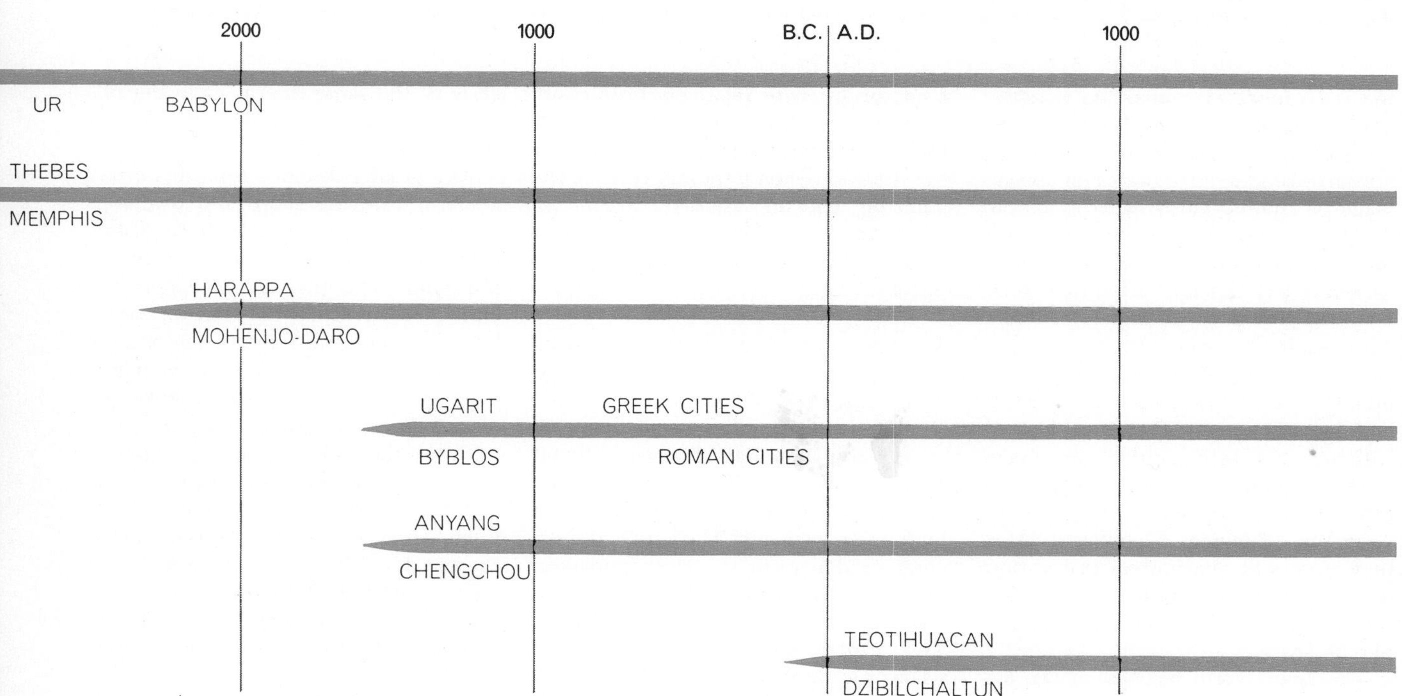

next appearance in the Nile valley, then extends to the Indus, to the eastern Mediterranean region and at last to China. In each area, the independently urbanized New World included, cities rose and fell but urban life, once established, never wholly disappeared.

TEOTIHUACÁN is an extensive urban site near modern Mexico City that flourished during the first millennium A.D. Only the center of the city is seen in the photograph, but the precise grid layout of the city is partly revealed. The full extent of the grid, based on 60-meter-square city blocks, is not yet known, but it continues for miles beyond the city center. Aerial and ground surveys of the region by René Millon of the University of Rochester show that the north-south axis of the city was formed by a broad avenue (the

the Inca, however, cannot be classified as truly urban. In spite of—perhaps because of—their possession of a mnemonic means of keeping inventories (an assemblage of knotted cords called a quipu) the Incas lacked any conventionalized set of graphic symbols for representing speech or any concepts other than numbers and certain broad classes of items. As a result they were denied such key structural elements of an urban community as a literate elite and a written heritage of law, religion and history. Although the Incas could claim major military, architectural and engineering triumphs and apparently were on the verge of achieving a civilized order, they were still quasi-urban at the time of the European conquest, much like the Dahomey, Ashanti and Yoruba peoples of Africa.

The New World teaches us two lessons. In Mesoamerica cities were created without animal husbandry, the wheel and an extensive alluvial setting. One reason for this is maize, a superior grain crop that produced a substantial food surplus with relatively little effort and thus compensated for the limited tools and nonriverine environment. In the Andean region imposing feats of engineering and an extensive division of labor were not enough, in the absence of writing, to give rise to a truly urban society.

In spite of considerable cultural diversity among the inhabitants of the Near East, the Orient and the New World, the early cities in all these regions had a number of organizational forms in common. The dominant pattern was theocracy—the king and the high priest were one. The elite had their chief residences in the city; moreover, they and their retainers and servants congregated mainly in the city's center. This center was the prestige area, where the most imposing religious and government buildings were located. Such a concentration had dual value: in an era when communications and transport were rudimentary, propinquity enhanced interaction among the elite; at the same time it gave the ruling class maximum protection from external attack.

At a greater distance from this urban nucleus were the shops and dwellings of artisans—masons, carpenters, smiths, jewelers, potters—many of whom served the elite. The division of labor into crafts, apparent in the earliest cities, became more complex with the passage of time. Artisan groups, some of which even in early times may have belonged to specific ethnic minorities, tended to establish themselves in special quarters or streets. Such has been characteristic of preindustrial cities in all cultural settings, from the earliest times to the present day. The poorest urbanites lived on the outskirts of the city, as did part-time or full-time farmers; their scattered dwellings finally blended into open countryside.

From its inception the city, as a residence of specialists, has been a continuing source of innovation. Indeed, the very emergence of cities greatly accelerated social and cultural change; to

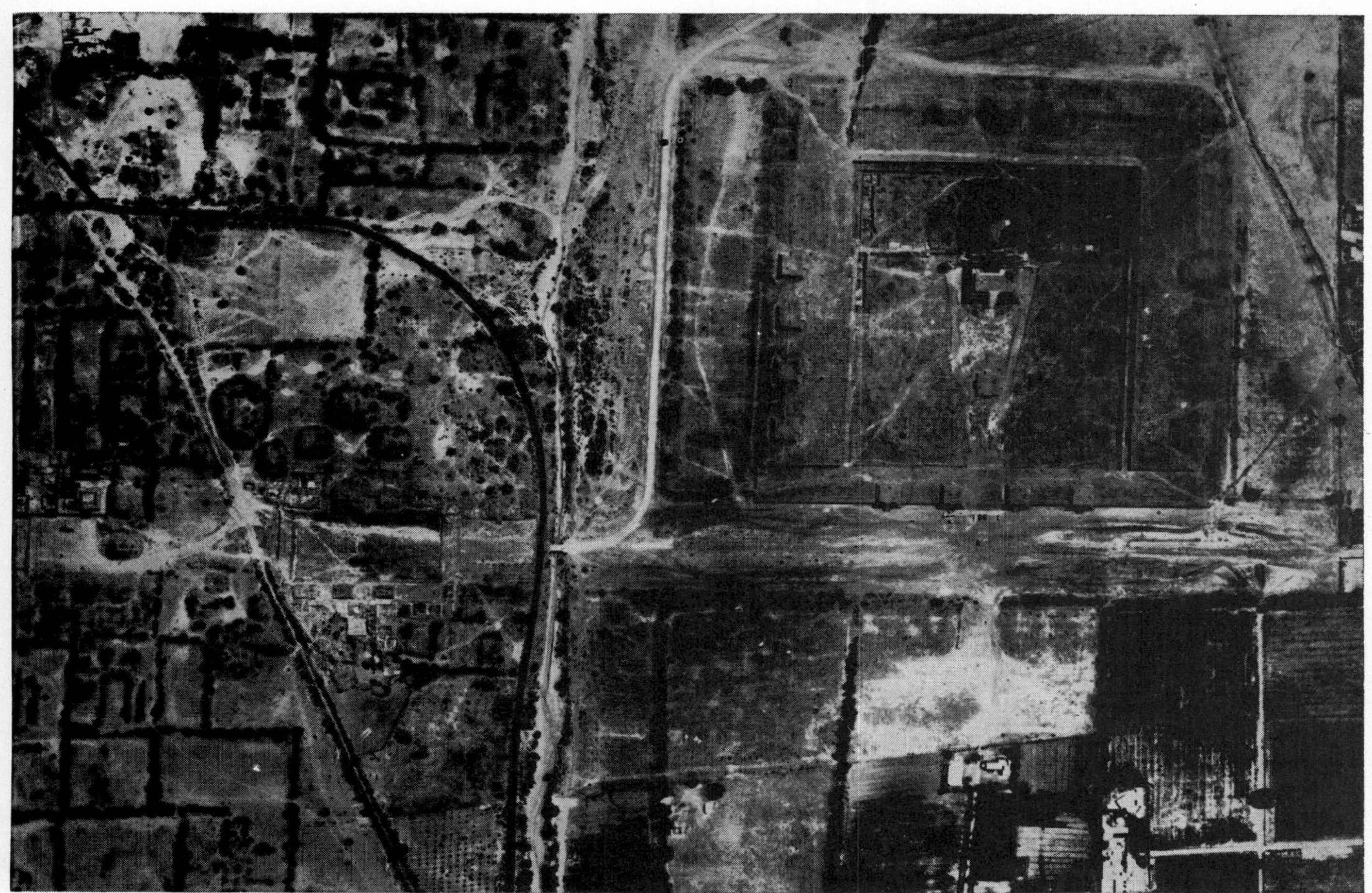

Street of the Dead) that starts at the Pyramid of the Moon (*far left*), runs past the larger Pyramid of the Sun (*left of center*) and continues more than three miles beyond the Ciudadela (*far right*). The east-west axis of Teotihuacán was formed by similar avenues that can be traced outward for two miles on either side of the central Ciudadela area. Although primarily a market and religious center for the surrounding countryside, Teotihuacán probably contained a resident population of 100,000 or more within its 16 square miles.

borrow a term from the late British archaeologist V. Gordon Childe, we can properly regard the "urban revolution" as being equal in significance to the agricultural revolution that preceded it and the industrial revolution that followed it. The city acted as a promoter of change in several ways. Many of the early cities arose on major transportation routes; new ideas and inventions flowed into them quite naturally. The mere fact that a large number of specialists were concentrated in a small area encouraged innovation, not only in technology but also in religious, philosophical and scientific thought. At the same time cities could be strong bulwarks of tradition. Some—for example Jerusalem and Benares—have become sacred in the eyes of the populace; in spite of repeated destruction Jerusalem has retained this status for more than two millenniums [see "Ancient Jerusalem," by Kathleen M. Kenyon; SCIENTIFIC AMERICAN, July 1965].

The course of urban evolution can be correctly interpreted only in relation to the parallel evolution of technology and social organization (especially political organization); these are not just prerequisites to urban life but the basis for its development. As centers of innovation cities provided a fertile setting for continued technological advances; these gains made possible the further expansion of cities. Advanced technology in turn depended on the increasingly complex division of labor, particularly in the political sphere. As an example, the early urban communities of Sumer were mere city-states with restricted hinterlands, but eventually trade and commerce extended over a much broader area, enabling these cities to draw on the human and material resources of a far wider and more diverse region and even bringing about the birth of new cities. The early empires of the Iron Age—for instance the Achaemenid Empire of Persia, established early in the sixth century B.C., and the Han Empire of China, established in the third century B.C.—far surpassed in scope any of the Bronze Age. And as empires became larger the size and grandeur of their cities increased. In fact, as Childe has observed, urbanization spread more rapidly during the first five centuries of the Iron Age than it had in all 15 centuries of the Bronze Age.

In the sixth and fifth centuries B.C. the Persians expanded their empire into western Turkestan and created a number of cities, often by building on existing villages. In this expansion Toprakkala, Merv and Marakanda (part of which was later the site of Samarkand) moved toward urban status. So too in India, at the close of the fourth century B.C., the Mauryas in the north spread their empire to the previously nonurban south and into Ceylon, giving impetus to the birth of cities such as Ajanta and Kanchi. Under the Ch'in and Han dynasties, between the third century B.C. and the third century A.D., city life took hold in most of what was then China and beyond, particularly to the south and west. The "Great Silk Road" extending from China to Turkestan became studded with such oasis cities as Suchow, Khotan and Kashgar; Nanking and Canton seem to have attained urban status at this time, as did the settlement that was eventually to become Peking.

At the other end of the Eurasian land mass the Phoenicians began toward the end of the second millennium B.C. to spread westward and to revive or establish urban life along the northern coast of Africa and in Spain. These coastal traders had by then developed a considerable knowledge of shipbuilding; this, combined with their far-reaching commercial ties and power of arms, made the Phoenicians lords of the Mediterranean for a time. Some centuries later the Greeks followed a rather similar course. Their city-states—actually in a sense small empires—created or rebuilt numerous urban outposts along the Mediterranean shore from Asia Minor to Spain and France, and eastward to the most distant coast of the Black Sea. The empire that did the most to diffuse city life into the previously nonurban regions of the West—France, Britain, the Low Countries, Germany west of the Rhine, central and even eastern Europe—was of course Rome.

Empires are effective disseminators of urban forms because they have to build cities with which to maintain military supremacy in conquered regions. The city strongholds, in turn, require an administrative apparatus in order to tap the resources of the conquered area and encourage the commerce needed both to support the military garrison and to enhance the wealth of the homeland. Even when a new city began as a purely commercial outpost, as was the case under the Phoenicians, some military and administrative support was necessary if it was to survive and function effectively in alien territory.

There is a significant relation between the rise and fall of empires and the rise and fall of cities; in a real sense history is the study of urban graveyards. The capitals of many former empires are today little more than ghostly outlines that only hint at a glorious past. Such was the fate of Babylon and Nineveh, Susa in Persia, Seleucia in Mesopotamia and Vijayanagar in India. Yet there are exceptions. Some cities have managed to survive over long periods of time by attaching themselves first to one empire and then to another. Athens, for example, did not decline after the collapse of Greek power; it was able to attach itself to the Roman Empire, which subsidized Athens as a center of learning. Once Rome fell, however, both the population and the prestige of Athens dwindled steadily; it was little more than a town until the rise of modern Greece in the 19th century. On the other hand, nearby Byzantium, a city-state of minor importance under Roman rule, not only became the capital of the Eastern Roman Empire and its successor, the Ottoman Empire, but as Istanbul remains a major city to this day.

In the light of the recurrent rise and decline of cities in so many areas of the world, one may ask just how urban life has been able to persist and why the skills of technology and social organization required for city-building were not

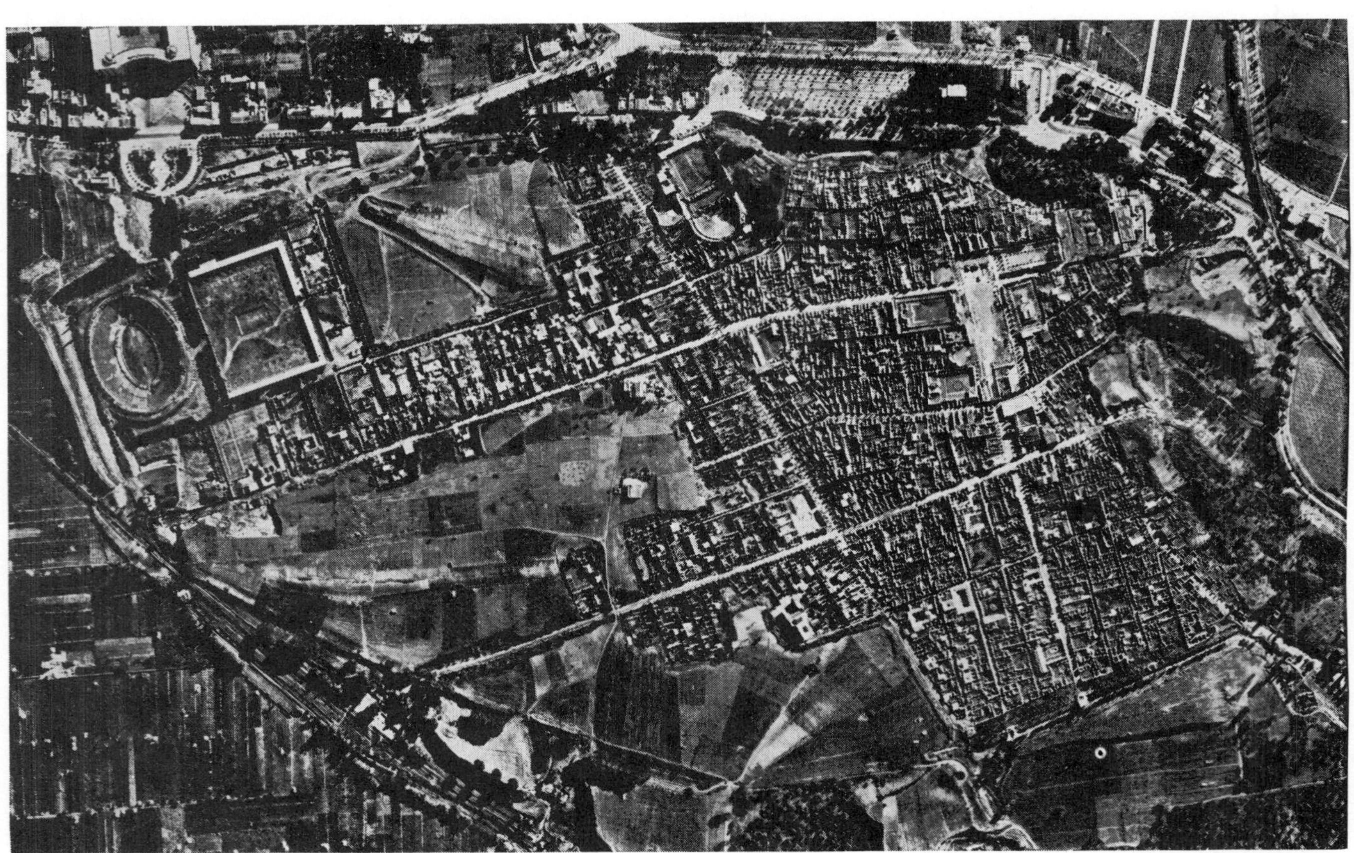

A ROMAN RESORT in Italy, Pompeii was buried by 18 feet of ash from Vesuvius in A.D. 79 after a lifetime of at least 400 years. Its rectangular ground plan was presumably designed by the Etruscans, who were among the city's first residents in pre-Roman days. Population estimates for the resort city are uncertain; its amphitheater (*far left*), however, could seat 20,000 people. Forgotten soon after its burial, Pompeii was rediscovered in 1748; systematic excavation of the site began in the middle of the 19th century.

lost. The answer is that the knowledge was maintained within the framework of empires—by means of written records and oral transmission by various specialists. Moreover, all empires have added to their store of skills relating to urban development as a result of diffusion—including the migration of specialists—from other civilized areas. At the same time various civilized or uncivilized subjects within empires have either been purposely educated by their conquerors or have otherwise gained access to the body of urban lore. The result on occasion is that the subjects challenge the power of the dominant ruling group.

The rise and fall of the Roman Empire provides a highly instructive case study that illuminates several relations between the life-span of cities and the formation and decline of empires. The Romans themselves took many elements of their civilization from the Etruscans, the Greeks and other civilized peoples who came under their sway. After Rome's northward expansion in western Europe and the proliferation of Roman cities in regions inhabited by so-called "barbarians"—in this instance preliterate, or "noncivilized," peoples—the Roman leaders were simply unable to staff all the bureaucratic posts with their own citizens. Some of the preliterates had to be trained to occupy such posts both in their own homelands and in the cities on the frontier. This process made it possible for the Romans to exploit the wealth of conquered regions and may have pacified the subjugated groups for a time, but in the long run it engendered serious conflicts. Eventually the Ostrogoths, Vandals, Burgundians and others —having been partially urbanized, having developed a literate elite of their own and having acquired many Roman technological and administrative skills—turned against the imperial power structure and engineered the collapse of Rome and its empire. Nor is this a unique case in history; analogies can be perceived in the modern independence movements of such European colonies as those in Africa.

With the breakup of the Roman Empire, not only did the city of Rome (which at its largest may have had more than 300,000 inhabitants) decline markedly but many borderland cities disappeared or shrank to small towns or villages. The decline was dramatic, but it is too often assumed that after the fall of Rome cities totally disappeared from western Europe. The historian E. Ewig has recently shown that many cities continued to function, particularly in Italy and southern France. Here, as in all civilized societies, the surviving cities were the chief residences and centers of activity for the political and religious elite who commanded the positions of power and privilege that persisted during the so-called Dark Ages.

A ROMAN OUTPOST in Syria, Dura Europos was founded on the Euphrates about 300 B.C. by the Seleucid successor to Alexander the Great. At first a center of Hellenism in the East, it was later a Roman stronghold until Valerian lost it in A.D. 257. Yale University archaeologists have studied the site since 1922; finger-like ramps are their excavation dumps.

In spite of Rome's decline many of the techniques and concepts associated with literate traditions in such fields as medicine and astronomy were kept alive; this was done both in the smaller surviving urban communities of Europe and in the eastern regions that had been ruled by the Romans—notably in the cities of the succeeding Eastern Roman Empire. Some of the technology and learning associated with Rome also became the basis for city life in the Arab empires that arose later in the Near East, North Africa, Spain and even central Asia. Indeed, the Byzantine and Arab empires—which had such major intellectual centers as Constantinople, Antioch, Damascus, Cairo and Baghdad —advanced beyond the knowledge inherited from antiquity. The Arabs, for example, took from the Hindus the concept of zero and the decimal system of numerals; by utilizing these concepts in both theory and practice they achieved significant advances over the knowledge that had evolved in the West. Eventually much of the new learning was passed on to Europe, where it helped to build the foundations for the industrial revolution.

In time Europe reestablished extensive commercial contact with the Byzantine and Arab empires; the interchange that followed played a significant role in the resurgence of urban life in southern Europe. The revitalization of trade was closely associated with the formation of several prosperous Italian city-states in the 10th and 11th centuries A.D. Venice and other cities eventually were transformed into small-scale empires whose colonies were scattered over the Mediterranean region—a hinterland from which the home cities were able to extract not only many of their necessities but also luxury items. By A.D. 1000 Venice had forged com-

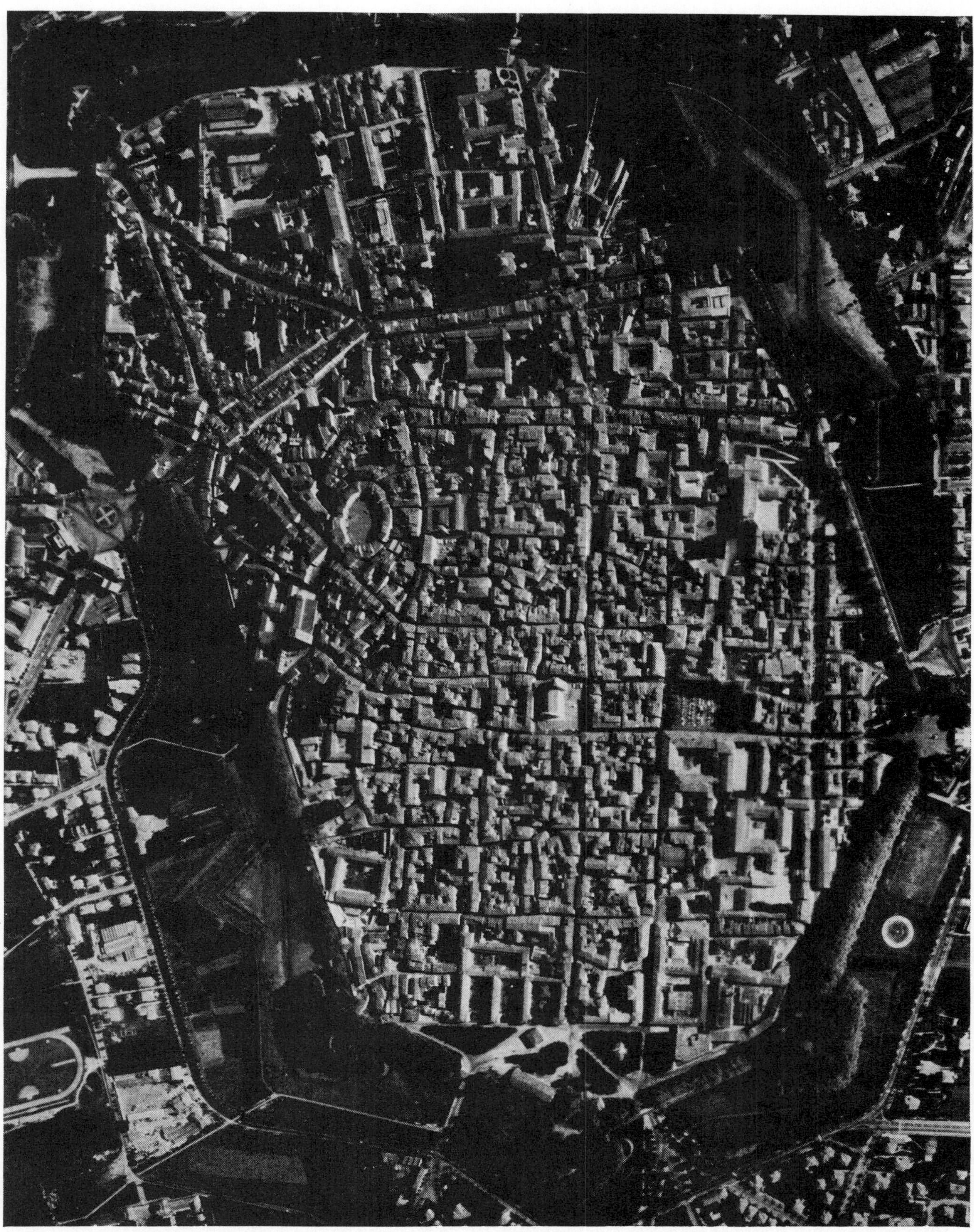

A RENAISSANCE CITY, Lucca in northern Italy is no longer contained within the bastioned circuit of its walls, which were begun in 1504 and completed in 1645. Lucca's seesaw history is like that of many other southern European cities. A Roman town during the Punic wars, it was the site of Caesar's triumvirate meeting with Pompey and Crassus in 60 B.C. and was pillaged by Odoacer at the fall of the Roman Empire in A.D. 476. A fortress city once again by the seventh century A.D., Lucca had become a prosperous manufacturing center, specializing in the weaving of silk textiles, by the 12th century. It continues to produce silk and other textiles today.

mercial links with Constantinople and other cities of the Eastern Roman Empire, partly as a result of the activities of the Greek colony in Venice. The Venetians were able to draw both on the knowledge of these resident Greeks and on the practical experience of sea captains and other specialists among them. Such examples make it clear that the Italian city-states were not merely local creations but rather products of a multiplicity of cultural forces.

Beginning at the turn of the 11th century A.D. many European cities managed to win a kind of independence from the rulers of the various principalities and petty kingdoms that surrounded them. Particularly in northern Italy urban communities came to enjoy considerable political autonomy. This provided an even more favorable atmosphere for commerce and encouraged the growth of such urban institutions as craft guilds. The European pattern is quite different from that in most of Asia (for instance in India and China), where the city was never able to attain a measure of autonomy within the broader political structure. At the same time the extent of self-rule enjoyed by the medieval European cities can be exaggerated and often is; by the close of the Middle Ages urban self-rule was already beginning to be lost. It is therefore evident that the political autonomy of medieval cities was only indirectly related to the eventual evolution of the industrial city.

It was the industrial revolution that brought about truly far-reaching changes in city life. In some nations today, as Kingsley Davis notes in his first introduction, the vast majority of the inhabitants are city dwellers. Nearly 80 percent of the people in the United Kingdom live in cities, as do nearly 70 percent of the people of the U.S. Contrast this with the preindustrial civilized world, in which only a small, socially dominant minority lived in cities. The industrial revolution has also led to fundamental changes in the city's social geography and social organization; the industrial city is marked by a greater fluidity in the class system, the appearance of mass education and mass communications and the shift of some of the elite from the center of the city to its suburban outskirts.

Although there are still insufficient data on the rise of the industrial city—an event that took place sometime between 1750 and 1850—and although scholars disagree over certain steps in the process, the major forces at work in the two or three centuries before the industrial city emerged can be perceived clearly enough. Viewed in the light of Europe's preindustrial urban era, two factors are evident: the expansion of European power into other continents and the development of a technology based on inanimate rather than animate sources of energy. The extension of European trade and exploration (which was to culminate in European colonialism) not only induced the growth of cities in Asia, in parts of nonurban Africa and in the Americas but also helped to raise the standard of living of Europeans themselves and made possible the support of more specialists. Notable among the last was a new occupational group—the scientists. The expansion abroad had helped to shatter the former world view of European scholars; they were now forced to cope with divergent ideas and customs. The discoveries reported by the far-ranging European explorers thus gave added impetus to the advance of science.

The knowledge gained through the application of the scientific method is the one factor above all others that made the modern city possible. This active experimental approach has enabled man to control the forces of nature to an extent undreamed of in the preindustrial era. It is true that in the course of several millenniums the literate elite of the preindustrial cities added significantly to man's store of knowledge in such fields as medicine, astronomy and mathematics, but these scholars generally scorned mundane activities and avoided contact with those whose work was on the practical level. This meant that the scholars' theories were rarely tested and applied in the everyday realm. Moreover, in accordance with prevailing religious thought, man was not to tamper with the natural order or to seek to control it, in either its physical or its social aspect. For example, medical scholars in Greek and Roman cities did not dissect human cadavers; not until the 16th century in Europe did a physician—Andreas Vesalius of Brussels—actually use findings obtained from dissection to revise ancient medical theories.

In the field of engineering, as late as the 17th century most advances were made by artisans who worked more or less on a trial-and-error basis. With the development of the experimental method, however, the learning of the elite became linked with the practical knowledge of the artisan, the barber-surgeon and the like; the result was a dramatic upsurge of knowledge and a fundamental revision of method that has been termed the scientific revolution. Such was the basis of the industrial revolution and the industrial city.

That the first industrial cities appeared in England is hardly fortuitous; England's social structure lacked the rigidity that characterized most of Europe and the rest of the civilized world. The Puritan tradition in England—an ethical system that supports utilitarianism and empiricism—did much to alter earlier views concerning man's place in nature. In England scholars could communicate with artisans more readily than elsewhere in Europe.

The advent of industrialism brought vast improvements in agricultural implements, farming techniques and food preservation, as well as in transportation and communication. Improved water supplies and more effective methods of sewage disposal allowed more people to congregate in cities. Perhaps the key invention was the steam engine, which provided a new and much more bountiful source of energy. Before that time, except for power from wind and water, man had no energy resources other than human and animal muscle. Now the factory system, with its mass production of goods and mechanization of activity, began to take hold. With it emerged a new kind of occupational structure: a structure that depends on highly specialized knowledge and that functions effectively only when the activities of the component occupations are synchronized. This process of industrialization has not only continued unabated to the present day but has actually accelerated with the rise of self-controlling machines.

The evolution of the industrial city was not an unmixed blessing. Historians have argued through many volumes the question of whether the new working class, including many migrants from the countryside, lost or gained economically and socially as the factory system destroyed older social patterns. Today, as industrialization moves inexorably across the globe, it continues to create social problems. Many surviving traditional cities evince in various ways the conflict between their preindustrial past and their industrial future. Nonetheless, the trend is clear: barring nuclear war, the industrial city will become the dominant urban form throughout the world, replacing forever the preindustrial city that was man's first urban creation.

The Planning of a Maya Ceremonial Center

30

by Norman Hammond
May 1972

The center at Lubaantún in British Honduras called for a huge investment in labor and materials. When a choice had to be made between cutting costs and adhering to the plan, the plan won out

Among the pre-Columbian civilizations of the New World the Aztec and Inca empires that the conquistadors overthrew are commonly believed to have been the most advanced, but this distinction may well belong to the Maya, whose culture reached its apogee in the first millennium of the Christian Era during what is known as the Classic period. The brilliance of Maya aesthetics is apparent in Classic stucco work, vase-painting and fresco; the intellectual achievements of the Classic period include not only a written language but also calendric and astronomical studies of a high order. Classic Maya civilization was centered in the lowland jungle province of Petén in Guatemala and in adjacent Belize (British Honduras), extending northward and westward into Mexico and southward and eastward into Honduras and El Salvador.

The civilization of the Classic period flourished within a surprisingly loose framework compared, for example, with the partly contemporaneous pre-Columbian culture centered on Teotihuacán a few hundred miles away in the Valley of Mexico. In the first half of the first millennium the rulers of Teotihuacán built one of the largest and most precisely planned urban complexes known in ancient times [see the article "Teotihuacán," by René Millon, beginning on page 115]. Where the Maya held sway in the tropical lowlands, however, there were no such cities. The numerous population was scattered among widely dispersed farmers' hamlets. Living in relative isolation and sheltered in dwellings built of perishable materials, the great majority of the Maya supported themselves by raising crops (principally maize and beans) in forest clearings they prepared for planting by the slash-and-burn method. At intervals were a few clusters of more permanent structures built of stone, but these were not cities in any conventional sense; the most spectacular of their masonry edifices are lofty pyramids like those the first Spaniards saw used as temples in Aztec Mexico. As a result it has become customary to call these clusters of stone buildings "ceremonial centers."

From an economic viewpoint the construction of a Maya ceremonial center constituted an enormous investment in energy and materials. More than a century of archaeological investigation has shown that within a range of regional variation the centers are all much alike architecturally. Where uneven terrain had to be leveled, this was achieved by building foundation platforms of rough stone rubble retained by masonry walls. Rising from these foundations are stone structures arrayed around a number of open plazas.

Each structure consists of a freestanding masonry wall that encloses a more or less rectangular area, filled with rubble up to the height of the retaining wall; in general the greater the area enclosed, the higher the wall. On top of these structures stood superstructures of various kinds. It is customary to call the superstructures on high pyramidal substructures "temples" and those on lower and more extensive substructures "palaces." Most of the superstructures on lower and smaller substructures, having been made of perishable materials, have entirely disappeared; many are known to have been residences, whereas others are buildings of unknown purpose.

Amid the cluster of interconnected plazas with structures grouped around them, each Maya center is likely to have one or more "ball courts." Unlike the term palace, the term ball court is not guesswork. It is known from sculptured monuments that these distinctive structures were used for playing a game that might be described as a cross between volleyball and soccer. Each ball court consists of a pair of steep rubble mounds faced with masonry; these mounds form the sides of a long, narrow field of play where the Maya engaged in the ritual contest they called *pok-ta-pok*.

In most Maya centers built during the Classic period the plaza in front of the major temple pyramid contained sculptured stone monuments that archaeologists call by the Greek name "stelae." These bear the images of rulers, some of them shown with their captives, and long hieroglyphic inscriptions that seem to contain historical information. The portions of the inscriptions that record dates in Maya calendric notation can be read. The dates inscribed on stelae and on sculptured altars at the Classic sites of Piedras Negras and Yaxchilán, two ceremonial centers on the Usumacinta River in the Petén region, and Quiriguá, a third center to the southeast, seem to record events in the lives of several rulers. The first of these dated monuments was erected during the third century of the Christian Era and the last at the end of the ninth century.

The emphasis in recent years on settlement-pattern research in the Maya area has resulted in the common presumption that the location and layout of ceremonial centers and the distribution of settlements around them are due solely to environmental dictates, without the deliberate planning apparent in such places as Teotihuacán. On the other hand, the social investment in labor and materials required for the construction of such a center suggests that a certain amount of consideration must have gone into the work: the marshaling of labor, the specification of dimensions, the collecting of vast amounts of rubble fill and masonry facing blocks, and the feeding of all these things into the construction program. The successful integration of such elements and the abilities of a range of specialized artisans argues strongly in favor of a preordained plan, and one that specified the layout and subsequent function of the site.

My opportunity to seek evidence for Maya planning came recently. The occasion was the surveying and excavation of Lubaantún, a small Maya ceremonial center in the Rio Grande basin of southern Belize. Field studies were pursued there, primarily under the sponsorship of the University of Cambridge and the Peabody Museum of Archaeology and Ethnology of Harvard University, in 1970. Three main programs were undertaken. The first was the detailed mapping of the center and of a sample of the surrounding settlement area; this work was done by Michael Walton, a professional architect, and Basilio Ah, a local Mopan Maya Indian with previous mapping experience. The second program called for excavation at the center to determine both the sequence of construction and the dates of occupation. The third was an ecological survey of the Rio Grande region, including a study of the local geology by John Hazelden of the University of Cambridge, to determine what kinds of natural resources—building stone, materials for tools, forest products for construction, plants for medicine and ritual, wild game and other foodstuffs—were or had once been locally available.

Lubaantún lies in the foothill zone of the Maya Mountains [*see illustration on opposite page*]; it occupies a long sloping ridge that runs from north to south. To the east and west the ridge falls away steeply and is bounded by creeks. The slope of the ridge is gradual, eventually descending sharply to the level of the Rio Columbia, a branch of the Rio Grande that passes a few hundred meters south of the site. Stream erosion has carved the surrounding land into a maze of low, round-topped hillocks; as a result the ridge is the only fairly level tract of any size in the area.

The region around Lubaantún is well endowed with natural resources. The Rio Columbia contains an abundance of freshwater mollusks. It also provides a waterway, navigable by canoe, that runs via the Rio Grande all the way to the Caribbean; the seacoast is some 25 kilometers east of Lubaantún as the crow flies. Hazelden's survey showed that thinly bedded sandstone, limestone and siltstone are available along the riverbanks and in the nearby foothills, and that all the stone needed for the center could have been quarried within a radius of three kilometers. Potter's clay is also found along the river, and such forest products as copal gum, valued by the Maya as incense, can be gathered on the wooded coastal plain. Moreover, the foothill zone where Lubaantún is situated has some of the most fertile soil in all southern Belize. There is game in the hills and on the coastal plain, waterfowl in swampy areas, and mollusks, crustaceans and fish along the coast. The canoe route to the coast covers 90 kilometers, or almost four times the straight-line distance, and might be thought to have been traveled infrequently by the people of Lubaantún. When Elizabeth S. Wing of the Florida State Museum analyzed the animal remains we recovered at the ceremonial center, however, she found that nearly 40 percent of them were of marine origin.

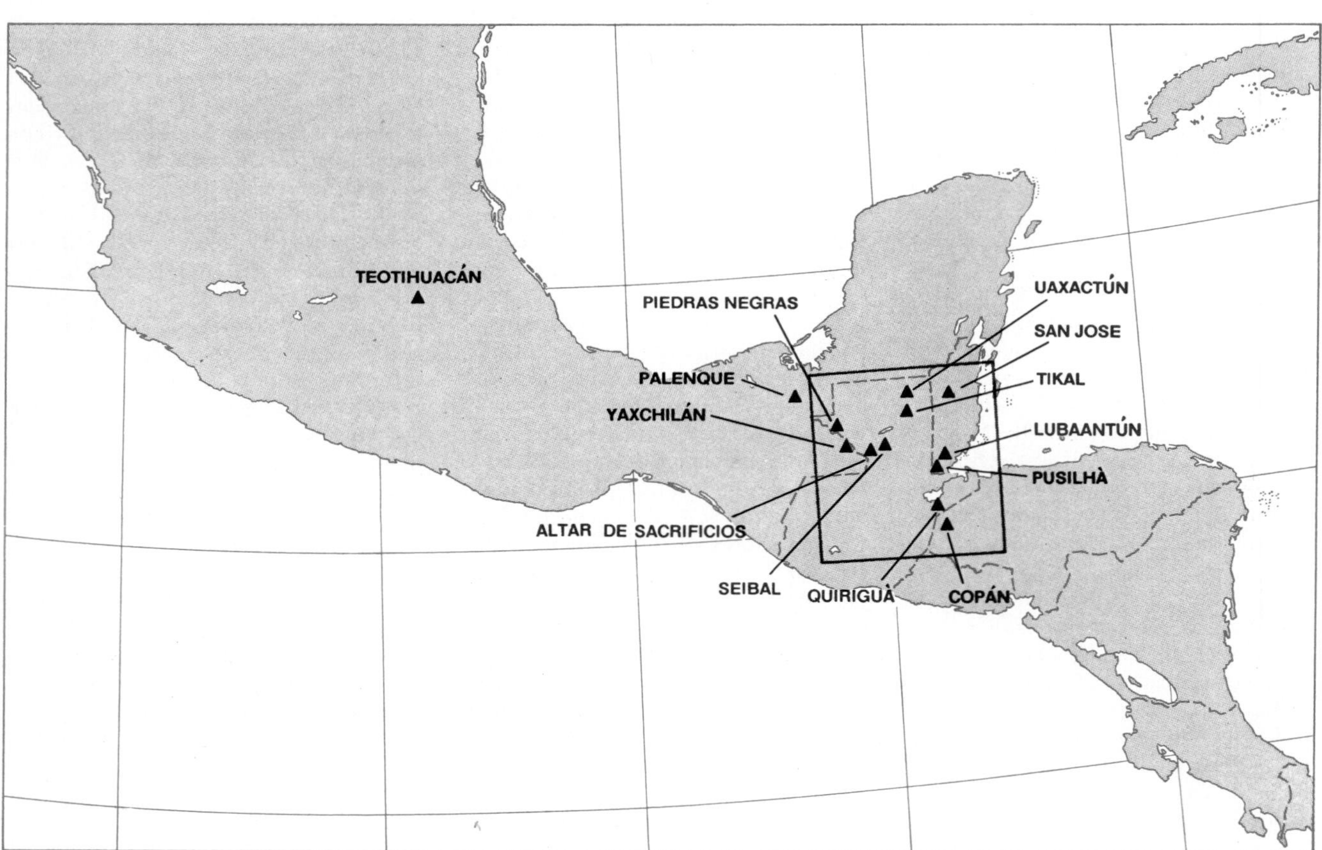

PETÉN LOWLANDS of northern Guatemala border on Mexico to the north and west and on Honduras and British Honduras to the south and east. Twelve lowland Maya centers of the Classic period are shown; the region is shown in more detail on the opposite page.

Our excavations showed that when the Lubaantún center was founded early in the eighth century, it consisted of a single large platform covering an area of some 2,500 square meters on the part of the ridge that was later occupied by an open plaza we have designated Plaza IV [*see "b" in illustration on pages 286 and 287*]. On the north side of this first platform stood a series of narrow rubble-filled substructures faced with stone. We were surprised to find that the original construction had begun so late; by early in the eighth century the Late Classic florescence of Maya civilization was already at its height. As will be seen, the lateness of the date has important historical implications.

In any event the first platform at the center was almost completely buried under later construction. In the second phase of the work two more large platforms were built north and south of the first, and large plaza areas were laid out beyond the north platform [*see "c" in illustration on pages 286 and 287*], quadrupling the area of Lubaantún. At one side of the north platform, facing what was later to be Plaza IV, the builders raised their first temple pyramid. We have designated it Structure 12. Its present size is the result of later construction that has entirely engulfed the original pyramid. Construction of a ball court on the southern extension completed the second-phase work at Lubaantún.

The first undeniable evidence that planning outweighed expediency in the building of the center appeared during the third phase of construction. Early work during the third phase had extended the north platform southward until it covered most of the 2,500-square-meter platform built in the first phase. It was then decided to enlarge the first pyramid and add two new ones. The size of these, as planned, meant that space in the center of the site was going to be very short indeed; for the first time a crucial decision was forced on the rulers of Lubaantún. Was the site to be extended still farther north and south along the ridge, where the shallow curve of the crest meant that a large surface area could be gained with the construction of a relatively shallow platform? Or was centralization more important than economy and should the center be expanded laterally even though the acquisition of a small area meant the construction of high platforms and the investment of a prodigious amount of labor and material resources? The latter decision was taken, and the growth of Lubaantún changed

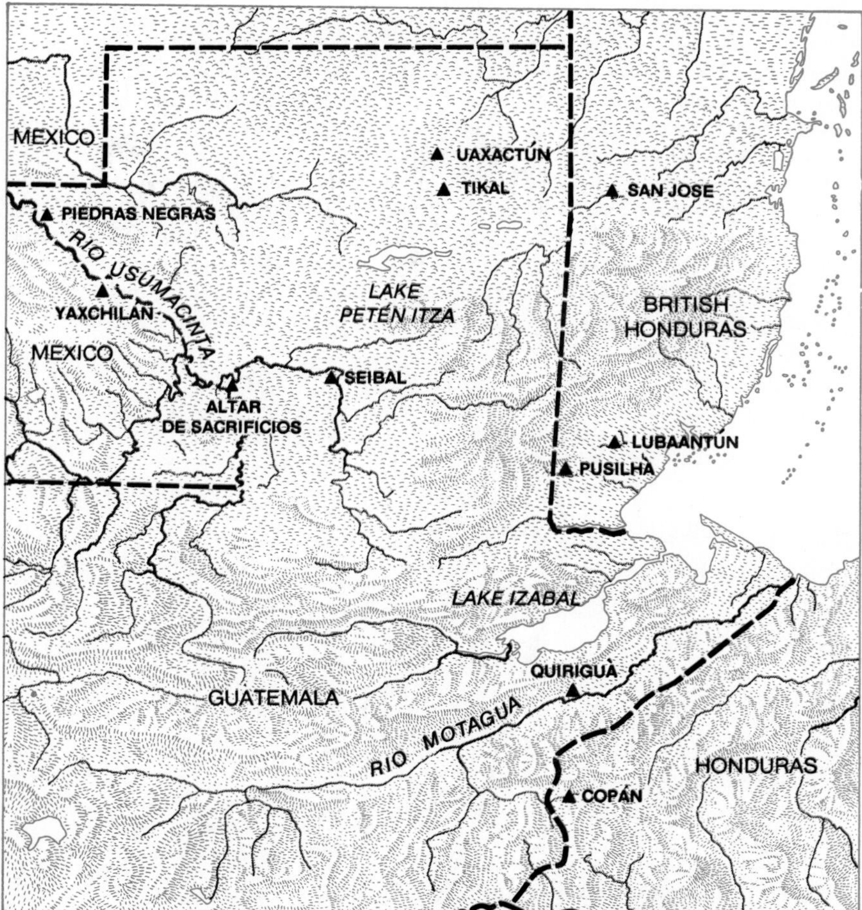

LUBAANTÚN IS SITUATED in the foothills of the Maya Mountains, an isolated highland area in southern British Honduras. It is among the last of the centers built by the Maya.

from modification of the local topography to the creation of an artificial topography [*see "d" in illustration on pages 286 and 287*]. The retaining walls that gained the builders six meters' horizontal space to the east and west are multiterraced and more than 11 meters high. The amount of rubble that fills the space between ridge slope and wall must exceed 3,000 cubic meters. It is hard to imagine clearer proof that the planned layout of Lubaantún was sufficiently important to force the builders to overcome the limitations of local topography.

In the fourth phase of construction at the center still more artificial topography was created. Just beyond the newly extended main platform was a gully cut by a small stream on the west side of the ridge. This watercourse was now covered by rubble-filled platforms, forming a series of broad plazas that led down the steep slope almost to the bank of the creek at the bottom [*see "e" in illustration on pages 286 and 287*]. Whether the most southerly part of this extension was built during the fourth phase or the fifth remains uncertain. In any event the major enterprise during the fifth and final phase of construction at Lubaantún was the refurbishing of the central part of the site. Broad staircases were built at the north and south ends of Plaza V, and a second ball court was constructed on a new platform east of the plaza. At the same time a new staircase was added to Structure 12, the largest of the temple pyramids at the site.

The building of Lubaantún, which had been in progress for between 100 and 150 years, was now essentially complete. Begun early in the eighth century, the work ended not long before the ceremonial center was abandoned sometime between A.D. 850 and 900. The plan of Lubaantún that we have now is a palimpsest, so to speak, of all five periods, but it is essentially the plan of the site as it was functioning at the time of its abandonment. It is only at this period that we can fully comprehend the zonal structure and traffic pattern within the ceremonial center.

As a result of the mapping project we

know not only the total number of edifices that were built at Lubaantún but also exactly where they stood in relation to one another and the exact dimensions of each. The structures range in height from as little as 20 centimeters to more than 12 meters and in basal area from 40 square meters to more than 500 square meters. As at other Maya ceremonial centers, each structure served as a foundation for some kind of superstructure. Elsewhere a number of these superstructures, in particular the temples and palaces, were built of stone and still survive. At Lubaantún, however, all the superstructures apparently were built of wood and no longer exist. They presumably had walls of poles and roofs of palm thatch, like the Maya houses in the vicinity today. Fragments of the clay that was daubed on the pole walls of one temple have been preserved by fire; the impressions show that the poles were a little over three inches in diameter.

When we compared the dimensions of the various foundation structures, we found that they fell into four distinct clusters. The pyramids are at the top of the scale; the smallest of the three has a basal area of more than 500 square meters and is more than five meters high. Our system of classification placed structures this large or larger in the "religious" category. At the bottom of the scale are numerous small, low structures, all less than 1.2 meters high and 100 square me-

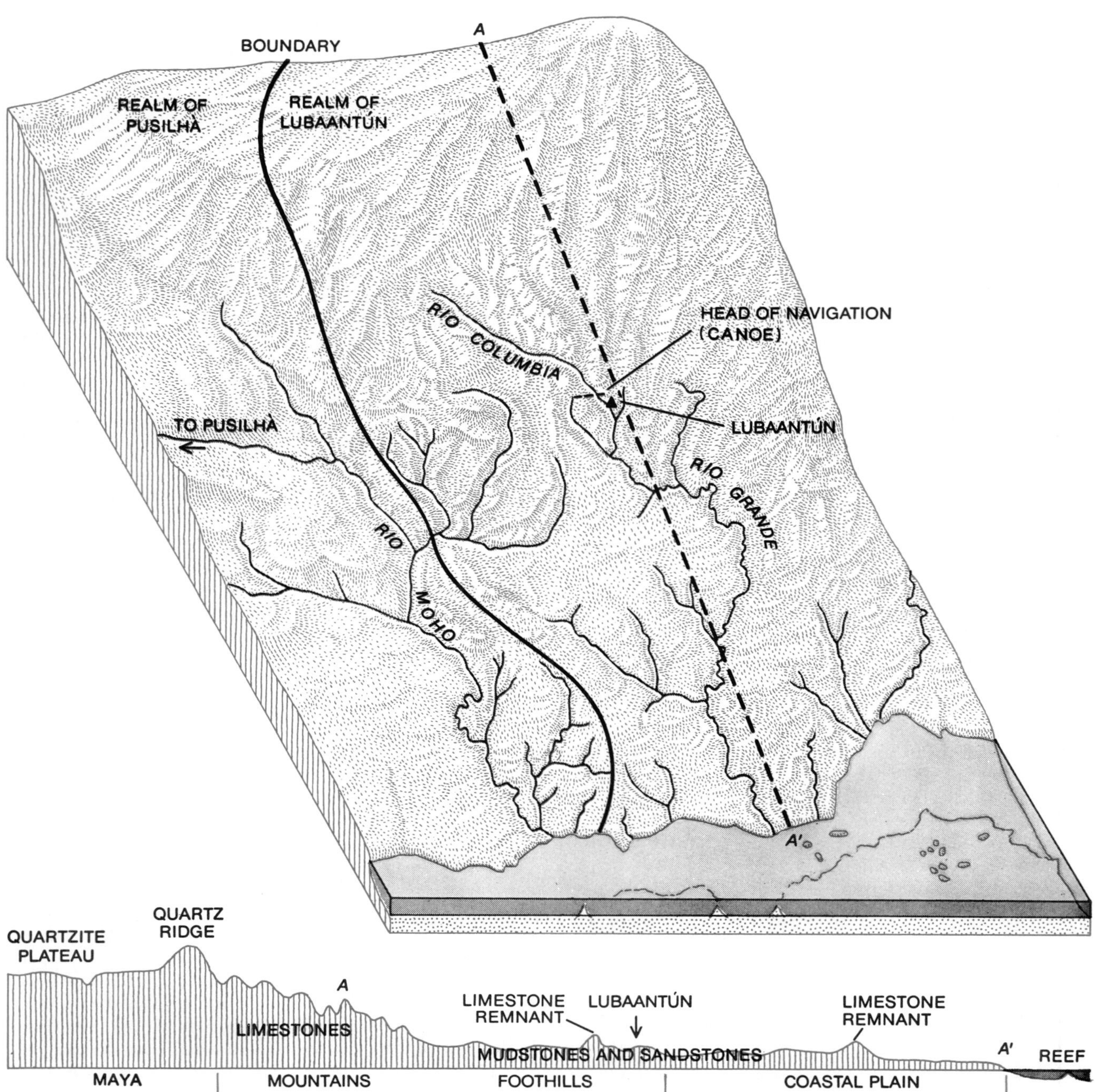

REALM OF LUBAANTÚN extended northwest some 25 kilometers from the foothills of the Maya Mountains to the highland plateau and southeast another 25 kilometers to the low-lying Caribbean coast and the sheltered waters of the barrier reef offshore (*see cross section at bottom*). The region controlled by the ceremonial center consisted of some 1,600 square kilometers, and the population may have numbered 50,000. The soil in the foothills was fertile, and the realm was rich in raw materials and wild foods.

ters in area. We assume that they were house foundations and have classified them as "residences." Between these extremes are two groups of structures with dimensions that overlap with respect to area but not with respect to height. The structures of the smaller group range from more than 1.2 meters in height to less than two meters; none is less than 150 or more than 280 square meters in basal area. On the basis of size and location we have dubbed this group of structures "elite residences." The structures of the larger group, ranging in height from two to 3.6 meters with a basal area as large as 330 square meters, include the two Lubaantún ball courts and a number of other structures that are neither obviously residential nor obviously ritual. We have placed all of them in a nonspecific category: "ceremonial structures."

When we marked the structures on the site map according to this four-category classification, an interesting correlation emerged. The structures surrounding any particular plaza usually belonged in the same category. Plaza IV, with its three pyramids, is a prime example; it is the only one of the 20 plazas at Lubaantún that belongs in the "religious" category. Furthermore, the five plazas immediately contiguous to Plaza IV all belong to the "ceremonial" category, and six of the seven most remote plazas at the site fall in the "residential" category. The master plan for Lubaantún seems to have called for a religious core surrounded by an inner zone of ceremonial plazas and an outer zone of residences. Such a layout follows a simple concentric-zone model, modified at Lubaantún only by the requirements of topography.

Common sense suggests that the traffic plan for such a concentric-zone model would call for residential areas with low accessibility and public areas with high accessibility. Religious areas would be either accessible or secluded depending on the nature of the cult. For example, if access to a central religious area was restricted, this fact would suggest worship of an exclusive and elitist nature.

In order to test this hypothesis we conducted a topological analysis of the potential traffic flow at Lubaantún without regard for the presumed functions of the plazas as deduced from the categories of structures surrounding them. Our first step was to reduce the pattern of the major plazas and their interconnections to a planar graph [*see graph in bottom illustration at right*]. The graph en-

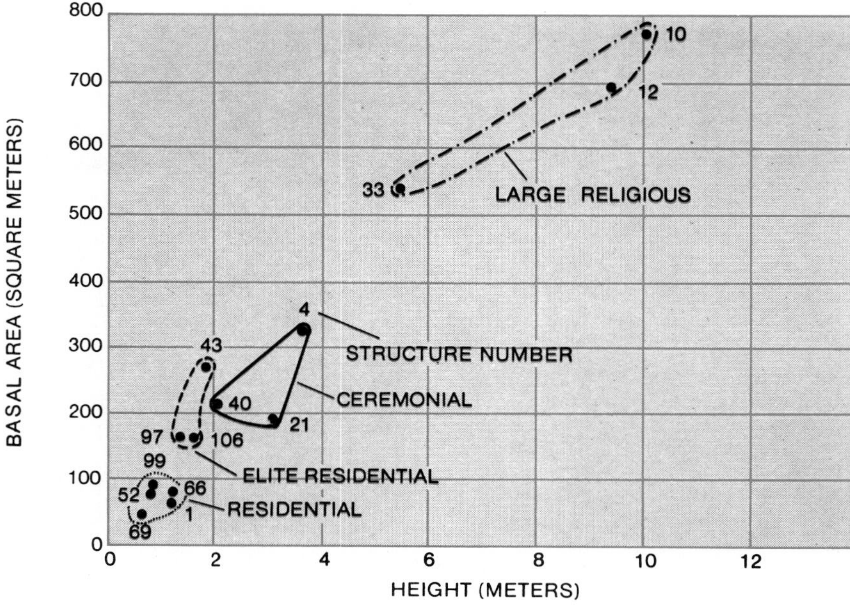

MEASUREMENT OF THE STRUCTURES at Lubaantún showed a proportional relation between height and basal area. When both measurements are plotted on a graph, the structures typically fall within one of four clusters. The pyramids of Plaza IV cover the most area and are the highest of all the structures at the site. Adjacent to the more remote plazas were the lowest and smallest structures; these had presumably been house foundations. Of the structures in two intermediate clusters, the higher were probably foundations for buildings that served "ceremonial" purposes; the lower may have been occupied by the elite.

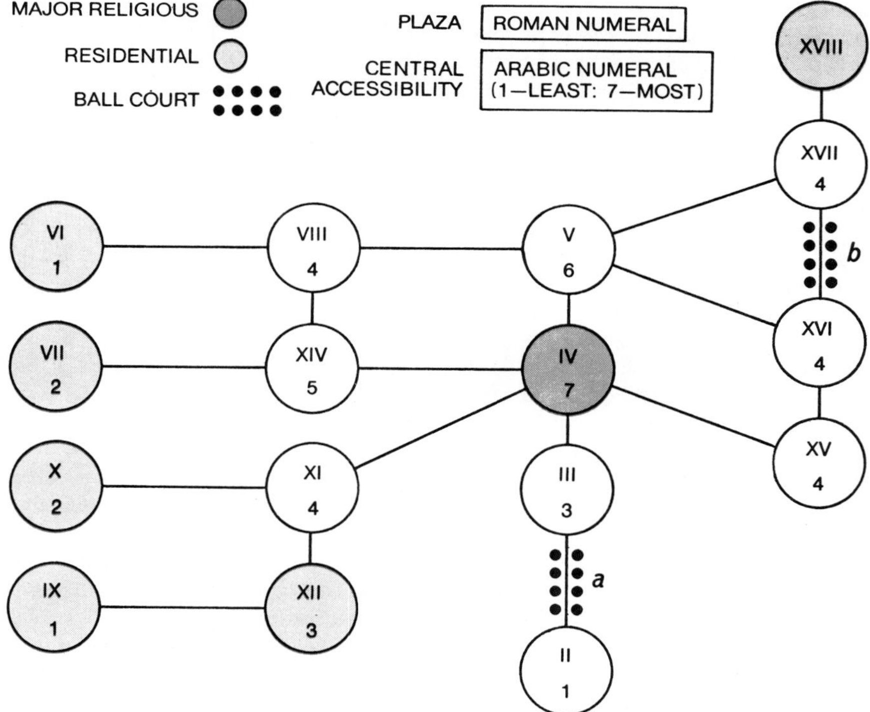

PLANAR GRAPH OF THE PRINCIPAL PLAZAS at Lubaantún and their interconnections allowed a topological analysis of the accessibility and centrality of each. An index of central accessibility showed that Plaza IV, the religious center of the site, was the most centrally accessible, with a maximum index value of 7. Of the eight least accessible plazas, all with an index value no greater than 3, six were bordered by small, low structures that were probably occupied by houses. A major difference is evident between the first ball court at the site, which was quite private (*a*), and the second, which was more public (*b*).

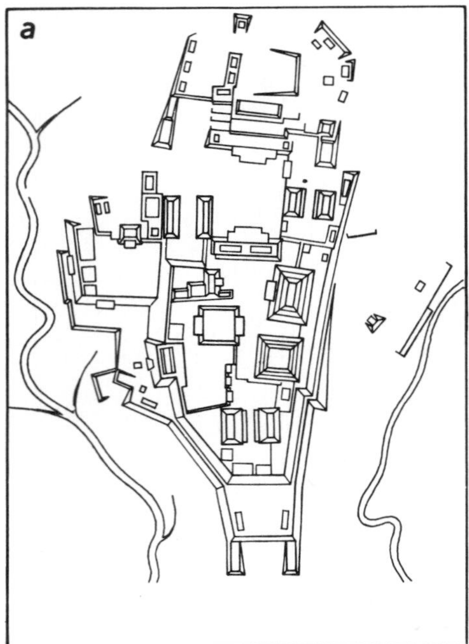

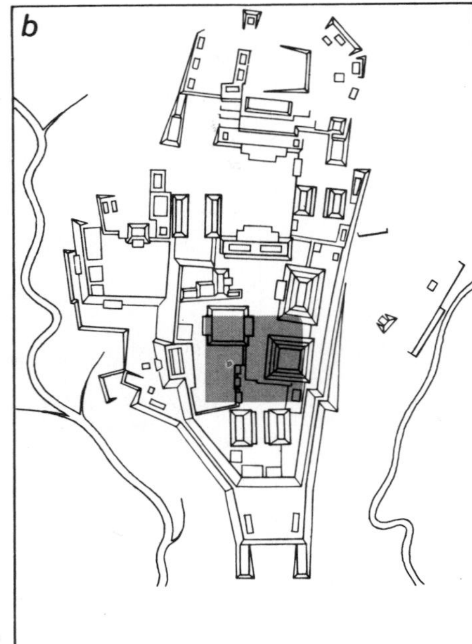

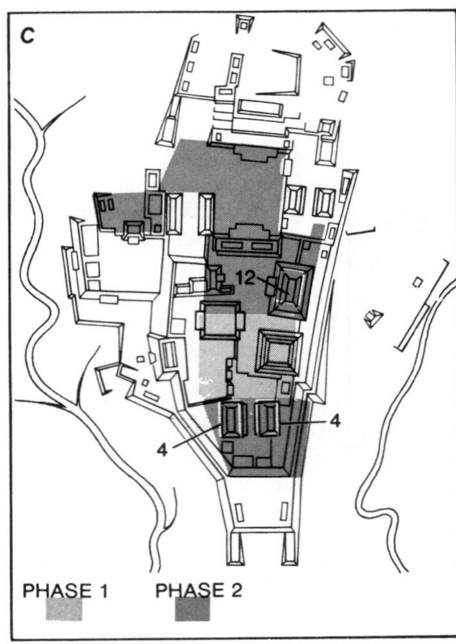

LUBAANTÚN GREW in the five phases outlined in this sequence of illustrations. The center after its completion is shown schematically at far left (*a*). In the first construction phase (*b*) a rectangular platform covering 2,500 square meters was built astride the north-south ridge that forms the long axis of the site. During the second phase (*c*) another platform was added to the south of the first, and plaza areas and a third platform were added to the north. The first pyramid at the site was built on one side of the north platform and the first ball court was built on the south platform. During the third phase (*d*) a southerly addition to the north plat-

abled us to calculate for each plaza an index of centrality and an index of accessibility. Combined, these indexes provided a rating of central-accessibility that ranged from a minimum value of 1 to a maximum value of 7.

We then compared the topological analysis with our estimates of the functions served by the various plazas. Our hypothesis of low accessibility in residential areas was confirmed. The most secluded of all the plazas, with the minimum rating of 1, were the plazas numbered VI, IX and XVIII, which we had classified as residential, and Plaza II, which we had classified as ceremonial. The next most secluded, with ratings of 2 or 3, were the residential plazas numbered VII, X and XII and a second ceremonial plaza, Plaza III. The most centrally accessible plaza at the site, with the maximum rating of 7, proved to be Plaza IV, the religious center of the site.

The fact that two ceremonial plazas, Plaza III and Plaza II, were among those with minimal accessibility ratings meant that the site layout called for a striking decline in accessibility southward along the central axis of Lubaantún. The accessibility rating of Plaza III is four points lower than the rating of its neighboring plaza to the north, and the rating of Plaza II is the minimum possible. Since these two plazas form the end zones of the first ball court built at Lubaantún and because the ball court can only be reached by way of Plaza IV, the site's religious center, the question arises: Were playing and watching the ball game restricted activities?

It is known from early Spanish accounts that the Maya ball game had ritual overtones; sculptures at Chichén Itzá indicate that some matches even ended with the sacrifice of the losing players. Taking this evidence and the restricted access at Lubaantún into consideration, it seems probable that if any part of the religious practice during the early days at the ceremonial center was confined to the elite, that part was the ball game.

The Spanish accounts, however, indicate that for all its ritual overtones the ball game was open to public view. This suggests that the fact the second ball court at Lubaantún, the one constructed late in the history of the center, is located in a much more public part of the center is significant. The second court lies just off Plaza V, a highly accessible area: plazas XVII and XVIII, which are its end zones, also rate high in accessibility. Perhaps a change in Maya attitudes regarding the esoteric nature of the game occurred in the interval between the building of the first court and the building of the second. If that is what happened, the trend toward a more public ritual that seems evident in the middle of the ninth century at Lubaantún persisted throughout the post-Classic period and on down to the time of the Conquest.

In summary, the traffic-flow analysis confirmed our commonsense hypothesis that the center's residential areas were secluded and its public areas more accessible. Concerning the question of whether the religious observances were public or restricted, common sense had identified Plaza IV, with its three pyramids, as the religious center of Lubaantún. By showing that Plaza IV was also the most accessible plaza at the site, traffic analysis suggests unrestricted public access to religious activities.

Plaza V, just to the north, ranks next in accessibility. This open area, with its broad stairways, is perhaps the most spacious of all the plazas at Lubaantún, and its high accessibility strengthens our suspicion that, with or without the contiguous Plaza VIII, this was the marketplace for the center. Finally, the fact that for a century or more the only ball court at Lubaantún was an area with sharply restricted access suggests that, at least until very late in Classic times, the ball game was confined to an elite group within a well-stratified society.

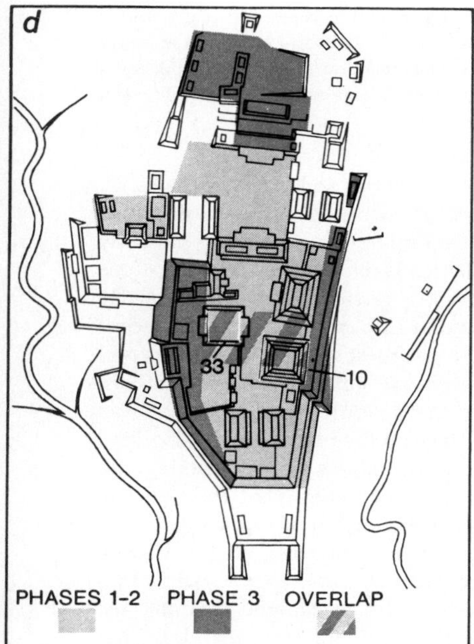

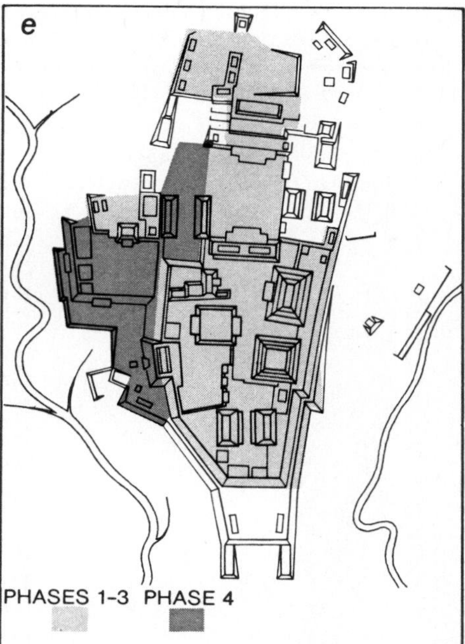

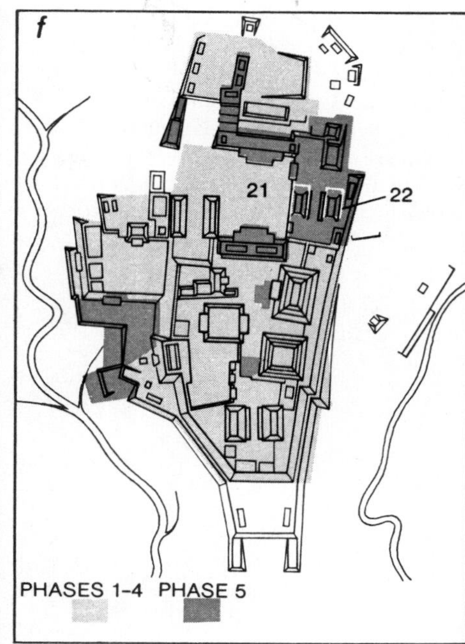

form covered up most of the first-phase platform at the site, and adequate foundations for two more pyramids were provided by new platforms built over the steep east and west slopes of the ridge. Construction in the fourth phase (*e*) included a series of platforms on the west slope that descended almost to the creek at the bottom of the ridge. In the final phase the main construction (*f*) consisted of a second ball court east of Plaza V and new staircases for Plaza V and for Structure 12, the first of the pyramids at the center. Growth of the center to the east and west regardless of the immense cost indicates the builders' adherence to a fixed plan.

Perhaps it is not too much to propose here a wider archaeological application of assessments of this kind. Analysis of the centrality and accessibility of the different areas that make up "palace" complexes in, for example, Mesopotamia or Crete or Mycenaean Greece might suggest functions quite different from those enshrined in long accepted but essentially poetic phrases such as "the queen's antechamber" or "lustral area."

Why was Lubaantún built where it was? The answer to the question is suggested by the results both of our mapping and ecological surveys and of our excavations. These show that the influence of the ceremonial center was felt not only adjacent to but well away from the site itself. Most of the low, round-topped hills on all sides of Lubaantún are surmounted by small masonry and rubble platforms; the dressed-stone retaining walls are one or two meters high and the rubble serves to level off the summit. These structures, on a smaller scale, are exactly like the great platforms at Lubaantún. Furthermore, they support house foundations in numbers sufficient to indicate that 1,200 to 1,300 people resided within a one-kilometer radius of the ceremonial center. This is scarcely a large population, but it is as densely concentrated as the local topography permits.

These hill platforms and house foundations represent a social investment in labor and materials that, although it is dispersed, is comparable to the more concentrated investment that produced the complex structures of the ceremonial center. The scale of the work also implies an adequate supply of food for the inhabitants of the district, which suggests in turn that location of the center in the belt of fertile soil along the foothills of the Maya Mountains was scarcely accidental.

Why was the center built, however, at precisely this place? The soil zone extends a considerable distance to both the northeast and the southwest, which suggests that factors in addition to the prospect of good crops must have entered into the decision to build the center here. One of the factors must have been the propinquity of the site to the Rio Columbia. Not only was the stream a source of water and the mollusks from it a reliable source of protein (their shells appeared by the thousands in our excavations) but also the head of navigation by canoe lies near Lubaantún. Goods coming upstream from the Caribbean would have been transferred from canoe to porter in this area. Moreover, this spot is also where the main overland trail along the base of the foothills crosses the river. Lubaantún was thus in a position to control canoe traffic to and from the coast and overland traffic along the foothills. In effect, the center dominated the entire Rio Grande basin, a "realm" extending for some 50 kilometers from the high plateau of the Maya Mountains southeastward to the Caribbean shore. The entire realm is some 1,600 square kilometers in extent; its population may have numbered as many as 50,000.

Our excavations made it clear that Lubaantún was the center of a flourishing regional marketing system. From the Maya Mountains came the metamorphic rock used to make not only axe heads of stone but also the *manos,* or stone rollers, and *metates,* or shallow stone troughs, that are used together to grind maize. From the Caribbean coast, which was as far away in the opposite direction, came marine shells used for ornaments and the seafood that forms such a high percentage of the animal remains at the site. In addition, trade extended far beyond the frontiers of the realm. Two sources in the highlands of Guatemala, identified by Fred H. Stross of the University of California at Berkeley, provided obsidian, which can be flaked into fine blades with a razor-sharp edge. Also from the highlands came tripod *metates* made of lava. From the south came plumes from the cock quetzal to adorn the rulers of Lubaantún and from an unidentified highland source came jade for their jewels.

In exchange for these imports the inhabitants of Lubaantún evidently traded the beans of the cacao tree, which are used to make chocolate and were the universal currency of Middle America in pre-Columbian times. As I have noted, the soil around Lubaantún is fertile. A study of all the soils in the region in terms of their utility to the Maya of the Classic period was conducted recently by Charles Wright of the United Nations Food and Agriculture Organization. He found that Lubaantún stands in the center of the largest zone of top-quality soil for cacao-tree culture in all of southern Belize. As Spanish records attest, cacao beans were traded between this lowland area and the highlands of Guatemala in post-Conquest times. That the tree and its fruit were known in Lubaantún is apparent from a figurine of the Classic period excavated there; it depicts a musician wearing a cacao-pod pendant [*see illustration at left*]. It seems clear that the prosperity of the realm was in large measure due to its possession of one of the sources of this scarce product, which was in constant demand. The trade with the Guatemalan highlands, where a completely different range of resources was available, was in many ways a form of economic symbiosis, existing for the mutual benefit of both partners and fostering diplomatic as well as commercial contacts that it was mutually useful to maintain.

CEREMONIAL CENTER at Lubaantún consisted of 11 major structures and many minor ones grouped around 20 plazas. A number of these are identified in the map on the opposite page by Arabic and Roman numerals respectively. Construction of the center began in the eighth century after Christ, late in the Classic Maya period, and continued for 150 years.

MUSICIAN WEARING A PENDANT in the form of a pod from the cacao tree is the subject of a figurine of the Classic period found at Lubaantún. Evidence that cacao was known to the people of Lubaantún, taken together with evidence that local soils are particularly suited to raising cacao trees, suggests that cacao beans were exchanged for foreign imports.

The question of why Lubaantún was built when it was remains unanswered. The entire Rio Grande basin appears to have been unoccupied territory until the eighth century, when the center was founded. So far not a single object made before Late Classic times, not even a potsherd, has been discovered at any site in the region. To the southwest of the Rio Grande basin another Maya site, a ceremonial center named Pusilhà, has been discovered in the basin of the Moho River. Some 20 stelae have been found there; the dates they bear range from A.D. 573 to 731. Pusilhà was therefore functioning as a ceremonial center during all of the seventh century. Moreover, the most recent of the Pusilhà stelae dates and the presence there of Lubaantún-style figurines show that the center was still occupied well after the foundation of Lubaantún.

Pusilhà was flourishing before Lubaantún was even built. This fact has given rise to a number of cause-and-effect hypotheses. According to one of them, the Maya who built Lubaantún were former residents of the Pusilhà realm who migrated northward as a re-

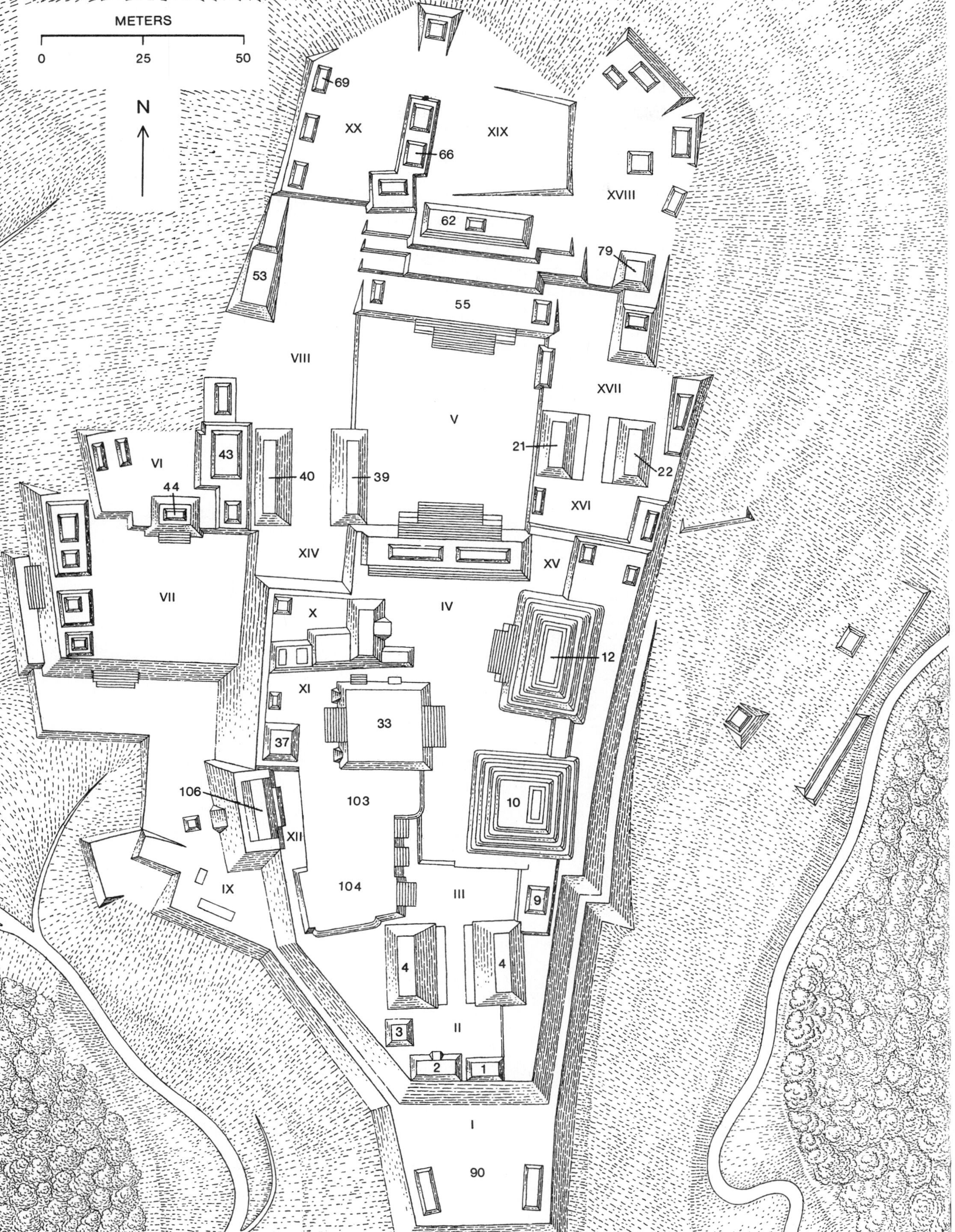
METERS
0
25
50
N
XX
XIX
XVIII
69
66
62
79
53
55
VIII
XVII
V
VI
43
40
39
21
22
44
XVI
XIV
XV
VII
X
IV
12
XI
33
37
10
106
103
XII
IX
104
III
9
4
4
3
II
2
1
I
90

sult of population pressure or political expansion within or beyond that realm. Another hypothesis, first advanced in 1938 by Sylvanus Griswold Morley, suggested that political control had been transferred from Pusilhà to Lubaantún in the eighth century, the time when the Maya at Pusilhà ceased to raise stelae. According to the Morley hypothesis, the halt in stela-raising was evidence that the use of Pusilhà as a ceremonial center had also ceased.

The Morley hypothesis, applied more generally, has been the controlling model for much of the speculation about the collapse of Classic Maya civilization. In this view the end of the "stela cult" at each ceremonial center marked the end of the religious, political, administrative and commercial control exerted by the realm's rulers. Our studies at Lubaantún cast doubt on that line of speculation. Although this Late Classic ceremonial center exerted control over a wide realm for some 150 years, not one stela, sculptured or plain, appears to have been raised there. It thus seems clear that the presence of the stela cult was not crucial to the exercise of effective religious, political and commercial control. If a center such as Lubaantún could flourish without instituting such a cult, then other ceremonial centers could have continued to exercise authority after stelae were no longer raised. Excavation at Maya sites of the Classic period to obtain articles for carbon-14 or thermoluminescence analysis might well shed more light on the decline of Maya civilization than do hypotheses that depend on the terminal dates preserved on stelae.

The stelae cult might better be viewed as a product of ideological fashion than as an integral part of the social and economic infrastructure that supported the culture of the Maya for more than 2,000 years. Maya ceremonial centers, if Lubaantún is a fair example, drew their power not so much from the gods as from the integration of a broad range of economic resources. The economic effort may often have included, as it did at Lubaantún, the exploitation of a commodity in great demand. Seen in this light the Maya ceremonial center seems to have been more the focus of a regional marketing system and, as a result, a seat of administrative and political power than the headquarters of a primarily religious institution. In almost every aspect except population density the Maya centers equate in form and function with the preindustrial cities of the Old World.

The Flow of Energy in a Hunting Society

31

by William B. Kemp
September 1971

Early man obtained food and fuel from the wild plants and animals of his environment. How the energy from such sources is channeled is investigated in a community of modern Eskimos on Baffin Island

The investment of energy in hunting and gathering has provided man's livelihood for more than 99 percent of human history. Over the past 10,000 years the investment of energy in agriculture, with its higher yield per unit of input, has transformed most hunting peoples into farmers. Among the most viable of the remaining hunters are the Eskimos of Alaska, Canada and Greenland. What are the characteristic patterns of energy flow in a hunting group? How is the available energy channeled among the various activities of the group in order for the group to survive? In 1967 and 1968 I undertook to study such energy flows in an isolated Eskimo village in the eastern Canadian Arctic.

I observed two village households in particular. When I lived in the village, one of the two households was characterized by its "modern" ways; the other was more "traditional." I was able to measure the energy inputs and energy yields of both households in considerable detail. (The quantitative data presented here are based on observations made during a 54-week period from February 14, 1967, to March 1, 1968.) The different patterns of energy use exhibited by the two households help to illuminate the process of adaptation to nonhunting systems of livelihood and social behavior that faces all contemporary hunting societies.

For the Eskimos the most significant factor in the realignment of economic and social activity has been the introduction of a cash economy. The maintenance of a hunting way of life within the framework of such an economy calls for a new set of adaptive strategies. Money, or its immediate equivalent, is now an important component in the relation between the Eskimo hunter and the natural environment.

The village where I worked is one of the few remaining all-Eskimo settlements along the southern coast of Baffin Island on the northern side of Hudson Strait [*see illustrations on next page*]. In this village hunting still dominates the general pattern of daily activity. The economic adaptation is supported by the household routine of the women and is reflected in the play of the children. Villages of this type were once the characteristic feature of the settlement pattern of southern Baffin Island. Within recent years, however, many Eskimos have abandoned the solitary life in favor of larger and more acculturated settlements.

The community I studied is in an area of indented coastline that runs in a northwesterly direction extending from about 63 to 65 degrees north latitude. The land rises sharply from the shore to an interior plateau that is deeply incised by valleys, many containing streams and lakes that serve as the only routes for overland travel. At these latitudes summer activities can proceed during some 22 hours of daylight; the longest winter night lasts 18 hours. Perhaps the most noticeable feature of the Hudson Strait environment is tides of as much as 45 feet. Such tides create a large littoral environment; bays become empty valleys, islands appear and disappear and strong ocean currents prevail. In winter the tides build rough barriers of broken sea ice, and at low tide the steeper shorelines are edged with sheer ice walls. In summer coastal navigation and the selection of safe harbors are difficult, and in winter crossing from the sea ice to the land tries the temper of men and the strength of dogs and machines.

The varying length of the day, the seasonal changes of temperature, the tides and to some extent the timing of the annual freeze-up and breakup are predictable events, easily built into the round of economic activity. Superimposed on these events is the variability and irregularity of temperature, moisture and wind, which affect the pattern of energy flow for the community on a day-to-day basis. In winter the temperatures reach −50 degrees Fahrenheit, with a mean around −30. In summer the temperature may climb above 80 degrees, although temperatures in the low 50's are more typical. Throughout the year there may be large temperature changes from one day to the next. Midwinter temperatures have gone from −30 degrees to above freezing in a single night, bringing a thaw and sometimes even rain.

The heaviest precipitation is in the spring and fall, and strong winds can arise any day throughout the year. Winds of more than 40 miles per hour are common; on four occasions I measured steady winds in excess of 70 m.p.h. Speaking generally, the weather is most stable in March and April and least stable from late September into November.

Within this setting the Eskimos harvest at least 20 species of game. All the marine and terrestrial food chains are exploited in the quest for food, and all habitats—from the expanses of sea ice and open water to the microhabitats of tidal flats, leeward waters and protected valleys—are utilized. Traditionally the Eskimos of southern Baffin Island are mainly hunters of sea mammals: the small common (or ring) seal, the much larger bearded seal and on occasion the beluga whale and the walrus.

Survival in such a harsh environment has two primary requirements. The first is an adequate caloric intake in terms of food and the second is maintenance of a suitable microclimate in terms of shelter and clothing. In the village where I worked the Eskimos met these require-

BAFFIN ISLAND extends for nearly 1,000 miles in the area between the mouth of Hudson Bay and the Greenland coast. The villagers' hunting ranges lie within the black rectangle.

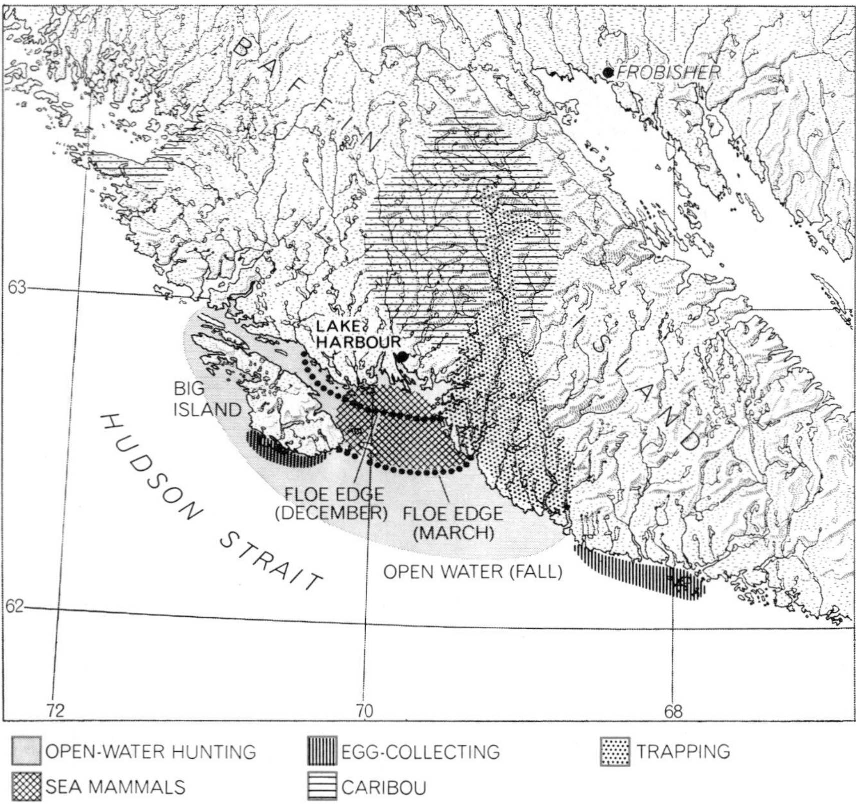

HUNTING RANGES of one Eskimo village in southern Baffin Island change with the season. The most productive months of the year are spent hunting in coastal waters. Trapping and caribou hunting, generally winter activities, carry the hunters into different areas.

ments by hunting and trapping and by buying imported foods and materials. They also bought ammunition for their guns and gasoline for two marine engines and two snowmobiles, transportation aids that increased their hunting efficiency. The money for such purchases was obtained by the sale of skins and furs (products of the hunt) and of stone and ivory carvings (products of artistic skill and of the Eskimos' recognition of consumer preferences). Because government "social assistance" and some work for wages were available, certain individuals had an occasional source of additional cash.

The daily maintenance of life in the village called for an initial input of human energy in the pursuit of game, in the mining of soapstone and in the manufacture of handicrafts. The expenditures of human energy for the 54-week period were 12.8 million kilocalories. They were augmented by expenditures of imported energy: 10,900 rounds of ammunition and 885 gallons of gasoline. The result was the acquisition of 12.8 million kilocalories of edible food from the land and seven million kilocalories of viscera that were used as dog food. To this was added 7.5 million kilocalories of purchased food. By eating the game and the purchased food the hunters and their dependents were able to achieve a potential caloric input of 3,000 kilocalories per day, which was enough to sustain a level of activity well above the maintenance level. The general pattern of energy flow into, through and out of the village is shown in the illustration on pages 294 and 295.

During my stay the population of the village varied between 26 and 29. The people lived in four separate dwellings. One, a wood house, had been built from prefabricated materials supplied by the government. The other three were the traditional *quagmaq:* a low wood-frame tent some 20 feet long, 15 feet wide and seven feet high. These structures were covered with canvas, old mailbags and animal skins and were insulated with a 10-inch layer of dry shrubs. Inside they were lined with pages from mail-order catalogues and decorated with a fantastic array of trinkets and other objects. The rear eight feet of each *quagmaq* was occupied by a large sleeping platform, leaving some 180 square feet for household activities during waking hours. The wood house (Household II) was occupied by six people comprising a single family unit. One *quagmaq* (Household I) was occupied by nine people: a widower, his son, three

BEARDED SEAL (*left*) is a relatively uncommon and welcome kill. It weighs more than 400 pounds, compared with the common seal's 80 pounds, and its skin is a favorite material. Flat-bottomed rowboat (*rear*) is used to retrieve seals killed at the floe-ice edge.

daughters, a son-in-law and three grandchildren.

The *quagmaq* was heated in the traditional manner with stone lamps that burned seal oil. The occupants of the wood house heated it with a kerosene stove. In a period when the highest outdoor temperature during the day was −30 degrees, I measured the consumption of fuel and recorded the indoor temperatures of the wood house and the *quagmaq*. The *quagmaq* was heated by three stone lamps, two at each side of the sleeping platform and one near the entrance. In a 24-hour period the three lamps burned some 250 ounces (slightly less than two imperial gallons) of seal oil. The fat from a 100-pound seal shot in midwinter yields approximately 640 ounces of oil, which is about a 60-hour supply at this rate of consumption. The interior temperature of the *quagmaq* never rose above 68 degrees. The average was around 56 degrees, with troughs in the low 30's because the lamps were not tended through the night.

In the wood house the kerosene stove burned a little less than three imperial gallons every 24 hours. This represented a daily expenditure of about $1 for fuel oil during the winter months. (Since 1969 this cost has been fully subsidized by the government.) The interior temperature of the house sometimes reached 80 degrees, and the nightly lows were seldom below 70. One result of the difference between the indoor and outdoor temperature—frequently more than 100 degrees—was that the members of Household II complained that they were uncomfortably warm, particularly when they were carving or doing some other kind of moderately strenuous work.

Before the Eskimos of southern Baffin Island had acquired outboard motors, snowmobiles and a reliable supply of fuel they shifted their settlements with the seasons. Fall campsites were the most stable element in the settlement pattern and were the location for the *quagmaq* shelters. During the rest of the year the size and location of the camps depended on which of the food resources were being exploited.

The movements of settlements to resources served to minimize the distance a hunter needed to travel in a day. Thus little energy was wasted traversing unproductive terrain, and good hunting weather could be exploited immediately. This is no longer the practice. Long trips by the hunters are common, but seasonal movements involving an entire household are rare. Therefore the location of the village never shifts. The four dwellings of the village I studied are more or less occupied throughout the year. Tents are still used in summer, but they are set up within sight of the winter houses. There is a major move each August, when the villagers set up camp at the trading post, a day's journey from the village. There they await the coming of the annual medical and supply ships and also take advantage of any wage labor that may be available.

The hunters' ability to get to the right place at the right time is ensured by a large whaleboat with a small inboard engine, a 22-foot freight canoe driven by a 20-horsepower outboard motor, and the two snowmobiles. In addition the villagers have several large sledges and keep 34 sled dogs. The impact of motorized transport (particularly of the marine engines) on the stability of year-round residence and on the increase in hunting productivity is evident in the remark of an older man: "As my son gets motors for the boats, we are always living here. As my son always gets animals we are no longer hungry. Do you know what I mean?"

The threat of hunger is a frequent theme in village conversation, but the oral tradition that serves as history gives little evidence of constant privation for the population of southern Baffin Island. Although older men and women tell stories of hard times, the fear of starvation did not generate the kind of social response known elsewhere. In the more hostile parts of the Arctic female infanticide was common well into the first quarter of this century. The existence of the practice is supported by statistical data compiled by Edward M. Weyer, Jr., in 1932. For example, among the Netsilik Eskimos the ratio of females to males in the population younger than 19 was 48 per 100; in the Barren Grounds area the ratio was 46 per 100.

Census data from Baffin Island in 1912 indicate that female infanticide was not common along the southern coast. In that year a missionary recorded the population for the region; the total was some 400 Eskimos. Among those younger than 19 there were 89 females per 100 males. Among those 19 or older the ratio was 127 females per 100 males; hunters often had short lives. The vital statistics that have been kept since 1927 by the Royal Canadian Mounted Police support the impression that death by starvation was a rare occurrence on southern Baffin Island. On the other hand, hunting accidents were the cause of 15 percent of the deaths. The causes of trouble or death most usually cited by the villagers were peculiarities of the weather, ice conditions and mishaps of the hunt. Starvation was commonplace in the dog population, but for human groups disasters were local. A 75-year-old resident of the southern coast was able to recall only one year when severe hunger affected a large segment of the population.

A major factor in reducing the possibility of hunger is the Eskimos' increasing access to imported goods. Although store foods are obviously of prime importance in this respect, energy in the form of gasoline for fuel is also significant. The snowmobiles in the village are owned by an individual in each household, but all the hunters help to buy the gasoline needed to run these machines and the marine engines. The two snowmobiles consumed about twice as much fuel as the two boat motors. A snowmobile pulling a loaded sled can run for about 35 minutes on a gallon of gasoline. A trip from the village to the edge of the floe ice 10 miles away took 55 minutes in each direction and cost nearly $3.

Variations in fuel purchases are not necessarily correlated with variations in hunting yield or cash income. Debt can be used to overcome fluctuations in income, and the desire to visit distant relatives may be as important a consideration as the need to hunt. The largest monthly gasoline purchase was made in September, 1967. Wages paid for construction work were used to buy a combined total of 170 gallons of gasoline.

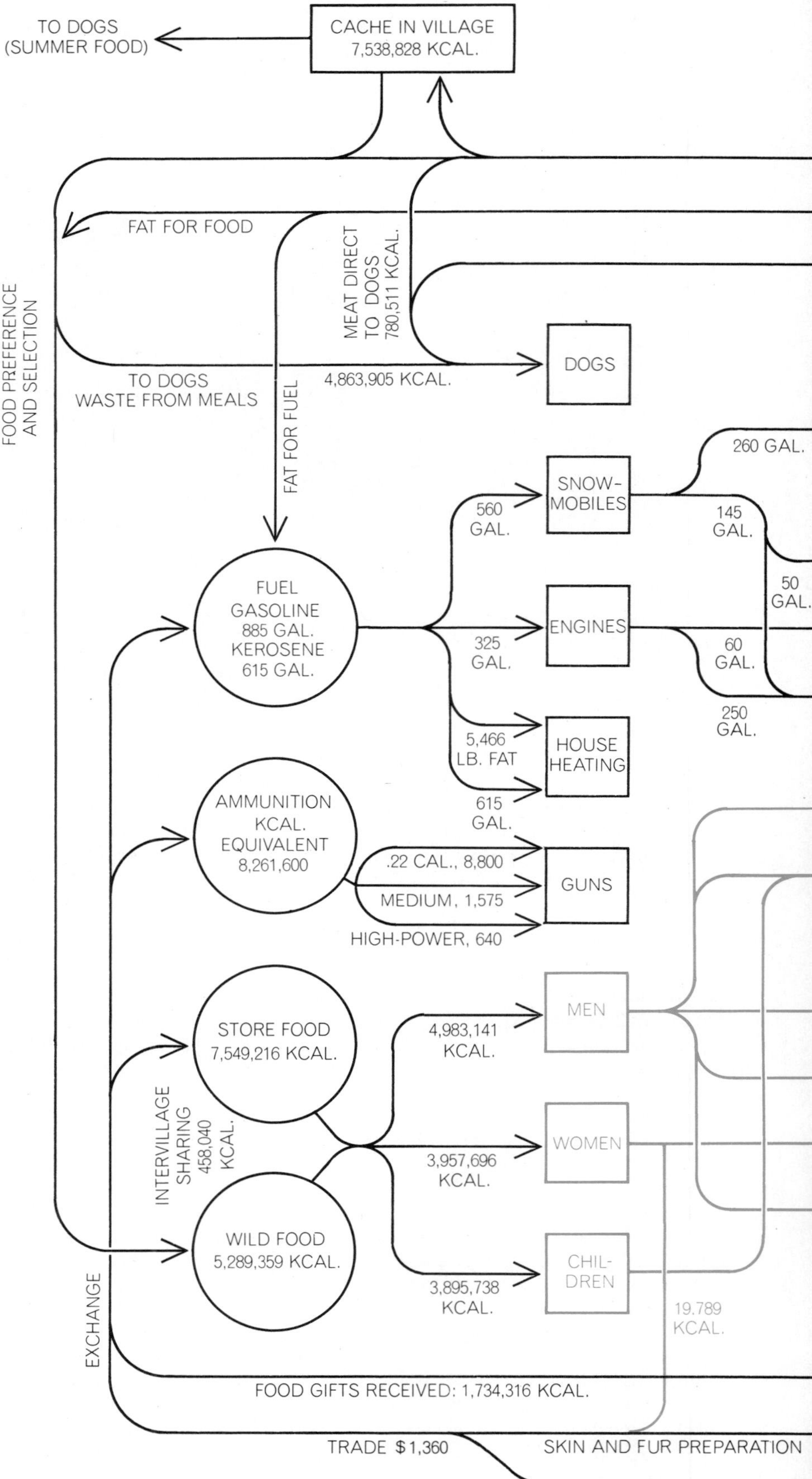

FLOW OF ENERGY within two hunting households is outlined in this diagram. The inputs and yields were recorded by the author in kilocalories and other units during his 13-month residence in an Eskimo hunting village. The input of imported energy in the form of fuel and ammunition, along with the input of native game and imported foodstuffs (*far*

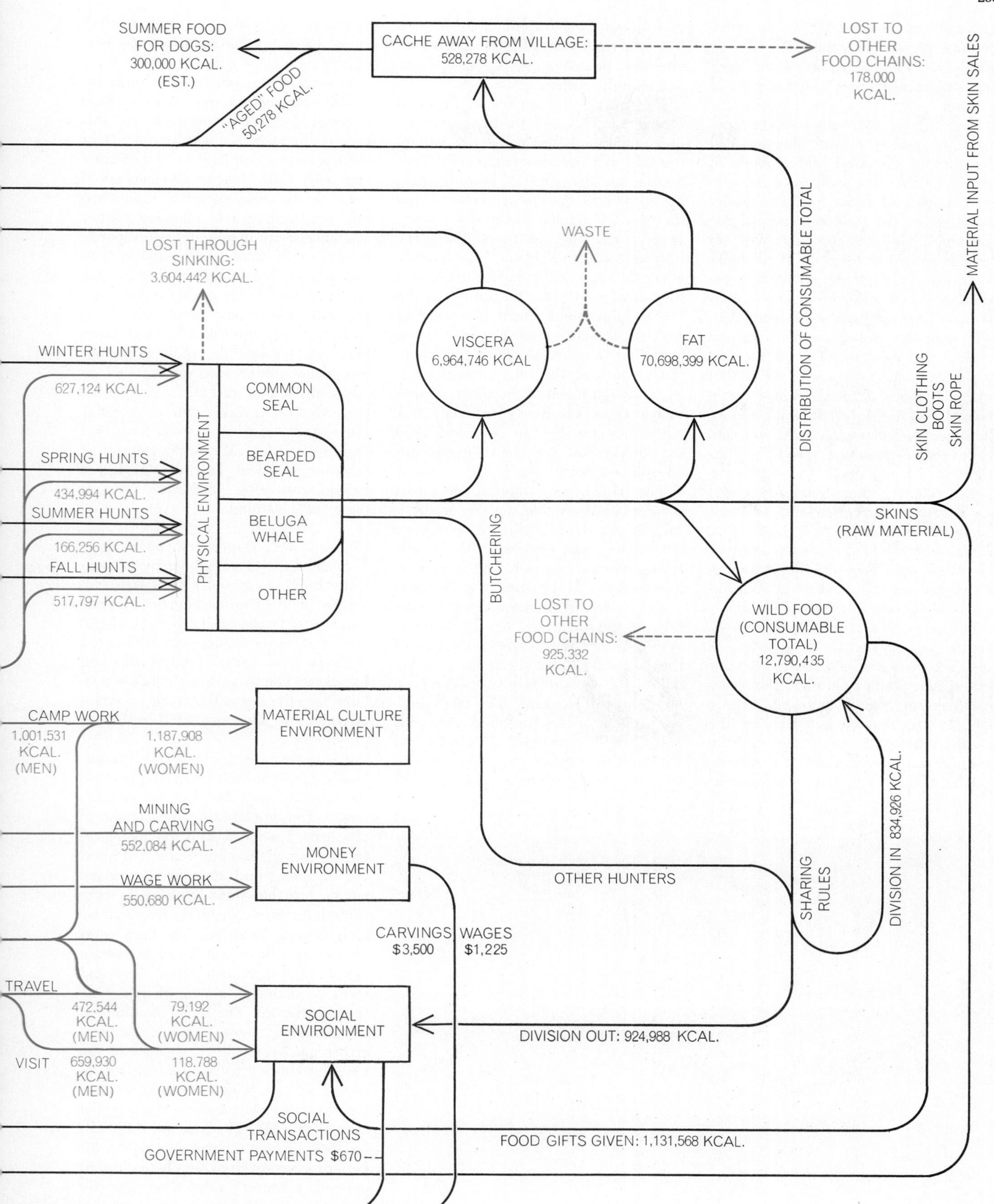

left), enabled the four hunters and their kin (*left, color*) to heat their dwellings and power their machines (*left, black*), and also to join in many seasonal activities (*colored arrows*) that utilized various parts of the environment in the manner indicated (*right*). The end results of these combined inputs of energy are shown as a series of yields and losses from waste and other causes (*far right*). The net yields then feed back through various channels (*lines at borders of diagram*) to reach the starting point again as inputs.

This fuel was utilized for the intensive hunting of sea mammals in order to make up for a summer when the Eskimos had been earning wages instead of hunting.

Hunting was a year-long village occupation in spite of considerable seasonal variation in the kind and amount of game available. An analysis of the species represented in the Eskimos' annual kill confirms the predominance of sea mammals. The common seal (with an average weight of 80 pounds) provided nearly two-thirds of the villagers' game calories. When one adds bearded seals (with an average weight of more than 400 pounds) and occasional beluga whales, the sea mammals' contribution was more than 83 percent of the annual total. Caribou accounted for a little more than 4 percent of the total, and all the other land mammals together came to less than 1 percent. Indeed, the contribution of eider ducks and duck eggs to the villagers' diet (some 7 percent) was larger than that of all land mammals combined. The harvest of birds, fish, clams and small land mammals may not contribute significantly to the total number of calories, but it does provide diversity in hunting activities and in diet.

The common seal is hunted throughout the year and is the basic source of food for both the Eskimos and their dogs. From January through March sea mammals are hunted first at breathing holes in the sea ice and then at the boundary between open water and the landfast ice. The intensity of sea-mammal hunting during the winter months varies according to the amount of food left over from the fall hunt and the alternative prospects for trapping foxes and hunting caribou.

In winter some variety in the food supply is provided by the hunting of sea birds and small land mammals, but for the most part seal meat remains the basic item in the diet. In April hunting along the edge of the floe ice is intensified, and the canoe is hauled to the open water beyond the floe ice for hunting the bearded seals. In May and June hunting along the edge of the floe ice (on foot or by canoe) continues; the quarry is the seal and the beluga whale. In late spring seals are also stalked as they bask on top of the ice. By the middle of July open-water hunting is the most common activity, although much of the potential harvest is lost because the animals sink when they are shot. In 1967 and 1968 the villagers lost five whales, five bearded seals and 47 common seals.

The sinking of marine mammals serves to illustrate the interplay of physical, biological and technological factors the hunter must contend with. In late spring the seal begins to fast and therefore loses fat. At the same time the melting of snow and sea ice reduces the salinity of the surface waters. These interacting factors reduce the buoyancy of the seal, and a killed seal is likely to sink unless it is immediately secured with a hand-thrown harpoon. The high-powered rifle separates the hunter from his prey; it may increase the frequency of kill but it does not increase the frequency of harvest. In 30 hours of continuous hunting on July 20 and 21 only five out of the 13 seals killed were actually harvested.

From May through July the hunts are usually successful, even with sinkage losses as high as 60 percent. It is at this time of the year that a large amount of meat goes into dog food for the summer and early fall. Meat is also cached in areas the Eskimos expect to visit when they are trapping the following winter. The caches are deliberately only partly secured with rocks; their purpose is to bait areas of potential trapping. In May the variety of foods begins to increase. Seabirds, ptarmigans, geese, fish, clams and duck eggs are taken in large numbers and become the most important component of the food input. Only an occasional seal or the edible skin of a beluga whale is carried home to eat. The great variety of small game is consumed within a few days. With the exception of duck eggs, about half of which are cached until after Christmas, none of these foods is stored.

In September the sea mammals again become the primary objective. Open-water hunting continues until early November, when the sea begins to freeze. Just before freeze-up the beluga whales pass close to the village and are hunted from the shore with the aid of rifles and harpoons. The success of the fall whale-hunting is the key to the villagers' evaluation of the adequacy of their winter provisions.

As the sea ice thickens and extends, hunting seals at their breathing holes in the bays becomes the most common activity. The unfavorable interaction of physical, biological and technological factors that affects open-water seal-hunting in spring and summer is reversed where breathing-hole hunting is concerned. As the sea begins to freeze, some seals migrate away from the land in order to stay in open water. Others remain closer to the shore, using their claws and teeth to maintain a cone-shaped hole through the ice. The seal's breathing is now confined to specific points the hunter can easily find on the surface of the ice. The hunting technique calls for locating the breathing holes and distributing the available men to maximize the chance of a kill. The hunting skill calls for the patience to wait motionless for periods of as much as two hours and to depend on hearing rather than sight. By mid-December the new ice is covered by a deep layer of drifting snow, and the breathing holes become harder to locate. The Eskimos then move out to the edge of the floe ice and the seasonal cycle be-

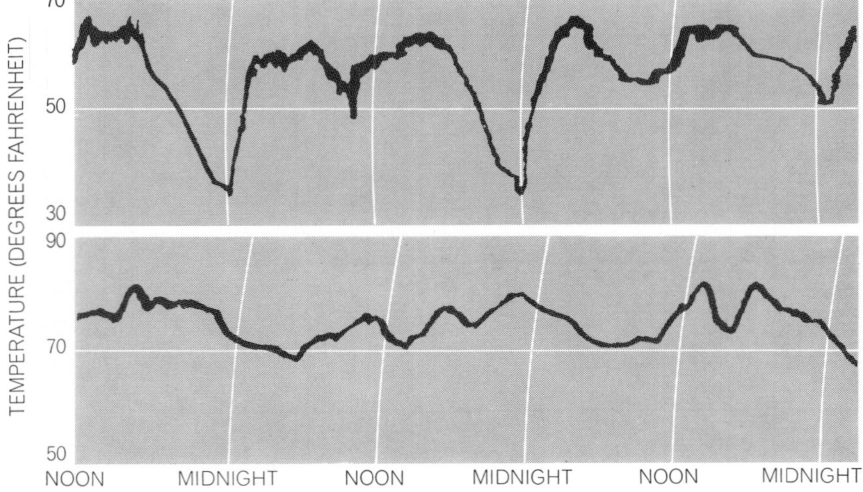

CONTRASTING METHODS of heating maintained different house microclimates with the consumption of different amounts of fuel. In Household I (*top*), the more traditional one, the use of three lamps that burned seal oil produced an average temperature of 58 degrees F. A kerosene stove (*bottom*) in the more modern Household II kept the average closer to 75 degrees. As a result Household II used three gallons a day to the other's two.

gins anew.

The analysis of hunting success on a month-to-month basis shows great variability in the total caloric input and in each member's contribution to the total [*see illustration on page 300*]. The peak hunting months for the two households were June (some 2.5 million kilocalories), October (more than three million) and November (2.9 million). Stockpiling provides the motivation for the big October and November kills. Game taken in these months will remain frozen and unspoiled through the winter and will help to feed the hunters and their dependents in February, March and April.

In the fall days grow short and winds often restrict the choice of hunting areas. Daylight hours are utilized to the full, and the evening darkness is filled with the sound of the hunters struggling to get their catch across the difficult terrain of the tidal flats. In this period almost all the food is brought back to the village; it is stored in a small meat house, on elevated platforms, under the hulls of old boats and on top of the wood house. A few of the seals shot in early fall are cached on the land in order for the meat to "age." These carcasses are retrieved in the spring, and the meat is considered one of the more flavorsome food inputs.

The large kill in June results from the fact that the daylight hours are at a maximum and that there is a much greater choice of resources. If weather conditions hamper open-water hunting, basking seals can be pursued. Under conditions of severe wind or poor ice, spearfishing for arctic char is possible and duck eggs can be collected. Summer hunts last for three or four days; the hunters sleep during the few hours of least light or during brief pauses in the hunt. Game killed in June will thaw in the summer months, so that almost all the two million kilocalories of sea mammals harvested that month is destined for the dogs.

Compared with the high caloric inputs of the spring and fall, winter hunting is much less productive in terms of total harvest. For example, February, 1967, was only a fair hunting month for Household I and a very bad month for Household II. The combined kill (more than 70 percent common seals) provided only 166,500 kilocalories of food; more than 90 percent of the total was taken by Household I. A month of low food input does not, however, mean hardship. Such a February is an example of the important role storage plays in the villagers' management of energy resources. The fall hunt had provided enough food for the winter, and as a result in February the villagers did more visiting than hunting. Visiting is therefore one mechanism that takes hunters out of the productive sector of the economy and creates a better balance between energy availability and energy need. The same pattern holds true throughout the winter months, so that the 500,000 calories that was harvested from February through April was as much a caloric expression of leisure as it was of poorer hunting conditions. The differential hunting success of individuals or of households in the month of February did not greatly influence energy distribution within the social unit. Although one hunter may have more skins to trade, food is stored in bulk and is generally available to all.

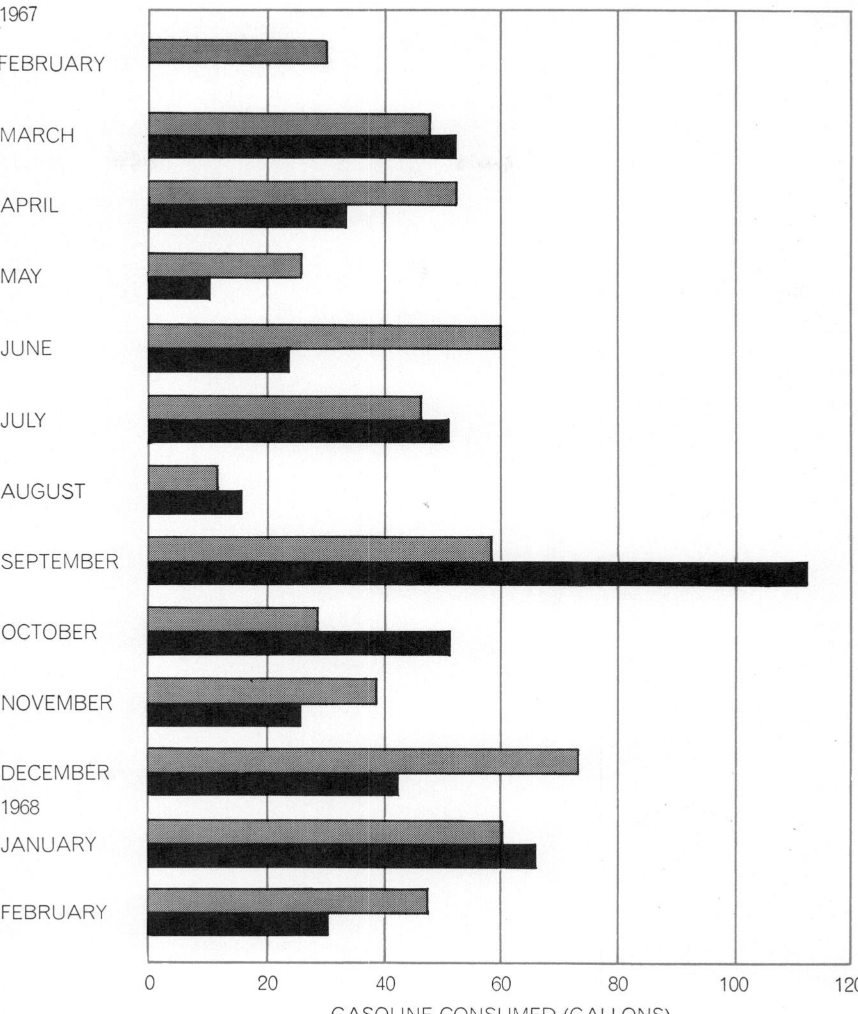

GASOLINE CONSUMPTION by two Eskimo households is shown over a 12-month period. The fuel was used to power the two snowmobiles and the marine engines that greatly increased the villagers' hunting efficiency. Purchases by the three hunters of Household I are shown in black and those by the single hunter of Household II are in gray. Gasoline is second only to imported food among the exotic energy inputs to the Eskimo hunting society.

The records show that although caribou are hunted only occasionally, the animals are then present in substantial numbers. In the lean February of 1967 caribou made up some 7 percent of the kill, providing about 11,000 kilocalories of food. The following month caribou comprised more than 37 percent of the kill, amounting to a total of 90,000 kilocalories. After that caribou were almost absent from the villagers' diet until January, 1968, when they furnished nearly 70 percent of the kill for a yield of 245,000 kilocalories.

Today no Eskimo community depends exclusively on hunting for its food. Each day the adults of the village consumed an average of half a pound of imported wheat flour in the form of a bread called bannock, a pan-baked mixture of flour, lard, salt and water. Bannock has long been an Eskimo staple; it is eaten in the largest quantities where hunting has

fallen off the most.

In addition to this basic breadstuff the villagers consumed imported sugar, biscuits, candy and soft drinks, and they fed nonnursing infants and young children a kind of reconstituted milk. A daily ration consisted of 48 ounces of water containing 1.2 ounces of dry whole milk and 1.7 ounces of sugar.

I kept a 13-month record of the kind and amount of imported foods bought by the two households. During this period the more traditional household bought store foods totaling almost 3.3 million kilocalories and the more modern household store foods totaling 3.75 million kilocalories. The purchases provided 531,000 kilocalories of store food per adult in Household I and 477,300 per adult in Household II. The larger number of adults in Household I is reflected in the size of its flour purchase, which made up 53 percent of the total, compared with 40 percent in Household II. The larger purchase of lard by Household II (23 percent compared with 10 percent) is a measure of preference, not consumption. Household I prefers to use the fat from whales for bannock; hence its smaller purchase [*see illustration on page 301*]. The consumption of the third imported staple—sugar—was about the same in both households.

The quantities of store food that were bought from month to month showed substantial variations. In March, 1967, the store purchases of the two households rose above one million kilocalories because both households received a social-assistance payment. In February, 1968, social assistance was again given each household, and as before the money was used to buy more than the average amount of food. The rather high caloric input from store food in September, 1967, is attributable to money available from wage labor.

Store foods, unlike food from the land, are not stockpiled and they are not often shared. Except for the staples and tea, tobacco and candy, there is no strong desire for non-Eskimo foods. When vegetables are bought, it is usually by mistake. Canned meats, although occasionally eaten, are not recognized as "real" food. The villagers like fruit, but it is never bought in large quantity. Jam, peanut butter, honey, molasses, oatmeal and crackers all find their way into the two households. They are consumed almost immediately.

The data on food input support the general findings from other areas that show the Eskimo diet to be high in protein. At least in this Eskimo group, even though imported carbohydrates were readily available and there was money enough to buy imports almost ad libitum, the balance was in favor of protein.

Over the 13-month period the villagers acquired 44 percent of their calories in the form of protein, 33 percent in the form of carbohydrate and 23 percent in fat. Almost all the protein (93 percent) came from game; 96 percent of the carbohydrate was store food. The figures suggest how nutritional problems can arise when hunting declines. As store-food calories take the place of calories from the hunt, the change frequently involves increased flour consumption and consequently a greater intake of carbohydrate. This was the case in Household II during September, 1967, a period when the family worked for wages. The caloric input remained at 2,700 kilocalories per person per day, but 62 percent of the calories were carbohydrate and only 9 percent were protein.

A framework of social controls surrounds all the activities of the village, directing and mediating the flow of energy in the community. For example, even though all the inhabitants are ostensibly related (either by real kinship or by assigned ties), the community is actually divided into two social groups, each operating with a high degree of economic and social independence. Food is constantly shared within each social group, and the boundary between groups is ignored when a large animal is killed.

Village-wide meals serve to divert a successful hunter's caloric acquisitions for the benefit of a group larger than his own household. The meal that follows the arrival of hunters with a freshly killed seal is the most frequent and the most important of these events. It is called *alopaya,* a term that refers to using one's hands to scoop fresh blood from the open seal carcass. The invitation to participate is shouted by one of the children, and all the villagers gather, the men in one group and the women in another, to eat until they are full. The parts of the seal are apportioned according to the eater's sex. The men start by eating a piece of the liver and the women a piece of the heart. The meat from the front flippers and the first third of the vertebrae and the ribs goes to the women. The men eat from the remaining parts of the seal. This meal, like almost all other Eskimo meals, does not come at any specific time of the day. People eat when they are hungry or, in the case of village-wide meals, when the hunters return. If anything remains at the end of an *alopaya* meal, the leftovers are divided equally among all the families and can be eaten by either sex.

Whaleboats and freight canoes began to replace the kayak for water transportation in southern Baffin Island some 30 years ago; by the end of the 1950's outboard motors had been substituted for oars and paddles. The latter change, which made possible more efficient open-water hunting, coincided with a high market price for sealskins. In the early 1960's a single skin might bring as much as $30, and the value of the annual village catch was between $3,000 and $4,000. The good sealskin market enabled the villagers to buy their first snowmobile in the fall of 1963. A decline in skin prices that began in 1964 has since been offset to some extent by the growth of handicraft sales and by the availability of work for wages.

As a result of these new economic inputs a new kind of material flow is now observable. It consists of the movement of secondhand non-Eskimo goods. The flow is channeled through a network of kinship ties between individuals with an income higher than average and those with an income lower. By 1971 anyone who wanted a snowmobile or some other item of factory-made equipment could utilize this network and get what he wanted through a combination of salvage, gift and purchase.

For the individual the exploitation of economic alternatives and the pattern of activity vary according to taste and life-style. Although life-style is in large degree dictated by age, the effect within the village is integrative rather than disruptive. A son's snowmobile gives the father the advantage of a quick ride to the edge of the floe ice, and the son can rely on the father's dogs to tow a broken machine or to help pull heavy loads over rough terrain. The integration extends to areas beyond the hunt. At home it is not unusual to find the father making sealskin rope or repairing a sledge while the son carves soapstone. Neither considers the other's work either radical or impossibly old-fashioned.

Social controls also affect the expendi-

BLEAK TERRAIN of the Canadian Arctic is seen in the aerial photograph on the opposite page. The steep shore and treeless hinterland are part of an islet in Hudson Strait off the coast of southern Baffin Island. By hunting sea mammals the Eskimos of the region can obtain enough food and valuable by-products to keep them well above the level of survival.

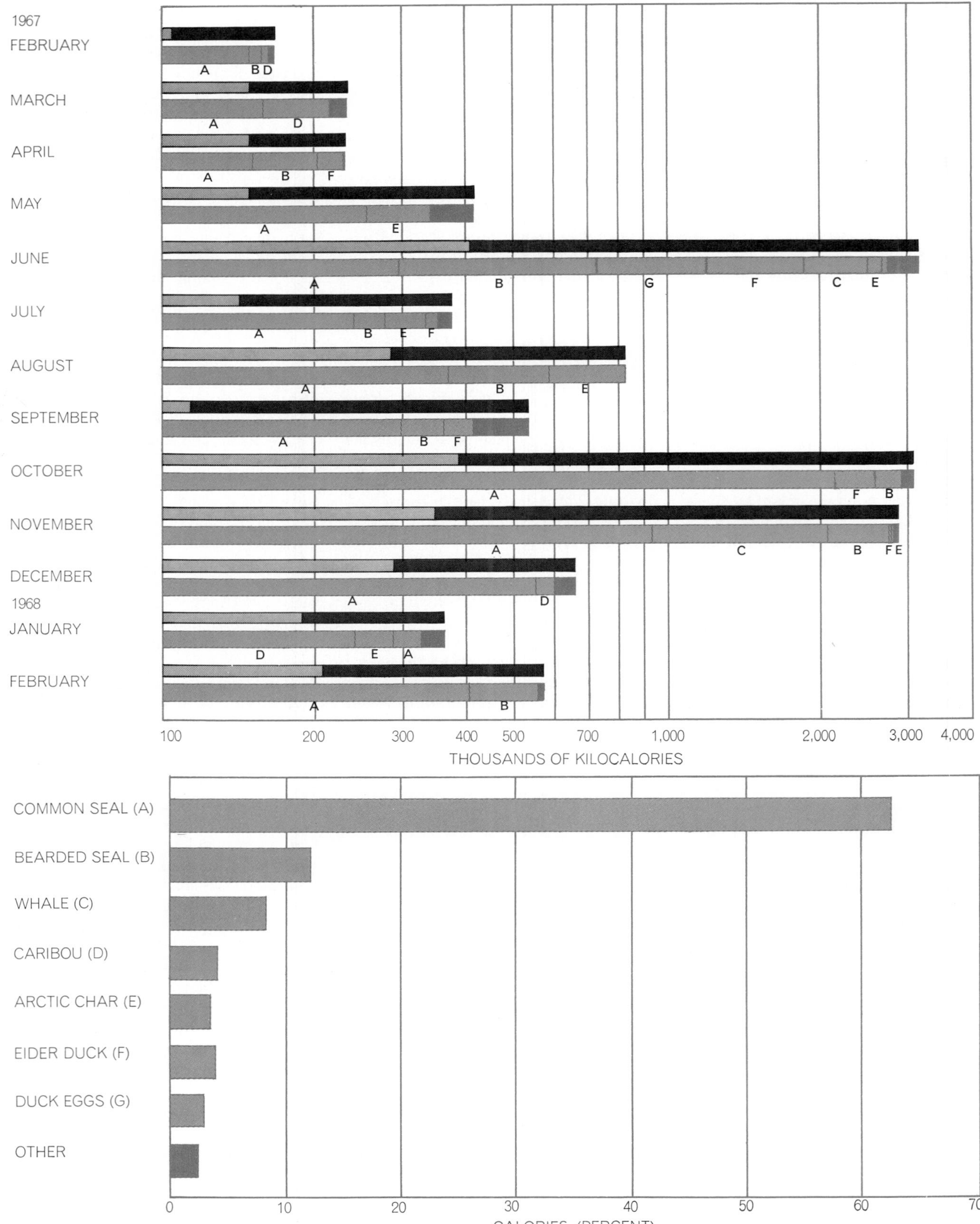

HUNTERS' BAG varies considerably from month to month as a result of chance and preference and also because of seasonal fluctuations. The top graph shows the wild foods acquired by Household I (*black*) and Household II (*gray*) in the course of 13 months. A fish known as arctic char, birds such as murres, geese and ducks, duck eggs and even berries add variety to the Eskimo diet from April through October, while caribou contribute to the smaller game bag of winter months. The 13-month totals, however, show that sea mammals (the common seal in particular) provide most of the Eskimo households' consumable kilocalories (*bottom graph*).

ture of personal energy within the household. The losers are the teen-age girls. Among the men of the village there is little emphasis on authority structure or leadership; decision-making is left to the individual. Choices for the most part converge, so that joint efforts are a matter of course. Among the women, however, authority structure is emphasized. A girl is subordinate not only to the older women but also to her male relatives. One can make the general statement that those who because of sex, age and kinship ties are most subject to the demands of others expend a disproportionate amount of energy in household and village chores.

One series of social controls has been radically altered by the introduction of non-Eskimo technology, energy and world view. These controls are the beliefs and rituals relating the world of nature to the world of thought. In the traditional Eskimo society the two worlds were closely related. All living organisms, for example, were believed to have a soul. In his ritual the Eskimo recognized the fragility of the Arctic ecosystem and sought to foster friendly relations with the same animals he hunted for food. Obviously the friendship could not be a worldly one, but it did exist in the realm of the spirit. A measure of the strength of this belief was the great care taken by the Eskimo never to invite unnecessary hardship by offending the soul of the animal he killed.

Today ritual control of the forces of nature and of the food supply has almost disappeared; technology is considered the mainspring of well-being. Prayers may still be said for good hunting and good traveling conditions, and the Sunday service may include an analysis of a hunting success and even a request for guidance in the hunts to follow. Hunting decisions may also be affected by dreams. None of these activities, however, has the regulatory powers of the intricate symbols and beliefs of earlier times. The hunters complain of a change in the seals' behavior. Nowadays, they say, only the young animals are curious and can be coaxed to come closer to the boat or the edge of the floe ice. The mutual trust between man and his food supply has evidently been lost in the report of the high-powered rifle and the rumble of the outboard motor.

What conclusions can we draw from the analysis of energy flows in a hunting society? The Eskimos do not differ from other hunters in that the processes surrounding the quest for food involve much more than a simple interplay of

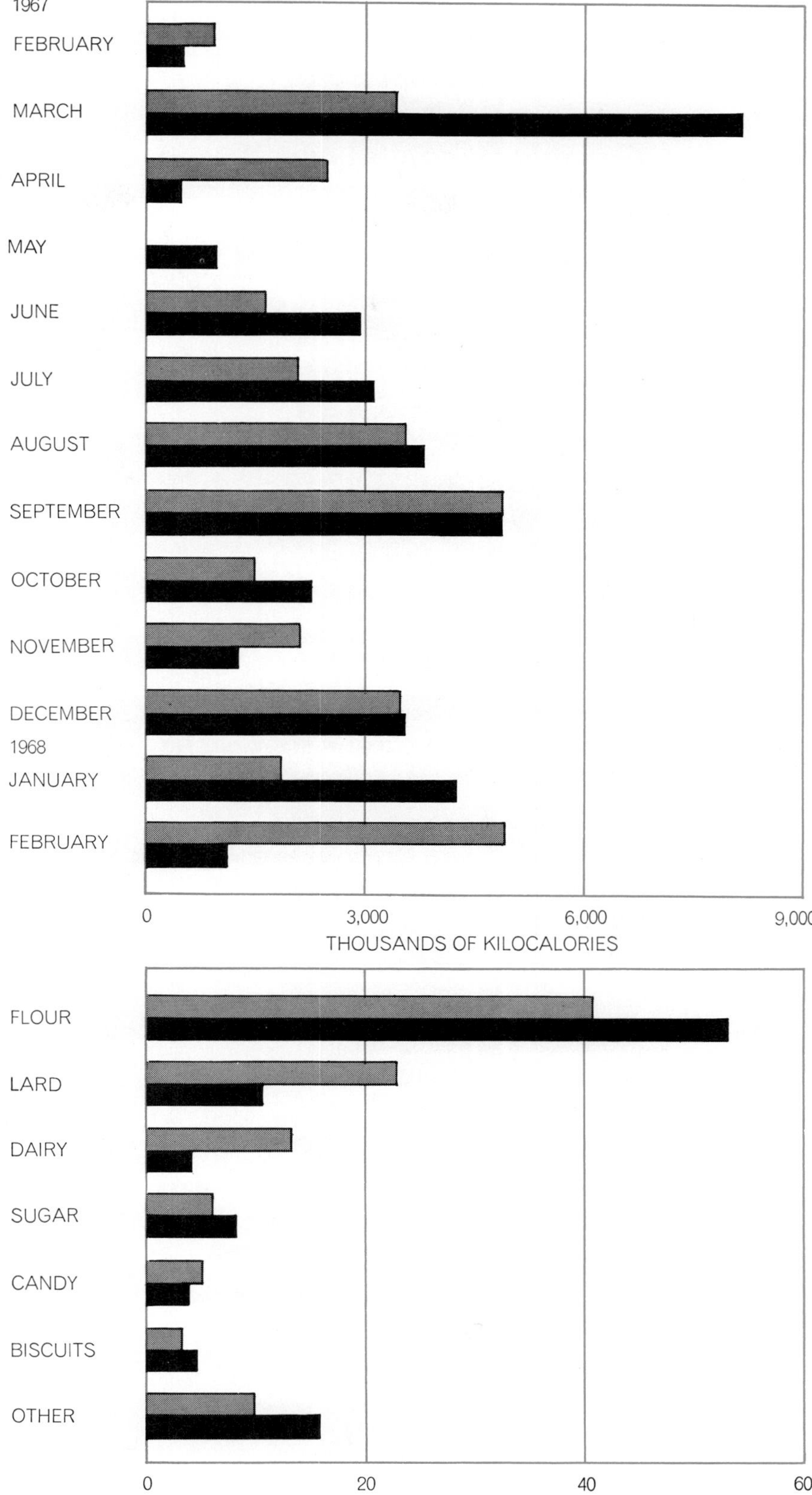

PURCHASES OF IMPORTED FOOD also show large monthly variations. The top graph shows the kilocalorie values of staples such as flour, lard and sugar and of lesser items such as powdered milk, biscuits, soft drinks and candy acquired over 13 months by Household I (*black*) and Household II (*gray*). Most of the flour and lard went to make a kind of bread called bannock. The 13-month totals (*bottom graph*) show how the two households differed in the percentage of all store-food purchases that each allotted to flour and to lard.

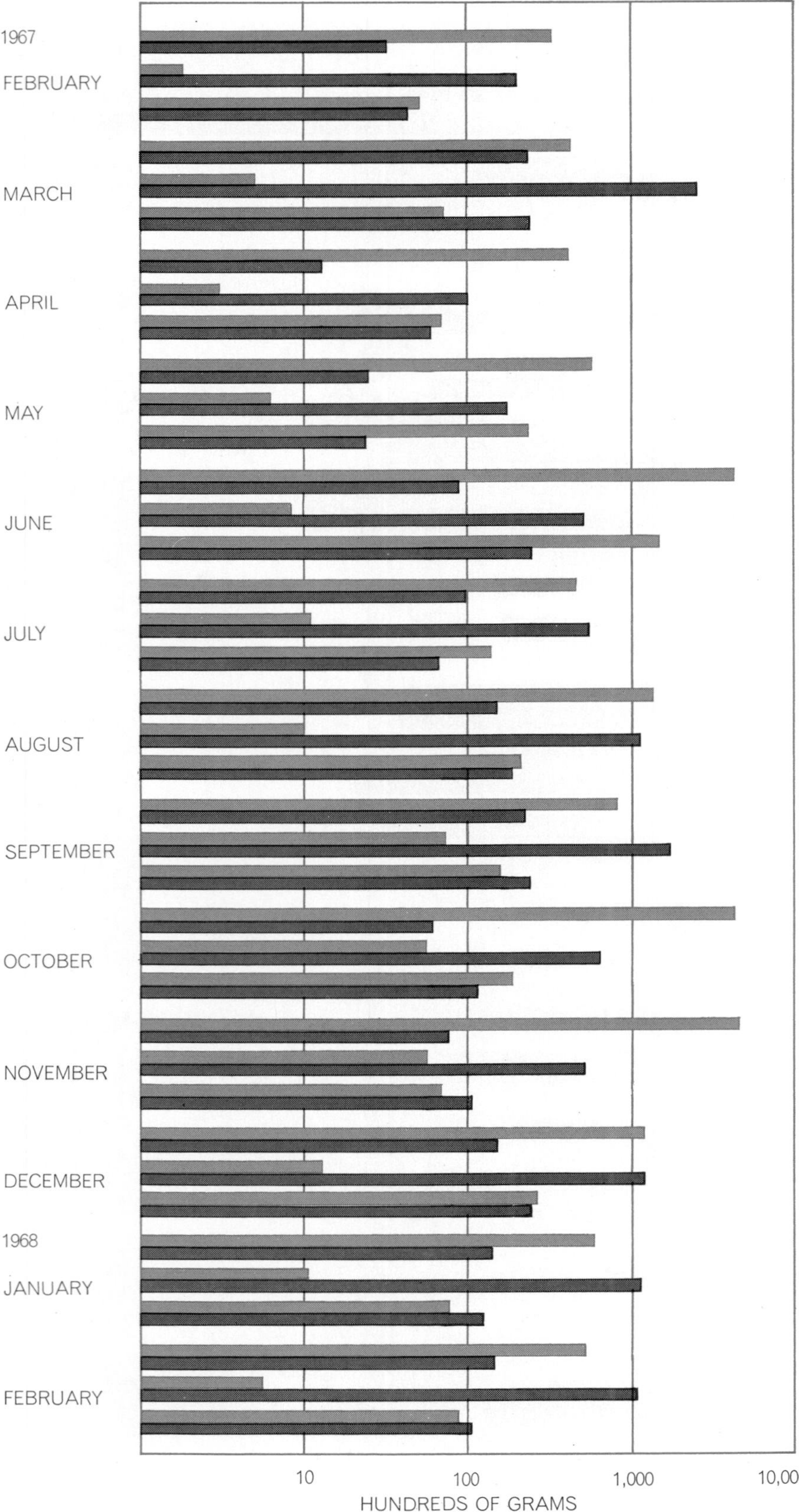

COMPOSITION OF DIET is presented for a 13-month period in terms of monthly acquisitions of protein (*top pair of bars*), carbohydrate (*middle pair of bars*) and fat (*bottom pair of bars*), measured in hundreds of grams. The colored bar of each pair indicates the number of grams acquired by hunting and gathering and the black bar indicates the number acquired in the form of store food. Protein outranked the others in total acquisitions: 2.1 million grams, compared with 1.1 million grams of carbohydrate and .7 million grams of fat.

environment and technology. There are many times when a technological advance is fatal to an ecological balance; this was particularly evident in the near-extermination of the caribou herds west of Hudson Bay with the introduction of the rifle and the relaxation of traditional beliefs. In southern Baffin Island, however, there is not yet any evidence of a trend toward "overkill." At the same time that motorized transport has enhanced the ability to kill game, other social and economic factors have acted to reduce the amount of time available for hunting and have kept the kill within bounds. Snowmobiles give quick access to the edge of the floe ice; they also make it easy to visit distant kinsmen. A regular day of rest on Sunday has a religious function; it also contributes to the management of energy resources.

Do hunting societies have a long-term future? In the case of the Eskimo one can reply with a conditional yes. The universal pressure on resources makes continued exploitation of the Arctic a certainty, and Eskimos should be able to profit from these future ventures. Already it is possible to see three distinct groups emerging within Eskimo culture. One of them consists of the wage earners in the larger communities. Another, which is just beginning to make its appearance, is an externally oriented group that seems destined to regulate and control the inputs from the outside world: the non-Eskimo energy flows and material flows that, as we have seen, now play a vital part in the hunters' lives.

Finally, there is a third group, small in numbers but vast in terms of territory, made up of the hunters who will continue the traditional Eskimo participation in the fragile, far-flung Arctic ecosystem. There will be linkages—exchanges of materials and probably of people—between the wage earner and the hunter. Those who choose to live off the land may appear to be the more traditional of the three groups, but their lives will be dynamic enough because the variables that define the hunting way of life are constantly changing. If a snowmobile is perceived to have greater utility than a dog sled, then the ownership of a snowmobile will become one of the criteria defining the traditional Eskimo hunter. With the outward-oriented Eskimos providing stability for the three-group system through their control of exotic inputs, the northern communities should be able to evolve further without developing disastrous strains. But the fundamental linkage—the relation between the hunter and the Arctic ecosystem—will remain the same.

VI

EPILOGUE: CONTEMPORARY ISSUES

VI EPILOGUE: CONTEMPORARY ISSUES

INTRODUCTION

The two articles here remind us of two major concerns in New World archaeology. The first is the ever more rapid and extensive destruction of the record of the past. The building of highways, canals, pipelines, suburban tracts, shopping centers, dams, and reservoirs destroys hundreds, if not thousands, of sites each year. At the time Roberts wrote "A Crisis in U.S. Archaeology," a handful of archaeologists were faced with the task of salvaging what they could from the largest sites. Since funds for this task were sporadic and inadequate, many of the largest sites were lost, but even more less striking ones. Thus the record of adaptation and change of many prehistoric Indian cultures has disappeared, never to be read.

The archaeologist Charles McGimsey, Director of the Archaeological Salvage Program of the State of Arkansas, has suggested a powerful simile. An archaeologist faced with salvaging the record of a past culture is like an historian in an archive containing thousands of books. He can select only one, and solely on the basis of its external appearance. As soon as the book is chosen, the rest are immediately burned. The scene is repeated in countless rooms.

Although this crisis is still as real as ever, the means for dealing with it have improved somewhat. Greater emphasis is placed on preservation of historic and prehistoric sites. Some archaeological parks have been created. More systematic planning and regional development are producing more complete inventories of sites. Greater lead time is being gained, during which to assess the significance of threatened sites and, if necessary, to plan and execute extensive salvage programs. Sites are still "salvaged" on twenty-four-hour notice by volunteer crews, while impatient bulldozers idle beside them. But, one hopes, this is becoming less frequent. Greater planning is now being backed by a variety of local, state, and federal laws.

Better and more consistent funding, the training of more professional archaeologists, the recruiting and training of interested amateurs, and the development of more efficient means to sample, excavate, and record data will continue to contribute to more effective recovery of data. Equally important is the support of analysis, publication, and archiving of data after excavation. Archaeologists are developing institutions which are more adequate to cope with these increased challenges. The crisis today is as great as in 1948. But the enlightened concern for the record of the past by the public in general, and by governments in particular, together with the active participation of archaeologists in planning, preservation, and salvage, has grown. This gives hope that the record of achievement of the Indians of the New World will not continue to disappear without chroniclers.

Oliver LaFarge, in "The Enduring Indian," reminds us of the strength and resiliency of native American cultures. Their ability to adapt to enormous pressures from their social environment—political, economic, military—as well as to the radically new natural environments to which many were "removed," testifies to this. The cost in lives, in property, and in individual happiness has been great. Yet native American cultures remain. Their ancestors made major contributions to world culture; their art and their domesticated crops are well-known examples of this. Today their potential contribution is as great. They provide a body of knowledge from which we can learn new ways of perceiving our relationships with ourselves and with our natural world.

The wish of native Americans to achieve respect and economic success, but at the same time to maintain cultural unity within the national societies of the New World, is stronger than ever. So is their concern that the material record of their achievements be respected and preserved, and here there is potential for conflict with New World archaeologists. Unrestrained excavation on the one hand, and no excavation on the other, are incompatible demands, but compromise to attain common ends is possible. Many native Americans are coming to realize that the chronicle of their history depends on careful and sympathetic recovery of their material record. And New World archaeologists are coming to recognize, to understand, and to honor the legitimate desire that this heritage be preserved.

EARTH-MOVING MACHINE working on a slope at the Medicine Creek Reservoir in Nebraska is an indication of the archaeologists' haste. Here they have uncovered the sites of three dome-shaped houses built by Indians some 500 to 600 years ago. The original post holes made by the inhabitants have been dug out again by hand.

A Crisis in U.S. Archaeology

by Frank H. H. Roberts
December 1948

The damming of rivers will shortly flood the valleys where lived the aboriginal Americans. Archaeologists must work fast to save what they can of the remains

DURING the past two years archaeologists have been scraping away at the river basins of the U. S. with an anxious haste that suggests Noah's preparations for the Flood. Their search parties have prospected thousands of miles of the North American watershed, searching for traces of its prehistoric inhabitants, and have staked out hundreds of sites for excavation. They are so pressed for time that in some places they are digging with bulldozers instead of with the customary archaeologist's spade. The objective of this activity—perhaps the most massive and most unleisurely excavation project in archaeological history—is to unearth as much as can be saved of North America's prehistoric remains before it is too late. For the archaeologists are actually working against the deadline of a series of impending floods that soon will bury the civilizations of the aboriginal Americans beyond recovery.

The reason for this state of affairs is the Federal government's nation-wide river development program. Its numerous projects for flood control, irrigation, hydroelectric power and navigation will inundate most of the archaeological sites in the U. S., many of which, unfortunately, are still completely unexplored. The American aborigines, like the inhabitants of other lands, generally lived along river banks, where there were fields for raising crops and good locations for camps and villages, where game, fowl and fish abounded and where easy transportation by water was at hand. For this reason, about 80 per cent of the archaeological remains in this country are located in places where the damming of rivers and the formation of reservoirs will obliterate them for all time.

The archaeologists of the U. S. have thus been suddenly presented with a problem of appalling dimensions. The construction of dams is going ahead so rapidly that they have only a few short years to carry out explorations which would ordinarily take several generations.

Early in 1945 they began to organize their forces. Within a year there was mobilized a large cooperative enterprise supported by the Army Corps of Engineers, the Bureau of Reclamation, the National Park Service (which is charged by law with responsibility for the preservation of archaeological sites) and the Smithsonian Institution. The National Research Council's Committee on Basic Needs in American Archaeology, the Society for American Archaeology. the American Anthropological Association and the American Council of Learned Societies formed an independent Committee for the Recovery of Archaeological Remains (including also paleontological remains) to serve in an advisory capacity and to assist in planning a nation-wide survey and digging program for all the river basins where dam projects were in prospect. As the program progressed the committee helped to enlist scientists from many universities, museums and state societies in the cooperative effort. The Smithsonian was given chief responsibility for the scientific work, and the National Park Service agreed to keep it informed of all dam and reservoir projects and to make arrangements for surveys of the areas involved.

PROJECTILE POINT is brushed by archaeologist working in Angostura Reservoir area of South Dakota.

The archaeologists went to work first in the Missouri River Basin, where 105 river development projects had already been authorized. From field headquarters at the University of Nebraska, survey parties reconnoitered more than 13,000 miles of the basin and covered 94 reservoir areas. Meanwhile other parties began explorations in the Columbia-Snake Basin in Oregon, on the Etowah River in Georgia, the Roanoke in Virginia, the Brazos and Neches rivers in Texas, and in the Central Valley of California and the Arkansas drainage basin in Oklahoma. And other surveys, sponsored by individual universities, have been started or planned in a score of states from Florida to Oregon.

Thus far the central survey staff alone has located some 1,800 archaeological sites and recommended digging operations at 250 of them. Because of limited funds, large-scale digging has actually been undertaken at only nine sites: the Addicks Reservoir in Texas, Medicine Creek Reservoir in Nebraska, Angostura Reservoir in South Dakota, Heart Butte Reservoir in North Dakota, Boysen Reservoir in Wyoming, McNary Reservoir in Oregon, O'Sullivan Reservoir in Washington, Fort Gibson Reservoir in Oklahoma and the Tucumcari project in New Mexico. The cooperating universities, however, have undertaken a number of other excavations, and at many additional sites there has been preliminary test digging.

Some of these excavations are being made, with great haste, in places where the destruction of the sites by the engineers is imminent or, indeed, already under way. An example is the Medicine Creek project on the Republican River in Nebraska. There, for the first time in archaeological history, power machinery has been used on a large scale. Time and man power were so short that the archaeologists decided to risk utilizing heavy equipment, provided by the Bureau of Reclamation, to scrape away the earth covering buried villages. The experiment

SKELETON of a 70-year-old man is carefully uncovered in the same Medicine Creek Reservoir area that is shown on page 306. This region has been the most thoroughly worked of all those that will be inundated.

FLOORS of Indian houses are exposed in the Medicine Creek Reservoir area. Posts placed in the holes supported an earth-covered structure. The entrance was at rear center. The larger holes were employed for storage.

surpassed expectations; it was found entirely feasible to remove the overburden from large areas with practically no damage to the underlying remains. In five months this group accomplished as much work as would normally have taken a much larger crew two full seasons. It was therefore decided to use machinery at other sites.

The diggings have already yielded important and interesting information about the little-known prehistoric peoples of North America. Among the most significant finds have been those in the Columbia River Basin of the Northwest. There the diggers have unearthed at successive levels the buried remains of villages ranging in time from 4,000 years ago to the time of the Lewis and Clark expedition in the early 1800s. The two seasons of preliminary exploration in this relatively unknown area have turned up many camp and village sites, rock shelters and burial grounds. From the great wealth of buried material archaeologists hope to reconstruct a continuous history of the aboriginal occupation covering several thousand years. The Columbia Basin was the most important prehistoric travel route in the West; there is evidence of aboriginal trading up and down the river from the West Coast to the upper Missouri Basin.

In the Missouri Basin there have been finds of cultures much older than those on the coast. Indeed, some of the deep strata which have been exposed by streams cutting through the terrain promise to yield material belonging to the so-called Paleo-Indian, who is believed to have migrated from Asia to North America in the late Pleistocene period. Most of the sites in the Wyoming-Montana area contain no pottery—an evidence of very primitive culture. Farther east, in the western Dakotas, pottery begins to appear. In both areas great numbers of stone circles or tipi rings, marking tent sites, have been unearthed. But to the south, in northwestern Nebraska and northern Kansas, the predominant dwellings were pit houses, and in the eastern Dakotas there are many mounds and remains of villages—all suggesting a more sedentary, agricultural type of civilization.

SOME of the largest, best preserved and most impressive fortified Indian sites in the U. S. have been found along the main stream of the Missouri in the Dakotas. In some of the sites there are records of prehistoric floods, of silting and soil erosion, of recurrent droughts and of fluctuations in climate. The excavation and interpretation of the data contained in such sites should not only contribute to the story of the growth and development of the Plains Indians but also add considerably to our understanding of how the aboriginal people met and overcame climatic and other environmental conditions not unlike those of the present day. Part of this study has already been made at the Medicine

Creek Reservoir in Nebraska and at the Angostura Reservoir in western South Dakota.

The Medicine Creek area, thanks to the help of earth-moving machinery, to date is the most thoroughly explored of all the projects. Its remains consist mostly of house pits, middens (dumps for debris and refuse), cache pits where crops were stored, and burial grounds. The material already uncovered indicates that archaeologists will have to revise some of their long-held theories about the Indians of that area and their relationship to their environment. The finds show that these Indians practiced community planning and varied their housing architecture. They also shed new light on early developments in horticulture.

The Medicine Creek villages which have been excavated probably were occupied about 500 to 600 years ago. They certainly were never visited by white explorers, and so far it has not been possible to connect them with the Indian tribes that have lived in the area in more recent times. Each village consisted of a half dozen or more earth-covered, dome-shaped houses. The floors were slightly below ground level. Near the center of the large chamber in each house was the fireplace, with the smoke passing out through a hole in the roof. The entrance to the house was a tunnel-like passage, placed on the side away from the prevailing winter winds.

Each house probably was occupied by two or more families. Small underground pits inside and outside the houses were used for storage, and later as dumps for refuse. The remains show that these people raised corn, squash and beans, gathered wild fruits, berries and tubers, and hunted bison, deer, antelope and small game. They also depended a good deal on aquatic food; bone fishhooks have been found, and vast numbers of fresh-water mussel shells.

Just above these archaeological deposits is a thick layer of dust—evidence that the area suffered a period of severe droughts comparable to those which occurred in the Plains area a decade ago. During the drought period the Indians withdrew from the region. Later the weather improved and layers of good soil, now covered with sod, were deposited over the dust. This is just one of many proofs that cycles of good and bad times have been not uncommon in the area.

The fact that when white men first came to North America from Europe they found a virgin wilderness, apparently very sparsely populated, has fostered a wide impression that the continent had only a scanty human history. The current digging is amply demonstrating how wrong that impression is. It shows, as archaeologists have long suspected, that what is now the U. S. was peopled in ancient times by many diverse tribes occupying almost every region on the continent.

In California the present survey has un-

PIT DWELLING is dug out at the O'Sullivan Reservoir in Washington. This region was one of the most important prehistoric travel routes in U.S. Remains of villages dating from 4,000 years ago have been unearthed.

INTERIOR of pit house in the picture at the top of the page shows structural plan. Many such houses had a fireplace in the center, with a hole in the roof for a chimney. Man in rear sifts earth for small objects.

TIPI RINGS, circles of stones set on the ground to anchor Indian tipis, are plainly visible in the Tiber Reservoir area of Montana. These rings locate the sites of some comparatively recent settlements of the Indians.

FORTIFIED VILLAGE built by the Indians is still a rough outline beside the muddy main stream of the Missouri River. This site, visible at bottom center of this aerial view, will be inundated by the Oahe Reservoir.

earthed village sites, soapstone quarries, pictographic writing and pottery of peoples previously unknown. In Texas, camp and village sites have been found in many new areas. In Virginia and North Carolina there are a number of signs of what seems to be an eastern phase of the famous Folsom culture which flourished in the Western Plains during the closing days of the last Ice Age. At the Fort Gibson Reservoir site in Oklahoma there are valuable remains which are attributed to the great mound-building era, the period of cultural efflorescence which swept across the southern U. S. in the late pre-Columbian and early historic period.

THE flooding of river basins will of course bury many deposits of fossils as well as those of aboriginal cultures. Thus far reconnaissance in this field has been confined mostly to the Missouri Basin, but it is now being extended to other areas. On the whole the loss to paleontology will not be so serious as that facing archaeology, for fossils similar to those that will be inundated can in most cases be found in other locations. A few unique quarries will be flooded, however, and there are many valuable fossil remains in the Indian sites themselves. Archaeologists frequently find fossil bones and leaves which the Indians apparently collected as curiosities. They used them as ornaments and sometimes carved implements from them.

The nation-wide effort to salvage archaeological and paleontological materials, the largest coordinated project of the kind ever undertaken in this country, has made a good start, but a staggering amount of work remains to be done, and time is running out. The great problem is lack of funds. So far the work has been financed mainly by funds transferred from appropriations of the Department of the Interior and the Army Corps of Engineers. The money available has been so limited that in many critical areas where sites are about to be destroyed the necessary surveys and excavations cannot even be attempted. As the Federal river development program proceeds, the emergency will become more and more acute. The Committee for the Recovery of Archaeological Remains is making a yeoman attempt to obtain the increased financial backing that is greatly needed. Unless more active support is provided, much of the archaeological story of North America will be lost. It will take a great combined effort by Federal, state and local institutions to achieve even a fair sampling of the nation's archaeological resources and to save a minimum of its prehistoric record.

EXPLORATORY TRENCHES are dug in the lee of a cliff in the Oregon Basin Reservoir area. Indian villages were very likely established here for shelter. Layers of earth in village sites indicate that Indians lived under climatic conditions much the same as those of today. One layer indicates a long period of severe drought.

CAVE IS WORKED by a group of archaeologists in the Boysen Reservoir region of Wyoming. Deposits on the floor of the cave are carefully removed in layers. Each layer is separately sifted for artifacts. This process insures the segregation of characteristic artifacts left by the inhabitants of different periods and cultures.

The Enduring Indian

by Oliver La Farge
February 1960

Americans of European descent have always believed that the original Americans would somehow vanish. But despite slaughter, assimilation, disease and dislocation, Indians continue to maintain their identity

In 1954 a group of anthropologists, two of them American Indians, held a conference in Chicago. Their topic of discussion was the American Indian of today, and they considered in particular the idea (as they put it) "that assimilation of the American Indian into the normal stream of American life is inevitable, and that Indian tribes and communities will disappear."

On the basis of current and historical evidence they concluded: "This prediction is unwarranted. Most Indian groups in the United States, after more than 100 years of Euro-American contact and in spite of strong external pressures, both direct and fortuitous, have not become assimilated in the sense of the loss of community identity and the full acceptance of American habits of thought and conduct. Nor can one expect such group assimilation within any predictable time period, say one to four generations. The urge to retain tribal identity is strong and operates powerfully for many Indian groups."

The vanishing Indian, in other words, is not vanishing.

The general adherence to the contrary view has several motives. One is simple good will—the belief that there is no better fate for any group than to be melted down and totally fused into the general community, and that Indians must desire and eventually follow the same course as the Irish or the Italians. Another is wish-fulfillment. The white men who conquered what is now the U.S., with the exception of the Spanish of the Southwest, came here to settle, to occupy and use the country for all it was worth. They found an alien, primitive, sparse population holding the land. That population had to be evicted. It still holds land. It owns good pasture in areas where pasture is scarce, valuable timber, minerals and water. There are still large numbers of white men who desire this property and accordingly are inclined to believe that the Indians will, or must be made to, vanish.

More important in the thinking of the majority of Americans is the actual history of the decline in Indian population. In 1600 the Indian population of the area now embraced by the 49 states of the continental U.S. was, according to the best estimate, between 900,000 and one million. At its lowest ebb, around 1920, the Indian population was perhaps 350,000. This shrinkage was caused by European diseases, by conflict and, to a small degree, by assimilation.

The first European settlers on the Atlantic Coast, in New England and Virginia, needed and sought the Indians' friendship. Their racial attitude was tolerant; stable marriages between whites and Indians could occur, the most famous of which was that of John Rolfe and Pocahontas. But new settlers were constantly arriving, and the settlements were expanding. Pocahontas's father, Powhatan, found his people being crowded from their land. He attacked, but too late. The English counterattacked, and the Powhatan confederacy was shattered. In New England, Metacomet, commonly called King Philip, son of the Pilgrims' loyal friend Massasoit, organized a still more powerful attack, in the conviction that there was no hope for his people unless the white men were driven out. He too was defeated, after heavy fighting. He had tried for total war; the white men did the same. In a large region that was mostly wilderness, actual genocide was not possible. The Yankees nonetheless had a good try at it.

As settlement increased, the Indians became involved in the imperial wars between the European nations, the most important of which were between the French and the English. Warfare between tribes had usually been sporadic and to some extent a sporting proposition; now it became constant and deadly. Tribes on the losing side suffered heavily; some were wiped out. Throughout the Colonial period, moreover, colonists attacked individual Indian villages, often wantonly, killing everyone they could find.

War and disease eliminated a number of the Eastern tribes. In the North simple intermarriage helped the process along. In the South, however, the importation of Negro slaves raised the shibboleth of racial purity and brought the assimilation of Indians to a stop. An interesting indication of the change can be seen in the laws of Virginia, which forbid miscegenation between whites and Indians, and define an Indian by a proportion of Indian descent that, at the time the law was enacted, was just large enough not to include those who claimed

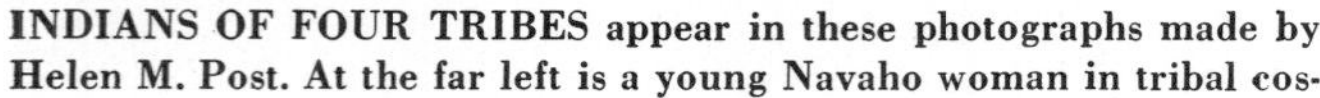

INDIANS OF FOUR TRIBES appear in these photographs made by Helen M. Post. At the far left is a young Navaho woman in tribal costume. Second from the left a member of the Crow tribe addresses a tribal fair. Third from the left is an old man of the Blackfeet

descent from Pocahontas. In many New England communities there are white men who are proud to claim an Indian ancestor; in the South there are separate communities of "Indians," for example, the Lumbees of North Carolina, who recently became famous for shooting up the Ku Klux Klan.

The once-powerful Narragansetts of Rhode Island no longer exist as a tribe; the Wampanoags are extinct; of the Pequots and Mohicans there remains a tiny handful in Connecticut. The Natchez nation of Mississippi and Louisiana is entirely gone. Still, when you call the roll of Eastern tribes, the surprising thing is that traces of so many of them still exist, some *in situ,* more of them west of the Mississippi.

These latter Indians were among the subjects of the "Indian removals," by which, in the first half of the 19th century, the young republic set out to clear the Indians from all the country east of the great river. Tribe after tribe was dumped across the river, or removed itself westward. A large concentration of them landed in what is now Oklahoma, to the surprise and distress of the Indians then occupying that region. West of the Mississippi, from Wisconsin to Texas, can be found what is left of one Eastern tribe after another, and in Oklahoma itself are some of the tribes that moved out of the very states in which these others were settled.

The Indian removals were accompanied by naked force, brutality and fraud. Before the Revolution the British Crown endeavored to honor the treaties and alliances it had made. But after the Revolution its Indian allies found themselves abandoned, their lands wanted by frontiersmen against whom they had fought all too well. Both Washington and Jefferson strove to check the frontiersmen, who were already going on the slogan that the only good Indian was a dead one, and for many years the Federal Government maintained at least the appearances of decency. The West moved ever farther from the seat of government and became ever more powerful politically. Getting Indians to sign treaties when blind drunk was standard practice; so was it to set up sham chiefs, sign treaties with them, and use these as an excuse for applying force. A rough and hardy people had to have that territory to expand into and intended to get it by whatever means.

The great pressure at that time was to clear the South of the powerful "Five Civilized Tribes": the Cherokees, Choctaws, Creeks, Chickasaws and Seminoles. The finding of some gold in Cherokee territory in Georgia intensified the drive. The Cherokees sought legal redress, leading to a famous decision by Chief Justice John Marshall in the case of Worcester *v.* Georgia. This decision, which found solidly for the Indians, was the cornerstone of later Indian law. But Andrew Jackson, himself a frontiersman and Indian fighter, was President. He said: "Marshall has made his decision; let him enforce it." The President commanded the troops; the troops marched in and moved the Cherokees, and after them the rest. Thousands died in the course of these removals; not a few were killed trying to defend their homes, or simply to encourage the others to hurry.

The intent was to settle all Indians on land white men would not want. But the white man kept moving westward, wanting new land. The Delawares, for instance, moved from the coast to the interior of Pennsylvania, then to Ohio. From there some wandered as far as Texas, hoping for better faith from the Spanish Government, then returned. In 1835 the main body was settled in Kansas on a reservation purchased with money paid for lands they had given up farther east. They were Christians. They fenced the land, built houses and a church, raised cattle and planted. But Kansas, it turned out, was fertile; in 1867 the Delawares were removed to Oklahoma and much poorer soil.

During the 1840's the white men's westward movement jumped over the "Great American Desert" to the West Coast, in the south gold-bearing, in the north richly fertile, in places both. There history repeated itself, with local varia-

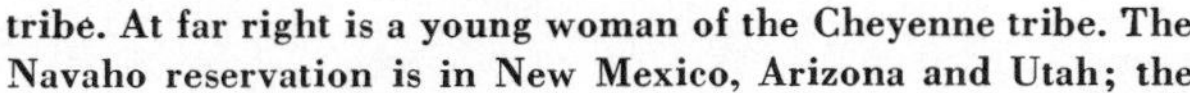

tribe. At far right is a young woman of the Cheyenne tribe. The Navaho reservation is in New Mexico, Arizona and Utah; the Crow, in southern Montana; the Blackfeet, in northern Montana; the Cheyenne, in southern Montana (*see map on next two pages*).

tions, and with the important difference that it was becoming more and more impracticable to try to settle all Indians in Oklahoma. Instead there developed the practice of giving them reservations in their native territories.

After the Civil War white men began to settle the Great Plains and the mountain country. As they closed in on the tribes of these regions they outdid them, on the whole, in treacheries and outrages. But it was no longer possible to be as openly ruthless with the Indians as it had been with the tribes that had been broken earlier. When gold was found in the Black Hills of South Dakota, country pledged to the Sioux by treaty, the Army honestly tried for a while to keep goldseekers from going in. Removals to Oklahoma did occur, as in the case of the Cheyennes of Montana, but the majority of the Western tribes received reservations where they had always lived.

In Arizona and New Mexico there were special circumstances. That region had been conquered by the Spanish. The Spanish did not come to colonize, to till the soil, but for imperial conquest in the grand manner. They did not break treaties, because they did not make them. They looked upon the Indians as their labor force and as souls to be won to God; they did not want to exterminate them, but needed them to make their empire pay. The Spanish Crown gave definite rights and protections to its Indian subjects. These were fully recognized by the Mexican Republic, and when the U. S. annexed the region after the Mexican War, they were written into the Treaty of Guadalupe-Hidalgo. Thus many of the sedentary, farming tribes of the Southwest are protected, especially in title to their land and in rights of self-government, by an international treaty.

The wilder, hunting tribes of that region occupied semidesert, or country that seemed hopelessly remote. Many of these, such as the Navahos and Apaches, had a high nuisance value, as did the strong Plains tribes, at a time when the East was beginning to balk at the cost of Indian wars. The demand for land in the Southwest was relatively weak until recently. As a result of all these factors the Indians of the Southwest received fairly ample reservations in their native territories.

By 1880 the major Indian wars were over, and most tribes were located on the reservations where they are now. There were hostilities after that. Some tribes were moved; some had yet to receive reservations, but the big job was done. The reservation and along with it the status of the Indian have changed considerably since 1880, but the essential terms of this arrangement still play a part in the lives of Indians today.

A reservation is a tract of land—part of a tribe's original territory or given in exchange therefor—set aside for the exclusive use of a tribe or group of Indians, and held in trust for them by the Federal Government. At first white men also conceived of reservations as areas within which a dangerous, hostile people could be confined. Most Indians were not citizens of the U. S.; as "Indians not taxed" they were excluded from the provisions of the Fourteenth Amendment to the Constitution. Whatever their theoretical rights may have been, they were *de facto* wards and subject to astonishing arbitrary controls over their personal and public lives. They could be, and occasionally were, punished for leaving their reservations; to this extent these areas could be considered as concentration camps of a very roomy kind, but even that is a past condition.

A long series of court decisions, going back to Chief Justice Marshall's Cherokee decision, has firmly established that, within the boundaries of the reservations, civil and criminal jurisdiction belong to the Federal Government and the tribe, with the states and territories excluded. Citizenship was extended to Indians gradually until 1924, when in recognition of their services in World War I Congress made all of them citizens. Since then it has been amply proven in the courts that there are no more "Indians not taxed," and that the Fourteenth Amendment applies to them all.

The courts have established that Indians are not wards, that they are American citizens endowed with all the rights deriving from their status as the original occupants of this country, including local self-government under Federal jurisdiction and Federal responsibility for their health and education while they reside in what is legally termed "Indian country." This combination of Federal and autonomous jurisdiction the Indians hold to be their most valuable and necessary right. When an Indian leaves "Indian country," his status is theoretically the same as anyone else's. But some states or local units frankly refuse to extend normal services to the Indian. Unless he goes far from home he usually encounters the prejudice, the discrimination, the unequal justice before the law that help explain why Indians have feared recur-

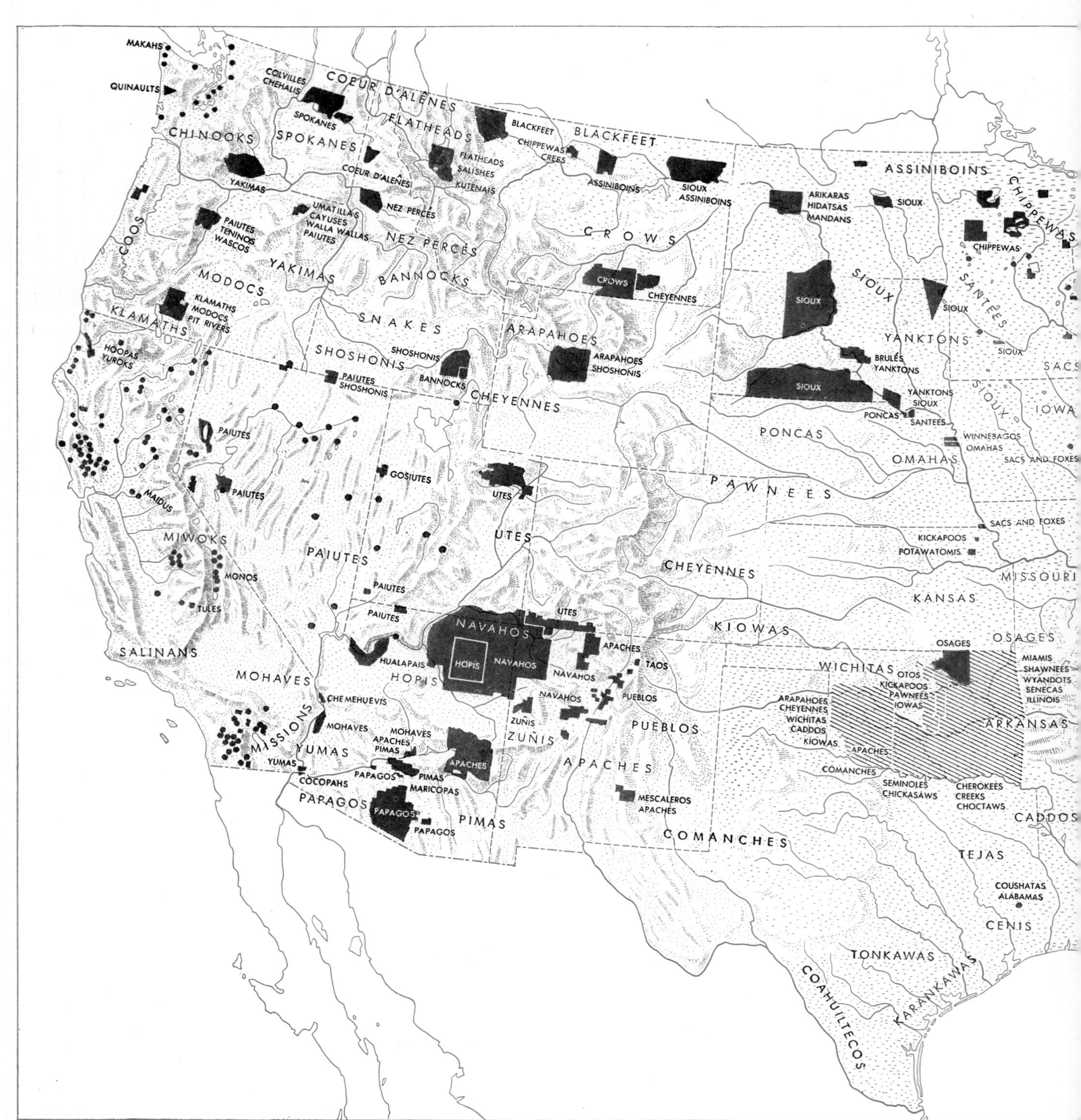

ORIGINAL AND PRESENT LOCATIONS of the principal American Indian tribes are shown in this map of the U.S. The general original location of the tribes is indicated by the large type; the present location (or locations) is given in small type. Indian reserrent moves to turn them over to state governments.

Indian trust-land cannot be alienated or rented without the consent of both the trustee and the beneficiary. It is tax-exempt, and so is income derived from it by its Indian owners, an enormous advantage. It is also called "restricted land," because it is inherent in the nature of the trust that the owners are not perfectly free to do as they like with it, beginning with losing it to satisfy debts. The trustee (the Government) is responsible for the proper use of the land and its conservation, which is no easy responsibility. There has been one case in which a tribe persuaded the Bureau of Indian Affairs to approve an arrangement it wanted for the sale of its timber. The arrangement was bad, and the tribe lost a great deal of money, whereupon it turned around and successfully sued its trustee for more than $1 million in damages.

All that has been said so far makes reservations and the status of a federally recognized Indian sound highly desirable, and in fact there are few such Indians who do not want to see their reservations and their Indian status continued. The restrictions, however, can be burdensome. The trustee is not an individual but a large bureaucracy that changes policy with almost every change of administration. The Government is trustee of a large part of Indian funds as well as of property. Its officials are educated, experienced; the beneficiaries are ignorant, inexperienced. Most Indians, although theoretically literate, are unable to handle the papers of quite simple business transactions without help. It is easy for the trustee, for technical reasons, to withhold funds, to block or promote Indian enterprises, to refuse assistance. Thus the Indians' legal situation has been partly negated by the realities.

As of 1880 the Indians owned 155 million acres of land, mostly guaranteed by treaties. As the West filled up, this land was coveted. The allotment system, culminating in the Allotment Act of 1887, became the device for subtracting land from the Indians' domain. Under this system tribes were high-pressured into surrendering title to their reservations, accepting instead individual allotments of land and ceding the "surplus" to the U. S. for a song. The trust periods on the individual allotments were limited, and when trust was removed, those tracts too could be obtained by non-Indians. The humanitarians of the time supported this system in the belief that individual ownership would break up the tribes and lead to assimilation. Outside the Southwest, between 1887 and 1933, when the process was temporarily halted, the Indians lost 93 million acres, with economically disastrous results in many places.

Allotment vests still further power in the trustee; it can extend or refuse to extend the trust period when it is due to expire. Once an allotment goes out of trust it becomes subject to taxation, and experience shows that it soon passes into

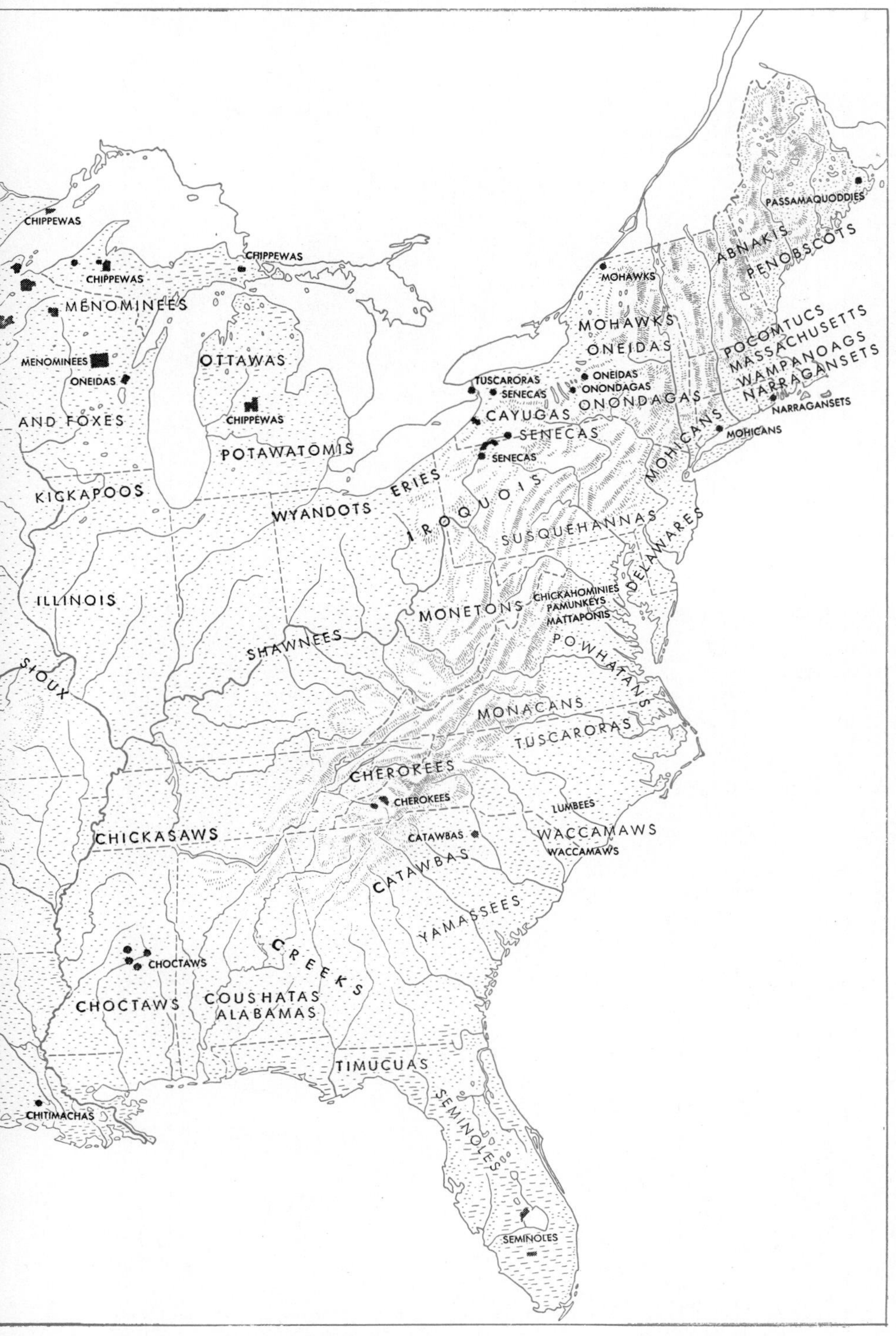

vations are denoted by areas or points in gray. Hatched area in Oklahoma was once reservation. Many Indians now live there with certain rights guaranteed by special legislation.

NAVAHO FAMILY is photographed at its home on Navaho Mountain, in a remote part of the Navaho reservation. At the left is the entrance to the family's hogan, a structure built of wood and earth. This photograph is reproduced through courtesy of *Farm Quarterly*.

NAVAHO SCHOLARSHIP COMMITTEE interviews Emily Roanhorse, who wishes to obtain schooling outside the reservation. The tribe has a trust fund of $5 million for this purpose, and each year sends some 200 students to colleges, universities and trade schools.

white ownership. There is also the matter of "key allotments," that is, tracts of land whose ownership controls the use of surrounding tracts. The key piece of land may have the only water in a large area of grazing land, or it may be the only means of access to a stand of timber. When a non-Indian gets hold of a key allotment, there is little the surrounding Indian owners can do but sell or lease to him at his price. For many years prior to 1953 Indian Bureau regulations established special safeguards over such parcels of land. Under the present administration, however, the field officials concerned were instructed to ignore the "key" consideration entirely when land was in line to be sold. This harsh injunction has recently been somewhat softened.

Indians sell their lands for various reasons. Many allotments are owned by persons, usually of mixed blood, who have permanently left their reservation and no longer care what happens to the tribe. They receive lease money, but prefer to get a lump sum in cash and have done with it. Many try to sell their land in order to obtain at least temporary relief from destitution, or because the states in which they live will not give old-age payments or other relief to persons owning property. Perhaps the principal cause is heirship: an allotment may now be owned by the numerous grandchildren and even great-grandchildren of the original allottee. There are actual cases of heirs who receive only one cent per annum in lease money. The natural tendency of the trustee and of the heirs is to get rid of the mess by selling the land outright.

As the land base dwindled, so did the Indian population, tactfully fulfilling white expectations. In this there were two principal factors. One was disease, fortified by malnutrition, entire lack of sanitation, and little or no medical or public-health service. The other was plain hopelessness, reflected in a declining birth rate. After the 1920 nadir, when the Indian population (including a few thousand Eskimos and Aleuts) had fallen to 350,000, the Indians began to increase. No improvement in their condition explains this development. One can only speculate that a new generation had come along that had made at least a partial adjustment to its wretched mode of life and was therefore less despondent and more inclined to reproduce than its predecessors had been.

The upturn was followed by developments that favored it. A major overhaul in the Indian health service was undertaken in 1926 under President Coolidge and was reinforced during the Hoover administration. During the Eisenhower administration Indian health was made the responsibility of the Public Health Service, and that transfer, with certain other innovations, leads to the hope that before too long health services to Indians will be comparable to those received by other Americans.

The Hoover administration also initiated reforms in education. Most education for Indians had been vocational; Indians were expected to be farmers, herders, manual workers and domestic servants, and they were schooled accordingly. Indian schools were places of virtual imprisonment, of harsh discipline, hard labor, hunger and a minimum of learning. Under President Hoover the schools actually became schools. To mention just one item, the provision of sufficient food for the children—initially by raising the allowance in 1931 from 11 to 28 cents a day—has meant a change in the physical potential of an entire generation. Further improvements have been introduced by succeeding administrations. The picture is still not perfect; there are still too many Indians who never get to school at all. But it is no longer surprising to find Indians in college, and one can detect the spread of a new self-confidence and new competence, still beginning, still uncertain, among the Indian people.

In the grievous problem of trust lands the Hoover administration adopted the policy of automatically renewing the trust periods as they expired. Under the administration of Franklin D. Roosevelt the Indian Reorganization Act offered all tribes authority to form recognized local governments with clearly defined powers and, if they wished, to become corporations under Federal charter, with financing available in a $10 million revolving loan fund. Further allotment of land was stopped; tribes were given all possible encouragement to buy land coming up for sale and to recapture ceded lands that had never been occupied. For the first time in history the total Indian estate increased, from 47 million to slightly more than 50 million acres. There was a distinct upturn in the Indian economy, and a quite dramatic increase in the number of Indians in professional positions, both in the Indian Bureau which administers their affairs and in private life. By and large the Federal Government seemed to accept the idea that Indian communities would continue, had a right to continue and that Indian progress should be based upon them.

In the second Truman administration Indian policy swung around abruptly, both in the Executive Branch and in Congress. Once again the Federal trustee set out to diminish the Indian land base, which one major official, speaking of an irritatingly persistent tribe, said was "a millstone around those Indians' necks." Once again it was hoped that the tribes, divested of their land, would disperse and that the individuals would disappear into the general population. The drive reached its peak during the first Eisenhower administration. But throughout this period one could see that the white men were uncertain. Thousands of acres of lands in various categories were added to a number of reservations by Congressional action, while administrative action caused disastrous thousands of acres to be lost to others.

Dispersal of the tribes was further promoted during this period by the device of "termination," in essence the passing of an act of Congress declaring that a given group of Indians is no longer Indian. All trust land then goes out of trust; local jurisdiction, self-government, all Indian rights are ended; and the early dissipation of the tribe is comfortably sure. Actually only a few tribes were terminated before Congress, reversing itself again, balked at the process. The most important of the terminated tribes are the Klamaths of Oregon and Menominees of Wisconsin, both of which were owners of large tracts of valuable timber.

In 1958 Secretary of the Interior Frederick A. Seaton announced what amounts to at least a three-quarter return to the policies of the Roosevelt period. Since then the Department of the Interior has given many tribes substantial help in holding their land and starting sound programs for self-advancement. The subordinate Indian Bureau, however, has not clearly identified itself with the new turn in policy. In the field one finds the superintendent and the tribal council on one reservation happily working out an effective program for retention and consolidation of land and for economic development, while on the next reservation the superintendent is facilitating the loss of land and blocking efforts to stop this loss. All in all, it must be rather bewildering to be an Indian.

Despite everything, the tribes are still here. The Indian population now numbers close to half a million, and is increasing by nearly 5 per cent per annum. In this half million I include an estimated 50,000 people east of the Appalachians who are not recognized as Indians by the Federal Government, but are so recognized by the states in which they live. By and large, the Indians are extremely poor. They live in scattered communities, few of which exceed 50,000 and many of which number less than 1,000. Their health is worse than that of any other racial group in the country—the average life-expectancy of the Papago Indians of Arizona, in a most salubrious climate, is 17 years. Yet the Indians and most of their communities are going to continue into the future.

This retention of identity is not rigid, nor is it necessarily antiprogressive. Except for a small and ever diminishing number of extremists who somehow dreamily hope to wave the white men away, Indians desire functional equality with other Americans. They are selective about the Indian cultural items to be retained; they want education; they want to progress as individuals and as communities. There is a constant movement of individuals out into the general society, as indicated by the presence of the two Indian anthropologists at the conference to which I have referred. On the other hand, prejudice in the white community is an important factor, often ignored, in fostering Indian identity. In most parts of the country where there are considerable concentrations of Indians, they suffer from discrimination that ranges from mild to violent. In many communities far from the South, Indians are flatly segregated, and even in the past 10 years white men have killed Indians with impunity.

Present Indian culture could be represented by a parallelogram of forces, in which the current attitudes, emotions, and ways of responding to situations are the product of the action upon each other of the aboriginal culture and the culture that the white man has brought or imposed. The Indians' old way of life differed enormously from that of the present. It was a rhythmic alternation of activities—hunting, fighting, planting, cultivating, harvesting, performance of ceremonies—with intervals of leisure. What they did went by the seasons, the positions of the sun, the occurrence of need. Those ways have been shattered, and little has been available to replace them. With some exceptions, especially in the Southwest, the outward manifestations of their cultures have been abandoned except as reminiscent public functions, assertions of identity, such as the pasteurized sun dances staged annually by many Plains tribes. Deep down the cultural stream runs strong and, it seems, cannot be choked off. An educated modern Sioux tribal official may tell you confidentially that some of the old men say he is *wakan*—touched by the influence of God—and that sometimes he wonders if this is not so. In the old days many tribes were contemptuous of the accumulation of property and of individual self-assertion; this pattern still inhibits Indians in competition for jobs and promotion, or in reciting and asking questions in college classrooms. When white advisers have had the sense to work with this trait, instead of fighting it, they find that it leads to strength in community endeavors and progress.

One effect of the Indians' historical experience has been a development of frustration, resentment and dependency—qualities that can too often be observed in modern Indians. At that conference of anthropologists the participants agreed that most Indians concur in these assumptions about their situation: "that Indians can expect no long-term consistency in policies affecting them; that the interests of the dominant society will take precedence over their own in any policy decisions; that Indians can do little to affect decisions concerning themselves; that the turning over of Indian affairs to the states is inevitable; and that state administration is more likely to be hostile to Indians than is the Federal administration."

These assumptions, although pessimistic, are realistic; in them I find a quality of despair. The Indians have been pushed around for anywhere from one to two centuries; they are despised and discriminated against; they are baffled, angry, frustrated. The last time they had something like an even break was in King Philip's War.

Yet the Indians have not given up. They strive for the right to be themselves. Unlike any other American minority, they did not come here seeking freedom and a good life; they were here and had both until white men arrived and took these from them. They are our ultimate aristocrats, and as a whole have no more intention of losing their identity than have the members of the Daughters of the American Revolution. They remain surprisingly good-natured and have extraordinarily little of the monolithic prejudice toward white men that white Americans commonly feel toward the dark races. They want tolerance, time and reasonable opportunity, and they absolutely refuse to vanish.

LIGE REEVES is one of three northern California Indians whose status is depicted in

BILL FRAZIER is also a resident of Round Valley. Younger than Lige Reeves, he has

ERNIE MARSHALL is a member of the Hoopa tribe, which lives 200 miles north of

these photographs by John Collier. Reeves's home (*left*) is in

Round Valley, into which remnants of seven tribes were driven. At right he sits with a daughter and a grandchild. Too old to do heavy farming, he lives mainly on relief. His allotted land is tax-free.

been able to develop his land into a thriving stock farm (*left*).

He and his wife (*right*), like other Indian residents of the valley, worry that their government-allotted land will be "terminated." This would force Indians who were unable to pay taxes to sell their land.

Round Valley. The Hoopa land, unlike that of the Indians of

Round Valley, has not been allotted to individuals but is owned by tribe. Rich in timber, it provides a good living to tribe members. At left is Marshall's home; at right he sits with son and grandson.

BIBLIOGRAPHIES

I CULTURAL AND THEORETICAL TRANSFORMATIONS

1. Culture History vs. Culture Process

AN INTRODUCTION TO AMERICAN ARCHAEOLOGY, VOLUME I: NORTH AND MIDDLE AMERICA. Gordon R. Willey. Prentice-Hall, 1967.

2. Cultural Evolution

SCIENCE OF CULTURE. Leslie A. White. Farrar, Straus & Young, 1949.

SOCIAL EVOLUTION. V. Gordon Childe. Henry Schuman, 1951.

THEORY OF CULTURE CHANGE. Julian Steward. The University of Illinois Press, 1955.

II THE ROMANTIC VISION

3. The Lost Cities of Peru

THE CALLEJON DE HUAYLAS OF PERU AND ITS MONUMENTS. Richard P. Schaedel. *Archaeology,* vol. 1, no. 4, pp. 198–202; December 1948.

4. America's Oldest Roads

THE TRAVELS OF PEDRO CIEZA DE LÉON, A.D. 1532–1550. Translated and edited by Clements R. Markham. Hakluyt Society, 1864.

III TIME-SPACE SYSTEMATICS: GAPSMANSHIP

5. Early Man in South America

EARLY CULTURAL REMAINS ON THE CENTRAL COAST OF PERU. Thomas C. Patterson. *Ñawpa Pacha,* no. 4, pp. 145–153. Institute of Andean Studies, 1966.

A LATE-GLACIAL AND HOLOCENE POLLEN DIAGRAM FROM CIENAGA DEL VISITADOR (DEPT. BOYACA, COLOMBIA). T. van der Hammen and E. Gonzales. *Leidse Geologische Mededelingen,* vol. 32, pp. 193–201; September 15, 1965.

LATE-PLEISTOCENE POLLEN DIAGRAMS FROM THE PROVINCE OF LLANQUIHUE, SOUTHERN CHILE. Calvin J. Heusser. *Memoirs of the American Philosophical Society,* vol. 110, no. 4, pp. 269–305; August 1966.

6. Early Man in the Andes

EARLY LITHIC INDUSTRIES OF WESTERN SOUTH AMERICA. Edward P. Lanning and Eugene A. Hammel. *American Antiquity,* vol. 27, no. 2, pp. 139–154; October 1961.

EARLY MAN SITE FOUND IN HIGHLAND ECUADOR. William J. Mayer-Oakes and Robert E. Bell. *Science*, vol. 131, no. 3416, pp. 1805–1806; June 17, 1960.

EVIDENCE OF A FLUTED POINT TRADITION IN ECUADOR. Robert E. Bell. *American Antiquity*, vol. 26, no. 1, 102–106; July 1960.

7. A Stone Age Campsite at the Gateway to America

THE ARCHEOLOGY OF CAPE DENBIGH. J. L. Giddings. Brown University Press, 1964.

THE BERING LAND BRIDGE. David Moody Hopkins. Stanford University Press, 1967.

8. Early Man in the West Indies

AN ARCHEOLOGICAL CHRONOLOGY OF VENEZUELA. J. M. Cruxent and Irving Rouse. *Social Science Monographs, VI: Vols. I and II.* Pan American Union, 1958, 1959.

THE ENTRY OF MAN INTO THE WEST INDIES. Irving Rouse. *Yale University Publications in Anthropology*, No. 61; 1960.

PREHISTORY OF THE WEST INDIES. Irving Rouse. *Science*, vol. 144, no. 3618, pp. 499–513; May 1, 1964.

PALEOHUNTERS IN AMERICA: ORIGINS AND DIFFUSION. Hansjürgen Müller-Beck. *Science*, vol. 152, no. 3726, pp. 1191–1210; May 27, 1966.

IV RECONSTRUCTIONS

Reconstructions of Events or Periods

9. Early Man in the Arctic

THE DENBIGH FLINT COMPLEX. J. L. Giddings, Jr. *American Antiquity*, vol. 16, no. 3, pp. 193–203; January 1951.

A PALEO-ESKIMO CULTURE IN WEST GREENLAND. Jorgen Meldgaard. *American Antiquity*, vol. 17, no. 3, pp. 222–230; January 1952.

RADIOCARBON DATING IN THE ARCTIC. Henry B. Collins. *American Antiquity*, vol. 18, no. 3, pp. 197–202; January 1953.

RECENT DEVELOPMENTS IN THE DORSET CULTURE AREA. Henry B. Collins. *American Antiquity*, vol. 18, part 2, pp. 32–39, January 1953.

10. A Transpacific Contact in 3000 B.C.

POSSIBLE TRANSPACIFIC CONTACT ON THE COAST OF ECUADOR. Emilio Estrada, Betty J. Meggers, and Clifford Evans. *Science*, vol. 135, no. 3501, pp. 371–372; February 2, 1962.

VALDIVIA—AN EARLY FORMATIVE CULTURE OF ECUADOR. Clifford Evans and Betty J. Meggers. *Archaeology*, vol. 11, no. 3, pp. 175–182; Autumn 1958.

11. An Archaic Indian Cemetery in Newfoundland.

THE CULTURAL AFFINITIES OF THE NEWFOUNDLAND DORSET ESKIMO. Elmer Harp, Jr. *National Museum of Canada*, Bulletin no. 200, Anthropological Series no. 67, pp. 1–183; 1964.

EVIDENCE OF BOREAL ARCHAIC CULTURE IN SOUTHERN LABRADOR AND NEWFOUNDLAND. Elmer Harp, Jr. *National Museum of Canada*, Bulletin no. 193, Contributions to Anthropology 1961–62, part I, pp. 184–261; 1964.

FIVE PREHISTORIC BURIALS FROM PORT AU CHOIX, NEWFOUNDLAND. Elmer Harp, Jr., and David R. Hughes. *Polar Notes*, no. 8, pp. 1–47; June 1968.

12. Teotihuacán

THE CULTURAL ECOLOGY OF THE TEOTIHUACÁN VALLEY. William T. Sanders. Department of Sociology and Anthropology, Pennsylvania State University. 1965.

INDIAN ART OF MEXICO AND CENTRAL AMERICA. Miguel Covarrubias. Alfred A. Knopf, 1957.

AN INTRODUCTION TO AMERICAN ARCHAEOLOGY, VOL. I: NORTH AND MIDDLE AMERICA. Gordon R. Willey. Prentice-Hall, 1966.

MESOAMERICA BEFORE THE TOLTECS. Wigberto Jiménez Moreno, in *In Ancient Oaxaca,* edited by John Paddock. Stanford University Press, 1966.

MEXICO BEFORE CORTEZ: ART, HISTORY AND LEGEND. Ignacio Bernal. Doubleday, 1963.

NORTHERN MESOAMERICA. Pedro Armillas, in *Prehistoric Man in the New World*, edited by Jesse D. Jennings and Edward Norbeck. The University of Chicago Press, 1964.

TEOTIHUACÁN: COMPLETION OF MAP OF GIANT ANCIENT CITY IN THE VALLEY OF MEXICO. R. Millon. *Science*, vol. 170, no. 3962, pp. 1077–1082; December 4, 1970.

TEOTIHUACÁN, MEXICO, AND ITS IMPACT ON REGIONAL DEMOGRAPHY. Jeffry R. Parsons. *Science*, vol. 162, no. 3856, pp. 872–877; November 22, 1968.

13. The Death of a Civilization

THE CONQUEST OF YUCATAN. Frans Blom. Houghton Mifflin, 1936.

THE DISAPPEARANCE OF CLASSIC MAYA CIVILIZATION. Jeremy Arac Sabloff, in *The Patient Earth*, edited by J. Harte and R. Socolow. Holt, Rinehart, and Winston, 1971.

THE RISE AND FALL OF MAYA CIVILIZATION. J. Eric Thompson. The University of Oklahoma Press, 1954; 2d ed., 1966.

14. The Hopi and the Tewa

CULTURE IN CRISIS: A STUDY OF THE HOPI INDIANS. Laura Thompson. Harper & Brothers, 1950.

THE HOPI-TEWA OF ARIZONA. Edward P. Dozier. *University of California Publications in American Archaeology and Ethnology*, vol. 44, no. 3, pp. 259–376. The University of California Press, 1954.

RESISTANCE TO ACCULTURATION AND ASSIMILATION IN AN INDIAN PUEBLO. Edward P. Dozier. *American Anthropologist*, vol. 53, no. 1, pp. 56–66; January-March 1951.

THE SOCIAL ORGANIZATION OF THE TEWA OF NEW MEXICO. Elsie Clews Parsons. *Memoirs of the American Anthropological Association*, no. 36; 1929.

Reconstructions of Historical Sequences

15. Early Man in the Andes

ANCIENT MAN IN NORTH AMERICA. H. M. Wormington. The Denver Museum of Natural History, 1957.

EARLY MAN IN THE NEW WORLD. Alex D. Krieger, in *Prehistoric Man in the New World*, edited by Jesse D. Jennings and Edward Norbeck. The University of Chicago Press, 1964.

AN INTRODUCTION TO AMERICAN ARCHAEOLOGY, VOL. I: NORTH AND MIDDLE AMERICA. Gordon R. Willey. Prentice-Hall, 1966.

16. The Origins of New World Civilization

ANCIENT MESOAMERICAN CIVILIZATION. Richard S. MacNeish. *Science*, vol. 143, no. 3606, pp. 531–537; February 1964.

THE CHINAMPAS OF MEXICO. Michael D. Coe. *Scientific American*, vol. 211, no. 7, pp. 90–98 (Offprint 648); July 1964.

DOMESTICATION OF CORN. Paul C. Mangelsdorf, Richard S. MacNeish, and Walton C. Galinat. *Science*, vol. 143, no. 3606, pp. 538–545; February 1964.

FIRST ANNUAL REPORT OF THE TEHUACAN ARCHAEOLOGICAL-BOTANICAL PROJECT. Richard Stockton MacNeish. Robert S. Peabody Foundation for Archaeology, 1961.

THE LOST CITIES OF PERU. Richard P. Schaedel. *Scientific American*, vol. 185, no. 2, pp. 18–23; August 1951.

MEXICO. Michael D. Coe. Frederick A. Praeger, 1962.

SECOND ANNUAL REPORT OF THE TEHUACAN ARCHAEOLOGICAL-BOTANICAL PROJECT. Richard Stockton MacNeish. Robert S. Peabody Foundation for Archaeology, 1962.

17. The History of a Peruvian Valley

AMERICA'S OLDEST FARMERS. Junius B. Bird. *Natural History*, vol. 57, no. 7, pp. 296–303, 334–335; September 1948.

CULTURAL STRATIGRAPHY IN THE VIRÚ VALLEY, NORTHERN PERU. William D. Strong and Clifford Evans, Jr. Columbia University Press, 1952.

THE GALLINAZO GROUP, VIRÚ VALLEY, PERU. Wendell C. Bennett. Yale University Press, 1950.

PREHISTORIC SETTLEMENT PATTERNS IN THE VIRÚ VALLEY, PERU. Gordon R. Willey. Smithsonian Institution, 1953.

18. The People of Pine Lawn Valley

THE SU SITE EXCAVATIONS AT A MOGOLLON VILLAGE, WESTERN NEW MEXICO. Paul S. Martin. Field Museum of Natural History, Chicago. Publications 476, 526 and 601, Anthropological Series, vol. 32, nos. 1, 2 and 3; 1940, 1943 and 1947.

THE MOGOLLON CULTURE OF SOUTHWESTERN NEW MEXICO. Emil W. Haury. Gila Pueblo, Medallion Papers, no. 19, Globe, Ariz.; 1936.

19. Underwater Archaeology in the Maya Highlands

ANTIQUITIES OF GUATEMALA. Eduard Seler. *Bureau of American Ethnology Bulletin*, no. 28, pp. 75–121; 1904.

LIMNOLOGICAL STUDIES ON SOME LAKES IN CENTRAL AMERICA. Chancey Juday. *Transactions of the Wisconsin Academy of Sciences, Arts, and Letters*, vol. 18, pp. 214–250; 1916.

LUGARES ARQUEOLOGICOS DEL ALTIPLANO MERIDIONAL CENTRAL DE GUATEMALA. Edwin M. Shook. *Antropologia e Historia de Guatemala*, vol. 4, no. 2, pp. 3–40; June 1952.

A NEW SURVEY OF THE WEST INDIES, 1648. THE ENGLISH-AMERICAN. Thomas Gage. Robert M. McBride, 1929.

THE SILENT WORLD. Captain J. Y. Cousteau with Frédéric Dumas. Harper & Brothers, 1953.

20. Prehistoric Man in the Grand Canyon

THE ABANDONMENT OF THE SAN JUAN REGION. Erik K. Reed. *El Palacio*, vol. 51, no. 4, pp. 61–74; April 1944.

CLIMATE CHANGE AND CULTURE HISTORY IN THE GRAND CANYON REGION. Douglas W. Schwartz. *American Antiquity*, vol. 22, no. 4, pp. 372–377; April 1957.

THE COHONINA CULTURE OF NORTHWESTERN ARIZONA. John C. Mc.Gregor. The University of Illinois Press, 1951.

DEMOGRAPHIC CHANGES IN THE EARLY PERIODS OF COHONINA PREHISTORY. Douglas W. Schwartz, in *Prehistoric Settlement Patterns in the New World*, pp. 26–31; 1956.

HAVASUPAI ETHNOGRAPHY. Leslie Spier. *Anthropological Papers of the American Museum of Natural History*, vol. 29, part 3, pp. 81–408; 1928.

21. The Iroquois Confederacy

THE ARCHAEOLOGY OF NEW YORK STATE. William A. Ritchie. The Natural History Press, 1965.

IROQUOIS CULTURE, HISTORY, AND PREHISTORY: PROCEEDINGS OF THE 1965 CONFERENCE ON IROQUOIS RESEARCH. Edited by Elisabeth Tooker. New York State Museum and Science Service, 1967.

THE DEATH AND REBIRTH OF THE SENECA. Anthony F. C. Wallace. Alfred A. Knopf, 1970.

Reconstructions of Strategies

22. Elephant Hunting in North America

ANCIENT MAN IN NORTH AMERICA. H. M. Wormington. The Denver Museum of Natural History.

THE PALEO-INDIAN TRADITION IN EASTERN NORTH AMERICA. Ronald J. Mason. *Current Anthropology*, vol. 3, no. 3, pp. 227–278; June 1962.

PREHISTORIC MAN IN THE NEW WORLD. Jesse D. Jennings and Edward Norbeck. The University of Chicago Press, 1964.

THE QUATERNARY OF THE UNITED STATES. Edited by H. E. Wright, Jr., and David G. Frey. Princeton University Press, 1965.

23. A Paleo-Indian Bison Kill

ANCIENT MAN IN NORTH AMERICA. H. M. Wormington. The Denver Museum of Natural History, 1949.

EARLY MAN IN THE NEW WORLD. Kenneth Macgowan and Joseph A. Hester, Jr. Doubleday, 1962.

THE HIGH PLAINS AND THEIR UTILIZATION BY THE INDIAN. Waldo R. Wedel. *American Antiquity*, vol. 29, no. 1, pp. 1–16; July 1963.

24. The Hopewell Cult

EXPLORATION OF THE MOUND CITY GROUP. William C. Mills. *Ohio Archaeological and Historical Quarterly*, vol. 31, no. 4, pp. 423–584; October 1922.

EXPLORATIONS OF THE SEIP GROUP OF PRE-HISTORIC EARTHWORKS. Henry C. Shetrone and Emerson F. Greenman. *Ohio Archaeological and Historical Quarterly*, vol. 40, no. 3, pp. 349–509; July 1931.

25. The Chinampas of Mexico

THE AGRICULTURAL BASIS OF URBAN CIVILIZATION IN MESOAMERICA. Angel Palerm. *Irrigation Civilizations: A Comparative Study*, Social Science Monograph I, pp. 28–42, Pan American Union, 1955.

DAILY LIFE AMONG THE AZTECS. Jacques Soustelle. Macmillan, 1962.

MEXICO. Michael D. Coe. Frederick A. Praeger, 1962.

26. Pre-Columbian Ridged Fields

THE ABORIGINAL CULTURAL GEOGRAPHY OF THE LLANOS DE MOJOS OF BOLIVIA. William M. Denevan. The University of California Press, 1966.

ANCIENT RIDGED FIELDS OF THE SAN JORGE RIVER FLOODPLAIN, COLOMBIA. James J. Parsons and William A. Bowen. *The Geographical Review*, vol. 56, no. 3, pp. 317–343; July 1966.

RIDGE OR "ERA" AGRICULTURE IN THE COLOMBIAN ANDES. Robert C. West. *Actas del XXXIII Congreso Internacional de Americanistas*, vol. 1, pp. 279–282; San Jose, Costa Rica, 1959.

27. Early Metallurgy in the New World

INDIAN LIFE IN THE UPPER GREAT LAKES: 11,000 B.C. TO A.D. 1800. George Irving Quimby. The University of Chicago Press, 1960.

LA MÉTALLURGIE EN AMÉRIQUE PRÉ-COLOMBIENNE. Paul Rivet and H. Arsandaux. *Travaux et Mémoires de l'Institut d'Ethnologie*, vol. 39, pp. 1–254; 1946.

PRE-HISPANIC METALLURGY AND METALWORKING IN THE NEW WORLD. Dudley T. Easby, Jr. *Proceedings of the American Philosophical Society*, vol. 109, no. 2, pp. 89–98; April 1965.

TREASURES OF ANCIENT AMERICA: THE ARTS OF THE PRE-COLUMBIAN CIVILIZATIONS FROM MEXICO TO PERU. S. K. Lothrop. Skira, 1964.

V ANALYSIS OF SYSTEMS AND PROCESSES

28. The Bering Strait Land Bridge

INSTABILITY OF SEA LEVEL. Richard J. Russell. *American Scientist*, vol. 45, no. 5, pp. 414–430; December 1957.

OUTLINE OF THE HISTORY OF ARCTIC AND BOREAL BIOTA DURING THE QUATERNARY PERIOD. Eric Hultén. Bokförlags aktiebolaget Thule, 1937.

RATE OF POSTGLACIAL RISE OF SEA LEVEL. F. P. Shepard and H. E. Suess. *Science*, vol. 123, no. 3207, pp. 1082–1083; June 15, 1956.

A THEORY OF ICE AGES. Maurice Ewing and William L. Donn. *Science*, vol. 123, no. 3207, pp. 1061–1066; June 15, 1956.

29. Origin and Evolution of Cities

THE AGRICULTURAL REVOLUTION. Robert J. Braidwood. *Scientific American*, vol. 203, no. 3, pp. 130–148 (Offprint 605); September 1960.

CITIES AND NATIONS OF ANCIENT SYRIA. Giorgio Buccellati. Istituto de Studi del Vicino Oriente, Universitá di Roma, 1967.

CITIES AND PLANNING IN THE ANCIENT NEAR EAST. Paul Lampl. Braziller, 1968.

THE CITY IN HISTORY: ITS ORIGINS, ITS TRANSFORMATIONS, AND ITS PROSPECTS. Lewis Mumford. Harcourt, Brace and World, 1961.

CITY INVINCIBLE: A SYMPOSIUM ON URBANIZATION AND CULTURAL DEVELOPMENT IN THE ANCIENT NEAR EAST. Edited by Carl H. Kraeling and Robert M. Adams. The University of Chicago Press, 1960.

THE CITY OF CHANG-AN. Jaqueline Tyrwhitt. *Town Planning Review*, vol. 39, no. 1, pp. 21–37; April 1968.

AN EARLIER AGRICULTURAL REVOLUTION. Wilhelm G. Solheim, II. *Scientific American*, vol. 226, no. 4, pp. 34–41; April 1972.

THE EVOLUTION OF URBAN SOCIETY. Robert McC. Adams. Aldine Publishing Co., 1966.

FOREST CLEARANCE IN THE STONE AGE. Johannes Iversen in *Scientific American*, vol. 194, no. 3, pp. 36–41. (Offprint 1151); March 1956.

THE MEDIEVAL TOWN. Fritz Rörig. The University of California Press, 1967.

A NEOLITHIC CITY IN TURKEY. James Mellaart in *Scientific American*, vol. 210, no. 4, pp. 94–104 (Offprint 620); April 1964.

THE ORIGIN OF CITIES. Robert M. Adams in *Scientific American*, vol. 203, no. 3, pp. 153–168 (Offprint 606); September 1960.

THE PREINDUSTRIAL CITY: PAST AND PRESENT. Gideon Sjoberg. The Free Press of Glencoe, Illinois, 1960.

URBANIZATION OF THE CLASSICAL WORLD. Norman J. G. Pounds. *Annals of the Association of American Geographers*, vol. 59, pp. 135–157; March 1969.

30. The Planning of a Maya Ceremonial Center

MAYA ARCHAEOLOGIST. J. Eric S. Thompson. Robert Hale, 1963.

LOCATIONAL ANALYSIS IN HUMAN GEOGRAPHY. Peter Haggett. Edward Arnold, 1965.

31. The Flow of Energy in a Hunting Society

THE NETSILIK ESKIMOS: SOCIAL LIFE AND SPIRITUAL CULTURE. Knud Rasmussen, in *Report of the Fifth Thule Expedition, 1921–24, No. 8*. Copenhagen: Gyldendalake Boghandel, 1931.

THE ESKIMOS: THEIR ENVIRONMENT AND FOLKWAYS. Edward Moffat Weyer, Jr. Yale University Press, 1932.

MAN THE HUNTER. Edited by Richard B. Lee and Irven DeVore. Aldine, 1969.

VI EPILOGUE: CONTEMPORARY ISSUES

32. A Crisis in U.S. Archaeology

RIVER BASIN SURVEYS. *Sixty-fourth Annual Report of the Bureau of American Ethnology*, pp. 12–27; 1948.

SYMPOSIUM ON RIVER VALLEY ARCHAEOLOGY. J. O. Brew and others. *American Antiquity*, vol. 12, no. 4, pp. 209–225; 1947.

33. The Enduring Indian

THE AMERICAN INDIAN RELOCATION PROGRAM. La Verne Madigan. Association on American Indian Affairs, Inc., 1956.

THE FIVE CIVILIZED TRIBES OF OKLAHOMA. Angie Debo. Indian Rights Association, 1951.

THE LAST TREK OF THE INDIANS. Grant Foreman. The University of Chicago Press, 1946.

A PICTORIAL HISTORY OF THE AMERICAN INDIAN. Oliver La Farge. Crown, 1956.

THEY CAME HERE FIRST. D'Arcy McNickle. J. B. Lippincott, 1949.

INDEX